ETHICS, INTEGRITY AND APTITUDE

For Civil Services Examination

G Subba Rao
IAS (1965)

P N Roy Chowdhury
IAS (1977)

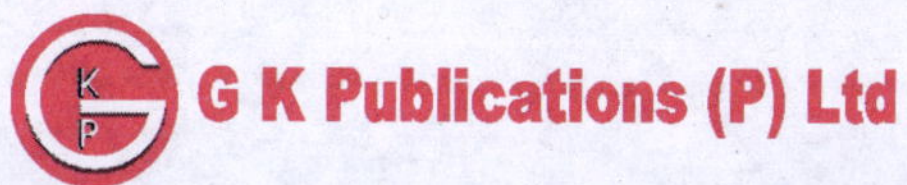

Title : Ethics, Integrity & Aptitude (For Civil Services Examination) 8e

Language : English

Authors : G Subba Rao, P N Roy Chowdhury

Typeset & Published by :

Career Launcher Infrastructure (P) Ltd.

A-45, Mohan Cooperative Industrial Area, Near Mohan Estate Metro Station,
New Delhi - 110044

Marketed by :

G.K. Publications (P) Ltd.

Plot No. 63, Sector-27A, Near Sector - 28 Metro Station, Faridabad, Haryana-121003

ISBN : 978-93-94168-24-4

Printer's Details : Printed in India, New Delhi.

About the Authors

Shri G Subba Rao is a retired IAS officer of the 1965 batch and has a long experience extending over four decades in governance and public administration. He has worked in diverse areas of development and regulatory administration at the Centre and in Gujarat, both at levels of policy making and implementation.. He was Chief Secretary, Government of Gujarat, during June 2001 to April 2003 and later Chairman, Gujarat Electricity Regulatory Commission from May 2003 to January 2008. He was Chairman, Gujarat State Police Complaint Authority, from July 2013 to July 2017.

Shri Rao holds an MA in Economics from Andhra University, MA in Rural Development from University of East Anglia, United Kingdom, and a post graduate diploma in Public Administration from the Indian Institute of Public Administration (IIPA), New Delhi. He has keen interest in Western philosophy.

Shri P. N. Roy Chowdhury has forty years of experience in teaching, public service and in highest levels of corporate management. He has a Masters in Applied Mathematics from Calcutta University. He taught in undergraduate Honours courses and later joined the IAS in 1977. In the middle of his career, he completed his M.Sc. in Finance from Strathclyde University, Glasgow, UK and an MBA from the University of Rochester, New York, USA.

At the time of retiring from the IAS in 2011, he was Additional Chief Secretary to the Government of Gujarat. Post retirement, he joined the Adani Group and is presently working with the Group as Advisor, Strategic Management. He has written a number of books–four of them in Gujarati, covering the requirements of the state Civil Services examination. He co-authored *Good Governance: Theories, Challenges and Case Studies* with Shri Subba Rao, IAS (retd) which is a unique, innovative and relevant book for our times.

Preface to the Eighth Edition

We are extremely happy to bring out the *Eighth* edition of our popular textbook *Ethics, integrity and Aptitude*. On this occasion, we express our deep gratitude to students and teachers for their continued support to our efforts.

In this edition, *we* made important changes in the text. We *deleted the chapter on Individual Ethics of Civil Servants* since its content is partly covered in the chapter on Codes of Ethics and Codes of Conduct. We *omitted the chapter on Code of Conduct for Ministers* because no question on it has so far been asked in the Ethics papers of the UPSC mains examination. We have *omitted the chapter Fight Against Corruption: Current Issues by transposing its materials after compression into the two other chapters in the text on corruption.* We have updated these two chapters by incorporating changes in laws bearing on corruption and related matters.

We have also *deleted the chapter on Utilization of Public Funds.* Although this topic finds a mention in Ethics paper syllabus, students would cover it in any case in their studies on Indian polity and Indian economy. Further, a question peripherally touching upon this subject was asked only once in the Ethics papers of the UPSC mains examination.

Publishers of this text bring out every year a book containing answers to all the papers of the UPSC civil services mains examination. That book also contains our answers given in this text to Ethics papers of the UPSC mains examination. In order to avoid this duplication, we have also omitted the chapter on Solved papers.

These omissions have helped in trimming the size of the text. However, no essential material content has been sacrificed.

We have *enlarged the glossary* and simplified its language.

We have substantially *revised the table in Introduction* outlining the milestones in development of ethical thought.

We have *extensively revised the text* in order to make it more lucid, simple and intelligible.

We are sure that with all the aforesaid revisions, the text will help students greatly in their UPSC examination preparation.

G Subba Rao

P N Roy Chowdhury

CONTENTS

18. Modern Ethical Conundrums 18.1–18.42

20. International Morality 20.1–20.32

INTRODUCTION TO ETHICS

DEFINITIONS OF ETHICS

Ethics has been defined in various ways. The purpose of a definition is to describe its subject concisely and yet completely. Although there are many definitions of Ethics, a common thread runs through them. They are in fact different ways of looking at Ethics. We begin our discussion with some common definitions of Ethics. These definitions will help us in getting an overview of Ethics which in turn will enable us to look at moral questions and issues in an appropriate perspective.

We often make moral judgements in many contexts of life. Such judgements require norms or standards of right and wrong. To take a simple example, X notices that Y, his neighbour, has forgetfully left his purse behind. X is strongly tempted to pocket the purse and the money, but he resists the temptation. In doing so, he makes a moral judgement i.e. that it is wrong to take what is not one's own. This example presents a simple moral problem. From this perspective, Ethics can be regarded as a study of moral problems which men face.

In another view, Ethics deals with conduct viewed as right or wrong, good or bad. Conduct in Ethics means 'moral conduct', or the 'moral life'. Elaborating this idea, we can say that Ethics gives a systematic account of our judgments about conduct viewed from the standpoint of right or wrong, good or bad. Ethics explains judgments about conduct by elucidating the principles on which such judgments rest. Conduct or the moral life has two aspects. One aspect refers to thoughts and feelings, ideals and motives of human beings, and to how they evaluate things and make choices. This aspect refers to the mental state of a moral being. The second aspect of conduct concerns its impact on human society. This aspect refers to the external effects of a moral being's actions. Human decisions and actions affect, either favourably or adversely, the wellbeing of others in society. Ethics uses this as a standard to judge decisions and actions as right or wrong.

Moral judgments consist of two parts. The first part is about what is done or the content of action. The second part relates to the attitude or the motive underlying an action. Not only should an action be good but its underlying intention or motive should also be good. Good action loses its sheen if done for some ulterior purpose. Similarly, a commonly admired quality like frankness by itself may not make people support an action when an individual plainly discloses his intention. If someone openly and brazenly admits that he is seeking public office for self-aggrandizement, people will condemn him.

Moral Judgements based on Content

Moral judgements, based on the content of morals, adopt two points of view – (1) 'higher' and 'lower' within the man's own self; and (2) his treatment of others. The first perspective contrasts a life of the spirit to the life of the flesh, the finer to the coarser, and the nobler to the baser. These two opposite tendencies are parts of human nature. Without the instincts for aggression, self-preservation and procreation, human beings would have perished. But in order to realise their full potential, men have to control these impulses and passions by other motives. Men can make the best of their (rational) life only by pursuing higher or ideal interests through a process of mental and moral discipline.

The second point of view for making moral judgements based on the content of morals relates to the treatment of others. In this conception, qualities like justice, kindness, and the Christian golden rule (Behave towards others as you would like them to behave towards you) are the right and good. Injustice, cruelty, selfishness are the wrong and the bad. These opposing qualities are known as virtues and vices.

Analysis of Intention : The Right and the Good

Right and good are often used interchangeably. But right and good approach conduct from two different angles.

In speaking of conduct as right, one judges it. The act is viewed with reference to a standard. The standard is thought of as a moral law which one ought to obey. Its authority is respected, and considered a check on human impulses and desires. An individual who recognizes such a law and uses it as a guide to his duty is considered conscientious. In doing his duty, he regulates his impulses, and shows self-control.

In thinking of conduct as good, one is approaching conduct from the angle of what is desirable. This is also a standard, but standard regarded as a desirable end rather than as a law. It is a chosen ideal with which one identifies, and not a law which one uses to control one's conduct. The conscientious man, viewed from this angle tries to discover the true good, and to form his ideals in its light, instead of following impulses or accepting any seeming good unthinkingly. The good man whose impulses are directed by ideals will be straightforward. In other words, he will not be moved to do the good act by fear of punishment, or by bribery. The man who regards the standard as a moral law will act similarly but out of a sense of duty, of respect for principles.

Thus, the term 'right' is used in the context of duty. The term 'good' is used in the context of ends or purposes. Further, right usually refers to decisions and actions; good refers to ends, motives and goals.

The Ends of Human Life

There are many ends which men may pursue in life. Some may seek wealth, independence, power, fame, knowledge, love, excitement or peace. Others may take interest in art and science; or in loving and serving others; or in development of social and political institutions. Some others pin their highest hopes on a life beyond death. The different ends men pursue lead to a question: Is there some ultimate ideal of life or some standard of judgment which enables one to say that one form of conduct is better than another? From this angle, Ethics is seen as a study of the ideals involved in human life.

Ethics has some connection with subjects like anthropology, sociology, economics, politics, history and biology. However, Ethics is distinct from them since unlike them it is not a matter of factual knowledge. It examines the nature of normative theories, and their application to practical moral problems.

Ethics is concerned with practical life and not merely with pure theories. It is normative and lays down rules or laws for defining ideal conduct. Ethics is not concerned only with the facts of the moral life but deals with the rules and ideals of the moral life. The former study is a part of sociology which deals with the general structure of societies. The latter study is Ethics. Sociology is a positive (or descriptive) science; Ethics is a normative (or prescriptive) science. But, of course, in dealing with Ethics, we cannot ignore morals which societies actually follow. In administrative contexts, approach to Ethics has to be practical. It has to be normative or rule-based dealing with real life administration and not with moral games or puzzles or abstract theoretical systems.

COMMON CONCEPTS USED IN EXPLAINING HUMAN ACTIONS

Ethics is also known as moral philosophy. (Incidentally, Philosophy is the source of complicated theoretical discussions found in Ethics.) As we have seen, Ethics discusses what is morally good and bad and what is morally right and wrong. The term 'Ethics' is also used in relation to systems or theories of moral values or principles.

Ethics discusses perennial questions that humanity faces. What manner of life should one lead? Should men pursue happiness, or knowledge, or virtue, or artistic pursuits like creation of beautiful paintings, musical compositions, architectural monuments and the like? If someone decides to pursue happiness, should it be his/her own or of society at large? Besides, Ethics seeks answers to specific problems men face. Can one be dishonest while pursuing a good cause? Can we justify a few wealthy people living in the lap of luxury in the midst of mass poverty? Can fighting wars be justified considering that they invariably lead to loss of innocent lives? Is it moral to clone human beings or destroy human embryos in medical research? What responsibilities do men owe to future generations or animals with whom they share the earth?

Ethics discusses basic issues of practical decision-making. It focuses on the nature of ultimate values and standards by which one can judge human action as right or wrong.

We now outline the common ethical concepts used to explain moral actions. These form the stock in trade of moral discussions, and help us in following them.

Appetites and Impulses

Appetites are blind drives towards particular ends. Satisfactions of appetite are often called pleasures; unsatisfied appetites are called pains. A pleasure-seeker is one who seeks the satisfaction of his animal appetites. Some schools of philosophy such as Epicureanism in ancient Greece and Charvakas in ancient India advocated pursuit of pleasure as legitimate goal of human actions. However, conduct as conceived in Ethics, has to be guided by rational considerations. Hence, appetites and impulses need to be brought under rational control.

Good

'Good' is a fundamental idea in Ethics. Good is anything which men consciously desire. Nothing becomes an object of desire unless it is consciously regarded as a good. Real desire is something considered as good, and consciously chosen as an end. Of course, men may adopt as ends objects which are only seemingly but not really good. 'What is good' is a topic much discussed in philosophy.

Wish

Men often have desires which are inconsistent or conflict with one another. In the process, some desires prevail over others. The term 'wish' refers to those desires that prevail and are effective. In Ethics, a wish is distinguished from definite act of will. Even when possessed of will, we may not act. 'Force of will' is the power of carrying resolutions into actions. Will implies that we not merely wish for something, but take active steps for getting hold of it – will contains an energising element. In an act of will, we do not look upon an end as a good to be sought; we regard it as an end to be brought about by us.

Purpose, Intention and Motive

The terms 'purpose', 'intention' and 'motive' are frequently used in explanations of human actions. An intention means any aim that is definitely adopted as an object of will. Motive means what moves men or causes them to act in a particular way. Men are sometimes moved to action by feeling or emotion. But moral judgments can be passed only on thoughtful actions or actions which aim at consciously examined ends. Moral activity or conduct is purposeful action; and action with a purpose is not simply moved by feeling: it is moved by the thought of some end to be attained. Hence, the motive or that which induces us to act is the thought of a desirable end. Men often understand what is good, but fail to pursue it. This happens because motives of human action are often partly or wholly irrational.

CHARACTER IN ETHICS

There is a close relation between an individual's desires, character and conduct. The desires of a person are not bits and pieces randomly thrown together, but form a system which is held together by certain moral ideas. Here, we ignore man's biological drives based on hunger, thirst and reproductive instincts as also the minimum amenities like shelter and clothing needed for human existence. An individual's desires reflect the dominant moral features of his character. It is from this point of view that one can understand the significance of a man's desires.

Human beings desire what they like; and what they like, Ruskin says, reveals what they are. In a way, an individual's desires shed light on his character and morals. Character consists in the continuous dominance of certain moral features in a man's conduct. It shows the moral universe which an individual occupies. A man of good character is one who is habitually guided by a sense of duty. A swindler is one who is constantly seeking means of defrauding others. A fanatic is one who is so completely dominated by a single thought that he shuts out completely other important points of view. Similarly, all other kinds of character may be described by reference to the ideas that are dominant in them. Accordingly, many writers define 'conduct' as the habitual modes of action that accompany a formed character. In a wider sense, conduct as used in Ethics refers to an individual's moral life – and not just to an individual's particular actions.

Ethics regards character as the most important aspect of human life. Occasional good deeds are of no great significance; they have to be performed habitually with few exceptions. Hence Aristotle emphasised that the formation of good habits is essential for cultivating a good character. Will is an expression of character. As expressed in the saying that "the tree is known by its fruit", good character shows itself in good acts of will. Accordingly, it is said that conduct refers to the habitual modes of action that accompany a formed character.

Generally, conduct corresponds to character. But it is sometimes said that a man's conduct depends upon his character and circumstances. By circumstances, we mean in general, a man's social surroundings such as lineage and upbringing, riches or poverty, health or disease, and so on. As we know, man's moral effort consists partly in holding on to ethical norms in adverse circumstances.

The above discussion points to two questions of morality. (1) What are ends to be pursued in life? (2) How can one pursue these ends? Or how can one strengthen his will to pursue the ends or ideals? Or what are the means by which one can cultivate right moral habits?

MODEL OF MORAL DECISION MAKING

Uptil now, we have outlined the definitions of Ethics and the terms commonly used in moral discussions. Ethics can be looked at from another point of view. In fact, the best way of approaching any subject is to consider the problems which it analyses. A simple way of understanding moral problems is to consider the manner in which we take moral decisions. The elements involved in moral decision-making can be represented as in the following format.

Model of moral decision making

Moral agent — X

Voluntary action or conduct — X picks Y's pocket

X's action is morally wrong — judgment

It is wrong to steal — moral standard

Religion, custom, law, social norm and the like — source of standard

With the help of the above model, we can get a simple overview of Ethics. Moral standards lie at the core of Ethics. As we shall see, many theories discuss different moral standards e.g. duty, social welfare and individual self perfection. Ethics also discusses the sources from which men derive their moral standards. Such sources are religion, laws, social customs and values imbibed at home or in school. Ethics also discusses the nature of the moral standards. For example, are moral standards objective or subjective? Are they based on intellectual analysis or simply derive from man's innate moral sense? Are moral standards absolute and universal or are they relative to social situations at given times and places? Are they amenable to logical analysis or are simply unanalysable intuitions or feelings? We will discuss these issues as we go along.

In our above example, the right course of action or right moral judgment can be easily seen. All will agree to the applicable moral standard. But situations often arise in which people differ on the applicable moral standard. Imagine a situation in which a man whose family is starving becomes desperate and breaks into a grocery store, and steals some items of food. What moral judgment should we pass on his action? We would tend to condone his theft out of a sense of natural sympathy for his suffering family. But those who take a stringent view of morality or adhere to absolute ethical standards will condemn the act of theft. "A theft", they will say "is a theft irrespective of the thief's personal circumstances". They are rigid moralists who apply strict standards in judging this act of theft.

For example the great philosopher Immanuel Kant would apply rigid ethical rules even in this type of cases.

Besides the stringency or leniency involved in their application, moral principles can conflict in some situations. In the example of the individual who steals food to feed his hungry family, two moral standards clash with each other. (1) Theft is wrong. (2) A householder must not let his family go hungry. This type of situation involving conflict between two equally valid moral standards is called an ethical dilemma. We discuss ethical dilemmas in a later chapter.

In addition, philosophers are fond of imagining situations which resemble moral puzzles. Suppose for example that a doctor has only a single dose of a life saving injection, and two patients in need of the injection are brought to him. To whom shall he administer the injection? What principles can regulate his choice of whom to save? The purpose of such puzzles is to show that commonly accepted ethical standards break down or fail to provide guidance to moral agents in some situations. In this way, the universal validity of moral standards may be questioned. Further, the idea may be to show that some decisions have to be taken, in the absence of any guiding principles, randomly or based on a moral agent's discretion.

ETHICAL IDEALS IN LIFE

Another area of Ethics deals with the ideal life which human beings should lead. There are various views about the chief good or aim of life. One such aim is pleasure, conceived as consisting simply in the gratification of the particular impulses as they arise. This is known as hedonism. Happiness is seen as another goal of life. Happiness is sought over the whole of one's life. It consists of enjoying various pleasures in moderation and in avoiding dissipation. The pleasures can consist of ties of family and friendship, intellectual interests, aesthetic enjoyments and spiritual pursuits. Some writers like Hobbes and Nietzsche have taken a radically different view arguing that people may pursue power or self assertion as an alternative goal.

There is a sublime conception of ideal human life. It holds that human impulses must be subjected to a moral law to encompass them in a rational system. This view emphasises the law of reason or of duty. The feelings which people experience in adopting this mode of life are very different from mere satisfaction of desires. Pursuit of self-interest leads to a type of satisfaction quite different from following duty; sensual enjoyments yield satisfactions different from those that arise from poetic or religious emotion. Carlyle describes such higher types of feelings as blessedness than as happiness. Spinoza uses the term beatitude in this sense. This form of happiness is found, according to Spinoza, in the "Intellectual Love of God," i.e. in the appreciation of the universe as the realisation of a spiritual principle. Spinoza says, that "happiness (beatitude) is not the reward of virtue, but virtue itself," i.e. it is an essential aspect in the attainment of the right point of view. A very different self is realised in each of these cases; and the accompanying feeling of self realisation is therefore different.

Moral ideal in these conceptions consists in some form of self-realisation i.e. in some form of the development of character; and the end is seen as moral perfection than as happiness. Moral life is viewed as a process of growth. According to Green, the essential element in the nature of man is the rational or spiritual principle. Man resembles animals in having appetites, sensations and mental images. However, all these, and everything else in man's nature, are modified by his reason. This is because man is rational, self-conscious, and spiritual. This is the essential aspect of human nature. The significance of the moral life consists in the constant endeavour to make this principle more and more explicit - to bring out more and more completely our rational, self-conscious, spiritual nature. Green says that men should attain a moral status which is most completely rational.

ETHICS BASED ON THEORY OF EVOLUTION

The previous view of self realisation as ethical end is highly sublime. Ethics based on biological evolution is mundane. Herbert Spencer is the chief exponent of these ideas. These theories of Ethics follow the pattern of explanation of biological evolution which Darwin gave in *The Origin of Species*. According to Darwin, the development of animal species takes place by means of a struggle for existence in which the fittest survive. This process is known as natural selection of biological species. Natural Selection is a process in which different species with characteristic structures (bodily forms) contend for supremacy. Some species survive in this process (which often stretches over millions of years) and become relatively permanent. In animal world, the struggle is both between individuals within species and between species. Certain individuals or sets of individuals happen to be born with peculiar natural gifts. These gifts turn out to be such as make them more fit to survive than other individuals; and accordingly they do survive, and transmit their characteristics to their descendants, while their less favoured rivals die out. In the process, some species disappear while the "more fit" survive. It should be understood that 'fitness' here refers to appropriate adaptation to environment, which ensures survival.

Moral theories based on ideas of biological evolution are no longer popular. But they are of historical interest as reflecting how theoretical models from biology were applied in Ethics. Moral thinkers found these models appealing since they contained the notion of development.

Unfortunately, Darwin's ideas were given a sinister twist in Social Darwinism. In simple terms, this doctrine argued that the ruthless struggle for existence found in nature should be replicated in human societies in the form of competition between individuals and social classes as a means of achieving greater progress. It dismissed humanitarianism and benevolence as pointless sentimentalism. Some writers identified Social Darwinism as among the tendencies that gave rise to Nazism.

Quite simply, human ethics cannot be reduced to or grounded in processes that are found in nature. As has been observed, "Ethics is about neither the origins nor the history of morals. It looks at human ideals and how they influence conduct. Now the ideal is what humanity hopes to be and determines the direction of human moral development."

Unlike earlier moral theorists of nineteenth century, modern moral thinkers view the relation between ethics and evolution differently. One group of thinkers believe that human beings were involved in intense struggle for survival, and that this left a lasting imprint on their mental makeup. In the evolutionary process men became aggressive, ruthless, and self serving. It needs enormous effort to overcome these anti-social qualities which got embedded in human nature in the process of evolution. The other group of thinkers believe that men acquired many beneficent and other-regarding qualities in the process of evolution - especially in relation to their family and group. They also emphasise that animal behaviour shows many instances of reciprocal altruism.

EXPOSITION OF ETHICS

An Analytical and Historical Perspective

Expositions of topics in modern textbooks are analytical. They explain the subject based on the concepts, principles and theories which currently hold the ground. No references are usually made to the history or evolution of ideas. While explaining electricity or magnetism, modern Physics texts do not discuss earlier theories which regarded electricity and magnetism as some sort of fluids. The earlier theories are of interest only to historians of ideas, and not to current practitioners.

The position of Ethics (and more generally of philosophy) is rather different in this regard. The central questions concerning human morals have been formulated by the ancient Greek philosophers and Indian sages. Although human society has since been transformed totally, the essential moral issues which men face continue to be the same. The identification, analysis and resolution of moral problems which the great thinkers of the past attempted have therefore continued to be relevant. Hence, textbooks on Ethics continue to refer to the work of the great philosophers of the past.

MILESTONES IN THE DEVELOPMENT OF ETHICAL THOUGHT

The milestones in the development of modern ethical thought are shown below. For sake of simplicity, we have given a compressed list. Many philosophes, sages, thinkers and literary men and women have contributed to the development of ethics. As we cannot cover all such writers, we have selected a few who made seminal contributions to moral philosophy.

Period	Philosopher/philosophic school	Central doctrines
1200 BCE to about 800 BCE	Periods of the four Vedas	The roots of Hindu ethical ideas can be traced to the Vedas. The Vedas are divided into three sections i.e. the Mantras, the Brahmanas and Upanishads. The mantras or hymns are found in four collections or Samhitas - Rigveda, Yajurveda, Samaveda and Atharvaveda. Three themes in Rigveda, the oldest Samhita, are nature worship, the concept of cosmic order and details of religious practices. Samaveda is a summary of Rigveda in musical form. Yajurveda contains the liturgy or mantras for undertaking the Vedic ceremonies. The Atharvaveda speaks more about Yoga, the human physiology, different ailments, social structure, spirituality, appreciation of natural beauty, and so on*.
800 BCE-600 BCE	Period of Upanishads	In Upanishads, the highest ethical purpose of man is seen as quest for self knowledge. It is another aspect of the search for ultimate reality.

Contd....

599 BCE - 527 BCE 563 BCE - 483 BCE	Mahavira (according to tradition) Gautama Buddha (according to tradition) Buddhism and Jainism	The two religions arose in opposition to the ritualism, formalism and caste divisions of Hinduism. They opposed animal sacrifices, preached non-violence and the need to contain human passions and cultivate serenity.
5th to 4th century BCE	Period of Ramayana	Essence of morality is conveyed in Ramayana through the noble character of Rama. Ramayana covers individual, social and kingly morality.
540 to 300 BCE	Period of Mahabharata	The *Mahabharata* discusses personal virtues and royal virtues. It also discusses statecraft, diplomacy, and contains the first account of Just War concept.
Fifth century to second century BCE	*Bhagavat Gita*	It is the most important Hindu religious text. It preaches that one should work sincerely without worrying about its likely outcome. It emphasises the centrality of dharma to human action. Its central theme is disinterested action.
Beginning around 481 BC	Sophism	Sophists are the first to deny the existence of universal, objective moral standards. This view called moral relativism argues that morality depends on conditions in particular societies, on historical circumstances and on intellectual attitudes.
470-399 BC	Socrates	One of the greatest ethical philosophers who not only discussed moral theories and concepts but also followed them in his life. He is famous for the view that knowledge is virtue. His ideas are contained in the dialogues which Plato wrote.

Contd....

428-348 BCE	Plato	Author of the Socratic dialogues such as the *Apology and the Republic*; great Idealist philosopher who denied the reality of the world of senses; considered reality to consist of eternal and unchanging Forms; known more as a philosopher and a political thinker than a moralist; identified fortitude, justice, prudence and temperance as cardinal virtues which underlie all human virtues.
384-322 BCE	Aristotle	First academic philosopher who wrote systematically on Ethics; author of *Nicomachean Ethics;* first writer who discussed virtue ethics; regarded virtue as a mean between two extreme qualities.
345 BCE-300 BCE	Kautilya's *Arthashastra*	It is probably the first treatise on statecraft, administration, war, diplomacy and state regulation of economy.
323 BCE (birth of Zeno, founder of Stoicism);	Stoics	Their morals are characterised by strict asceticism and severe austerity. Stoicism was popular also during Roman times.
341 BCE (birth of Epicurus)	Epicureans	They advocated happiness as the goal of life. Happiness does not imply craving for momentary pleasures. Happiness is something that has to be pursued rationally over one's whole life.
(354-430 AD)	St. Augustine, a great Christian theologian and moral thinker mentioned along with St. Thomas Aquinas	Author of *The City of God*; was influenced by Plato
1223-1274 AD	St. Thomas Aquinas	Great Catholic philosopher and author of *Summa Theologica*; was greatly influenced by Aristotle

Contd....

1469-1539	Guru Nanak	Nanak founded Sikhism which preached monotheism and human brotherhood Early intuitionists aka Cambridge Platonists:
1596-1650	Descartes	Founder of modern philosophy; his chief interest was in metaphysics; followed Stoicism
1588-1679	Hobbes	Materialist, not metaphysical, thinker; followed Epicureanism; Hobbes believed that men are highly egoistic and power-hungry.
Early intuitionists aka Cambridge Platonists:		
1617-88	Cudworth	Argued that the distinction between good and evil does not lie in human desires but is something objective that can be known by reason intuitively.
1614-1687	Henry More	Formulated moral axioms such as benevolence that could be recognized as self-evidently true.
1675-172	Samuel Clarke	Outlined the principle of equity deriving it from the golden rule: act towards others as you would like them to act towards you.
1671-1713	Shaftesbury	Founded the moral sense school. In its view, besides egoistic feelings, men possess other natural feelings such as benevolence, generosity, sympathy and gratitude that give them an "affection for virtue"—which Shaftesbury calls a moral sense. This naturally reconciles virtue and self-interest.
1694-1746	Hutcheson	Like David Hume, opposed intuitionists who grounded moral judgments in reason. Moral judgement rests on whether an action is agreeable or disagreeable to one's moral sense which is made up of one's sentiments.
1711-76	Hume	Considered reason as instrumental: it can show the best means of achieving our ends; it cannot formulate human ends; these depend on people's prior wants and desires. Hence, reason cannot give rise to moral judgments or motivate people to act.

Contd....

1723-91 1710-96	Richard Price and Thomas Reid	These two writers revived early intuitionism in a new form. They took the line that notions of right and wrong are simple, objective ideas that are directly perceived by reason and not further analyzable (or reducible) into anything else.
19th century	Utilitarianism	Shifted the earlier debate, from whether morality is based on reason or on feelings, towards which actions are right and which are wrong. This is a shift from metaethics to normative ethics.
1748-1832 1806-1873	Bentham J.S. Mill	These two utilitarian writers believed that the good is that which is beneficial to society or that which promotes human happiness. They defined the ethical end as the greatest happiness of the greatest number. Utilitarianism is a dominant school of ethics even today.
1838-1900	Sidgwick	Tried to reconcile common sense morality and utilitarianism. He showed that whatever was sound in common sense morality could be explained in terms of utilitarianism.
1836-82	TH Green	Introduced considerations of economic justice into utilitarianism. He also believed that the end of human life should be moral perfection.
1724-1804	Immanuel Kant	According to Kant, morality consists in following the command of duty or obligation or what one 'ought to' do. This approach to ethics is called deontological, as opposed to that of utilitarianism, which is called teleological. Kant believed that there is no place for emotions or sentiments in morality since these are irrational. Kant was impressed by the idea of moral law. In a famous passage, he says, *"Two things have always filled me with awe: the starry heavens above and the moral law within [me]"*

Contd....

	Continental European ethical writers	One major stream of European ethical tradition can be traced from Spinoza to Nietzsche (including Rousseau, Leibnitz, Hegel and Schopenhauer). Two philosophers from this tradition ---Kant as a proponent of deontological ethics, and Karl Marx as a political ideologue---are especially relevant to our discussions.
Nineteenth century India	Period of Hindu reformism	The famous reformers of this period, to name a few, are Raja Rammohan Roy, Ramakrishna Paramahamsa and Vivekananda.
Twentieth century developments		
1873-1958	George Moore	Viewed good as the name of a simple, unanalyzable quality; attempts to define it end in "naturalistic fallacy" (explained in the third chapter of our book). He considered good to consist in impersonal aesthetic and intellectual pursuits, genuine friendships and benevolent actions. He was an idealist utilitarian.
1877-1971	W.D. Ross	Identified prima facie duties that determine what moral agents concretely ought to do. A prima facie duty is binding unless in a given situation another duty seems more appropriate. Ross is well known for his discussion of ethical dilemmas.
1910-89	AJ Ayer	Propounded emotivism or the doctrine that moral judgments are neither logical nor mathematical truths nor statements of fact. They are, instead, merely emotional expressions of one's approval or disapproval of some action or person. As expressions of approval or disapproval, they can be neither true nor false.

Contd....

1919-2002	R.M. Hare	Held that ethics can be a matter for logical discussion, not merely of subjective preference. Morals can be universalized---applied to all---and morality can be reasoned about. Further, combination of values and factual statements can make moral discussions logical.
1921-2002	John Rawls	Tries to logically derive rights and liberties which liberals cherish, together with egalitarian principles. He grounds his assertion in the argument that liberal and egalitarian principles would be chosen by rational individuals placed in a certain hypothetical yet plausible social situation.
1938-2002	Robert Nozick	Was a famous conservative thinker whose views can be set in opposition to those of John Rawls.
		Twentieth century philosophers elaborated and evaluated utilitarianism in its two variants, act-utilitarianism and rule-utilitarianism. They have also analyzed deontological ethics in detail. During this period philosophers also developed metaethics or analytical ethics which focuses not on formulating moral systems or standards, but on analyzing the moral concepts or terms which are used in ethics and in ordinary language. Modern philosophers generally refrain from preaching morals. They think that the task of philosophy is to analyze and clarify concepts, and not to advocate morals.
Twentieth century	Gandhi	Needs no introduction.

* *It should be noted that historians and scholars are divided about the exact time of composition and the relative time sequence of Vedic and other Hindu treatises. Further, Vedas, Upanishads, Mahabharata, and Ramayana have been composed over long periods. The ancient Hindu writers did not mention exact historical times of composition. As a result, historians came up with different chronologies of events in ancient Indian history. Hence, readers may come across somewhat different time lines for ancient period than those given in the table.*

We discuss some of these thinkers and their ideas later in the text. Our intention at this stage is to show very broadly the main historical lines of development in Ethics. The overview of Ethics and the broad sweep of its historical development given above will provide useful background to students in their study of the subject.

CONTENTS OF THE BOOK

Now, we outline briefly the topics covered in the book and the best method of using it. The **second chapter** discusses the doctrines of moral scepticism. These doctrines question the value of Ethics and/or argue that Ethics as a study cannot be grounded in logic. We argue that such sceptical views are misconceived. This chapter also discusses the moral responsibility of human beings for their actions. The **third chapter** deals with the contributions of moral thinkers mainly from the West. It discusses the ideas of great moral thinkers such as Socrates, Plato, Aristotle, Epicureans, Stoics, Kant and utilitarians and twentieth century philosophers. The **fourth chapter** discusses ethical ideas from the Indian philosophical tradition. It discusses ethical ideas from Hinduism, Buddhism, Jainism, and Sikhism and of Gandhi. The **fifth chapter** discusses the lessons one can learn from the lives of great leaders, reformers and administrators.

Chapters 6-8 discuss the theoretical portions of Ethics included in the syllabus. The **sixth chapter** examines the sources of ethical guidance which are commonly identified as laws, rules, regulations and conscience. The **seventh chapter** discusses various human virtues (and vices) with reference to quotations from great thinkers about such virtues and vices. We adopted this approach to enable students to gain deeper insight into the nature of these moral qualities. This approach will also help students in answering examination questions which ask them to discuss or elucidate ideas contained in given quotations. Instead of asking a direct question on a theory, concept or doctrine, examiners embed it in a quotation and ask students to comment on it. By reflecting on the quotations and the discussions which follow, students will be in a better position to answer such questions. Moreover discussion in such cases will be greatly enriched when students use quotations or the central point of a quotation while elaborating a point of view.

The **eighth chapter** discusses ethical reasoning and moral dilemmas. Ethical reasoning is relevant to situations in which decisions are based on moral choices. One needs to think about the moral question, the circumstances which give rise to it, and the moral standards applicable to those circumstances. Moral dilemmas arise when two equally valid but divergent standards apply to a given situation. Questions based on case studies which outline the facts in a given situation and the likely alternative courses of action involve ethical reasoning and (at times) moral dilemmas. In answering these questions, students have to think of the central problem arising from the circumstances and the the moral or administrative principle best suited for its resolution.

Chapters 9 deals with the concepts of code of ethics, codes of conduct and official codes of conduct which apply to civil servants.

People are greatly exercised today over the problem of corruption in politics and administration. **Chapters 10 and 11** examine the phenomenon of corruption from different perspectives. **Chapter 10** discusses the existing administrative structure and the prevailing procedures for tackling corruption. It is commonly argued that there are several administrative and other impediments which slow down action against corruption. Corruption arises not only from the moral failings of public functionariest but also from the economic and political environment that often creates opportunities for corruption. It is necessary undertake reforms and bring about systemic changes to reduce scope for corruption. **Chapter 11** examines this theme. **Chapter 12** deals with Lok pal, the latest institutional mechanism, created for controlling corruption.

Public administration scholars advocate frequent, lively and effective contacts between people and administration. To enable people to understand public issues and to comment on them, they have to be given access to information. This is also a means of making administration transparent and reducing scope for malpractices. **Chapter 13** discusses the right to information which addresses these issues.

A large part of public administration is concerned with delivering services to citizens. Services include policing, sanitation, civic amenities, health and education. People often complain that administration fails in meeting their needs efficiently and in time. This administrative question is discussed in **Chapter 14** on citizen's charter. **Chapter 15** discusses corporate governance.

Three areas of the syllabus are from social psychology. **Chapter 16** covers various aspects of attitudes which include their sources, structure and psychological functions. It also discusses processes involved in persuasion and communication. **Chapter 17** is about political attitudes. This topic and ideology are studied in economics, political science, sociology, psychology and philosophy. We outline political attitudes and ideologies mainly relying on ideas from political science and based on contemporary Indian trends and discourse. This is because the previous examination questions on this subject were based on conventional approaches to the subject in political theory and on contemporary Indian political trends and topics. **Chapter 18** is about modern ethical conundrums. In this chapter, we discuss several current issues such as homosexuality, death penalty, gene therapy, animal rights and surrogacy. These problems have their origin in changing attitudes to human sexual mores, revolutionary changes in biotechnology, liberal critiques of traditional religious and other customary practices, and faint hearted misgivings in squarely facing the challenges thrown up by hardcore terrorist ideologies and movements.

Students tend to get confused about the approach they should adopt towards such issues. In this chapter, apart from discussing specific issues, we also indicate the manner in which students can analyse such issues.

Chapter 19 outlines the various concepts and theories of emotional intelligence. This topic is essentially about the skills which civil servants need in their interactions with public and colleagues. **Chapter 20** is on international morality which refers to the code of conduct which nations have to follow in dealing with one another. It discusses international morality on the basis of UN charter and the ideas of John Rawls. It covers various theories of international relations like idealism, realism, neorealism and neoliberalism. It discusses topics like just war, rules governing wars, pacifism, and regime changes brought about by external powers. It also examines the economic dimensions of international morality.

Chapter 21 contains detailed case studies which illustrate various moral and administrative principles. The structure of the case studies conforms to the UPSC questions pattern. We have indicated the possible answer choices and discussed the principles which help in selecting the correct answer. At the beginning of the chapter, we have also outlined a structured method which students can use in tackling the case studies.

Our discussion of the case studies are intended to stimulate the thinking of the readers. Students should learn to look at issues from diverse perspectives. The cases in various chapters as also the cases listed in this chapter will help students in preparing for examination questions which have similar format. They illustrate the likely question patterns and the possible methods of answering questions. Examiners will decide the length of the case study as also the length of the answer. Students should adhere to the word limits while answering questions.

Chapter 22 is a glossary of terms. It covers all the relevant and important concepts. It can be used as a reference or independently for revision before the examination.

We close with a piece of general advice on answering questions. Often, it may be possible to answer questions on Ethics and administration from a commonsensical point of view. We appreciate that commonsense is a crucial ingredient for success in almost all endeavours. At the same time, evaluators of UPSC exam will be definitely looking for depth and richness in an essay type answer. Answers can be enriched if references are made to their theoretical underpinnings; or to relevant supporting doctrines, concepts; or to ideas of moral thinkers. Students are advised to keep this in view while answering questions. The materials assembled in the text will help students in enriching their answers in the manner indicated.

REFERENCES

- John S. Mackenzie, M.A. — A Manual of Ethics
- Wilbur Marshall Urban, — Fundamentals of Ethics - An Introduction to Moral Philosophy
- William Frankena — Ethics
- John Dewey — Ethics
- BBC Ethics Guide — Ethics: a General Introduction
- Doug Erlandson — Ethics : A Jargon Free Guide for Beginners

(These are general text books on Ethics and can be consulted on various specific topics.)

CHALLENGES TO ETHICS AND MORAL ACCOUNTABILITY

INTRODUCTION

By and large, people take the tenets of common morality for granted. They seldom think critically about moral principles. Nor do they worry about the logical foundations of morality. Morality becomes an ingrained aspect of their mental processes. But this is not so in philosophy. One part of Ethics i.e. ethical theory or philosophical ethics is a part of philosophy. Philosophy (being concerned about foundations of human knowledge) subjects all its definitions, concepts, principles and doctrines to intense logical scrutiny.

Since the beginning of philosophical inquiry, some thinkers have expressed deeply sceptical views about Ethics. A sceptic is one who doubts the value of Ethics in human life or argues that ethical studies can have no logical foundations. Ethics in this view is devoid of logic. We may mention the ideas of Sophists of ancient Greece and of Charvakas of ancient India as examples of moral scepticism.

It is useful to begin our study of Ethics with the doctrines of secptical moral thinkers. It may seem that we are approaching the subject from a negative point of view. But anyone serious about study of ethics or concerned with morality has to first consider the secptical views on morality. It is difficult to proceed with the study of Ethics without addressing the main doctrines which raise doubts about its logical validity or utility.

SCEPTICAL DOCTRINES

In this chapter, we examine various points of view which for one reason or another seem to undermine the very idea of ethical studies. From the beginning of philosophical inquiry, one section of thinkers doubted the value of pursuing ethical studies. This line of thought has different strands. In one view, human nature is such that men cannot genuinely pursue moral goals. Another view holds that though men may be capable of pursuing higher ideals, it would not be in their best interests to do so. According to another strand of thought in this vein, men are incapable of pursuing moral goals since there are no fixed or objective moral criteria to distinguish the moral from the immoral. A further view holds that the actions of men are often determined not by their free will or volition but by external forces beyond human control. As a consequence, the idea of men freely choosing their actions and being responsible for such actions whether for good or bad makes no sense. There are many variations on these themes.

In simple terms, we can classify ethical doctrines into two categories: (1) those which doubt the logical validity or practical utility of ethical principles; and (2) those which propound moral doctrines such as utilitarianism or virtue ethics. Traditional textbook accounts of Ethics often present the doctrines which question the value of Ethics alongside doctrines which propound genuine systems of morality. The sceptical doctrines, strictly speaking, are not ethical theories but their refutations. When the two types of doctrine are juxtaposed, doubts are likely to arise in the minds of students causing bewilderment. It is, therefore, necessary to deal with and answer the negative arguments at the outset. Thereafter, one can discuss the major ethical systems.

PSYCHOLOGICAL EGOISM

We begin our discussion with the doctrine of psychological egoism. Egoism simply means that men are only concerned with their individual advantages, pleasures and welfare and have no concern or care for others. Egoism is the doctrine that human beings are innately selfish. An important part of morality is concern for welfare of others and a general feeling of benevolence. If human beings are inherently selfish, it will be impossible for them to practise morality. Their psychological makeup is such as to prevent them from acting morally. It can be seen that psychological egoism is not a doctrine about ethical behaviour; it is a psychological theory according to which men are so constituted that they always act in their selfish interest. It is not possible for them to act otherwise.

Criticisms of psychological egoism

Psychological egoism is often criticised. It is inconsistent with many common patterns of altruistic and other-regarding human behaviour. Many individuals go out of the way to help others. They help philanthropic causes through generous donations and devoted efforts. In many situations, people help others at the risk of their lives. Soldiers in battle situations sacrifice themselves for saving their comrades. Many parents struggle unmindful of personal comfort for the welfare of their children. There are many instances of mothers laying down their lives in an effort to protect their children.

Psychological egoists argue that such examples do not invalidate their position. The seemingly altruistic conduct is a manifestation of egoistic behaviour. Thus, in giving charity, an individual is satisfying his psychological need to feel superior to the persons in need. Or it may be the source of pleasure or of strong psychological compulsion. Thus a mother jumping into a pool to save her kid may be trying to avoid a sense of lifelong guilt feeling she would harbour if she had not made the rescue effort.

Psychological egoism portrays even acts of altruism and sacrifices as instances of satisfying one's impulses. This way of looking at things involves a strained interpretation of common occurrences. It also twists the meanings of commonly used words. It is a topsy turvy way of looking at things.

Psychological egoists also argue that one need not always act from motives which are consciously selfish. Our motives are often unconscious and we are unaware that they are selfish. While people may claim or seem to act in a selfless or altruistic manner, there are hidden selfish motives behind such external appearances.

This defence does not hold because it takes the matter away from the empirical field. Hidden motivations are unobservable, and are therefore, unverifiable. There is no way of determining whether they are true or false. It makes all actions of an individual selfish from the mere fact of his acting. It is like holding something as true by definition. There is no way of either proving or disproving the idea.

ETHICAL EGOISM

Ethical egoism is the view that people should in fact act according to their self interest. Ethical egoists argue that people do not often pursue their self interest, but that they should in fact do so. Acting in self interest means that we should do what maximises our happiness and minimises our unhappiness. This is a form of hedonism (derived from the Greek word "hedon" which means happiness or pleasure). Hedonism is a doctrine which proposes that one should maximise one's happiness and minimise one's unhappiness.

Not all ethical egoists are hedonists. There are many desirable goals other than happiness such as contentment, knowledge, power, love or freedom. In order to bring in all such goals which people pursue into discussion, the general term 'utility' is used. Utility can be defined as whatever makes the consequence of any action desirable; disutility is whatever makes the consequence of an action undesirable. Ethical egoism can be restated as the view that one should so act as to maximise his utility and minimise his disutility.

This view obviously goes against the normal trend of common thinking. If everyone adopts ethical egoism, it will result in universalisation of selfishness and self centredness. Many writers tone down their statements of ethical egoism to answer this criticism. Even while pursuing selfish ends, people have to ensure that they can pursue such ends over the long term. If people are too brazen or aggressive in pursuing their selfish ends to the extent of riding roughshod over others, they will meet with resistance; people will be wary of them and will avoid them. Then they cannot pursue their ends. Therefore, even while pursuing selfish ends, one has to be prudent and ensure that they do not lead to backlash from others.

In this way, ethical egoism leads to conduct which is morally acceptable. Thomas Hobbes (1588-1679), a famous political thinker, believed that men are essentially driven by very selfish, ruthless and aggressive tendencies. As a result, highly anarchic, violent and disorderly conditions prevailed in the 'state of nature' which is a stage of human existence before organised societies came into being. Hobbes describes human life in the state of nature as "solitary, poor, nasty, brutish and short". People would have realised that this state of affairs can be ended only by changing their selfish behaviour and by joining in a society which prescribes rules and laws in order to ensure that men control their aggressive selfish drives to factor in the concerns of others.

We may also mention Mandeville and Adam Smith in this context. Mandeville put forth the view that self interest is the sole criterion of rightness. Self preservation is the first law of existence. Even while working for the good of others, men have self interest in view. Paradoxical though it may seem, individuals in pursuing their self interest also promote the society's general interest. Adam Smith, in *The Wealth of Nations* extends this doctrine to the competitive market system. In this system, the consumers seek to maximise their satisfactions by purchasing the commodities they want. The producers wish to maximise their profits by meeting the demands of consumers. The self regarding actions of the myriad buyers and sellers are harmonised by an 'invisible hand' leading to maximum production and welfare.

Weaknesses of ethical egoism

Even after modifying ethical egoism into a form of enlightened (as opposed to crude) self interest, it has certain weaknesses. First, it leads to a conclusion that people can act selfishly or immorally when they are not being observed or when their actions cannot be detected. If X detects a purse that someone has dropped and if others are around, he will pick it up and return it to the owner. If nobody is around, he may be tempted to pocket it. Anyone adopting ethical egoism may not adopt moral principles as binding under all circumstances.

Another unacceptable feature of ethical egoism is that it may lead to ignoring the interests of future generations. For example, it is necessary to reduce greenhouse gas emissions to guard against climate change. The change will occur in the long term. Ethical egoism will imply that (since future generations are not around), there is no need to worry about them.

There is another problem with ethical egoism that one cannot publicly espouse it. We cannot make it known that we are ethical egoists, i.e. given anonymity we will quietly pursue our personal interests and ignore others. If everyone follows this course, then nobody can gain any advantage.

MORAL RELATIVISM AND MORAL OBJECTIVISM

The next challenge to ethics comes from the claim that moral judgments are relative to the individual or particular societies and are not universally applicable. Moral relativists are those who deny the existence of universal moral principles. The opposite position to moral relativism is called moral objectivism. It takes the position, that there are objective moral truths that some actions are right for all people at all times and that others are wrong for all people at all times. Theories of moral objectivism can be approximately divided into two categories: consequentialist (also known as teleological) and deontological). Consequentialist theories state that what makes an action right or wrong are the consequences which flow from it. If the consequences of an action are good, then it is good; otherwise it is bad. Deontological theories define the difference between good and bad actions on the basis of the quality of the action itself without considering its consequences. Thus truth telling is good and lying is bad regardless of the consequences that may follow. The problem with accepting relativism is that there will be then no fixed standard or criterion with reference to which actions can be evaluated as good or bad.

MORAL SUBJECTIVISM

Moral relativism can be stated in two forms: moral subjectivism and cultural relativism. Moral subjectivism argues that in the sphere of human behaviour what is true for one individual is not true for everyone else or even for anyone else. In this view, right and wrong is a matter of personal opinion. There is no way in which we can evaluate the views on moral questions held by people. If X says that same sex marriage is abhorrent and Y says that it is eminently desirable, there is no way of settling the dispute. It is morally unacceptable to X and morally acceptable for Y. There are no objective criteria to which we can appeal for settling the dispute.

Refutations of moral subjectivism

Moral subjectivism reduces morality to individual opinion and is at odds with commonsense ideas. There are two ways in which it can be refuted. First, it is self refuting. Secondly, people cannot hold on to this view all the time.

The first objection looks at the logical status of moral subjectivism and points out that it is self contradictory. Suppose I assert that all moral judgements are personal opinions. This assertion can be considered from two sides. It may be treated just as my personal opinion. Then it fails to establish what I assert - it is no more than my opinion.

We may alternatively treat the statement as a valid judgement about moral truths. The implication then follows that there is at least one objective judgement about moral truths. This objective judgement is that 'there are no objective moral truths'. This implication contradicts the position of the moral subjectivist.

That one cannot always be a moral subjectivist can be easily shown by referring to an example. We take it from Doug Erlandson's *Ethics: A Jargon Free Guide for Beginners.* Bertrand Russell, a famous British philosopher, argues in his book *Religion and Science* in favour of subjectivity of values or that moral judgements are matters of personal taste and preference. They are not objectively true or false just like one's statement about oysters as a food item. A little later he makes two further statements. One is that "hell, as a place of punishment for sinners, becomes quite irrational." The other is that, "it is the business of wise institutions to create harmony [between our interests and the interests of society] as far as possible."

How is Russell being inconsistent in his moral subjectivism? He does not say that in his personal view hell is irrational or that institutions which produce harmony are wise. He states what he believes as though he were stating objective truths. He wants readers to consider them in that light. It is impossible to continuously and unfailingly adopt moral subjectivism in human life or in academic discourse.

CULTURAL RELATIVISM

Cultural relativism asserts that within a given culture there may be moral standards that are true for that culture. But there is no objective standard of morality which transcends individual cultures and which can serve as a basis for evaluating individual cultures. Cultural relativism is also known as conventional relativism. This view is widely prevalent among anthropologists, sociologists and others but not among philosophers. Cultural anthropology began at the Columbia University and its chief proponents are Franz Boas, Margaret Mead, Ruth Benedict and Melville Herskovits.

These writers argue that various cultures of the world disagree on their conceptions of right and wrong. Some cultures practise polygamy whereas others condemn it. Eskimo culture permitted infanticide. This led cultural anthropologists to conclude that there are no moral standards which transcend a culture and by which the standards of a culture can be judged. There may be moral truths within a society but they are relative to and valid for that culture.

There are two ways of stating cultural relativism. One form is that what is considered as morality varies from culture to culture. The second form is that morality changes from society to society. *These two formulations need to be considered against the following two positions.*

(1) There is a universal standard of morality which transcends individual cultures and which enables us to judge the moral standards of any culture.

(2) There is no universal standard of morality by which we can judge the moral standards of individual cultures.

According to (1), we can look at the practices of a culture and determine whether they correspond to the universal standard. If slavery or infanticide is practised in a culture, it can be regarded as failing to measure up to the universal standard of morality. According to (2), no such evaluation is possible.

In the later part of the twentieth century, moral relativism has become increasingly popular. The main reasons for this popularity are the decline of religious belief in the West and the increasing awareness of cultural diversity in the world. Religion prescribes a morality that is independent and often opposed to human inclinations. Decline of religion has led to secepticism about objective morality. As Dostoevsky says, "If God doesn't exist, everything is permissible". Increasing knowledge of cultural diversity in the world has created doubts about objective morality. For example, anthropologist Ruth Benedict argued that this diversity shows that there is no single objective morality and that morality varies with culture.

Problems with cultural relativism

Cultural relativism leads to many unacceptable implications. There is no harm in admitting and even admiring the interesting diversity found in cultures. But some practices and value systems of cultures can be positively harmful. For example, a culture may try to marginalize or decimate a minority. It cannot be justified on the ground that it is admissible within that society's ethos. Even if one's own society is wanting in some ways, they will appear justifiable within its cultural context. This will run counter to the concept of moral progress in a society. There will also be no way of resolving the differences within any individual culture. Any idea that differences should be settled by majority will lead to odd results. What if the majority for one side is wafer thin? In that case, the view cannot become an accepted feature of the culture. From these points of view, cultural relativism is thus flawed.

Before proceeding to consider the next challenge to Ethics, we may mention the doctrines of emotivism. It is the view that moral judgements are simply expressions of an individual's emotions. If X judges that something is good, it means he approves of it and that it evokes happy feelings and thoughts in him. If X judges that something is bad, he disapproves of it and it evokes negative feeling in him. This view reduces good and bad to the level of individual emotions. As emotions, they will not be fit subjects of logical or objective discourse. As we have discussed emotivism in the section on twentieth century thinkers, we will not pursue it further here.

DETERMINISM AND HUMAN FREE WILL

The next challenge which we consider to Ethics arises from the doctrine of determinism. In brief, determinism holds that the decisions and actions of human beings are causally determined by external forces. Men are not autonomous agents who can decide on matters on their own. They have no free will or independent volition. Since men are not free agents, they cannot make conscious or deliberate moral choices. Men cannot choose between good and bad courses of action. They are not really responsible for their actions. As a consequence, the concept of human morality loses meaning. Men cannot be morally held responsible for their actions.

The question whether human beings have free will is one of the oldest debates in philosophy. This issue requires some explanation. In many human activities, we assume that men are able to act freely or according to their will. Thus a customer who orders paubhaji in a restaurant is acting freely. As compared to this type of action, many events in nature are not acts of freewill. For instance, the next occurrence of lunar eclipse cannot be willed by anyone. It depends on the paths of movements of celestial bodies, and it is entirely predictable. The paths of celestial bodies are fully causally determined. If human actions were fully predictable like solar eclipses, then we could say that actions of men are fully causally determined, and that men have no free will. But since human actions are not predictable, we say that men are capable of acting freely. This view is known as incompatibilism. It argues that human free will and causal determinism are incompatible. Determinism states that for any action or event at any time there exist causes which ensure that the said action or event and no other occurs. If an action is fully causally determined it cannot be an act of free will. And if it is an act of free will it cannot be fully causally determined. Some philosophers subscribe to determinism.

Determinism creates a problem because if human beings have no free will and if their actions are all causally determined, then they cannot be held responsible for their actions. If any action is merely the result of an individual's DNA, his current brain state and environmental factors, then the person has no control over it. His actions result from various external and internal causes, and he has no free will to select from a range of alternatives. In this situation, the idea of a moral agent acting freely and being responsible for his actions loses meaning. We can say that a person ought to do something only if it is within his power to do so.

Libertarianism, the opposite of determinism in philosophy, denies that determinism applies fully to human actions. We mentioned earlier that natural events are determined because they have natural causes. Human actions also have underlying reasons. These may seem comparable to natural causes, but are not so. Human reasons are derived from human mind, thought and will. Men have control over them in some measure. They are not always imposed on them. Therefore, men act freely most of the time.

Free actions

How should we look at the question of when men can be said to act freely? Free actions take place in situations which are characterised by absence of two factors. The two factors are external constraint and internal compulsion.

It is easy to give examples of situations with and without external compulsion. If X requests Y for a loan of five hundred rupees, and Y takes out the money and gives it to X, he is acting freely. Now, suppose that X is walking along a dark street. He is approached by a thief who holds a gun to X's head, and demands his purse. X hands him the purse. Obviously, X acted under an external constraint.

What is an internal compulsion? This arises from mental conditions which may be mild or serious. Obsessive compulsive disorder (OCD) provides an illustration. In this situation, individuals are unable to refrain from going on repeating certain acts. One example is compulsive checking. Some passengers travelling will go on checking whether or not their passports, boarding cards, tickets, and cash are in the pocket. Some people will check many times in order to ensure that they have secured the doors before retiring for the night. If one has OCD, then to that extent his actions may be determined.

From this view, it follows that the question of human free will is not dependent on causal determinism. Human free will has to do with presence or absence of external constraints and internal psychological compulsions. Men are acting freely when there are no external constraints or internal compulsions on them. In such situations, human beings are free moral agents and are responsible for their actions.

Up till now, we have looked at the principal doctrines which question the value or validity of Ethics. A closer examination shows that these doctrines fail to make a dent on ethical theory and practice. We can now proceed to an examination of the important ethical systems. But before doing so, we consider the question of human moral accountability in greater detail.

DETERMINANTS OF MORALITY

The phrase 'determinants of morality' generally appears in old accounts of morality. It discusses the extent of accountability or culpability of a moral agent for his wrong action. In many situations, an individual who commits an offence is obviously guilty. But there may be valid reasons on account of which the wrong doer may be fully or partially freed of responsibility for his wrong deed. Before discussing the determinants of morality, we need to briefly discuss this aspect.

The judgement of rightness and wrongness can be passed only on those actions which are voluntary. They have to be willed by the doer or intended by him. Sometimes, an action may occur without premeditation as when a gun goes off accidentally. The person who accidently fired the gun may be not held accountable except perhaps for negligence.

A moral agent's act is voluntary, if it is based on adequate knowledge and is fully willed. Whatever diminishes knowledge, or partially supplants the will, takes off from the voluntariness of the act. Three considerations are seen as reducing the voluntariness of the act - ignorance, uncontrollable emotion and fear. Now we will consider the three factors briefly.

If an act is done through ignorance, it goes out of the realm of volition. Nothing unknown can be willed. Of course, affected or pretended ignorance cannot be an excuse. When someone knows or should know that people are suffering, as when they are starving, he cannot claim ignorance. His claim is pretence. There is also crass ignorance which is when an individual takes no pains to gain knowledge in an area which is important to him. Thus, if administrators take no pains to learn about important areas of their work, they are guilty of crass ignorance. On the other hand, uneducated rural women with little access to information can be considered genuinely ignorant. One should remember that ignorance can never be an excuse for violations of law.

If a moral agent is overcome by emotions and loses control over his will, then his action becomes involuntary. This is a factor taken into account in law as when a criminal is given a lighter sentence if he commits a crime under sudden and grave provocation. Moral thinkers argue that passions are held in check by an individual's will and reason. When passions overpower the will, the action becomes involuntary. However, an individual has to rein in his emotions, and cannot let them go haywire. This will not be an excuse except in rare cases.

Finally, men may be driven into involuntary acts under duress or threats of violence. If someone holds a gun to the cashier's head and the cashier parts with money, evidently the cashier's act is involuntary. He incurs no guilt for the act though he did physically handover the cash.

Moral thinkers discuss this question to determine when acts are voluntary and when individuals can claim exemption from moral responsibility for their actions. We have considered the question from a general perspective. The question can be discussed also in relation to specific actions. The morality of any action is determined by three elements, the end in view, the means used, and the circumstances that accompany the use of the means. These three aspects of an action need to be examined in order to determine whether an action is right or wrong. This is the general approach, and the answer in any particular case will need detailed analysis. The expression 'determinants of morality' implies analysis of actions based on the three elements we mentioned earlier. The entry on this topic in UPSC syllabus refers to essence, determinants, and consequences of ethics in human actions. We have already mentioned the meaning of the expression 'determinants of morality'.

Essence of morality in this context means the difference between actions that are good and actions that are bad. In other words, it is what essentially separates a good action from a bad action. Discussions on determinants of morality in old Ethics text books cover the relation between good, bad and neutral actions. In what follows, we discuss the determinants of morality of individual actions based on the account given by Patrick J. Sheeran in *Ethics in Public Administration: A Philosophical Approach*. This account is largely based on ideas and terminology taken from medieval philosophy. Because of the antiquity of the ideas and the terminology, the discussion becomes obscure. Students need not puzzle themselves in trying to disentangle the indistinct thoughts. They should simply pick up the main ideas the topic covers. We have tried to explain these main ideas in simple language.

For morally evaluating an action, this account divides it into three parts: the object of the action; the circumstances under which an action takes place; and the purpose of the action.

Object of Action

Every action has an object which is its nature or essence. We need to note that this definition varies from the common meaning of 'object' in modern usage. One meaning of 'object' is target or victim or recipient, as in *target of unfair criticism*. Another meaning of 'object' is purpose, intention or aim. But in Sheeran's list of the three parts of an action, its purpose is separately mentioned as the third part. This approach of Sheeran in defining 'object' is that of scholasticism which following Aristotle defined objects, beings and things in terms of their essence. He defines an action as its essence or object. Readers may be unfamiliar with this terminology, but the ideas it conveys are fairly simple.

Every action has an object which defines it and sets it off from other actions. The object can be good, bad or indifferent i.e. neither good nor bad. Telling truth is good; uttering falsehood is wrong. Truth by its very nature is good; and lying by its very nature is bad.

The three principles which apply to any action are listed below:

1. An action whose object is by nature is bad will always remain so. Neither circumstance nor intention nor purpose can in any way alter the inherent or intrinsic badness of an action whose object is bad. As object here means essence, an act whose essential nature is bad will always retain its bad quality. From this angle, no circumstances or purposes can change the nature of a lie.

2. An action which is good can become bad because of circumstances or intention. Sex in wedlock for procreation is good. But having 'relationships' or flings or affairs is bad. For in the latter, the circumstances change and make a good thing bad.
3. An action that is indifferent (neither good nor bad) can become good or bad depending on circumstances or purpose. Running by itself is neither good nor bad. But a run to an ATM to rob it is bad. If the run is into a house on fire to rescue trapped children, it is good.

Circumstances of Action

By circumstances, we mean those features which lend abstract actions their individual, concrete content. They refer to the time and place of an action, to the agent carrying out the action and to the manner of doing the act. The rightness or wrongness of actions depends not on physical but moral circumstances. Opening a bank safe for withdrawing cash for transactions is a normal function; but opening a bank safe for theft is immoral (and a crime).

Some circumstances aggravate or increase the badness of an action. Misappropriating Rs 20, 000 from a widow's account is much worse than misappropriating the same amount from a rich stockbroker's account. Badness of an action gets aggravated in the former instance. There can also be extenuating circumstances which reduce the evil character of actions. If a robber acts like Robin Hood by stealing from the rich to help the poor, his robberies become less immoral. But in both examples, the actions retain their immoral character.

Circumstances are specifying when they make indifferent actions good or bad or impart a new type of goodness or badness to an action. Thus, when someone throws stones at random without aiming at any one, his actions are indifferent. But if he throws stones with a view to hit a dog or a cat, his action is immoral.

Purpose of Action

The end is the purpose that moral agents have in mind while performing an act or their intention in doing it. An action may have a single or multiple ends.

The manner in which purpose impacts the ethics of an action is outlined below.

1. An indifferent act becomes good or bad depending on its purpose. One may acquire computer skills to play games and while away time. This action is morally neutral. One may learn computer skills to help an old age home in its work. This is a good thing to do. One may learn computer skills with a view to hacking bank accounts. This is immoral.
2. An action that has a good object can become more or less good because of its purposes. If one gives a subscription to a deserving cause, it is a good action. But if one does it merely to get rid of the person seeking subscription, the action is not as good as before. If one gives the subscription with a view to later inciting the person seeking subscription into undesirable activities, the action is immoral.
3. An action which is inherently wrong may become a greater or lesser wrong depending on the purpose of the moral agent. Telling a lie is wrong. But telling lies to falsely implicate someone in a crime is a far greater wrong. But if someone lies to help an innocent man in trouble, the action is still wrong, but its gravity gets lessened. As before, an inherently wrong act can never become good. Further, bad means cannot be used to secure good ends. Both ends and means have to be good. To put matters in homely terms: A rotten apple stays more or less rotten. A good apple may become rotten. A nondescript apple may turn out to be good or bad.

RESPONSIBILITY OF MORAL AGENTS

Our preceding discussion focused on three factors which determine the morality of actions. It presupposed that the moral agents are responsible for the actions. They have carried out the acts. Men are responsible for their actions when they act out of their freewill, with knowledge of what they are doing and with intent of performing the action. They are the ones acting and doing things.

The effects of the action are attributed to one who physically performs the action. He is directly responsible for the action. Of course, one may cause an action to be performed through others - or commission the job - instead of directly undertaking it. Even then he is responsible for the consequences of the action to the extent he has foreseen them. He has a direct moral responsibility for such consequences. We will become responsible for the consequences of actions of others if we encourage, help and persuade them or if we remain silent when we could have advised them.

In administrative situations, officials often commit errors of commission and errors of omission. Error of commission means that one has committed an offence or wrongful act. He has been an active agent. The famous line from Macbeth, "The deed is done" refers to active commission of crime. Errors of omission are situations when people fail to perform their duty or what they are supposed to do in a particular role. If a father neglects his children but does not otherwise ill treat them, he is still guilty of not performing his duty as a parent. If a police officer happens to see a crime being committed but takes no action, he is guilty of an act of omission. Administrators generally try to avoid getting into messy situations or skirt decisions for which they may later be targeted or 'hauled over coals'. But if the matters or issues fall within their official domain, they have no option but to act in their best judgement. Otherwise, they will be guilty of dereliction of duty. They have to bite the bullet in such instances.

Many writers discuss the question about when a moral agent incurs responsibility for bad actions. They will, of course, be responsible if they had knowledge of the likely ill effects of the action. The standard applied is in fact more rigorous. Even if the moral agent has a vague inkling of the likely evil consequences of his action, he will be responsible. When a driver under influence of alcohol drives speedily along a crowded street, he will be liable if an accident takes place. Even if a sober person drives fast in such circumstances, he will be responsible for any accident.

But a good effect is attributed to only one who performs a good deed - not to others. Suppose that after a natural calamity, a government official organises a meeting and seeks donations for chief minister's relief fund. Many people make contributions. The credit goes not to the official who organised the meeting but to the donors.

CONSEQUENCES OF HUMAN ACTIONS

Acts with Double Effects

Now, we turn to the question of the consequences which follow human actions. There are some actions which have both good and bad consequences. These are known as acts with double effects. The problem is that it is difficult to decide whether such actions are good or bad.

For resolving such questions, moralists have proposed the following general principles.

- The action which produces the double effects must be either good or indifferent.
- If it is inherently bad, it can never become good, and will continue to be bad.

- The good effect must be direct i.e. it should not happen via a bad effect.
- The intention or purpose of the act must be good.
- There must be a reason or cause upfront for performing the action.
- The good effect must be proportionately much more than the bad effect.

In acts with double effects, the main problem is to decide whether the good effect is the outcome of the bad effect. In that case, the act becomes bad. If the good effect persists when the evil effect is removed, then the good effect is not caused by the evil effect. In case of doubt, one needs to make certain that the good effect is not subordinated to the bad one. The point to note is that for a double effect to be good, the good effect should not be caused by the evil effect.

A few examples will help in explaining the principle of double effect. St. Thomas Aquinas first formulated the principle, and illustrated it with an example of self defence. X is attacked by Y. While protecting himself, X kills Y. The good effect is that X saved himself. The bad effect is that Y got killed. Aquinas regarded the act as good since X did not intend to kill Y. It happened as an unintended consequence or by-product of his self defensive action. Aquinas, however, made it clear that the force used in self defence should not be excessive, but just sufficient to serve the purpose of saving X. The currently popular term 'collateral damage' refers to actions with double effects. It takes comic form in movie car chases in which villains pursue the hero and the heroine, but in the process, drive helter skelter the people sitting in wayside cafes.

Our next example is from the Stanford encyclopaedia of philosophy.

The terror bomber aims to bring about civilian deaths in order to weaken the resolve of the enemy: when his bombs kill civilians this is a consequence that he intends. The tactical bomber aims at military targets while foreseeing that bombing such targets will cause civilian deaths. When his bombs kill civilians this is a foreseen but unintended consequence of his actions. Even if it is equally certain that the two bombers will cause the same number of civilian deaths, terror bombing is impermissible.

As we mentioned earlier, actions with double effects should produce many more beneficial than harmful effects. This is the standard traditional philosophical view.

Criticisms of the Doctrine of Double Effect

- Moral agents are responsible for all the anticipated consequences of their actions.
- If moral agents can foresee two effects of their actions, they have to take moral responsibility for both effects. They cannot evade responsibility by deciding to intend only the effect that suits them or the good effects.
- Some people (those who believe in moral objectivism) argue that intentions of individuals are irrelevant, and that morality cannot decide the rightness or wrongness of an act by looking at the intention of the person who carries it out. In their view, some acts are objectively right or wrong, and the intention of the person who carries out those acts is irrelevant.
- However, most legal systems regard the intention of a person (or mens rea in legal terminology) is a vital element in deciding his culpability and the gravity of the crime, particularly in cases of causing death.

Case Study

Michael is a surgeon in the United States. On the issue of abortion, social opinion is sharply divided in the USA. There is one group of conservative, religious and pro life activists, who regard human life from its inception as sacrosanct. They totally oppose abortion in principle. They also belong to the right wing of the political spectrum.

The other group consists of liberals of various hues including women's rights activists. They are known as pro choice, and advocate that a pregnant woman should have full freedom to undergo abortion. For them, the decision of a woman to continue or terminate her pregnancy is her individual choice and not a matter of social or religious policy.

As a prolife protagonist, Michael believed that abortion was wrong, even in order to save the mother's life. So, he refuses to perform an abortion for Martha who fears that her pregnancy might endanger her health in some ways. Since Martha had faith in Michael's skills, she decides reluctantly to go to another clinic.

After a couple of years Martha is pregnant again and this time she is diagnosed with cancer, and goes to Michael for an operation. He agrees to perform a hysterectomy on Martha although the foetus might die in the process.

Question

1. Do you think that Michael's decisions show his moral inconsistency?

Discussion

In this case, we can apply the doctrine of double effect. It makes a subtle distinction between a result which a moral agent intends, and a result which follows as a side effect of what he does. In the first situation, the result (death of foetus) is a direct consequence of his action; he intends it. In the second situation, though he may foresee the result, he does not intend it.

This principle explains why Michael later agreed to perform the operation. Had he performed abortion, he would have intended the death of the unborn baby. This would be against his moral principle of valuing life. But in carrying out the hysterectomy to treat Martha's cancer, Michael would aim to save Martha's life while merely foreseeing the death of the foetus. It would be an unfortunate side effect. Performing an abortion, by contrast, would involve intending to kill the foetus as a means of removing risks to Martha's health.

Evidently, the distinction involved is rather fine. In certain situations, as in a war of self defence, even when one foresees human losses, one does not intend it. It is an unfortunate and unavoidable side effect. But these are exceptions. By and large, one has to avoid unacceptable levels of collateral damage.

Summary

- Since the beginning of philosophical inquiry, some thinkers have expressed deeply sceptical views about Ethics raising doubts about the value of Ethics in human life or arguing that ethical studies can have no logical foundations.
- Egoism simply means that men are only concerned with their individual advantages, pleasures and welfare and do not care for others.
- Psychological egoism is not a doctrine about ethical behaviour; it is a psychological theory according to which men are so constituted that they always act in their selfish interest.
- Ethical egoism is the view that people should in fact act according to their self interest. Ethical egoists argue that people do not often pursue their self interest, but that they should in fact do so.
- Ethical egoism can be restated as the view that one should so act as to maximise his utility and minimise his disutility.
- Even while pursuing selfish ends, one has to be prudent and ensure that they do not lead to backlash from others.
- The theories of Thomas Hobbes, Mandeville and Adam Smith can be considered as examples of ethical egoism.
- Even after modifying ethical egoism into a form of enlightened (as opposed to crude) self interest, it has certain weaknesses.
- Moral relativists are those who deny the existence of universal moral principles.
- Moral objectivism claims that there are objective moral truths, that some actions are right for all people at all times and that others are wrong for all people at all times.
- Moral relativism can be stated in two forms: moral subjectivism and cultural relativism.
- According to moral subjectivism, right and wrong is a matter of personal opinion.
- Cultural relativism asserts that within a given culture there may be moral standards that are true for that culture. But there is no objective standard of morality which transcends individual cultures and which can serve as basis for evaluating individual cultures.
- In brief, determinism holds that the decisions and actions of human beings are causally determined by external forces. Men are not autonomous agents who can decide on their own. They have no free will or independent volition.
- Determinism creates a problem for morality because if human beings have no free will and if their actions are all causally determined, then they cannot be held responsible for their actions.
- Men are acting freely when there are no external constraints or internal compulsions on them. In such situations, human beings are free moral agents and are responsible for their actions.
- For moral evaluation of an action, it is divided into three parts – its object, its circumstances, and its purpose.

- Every action has an object which is its nature or essence. An action whose object is by nature is bad will always remain so. An action which is good can become bad. An action that is indifferent (neither good nor bad) can become good or bad.
- Circumstances refer to the time and place of an action, to the agent carrying out the action and to the manner of doing the act.
- Circumstances can be aggravating, extenuating and specifying. Circumstances place actions in their situational contexts.
- The end is the purpose that moral agents have in mind while performing an act or their intention in doing it.
- An indifferent act becomes good or bad depending on its purpose.
- An action that has a good object can become more or less good.
- An action which is inherently wrong may become a greater or lesser wrong depending on the purpose of the moral agent.
- Actions with both good and bad consequences are known as acts with double effects. Ii it is difficult to decide whether such actions are good or bad. Moralists have proposed general principles for deciding the question. The standard view is that actions with double effects should produce many more beneficial than harmful effects.
- But one view is that moral agents cannot be absolved from responsibility in these cases. When they foresee the two effects of their actions, they have to take moral responsibility for both effects. They cannot evade responsibility by deciding to intend only the effect that suits them or the good effects.

Questions for self assessment

1. "*Ethics seeks to clarify the logic and the adequacy of the values that shape the world; it assesses the moral possibilities which are projected and portrayed in the social give-and-take*". Elucidate the two conceptions of Ethics mentioned in the statement. Which of the two conceptions is more relevant to public servants and why?
2. Some moralists proposed self interest as the sole criterion of rightness - a view which opposes the traditional belief that altruism is the essence of morality. Argue the case for and against the position that pursuit of self interest always harms social good.
3. What is psychological egoism? How does it differ from ethical egoism?
4. What is moral subjectivism? Many artists claim that common rules of morality do not apply to them. Do you agree?
5. What is moral objectivism?
6. What is cultural relativism? What are the problems which cultural relativism presents to morality?
7. According to a common moral principle, "An action whose object is by nature is bad will always remain so". X who has been a pickpocket for ten years has a change of heart and becomes a manual worker. Will he still be considered as 'bad'?

8. Discuss the following cases which are based on the doctrine of double effects.

   Case (a): A runaway trolley is rapidly heading towards a group who has no escape route. Someone pushes a bystander into its path in order to stop it and keep it from hitting five people on the track ahead.

   Case (b): A driver diverts a runaway trolley onto a track on which one man is standing, from its normal track on which five men are standing. His intention was to save the five on the main track. What is the moral difference between the two cases?

   [**Hint**: (a) The driver foresees the death of the one as a side effect of saving the five but does not intend it. Therefore, the theory of actions with double effects justifies it. (b) But pushing a guy under a trolley is murder.]

9. Suicide is courting death and is condemned by all religions. Imagine two actions. (i) X is fed up with life and commits suicide. (ii) A soldier throws himself on a live grenade to shield his brothers-in arms from its blast knowing full well that he will perish. How will you differentiate the situations?

   [**Hint:** The soldier merely foresees his own death; by contrast, X who commits suicide intends to bring his own life to an end. This is the position from the angle of the theory of action with double effects. We can think of the example of the soldier also as a moral dilemma in which a higher military duty overrides the prohibition against taking one's life.]

REFERENCES

- John S. Mackenzie, M.A. A Manual of Ethics
- William Frankena, Ethics
- Terry l. Cooper Handbook of Administrative Ethics (A collection of 34 essays by eminent public administration theorists).
- Doug Erlandson Ethics Basics A Jargon-Free Guide for Beginners (e book).

WESTERN MORAL THINKERS

SOCRATES

A brief Historical and Philosophical Prelude

For understanding the trends of ancient Greek moral philosophy, especially the departure which Socratic doctrines represent, it is necessary to begin with Sophism. Sophists shifted the focus of ancient Greek philosophy by giving it a practical orientation. Until then, Greek philosophy was predominantly metaphysical. It is not easy to say what the term 'metaphysics' means. In ancient Greek and medieval philosophy, it designated study of three areas.

One was 'being or existence as such'. What does this expression mean? For example, a cluster of stars, an elephant or an amoeba may exist. These are three individual instances or manifestations of existence. But what is existence in general or by itself disassociated from its individual examples? This subject is nowadays called ontology.

Secondly, metaphysics studied 'first causes of things'. We see many things and observe many phenomena in the world. These are produced by secondary or tertiary causes. These differ from the original or initiating cause of the universe which set it on its cosmic course. Some philosophers identified God with the First Cause.

Unchanging, permanent things constitute the third area metaphysics studies. The natural world we observe through our senses is continuously changing or is in constant flux. It represents "becoming" in Greek terminology and not being. Being is the unchanging reality that underlies the physical, material world. Greek metaphysics found expression in works of philosophers such as Parmenides and Heraclitus.

This philosophizing was done against the background of primitive, non-experimental and non-empirical science. Consequently, the philosophers confused themselves and their followers by conjuring up all sorts of philosophical riddles about the universe. (Wittgenstein compares this type of philosopher with a fly in a bottle, going on and on, buzzing about, without finding the exit. Incidentally, modern philosophers consider some problems about universe and nature as unresolvable even with present advanced state of knowledge. As is to be expected, the early speculations on the subject could make little headway and this led to scepticism about abstract philosophical thinking.

There was another reason which altered the social perspectives of Greeks. Around this time, the contacts of Greeks with the rest of the world began and changed their outlook. Earlier, Greeks believed that their morals and ideals are not merely the conventions of their own society, but are rooted in natural order. Their morals are not subjective views of a particular society but are objective and universal. The Greek thinkers began to wonder whether various national and local ways of life, customs, religions and moral codes which their contacts with outside world revealed are conventions or naturally given. They began to doubt the earlier view that Greek culture and morals are ideal and rooted in nature. Greek morality no longer seemed ideal or unique. Morals, it seemed, are neither universal nor absolute but are relative to a given society. As we shall see, Socrates opposed this sort of moral relativism.

Further, Sophists unlike the earlier Greek philosophers, had no interest in discovering objective truth about the external world. They were professional teachers who imparted skills which youth needed for pursuing lucrative occupations. The contemporary Greek city state opened out many opportunities of political advancement to talented youth. But for this purpose, the political aspirants had to cultivate skills of clever oratory for swaying the masses. Another avenue of making money in ancient Greece was through arguing in law suits which also presupposed oratorical skills. Sophists were itinerant professors who travelled from city to city and gave instruction to young men. They taught them grammer, interpretation of poets, the philosophy of mythology and religion, etc. Their main focus was however on rhetoric or on presentation of arguments in attractive and pleasing garb. This earned them a bad name. It seemed that Sophists taught the art of making the unjust appear the just cause. They also taught, so people felt, how to win law suits by hook or crook and how best to advance one's political career.

Sophists also dabbled in moral philosophy. Sophists put man at the centre of their doctrines. Protagoras, the most renowned sophist expresses this view in the following beautiful passage: "...man is the measure of all things, of those that are, that they are, of those that are not, that they are not." This may mean that the community, society or the whole of humanity is the standard or criterion of truth. However, Protagoras regarded moral judgements or valuations as relative. "For I hold that whatever practices seem right and laudable to any particular state are so for that State, so long as it holds by them." Sophists at times pushed this line of thinking towards extreme subjectivism: "what appears to you to be true is true for you, and what appears true to me is true for me".

On the contrary, Socrates believed that moral standards and judgements are universal and objective. People use common moral standards, and will therefore make a common moral judgement in similar moral situations. Socrates refuted the moral relativism of Sophists. To this end, he sought to give stable and fixed meanings or definitions to moral terms. This is the reason why he discusses moral concepts such as truth, courage and justice at great length.

However, many modern philosophers feel that ancient moral thinkers criticized Sophists too harshly. With this background, we now proceed to discuss Socrates.

Socrates As the First Systematic Moral Thinker

Socrates is the first systematic moral thinker in Western philosophical tradition. He belonged to the Athenian republic in ancient Greece. Early on, Athens was a city State but gradually became an empire. Socrates lived in the fifth century B.C. (469-399). To understand his ideas, we need to have some historical background of his times.

Around this period, Persians and Greeks were often at war. The Greeks won a notable victory at Marathon in the first Persian war. In the victories over Persia, Sparta, a city state and rival of Athens played a major role. While the Athenian republic was a democracy, Sparta was a military oligarchy. Under Pericles, a democratically minded ruler, Athens prospered and witnessed great artistic efflorescence. The famous ancient Greek dramatists - Aeschylus, Sophocles, and Euripides – belonged to fifth century B.C. Incidentally, Aristophanes, a comic poet of this time, lampooned Socrates in the drama Clouds.

The rivalry between Athens and Sparta resulted in the outbreak of the Peloponnesian War in 431 B.C. Sparta defeated Athens in the war, and set up in Athens, an oligarchic government, known as the Thirty Tyrants. Some of these tyrants (such as Critias, their head) had been pupils of Socrates. They were overthrown within a year and democracy was restored. The political atmosphere became poisoned in the wake of war, plague, defeat and amidst widespread suspicions about conspiracies and treacheries against government.

Trial of Socrates

It was at this time that Socrates fell foul of the political rulers in Athens. He was accused of corrupting the youth and of impiety towards gods. At the end of the trial, Socrates was condemned to death. Plato, a great philosopher and disciple of Socrates, gives a poignant account of the trial in *The Apology*. It is a great Platonic dialogue. In those times, philosophers used to write their treatises in the form of dramatic dialogues among the participants.

Philosophers have gleaned the moral doctrines of Socrates mainly from various dialogues which Plato wrote. Some of the famous Platonic dialogues, besides *Apology*, are: *Republic, Phaedo*, *Protagoras*, *Meno*, and *Gorgias*. Many philosophers think that the Socrates portrayed by Plato in his dialogues may not be historical but fictional. We can bypass this question and proceed straight to a few important details of Socrates's personality and then outline his moral theories.

Socrates was a man of modest means. In his younger days, he served in the army, and acquitted himself with courage and honour. He then settled down in Athens. He spent his time in disputation, and taught philosophy to the young without charging fees. He carried on his discussions in market places and other public forums. He was high-minded and was indifferent to worldly success. He was a saintly character with a beautiful soul. Far from being an arm-chair moral thinker, Socrates practised what he preached.

His trial and death have created a halo of moral heroism around him. He has been put on the same pedestal as Jesus, Galileo, and Sir Thomas More. In his tract, *On Liberty*, Mill wrote, *"Mankind can hardly be too often reminded that there was once a man named Socrates between whom and the legal authorities of his time there took place a memorable collision."* In modern terminology, Socrates would be called 'an anti-establishment thinker'.

Moral Concerns of Socrates

The philosophic interests of Socrates, unlike those of his predecessors, were ethical rather than scientific. He turned away from cosmic speculations and brought 'Philosophy down from Heaven to Earth'. He focused on human relations of life and on the various ways in which men in their different roles interact with one another. He thought that these alone lie within the compass of knowledge, and are capable of yielding lessons for proper conduct of life. He was a practical moralist in this sense.

According to Socrates, Ethics has an end or a standard; the precepts or means of achieving the end flow from ethical theory. But he did not precisely state what it is. The Greek philosophers developed the concept of the Summum Bonum at a later time. Summum Bonum is the highest good or the ultimate good according to which values and priorities are established in an ethical system. Socrates (and Plato) referred to the final end of conduct as 'the art of dealing with human beings'; 'the art of behaving in society'; and 'the science of human happiness'.

Socrates puts moral considerations above all else. The only worthwhile pursuit for men is virtue-the noble and the praiseworthy. Doing-well consists in excelling in whatever one does. Knowledge is a prerequisite for good behaviour. He preferred the pleasures of self-improvement and of duty as opposed to indulgences, honours, and worldly advancement. In '*Apology*', he reproaches men for pursuing wealth and glory more than wisdom and virtue. The soul can be perfected by acquiring virtues. In modern terminology, for Socrates, virtue is the highest psychological good and is always to be preferred to material good. Life is not worth living if soul is destroyed, and wrong doing corrodes it.

Unjust acts signify improper behaviour towards others. To quote his examples, it is unjust to rob temples, betray friends, steal, break oaths, commit adultery, and mistreat parents. Socrates opposed wrongdoing even when his life was at stake. His friends arranged for his escape from prison so that he can evade the death penalty. Socrates declined their offer saying that it would be unjust to do so. He said that we should not act wrongly or unjustly, even when others are unjust to us. As we saw before, Socrates shows admirable moral heroism by refusing to abandon his principles and by refusing to escape death through immoral means.

Socrates holds that no one knowingly does what is bad. This view is known as moral intellectualism. It means that only knowledge is needed to make men virtuous. Socrates thinks that men desire what is virtuous or good for them. If they desire bad things or act wrongly, it is due to their ignorance. In this conception, virtue is knowledge and ensures good action. Further, virtue is sufficient for happiness. It is noteworthy that in Christian (as in Hindu) ethics, a pure heart (not necessarily knowledge) leads to virtuous action, and can be found both among the ignorant and the learned.

Common experience shows that men often crave for things which they know are bad and pursue activities which they know are harmful. They drive recklessly or take drugs. Even saints, not to speak of ordinary mortals, succumb to worldly temptations. Moral knowledge by itself is inadequate to motivate men to be virtuous or follow the right course of action in a given situation. Hence, the Socratic conception is rather simplistic. Men often err knowingly and are unable to resist temptations. This is what the saying, "the spirit is willing but the flesh is weak" means. Thus Socrates has overlooked the complexities of moral psychology.

Aristotle criticizes the moral intellectualism of Socrates or the view that virtue is a kind of knowledge. Aristotle believes that the essence of moral life consists in cultivation of good habits. The two views can in fact be reconciled. Virtue involves both knowledge and habit. Virtue is, in fact, a perspective. The virtuous man lives continuously in a moral universe or simply follows moral duty. To live continuously in a moral universe is a habit; but simultaneously, it is a form of insight. The man who lives in a different universe sees things habitually in a different way through a differently coloured glass. To be virtuous, therefore, is to possess habitually a certain kind of knowledge or insight.

Virtue is both a kind of knowledge and a kind of habit. Habit as applied to moral character, is not mere custom. It is not comparable to habits such as one's walking or speaking style. Habits of moral significance are habits of deliberate choice. As deliberate choice depends on thought or reason, in order to choose the right, we must know the right. Thus, knowledge and habit both go into virtuous conduct.

Moderate Living

Socrates advocates mild asceticism. A philosopher need not give up all ordinary pleasures, but he should not be a slave to them. He must be entirely concerned with the soul, and not with the body. "He would like, as far as he can, to get away from the body and to turn to the soul." Philosophers, Socrates continues, try to dissever the soul from communion with the body, whereas other people think that life is not worth living for a man who has "no sense of pleasure and no part in bodily pleasure."

We also find in Socrates the religious ideas which devalue body and look upon it as an impediment to spiritual progress. "*It [body] needs food and is prone to disease. It fills us full of loves, and lusts, and fears, and fancies of all kinds, and endless foolery, and in fact, as men say, takes away from us all power of thinking at all*". Mental purity means freedom from slavery to the body and its needs. Socrates also thought that body is a hindrance to the acquisition of knowledge, and that sight and hearing are inaccurate witnesses: true existence, if revealed to the soul at all, is revealed in thought, not in sense.

The link between morality and theology was tenuous in Socrates' thought. Theology consists of study of philosophical and moral doctrines of a religion. Systematic religious thinking as for example in Judaism, Christianity or Buddhism did not exist in ancient Greece. Early Christian writers referred to Greek religious ideas as paganism. However, Christian writers were greatly influenced by Plato and Aristotle. Greeks worshipped many gods. Socrates was pious and reverential towards gods. So far as the gods administered the world in a right spirit, they would show favour to the virtuous.

Socratic Method

Socrates was a reflective moralist who analysed the moral categories then emerging into contemporary discourse. Platonic dialogues are discussions of definitions of ethical terms such as temperance or moderation, friendship, courage. Socrates consistently maintains that he knows nothing, and is only wiser than others in knowing that he knows nothing. His method of discussion consisted in putting a series of questions to others, and in the process, exposing their pretensions to knowledge. This could be the reason for the hostility which he provoked. In this connection, the following incident which Bertrand Russell cites is instructive.

He would ask such questions as: "If I wanted a shoe mended, whom I should employ?" To which some ingenuous youth would answer: "A shoemaker, O Socrates." He would go on to carpenters, coppersmiths, etc., and finally ask some such question as "who should mend the Ship of State?" When he fell into conflict with the Thirty Tyrants, Critias, their chief, who knew his ways from having studied under him, forbade him to continue teaching the young, and added: "You had better be done with your shoemakers, carpenters, and coppersmiths. These must be pretty well trodden out at heel by this time, considering the circulation you have given them"

Other Aspects of Socratic Thought

We need to consider only a few more aspects of Socratic morals. In one interpretation, the trial of Socrates is seen as a conflict between State power on one side and individual liberty and freedom of speech on the other. Whatever may be the status of contemporaneous law, the question arises about whether an individual can somehow put his own sense of conscience or moral integrity even above the law.

This is a perennial question in political theory. Even today, we have many activists who try to act as self appointed conscience keepers of the nation. They are often active on issues such as Naxalism, minority rights, secularism, tribal rights and environment. They also espouse the human rights of those accused of terrorism. In these matters, the question of balancing security threats to nation and human/individual liberties becomes important.

During his trial, Socrates says, "The unexamined life is not worth living." It means that a worthy life is possible only if we continually reflect on our thinking and remove contradictions and incoherence from it. This is a typically intellectual conception perhaps inapplicable to common people. But it reflects the sublime quality of Socratic thought. We referred to an interpretation of the trial of Socrates as a conflict between State (or political) power and freedom of speech. In another interpretation, it can be seen as the result of Socrates' highly individual quest for self perfection.

We may also note that Socrates has given a new direction to the then prevalent moral values. Greek epic poets, Homer and Hesiod, set out certain exemplary models of heroic virtue and civic life. The virtues of this tradition were the virtues of a warrior culture, of war-like peoples and men at war. This conception of the citizen contained certain notions of citizen loyalty and patriotism which were created and shaped by the poetic tradition going back to Homer. Socrates has replaced the traditional view of morality. Socratic conception of citizenship emphasises the individual's own powers of independent reason, argument and judgment. The Socratic citizen is unlikely to defer to or rely on such public goods as custom, authority and tradition.

Many centuries had to pass before the emergence of the modern State and its free citizens. Moral thought also went through many turns and twists over this long period. However, if we make due allowances for modern trends and tastes, the moral reaching of Socrates still holds its ground. The rigorous analysis of moral ideas which Socrates pioneered is a procedure which modern philosophy still follows. Conceptual analysis and clarification of ideas are parts of current philosophical practice. Modern philosophers adopt a positivist approach to morals which implies that they analyse but rarely commit themselves to a given moral code.

Summary of Socrates' Philosophy

- Socrates was the first systematic moral thinker.
- He led an exemplary life spending most of his time in philosophical discussion.
- He was accused of corrupting the youth and of impiety towards gods. At the end of the trial, Socrates was condemned to death.
- His trial and death have created a halo of moral heroism around him.
- Political activists like Henry David Thoreau, Gandhi and Martin Luther King were inspired by him.
- His pupil Plato, a great philosopher, outlined many Socratic ideas in the famous dialogues: *Apology*, *Republic*, *Phaedo*, *Protagoras*, *Meno*, and *Gorgias*.
- The philosophic interests of Socrates, unlike those of his predecessors, were ethical rather than scientific. He did not speculate on the origin and nature of the universe.
- According to Socrates, the only worthwhile pursuit for men is virtue-the noble and the praiseworthy.
- Unjust acts signify improper behaviour towards others.
- Socrates holds that no one knowingly does what is bad. This view is known as moral intellectualism.
- But this runs counter to the fact that men often err knowingly and are unable to resist temptations.
- Socrates advocates mild asceticism.
- Socrates was a reflective moralist who analysed the moral categories then emerging into contemporary discourse. Platonic dialogues are discussions of definitions of ethical terms such as temperance or moderation, friendship, courage.
- Socrates says, "The unexamined life is not worth living."
- Socrates had given a new direction to the then prevalent moral values. He shifted attention from heroic virtues. His conception of citizenship emphasises the individual's own powers of independent reasoning, argument and judgment.

PLATO

Introduction

Plato, whom many regard as the greatest philosopher, had a noble lineage. He was born in 429 B.C.- the second year of the Peloponnesian war and also the year of Pericles's death. He was a student of Socrates for eight years. He loved and admired Socrates. In some of his dialogues, he portrays Socrates as the very embodiment of virtue. After the execution of Socrates, he left Athens and lived in foreign lands for ten years. During this time, he met Euclid and learnt about Pythagorean ideas of mathematical mysticism. After returning to Athens, he founded the Academy (his school) and gathered around him a group of disciples including the great philosopher Aristotle. Plato died in his eighty first year.

Plato was not only a great philosopher but also a great literary genius. His dialogues are marked by deep mysticism and dazzling literary beauty. Plato's moral doctrines are similar to those of Socrates but contain a heavy admixture of metaphysics. Further, Plato introduced a political dimension into individual morals. In his famous dialogue *Republic*, Plato implies that only citizens of an ideal State or commonwealth can be moral. Critics complain that in the writings of divine Plato (as he was called by his admirers) logical thought is often overtaken by poetic fancy and that illiberal ideas masquerade in attractive literary costume.

In this section, we will briefly outline Plato's ethical ideas covering both individual morality and political ethics. But as an indispensable preliminary, we need to mention an aspect of his metaphysics, which is known as the theory of Ideas or Forms. Plato uses this theory in his writings on nature, dialectic [logic] and morals.

Plato's Metaphysics

Ancient Greek philosophers were greatly troubled by one aspect of the physical world. The world appeared to them as a kaleidoscopic picture of continuous change or flux. It seemed to be in a state "of constant becoming and continuous change, where things appear to be purely momentary, and in an incessant transition from the immediate past through the present into the future." Related to this was another problem that perception and sensation of things vary between individuals; and that sometimes the same individual has different perceptions and sensations about the same thing. Objects and things seemed to be "wholly wanting in constancy and stability". Many ancient philosophers thought that no reliable knowledge can be had of things which are in a state of such perpetual change. Heraclitus, for example, observed that we cannot step in and out of the same river for it would have changed in the meanwhile (or between our two steps). Some philosophers like Protagoras, however, believed that perception (or the deliverances of human senses) is knowledge of the empirical world as it is.

For Plato the external world, as given in senses, is only an appearance. He uses various expressions to describe the sensible and phenomenal world such as-the many, the divisible, the becoming, and non-being. The real world according to Plato is an abstract realm of eternal and unchanging Ideas or Forms. The objects and things of the physical world are appearances or phenomena which are like images of the Forms in the world of Ideas. Plato calls the Forms as archetypes and the objects of the material world as their copies or adumbrations. Plato believes that philosophers gain knowledge of the Forms (or being) through the intellectual perceptions of the soul.

Readers may wonder how the above piece of metaphysics ties up Plato's moral philosophy. To anticipate our discussion, Plato argues that since philosophers have an insight into Forms or reality, they should be the rulers of a State, or that alternatively rulers should become philosophers.

Bertrand Russell looks from a different perspective at the problem of continuous change in nature which bothered Greek philosophers. They felt that it prevents men from gaining certain knowledge. According to Russell, the problem which puzzled the Greek philosophers relates to universals or general terms used in language. Examples of general terms are roses, tables, chairs and the like. In modern language, these terms are concepts, and the objects which fall within the definition of any concept are assigned to it. There may be any number of instances of the concept 'rose'. Some philosophers believe that there is a form or essence underlying all such instances of a concept. They are called realists. Their opponents are nominalists who argue that one need not look beyond the individual instances of 'rose'.

Idea of Good

After this brief outline of the theory of Forms, we turn to Plato's moral ideas. For Plato the good has unconditional worth and is the source of worth in various things. He gives a sublime philosophical definition of the good: "It is the ultimate ground at the same time of knowing and of being, of the perceiver and the perceived, of the subjective and the objective, of the ideal and the real, though exalted itself above such a division." Plato regarded the idea of the good and God as identical.

Plato considers the good from three sides. First, he considers the good as Idea or good in itself as mentioned above. We may use the word 'good' to describe individual men and women, or things like paintings or actions involving valour or generosity. We may find instances of good in knowledge, truth, virtue and beauty. However, good in itself or in its abstract form has to be distinguished from its individual instances. Secondly, good has an individual aspect. The previous examples we cited of examples of good fall in this category. Thirdly, good can be the quality of a collective or of a group. Plato for example considers good as an attribute of the State he portrayed in *The Republic*. We will shortly consider the constitution which Plato outlines in the *Republic*.

Any discussion of the highest good has to consider the conception of pleasure. The doctrine of hedonism proposed that pleasure is the true good. Plato rejects hedonism because pleasures are indeterminate and relative. Further, pursuit of impure pleasures often results in pain and misery. Plato, however, admits pleasure as an ingredient of the good by showing the necessary connection between virtue and true pleasure. True and enduring pleasure is found in the exercise of reason and in the possession of truth and goodness. Good life is virtuous life largely made up of intellectual studies and rational action accompanied by some, pure aesthetic pleasures. Plato's conception of pleasure is thus spiritual and intellectual.

Theory of Virtue

Plato's theory of virtue follows the Socratic doctrine. He identifies virtue with knowledge. From this it follows that virtue is teachable, and that men can learn morality just as they can learn any other subject. Morality is not an innate quality or a contingent gift of nature. Moral beings are not born but made through education.

Plato makes a fourfold division of morals, and associates them with different parts of the soul. The four virtues are wisdom or prudence, valour, temperance and justice. Plato regards the virtues as forming a complex unity-the one can be manifold, or the manifold one. This may seem like philosophical word play, but implies that virtues share common features and look similar from several perspectives. Plato accords a privileged position to justice as the overarching virtue.

Plato divides soul into three parts-rational, spirited and appetitive. Wisdom or prudence is virtue of reason, the first part of the soul. Wisdom is the directing or measuring virtue. For instance, without it, courage will become a rash impulse, and quiet endurance will degenerate into stony indifference.

Valour is the virtue of spirit, the second part of the soul. Valour preserves the rational intelligence which is often beset with anxieties in its struggle against pain and pleasure, desire and fear. The third part of the soul consists of biological appetites. It is necessary to control their propensity towards excess. Temperance regulates human passions and signifies the submission of non-rational elements to reason.

Justice refers to the harmonious functioning of the related elements of the soul - the appetitive, the spirited and the rational. Justice in Plato's sense makes an individual concentrate on his duties; it can be thought of as the sense of duty. As we shall see, in the ideal commonwealth of Plato, every citizen will perform his assigned duties without craving for the (more attractive or powerful) roles of others.

Plato's Republic

As mentioned earlier, Plato considers that individual virtue is possible only for citizens of a moral State. Plato's dialogue, *Republic*, is a vision of such an ideal political society or commonwealth; it is the earliest political utopia. Plato proposes a constitution in which philosophers will be the kings or rulers. He holds that until philosophers are made kings, or kings and princes acquire philosophical wisdom, no solutions can be found for the political ills of States. Prima facie, Plato's suggestion of handing over State power to speculative philosophers sounds strange.

Political thinkers have identified the reasons which led Plato to his vision of the ideal commonwealth. He was reacting against the troubled political conditions in Athens after its defeat in the Peloponnesian war. In modern terminology, Athens then was a failed State. The capital penalty imposed on Socrates would have exacerbated Plato's dislike for democracy which had then degenerated into mob rule. Being an aristocrat, Plato had a natural antipathy towards democracy. Most importantly, Plato was impressed by the myth of Sparta. Sparta was a military autocracy controlled by an oligarchy. Plutarch in his *Life of Lycurgus* gave a glowing, romantic and fictional account of the Spartan State and created the myth of Sparta which impressed Plato. *The Republic* contains many features of the Spartan State which Plutarch narrated.

The citizens of the Republic are to be divided into three classes: the common people, the soldiers, and the guardians. Only the guardians are to exercise political power. The legislator (or the author of the constitution) will select the first group of guardians. Afterwards, the guardians will succeed by heredity. The main problem is to ensure that guardians will follow the intentions of the legislator.

To secure this end, Plato proposes a series of political, economic, educational and other measures.

As acquisitive instincts and family ties lead to corruption, the Republic will have neither private property nor the family system. There will be community living and common eating. Women and children will be commonly shared. Children will be taken away from parents at a certain age and will be raised by the State. Weak and infirm children will be exposed to death at birth.

Plato gives extensive details about the proper type of education. Education will consist of culture and athletics (gymnastics). There will be austere training of the body. Both boys and girls will participate in physical training. Girls will also be trained in all military arts and will be conditioned to be brave. The education will inculcate gravity, decorum and courage. The education, it is evident, is a form of rigorous military training.

Plato proposes strict censorship over literature, drama and music. Even Homer who attributes immoral behaviour to Gods is to be banned. Tragic dramas with their pathos which may undermine courage and military virtue are to be banned. Cheap comedy, pantomime and buffoonery will find no place in the Republic. Plato is severe on poets too. Military music which serves to embolden soldiers and the general populace will be encouraged.

Plato doubts whether people will readily accept his proposed State. He hopes that people can be convinced through "one royal lie". It will consist in propounding and propagating the myth that God has created men of three kinds - rulers (guardians), military class and the common citizenry. If people accept the inequalities and the class system as part of a divinely ordained order, there will be no dissatisfaction or social unrest. The Republic will enjoy political stability.

Plato explains his second conception of justice after describing the three classes of the ideal common wealth. The wisdom of the State resides in the small class of guardians; the courage of the State in the auxiliaries; (soldiers) and the temperance of the State in the subordination of the governed to the governing. The justice of the State consists in that everyone attends to his business without interfering with anyone else's. The individual is just when all the parts of his soul function harmoniously with due subordination of lower parts to the higher parts. Similarly, the State is just when all its classes and their individual members perform their due functions diligently. Political injustice, on the other hand, exists in a meddlesome and restless spirit, which leads to one class interfering with the business of the other. As Bertrand Russell observes humorously, that everyone should mind his own business is an admirable dictum, but it hardly, fits into modern concept of justice based on equity, impartiality and fair play.

Criticism of Platonic Ideas

For many centuries, philosophers lavished fulsome praise on Plato's *Republic*. It was seen as an odyssey of the free intellect; a sublime expression of political ideals freed from narrow, personal interests of the individual. Although the then Athenian State was in utter moral decline, Plato seemed to have expressed its Form or its true but deeply buried moral foundations. It was recognised that the political institutions of the Republic subordinate the individual to the political society. But it was considered a necessary corrective to unchecked individual licentiousness. The volitions of the individual and requirements of State power have to be reconciled to ensure political stability.

In modern times, political thinkers have attacked Plato's ideas. They are seen as offensive to the modern democratic temper. Bertrand Russell traces the ancestry of fascism to Plato. Karl Popper includes Plato among the three great intellectual enemies of open society - the other two being Hegel and Marx. Open society, according to Popper is representative democracy with full panoply of individual freedoms. We may note the main charges which modern writers level against Plato.

In spite of Plato's fine talk, his Republic is a hereditary military oligarchy. It is essentially based not on democratic but on aristocratic principle. Political power vests with the guardians. A large section of the population - farmers, artisans and traders - will be permanently excluded from political power. This will be a permanent dispensation with no possibility of change. Plato's Republic seems to reflect his subconscious aristocratic wish that the democratic tendencies should be stifled.

It may appear that the Republic will be ruled by saintly guardians imbued with Platonic ideals. As ideals represent impersonal ethics, there may seem no great objection to rule of the enlightened philosophers. It may seem preferable to the messy democratic systems often driven by venal greed and power lust of politicians. The difficulty is that there may be no unanimity or consensus on even the most enlightened ideology. Ideology expresses the desires, hopes and the world view of a social group. There can be conflicting ideologies. The second half of the twentieth century is a tale of the conflict between Western capitalism and communism. There can be clash on morality for instance as between that of a Christian saint and of Nietzsche's superman. Ideals cannot be often disassociated from the class, status or nation of an individual. The ideology of the guardians will have no relation to popular desires or hopes; at best guardians will implement Plato's ideals.

Plato's concept of justice, unlike modern democratic theory, has no connection with equality. Justice implies that citizens accept their status as guardians, soldiers, farmers, artisans or traders, and perform their assigned roles. This conception allows inequalities of power and privilege to exist without injustice. Plato sees no injustice in the rule of hereditary guardians since they are best fitted to rule because of their knowledge and training. Plato's view on this question is misconceived. In society, certain occupations like those of doctors, lawyers, navigators and accountants, require acquisition of professional skills. But those who seek political office need no such qualification - the common denominator of citizenship is sufficient for aspiring political leaders. Plato's view in this matter rests on a false analogy.

Plato argues that the guardians possess the knowledge of moral Ideas of the abstract realm. Leaving aside the question whether such an ideal realm in fact exists, we need to note another difficulty with Plato's conception. Plato, and for a long time many philosophers, mixed up factual statements and moral judgments. Factual statements are verifiable and objective. They are about events or features of the world whose veracity can be directly or indirectly checked. For example, experimental data are statements of fact. Knowledge of the physical world largely consists of factual statements of science.

Moral judgments and theories with which Plato is concerned are distinct from facts. We will discuss the nature of moral judgments later. But it is easy to see that morals are not directly linked to an objective external reality. They are essentially about desirable human conduct and ways of living. While there can be agreement in principle about facts - X is true or false - it is not so with morals. As we have noted, people disagree about morals which ultimately depend on one's ideals, preferences and ends. In this sense, morals cannot be equated with knowledge. In modern terminology, one has to distinguish between judgments of facts and judgments of value. Agreement on facts rests on standard verification procedures. Moral agreements are matters of consensus.

We may note a few more unattractive features of Plato's Republic. It smacks of totalitarian and autocratic rule. Plato is ready to use the 'royal lie' to deceive the gullible population. He introduces censorship which is against the principle of liberty. His proposals for abolishing family system are weird. He virtually abolishes the private moral space of the individual. He experiences his activities and pleasures not as an antonomous individual but as a part of the social organism. He is submerged in the State.

As we noted earlier, Plato's views on virtue are derived from Socrates. He places them within the framework of his theory of Forms. As a result, he injects an air of mysticism into them. Plato conceives an individual's moral life as dependent on the ethical constitution of the State. Hence any discussion of Platonic virtue cannot be separated from political ethics. Plato is generally seen more as a political thinker than as a moralist. His ideal political commonwealth is an outgrowth of his disenchantment with democracy and common populace ('the great unwashed' in the words of a political philosopher) and his desire to ensure the continued existence of an aristocratic State. Notwithstanding the glittering phrases he uses, his ideal commonwealth is essentially a closed military-aristocratic oligarchy. It contains features characteristic of modern dictatorships. As such, the Platonic political temper runs counter to modern liberal political thought. However, his account of individual virtue is still an inspiring ideal.

Summary of Plato's Philosophy

- Plato's political outlook was greatly influenced by the defeat of Athens in the Peloponnesian war and the death sentence on Socrates. His views became anti- democratic.
- Plato regards the external world, as given in senses, as only an appearance.
- The real world is an abstract realm of eternal and unchanging Ideas or Forms.
- Plato calls the Forms as archetypes and the objects of the material world as their copies or adumbrations.
- For Plato the good has unconditional worth and is the source of worth in various things.
- Plato rejects hedonism because pleasures are indeterminate and relative.
- Plato makes a fourfold division of morals, and associates them with different parts of the soul. The four virtues are wisdom or prudence, valour, temperance and justice.
- Plato divides soul into three parts as rational, spirited and appetitive. He associates different virtues with each part of the soul. He injects an air of mysticism into moral discussions.
- Justice refers to the harmonious functioning of the related elements of the soul– the appetitive, the spirited and the rational.
- Plato's dialogue, *The Republic*, is a vision of an ideal political society or commonwealth; it is the earliest political utopia.
- Plato proposes a constitution in which philosophers will be the kings or rulers.
- Plutarch in his *Life of Lycurgus* gave a glowing, romantic and fictional account of the Spartan State and created the myth of Sparta which impressed Plato. Sparta was a military dictatorship.
- The citizens of the Republic are to be divided into three classes: the common people, the soldiers, and the guardians. Only the guardians are to exercise political power.
- The Republic will have neither private property nor family system.
- Guardians will be hereditary and will be educated with rigid discipline for instilling in them military skills and culture.

- Plato proposes strict censorship of literature, drama and music.
- His republic is a hereditary military oligarchy. It smacks of totalitarian and autocratic rule. In it, the individual will be submerged in the State.
- In modern times, political thinkers have attacked Plato's ideas. They are seen as offensive to the modern democratic temper. Bertrand Russell traces the ancestry of fascism to Plato. Karl Popper includes Plato among the three great intellectual enemies of open society - the other two being Hegel and Marx.
- The ideology of the guardians will have no relation to popular desires or hopes; at best guardians will implement Plato's ideals.
- The individual is submerged in the State.

ARISTOTLE

Biographical Sketch

Socrates, Plato and Aristotle are the triumvirate of great ancient Greek philosophers. Aristotle was born in 384 B.C. at Stagirus, a Grecian colony in Thrace. Nichomachus, his father, was the court physician of the Macedonian king. Aristotle lost his parents early in life. He then went to Athens and studied under Plato for twenty years. In the Academy, Aristotle showed an indefatigable zeal for learning. After Plato's death in 347 B.C., Aristotle left Athens. He stayed in the royal court at Atarneus for three years. When its king was killed by Persians, he went to Mytilene and lived there for many years. From there he went to Macedonia at the invitation of King Philip to tutor his son, the famous Alexander, who was then thirteen years old. He supervised Alexander's studies for five years. He then returned to Athens and founded his own school of philosophy at a place called Lyceum.

Approach

In his philosophical temper, Aristotle differed sharply from Plato. Plato, the founder of philosophical idealism, soared high above the world of sense and mundane human affairs. In contrast, Aristotle is a down to earth practical thinker, who placed morals within the frame of ordinary human life. Aristotle sticks to the factual and the concrete, and stays within the bounds of actual human experience. Aristotle criticized many Platonic theories, and was even accused of being ungrateful to his teacher. However, Aristotle's criticism was free from personal rancour. He called himself a friend of Plato, but a greater friend of truth.

In his famous treatise, *Nicomachean Ethics*, Aristotle mainly discuses two aspects of Ethics-happiness and virtues. We outline his ideas on these themes. Two interesting points however may be mentioned here. For Aristotle, happiness and virtue go together. The idea that a virtuous man should lead miserable life somehow does not appeal to Aristotle. In later philosophy, the fact that the paths of happiness and virtue may diverge is clearly recognised. Secondly, Aristotle does not discusss the idea of duty which later assumes great importance in Ethics. Discussion of virtues is his abiding contribution to Ethics.

Summum Bonum

In his ethics, Aristotle discusses the *summum bonum* which is the final end towards which human activity is directed. Every human act has an end or aim. But many ends are means to other ends or ways of achieving the other ends. But finally, we reach an end which is ultimate and does not serve as a means to any other end. This is *summum bonum.*

Thus X may want to become a trader. Accordingly, he may buy a store in a mall. He may fill the store with wares he wants to sell for profit. He will do many things for the success of his business. If his business prospers, he will become rich. Riches will enable him to satisfy his material wants. And this satisfaction will make him happy. We can arrange X's actions in a series.

Buy store → stock it with wares → sell the wares → make profit → amass money → buy things → Satisfy material wants → feel happy.

In this simple example, the final end of all of X's actions is happiness (as he conceives it), and is the summum bonum. In this example, happiness completes the series. We can symbolize actions here as A_x and their ends as E_x. Then we have, A_1– E_1, A_2– E_2, A_3– E_3 and A_4– E_4. In this series, the end of action at one stage becomes the means for achieving the goal at the next stage. Thus E_1 becomes A_2; E_2 becomes A_3; and E_3 becomes A_4. We can think of the series of actions as comprising intermediate ends and a final end.

His Concept of Happiness

This is only the beginning of the story. People attach different meanings to 'happiness'. For instance, instead of spending money on material means of pleasure, X may donate to charities or go on pilgrimages. These actions will also make him happy. As the meaning or connotation of happiness may differ for different individuals, the concept of happiness has to be defined.

Aristotle defines happiness with the help of his philosophical principles. For Aristotle, every being in nature has its proper end, and its achievement is the special function of that being. The adequate performance of the special function is the good for any being. Sensation is the special function of animals, and hence sensual pleasures cannot be the good for man. Reason is the special function of human beings. Therefore, summum bonum or ultimate good for men is to be found in the life of reason.

Aristotle, however, does not wholly exclude what many would regard as sources of happiness. Aristotle believes that higher beings in nature possess the faculties of lower beings. Although man is a creature of reason, he still has the appetites of plants and the sensations of animals. As these are built into human nature, Aristotle divides virtues into two categories, as intellectual and ethical.

His Concept of Virtues

Moral virtues, for Aristotle, are to be distinguished from intellectual virtures. Moral virture has to do with feeling, choosing and acting well. Intellectual virtue is identified as a kind of wisdom acquired from teachers. It has to do with contemplation of the natural world, metaphysics and learning subjects like mathematics and logic.

The highest virtues belong to the life of reason or intellect. Philosophical contemplation forms part of this life. Aristotle designates these intellectual virtues as dianoetic. Ethical virtues consist in the subordination of human passions and appetites to reason. Intellectual virtues rank higher than ethical virtues because they are allied to man's special function as a rational creature. Another reason for their superiority is that thinking man resembles God whose life is one of pure thought. Intellectual and ethical virtues together constitute happiness. These are the absolute values for humanity.

Being a practical thinker, Aristotle recognises that even a virtuous man cannot be happy if circumstances conspire against him. Poverty, sickness and misfortune will make even a virtuous man miserable. Riches, friendships, health and good fortune, though not the same as happiness, contribute to it. To this extent, Aristotle acknowledges that the outward conditions of one's life can influence happiness.

Ethical Virtues

As between intellectual and ethical virtues, Aristotle discusses the latter at length. As we saw, ethical virtues consist in control of emotions by reason. Aristotle opposes the Socratic view that knowledge of morals is sufficient to make a man virtuous. Socrates overlooks the fact that it is hard to control human passions. A man may reason correctly and discover the correct moral course. However, he may be overwhelmed by his emotions and take the unethical route. The saying, "The spirit is willing, but the flesh is weak" sums up this situation.

How then to bring the wayward passions under the control of reason? According to Aristotle, the unruly human passions can be disciplined only by constant exercise of self control. With constant practice, virtuous conduct becomes a habit. Habit is of great importance in morality. It is by steadfast pursuit of morality that man becomes moral. "Virtue renders virtue easy".

We may now consider the reason why Aristotle rejects the ascetic ideal. The ascetic wants to completely eliminate appetites and passions from human heart. But it is not possible since they are essential attributes of human nature. As we noted earlier, higher forms of being include the faculties of lower forms of being. Virtue presupposes the operations of both reason and passions. If reason is to control passions, they have to be present. Aristotle regards passions as the matter of virtue and reason as its form. If passions, as ascetics propose, are extirpated, virtue will become an empty shell or a concept without content.

Golden Mean and Common Virtues

Aristotle's views on asceticism reflect his tendency to avoid extreme positions. In fact, virtue according to him implies moderation. Aristotle's celebrated doctrine of virtue defines it as the mean between two extremes. Every virtue lies in between two vices. For example, courage is a virtue which lies between the two extremes of cowardice and foolhardiness. Aristotle uses the terms 'defect' and 'excess' to describe the extremes or vices within which each virtue lies. But we can ignore these terms. We need to consider only the examples which Aristotle gives. While there are innumerable virtues, Aristotle mentions certain popularly recognised types of good action common in human life.

We tabulate some common virtues and their extremes in the following table:

Virtue	Extreme (1)	Extreme (2)
Courage	Cowardice	Rashness
Munificence (generosity)	Pettiness	Vulgar profusion
Good temper	Spiritlessness	Irascibility
Politeness	Rudeness	Obsequiousness
Modesty	Shamelessness	Bashfulness
Temperance	Insensibility	Intemperance
Liberality	Meanness	Prodigality
Proper pride	Humility	Vanity
Ready wit	Buffoonery	Boorishness

Some virtues, we can see, do not fit into this scheme. Wisdom, truthfulness and impartiality are among these.

Aristotle gives no criterion or rule for determining the correct mean which constitutes the virtue. The choice of mean is not like bisecting a straight line or calculating the average of two numbers. The choice depends on the individual and the circumstances of any particular case. It results from the good judgment of the individual or on his good sense and tact. Aristotle means that the mean varies from individual to individual depending on circumstances. For example, in acts of charity, the mean will be higher for a rich man than an ordinary man. Even an ordinary householder has to help his parents in need. In short, Aristotle believes that general rules cannot cover the wide range of possible situations of life.

Aristotle's Magnanimous Individual

We may briefly note the type of individual whom Aristotle calls as 'high-souled' or 'magnanimous' or 'proud'. He is a person who embodies the virtues of nobility. He is seen as good in the highest degree. He will be great in virtues such as valour, generosity, loyalty and dignity. The magnanimous morality may be impossible without nobility and goodness of character. The magnanimous man will be mainly concerned with maintaining his honour and dignity. Aristotle's portrait is evidently that of aristocratic virtue. Popular admiration for aristocratic and heroic virtues has declined with the growth of democratic sentiment. Bertrand Russell observes that virtues of the magnanimous man largely depend upon his having an exceptional social position. Hence, in the modern mind, these virtues of nobility get associated with hereditary privilege and inequality.

His Concept of Justice

For Aristotle, justice is a virtue of the State and not of the individual. He mentions two types of justice: distributive and corrective. His concept of distributive justice should not be understood in the modern egalitarian sense. Distributive justice in its modern sense seeks to reduce extreme inequalities in wealth and income. It may include provision for meeting the minimum needs of the poor. However, in Aristotle's thinking, distributive justice refers to rewarding people according to merit. Honours and rewards have to be assigned based on the worth of individuals. Those who are more meritorious will get higher rewards. Aristotle's view can be seen as an advice to rulers that they should reward meritorious individuals rather than psychophants and time servers.

Corrective justice has to do with inflicting punishment for wrong doing. Anyone who gains undue profit by unfair means should be made to suffer corresponding loss through a fine or penalty. Justice consists of general principles which cannot cover all the possible situations (cases) which arise in social life. Equity consists in adapting general rules to special circumstances.

His Concept of Freedom of Will

Aristotle upholds the freedom of human will. He criticizes Socrates for rejecting freedom of will. Socratic doctrine of knowledge as virtue implies that people who know what is right will necessarily follow it. Hence right action is the outcome, not of voluntary choice but compulsion. Aristotle argues that freedom of human will implies that men can choose between good and evil. The correct moral choices follow from the exercise of reason. Human choices are voluntary, except in situations such as when a robber compels at gun point a bank manager to open the cash chest. In Socratic conception virtuous actions appear as involuntary - necessarily flowing from knowledge. However, the question of human freedom of will has become enmeshed in many philosophical controversies. Freedom versus predestination is one such controversy. The question has acquired new dimensions with advances in physical science, neuroscience, sociology and psychology. We need not pursue this matter, but may note that virtuous action presupposes some freedom of choice.

Politics and State According to Aristotle

Aristotle believes that Politics (political science) is a division of Ethics. Politics is the ethics of the State. An individual's morality finds its end in the State, and is not possible without State. Welfare of citizens is the objective of the State, and people can be happy and virtuous only in a State. Man is a political animal. The State educates men in (civic) virtues and provides opportunities for exercising virtues.

Discussing the origin of the State, Aristotle notes that historically the family arose first and that it was followed by village communities and finally by the State. It is necessary to remember that the Greek idea of State did not extend beyond the city. Aristotle holds that the historical origin of State is not relevant for understanding the nature of the State.

The State is an organism with a life and reality of its own. The State is not a mechanical aggregation of individuals like a heap of stones. The individuals who are parts of the State are also organisms. The State has a purpose of its own. The individuals also have their ends. But the individual ends are included in the end of the State. To put it differently, in the State both the whole and the parts are real; the whole has its end, life and rights; similarly, each part has its life, end and rights.

Aristotle rejects both the collectivist and individualist conceptions of the State. The individualist view of State rejects the reality of the whole along with its ends. Only the individuals composing the State have ends and are real. The State exists as an external entity for the individual for ensuring his life, property and social amenities. Only individual life and purpose count. This became known as the Social Contract Theory later with the State seen as the outcome of a contract between individuals in search of security. Modern individualism is also based on similar views.

While individualist view denies the reality of the whole, Plato denies the reality of the individual. The Platonic State is omnipotent, and its individual citizen is obliterated by its might. As we saw, Plato proposes a community of wives and rearing of children in State nurseries from the first year of their birth. Aristotle holds that the family, as an individual unit and organism in its own right within the State, has absolute rights and cannot be obliterated. Plato considers the State as a homogenous entity, and denies the rights of its individual parts. As in other aspects of morality, Aristotle takes a more balanced view of State giving due importance both to government and citizens. His views on the relations between the state and the individual largely correspond to modern trends in spirit though not in their phraseology. Aristotle then proceeds to discuss different constitutions or State systems like monarchy, aristocracy and democracy. However, we need not pursue these matters which concern politics rather than ethics.

Criticism of Aristotle's Views

Various points of criticism have been urged against Aristotelian ethics. Many of these points are based on modern perspectives. The Aristotelian State confines its benefits and privileges to a chosen few. Democratic thinkers hold that so far as the state is concerned, the goods are power and property. Democratic sentiment demands that power and property should be widely shared in any society. It seems that for Aristotle what is best is essentially only for the few magnanimous men and philosophers. The bulk of the population is turned into means for the production of a few rulers and sages. Kant, a great philosopher whom we will discuss later, maintained that every human being is an end in himself, and this is also the view of democratic theory. As we shall see, in the Utilitarian theory, the prescribed end of action is maximizing of pleasure, irrespective of who its recipients may be. But the ancient Greek thinkers had a different conception of 'justice'. For them, each thing or person had its or his proper sphere, to overstep which is 'unjust'. Some men, in virtue of their character and aptitude, have a wider sphere than others, and there is no injustice if they enjoy a greater share of happiness.

In Aristotle's thought, there are other instances of acceptance of inequality which is repugnant to much modern sentiment. For example, Aristotle accepts slavery; he takes it for granted that husbands are superior to wives and fathers to children. These views are anathema to modern youth and feminists.

As noted before, Aristotle held that virtue lies in shunning extreme emotions, acts, thouths and ideas. He was also a down to earth thinker who wrote in an academic style. As a result, his writing and ideas are rather placid. He went along with the prevailing political and social mores of his time. All these injected an air of conservatism into his writings.

Many thinkers on the other hand want to bring about revolutionary changes in the world. Their writings are full of sound and fury. Many modern novelists have shown with great dramatic intensity the play of violent feelings and emotions in human life. They depict relations for example, between men and women with great passion with all attendant pleasures, pains and perils. Compared to such writing, Aristotle's works both in their content and style seem tepid, rather like a weak cup of tea.

Bertrand Russell accuses Aristotle of conventionality and smugness or what could be called petty bourgeoisie morality. To quote Russell:

More generally, there is an emotional poverty in the Ethics, which is not found in the earlier philosophers. There is something unduly smug and comfortable about Aristotle's speculations on human affairs; everything that makes men feel a passionate interest in each other seems to be forgotten. Even his account of friendship is tepid. … all the more profound aspects of the moral life are apparently unknown to him. He leaves out, one may say, the whole sphere of human experience with which religion is concerned. What he has to say is what will be useful to comfortable men of weak passions; but he has nothing to say to those who are possessed by a god or a devil, or whom outward misfortune drives to despair.

Russell's observations while interesting hardly do justice to Aristotle. We should not expect to find characters from Dostoevsky, Albert Camus or Emile Bronte in *Nicomachean Ethics*. The novelists we mentioned depict characters who find themselves in situations of great trouble, stress and anguish, and who also tend to go breserk in their responses and reactions. Many of them are rebels on the fringes of society. Neither such situations nor characters usually figure in morals of common life or in administrative situations. In fact, the coolness, composure and balance found in Aristotle can be a model even for modern day civil servants.

Summary of Aristotelian' Philosophy

- Aristotle is a systematic academic philosopher. His approach, unlike that of Plato, is down to earth and commonsensical.
- He wrote the treatise *Nicomachean Ethics*.
- He propounded the concept of Summum bonum or the ultimate objective which men seek. He identified it with refined intellectual pleasures and philosophical contemplation.
- Aristotle, however, does not wholly exclude what many would regard as common sources of happiness like friendship, family bonds and creature comforts.
- Aristotle makes a distinction between intellectual and ethical virtues.
- The highest virtues belong to the life of reason or intellect.
- Ethical virtues consist in the subordination of human passions and appetites to reason.
- Aristotle regards passions as the matter of virtue and reason as its form. If passions, as ascetics propose, are extirpated, virtue will become an empty shell or a concept without content.
- Aristotle opposes the Socratic view that knowledge of morals is sufficient to make a man virtuous.
- According to Aristotle, the unruly human passions can be disciplined only by constant exercise of self-control.
- Aristotle's celebrated doctrine of virtue defines it as the mean between two extremes. Every virtue lies in between two vices.
- The choice of mean is not like bisecting a straight line or calculating the average of two numbers. The choice depends on the individual and the circumstances of any particular case. It results from the good judgment of the individual or from his good sense and tact.
- He mentions two types of justice: distributive and corrective.

- Distributive justice refers to rewarding people according to merit.
- Corrective justice has to do with inflicting punishment for wrong doing.
- Aristotle upholds the freedom of human will.
- The correct moral choices follow from the exercise of reason.
- Politics is the ethics of the State. An individual's morality finds its end in the State, and is not possible without State.
- Aristotle rejects both the collectivist and individualist conceptions of the State.
- Criticisms of Aristotle:
- (i) The Aristotelian State confines its benefits and privileges to a chosen few. (ii) In Aristotle's thought, there are other instances of acceptance of inequality which is repugnant to much modern sentiment. (iii) Aristotle's ethics are marked by conventionality and smugness.

POST ARISTOTELIAN PHILOSOPHERS

Background

After Aristotle, ancient Greek philosophy lost its originality and vigour, and entered a phase of decay. Political, social and moral environment no longer sustained the creative impulses in philosophical thought. Greek city States with the exception of Sparta came under the rule of Macedonia. They never recovered their former independence. Greece later became a province of Rome. In any case, the 'delicate and beautiful' Greek civilization had lost its internal moral and social vitality.

In this period, philosophy is mainly concerned with helping the individual in escaping from the travails of life. It revolves around man in his personal capacity – around his destiny and spiritual welfare. Philosophy becomes a source of consolation for the troubled mind, a safe mooring for men escaping from the storms of life.

Their Approach

Because of their exclusive interest in the individual subject, philosophers became obsessed with ethical questions. Earlier, philosophers like Xenophanes and Anaxagoras made bold speculations about the origins and nature of the universe. But philosophers who followed Aristotle showed little interest in cosmogony. This approach narrowed their thought. For no individual who worries too much about himself and who is unable to lose himself in reflections about universe or in larger causes can produce original ideas. Thus the later Greek thinkers could not produce anything comparable to the all-embracing, great metaphysical systems of Plato and Aristotle.

The post-Aristotelian philosophers subordinated other branches of knowledge such as physics, metaphysics and logic to ethics. These areas merely provided the premises for their moral arguments, and held no intrinsic interest to them. They advocated, as we shall see, extreme and one-sided moral doctrines. Even in the central branch of philosophy or theory of knowledge, they introduced subjectivity. Truth was no longer considered objective and independent of one's personal desires or aspirations. Truth became an expression of personal opinion: nothing is true or moral in itself but opinion makes it so. In a similar vein, a group of philosophers known as sceptics denied the possibility of acquiring knowledge. This is another instance of one-sided philosophy. For it is one thing to recognise the difficulty of acquiring knowledge. But it is a totally different thing to deny the possibility of any knowledge. The irrationality of philosophical thought of this period is also illustrated in Neo-Platonism, "with its fantastic paraphernalia of sorcery, demons and demi-gods." In what follows, we shall outline the two famous Post-Aristotelian philosophies, namely Epicureanism and Stoicism.

EPICUREANISM

Epicureanism and stoicism were the two great schools of moral philosophy that followed Aristotelian philosophy. They were founded almost at the same time. Epicureanism derives its name from its founder Epicurus (342 - 270/71B.C.) Although the school of Epicurus survived for six centuries, his followers made no significant changes in his doctrines. Lucretius, the famous ancient Roman poet, expressed Epicureanism in verse form in *De Natura*.

Obstacles to Happiness

Epicurus regarded pursuit of happiness as the chief aim of life. We shall presently discuss his concept of happiness. Epicurus first traces the sources of human unhappiness. For a modern mind, it would appear that unhappiness arises from lack of means needed to satisfy material wants. Thus a man without a house, TV, refrigerator and car is likely to be unhappy. Realistically speaking, men in any historical period will crave for the material comforts and amenities then available. Along with material comforts men need family ties, friendships and spiritual consolations.

Epicurus, however, identifies popular religion as the chief obstacle to human happiness. For it haunts human mind with fears of gods, death, retribution and hell. Consequently, men live in a constant psychological state of trepidation and anxiety. To rid men of these fears, Epicurus proposes a materialist philosophy which depicts the cosmos as a mechanical system governed by natural causes and not by gods or any corporeal beings. Unlike Stoics, he endows men with free will, which they can exercise in pursuing happiness during their brief terrestrial existence.

Epicurus borrows his philosophy from Democritus. Democritus also formulated the ancient form of atomic theory. Epicurus applies this theory to human soul. He regards human soul, as everything else in the universe, to be composed of atoms. The atoms in the soul are scattered at death with no possibility of future life. This doctrine enables Epicurus to dispense with both joys of paradise and terrors of hell.

Epicurus describes death as a blessing, a release from the travails of life on earth. Men need not fear death. "For if death is, we are not; if we are, death is not." Death is the end of all feeling and consciousness. Hence, there is no need to fear a future state of which we will have no feeling when it comes.

Epicurus then proceeds to remove fears of divine intervention in human affairs. Ancient Greeks believed that gods punish men for their sins or pride (hubris). If a man achieves great success and feels proud, gods may suddenly bring him crashing down. Epicurus could have addressed these fears by advocating atheism or by denying the existence of God. But he accepts the existence of gods. He pictures gods as leading an immortal, serene and blessed life in the outer space. They live in a state of beatific joy, and never concern themselves with human affairs.

Happiness

As we noted earlier, the Epicurean doctrine advocates that men should pursue happiness. In this view, they followed the earlier school of Cyrenaics. Whereas Cyrenaics regarded happiness as pursuit of gross pleasures, Epicureans adopted a pure and noble conception of happiness. In this sense, happiness is an end by itself, and it is the only good. Pain is the only evil. For Epicureans, morality becomes an activity which gives pleasure. Virtue has no intrinsic value; it derives value from the pleasure which accompanies virtuous actions. These ideas in sum constitute the Epicurean ethical system.

A good part of Epicureanism consists in elaborating or clarifying the various aspects of happiness. Happiness does not mean momentary physical or mental pleasure. Happiness is joy which lasts for the whole life. Men should avoid momentary pleasures which may often lead to greater pains later. They should not be slaves to particular pleasures and desires. They have to master their passions. They need to abandon present pleasures which lead to future pain, and be ready to undergo present pain for sake of future joy.

There is also a streak of prudence in Epicureanism. Bertrand Russell says:

It was a valetudinarian's [or a sick man's] philosophy, designed to suit a world in which adventurous happiness had become scarcely possible. Eat little, for fear of indigestion; drink little, for fear of next morning; eschew politics and love and all violently passionate activities; do not give hostages to fortune by marrying and having children; in your mental life, teach yourself to contemplate pleasures rather than pains.

Epicureanism distinguishes between physical and mental pleasures. Mental pleasures are superior to physical pleasures. Body feels physical pleasures only during their duration. Physical pleasures are ephemeral. Mental pleasures arise from remembrance. Recollection of past joy is a present delight and anticipation of future pain is a present anxiety. Therefore, to be happy, one has to cultivate mental serenity.

Cultivating Serenity

Men should condition their minds to rise above physical pain and adversity. They should not rely on external conditions for their happiness. They should find joy in their own hearts. Rather extravagantly, Epicureans claim that a man on rack (a medieval instrument of torture) can be happy. If we leave out the hyperbole, we can see in the Epicurean idea, a conception of happiness as an inner mental state. Its link with outward circumstances is slender. While regarding happiness as spiritual, Epicureans recognised the innocent pleasures of senses. They particularly valued friendship.

The Epicurean conception of happiness is often called negative. Happiness is neither active joy nor tingling excitement. Epicureanism sought rather an absence of pain, mental serenity and calm spirit untroubled by fears and anxieties. "Absence of pain is in itself pleasure, indeed in the ultimate analysis the truest pleasure." Active joy is beyond human reach; man should avoid pain and lead quiet and contented life.

Epicureans cautioned against multiplying one's wants. Increasing wants are hard to satisfy and intensify one's unhappiness. One should, therefore, lead a simple life. Epicurus reputedly lived most of the time on bread and water. The route to happiness lies through moderation, simplicity and cheerfulness.

Epicureans did not preach exalted or noble morality. However, they were kind and benevolent. They said that it is better to extend than to receive kindness. Their morality is soft without stern calls to duty or harsh ethical commands. It is gentle and amiable.

Evaluation of Epicureanism

Epicureanism arose at a time when the Greek world was in decline. People had lost faith in their society and its institutions. They were insecure and had no assured means of living. They lived in constant danger of violence from invaders or from local tyrants. Active public service in politics, government and army became nearly impossible. In the environment of uncertainty, people withdrew into their private, personal life. Epicureanism is a recipe for individual happiness in a troubled world.

Epicureanism is hardly a philosophy suited to energetic, dynamic and self-confident societies or individuals. It advises men to seek peace and quiet, and to detach themselves from the problems of the world. It urges men to be prudent even in pursuing happiness. Essentially it encourages men to avoid the troubles and travails of life. It hinders an active political, economic and social life. It discourages men from optimistically planning for the future welfare of their family and society.

But no man can improve himself or others without necessary effort and commitment. In the process, he will often encounter problems and troubles. However, these hurdles have to be crossed. Fortunately, men are by nature hopeful; hope springs eternal in human heart. Epicureanism was a creed which appealed to a small group of philosophers and men of letters. It did not percolate to the masses. Historically Epicureanism was overtaken by Roman ideals of duty and heroic virtue. Further, Christianity preached the ethic of strenuous work and gave hope of posthumous redemption to men.

Summary of Epicurean Philosophy

- After Aristotle, ancient Greek philosophy lost its originality and vigour.
- In this period, philosophy is mainly concerned with helping the individual in escaping from the travails of life.
- Philosophers became obsessed with ethical questions. This approach narrowed their thought.
- The post-Aristotelian philosophers subordinated other branches of knowledge such as physics, metaphysics and logic to ethics.
- Epicureanism and stoicism were the two great schools of moral philosophy that followed Aristotelian philosophy.
- Epicurus regarded pursuit of happiness as the chief aim of life.
- Epicurus identifies popular religion and superstitions as the chief obstacles to human happiness.
- Democritus's materialist doctrine of atoms enables Epicurus to dispense with both joys of paradise and terrors of hell.
- He pictures gods as leading an immortal, serene and blessed life in the outer space. They live in a state of beatific joy, and never concern themselves with human affairs. Men need not fear gods.

- Epicureans adopted a pure and noble conception of happiness. In this sense, happiness is an end by itself, and it is the only good. Pain is the only evil.
- Mental pleasures are superior to physical pleasures.
- Men should condition their minds to rise above physical pain and adversity.
- Epicureanism sought absence of pain, mental serenity and calm spirit untroubled by fears and anxieties. Epicureanism is a recipe for individual happiness in a troubled world.
- Epicureanism is hardly a philosophy suited to energetic, dynamic and self-confident societies or individuals.
- Epicureanism was overtaken by Roman ideals of duty and heroic virtue. Further, Christianity preached the ethic of strenuous work and gave hope of posthumous redemption to men.

STOICISM

Founders

Zeno (342-270 B.C.) was the founder of the Stoic School. He was followed by Cleanthes and Chrysippus. Stoicism flourished for many years not only in Greece but also in Rome. The famous Roman Stoics were Marcus Aurelius, Seneca and Epictetus. We need only, however, discuss the central ideas of Stoicism to which all Stoic thinkers subscribed.

Philosophical Underpinnings

Stoicism rejected the idealism of Plato. According to stoicism, knowledge consists of the sense impressions which get imprinted in the mind. Mental activity is solely limited to these materials received from senses. This is in opposition to the Platonic view that mind is the source of knowledge and that senses are sources of error and illusion. Stoics denied the reality of the Platonic Forms or concepts. Concepts are simply ideas in the mind which are formed by noting the common features shared by particular objects like chairs, tables or bricks. Concepts have no existence outside human mind.

Knowledge refers to objects which senses perceive and convey as impressions to mind. Truth means the correspondence of sense impressions to objects. How can one be sure that sensory images are faithful copies of objects? The Stoic answer to this question is that objects which are real, produce an intense feeling in the mind. This creates a conviction of truth in the perceiver's mind. Thus truth becomes a subjective concept linked to one's feeling. Truth cannot in any case lie in concepts which are mental creations.

Stoics combined their faith in knowledge as derived from senses with materialism. They denied the existence of non-material entities. Plato located knowledge in thought and reality in Forms. Stoics place knowledge in (to use a modern phrase) what sense data reveal or in material realm. They regard human soul and God as material. Without getting into arcane philosophical discussion, we may simply note that Stoics reasoned that the universe is a unity and cannot, according to Stoics, consist of two distinct principles-one material and the other non material or spiritual. They felt that no interactions can occur between entities governed by such disparate principles.

In spite of their materialism, Stoics regarded God as absolute reason governing the universe. Two conclusions follow from this view. One is that the world has a purpose, and is marked by order, harmony, beauty and design. It implies that world is governed by strict necessity of cause and effect. The second conclusion is that freedom of will cannot exist in a world governed by necessity. Men imagine that they generally act voluntarily. But this is only their manner of speaking and does not mean the absence of necessity.

Reason as a Stoic Ethic

The Stoic ethic is built around two premises. One is that the universe is governed by absolute laws without any exceptions. The other is that reason is the essential attribute of man. The Stoic exhortation that 'one should live according to nature' sums up the two premises. This exhortation means that men should live according to nature and their reason.

The idea that men should follow the laws of nature may not amount to much. The belief that nature reveals or sanctions certain morals hardly seems credible to modern men. Belief in nature as a source of human laws or morals has virtually disappeared. Further, men can do little or nothing about the operation of natural laws like those of gravitation or conservation of mass.

The second idea that reason should govern conduct is readily intelligible. Stoics define virtue as the life according to reason. Morality consists in rational action. Men should follow not their inclinations or caprices but their reason. The wise man subordinates his life to the life of the whole universe of which he is an infinitesimally small part.

The idea that individual morality ought to be grounded in reason is not new. It is found in both Plato and Aristotle. But in many ways, Stoics have pushed this point to absurd lengths and reached odd conclusions. Although Aristotle regarded reason as the guide to human conduct, he recognised passions and appetites as embedded in human nature. He, therefore, proposed that emotions should be brought under the control of reason. He did not prescribe that they should be eliminated. In contrast, Stoics recommend extremely rigorous asceticism which runs counter to ordinary human nature.

Stoics and Emotions

Similarly, although Aristotle recognised that virtue alone has intrinsic value, he allowed some space for external circumstances and comforts in the good life. But Stoics are quite unrelenting in their attitude. In their doctrine, virtue alone is good, only vice is evil, and all else is a matter of absolute indifference. This approach means that poverty, ill health, suffering and death are not evils. Wealth, sound health, joy and life are not goods. Pleasure is not a good, and needs to be shunned. The sole happiness is virtue. But virtue has to be practised not as a means to happiness but as a duty. Stoics did not regard suicide as a vice since life has no value.

As virtue is based on pure reason which is knowledge, sciences have only an instrumental value as foundations of morality. Here we may recall the use to which Epicureans put a scientific doctrine such as atomism i.e. mainly to remove men's fears about life after death. The chief virtue from which other virtues arise is wisdom. The expressions 'wise man' and 'good man' are synonyms. The four cardinal virtues - bravery, insight, self control and justice - originate from wisdom. Any wise man will ipso facto have these virtues. Here, we need to note another strange view of stoicism. The wise man possesses all virtues, and a fool has no virtue at all. The society is divided into the wise who are absolutely virtuous and the unwise who are totally sinful. We would now call this a black or white view which ignores the shades of grey - as prevalent in morals as elsewhere in human life. The wise man becomes the embodiment of perfection. He can fit into any ideal type - such as a king, prophet, scholar or general.

As is to be expected, the stoics were compelled to dilute their extreme views in some ways. Since extirpation of passions (besides being impossible) will lead to total inactivity, they permitted mild and rational emotions. Among the things classified as matters of indifference, they allowed for some choice. Thus a wise man may prefer health to sickness. Finally, instead of branding every one as either good or bad, they conceded that heroes and statesman of history are touched by evil in a lesser degree than common men.

There is one aspect in which Stoics were far in advance of their times - that is in their cosmopolitanism. They based this conviction on two grounds. The world is one and is ruled by one God. The other ground is that men essentially share the same nature in being rational. As an eminent scholar observes "...there is something grand and noble about their zeal for duty, their exaltation above all that is petty and paltry, their uncompromising contempt for all lower ends". According to Schwegler, their merit was that "in an age of ruin they held fast to the moral idea".

The Stoic Message

The Stoic message[is] that what is important is the pursuit of wisdom and virtue, a quest that is open to all human beings because of their common capacity for reason, no matter what the external circumstances of their lives.

Today, the most common meaning of the word stoic is a person who remains unmoved by the sorrows and afflictions that distress the rest of humanity. ... Plato held that human passions and physical desires are in need of regulation by reason. The Stoics went farther: they rejected passions altogether as a basis for deciding what is good or bad. Although physical desires cannot simply be abolished, the wise person will appreciate the difference between wanting something and judging it to be good. Only reason can judge the goodness or badness of what is desired. If one is wise, he will identify himself with reason rather than with desire; hence, he will not hope for the satisfaction of physical desires or worry that they might not be satisfied. The Stoic will feel physical pain as others do, but he will know that physical pain leaves the true reasoning self-untouched. The only thing that is truly good is to live in a state of wisdom and virtue. In pursuing such a life, one is protected from the play of fortune that afflicts those who aim at physical pleasure or material wealth, for wisdom and virtue are matters of the intellect and under the individual's control. Moreover, if matters become too grim, there is always a way of ending the pain of the physical world. The Stoics were not reluctant to counsel suicide as a means of avoiding otherwise inescapable pain.

Perhaps the most important legacy of Stoicism, however, is its conviction that all human beings share the capacity to reason. This led the Stoics to a fundamental belief in equality, which went beyond the limited Greek conception of equal citizenship. Thus, Seneca claimed that the wise man will esteem the community of rational beings far above any particular community in which the accident of birth has placed him, and Marcus Aurelius said that common reason makes all individuals fellow citizens. The belief that the capacity to reason is common to all humans was also important because from it the Stoics drew the implication that there is a universal moral law, which all people are capable of appreciating. The Stoics thus strengthened the tradition that regarded the universality of reason as the basis on which to reject ethical relativism.

(Peter Singer, Adapted from Encyclopaedia Britannica)

Summary of Stoic Philosophy

- Zeno (342-270 B.C.) was the founder of Stoicism. The famous Roman Stoics were Marcus Aurelius, Seneca and Epictetus.
- Stoicism rejected the idealism of Plato. Concepts have no existence outside human mind.
- The world has a purpose, and is marked by order.
- Freedom of will cannot exist in a world governed by necessity.
- Men should follow not their inclinations or caprices but their reason.
- Stoics push to great lengths their opposition to pleasures and the need to control human passions.
- Stoics recommend extremely rigorous asceticism which runs counter to ordinary human nature.
- Stoics are quite unrelenting in their attitude. In their doctrine, virtue alone is good, only vice is evil, and all else is a matter of absolute indifference.
- The wise man possesses all virtues, and a fool has no virtue at all. This is a strange view.
- Stoics were far in advance of their times in their cosmopolitanism.

UTILITARIANISM

Introduction

Jeremy Bentham (1748-1832) gave the first systematic account of Utilitarianism in *Introduction to The Principles of Morals and Legislation*. Later thinkers like John Stuart Mill and Henry Sidgwick revised the original version of Utilitarianism to meet the criticisms it faced. In the process, the original ideas of utilitarianism underwent change, and the doctrine became more varied.

Main Tenets

Utilitarianism proposes that human actions should aim at promoting the greatest happiness of the greatest number of people. According to Bentham, "Nature has placed mankind under the governance of two sovereign masters, pain and pleasure. It is for them alone to point out what we ought to do, as well as to determine what we shall do". Let us suppose that in a given situation, a moral agent faces three alternative courses of action A_1, A_2 and A_3. Which one of these should he select? Utilitarianism answers that the moral agent has to choose that one which maximises the pleasure and minimizes the pain. The right action for an individual to perform on any occasion is that which will produce the greatest pleasure and the least pain to those affected by it including himself.

In the words of J.S. Mill (1806–1873), the utilitarian principle is " . . . that actions are right in proportion as they tend to promote happiness; wrong as they tend to produce the reverse of happiness. By happiness is intended [meant] pleasure, and the absence of pain; by unhappiness, pain, and the privation [deprivation] of pleasure." Mill believes that pleasure is necessarily a good i.e. anything that leads to happiness is good. Utilitarianism as an ethical rule of conduct applies to individual moral agents, institutions and governments. Further, good life according to utilitarianism will be one spent in maximizing the happiness and minimizing the pain in the world.

Bentham elaborated a 'hedonic calculus', which distinguishes between different aspects of pleasure and pain. He thought that pleasures from various sources can be measured and compared. The seven aspects of pleasure are – its intensity or strength; its duration or length; its certainty; its nearness in time (how soon or how late); its fecundity or likelihood of leading to other pleasures; its purity or freedom from pain; and its extent or the number of people it will include. Incidentally, utilitarians tend to use 'happiness', 'pleasure', 'utility' and 'welfare' interchangeably.

Mill gives an argument to show that happiness is the ultimate value. X is visible if people can see it; Y is audible if people can hear it. Likewise, happiness or utility is desirable if people desire it. And, common experience shows that people desire it. However, Mill's argument is invalid. In the first part of the argument, 'see' and 'hear' mean 'capable of being seen' and 'capable of being heard'. But 'desire' can be interpreted in two ways: 'capable of being desired' and 'worthy of being desired'. It is the latter meaning that is relevant in determining whether a desire is moral.

Utilitarianism, Egoism and Altruism

Before proceeding further, we need to note the relation between egoism, altruism and utilitarianism. Utilitarianism does not imply or endorse an egotistical attitude to life. It does not give any special status to the pleasure or happiness of the individual whose actions it is to guide. Bentham says that in applying the principle, each individual is to count for one and no one for more than one. The moral agent's own pleasures (and pains) will be exactly on par with those of others affected by the action.

Egoism or self-centeredness is an attitude by which an individual gives a privileged status to his own welfare. As opposed to this, Utilitarians treat everyone's welfare as equal. Hence, Utilitarianism is not an egotistical doctrine.

But at the same time, Utilitarianism is not altruistic. Altruism is the doctrine that the interests of others should be put before our own interests. Altruism is often considered central to morality. This is because Christianity which influenced Western moral traditions, strongly regards self-denial as a virtue. However, if what counts is happiness in general, one's own happiness is as important as anyone else's. But it is not any more important. This feature of utilitarianism is usually called its attitude of 'generalized benevolence', which differs from both altruism and egoism.

The relation between utilitarianism and egoism was seen clearly by later thinkers. However, when Bentham propounded utilitarianism, critics felt that he had elevated human selfishness to the status of a moral principle. Utilitarians then elaborated and clarified their concept of pleasure to include general happiness in it. However, this was seen as unconvincing. John Dewey argues:

"There is, accordingly, no direct road from individualistic hedonism (private pleasure) to universalistic hedonism (general pleasure). … Happiness is always a particular condition of one particular person. Whose happiness is desirable and to whom? Because my happiness is intrinsically desirable to me, does it follow that your happiness is intrinsically desirable to me? Indeed, in the hedonistic psychology, is it not nonsense to say that a state of your feeling is desirable to me?"

While recognizing the difficulty involved in the transition from individual happiness to general happiness, utilitarians argued that human beings are not utterly selfish and indifferent to the happiness of their fellow men. This is so because sympathetic and social feelings are naturally ingrained in human character; further, men become enlightened in some degree due to education and culture. These factors enable men to transcend their egoism.

Concept of Happiness

Critics also found fault with utilitarianism for what they regarded as its vulgar conception of happiness. Responding to such criticism Mill observes that in seeming to imply "that life has...no higher end than pleasure" utilitarianism is a "doctrine worthy only of swine." Mill says that "the accusation supposes human beings to be capable of no pleasures except those of which swine are capable." He introduces a distinction between higher and lower pleasures, with higher pleasures, including mental, aesthetic, and moral pleasures. Higher pleasures differ from lower pleasures not in degree (amount of pleasure) but in kind (as a different order of pleasure). He also says that "to do as you would be done by, and to love your neighbour as yourself, constitute the ideal perfection of utilitarian morality." In this way, he includes the Christian golden moral rule in utilitarianism.

Utilitarians argue that happiness or utility is the only end that people seek. This view fails to explain many aspects of human conduct. It does not explain the selfless care of parents for children, the sacrifice of soldiers for their comrades in arms and the asceticism of saints. Utilitarians try to explain these examples by saying that some people derive happiness by making sacrifices for others. However, acts of sacrifice and altruism cannot be explained as attempts at deriving personal pleasure. In such acts, people sacrifice personal happiness for other ends. Thus people value other things as ends in themselves and not as means to happiness.

Measuring Happiness

We have so far considered two criticisms which question the utilitarian ethical criterion, namely happiness. But even if we accept happiness as the ultimate value, it gives rise to a problem. Maximization of happiness involves measuring happiness, adding happiness and comparing happiness. There are no units (like grams) for measuring happiness. Hence happiness which arises from various actions cannot be added. Further, the happiness which individuals derive from the same action or from different actions cannot be compared. Thus the pleasure which Hari gets from drinking a cup of coffee cannot be compared with the pleasure which Giri gets from drinking an identical cup of coffee. This is because happiness is an individual's state of mind. In economics, this is known as the problem of interpersonal comparability of utility.

Utilitarians answer this point in the following general terms. It is true that happiness is not amenable to mathematical calculations. However, people have an intuitive sense of relative degree of utility or pleasure which can be derived from various things. Everyday human decisions involve comparing pleasure or happiness or utility. Utilitarian doctrine involves ranking of different human pleasures, and taking a broad view of the circumstances in which they will be higher or lower.

Untenable Results of Utilitarianism

We now turn to a different type of problem which utilitarianism involves. Philosophers have cited instances in which application of the utilitarian principles leads to totally unacceptable moral consequences. The situations are imaginary, but they serve as counter examples to show the inapplicability of utilitarian rules of conduct. Their purpose is to show that general moral principles have exceptions.

One such scenario imagines three eminent men - Nobel laureates in physics, medicine and genetics - who are critically ill, and in desperate need of organ transplant. One needs a kidney; another needs a heart; and the third a pancreas. But the needed organs are unavailable. As surgeons are agonizing over the problem, a completely unconscious drunken tramp without family, friends or home is brought to the hospital. The surgeons decide to remove the organs from the tramp and transplant them in the three noble laureates. Let us assume that the surgeons are assured of legal immunity for their act.

The question is whether utilitarianism can justify the act of the surgeons. In answering the question, let us ignore all moral principles other than utilitarianism. We need to isolate all other moral criteria and see the answer which we get from the utilitarian criterion. As we know, this involves calculating the total pleasure or utility to society from two alternatives: (i) removing the tramp's organs and transplanting them in the bodies of the noble laureates and (ii) allowing the tramp to walk away after he regains consciousness. It is clear that the social utility or happiness of alternative (i) will clearly exceed that of alternative (ii). For after all, what is the worth of a tramp's life compared to that of three Nobel laureates?

In this example, we have ended with a moral evaluation which no civilized society will accept. The example delineates a situation involving a single act. We understand 'act' here as comprising a single moral transaction. We should not get distracted by the ordinary meaning of 'act' involving various activities of doctors and nurses before, during and after operations. The situation which the example depicts is known as 'act utilitarianism'. Act utilitarianism refers to the moral evaluation of individual actions. Obviously, when utilitarianism is applied to individual acts, it yields unacceptable results.

Act Utilitarianism and Rule Utilitarianism

To avoid counter-examples of this kind, a distinction is usually made between 'act' utilitarianism and 'rule' utilitarianism. Act utilitarianism, the version of Bentham, says that every action must accord with the greatest happiness principle. Rule utilitarianism (which Mill mentioned) says that one should act in accordance with those rules of conduct that are most conducive to the greatest happiness. This distinction implies that in certain circumstances an obviously abhorrent act would contribute more to the general happiness than another decent act. But the abhorrent act loses its utilitarian sanction because it is contrary to a rule which itself is most conducive to the greatest happiness.

We can now examine our example from other angles - first from the point of view of law which is only a set of rules backed by State sanction. Killing an individual for his body organs is murder, pure and simple. It is a legal crime. Even if the surgeons can escape the law, they are guilty of a grave breach of morality. In almost all systems of morals, human life is sacrosanct. Moreover, surgeons are bound by the Hippocratic Oath which prescribes that a physician should only help a patient and never harm him. Even if they want to help the noble laureates, it cannot be at the cost of another human being.

The example contains an element of moral dilemma. However, in a genuine moral dilemma any decision involves choice between two or more equally important moral criteria. Hence the moral agent finds himself on the horns of a difficult moral dilemma. In our example, the choice is quite clear. The surgeons ought not to harm the drunken tramp even to save the lives of noble laureates.

Before leaving the example, we can restate rule utilitarianism. Men have to be guided by general rules. And the only acceptable criterion for general rules is a utilitarian one: *act in accordance with those rules which, if generally acted upon, will lead to the greatest happiness*. Rule utilitarianism is immune to the type of counter-examples which can be easily brought against act utilitarianism, because it can explain, always in terms of utility, why some actions are forbidden in general, even if they satisfy the greatest happiness principle.

Teleological and Deontological Moral Theories

At this stage, we can conveniently consider the manner in which utilitarianism approaches morals. Normative ethical theories are classified as teleological and deontological. These two types of theories differ in how they determine the moral worth of an action – whether an action is morally right or wrong, permissible or impermissible. The teleological approach is also called "consequentialism".

It determines the moral worth of any action by the consequences or outcomes of that action. An action is good if its consequences are good; an action is wrong if its consequences are bad. Hence, for judging an action morally, we have to consider its actual or likely results. Ethical egoism and utilitarianism are teleological.

In contrast to the teleological approach, the deontological approach rejects that the moral worth of any action depends on its consequences. Deontological approach to ethics holds that moral agents have to rigorously fulfil their moral duties or obligations unmindful of the consequences. Moral agents have to honour human rights and meet moral obligations even at the cost of an optimal outcome. Deontology argues that the moral worth of an action does not depend on its consequences, but that a different criterion should be used.

Utilitarianism as Consequentialism

Utilitarianism involves another question in that it requires a moral agent to foresee the consequences of his action. In any given situation, he has to consider the available alternative courses of action and select that course which will result in the maximum utility or the minimum disutility. But the consequences of acts are difficult to foresee. Let us look at an example which Gordon Graham gives in *Eight Theories of Ethics*.

Historians tell us that the event which triggered the First World War was the assassination of Austrian Archduke Ferdinand in Sarajevo. Leaving aside the deeper causes of the War, let us assume that the assassination caused the War. The assassins succeeded because of a mistake of the Archduke's driver, who drove up to a dead end and was forced to turn back. As the car halted in order to turn, the assassins got the opportunity of firing at the Archduke. Thus, had the driver not made the fateful error, Ferdinand would have been driven safely home. Of course, this did not happen. We have imagined a historical 'might have been' in the example.

We can arrange the momentous consequences of the driver's mistake schematically. Archduke's death → outbreak of the First World war → slaughter of millions → Russian revolution → Treaty of Versailles → its harsh treatment of Germany → dissatisfaction in Germany → rise of Hitler → holocaust and the Second world War → development of nuclear weapons → dropping of atomic bombs on Hiroshima and Nagasaki. In taking a wrong turn into the blind alley, the driver appears to have committed the greatest error in history.

The example deliberately exaggerates the consequences of the driver's mistake to highlight the problems in tracing the consequences of actions. First, consequences form a series; or an action leads to secondary effects like the ripples which a stone dropped into a pond creates. The first effect leads to a second effect, the second to a third and so on. This problem, though difficult, is not intractable. For practical purposes, we have to draw a somewhat arbitrary line when estimating consequences. Normally, the range of consequences for deciding whether an action is good or bad will be short for many actions.

Besides the unending chain of consequences, one has to consider the agent's responsibility. In analyzing problems, it is often necessary to separate consequences from responsibility. Ordinarily, people will be disinclined to pin responsibility on the driver in the example for the cataclysmic consequences. It is unreasonable to say that people have acted badly because of consequences which were not merely unforeseen but unforeseeable.

Forecasting Consequences of Decisions

In studying the consequences, one has to distinguish between expectations and outcomes, or between anticipated and actual consequences. When contemplating any action, we visualize *ex ante* or beforehand its likely consequences; but actions are assessed *ex post facto* based on their actual consequences. But while making decisions, we cannot rely on hindsight.

How do we then make decisions whether in moral or other contexts? The answer is that we have to rely upon generalizations about cause and effect and follow general rules. We estimate the likely consequences of a proposed course of action on the basis of past experience, and we summarize our experience in useful general rules of conduct. In simple terms, we have to project the likely consequences of an action, based on past experiences of similar events. These are embodied in general rules which point to cause and effect relations. Action X is likely to have such and such consequences. For example, we know that driving at breakneck speed will cause accidents and injure people.

Moral agents have to diligently consider the consequences of their actions. For instance, one will be irresponsible in pushing boulders from a hill top without looking down. As we mentioned before, one has to predict the likely consequences based on experience of similar actions in the past. In uncertain situations, one has to rely on the relative probabilities of different alternative actions. These probabilities can be derived from accurate statistics, if available. Otherwise, one has to rely on intuitive sense of probabilities. Utilitarianism casts a responsibility on the moral agent to seek diligently the available information and make informed decisions for maximizing welfare. Any one making decisions without considering conscientiously the available information will fall short of the moral standards.

Moral Responsibility

Here, we need to separate two questions which arise in situations involving moral decisions. One question is how to select an appropriate course of action. As we have seen, moral agents, according to utilitarian principles will have to follow the principle of the greatest happiness. The second question is about the responsibility of the moral agent - whether he deserves praise or blame for his action. We are only too ready to fasten blame on others, especially when things go wrong.

Utilitarians argue that moral agents should not be blamed straightaway for the bad consequences of their actions. The question is whether their actions are well-intentioned or not. The presumption is that actions undertaken in good faith are likely to have good consequences. However, one has to bear in mind the caution that the path to hell is paved with good intentions. As we have seen, people are under a moral obligation to be diligent in foreseeing the likely outcomes of their actions. However, if they have taken adequate care, they cannot be held responsible for the bad consequences of their acts. This is the concept of *bona fide* error.

Egalitarian Justice

Many writers argue that utilitarianism ignores the distributional aspects of happiness or utility. What this means is that not only total happiness or welfare but its distribution among members of society is important. Socialism, for example, advocates that wealth and income should be equally distributed in any society. As happiness and welfare are connected, the total social welfare has to be equitably shared. Otherwise, it is likely that the happiness of a tiny minority of the rich will be more than offset by the pain of the majority of the poor.

The early utilitarian thinkers generally ignored the distributional aspect of happiness or welfare. However, JS Mill took a more egalitarian view in such matters. Utilitarianism may not logically support any particular pattern of wealth distribution. One way to make a case for equality from utilitarianism is through the economic theory-diminishing marginal utility. In simple terms, this theory states that as a consumer goes on increasing the consumption of any commodity, the utility or satisfaction he derives from the extra units of its consumption goes on decreasing. Consequently, transfer of commodities from those who have too many (say R) to those who have too few (say P) will increase total satisfaction. For the satisfaction gained by P will be much more than the satisfaction lost by R.

According to economists, this argument will not apply to wealth redistribution because wealth is not a single commodity but represents command over commodities in general. In that case, the law of diminishing marginal utility will not apply. Increasing happiness through redistribution of wealth can be also logically challenged since interpersonal comparisons of utility or happiness are disallowed in economic theory. But these are theoretical considerations since egalitarianism is a moral value which many societies have adopted. Even at theoretical level, John Rawls makes a case for distributional justice in *A Theory of Justice*.

Political Rights

Mill separates justice in the sense of just action of an individual from other spheres of morality. Justice casts certain duties on us which others can expect as a matter of right. Just action is something which it is not only right to do, and wrong not to do, but which some individual person can claim from us as his moral right. X has no right to Y's charity, though Y would do well to be charitable. But X has a right that Y should do him no harm or that Y should repay him his debt.

According to critics, political rights of individuals cannot be adequately explained within the framework of utilitarianism. Mill argued that society ought to defend the individual rights of citizens, and gave social utility as the rationale of such defence. John Rawls, a famous twentieth century thinker, criticized the utilitarian approach on the ground that individual rights may be violated in the name of general social good.

Summary of Utilitarianism

- Utilitarianism regards happiness as the guide for human actions.
- Individuals, institutions and governments should try to maximise happiness and minimize pain.
- Good life is one which aims at achieving the maximum happiness for oneself and others.
- Utilitarianism is neither egoism nor altruism.
- Philosophers criticized utilitarianism as promoting selfish motives and gross pleasures.
- Mill introduced the concept of qualities or grades of pleasure to answer the critics. Mill gives a proof to show that desire for pleasure is a part of human nature.
- Utilitarians unconvincingly try to explain human behaviour involving self-sacrifice and heroism as pursuit of happiness.
- Utilitarianism faces problems since happiness is a subjective, non measurable mental state.
- Philosophers make a distinction between 'act' utilitarianism and 'rule' utilitarianism.
- Act utilitarianism involves maximisation of happiness in each action.
- Rule utilitarianism consists in following general rules which will maximise human happiness.
- Act utilitarianism can lead to actions contrary to common morality.
- Utilitarianism is a teleological as distinct from deontological theory.
- Deontological theories focus on following moral rules without regard to their consequences.
- Teleological theories concentrate on the good or bad consequences of action.
- It is difficult to foresee consequences of actions.
- Moral agents should diligently consider the likely outcomes of action based on experiences of similar actions in the past.
- Irrespective of consequences, acts done in good faith are justified.
- Utilitarianism ignores the distributional aspects of happiness or welfare.
- Individual rights cannot be adequately explained by utilitarianism.

KANTIANISM

Duty as Moral Criterion or Standard

Immanuel Kant (1724-1804) was a great German philosopher. He formulated a moral theory grounded in the idea of duty. It is a deontological theory. "Deontology" is derived from the Greek roots *deon* = duty + *logos* = reason. From these words, we can see that in deontological theories an action is seen as moral in virtue of its being a duty 'obligation or obedience to moral laws'.

We may associate 'duty' for example with military duty. But duty in this sense is derived from a military code. Kant's concept of moral duty is much wider; it is an outcome of an individual's rational thought. Human actions may lead to good or bad consequences. But these do not determine the moral worth of actions. In other words, an action which leads to undesirable consequences may be moral; and an action which leads to good consequences can be immoral. Consequences have nothing to do with moral obligation or duty, which alone counts for determining whether an action is moral or otherwise. In short, an action is moral if it is the outcome of a moral agent's sense of duty.

Kant says that when any individual acts intentionally in a particular way in a given situation, he sets up a rule of conduct for others. It is the rule which underlies his action. Intentional action is not based on blind impulse but on rational thought. Such actions are in conformity with his moral duty. If a moral agent acts according to his duty, he can rationally recommend such actions for others.

Another way of expressing this prescription is that one should obey the moral law. This raises the question of what the moral law or duty is for the individual. Kant does not enumerate a set of rules or moral duties. He describes the moral law in a formal and abstract way; the moral agent perceives his duty in any given situation by applying the formal law. As Kant's account of the moral law is complicated, let us follow it with the help of the following example.

(i) *X borrows Rs 50,000 from Y with a promise that he would return the amount in six months.*

(ii) *After six months, X may either (a) return the amount or (b) evade payment.*

(iii) *In either case, he sets up a rule of conduct applicable not only to him but to everyone.*

(iv) *In (a), the rule or principle of conduct is 'loans should be repaid on time'.*

(v) *In (b), the rule or priniciple is that loan repayment should be evaded.*

(vi) *X can recommend in good faith that everyone should adopt (a) as a rule of conduct. In Kant's phrase: X can recommend that it should be adopted as a universal law. Obviously, this universal law will be rational in that it creates trust among people and promotes business and commerce.*

(vii) *The rule or principles underlying (b) cannot be recommended in good faith for universal adoption. For it will destroy trust between people, commerce and economic progress.*

Kant says that people should follow such rational universal principles without relying on personal sentiments which usually misguide them.

Categorical Imperative

From the above reasoning, Kant derives a universally valid moral rule of action known as the Categorical Imperative. When a moral agent acts rationally, his action is based on a rule or maxim. The rule regulates his action. If a debtor evades repayment of his loan, he will be acting on the maxim: "one should evade loan repayment whenever one can". When as a rational agent he acts on this maxim, he is making an implicit recommendation that others should follow the very same maxim. Now a rule or maxim that everyone must follow would be a law, a rule of action that is universal or applicable to everyone. This is what Kant means by a universal law. From this reasoning, it follows that an intentional action is rational and thus morally permissible only if one could rationally recommend it to others. This is the same as saying that a moral agent's action is rational and morally permissible only if he could will that the maxim of his action become a universal law.

Kant's categorical imperative can be paraphrased as: A rational moral agent *should never act except in such a way that he can also will that the maxim of his action become a universal law.* This formulation is known as the universal law version of the categorical imperative. In Kant's own words, the categorical imperative can be expressed as: "So act that the maxim of your will might always hold as a principle of universal law".

We can derive many common rules of morality from Kant's formulation of the categorical imperative. 'One ought not to steal'. 'One ought not to injure others'. 'One should be kind to others.' In following such maxims, we can also wish that other members of society should follow those maxims for it would obviously be in our interest. However, we should not look upon Kant's theory as resting upon enlightened self-interest or recognition of the social advantage in following common rules.

Categorical Imperative and Rule Utilitarianism

In this regard, we can note the difference between Kant's categorical imperative and rule utilitarianism. Both rely on universally applicable rules of conduct. Rule utilitarian considers the probable consequences of such rules in terms of likely happiness. Kant considers whether the rule underlying a moral agent's action can be adopted in general social interest and in his own interest. Rule utilitarianism is empirical in that its moral worth depends on its likely consequences. Kant considers moral judgments as *a priori*, that is to say, judgments we can make without reference to what happens in the world. Mathematical propositions such as 3+2 =5 are *a priori* propositions. Kant says that one can evaluate moral actions without knowing the place or time of their occurrence or their consequences. It all depends on whether actions are based on maxims which can become rational universal rules of conduct. There is, however, an empirical side to Kant's categorical imperative. One should be able to formulate precisely and clearly the maxim or rule which underlies an agent's action. Only then can one determine whether it can be elevated to the status of a rational rule which all members of society can follow.

Besides the categorical imperative, Kant refers to hypothetical imperatives. Categorical imperative is an absolute command to be obeyed for its own sake. Hypothetical imperatives are technical means to other ends and have an instrumental value. A surgeon has certain skills which he uses for alleviating human suffering. A statesman has certain acumen which he uses for promoting general welfare. This sort of skill or acumen belongs to hypothetical imperatives. Hypothetical imperatives subserve other ends; categorical imperatives have their ground in themselves.

Second Formulation of Categorical Imperative

The categorical imperative has another form which holds that human beings are ends in themselves. In other words, men cannot be treated as instruments for securing any supposedly higher ends. This view will condemn the mass killings of Jews under Hitler and of Russian Kulaks by Stalin. In Kant's words this formulation of categorical imperative is: "*So act as always to treat man, both in your person and that of another, as an end and never solely as a means.*" Kant recognises that everything in the world, including man, may be used as a means. Man is the only rational being we know. Anyone who uses the categorical imperative is himself an ultimate end. Thus we find in Kant a clear enunciation of humanism. However, Kant has strong religious feelings-though ironically, he gave the first clear proofs demolishing the arguments for God's existence. Kant's view that men should not be treated as means but as ends in themselves encapsulates the modern day ideas on human rights.

Austere Morality of Kant

It is clear that Kant's moral philosophy is austere. He sees a constant struggle between human inclinations and duties. Nature does not endow men with innate 'pure spirits'. According to Kant, it is "sheer folly to flatter oneself into relying on an innate goodness of soul that requires neither spur nor check, nor even any commandment and so to forget one's duty". Relying only on mere feeling for the right will destroy human morality. While valuing good inclinations, uprightness of heart and a beautiful soul in man, Kant says that these must be sustained by a clear sense of duty. Ethical law for rational but imperfect beings cannot be a law of holiness but a law of duty.

Kant describes duty in his following famous passage: "Duty-word sublime and strong that implies nothing that pleases or charms ... nothing that threatens or inspires fear; your power is merely to establish a law before which all desires fall silent and which still is admitted to the chamber of the heart where it is held in reverence even if it is not obeyed."

Kant traces the origin of moral law to man's rationality or reason. He rejects education, civic constitution, inner perfection and God's will as sources of moral law. All these imply man's dependence on external sources or heteronomy. Kant affirms the autonomy of human reason and locates the moral law in it. In Kant's phrase, man has a self-legislating capacity.

Criticism of Kant's Theories

Notwithstanding its high moral tone, Kantianism has not escaped criticism. Philosophers have criticized its 'formalism'. It resembles an abstract formula. It contains few concrete moral directions or guidelines. Men get no direct instruction on what is right or what they should do to become good and contribute to a just society. Kant's categorical imperative resembles a general formula. For those unversed in moral reasoning, applying categorical imperative to variable, individual moral situations they face will not be simple or self-evident. They would be left groping for answers.

Although Kant downplays material values, he recognizes that their experience that creates moral motivation in men; it is their experience which creates moral motivation in men. The ascending hierarchy of material values, which in one sense indicates moral progression is shown in the following table.

Type	Material value
Sensuous	Pleasant, unpleasant
Vital	Noble, base
Spiritual	Beautiful-ugly, right, wrong
Summit	Holy, unholy

Kant's ethics rest on abstract laws or pure principle, without regard to the results which can follow from rigid adherence to principles. Philosophers continue to have a debate on principles versus results. Many thinkers argue that men are not to be judged by their principles alone, but are answerable for their actions. Kant's moral law resembles the injunction: *"do what is right and leave the consequences to God"*. As Karl Jaspers says, "*Those opposed to it can point to the evil that can be done in the name of moral principles. They can point to the violent men whose moral judgments have served their manifest desire to command and torment other men. They can evoke teachers of morality who have been the basest of men because they have used morality as a weapon by which to achieve immoral power and prestige.*"

Kant's emphasis on abstract laws leads him into extreme positions. He says that ethical laws "command unconditionally, regardless of what the outcome may be; indeed, they demand that we leave the outcome wholly out of account, when a particular action is being considered." What need men have "to know the outcome of their moral commissions and omissions? It depends on the course of the world. For them it is enough that they do their duty." In this spirit, Kant argues that we cannot tell lies under any circumstances, even for saving someone's life.

Many historical examples show how devout religious reformers became fanatical and promoted violent policies. The destructive Thirty Years War that ravaged central Europe had its origins in relentless pursuit by Protestants and Catholics of their exclusivist theocratic agendas. The rival protagonists were pursuing principles unmindful of their unethical or even disastrous consequences. Similar fanatical pursuit of principles led to Inquisition and religious persecution. From the political sphere, examples would be the violence of the reign of terror during French revolution and violence during the Chinese Cultural Revolution. Further, even reformers heading religious institutions often turned out to be insensitive and tyrannical.

In Kant's view, morality is its own reward, and one is always obliged to do what one should. This obligation to follow law does not cease even if others disobey the law. One is bound by moral law even when there is no reciprocal obedience to law from others. This creates a difficult situation. To quote Karl Jaspers again: "*Where men wield total terrorist power or serve it or take advantage of it in their actions, am I not justified in treating them as wild beasts? … Is the categorical imperative not blunted, if instead of speaking in its own right, it is translated into abstract injunctions such as: Never lie or: everyone who belongs biologically to species "man" is a rational being and must be treated as such, even when to do so involves the risk or even the certainty that I myself or those I love will perish as a result.*" Further, "*Do complete openness to reason, boundless patience, tireless striving for mutual understanding presuppose favourable situations and a consciousness of my own strength without which they become form of criminal self-destruction*?"

These observations of Karl Jaspers are part of his critique of Kant's ethical ideas from another viewpoint. They are also relevant to contemporary situations. Because of an unbalanced and one-sided tilt towards liberal ideology, civil liberties, human rights and general permissiveness, responses of democratic societies towards terrorist attacks and national security have become half-hearted and weak-kneed. Karl Jaspers points out that such Kantian theoretical and ivory tower ethical approaches–whether from State agencies or social groups---can prove self-destructive. Their relevance to Indian situation is too obvious to need specific mention.

Moral law, as Kant conceives, arises from human rationality. However, it operates and has its effect in the social world of human experience. Hence moral laws cannot be conceived in a Platonic world and implemented in society without taking into account their results. They have to be linked to the contexts of human existence. In a way, Kant conceives and abandons moral law in a world of pure thought.

Summary of Kantian Philosophy

- Kant formulated a moral theory grounded in the idea of duty. It is a deontological theory.
- Consequences have nothing to do with moral obligation or duty which alone counts for determining whether an action is moral or otherwise. In short, an action is moral if it is the outcome of a moral agent's sense of duty.
- Kant derives a universally valid moral rule of action known as the Categorical Imperative.
- Kant's categorical imperative can be paraphrased as: A rational moral agent *should never act except in such a way that he can also will that the maxim of his action become a universal law.* This formulation is known as the universal law version of the categorical imperative.
- Categorical imperative and rule utilitarianism are very different. Rule utilitarianism is based on the consequences of actions; categorical imperative is based on universal moral laws and ignores consequences of actions. For Kant, moral judgments are a priori; they are empirical in rule utilitarianism.
- Hypothetical imperatives are technical means to other ends and have an instrumental value.
- The categorical imperative has another form which holds that human beings are ends in themselves. In other words, men cannot be treated as instruments for securing any supposedly higher ends.
- This formulation of categorical imperative is: "*So act as always to treat man, both in your person and that of another, as an end and never solely as a means.*"
- Kant's moral philosophy is austere. He sees a constant struggle between human inclinations and duties.
- Kant traces the origin of moral law to man's rationality or reason. He rejects education, civic constitution, inner perfection and God's will as sources of moral law.
- Kant's emphasis on abstract laws leads him into extreme positions.
- Kant's ethics rest on abstract laws or pure principle without regard to the results which can follow from rigid adherence to principles.
- Moral laws cannot be conceived in a Platonic world and implemented in society without taking into account their results.

VIRTUE ETHICS

We discussed Utilitarianism and Kantianism in the previous two sections. Utilitarianism is a part of teleogical ethics. It is one form of consequentialism in which an action is judged based on its consequences, whether they are good or bad. Kantianism is a kind of deontology. It judges actions as good or bad based on whether or not they are in accordance with the moral agent's duty.

There are other approaches to ethics besides utilitarianism and deontology. One such approach is virtue ethics which goes back to Aristotle and which has seen a revival in late twentieth century. Virtue ethics propounds the view that while doing right things is important, it is equally or more important to be a virtuous person.

Virtues and vices

Aristotle is regarded as the first systematic proponent of Virtue ethics. Virtue can be defined as an excellence of character which leads one to act in a morally praiseworthy manner. A person who possesses the virtue of kindness will behave kindly towards others. He will not act kindly mainly because he thinks that it is his duty do so or because he calculates that acting kindly will maxmimise total utility in society. He acts kindly because he possesses the virtue of kindness. According to virtue ethics, the truly moral person is a virtuous person. He has internalized virtues and has a moral character.

Vice is the opposite of virtue. It is an acquired weakness of character which makes one act in a morally blameworthy manner. In this way, bad acts arise from one's moral weakness.

Virtue theory makes a distinction between moral virtues and non-moral virtues. Moral virtues include kindness, benevolence, compassion, honesty, conscientiousness and gratitude. Examples of non-moral virtues are self-control, patience, courage, endurance, perseverance and so on. Non-moral virtues can be used for bad ends. For example, one may show great courage in robbing a bank. Moral virtues promote a moral life.

We have already discussed the chief elements of Aristotle's ethics. To recapitulate briefly, they consist of the following:

- The aim of men should be to achieve 'eudaimonia" which can be interpreted as happiness or flourishing.
- As social creatures, men can achieve this goal by living in communities.
- As rational creatures, men have to lead a life of reason.
- Such life requires cultivation of moral virtues and intellectual virtues. This involves continuous practice.
- Virtue is a golden mean between two extremes and it can be found through practical wisdom.

Aristotle argues that developing a moral character by becoming a virtuous person is more important than knowledge of moral principles. Aristotle acknowledges the role of rules and principles as guides to action. However, the virtuous person will observe the rules voluntarily and without effort. Mere knowledge of moral principles and accepting them intellectually is not sufficient to make a person moral.

Virtue Ethics and Rule-based Ethics

Virtue ethics can be contrasted with rule-based ethics like utilitarianism. In rule based ethics, the moral agent appears simply in the role of someone just applying rules mechanically. Rule based ethics ignore his motive in wanting to be moral. Virtue ethics trace his moral actions to his motivation arising from his virtuous character. Moral individuals are not simply those adept at seeing what courses of action conform to categorical imperative or lead to the greatest happiness of the greatest number. Virtue ethics portrays moral persons as those who genuinely take pleasure in doing right things. They are not unwillingly propelled into good acts by a grim sense of duty or stoic resignation. Such acts come naturally to them. In this way, virtue ethics gives a more attractive perspective to the acts of virtuous people. While it is important to follow moral courses of action, it is more important to be a genuinely moral person.

Weaknesses of Virtue Ethics

Notwithstanding the above attractive features of virtue ethics, critics have also pointed to its weaknesses. Virtue ethics assumes that men are naturally good or at least are morally neutral. Hence, they can acquire a moral character through practice. But in some traditions (e.g. Christianity) men are considered as sinful and evil and that their redemption depends on divine grace. If this view is accepted, virtue ethics becomes weakened.

It it also argued that often men lack the knowledge necessary in order to become virtuous. In this regard, we may consider the case of ancient Greek ethics. Socrates, Plato and Aristotle produced profound and sublime ethical systems. But they have accepted the then prevalent system of slavery. To this extent, their ideas were historically conditioned and failed to transcend the contemporaneous conceptions.

Another difficulty is that even after cultivating a moral character, one may not know what virtue involves in a particular situation. Thus kindly persons may show misplaced generosity to undeserving people who may not really be in need. In such situations, one may have to rely on certain rules and principles.

Finally, there may be differences on what is and what is not a virtue. Aristotle considered pride as a virtue. While propounding this view, he had in mind the nobility and the military classes. Their moral codes placed emphasis on valour and taking pride in military traditions. However, Christianity regards pride as a sin.

In spite of the above weaknesses of virtue ethics, it provides the needed corrective to moral perspectives based on rule based ethics such as consequentialism and deontology.

Natural law ethics

Natural law ethics provides another important perspective on Ethics. Its origins go back to Aristotle and the Stoics. In Greek tradition, there was a tendency to set up an opposition between nature and society and contrast natural laws with social conventions. Natural law philosophy was fully developed by the medieval philosopher St. Thomas Aquinas. We have discussed an important part of natural law ethics---the doctrine of double effects---in the previous chapter. We will discuss the views of Thomas Aquinas on law in the sixth chapter. In this chapter, we outline the central features of natural law ethics.

Aquinas says that every natural object has a natural purpose or function. For example, the purpose of heart is to circulate blood. When natural objects perform their purposes, the resulting situation is wholesome, and one which has a natural value. But when natural objects are unable to perform their natural functions or achieve their natural purposes, the resulting situation is undesirable.

All living things share the natural value of preserving life. Living things ultimately die. But so long as they are alive, their parts serve the purpose of maintaining life. As life is a natural value, attempts to preserve it are good. Duty of preserving human life (and indeed all life) is basic to natural law ethics and sets it apart from other approaches to ethics. It is the main tenet of its morality. Morality imposes an obligation to preserve the lives of other people and of human species in general. It opposes those practices that prevent procreation such as abortion and sterilization. Roman Catholic religious principles are mainly based on the theological doctrines of Aquinas. Natural law ethics are the main reason why Roman Catholic Church opposes artificial means of birth control. These means defeat the natural function or purpose of sexual intercourse.

Another important tenet which Aquinas propounds is that human beings as rational creatures have a natural purpose of leading a life of reason. They need to distinguish between the rational and the irrational. Men have this ability. Rational actions which promote life and reason are morally right. Irrational actions are morally wrong.

Many conclusions follow from the above conception. As preservation of human species is part of man's natural function, men should do such things which promote the proper function of humanity. As human beings flourish in a well-ordered society, morality requires that we do things which promote social order. As a result, telling truth, keeping promises, and doing such other things as promote mutual trust become moral duties.

For a similar reason, it becomes a moral duty of people to support institutions such as marriage and civil government, which promote social stability. Aquinas argues, as we shall see later, that people need not support a government which is unable to perform its function of maintaining social order and harmony. Natural ethics lends support to duties from the perspective of maintaining social stability. Thus, property rights of others have to be respected. General social welfare has to be promoted by helping those in desperate need.

Natural law ethics lead to moral norms which are similar to those which follow from utilitarianism and deontology. However, natural law ethics derives its moral principles from the natural value of life and the need for stable social life. It does not refer to utility or duty as a driver of morality.

Natural law ethics concedes that in certain circumstances one may have to deprive individuals of their life. If a mad killer is going on rampage, police will be justified in killing him. The action of police will be justified on the basis of the principle of forfeiture. What this means is that the killer loses his natural right to life because of his going on a killing spree. No justification on utilitarian grounds is given for the action of police. We may mention that war, which leads to enormous loss of human life, is also justified in certain circumstances in natural law ethics. The idea of just war has been propounded by Augustine. It is essentially a defensive action taken to protect the nation against the aggressor.

Criticisms against natural law ethics

The doctrine of double effects is an offshoot of natural law ethics. It envisages situations which involve damage (including loss of life) happening in the course of a justifiable action. We have already discussed this doctrine and the criticisms levelled against it.

Now, we will outline the other criticisms against natural law ethics. Promoting natural purpose and functions may not always be desirable. Sting of female mosquitoes spreads malaria. Various measures are taken to destroy the habitats of these mosquitoes. But such measures may seem to violate natural law ethics. Another example could be the removal of poisonous weeds.

Many features of nature are unattractive. For example, animal kingdom consists of many predators and their prey. Killing and violence mark natural life. This led British poet Tennyson to speak of "nature red in tooth and claw". According to Darwin, natural evolution of species involves struggle for existence between species. Often the weak members are eliminated in the process. Hence, natural processes may not yield morally acceptable principles.

Another problem with natural law theories is that they pick and choose what they regard as natural. All natural organisms decay and die. Death is also a part of nature. But does it mean that we should promote or hasten death in certain circumstances? Natural law ethics oppose this suggestion. Many will regard their position as morally justified. But it may be inconsistent with their approach of favouring natural processes and functions.

Other Strands

We have discussed the principal systems of ethics. There are a few other strands which need a mention. Many thinkers argue that morality is a matter of human intuition. Intuition is an unexplainable faculty yielding correct moral judgements. We will discuss this aspect further while considering conscience as a guide to morality.

Philosophers also differ on whether morality is derived from human reason or human sentiments. This discussion distinguishes sharply between the reasoning faculties and emotional feelings of human beings. There is little doubt that many human virtues are rooted in emotions. We discuss these aspects in detail in another context. However, we may note at this stage that rationality and reasoning are important in critically evaluating moral principles. It may be risky to rely only on sentiments. At times emotional responses turn out to be undesirable.

Summary of Virtue Ethics

- Virtue ethics propounds the view that while doing right things is important, it is equally or more important to be a virtuous person.
- According to virtue ethics, the truly moral person is a virtuous person. He has internalised virtues and has a moral character.
- Aristotle gave the first systematic account of virtue ethics.
- Virtue ethics portrays moral persons as those who genuinely take pleasure in doing right things.
- In rule based ethics, the moral agent appears simply in the role of someone just applying rules mechanically.

Following criticisms can be made against virtue ethics.

- Virtue ethics assumes that men are naturally good or at least are morally neutral—an assumption which is questionable.
- Often men lack the knowledge necessary in order to become virtuous.
- There may be differences on what is and what is not a virtue.
- Even after cultivating a moral character, one may not know what virtue involves in a particular situation.

Summary of Natural Law Ethics

- Summary of natural law ethics
- Aquinas says that every natural law has a natural purpose or function.
- When natural objects perform their purposes, the resulting situation is wholesome, and one which has a natural value. But when natural objects are unable to perform their natural functions or achieve their natural purposes, the resulting situation is undesirable.
- As life is a natural value, attempts to preserve it are good. Duty of preserving human life (and indeed all life) is basic to natural ethics and sets it apart from other approaches to ethics.
- Human beings as rational creatures have a natural purpose of leading a life of reason.

Many conclusions follow from the above conception.

- For a similar reason, it becomes a moral duty of people to support institutions such as marriage and civil government, which promote social stability.

Following criticism can be made against natural law ethics

- Promoting natural purpose and functions may not always be desirable.
- Natural processes and functions may not yield morally acceptable principles.
- Natural law theories pick and choose what they regard as natural.

MORAL THINKERS OF THE TWENTIETH CENTURY

Introduction

Moral philosophy took a different turn in the twentieth century. Many philosophers gave up the earlier prevalent practice of prescribing or espousing particular moral systems. Instead, they tended to subject prevailing moral theories to close epistemological scrutiny. From this angle, they raised questions about the logical foundations of moral theories. What are the categories or concepts used in moral theories? What are the meanings commonly attached to such moral terms? What is the logical status of statements or propositions used in moral philosophy? Can moral arguments be accorded logical status? Their approach can be described as 'discussions about moral discussions'. This approach is known as meta-ethics. In this process, the normative has tended to recede to the background.

G. E. Moore

Ideal Utilitarianism

In his famous work, *Principia Ethica*, Moore propounded three doctrines: ideal utilitarianism; naturalistic fallacy; and moral intuition. Moore says that utilitarian moral standard can connect ethics to human conduct. When raising the practical question "What ought I to do?" one must always base his decision on whether the action will be the cause of the good or bring about good effect. From this it follows "that 'right' does and can mean nothing but 'cause of a good result,' and is thus identical with 'useful.'" The final determination of the useful (i.e., the good) was, as we shall see, for Moore a kind of intuition. It is through intuition that one 'sees' the intrinsic value of morally practical actions. Moore also identifies three types of desirable conduct. These consist of impersonal aesthetic and intellectual avocations; warm human friendships; and benevolent actions towards others. Some writers criticized Moore of ignoring class divisions, social conflicts, and thinking only about a small group of well off intellectuals.

Intuitive Perception of Goodness

Moore also discusses the nature and status of 'goodness', the chief moral trait. He says that it should not be mixed up or confused with natural properties of things. It is unanalyzable and indefinable. He gives an example of yellow light. In physics, it is identified with a particular wavelength of light. But we perceive yellowness as a quality directly without the paraphernalia of scientific terminology. Similarly, we also perceive goodness directly or intuitively. For Moore, goodness is a matter of intuitive moral perception. Aa a consequence of this, for Moore 'good' is a simple notion; just as 'yellow' is a simple notion. 'Good' is not to be defined in terms of anything outside itself, but this does not make it impossible for us to see or to grasp, any more than the colour yellow.

Naturalistic Fallacy

Moore's phrase "naturalistic fallacy" became very popular. The naturalistic fallacy consists in identifying goodness (or other moral qualities) with natural properties of things. For instance, identifying the good with the pleasurable involves a naturalistic fallacy. Moore argues that in fact no description of natural properties ever logically commits one to an ethical judgment. Thus, even if it is true that "X is pleasurable" (or that it is a naturalistic statement), one can always ask, "but is it good?" Its goodness does not logically follow. Thus naturalistic fallacy leads to logically inadmissible procedures.

Sir David Ross

Sir David Ross's ideas are propounded in his book *The Right and the Good*. Ross's ideas are largely a response to the type of utilitarianism found in Moore's *Principia Ethica*. Moore says that "right means productive of the highest good." For Ross, what makes a right act right is not the principle of utility but an overriding moral duty that might sometimes conflict with Moore's "ideal utilitarianism". Moore, for instance, says "in effect, that the only morally significant relation in which my neighbours stand to me is that of being possible beneficiaries by my action." This leads at times to breaking other important moral principles. Suppose a group of young men become lazy, and begin to live on charity, though they can earn a living thorough manual labour. A charitable person helps them to continue living in their indolent way. His generosity is misplaced and tends to displace the virtue of self reliance in the young men.

Prima facie Duties

Ross holds that moral agents have certain duties that are not based upon the consequences of their adoption, but on the rightness of their adoption. This is, of course the difference between approaches based on consequences of action (as in utilitarianism) and the inherent moral worth of an action (as in deontology). Ross calls such general principles *prima facie* duties in light of the fact that, "all things being equal" i.e., no other opposing circumstances present, we ought to follow the principle. For example, all things being equal, we ought to keep promises.

Conflict between Duties

But moral situations can be complex with a conflict of prima facie duties. On this account, Ross holds that in such situations the actual duty of moral agents will be that which is right for the particular situation. For instance, while keeping promises is a prima facie duty, in certain situations, it is outweighed by another prima facie duty. Ross uses the example of breaking a trivial promise of meeting a friend in order to prevent a serious accident. He writes in this connection:

"... *besides the duty of fulfilling promises I have and recognise a duty of relieving distress, and that when I think it right to do the latter at the cost of not doing the former, it is not because I think I shall produce more good thereby but because I think it the duty which is in the circumstances more of a duty.*"

In this case the latter duty is our actual duty, though both *prima facie* duties maintain their deontological nature. Ross's explanation of 'right action' removes the emphasis on "utility" in Moore's ethics. It emphasises the notion of a moral agent's duty to do the right thing.

The views of Moore and Ross reflect the spirit of the classical debates between the utilitarians and the Kantians. Moore prefers a notion of action based upon the consequences of bringing more good than evil into the world. Ross proposes a conception of action based upon the morally good person's fulfilment of his sense of duty in light of what is ethically right. As we shall see, the ideas of Ross are of particular importance in questions involving ethical dilemmas.

A.J. Ayer

Strictly speaking, A.J. Ayer is not a moral thinker. He belongs to a philosophical school called logical positivism. The main aim of logical positivists is to remove metaphysical speculations from philosophy. They proposed a criterion of truth which permits only certain categories of statements into philosophy. This view has important implications for moral discussions.

Types of propositions

For understanding these ideas, we need a brief background of 'proposition' as it is understood in logic and philosophy. Proposition is any statement which is either true or false. It cannot be both, for that will involve a contradiction - a cardinal sin in logic. The same proposition can be expressed in different verbal forms as different sentences with the same meaning.

The types of propositions are shown in the following table:

Type of propositions	Broad meaning	Example
Empirical or factual	Refer to physical, biological and social world	Moon is a satellite of earth.
Logical	Figure in logical reasoning	If a = b, and b = c, then a = c.
Mathematical	Derived through mathematical demonstration or proof	$(a + b)^2 = a^2 + 2ab + b^2$
Ethical	Refer to ideal conduct	Be respectful to your elders.

According to Ayer, only the first three types of statements are meaningful. Ayer propounded the criterion of truth as verification: that the meaning of a statement is the manner of its verification. What it means simply is that if there are no means of checking a statement's truth in practice or in principle, it should not be treated as a proposition. Logical and mathematical statements (analytic statements) are meaningful since they express the necessary truths of logic and mathematics derived through proofs.

Moral Emotivism

Ayer says that ethical statements as also statements of metaphysics, theology and many literary expressions are 'meaningless'. It means that they have no status as propositions or they are pseudo-propositions. As regards the status of ethical statements, Ayer says that they are merely expressions of emotions. Hence, this doctrine is known as emotivism.

Ayer expounds his ideas in *Language, Truth and Logic*. It is written in a clear, lucid and elegant style. Even general readers can easily read and understand it with a little effort. However, the book contains no substantial discussion on ethics. The question which Ayer raises is epistemological or concerns theory of knowledge: what kind of propositions can be considered part of philosophy?

C.L. Stevenson

Nature of Ethical Judgements

Stevenson worked out in greater detail the implications of emotive theory of ethics. He develops emotivism into a theory of ethical language according to which moral judgments do not state any sort of fact, but rather express the moral emotions of the speaker and attempt to influence others. When anyone says that something is good or bad, or right or wrong, it seems on the face of it, that he is describing, attributing to the thing some property, that is goodness or badness, or rightness or wrongness. But according to Stevenson moral judgments do not describe at all. In other words, they are not about facts. Uttering moral sentences has a different function: to express emotions, and to influence or invite others to share them. "Moral judgments are concerned with recommending something for approval or disapproval; and this involves something more than a disinterested description."

People often pass moral judgments that something is good or bad. Such statements simply reflect whether they like or dislike that thing. The purpose of such statements is to persuade the audience to adopt the attitude of the speaker. Moral expressions are, due to their strong emotive content, particularly well suited for such persuasion.

Stevenson here argues that moral judgments are simply a cover for the attempts which people make to persuade one other into adopting a particular normative attitude. For example, saying "dowry taking is wrong," is just a very strong way of stating that the speaker disapproves of dowry taking. The purpose of the statement is to evoke similar disapproval from others. It thereby attempts to influence the future conduct of both speakers and listeners.

Persuasive Definition

Stevenson introduced the phrase "persuasive definition" which has become very popular. It refers to a situation often found in ethical argumentation. It involves use of expressions that have two particular characteristics:

(i) having emotive overtones/meanings (positive or negative)

(ii) being vague in their descriptive content

Some examples of such terms are democracy, freedom, repression and terrorism. In discussions, one party gives a positive spin to the 'definition' of his cause, and a negative one to the opponent's. The persuasive definition uses the inherent vagueness of a term, which gives room for many possible definitions, facilitating clever use of emotively charged expressions. Thus terrorism may be described as heinous by one side and as legitimate response to intolerable oppression by the other.

Stevenson extends the distinction between facts and values (ethical norms) in ethics as a distinction between beliefs and attitudes. Beliefs belong to the realm of facts. Attitudes refer to the psychological states of approval or disapproval. Attitude can never, in principle, be reducible to a "disinterested description." Our attitudes are neither true nor false but simply beyond the sphere of facts.

Ayer and Stevenson belong to the twentieth century Anglo-American positivistic tradition. Positivism refuses to engage in moral discussions. It makes no moral assumptions; nor does it pass moral judgments on things, individuals, events and institutions. It aims at dispassionate factual analysis. It strictly follows the distinction between facts and values. We now look at moral philosophers who tried to get over the distinction between facts and values.

R.M. Hare

Prescriptivism

R. M. Hare's moral theory is known as prescriptivism. Hare first presented his theory in *The Language of Morals*. Hare rejected the prevailing theory of emotivism, which maintained that moral statements are merely expressions of individual preference. For Hare, moral statements are prescriptions or guides to conduct. They are universalizable i.e. they apply to everyone.

Suppose I am prescribing, for myself and others, the command of, for instance, not harming others. That type of prescription demands my acting in accordance with it. First, the very language of morals involves a commitment to conduct. Secondly, our reasoning about the ethical situation contains the principle of universality.

The universal applicability of moral judgments can be illustrated in the following example. Consider the judgment, "A ought to do X to B and C". When universalized, it also implies the judgments

"B ought to do X to A and C" and "C ought to do X to A and B"

Irrespective of who the benefactors and beneficiaries are, the moral judgment will still apply. Or one must accept the moral judgment irrespective of what one's individual preferences are i.e. whether one is A rather than B or C.

According to Hare, natural language has a particular logical aspect. It generally expresses moral judgments using the term "ought" or by saying what is "right". Such moral judgments are binding on all people and have overriding force.

Hare avoids broader metaphysical or epistemological considerations. Such considerations lead moral discussions astray. As we have noted earlier, (for example with Ayer and Stevenson) reasoning about ethics has become an investigation into ethical reasoning. There is virtually no moral content in such discussions.

Form of Moral Arguments

We will now give a simple version of Hare's conception of a moral argument. As we noted before, some philosophers reject the very possibility of moral arguments. According to Hare, if the premises contain moral terms along with factual statements, a valid argument will result. The basic form of the argument is shown below.

All animals in distress ought to be helped.

This dog is in distress.

This dog should be helped.

The main point to note is that moral arguments are not irrational but fall within reasonable discourse.

Two-level utilitarianism

Hare argues that human beings, depending on their intellectual endowments, rely on their intuitive moral beliefs or on critical thinking. In either case, the fundamental human moral beliefs are the same. But men differ in their critical reasoning abilities and in their ability to recognise the moral components of a situation and reaching the appropriate moral judgments. In other words, while making moral judgments, some people follow their moral intuitions, and others rely on their reason.

This leads Hare to the conception of two-level utilitarianism. Intuitive level of thinking implies that moral decisions are based on rule utilitarianism. People use prima facie principles which apply to common, general types of situations or occurrences. People follow this approach when there is no time for critical thinking or when they do not trust their critical faculties.

Critical level thinking implies act utilitarianism. Here, an individual analyses the likely consequences of an individual action, and considers whether on balance they will be good or bad. Act utilitarianism comes into play (i) in unusual cases; (ii) when prima facie principles are in conflict; (iii) when it is clear that utility can be maximised by adopting a particular course and one is sure that it is in fact so.

In conclusion, we may note that Hare regards ethical expressions as meaningful. He shows that there can be reasoned discussions about morals. He believes that the language of morals is prescriptive and provides universalizable imperatives applicable to particular circumstances.

John Rawls

Unlike analytical philosophers, contemporary thinkers discuss moral questions. John Rawls is one such philosopher. His book *A Theory of Justice* has strongly influenced thinkers in moral philosophy, political science and public administration. In this book, Rawls provides a rational justification for creating a just society.

John Rawls argues that adoption of the following two fundamental principles would create a just and ethical society:

1. Each person is to have an equal right to the most extensive system of equal basic liberties compatible with a similar system of liberty for all.
2. (i) Social and economic inequalities are to be arranged so that they are to the greatest benefit of the least advantaged. (ii) Access to public offices and positions should be open to all under conditions of fair equality of opportunity subject to exception in (i).

The first principle ensures civil liberties to all. Principle 2 (i) is similar to what is called 'positive discrimination'. It means that while unequal treatment of individuals is generally undesirable, it is justified for helping those people who suffer from disabilities which are not of their making.

Rawls explains how this outcome will come about or how rational people would choose it. He starts with a social tabula rasa or a clean state preceding the origin of social arrangements. He envisages how people would derive their preferences in such situation. He introduces a theoretical "veil of ignorance". It ensures that all the "players" in the social game would be placed in a particular situation. Rawls calls it the "original position." In this position, everyone only has a general knowledge about the facts of "life and society". Therefore, each player is to make a "rationally prudential choice" concerning the kind of social arrangements they would want to live under. As the players have no specific information about themselves, they cannot adopt a partisan or self-regarding view. In simple terms, as they do not know what their situation in the society would be, people opt for social arrangements that would ensure them minimum comfort levels even in the worst-case scenario. They are forced to adopt a generalized point of view akin to the moral point of view.

In this manner, a just social order gets created even though people act out of prudence and not out of a sense of morality. In the hypothetical situation Rawls envisages, people operate under a veil of ignorance about future. And, while attempting to cover the unknown risks they face, people opt for a social set up with a degree of egalitarianism. Rawls calls this "rational choice within a veil of ignorance". Rawls argues that given his assumptions people would prefer liberal societies with freedoms and liberties based on equality of opportunities, but with due allowance to the problems of various disadvantaged groups.

Rawls says: All social primary goods-liberty, opportunity, income and wealth, and props for an individual's self-respect-are to be distributed equally unless unequal distribution of any or all of these goods is to the advantage of the least favoured. The rationale of Rawls arguments can be simply stated. As we do not know where circumstances or fate will put us in social order, it is better to opt for arrangements that will assure us our minimum needs. This is how John Rawls rationally justifies egalitarian, distributive and inclusive policies. They are not subjective preferences. They do not involve any value judgements. If you place rational individuals who can reason objectively in a certain social situation, they will choose such policies.

Criticism of views of Rawls

But how can we question this approach? If we accept the premises and assumptions of Rawls his conclusions will follow. But his argument is hypothetical; it is based on suppositions. In any real society, we cannot start with a kind of ground zero situation, as he does. A society has a history; it is divided into economic classes with established, inherited positions which have legal sanction. These initial conditions in which individual find themselves cannot be wished away or cancelled. They are not just undesirable or unjust situations. They represent the acquired rights of people. This does not mean that we should oppose all reforms or attempts at uplifting the poor and the disadvantaged. They have to be carefully and cautiously worked out through moderate political and economic policies.

A counter view

Robert Nozick opposes redistributive policies which the above version of a just society implies. He claims that if the world were wholly just, the only people entitled to hold anything (or property) would be those who had justly acquired what they possess. Possession of property could be by some original act of acquisition; or through transfer from someone who had got it through an original act of acquisition or by purchase from a legitimate owner.

He gives an example, 'Why are you entitled to use that sea shell? 'I picked it up on sea shore where it belonged to no one and there were plenty left for everyone else.' This is a just act of original acquisition. Or 'Some one else picked it up on the sea shore and freely sold it or gave it to me'. There could be intermediate legitimate sales and purchases between an owner and his property. Nozick represents the conservative position justifying property rights. He regards them as natural and inalienable rights. State cannot deprive individuals of such rights.

This is an appropriate point to close our discussion on major twentieth century moral thinkers. We considered the main trends of their thought. There are other thinkers, but any discussions of them will take us beyond the scope of our topic. As we saw, till about sixties, barring a few, philosophers adopted a positivistic approach. They analysed moral concepts and provided little moral guidance for practical situations of life. Their work has no normative content. This approach is hardly relevant to practicing administrators who need to be committed to certain moral values. They cannot simply assume the role of moral analysts. This does not mean that we can ignore twentieth century moral thinking. It has illuminated many moral concepts and moral arguments. This knowledge can help in analysing the moral dimensions of many practical administrative situations.

Summary

- Many twentieth century philosophers gave up the earlier prevalent practice of prescribing or espousing particular moral systems. Instead, they tended to subject prevailing moral theories to close epistemological scrutiny.
- Moore propounded three doctrines: ideal utilitarianism; 'naturalistic fallacy'; and moral intuition.
- The naturalistic fallacy consists in identifying goodness with some natural property.
- One of the tenets of modern logic is that propositions of fact have to be separated from propositions of value.
- But if good is considered a natural property, one can draw moral judgments from factual statements. Arguments containing factual notions of pleasure in the premises could logically entail conclusions containing ethical judgments. This is an illicit procedure.
- Moore held that we see or recognise good through a process of moral intuition.
- Moore's version of utilitarianism is idealistic because he rejects hedonism.
- Moore says that "right means productive of the highest good." For Ross, what makes a right act right is not the principle of utility but an overriding moral duty that might sometimes conflict with Moore's "ideal utilitarianism".
- This may imply that at times moral principles can be broken.
- Moral agents have certain duties that are not based upon the consequences of their adoption, but on the rightness of their adoption. Ross calls such general principles prima facie duties.
- But moral situations can be complex with a conflict of prima facie duties. On this account, Ross holds that in such situations, the actual duty of moral agents will be that which is right for the particular situation.
- A.J. Ayer belongs to a philosophical school called logical positivism.
- Ayer says that as the propositions of ethics fail to reduce to statements capable of empirical verification, they fall under the category of pseudo-propositions and are not literally significant. They are merely expressions of emotions.
- Ayer's work contains no substantial discussion on ethics. The question which Ayer raises is epistemological or concerns theory of knowledge.
- According to Stevenson, moral judgments do not state any sort of fact, but rather express the moral emotions of the speaker and attempt to influence others.
- Moral judgments are not about facts. Uttering moral sentences has a different function: to express emotions, and to influence or invite others to share them.
- The purpose of such statements is to persuade the audience to adopt the attitude of the speaker.
- Stevenson also argues that moral judgments are simply a cover for the attempts which people make to persuade one another into adopting a particular normative attitude.

- ¤ Stevenson introduced the concept "persuasive definition".
- ¤ Ayer and Stevenson belong to the twentieth century Anglo-American positivistic position. Positivism refuses to engage in moral discussions.
- ¤ Hare rejected the prevailing emotivism, which maintained that moral statements were merely expressions of individual preference. For Hare, moral statements are prescriptions or guides to conduct. They are universalizable i.e. they apply to everyone.
- ¤ Some philosophers reject the very possibility of moral arguments. According to Hare, if the premises contain moral terms along with factual statements, a valid argument will result.
- ¤ Moral judgments use the term 'ought' and say what is 'right'. Such moral judgments are binding on all people and have overriding force.
- ¤ Hare introduced the conception of two-level utilitarianism. Intuitive level of thinking implies that moral decisions are based on rule utilitarianism. Critical level thinking implies act utilitarianism.
- ¤ Hare believes that common morality, professional ethics and personal morality have their roots in intuitive beliefs.
- ¤ Analytical philosophers refrain from propounding any world views, social philosophies or moral systems. They focus on the meanings of terms or clarification of concepts used in philosophy and sciences.
- ¤ John Rawls argues that the adoption of two fundamental principles of justice would guarantee a just and morally acceptable society.

PRACTICE QUESTIONS

1. "The unexamined life is not worth living". How would you interpret this statement of Socrates?
2. "Knowledge is virtue". Elucidate
3. To what extent are Socratic virtues applicable in modern administrative contexts?
4. How relevant are Plato's political ideas to modern democratic societies?
5. "Plato's idea that philosophers should be rulers really means that power should rest with committed experts than with bumbling, corrupt politicians." Comment
6. "Plato's Republic makes a case for totalitarian dictatorship in glowing literary phrases." Examine.
7. "Be brave, be brave, but do not be too brave". How will you theoretically justify this advice?
8. "Virtue renders virtue easy." Elucidate.
9. "Can we regard as morally satisfactory a community which, by its essential constitution, confines the best things to a few, and requires the majority to be content with the second-best?" Examine in the context of doctrines of Plato and Aristotle.
10. "Epicureanism advocates pursuit of vulgar pleasures". Do you agree?

11. Can Epicureanism and Stoicism be suitable models of virtue for modern civil servants?
12. Examine the view that Epicureanism is a form of escapism.
13. What is the difference between teleological and deontological ethical theories?
14. Outline the difference between act utilitarianism and rule utilitarianism. How is rule utilitarianism superior to act utilitarianism?
15. Which doctrine of Kant lends support to ideas of human dignity and human rights? How?
16. What is the justification of Kant's principle of categorical imperative?
17. Kant argued that one should not tell lies even to protect innocent people. How does Kant reach this position? Is it justified?

REFERENCES

- Bertrand Russell, A History of Western Philosophy (chapters on Ancient Greek philosophers discussed in this chapter)
- A History of Western Philosophy 1 Classical thought (OPUS paperback) Terence Irwin

Ethical Ideas in Indian Philosophical Tradition

HINDUISM

It is hard to propound Hindu ethics in a few paragraphs. They date back to Vedic period and have gone through a long period of evolution. They come from many sources, such as Vedas, Upanishads, Dharmasastras, Puranas, epics, itihasas and the like. Hindu doctrinal content has not been consolidated in a single text - though *Bhagavat Gita* comes closest to it. Hindu scriptures have received varying interpretations. Hindu saints and reformers altered many Hindu practices. However, we will briefly outline what are commonly considered the central Hindu doctrines with a focus on their moral content.

Four Principal Moral Ends

We can begin with the Hindu conception of the four principal moral ends of life – *Dharma* (moral law), *Artha* (wealth), *Kama* (desire), and *Moksha* (salvation). The moral ends enable men to lead a happy moral life and also attain salvation after death. *Dharma* signifies the rational control of human passions, appetites and desires. *Dharma* is the correct way in which a human being has to fulfil his personal, social and moral needs.

Commentators hold two views on the nature of *dharma* or moral law. Some hold that it is a command of God. God's prescriptions cover moral actions; God's prohibitions refer to evil deeds which men should avoid. Other writers consider that moral law is an imperative which men have to follow without exceptions. It is not embodied in God; it is, however, a moral ideal which transcends the physical world of space and time. In fact, its moral perfection lies beyond human reach; men can only strive towards that moral ideal. As we shall see, the general and specific duties of men in common life are found in Varnashrama dharma.

Artha and *Kama*

Before considering *dharma* in more detail in the form of virtuous behaviour, we may outline the concepts of *Artha* and *Kama*. *Artha* in the sense of wealth stands for material means of well being. A householder needs a minimum of wealth to maintain his family and to meet its wholesome desires. *Artha* is not an endorsement of the greed at the root of an acquisitive society. It recognises the need for money to ensure a minimum living standard and to pursue artistic and aesthetic activities.

Although *Kama* is desire, one can regard it as happiness arising from satisfaction of wants. The reference is not to endless desires but to those which are common to men living within family. They need not be the wants of the individual but of the whole family including children. In Hindu ethics happiness is subordinated to dharma or virtue. Moral conduct creates *Punya* or beneficial Karmic effect. Bad conduct creates *papa* or evil karmic effects. *Punya* leads one to heaven and *papa* to hell. But these states of existence seem impermanent since men will be reborn after their *papa* or *Punya* lapse.

Dharma and *Moksha*

Dharma in its form as virtue is the ultimate value or the end in itself. It resembles the summum bonum of the Aristotelian philosophy. The ultimate goal of Hindu religion is that soul should be liberated from the constraints of the physical world and its myriad problems. In this state, human soul transcends its empirical self and loses its worldly content. Although it is difficult to visualize this state, it can be thought of as soul without the troubles, anxieties and disturbances which characterize its earthly existences.

Moksha is conceived somewhat differently by different writers. *Moksha* means that the self lives in its pure spiritual form or essence. It is free from the encumbrances of the physical world of senses or of the material universe of space and time. Soul loses its vital and intellectual properties which it had while inhabiting the body. It becomes eternal and immortal. In Sankara's interpretation, the soul merges with *Brahman*. Ramanuja says that it is in essential community with God. It realises infinite beatitude in God.

Varnashrama Dharma

The above account of Hindu ethics, it is clear, relates to the individual, the way he should enjoy his earthly existence within the bounds of *dharma* and prepare himself for *Moksha*. Hinduism also has an ethic which links an individual's morals to his membership of a social group. It is the famous *Varnashrama dharma*. In this version, society is divided into four occupational groups. The Brahmins have to master Vedas, practise religious ceremonies, and promote spiritualism in society. They are the guardians of the society's academic and spiritual traditions. The *Kashtriyas* are the warrior class. They have to acquire military skills and defend the society against internal and external threats. The *Vaishyas* are the trading community who has to carry on commerce and industry. The *Shudras* are the artisans and craftsmen who create the amenities of civilization.

Apart from the morals arising from one's station in society, there are duties which have to be performed at different stages of life. Thus a student (*Brahmachari*) has to lead a pure, chaste life, learn Vedas, and imbibe knowledge from teachers. A man has to marry and raise a family for his happiness and social good. In the next stage of *Vanaprastha*, one has to dedicate himself to solitary prayer and meditation. In the final stage, man has to become a wandering monk (*sanyasin*), living on alms and devoting himself to service to society and God.

Obviously, the occupational patterns of society today scarcely resemble those of ancient India. The point that is still valid is that one has to faithfully work in one's field of occupation. Thus, a soldier, fire officer or a teacher has clearly demarcated duties. As for the duties appropriate to different life stages, they have to be adopted with due regard to the enormous changes which the ancient society has undergone. The stage-of-life duties have to be related to the context of the modern society.

Countless volumes have appeared on caste in India. They are generally very critical of caste system. That the caste system has created divisions among Hindus is a fact which received constant emphasis from leaders of national movement and religious reformers. Mahatma Gandhi in particular worked hard for removing the practice of untouchability.

BHAGAVAT GITA

Main Message

The Hindu ethics are clearly stated in the *Bhagavat Gita*. Although the treatise is set against the background of the self doubts which a warrior develops before the commencement of the battle, its message encompasses the whole of human life. *Bhagavat Gita* prescribes that man should perform his duty without any desire for its fruits, without attachment and aversion, and without getting distracted by selfish and base motives. In brief, duty has to be performed for its own sake. Ultimately, duties have to be performed for realizing the vision of God. Duties are performed for the welfare of humanity and for the good of all living creatures. *Gita* preaches that the aim of our efforts is not happiness but good; personal and social good are the same. In achieving the highest good, man realises the vision of God.

Gita's message is that the whole basis of a man's life lies in action. There can be no life without action. A state of inaction is virtual death. *Gita* advocates neither quietism nor withdrawal from life. However, the action has to be based on one's duty.

The *Gita* does not prescribe asceticism for it is also concerned with performance of duties in society. It does not say that men should get rid of all emotions. One has to control bad emotions such as – attachment, aversion, illusions, fears, lust, grief, anger, hatred, malice and envy. What we would call positive emotions are to be cultivated. These include universal goodwill and benevolence, kindness towards people in trouble, magnanimity, serenity, indifference to worldly concerns, and love and devotion to God. Of course, God is to be reached by serving fellow men. Unlike in Buddhism and Jainism, God is central to the moral system of the *Gita*.

Paths to Salvation

According to the *Gita*, there are three paths to the realisation of God. *Karmayoga* consists in performing one's duties disinterestedly (*nishkama karma*) in the service of God. *Bhakti yoga* is the route of devotion to God. *Jnana yoga* is the approach to God based on attaining the enlightenment of soul through sacred knowledge. Jadunath Sinha says that *Bhagavat Gita's* message is closer to Green's Eudemonism than to Kant's rationalism or asceticism. Eudemonism is an ethical doctrine that characterizes the value of life in terms of happiness. Happiness here has to be understood in its most sublime forms.

Virtues

Gita associates a man's station in life, his *Varna*, and his psychological attributes. In other words, a warrior will have a mindset which differs from that of a *Brahmin* and a *Vaishya*. It may seem strange that the mental characteristics or psychological nature of an individual should be linked to his *Varna* or profession. But we know from experience that one's profession does leave a mark on one's character. We may think of psychological types in modern terms. Thus, a military officer will tend to behave in a particular manner. Similarly, politicians and businessmen have characteristic ways of acting. The link between the caste of an individual and his occupation has disappeared even in ancient India. Even Varna membership was no longer a matter of birth, but involved considerable mobility. But leaving aside these factual matters, we can conclude that a man's vocation broadly determines his duties and attitudes.

The following table shows the virtues which the *Gita* mentions as characteristic of the three principal groups of the society. Although the association is between Varna and virtues, in the modern context, we can regard these as lists of virtues broadly associated with occupations.

Brahmins	Kashtriyas	Vaishyas
Control of senses	*Heroism*	*Commercial skills*
Control of mind	*Spiritedness*	*Organisationalabilities*
Tranquillity	*Steadfastness in battle*	*Economic insights*
Austerity	*Generosity*	
Purity	*Firmness*	
Magnanimity	*Sovereignty*	
Knowledge	*Military skills*	
Wisdom		
Faith		

We can see that many of the virtues are relevant to different contexts of modern life.

We may note the parallel between the association of virtues with castes and the virtues which Plato considered necessary for different classes in *The Republic.* Thus, philosopher-kings possess wisdom; the soldiers possess courage and martial virtues. Traders embody economic values and temperance is a virtue desirable in all the classes.

Action without Craving

The duties which the *Gita* enjoins are to be performed without any craving for the expected results. A sense of duty should motivate men to action. Their moral duty extends to performing the needed actions; the outcome of their actions depends on divine will. Hence, they have to perform their actions in a calm and composed manner without getting anxious about the likely outcomes. Concern about the probable results of action, their success or failure, leads to bondage. If one acts without desire for what the action will bring about, then he acts like a *Sanyasi* or *Yogi*. This is in fact the *Gita's* path to salvation through action.

Positive and negative emotions

As we saw above, the *Gita* mentions the virtues which an individual possesses by virtue of his occupation. The *Gita* also lists the desirable positive emotions and the undesirable negative emotions. We can also regard them as generalized lists of human virtues and vices. We outline them below.

- Affection, animosity, attachment, aversion, selfishness, arrogance, jealousy, greed, hypocrisy, malice and similar emotions should never drive our actions.
- While doing our duties, we should ensure that our mind remains serene and composed.
- We should not be obsessed with anxieties about success or failure, happiness or misery, victory or defeat, profit or loss and glory or humiliation which our actions may bring about.
- We should not get unduly buoyed up by success or overly depressed by failure. We should learn to take such things in our stride.
- Human beings, by their very nature, tend to be selfish. But we should sublimate our selfish propensities by directing them towards service to God and society.
- We should not venerate only the external religious symbols. Mechanical observance of liturgical rules or strict adoption of rituals does not constitute the essence of religion. It is necessary to discipline our heart and purify our desires so that our desires flow along moral channels. Sacredness and purity ought to become the attributes of our souls.
- Men should not opt out of the challenges of personal and social life. They should not fall into escapism or seek false anodynes. Ideas like divine will or destiny should not be used as pretexts for inaction. Men cannot know divine will. They have to perform their duty without thinking about other matters.

We have outlined the negative emotions and the way to avoid them. Now, we look at the positive virtues which men should cultivate. For easy reference, we have put them in a tabular form.

Humility	*Kindness*	*Magnanimity*	*Forthrightness*
Respecting teachers	*Purity*	*Steadfastness*	*Self control*
Indifference to material pleasures	*Detachment*	*Sensitivity to human condition and human suffering*	*Benevolence*
Contentment	*Mental balance*	*Wisdom*	*Charity*
Truthfulness	*Control over senses*	*Concern for all sentient eings*	*Compassion*
Determination			

Comparison with Western Moral Ideals

Philosophers have compared the ethical system of *Gita* to moral systems of the Western philosophy. The system of *Gita* does not follow hedonism – which regards happiness as the end of life. Happiness can be given a refined meaning as aesthetic or cultural enjoyment. But even so, it is not covered in *Gita's* message. Nor does it correspond with utilitarianism in any of its forms. However, promoting human welfare is an object which men have to keep in view while performing their duties. As we emphasised, *Gita* rules out ennui, escapism, quietism or other forms of inertia. It propounds an ethic of action based on duty. In this form, it is eminently suitable for people active in various spheres of life.

As Kantianism is also based on 'duty', *Gita's* message has been compared to it. We need not delve deep, into this aspect. Suffice it to say that Kant's system is worked out without reference to God, whereas realisation of God is a constantly running theme of *Bhagavat Gita*. Further, though Kantianism differs from hedonism and utilitarianism, it centres on the individual. Concerns of general social welfare hardly find a direct mention in it. *Bhagavat Gita* abounds in references to welfare of human kind and of the whole of living creation.

Other Aspects of *Gita's* Moral Message

We may note the other main features of the moral preaching of the *Gita*. At one level, *Gita's* message is addressed to those who are totally concerned with realisation of God. Hence, *Gita* has passages in which one is advised to avoid excessive attachment to one's family and close kith and kin. One is also told to treat his family members at par with others. Such idealistic injunctions and a pronounced 'other worldliness' may create an impression that the message of *Gita*, though sublime, is unsuited to the normal situations of social life. The paths of devotion and of knowledge for realizing visions of Brahman also may seem remote from every day human concerns. Like the moral messages of other religions, they appear against settings of ancient societies. However, no religious belief remains static, but is interpreted to suit changing times. The message of *Gita*, rooted as it is in the concept of human duty, is universal and timeless in its appeal and relevance.

MORAL CRITERIA AND CONCEPTS

While discussing Hindu ethics, we need to consider some other aspects. First, Hindu scriptures and moral treatises contain explanations of human conduct, and the reasons why men fare so differently in their lives. Some succeed; others fail; some become rich; others stay poor; some are born with a silver spoon in the mouth; others take birth in a cottage; and some are happy; and others are miserable. Secondly, the treatises explain the motive springs of human action. Thirdly, they contain moral concepts and moral standards. We begin with explanations of human conduct.

To those acquainted with accounts of human motivation, behaviour and action in modern psychology, the explanations of ancient writers will seem strange. They tend to be simplistic; use unreal concepts, and introduce non verifiable or supernatural elements. Even with these limitations, they reveal an intuitive insight into human psyche. To understand ancient writers, we have to enter their social world using historical and psychological imagination.

According to ancient writers, men have freewill. They can decide whether or not to follow the moral law. The classification of right and wrong is based on scriptures. Right is that which scriptures prescribe; wrong is that which scriptures prohibit. Man acquires merit or virtue by doing good deeds; he collects demerit or vices by following evil. Virtues and vices are predispositions (to act) which get lodged in men's souls. They produce their results, good or bad, usually with a time lag either in this or next life. These are the causes of our happiness or misery. The chain consists of:

Good deed → merit → happiness; and

Evil deed → demerit → misery

One can overcome demerits by doing good acts; and one can also lose merit by committing sinful acts. There is a continuous cycle of births and deaths. It consists of birth, life, good deeds, bad deeds, merits, demerits, death, transmigration of soul, and rebirth. Release from this perpetual cycle comes through realisation of God through one of the three paths to salvation. This is the law of karma which many writers regard as the corner stone of Hindu philosophy.

Continuing with this explanation of human conduct, we find that our actions arise partly from our merits and demerits, and partly from our autonomous volitions. Action based on human will is *purushakara* or *purushardha*. Merits and demerits from earlier life are *daiva.* They are invisible entities or *adrishta.* They are like random variables, and influence our life. They need to be distinguished from fate or destiny which is preordained and decided by an external agency without any reference to man. But *adrishta* is based on man's own actions; they are predispositions of soul which man's own actions have created. There is another meaning of *daiva,* as when we say that our success in an enterprise is due to divine will. Our voluntary efforts succeed only when endorsed by divine will or "*insha Allah*" (God willing). *Purushardha* and *daiva anugraha* (divine grace) are necessary for success.

Law of Karma

Law of karma is a matter of faith. It is not an empirical (grounded in human experience) theory; nor is it verifiable. An attempt to establish a statistical correlation between good deeds and merit and bad deeds and demerit is impossible. We do not know what happens to the soul, if there is one, after death. In modern psychology, human consciousness is considered a psycho-physiological phenomenon. So death may be the end of everything.

Apart from the scientific veracity of the law of *karma,* it has other disadvantages. Of course, the conflict between science and religion is not confined to any particular religion. The doctrine of *karma* had other consequences. Though it is not the same as fatalism, and though the effects of bad deeds can be overcome, it has created a negative or fatalistic outlook. People concluded that their prospects in life are largely predetermined. They underestimated the value of and the need for human initiative and self driven effort.

Karma theory leads to social and economic conservatism. Human suffering, poverty and social inequalities appear as consequences of demerits of the victims. The incentive for good works suffers as a consequence. Concerted social action for tackling existing evils gets discouraged. Actually, these unfortunate conclusions follow from a false interpretation of *karma* theory. As we saw, *Bhagavat Gita* is a gospel for action. In modern times, Swami Vivekananda worked indefatigably to remove these cobwebs from the Hindu psyche.

Manu's Ideas

Manu (much reviled in modern times) regarded the customary law of the society as the standard. It is called *achara.* It is sanctified by practice over many generations, and becomes part of social memory. Those who follow it faithfully live for long and are happy. They achieve good things. On the contrary, those who flout *achara* fare ill.

According to Manu, the customary law has to be in consonance with Vedas which are the divine source of law. For Manu, Vedas provide the moral standard. He also recognises conscience as a source of law. When we perceive an act as in keeping with our conscience, we feel a sense of ease. When we violate the promptings of conscience, we feel uneasy. We are all familiar with feelings of guilt, generally over minor transgressions. Sigmund Freud, the founder of psychoanalysis, speaks of a 'super ego', which represents the moral codes implanted in us at home and school. We feel mentally uneasy when we act against the dictates of the super ego.

Mahabharata

According to *Mahabharata*, Vedas which reveal divine law, and Smritis, which reveal customary law are the sources of our morals. Virtue is defined in terms of customary conduct. Those actions which generally receive common approbation are virtuous; those actions which receive social opprobrium are wrong. Acts which carry social approval should be done; acts which carry social censure should be avoided.

As we saw, our conduct should conform to dharma. *Mahabharata* refers to many dimensions of dharma. *Dharma* is something common to the conduct of virtuous individuals in many places. *Dharma* always carries the sanction of conscience. It is good and promotes the welfare of humanity. The different sides of *Dharma* are Vedic injunctions, customary conduct, voice of conscience and whatever promotes social welfare. In case of conflict between these, Vedic injunctions become ultimate arbiters.

Ramayana contains similar ideas on morality. Whether an action is right or wrong has to be decided having regard to Vedic law, reason, customary behaviour of virtuous persons and social norms. Vedas will, however, prevail in case of conflict among these criteria. Devotion to the good of humanity is seen as the highest virtue.

Samyama

Indian ethics consider moderation (*samyama*) as a moral standard. We can find these ideas in Buddhism, Jainism and Hinduism. Samyama finds expression in the following moral ideas which Buddha preached;

- Men should not seek sensual pleasures in excess; however, they need not also extinguish all material desires.
- A virtuous life is a life of moderation which avoids both hedonism and asceticism.
- Men should be benevolent, control their will and spend time in serene meditation.
- Jainism expresses similar ideas.
- Excessive pleasures which undermine the moral basis of the soul and upset its balance are bad.
- Natural instincts, passions and impulses should not be totally curbed, but regulated by reason for harmonious living.

Bhagavat Gita places great emphasis on temperance.

The extremes which *Gita* mentions are:

Over eating – fasting
Overwork – inactivity
Over sleeping – sleeplessness

Gita stresses that moderation is the key to mental discipline.

In Indian ethics, both political law and divine law are mentioned as moral standards. These standards are external. Charvakas considered king's commands as laws. A king represents the highest political authority or sovereignty. The laws that he proclaims become the moral standards. To obey a king's law is right; and to defy a king's law is wrong.

However, this view is opposed by many authoritative treatises. According to the *Nyaya Vaisheshika*, the divine law or the God's command is the moral standard. God is the creator and sustainer of the world. He created the world as a moral order and governs accordingly. The divine laws are contained in the Vedas. It is to these that one should look up to for moral guidance. *Bhagavat Gita* and *Mahabharata* take similar positions.

According to *Bhagavat Gita*, in the human world, social welfare is the greatest good. Men have to act according to their duties to promote human welfare; in this manner, they also make personal spiritual progress. Wise men should perform work without hoping for personal gain and for general good. Sankaracharya interpreted social welfare as social regeneration. The degenerate individuals have to be reformed and turned away from evil.

We may also note that *Pravitti* and *Nivritti* are two modes of moral life which Sankaracharya mentions. The former refers to personal morality as applicable to empirical world. The latter signifies the withdrawal of spiritually inclined individual from worldly preoccupations. He detaches himself from all activities and avocations; and concentrating on his self, he seeks a vision of the Godhead. These standards refer to an individual's religious practice than to practical ethical problems or standards.

JAINISM

Jainism dates back to sixth century B.C. Its founder, Mahavira, is a contemporary of Buddha. Like Buddhism, Jainism also rose partly in reaction to the ritualism which marked Vedic religion. Elements of Jain teaching such as ahimsa, including opposition to animal sacrifices found expression even during Vedic period. Mahavira like Buddha admitted people from different ranks of society into Jainism. Unlike Buddhism, Jainism has survived in India throughout history despite the vicissitudes it faced. This is due to the strict adherence of Jains to their religious discipline. In Jainism, strict moral discipline is seen as the route to salvation. In its course, Jainism separated into two sects – Swetambaras and Digambaras. Swetambaras wear clothes, and Digambaras go without them.

Ahimsa

Ahimsa is a core moral principle of Jainism. It lays down that no existent being with life or the essence or potential of life should be injured. Injury is defined as its destruction, subjection or denial of its living essence or potential. Jain principle of *Ahimsa* in turn follows from the fact that sentient creatures are vulnerable to pain and sorrow. Just as pain and sorrow are undesirable to human beings, so are they to other creatures which breathe, live and possess the essence of or potential for life.

Path to Salvation

For a Jain, life is a spiritual odyssey towards divine consciousness. This state is attained when men secure release from the bonds of karma. Ratnatraya or three ornaments open the path to salvation. These are–Samyak darshan or right faith, Samyak Jnana or right knowledge and Samyak charitra or right conduct. The ultimate objective of spiritual efforts is to find freedom from the misery of the world in which one's soul is enmeshed.

Five Moral Principles

Jainism prescribes moral principles both for householders and monks. The codes for monks are more rigorous. The five common moral principles applicable both to monks and householders consist of: refraining from violence towards any living things; speaking the truth; refraining from theft; shunning adultery; and eschewing greed for material wealth.

We need to briefly elaborate the five moral ideas as understood in Jainism. As we saw before, killing or hurting any living creature constitutes violence. Life in nature is equal; harming big or small animal life is equally bad. Violence includes not only physical injury to others but also emotional harm through bad behaviour or offensive language. Jainism accepts that householders cannot lead a life which causes no harm at all to sentient beings. A householder must therefore try to minimize the injury he causes to others. Eating animal flesh in any form is strictly forbidden.

Jain conception of truth means faithful rendering of the visual and verbal evidence in one's possession. One cannot depart from truth even for saving oneself. This injunction is similar to Kant's Categorical Imperative which is absolutely inviolable. However, one can make an exception to this rule from an altruistic angle with a view to prevent harm to others.

The concept of stealing is wider than its current legal meaning. It includes directly stealing something or asking others to steal it. Use of false measures or weights, and receiving of stolen property are also forms of stealing. One should return, when he finds any lost property, to its owner. Keeping such property for one's use is a form of theft.

The fourth principle enjoins that a married person should not cast covetous glances at women. He should treat them respectfully. This rule of Brahmacharya applies to all men.

The fifth ethical principle urges men to curb their acquisitive instincts. Naturally, a householder needs a minimum income and wealth to support his family. He should not, however, get greedy and develop an inordinate love for wealth. This propensity invariably leads to dissatisfaction and suffering. Households should restrain their wants, and lead a simple, contented life.

The concept of God or a supreme being governing the universe is lacking in Jainism. The world, in its view, is governed by natural laws. In this regard, Jainism has a parallel in Stoicism. Another affinity with Stoicism consists in its advocacy of austere bodily and mental discipline. Jains are advised to ignore the superstitious beliefs popular among people. They should avoid the practice of performing rituals and ceremonies for pleasing gods.

Pride

In their pursuit of self-perfection, men have to abandon pride. In a way, this idea also finds an echo in Christianity - pride is one of the seven deadly sins. Jainism traces human pride or arrogance to eight sources. Men usually take pride in their intelligence, their beauty, their noble family, their caste, their physical and mental strength, their magical powers, their mode of temple worship and their tapas (prolonged meditation) and yoga. One has to give up arrogance on these counts. Unless one gives up pride, he cannot become pure and humble in heart, and attain to divine consciousness.

The Jain monks have to follow a more austere code than householders. They cannot live long at a place and have to lead a peripatetic life. They have to expose themselves to the elements in order to steel themselves against hunger, thirst, cold and heat. By leading an intensely austere life, based on sound moral and aesthetic principles, by making their hearts pure and humble, they become "jina" or spiritual conquerors.

BUDDHISM

Life of Buddha

Siddhartha was born about 583 BC near Nepal. His father, King Suddhodana, was head of the Shakya clan. His mother, Queen Maya, died shortly after his birth. Suddhodana wanted his son to become a great warrior. He raised Siddhartha in great luxury and shielded him from knowledge of death and human suffering. Till his twenty ninth year, Siddhartha knew little of life outside the palace walls.

One day, overcome by curiosity Siddhartha made several trips in a chariot through the countryside. In these trips, he met with disturbing sights of an aged man, a sick man, and a corpse. The grim pictures of old age, disease, and death upset him greatly. Later, he saw a wandering ascetic who had renounced the world and sought release from fear of death and suffering.

He returned to palace life for a while, but found little pleasure in it. The news of his son's birth also did not cheer him. One night he wandered in the palace alone, and was seized by a sense of futility of his luxurious life. He left the palace, shaved his head, changed his prince's clothes for a beggar's robe, and began his search for enlightenment.

Siddhartha held discourses with renowned teachers, and learnt religious doctrines and meditation. Still, he found no answers to his doubts and questions. He and his first five disciples then began looking for enlightenment on their own. They sought freedom from suffering through physical discipline, enduring pain, holding their breath, fasting nearly to starvation. Finding no release, Siddhartha tried the Middle Way. He realised that the path of liberation was through discipline of mind. He found enlightenment while meditating beneath a sacred fig, known later as the Bodhi Tree. His spiritual struggle was mythologized as a great battle with Mara, a demon whose name means "destruction" and who represents the human passions.

Conceptual framework of Buddhist thought

Four Noble Truths

The essence of Buddha's teaching is contained in the Four Noble Truths. He enunciated them in the first sermon which he gave to his five old ascetic colleagues at Sarnath. The Four Noble truths set out the path for an individual's enlightenment.

The four truths are:

- The truth of dukkha
- The truth of the origin of the dukkha
- The truth of cessation of dukkha
- The truth of the path leading to the cessation of dukkha

Truth of Dukkha

Three Types of Dukkha

The meaning of dukkha is suffering, anxiety and dissatisfaction. This Pali term has wider connotation than its Sanskrit counterpart which means 'suffering'. Buddhist thought refers to three types of dukkha.

Dukkha-dukkha means the dukkha of ordinary suffering. This is the pain associated with giving birth, growing old, physical illness and the process of dying.

Viparinama dukkha is the dukkha produced by change. It denotes the anxiety or stress in trying to hold on to things that are continuously changing.

Samkhara dukkha is the dukkha of conditioned states. It arises from a realisation that all forms of life are characterised by impermanence and flux. In this sense, dukkha indicates a lack of satisfaction which arises from feeling that things never measure up to our expectations or standards.

The focus on dukkha is not pessimistic. The purpose is to understand the nature of dukkha with a view to transcend it. Buddha recognised that that the world offers both happiness and unhappiness. However, the states of happiness are transitory and changing. Hence, whatever we experience in the world leaves us with a sense of dissatisfaction. Unless we gain an insight into what gives us happiness and what is unable to do so, we will continue in a state of unhappiness. We look for happiness in external things rather than in our internal feelings and attitudes. As all sources of happiness are transient, any feeling of happiness is accompanied by dissatisfaction. We have to recognise this to start looking for real happiness.

Origin of Dukkha

The origin of dukkha is traced to craving (tanha) conditioned by ignorance (avijia). Hankering runs along three tracks:

¤ Craving for sense pleasure which is craving for sense objects that give pleasant sensations or carving for sensory pleasures.

¤ Craving consists in the desire to be something, to unite with an experience. It includes craving for continuity, to be a being that has a past and a future, and the desire to prevail and dominate others.

¤ 'Craving not to be' signifies a desire not to experience the world, and to be nothing, a wish to be separated from painful feelings.

¤ Ignorance can be interpreted as ignorance of the meaning and implications of the four noble truths. It implies a misunderstanding of the self and reality.

Cessation of Dukkha

The third noble truth is cessation of all the unsatisfactory experiences and their causes in a manner that they cannot recur. It refers to final absence or non-arising of things that cause suffering. Cessation of dukkha is the objective of Buddhist spiritual practices. Having eradicated the sources of suffering i.e. craving and ignorance, one feels liberated. This is also the state of nirvana. By removing causes of suffering from the mind, one can experience temporary nirvana. The more serene the mind, the greater the nirvana it experiences.

Path Leading to the Cessation of Dukkha

Eightfold Path

The fourth noble path is the way to end dukkha. It is called the eightfold path. It consists of: Right Understanding; Right Thought: Right Speech; Right Action; Right livelihood; Right Effort; Right mindfulness; and Right concentration. The first three paths help in understanding the nature of dukkha. The fourth path is a practical means of overcoming dukkha. The paths are interconnected and constitute a way of living. The wheel of *Dharma* pictorially depicts the eightfold path.

Right view is the intellectual aspect of wisdom. It implies penetrating the outward aspect of things, understanding the transient and imperfect nature of worldly objects and ideas, and understanding the law of karma and karmic conditioning.

Right intention refers to the type of psychic energy which controls human actions. It is commitment to moral and mental self-improvement. There are three kinds of right intention (i) resisting the pull of craving; (ii) resisting feelings of anger and aversion; and (iii) avoiding thoughts and actions which involve violence, cruelty and aggression and cultivating compassion.

Right speech is route to moral discipline which sustains other virtues. Right speech consists of the following:

- To abstain from telling lies and speaking deceitfully
- To avoid malicious or slanderous speech
- To refrain from using harsh words which hurt others
- To abstain from idle chatter that lacks purpose or depth

Right action includes: acting kindly and compassionately; to be honest; to respect the belongings of others; and to avoid sexual misconduct.

Right livelihood implies that one should follow righteous means of earning bread and that wealth has to be earned only through legal and nonviolent ways. Buddha suggests that the following occupations should be avoided:

- Dealing in weapons
- Dealing in living things such as slave trade or rearing animals for slaughter
- Working in meat production or butchery
- Selling intoxicants or poisons

Right effort refers to psychic energy which produces either wholesome or unwholesome mental states. It can lead, for example, to aggression, envy, desire and violence. But the same energy can lead to self-discipline, honesty, altruism and compassion. One has to control mind through right efforts. These are:

- To prevent any unwholesome states from arising in the mind
- To banish unwholesome states which have arisen in the mind
- To arouse wholesome states in the mind
- To sustain the wholesome states present in the mind

Right mindfulness refers to the cognitive processes through which we understand things. We receive sense impressions through perception. Our cognitive processes act on the bare impressions and interpret those using concepts and our earlier experiences. In this way, we end up creating complex interpretive schemes. The original impressions and associated thoughts can get distorted in this process. Buddha says that we should perceive clearly and should not get carried away by the working of intellectual processes. For this purpose, he recommends four foundations of mindfulness:

- Contemplation of the body
- Contemplation of feeling (repulsive, attractive or neutral)
- Contemplation of the state of the mind
- Contemplation of the phenomena

Right concentration signifies single-pointedness of the mind in which all mental faculties are unified and directed towards a single object. The right concentration has to be on wholesome thoughts and actions. Buddhists try to achieve right concentration through practising meditation. This leads to a mental state without passions, with self-control and tranquillity.

Buddhists believe that to concentrate on complete self-realisation, men need to follow three golden rules:

(i) Taking refuge in Buddha

(ii) Taking refuge in *Dharma*

(iii) Taking refuge in Sanga (company of enlightened)

Prescriptions for Family and Society

Buddhism prescribes various morals for harmonious family and social life. Parents are enjoined to provide intellectual education to children and bequeath property to them. Children should take care of their aged parents. Disciples have to respect their teachers. Teachers have to instruct pupils in arts, sciences and virtues. It is a husband's duty to treat his wife affectionately, provide her needs, and observe marital fidelity. The wife has to manage the household wisely and frugally, be faithful and loving towards her husband. The master should treat his servants well, pay adequate wages and give periods of rest. The servants should be faithful, contented and serve their masters cheerfully. People should acquire qualities of liberality, courtesy, kindness and selflessness.

Non-Violence and Peace

In the end, we may note the important features of Buddhist morals. Buddha preached that everyone should cultivable happiness and serenity; and that no one should despise or injure another. Men should overcome hatred with love, and evil with good. Otherwise, hatred and evil will only grow. Returning good for good is great, but returning good for evil is greater. Buddha anticipates the injunction of Christ that violence should not be met with violence.

A man who imposes his view on others violently is unjust. A man who distinguishes between right and wrong, and who leads men not through violence, but by law, righteousness and equity is just. An Arya is cultured not because he kills animals but because he does not injure them. Only a person who refrains from injuring others by word or deed deserves the title of 'Brahmin'. Barbarism is characterised by violence and culture by compassion and non-violence.

Buddhism emphasises the need for purity of heart; mere externally decent conduct is of no avail. Men should free themselves from malice, greed and delusion. Anger, jealousy, and evil emotions have to be eschewed.

Middle Course

Buddhism steers a middle course between extreme self-denial and excessive pursuit of material pleasures. Selfishness creates cravings which become a source of suffering; it is only by regulating such cravings through self-discipline that men can enter the path to enlightenment. At the same time, Buddha does not advocate rigorous asceticism, and mortifying the body. Physiological needs of body like food, clothing, and minimum comforts of existence are necessary. Otherwise, the mind will fail to reach the composure necessary for meditation. We can compare Buddha's approach to that of Aristotle's golden mean which avoids extremes of human conduct.

Buddha preferred the life of a monk to that of a householder. He strikes a balance between hedonism and asceticism. It does not lead to quietism or passive withdrawal from social life. He recommends an active and good life in the service of humanity.

Altruism

Buddhism has a strong streak of altruism. It advocates universal compassion, benevolence and kindness to all life forms. It reacted against cruel animal sacrifices, rigid occupational classification of society, and religious metaphysics. Buddha did not discuss God and soul in detail as Hindu scriptures do. He moved away from mere ceremonialism to ways of reducing human misery and increasing human happiness. Many writers regard Buddhism as informed by moral rationalism.

Buddhist approach also relies on a rational outlook. Men need to be self-conscious and live in the present in a calm frame of mind. They have to avoid activities which cause suffering. They need to shun activities which result in remorse and anxiety.

GANDHIAN ETHICS

Gandhian thought covers many aspects of human life. Gandhi, as leader of Indian national movement, and as prolific writer has commented on very many things. His thought is multi-dimensional and covers political, social, economic, religious and ethical aspects of human life. His ideas emerged partly from his inner religious convictions, partly from the exigencies of forging strategies for a mass political movement and partly from the influence of others such as Tolstoy, Carlyle and Thoreau. Gandhi was also influenced by ethical principles embedded in Buddhism, Jainism, Hinduism and Christianity. It is impossible to cover all aspects of Gandhian thought within a short span. However, we will discuss those aspects of Gandhian thought which have a special bearing on ethics.

There is of course a difficulty in that no part of Gandhian thought can altogether be separated from ethics. His ideas are generally expressed in moral categories or terminology. Ethical theories provide the underpinnings for Gandhian thought in any sphere. Evolution of Gandhian ideas took place within a matrix of non-violent mass political struggle. In the process, they went through some twists and turns. Any general outline of Gandhian ethical ideas has to concern itself with the major ethical streams which flow through them. We will now consider the major moral themes embedded in Gandhian thought.

Gandhi is not an academic thinker. Further, as a mass leader, he was concerned more with praxis or practice than with theory. He had to communicate with untutored masses. Although his thoughts are not illogical, they are based on premises whose truth is taken for granted. These premises are essentially the core moral values to which Gandhi subscribes. Gandhi has a feeling of inner certainty about them. Based on such values, Gandhi has created a moral system which also served as the framework for his political practice. In this sense, Gandhi's ethics and his political action are intertwined.

Faith in God

Gandhi has a deep and abiding faith in God, and has written extensively about his conception of God. However, these ideas, really speaking, belong to theology or religious theory. So, we need not discuss the nature of God in Gandhian thought. But a few words on the subject are necessary since Gandhi derives his political ideology from his desire to realise God. His conception of God-though Gandhi was fond of Lord Rama-is not derived from any particular religion. He regards God as an impersonal force and benevolent governor of the world. God is present (or immanent) in every human soul.

We will now consider how Gandhi's chief moral ideas and practices follow from his conception of God. It is impossible to establish clear logical links in his thought processes because the ideas involved are mystical. In other words, they belong to religious mysticism than to pure logic. Gandhi considers that the ultimate goal of man is to realise the vision of God. And realisation of God is impossible unless one follows the path of truth, love, non violence and service to humanity.

Gandhi narrates various divine attributes and posits equivalence between these individual attributes and God. Incidentally, God in Hindu conception is eternal, all knowing, all powerful and absolutely benevolent. God has no form or qualities – Nirguna, Nirakara Brahman. The representations of God in Hindu temples are symbolic. The Christian God is personal, and has the triune form of Father, Son (Christ) and Holy Spirit (Christ's appearance in spiritual form after his crucifixion).

Returning to Gandhi's conception of God, we may note that Gandhi regards God as Truth, Love, Fearlessness, and the source of Light and Life. He says that God and his Law are the same. God is also Truth-Knowledge-Bliss (Sat-Chit-Ananda).

Ethical Conduct

Gandhi draws several conclusions from these equivalences. Men should emulate, to the extent they can, the divine attributes in their conduct. Of course, as human beings, men can never reach the perfection of divine virtues. However, they should strive with all their strength to follow the virtues of truth, love, nonviolence, tolerance, fearlessness, charity and service to mankind. Men have to uphold the right, regardless of the personal consequences they may face. As we shall see, Gandhi urges Satyagrhis (those keen in pursuit of truth or a right cause or nonviolent protestors) to adopt these virtues.

As mentioned above, Gandhi equates God with truth and love. Love is another name of nonviolence. Gandhi regarded that men should be guided by the objective of realizing the vision of God. This aim should inform all their activities–personal, political or social. Now, as God is truth and love or nonviolence, practising these two virtues is the way to reach God.

Truth

Gandhi equates God also with truth. He designated his religion as 'religion of truth'. To start with, Gandhi used to say that God is truth. Later, he changed it to 'truth is God' to show that truth constitutes the divine essence. He uses a metaphor to explain his meaning. Individual man is like a spark of truth. When all the sparks combine, they result in an indescribable divine conflagration.

Gandhi's metaphor is rather obscure. In modern logic, truth and falsehood are the properties of propositions. Modern philosophers subscribe to two theories of truth. One is called the correspondence theory of truth. It says that a statement is true if what it alleges describes an existing state of affairs in the world. A true statement corresponds to some fact in the world. For example, 'there is a dog near the gate'. This statement will be true if there is *really* a dog near the gate.

The second conception of truth is based on coherence theory. It says that a statement is true if it is consistent with a system of ideas or beliefs that one holds. In other words, a true idea is part of a consistent set of beliefs. In the first view, truth reduces to a question of empirical verification. In the coherence theory, truth is a matter of logical consistency.

Gandhi's idea of truth is not taken from epistemology or theory of knowledge. He views truth in the form it often takes in lofty discussions of religion, theology and metaphysics. It is an ideal of human conduct; it shows how men should order their social, political and economic world. It applies to entities such as political or social causes and movements. Thus Gandhi regarded that the Indian struggle for independence stands for truth because it represents a just struggle for national and individual autonomy. Truth in this sense is not amenable to strict logical analysis. It is part of what we would now call 'a value system'. However, one can examine whether the things described as 'truth' form part of a consistent set of ideas. There is no doubt that 'truth' in this meaning fits into the larger canvas of Gandhian thought.

Incidentally, we may note here Tolstoy's influence on Gandhi. Tolstoy says, "The heroine of my writing is she, whom I love with all the force of being. She who always was, is and will be beautiful is truth." Gandhi announces: "I am devoted to nothing but truth and I owe no discipline to anybody but truth."

Service to Society

There is another way in which Gandhi's concept of God underpins his practical actions. As we have already noted, realisation of vision of God ought to be man's principal aim in life. The only way to see God is through his creation and by identifying oneself with it. This is possible only through service to humanity. Gandhi speaks in this context of merging oneself with humanity and of regarding oneself as a part of a larger whole. Gandhi's emphasis on social service also follows from this view. There is no escape from social service to those in search of divine vision. It has to be the be-all and end-all of their life.

For Gandhi, human brotherhood and oneness follow from the unity of life. As part of God's creation, men share the same life. There can be no real differences between them. From this angle, distinctions based on gender, caste, creed, language and nationality are trivial; what counts is the underlying unity of life of mankind. One can see that the principle of unity of life leads to Gandhian concepts of secularism or religious toleration, human equality, and explains his life long battle against untouchability.

Purity of Heart

As Gandhi identified God with virtues, it follows that men should be pure in heart. Gandhi insisted on cleanliness even in its physical manifestations. The Ashrams and their surroundings had to be spic and span with no litter, dirt or filth. He believed in the adage that cleanliness is next to godliness. Morally, Gandhi advocated self-purification. This is part of the personal morality derived from religion. Modern readers will feel that Gandhi pushed some ideas to excess. He had a natural revulsion to non vegetarian food. His autobiography shows that his onetime secret consumption of meat in childhood proved traumatic. He also appears to have been troubled by the normal sexuality which is part of marriage.

Ends and Means

More importantly, Gandhi firmly believed that even for attaining noble objectives, men have to only adopt good means. No good can follow from bad deeds, even if they are well intentioned. In this regard, we may also recall the saying that, "The path to hell is paved with good intentions". This is known as the 'ends and means' debate. Some writers (e.g. Machaivelli) argue that bad means can be used to achieve good ends. What matters is the end. The sacrifices which society bears in adopting evil means are compensated by the noble ends which are attained.

However, few thinkers now support the view that ends justify the means. Human experience has shown that in the name of pursuing noble ends, untold misery and suffering have been inflicted on innocent men and women. This happened during religious wars which Catholics and Protestants fought in Europe during the sixteenth century. A more recent example is from Soviet Union. Stalin pursued an utterly ruthless policy of collectivization of private farm holdings in pursuit of communist ideology, and in the process massacred millions of Kulaks or Russian peasants. For pursuing the putative ideals, Stalin used evil means unmindful of their terrible human costs.

Gandhi constantly emphasised that means have to be pure. This follows *ipso facto* from the conception of God as the embodiment of virtues. In following unethical means in any matter, we will be acting in opposition to divine injunctions. He regarded ends and means as interchangeable terms.

Human Nature

Now, we proceed to a consideration of the main concepts associated with Gandhian thought. First, we outline the idea of non violence or ahimsa. Before doing so, we need to briefly outline Gandhi's conception of the moral order in the universe. The world is such that men can realise their moral ideals. Man has a divine spark in him. As a spiritual being, he cannot follow the mores of animal life or its ruthless struggles. Violence and self-assertion are alien to him. Rather he is benevolent with a desire to help others. The will to power-the desire to subjugate and crush others-is not a part of his nature. He is gentle, humble, kind, generous, loving and considerate. Gandhi sides with those philosophers like Rousseau and David Hume, who regard man as inherently good and benevolent. His conception of humanity is radically opposed to those thinkers who regard man as essentially selfish and bent upon imposing his will ruthlessly on others. Gandhi also believed that men are reasonable, willing to see the viewpoints of others, and partly accommodate their viewpoints through rational discussion.

Ahimsa

Gandhi explained ahimsa in negative and positive terms. The negative view of ahimsa implies the following.

- It is refraining from killing or injuring others.
- One should not harm anyone by thought, word or deed.
- Violence has to be shunned in all its aspects.

The positive view embraces the following aspects.

- Non-violence does not just mean that one avoids injuring others. One should also show overflowing love to mankind and all living beings.
- Ahimsa is closely linked to truth, and to man's search for God. As God is truth and love and as love is ahimsa, man can realise God only by pursuing ahimsa. Gandhi regards truth and non-violence to be inseparable.

Many prerequisites are necessary for steadfast pursuit of ahimsa. Foremost among these are truthfulness and fearlessness. Men need only fear God and no one else. If men obey God, they need not worry about any human agency. From this follows the doctrine of Satyagraha which denotes fearless pursuit of truth. Satyagraha is the name which Gandhi gave to the peaceful protests against British rule in India.

Ahimsa requires complete self-purification. It also needs faith in the existence of soul which is distinct from body. *Ahimsa* is described as 'soul force', 'power of Atman', 'power of love' and utter selflessness.

Selflessness in turn signifies total indifference to body. It seems that Gandhi's aim is to strengthen the resolve of the freedom fighters, and to encourage them to be prepared to undergo bodily pain.

Anger and hatred are the opposite poles of ahimsa. Hatred is a very subtle form of violence. Men should rather win over their enemies by love. One should not react to violence with counter violence. *Ahimsa* means that one's love should be extended to one's enemies. It is similar to Christ's injunction: Love thy enemy.

Non-violence, in its active sense, includes truth and fearlessness. Gandhi insists that non-violence is not a creed of inaction. Nor is it for the weak or the timid. Non-violence does not signify meek acceptance of evil. It is better to be violent than to be cowardly. Gandhi naturally feared that nonviolence may become a convenient alibi for avoiding confrontation with the British rulers.

Non-violence requires humility for it relies solely on God. One does not use any physical means to resist force. Non-violence is superior to vengeance which is based on apprehended harm. Vengeance is better than meek surrender to superior force. But forgiveness is the best for it shows strength and courage. In sum, many qualities – such as truthfulness, selflessness, absence of anger, pride and hate, benevolence, altruism, courage, magnanimity, humility and total submission to God – are comprised in nonviolence.

Non-violent Non-cooperation

Gandhi advocated that evil should be tackled by means of non-violent non-cooperation with it. One should hate the evil deed but not its perpetrator. The logic for this belief is that men are the children of the same God, and that attacking even a single individual is an attack on the whole of humanity. If all cooperation with evil is withdrawn, it will have nothing to act upon.

This logic applies to individuals as well as to institutions and systems. To fight an unjust system Gandhi advocated non-violent non-cooperation. To fight the British imperial rule, Gandhi relied on civil disobedience and passive resistance. Gandhi borrowed the idea of civil disobedience from Henry Thoreau, a famous American thinker. Thoreau's books relevant in this context are *Resistance to Civil Government* and his autobiography *A Yankee in Canada.* A civil resistor simply ignores the authority of the government. He opposes the unjust laws imposed on him without resorting to violence.

Gandhi traces all social, political, economic and religious problems to violence. Non-violence holds the key to the solution of these problems. Gandhi argues that non-violence can be a potent weapon in the hands of masses. Non-violent non-cooperation of masses is not a rebellion; it is a revolution – but an evolutionary revolution. Gandhi considered such mass movements as bloodless revolutions in the sphere of spirit and thought.

Gandhi often resorted to fasting as a weapon of Satyagraha. He thought that fasting has a spiritual value and that it heightens the effect of prayer. For those who believe in nonviolence, it is an ultimate weapon. In extreme situations, a Satyagrahi should be prepared to fast unto death.

Qualities of a Satyagrahi

A Satyagrahi is the foot soldier of the passive resistance movement. He has to embody the virtues of truth and nonviolence. The effectiveness of the civil disobedience movements will depend on him; he will also be on display as a model of Gandhian values. Gandhi prescribes various virtues which a Satyagrahi needs to cultivate.

A Satyagrahi should be truthful, nonviolent, honest, and eschew material possessions and sexual desires. Realisation of God is impossible if one does not eradicate sexual desire. Sexual act in so far as it promotes procreation is noble. Any other use of it is a sin. Brahmacharya (avoiding sexual activity) has to be observed in thought, word and deed–*Mano, Vacha, Karmani*.

Gandhi prescribes a severe code for the Satyagrahi which includes harsh moral discipline, control of senses and ascetic self-denial. The qualities which a Satyagrahi has to cultivate are shown in the table below.

Humility	*Silence*	*Renunciation*
Self-sacrifice	***Thought control***	***Non-violence***
Universal benevolence	***Non use of drinks and drugs***	

He should earn his living; he has to do manual work and cut down his wants to bare necessities. He should show respect to all men and women and to all religions. He has to discharge his duties diligently without making undue claims. He should be like an enthusiastic voluntary soldier ever ready to undertake onerous tasks.

In this connection, we may recall the 11 vows which residents of Kochrab and Sabarmati ashrams had to observe,

The vows were:

- Satya: Truth
- Ahimsa: Non-violence
- Brahmacharya: Celibacy
- Asvada: Control of the palate
- Asteya: No stealing
- Aparigraha or Asangraha: Not having personal possessions
- Sharira Sharama: Physical labour
- Swadeshi: Indigenization
- Abhaya: Fearlessness
- Asprishyaatanivarana: Removal of untouchability
- Sarva Dharma Sambhava: Respect for all religions

The first five were the most important and are found in all religions. Bapu called them 'Panch Mahavratas'. The world may have seen Gandhi as a freedom fighter and political leader, but in his heart he was a 'sadhak' - one who is in search of God. He believed that the service of humankind was the best way to realise God, which was the driving force behind most of his rules.

Gandhi's Economic Ideas

Introduction

Gandhian ethics cover economic sphere also. Gandhi says that everyone should earn his bread with his own hands or through manual labour. He calls it bread labour, and it alone gives man his right to eat. It is impossible for a few to amass wealth without exploiting the rest. Exploitation is a form of violence. As men have a right to live, they are entitled to the means of securing food, shelter and clothing.

Gandhi does not propose drastic or violent means of bringing about economic equality. Ideally, wealth should be distributed equally among all members of the society. As this is impracticable, Gandhi proposes that wealth should be shared equitably. He urges that people should reduce their wants and live a simple life. This process will release resources which can be used to help the poor.

Doctrine of Trusteeship

Gandhi has introduced a concept in which the rich are regarded as trustees of wealth. Ultimately, as all property belongs to God, the excess or superfluous wealth which the rich possess belongs to society and should be used for supporting the poor. Wealthy people have no moral right to what is more than their proportionate share in national wealth. They simply become trustees for the disproportionate share of God's property they hold. They have to use it for helping the poor.

Gandhi and Marx

Gandhi opposes forcible distribution of wealth since it will lead to violence. He therefore proposes that the wealthy have to hold their excess wealth as trustees and help the poor. This view differs sharply from communist and socialist ideologies. Karl Marx argued that capitalists and workers (or rich and poor in general terms) are antagonistic classes and that there is an ongoing class war between them. Marx advocates communist revolution through violent overthrow of the capitalist State. Gandhi favours class harmony, nonviolence and voluntary sharing of wealth by the rich.

Gandhi also identified what he called as seven social sins. These are politics without principles; wealth without work; commerce without morality; education without character; science without humanity; pleasure without conscience and worship without sacrifice.

Religious Tolerance

Gandhi was the greatest advocate of religious tolerance. He preached equality of religions based on the following principles:

- ¤ God is unfathomable and unknowable and reigns above us all.
- ¤ God reveals himself in many ways all the time and evokes human religious sentiments.
- ¤ Nonviolence is a central theme of all religions.
- ¤ All religions are prone to errors and imperfections.
- ¤ All religions are continually evolving towards realisation of higher truth.

Gandhi regarded that the essence of Christianity lies not in Christology but in its conception of ethics as the means to truth. Boundless love and absence of retaliatory violence are fundamental tenets of Christianity.

In the present time, the Gandhian emphasis on communal harmony is especially relevant to national integration. Gandhi did not merely pay lip sympathy to communal harmony. He considered it as a means of promoting an unbreakable bond of brotherhood between followers of different religions. It has to be rooted, according to Gandhi, in equal respect for all religions. One must show for other religions the same regard he accords to his own. If people adopt this attitude, religion will no longer be a source of discord but of harmony. All religions preach that men should live harmoniously.

Summary

- ¤ The Hindu conception of the four principal moral ends of life consists of – Dharma (moral law), Artha (wealth), Kama (desire), and Moksha (salvation).
- ¤ Dharma is the correct way in which a human being has to fulfil his personal, social and moral needs.
- ¤ Some hold that it is a command of God. Other writers consider that moral law is not embodied in God, but that it is a moral ideal which transcends the physical world of space and time.
- ¤ Artha in the sense of wealth stands for material means of well-being.
- ¤ Kama refers to desires common to men living within family fold.

- Hindu ethics subordinate happiness to dharma or virtue.
- The ultimate goal which Hinduism prescribes is that soul should be liberated from the constraints of the physical world and its myriad problems.
- Moksha means that the self lives in its pure spiritual form or essence free from the encumbrances of the physical world of senses or of the material universe of space and time.
- Hinduism also has an ethic which links an individual's morals to his membership of a social group. It is the famous Varnashrama dharma.
- Apart from the morals arising from one's station in society, there are duties which have to be performed at different stages of life - Brahmacharya, Grihastha, Vanaprastha and Sanyas.
- In modern age, it means that one has to faithfully work wherever one is employed.
- Bhagavat Gita is the chief religious and moral treatise of Hindus.
- Bhagavat Gita prescribes that man should perform his duty without any desire for its fruits, without attachment and aversion, and without getting distracted by selfish and base motives. In brief, duty has to be performed for its own sake. Duties are performed for the welfare of humanity and for the good of all living creatures. Ultimately, duties have to be performed for realizing the vision of God.
- One has to control bad emotions such as - attachment, aversion, illusions, fears, lust, grief, anger, hatred, malice and envy. What we would call positive emotions are to be cultivated. These include universal goodwill and benevolence, kindness towards people in trouble, magnanimity, serenity, indifference to worldly concerns, and love and devotion to God.
- Unlike in Buddhism and Jainism, God is central to the moral system of the Gita.
- According to Gita, there are three paths to the realisation of God - through action, devotion and knowledge.
- Gita associates a man's station in life, his Varna, and his psychological attributes. Experience shows that one's profession generally leaves a mark on one's character. Modern psychology also refers to human psychological types.
- Virtues which the Gita mentions are characteristic of the three principal occupational groups of the society. In modern terms, they can be associated with intellectual, heroic and commercial virtues.
- Comparison of Hindu ethics with Western moral ideals like hedonism, utilitarianism or Kant's ideas of duty is generally inappropriate.
- Bhagavat Gita mentions both positive and negative emotions.
- At one level, Gita's message is addressed to those who are totally concerned with realisation of God. Such idealistic injunctions and a pronounced 'other worldliness' may create an impression that the message of Gita, though sublime, is unsuited to the normal situations of social life. But the message of Gita, rooted as it is in the concept of human duty, is universal and timeless in its appeal and relevance.
- To understand ancient Indian writers, we have to enter their social world using historical and psychological imagination.

- Law of karma is a matter of faith. It is not a verifiable scientific idea.
- Karma theory leads to social and economic conservatism. Though it is not the same as fatalism, and though the effects of bad deeds can be overcome, it has created a negative or fatalistic outlook. In modern times, Swami Vivekananda worked indefatigably to remove these cobwebs from the Hindu psyche.
- Manu regarded the customary law of the society or achara as the standard. It is sanctified by practice over many generations. For Manu, Vedas provide the moral standard. He also recognises conscience as a source of law.
- Indian ethics consider moderation (samyama) as a moral standard. We can find these ideas in Buddhism, Jainism and Hinduism.
- In Indian ethics, both political law and divine law are mentioned as moral standards.
- Jainism dates back to sixth century B.C.
- Like Buddhism, Jainism also arose partly in reaction to the ritualism which marked Vedic religion.
- Ahimsa is a core moral principle of Jainism. It lays down that no existent being with life or the essence or potential of life should be injured.
- For a Jain, life is a spiritual odyssey towards divine consciousness.
- The five common moral principles applicable both to monks and householders consist of: refraining from violence towards any living things; speaking the truth; refraining from theft; shunning adultery; and eschewing greed for material wealth.
- The concept of God or a supreme being governing the universe is lacking in Jainism. The world, in its view, is governed by natural laws. In this regard, Jainism has a parallel in Stoicism. Another affinity with Stoicism consists in its advocacy of austere bodily and mental discipline.
- In their pursuit of self-perfection, men have to abandon pride. In a way, this idea also finds an echo in Christianity – pride is one of the seven deadly sins.
- Jainism traces human pride or arrogance to eight sources.
- The essence of Buddha's teaching is contained in the Four Noble Truths.
- The four truths are: the truth of dukkha; the truth of the origin of the dukkha; the truth of cessation of dukkha; and the truth of the path leading to the cessation of dukkha.
- The three types of dukkha are: dukkha of ordinary suffering; the anxiety or stress in trying to hold on to things that are continuously changing; and the dukkha of conditioned states.
- The purpose of understanding the nature of dukkha is to transcend it.
- The origin of dukkha is traced to craving (tanha) conditioned by ignorance (avijia). Craving runs along three tracks - all linked to attachment to sensual pleasures and worldly objects.
- The third noble truth is cessation of all the unsatisfactory experiences and their causes in a manner that they cannot recur.
- Cessation of dukkha is the objective of Buddhist spiritual practices.
- The fourth noble path is the way to end dukkha. It is called the eightfold path.

- It consists of: Right Understanding; Right Thought; Right Speech; Right Action; Right Livelihood; Right Effort; Right Mindfulness; and Right Concentration. The first three paths help in understanding the nature of dukkha. The fourth path is a practical means of overcoming dukkha.
- Right view is the intellectual aspect of wisdom.
- Right intention is commitment to moral and mental self-improvement.
- Right speech is route to moral discipline which sustains other virtues.
- Right action includes: acting kindly and compassionately; to be honest; to respect the belongings of others; and to avoid sexual misconduct.
- Right livelihood implies that one should follow righteous means of earning bread and that wealth has to be earned only through legal and nonviolent ways.
- Right effort refers to harnessing psychic energy towards production of wholesome mental states.
- Buddha says that we should perceive the world clearly and should not get carried away by the working of intellectual processes. For this purpose, he recommends four foundations of right mindfulness.
- These are contemplation of body, of feeling, of state of the mind and of the phenomena.
- Right concentration signifies single-pointedness of the mind in which all mental faculties are unified and directed towards a single object. This leads to a mental state without passions, to self-control and tranquility.
- To concentrate on complete self-realisation, men need to follow three golden rules of taking shelter in Buddha, in Dharma and in Sangha.
- Buddhism prescribes various morals for harmonious family and social life.
- Buddha preached that everyone should cultivate happiness, security and peace.
- Buddhism steers a middle course between extreme self-denial and excessive pursuit of material pleasures.
- Buddhism has a strong streak of altruism. It advocates universal compassion, benevolence and kindness to all life forms.
- Buddhist approach is based on a rational outlook.
- Gandhian thought is multi-dimensional and covers political, social, economic, religious and ethical aspects of human life. His ideas emerged partly from his inner religious convictions, partly from the exigencies of forging strategies for a mass political movement and partly from the influence of others such as Tolstoy, Carlyle and Thoreau.
- Ethical theories provide the underpinnings for Gandhian thought in any sphere. Evolution of Gandhian ideas took place within a matrix of non-violent mass political struggle. In the process, they went through some twists and turns.
- Gandhi has a deep and abiding faith in God, and has written extensively about his conception of God.

- He regards God as an impersonal force and benevolent governor of the world. God is present (or immanent) in every human soul.
- Gandhi considers that the ultimate goal of man is to realise the vision of God. And realisation of God is impossible unless one follows the path of truth, love, non-violence and service to humanity.
- Men should emulate, to the extent they can, the divine attributes in their conduct.
- Gandhi equates God with truth and love; as God is truth and love or nonviolence, practising these two virtues is the way to reach God.
- Gandhi equates God also with truth. He designated his religion as 'religion of truth'
- Truth for Gandhi is not an epistemological concept; it is part of what we would now call 'a value system'.
- Tolstoy influenced Gandhi in his thinking on truth.
- Gandhi preached that the only way to see God is through his creation and by identifying oneself with it. This is possible only through service to humanity.
- For Gandhi, human brotherhood and oneness follow from the unity of life. As part of God's creation, men share the same life.
- As Gandhi identified God with virtues, it follows that men should be pure in heart. Gandhi insisted on cleanliness even in its physical manifestations.
- Gandhi firmly believed that even for attaining noble objectives, men have to adopt only good means.
- Gandhi constantly emphasised that means have to be pure. This follows ipso facto from the conception of God as the embodiment of virtues.
- Man has a divine spark in him. Gandhi also believed that men are reasonable, willing to see the viewpoints of others, and partly accommodate their viewpoints through rational discussion.
- Gandhi explained ahimsa in both negative and positive terms. These have been mentioned earlier as points.
- Ahimsa requires complete self-purification. It also needs faith in the existence of soul which is distinct from body. Ahimsa is described as 'soul force', 'power of Atman', 'power of love' and utter selflessness.
- Many prerequisites are necessary for steadfast pursuit of ahimsa. Foremost among these are truthfulness and fearlessness. Men need only fear God and no one else.
- Gandhi advocated that evil should be tackled by means of non-violent non-cooperation with it. One should hate the evil deed but not its perpetrator.
- If all cooperation with evil is withdrawn, it will have nothing to act upon.
- Gandhi argues that non-violence can be a potent weapon in the hands of masses. Non-violent non-cooperation of masses is not a rebellion.
- A Satyagrahi is the foot soldier of the passive resistance movement. He has to embody the

virtues of truth and non-violence. Gandhi prescribes various virtues which a Satyagrahi needs to cultivate.

- Gandhian ethics cover economic sphere also.
- Gandhi says that everyone should earn his bread with his own hands or through manual labour. He calls it bread labour, and it alone gives man his right to eat.
- It is impossible for a few to amass wealth without exploiting the rest.
- Gandhi has introduced a concept in which the rich are regarded as trustees of wealth. Ultimately, as all property belongs to God, the excess or superfluous wealth which the rich possess belongs to society and should be used for supporting the poor.
- Gandhi's ideas on economics differ radically from Marxian ideas.
- Gandhi was the greatest advocate of religious tolerance. He preached equality of religions based on certain fundamental principles.
- In the present time, the Gandhian emphasis on communal harmony is especially relevant to national integration. Gandhi did not merely pay lip sympathy to communal harmony. He considered it is a means of promoting an unbreakable bond of brotherhood between followers of different religions.

PRACTICE QUESTIONS

1. What are the four moral ends of Hinduism? Outline them in brief
2. How can we interpret Varnashrama dharma in the modern context?
3. Briefly distinguish Hindu ethics from hedonism, utilitarianism and Kantianism.
4. What is the law of karma? Can it come in the way of individual initiative and effort?
5. Some thinkers consider that Hinduism is too metaphysical and other worldly. Do you agree? Give reasons in support of your answer.
6. Are there any aspects of Hindu ethics which are relevant to modern administrators?
7. What are the positive moral principles which can be derived from Hindu ethics?
8. What are the five moral ideas which Jainism emphasises?
9. Briefly outline the differences between Jain and Hindu ethics.
10. What are the four noble truths of Buddhism? Discuss briefly.
11. Outline briefly the eightfold path to enlightenment which Buddha preached.
12. Discuss some parallels between Buddhism and modern ideas on emotional intelligence.
13. What aspects of Buddhist teaching are based on human rationality?
14. What is the relevance of Buddha's message to modern Indian society?
15. Outline briefly how Tolstoy, Ruskin and Thoreau influenced Gandhi.
16. How did Gandhi's conception of God influence his ideas and actions?
17. Briefly discuss Gandhi's concept of non-violence. Has it any relevance in dealing with Naxalite movement?

18. Discuss Gandhi's ideas on truth.
19. Explain Gandhi's concept of Satyagraha. Do you think that Gandhi adopted it only as a political strategy since India could not hope then to fight against the might of the British Empire?
20. Briefly discuss Gandhi's concept of non-violent non-cooperation.
21. Explain briefly the concept of trusteeship which Gandhi proposed? Is it realistic?
22. Write short notes on; (i) Nishkama Karma (ii) Achara (iii) dharma (iv) karma (v) 'pride' in Jain morality (vi) origin of dukkha (vii) Right Speech (viii) Right Livelihood (ix) samyama (x) soul force (xi) bread labour.

REFERENCES

- Jadunath Sinha, A Manual of Ethics
- S. Radhakrishnan, The Hindu View of Life
- Cambridge University, The Ancient History of India (older text)
- Surendranath Dasgupta, A history of Indian Philosophy Volume 1

Lessons from the Lives of Great Indian Leaders, Reformers and Administrators

INTRODUCTION AND APPROACH

We need to begin this chapter with a few prefatory remarks. The verbatim reproduction of UPSC's description of the topic is 'Human values - lessons from the lives and teachings of great leaders, reformers and administrators'. This topic is open-ended in the sense that it is difficult to determine its contours. Further, the number of such men and women being large, one can discuss only a selected few as representative exemplars. The treatment has to briefly cover both their lives and ethical messages.

One has to further consider the three categories - leaders, reformers and administrators. Some individuals have combined these roles. Among leaders, those who spearheaded our national independence movement deserve special mention. Students will be familiar with their names: Gandhi, Nehru, Vallabhai Patel, Subhas Chandra Bose, Dadabhai Naoroji, Tilak, Gokhale, Maulana Azad, Ambedkar, Rajagopalachari, Tanguturi Prakasam, Subhramanya Bharati and many others. Students would have learnt about their lives, sacrifices and ideas while reading about Indian independence movement. It is, therefore, unnecessary to discuss them here.

Reforms can be political, social, economic, religious moral or ethical. Religion and ethics are closely connected, and accordingly, we concentrate on such reforms. Moreover, historians have especially focused on social and religious reforms in Indian society in the nineteenth century. Raja Ram Mohan Roy, Ramakrishna Paramahamsa and Swami Vivekananda are the foremost figures of this reform movement. We also need to go back in history and consider the saints associated with *Bhakti* movement. They emphasised simple devotion to God and cultivation of virtue. They tried to break caste barriers and promote social unity. Their messages have particular relevance to contemporary Indian society.

'Administrators' may mean members of bureaucracy as in modern sense, or in a historical context, able or benevolent rulers in Indian history. They can be from ancient, medieval and modern periods. As examples, we can think of Kautilya, Asoka, Shershah, Raja Todarmal, Rani Ahalyabai, enlightened rulers of Baroda and Mysore princely states, Sir Thomas Munro and M. Visveswarayya. From an examination point of view, rulers or administrators of post-independence period can be ignored. It is better to concentrate on historical figures distant from us in time.

UPSC gave the following model question from this area for the guidance of students: Which great Indian personality has inspired you as a role model and how have you been able to benefit in your life by such an inspiration? Although we cannot assume that questions of only this pattern will be asked, we can draw one conclusion from it. Questions may not be set by name on a particular leader, reformer or administrator. They may ask candidates to explain how they have been influenced by any great personality or what lessons his life teaches us. This is only our conjecture. Incidentally, in GS 4 paper of UPSC 2020, a question was asked on Savita Phule by name.

The following question from this topic was asked in GS 4 Paper in examination of 2014: Q4 (a) Which eminent personality has inspired you the most in the context of ethical conduct in life? Give the gist of his/her teachings giving specific examples; describe how you have been able to apply these teachings for your own ethical development.

The following question from 2017 paper is also from this part of the syllabus:

Q5. (a) "Great ambition is the passion of a great character. Those endowed with it may perform very good or very bad acts. All depends on the principles which direct them." - Napoleon Bonaparte. Stating examples mention the rulers (i) who have harmed society and country, (ii) who worked for the development of society and country.

Thus examiners may interpret the topic in various ways and ask questions to test the understanding and analytical skills of candidates.

In this regard, we make a suggestion which students will find useful. Whenever they happen to read about a prominent historical personality, they can ask themselves whether he or she can be placed among great leaders, reformers or administrators. If they think so, they should jot down brief details of the life and teachings of such personalities. They can use index cards, one for each individual, to enter such details. They should remember these details.

HUMAN VALUES

There is another point which we need to consider. This topic is mentioned under the rubric or heading 'human values'. What are human values? What are the doctrines from which human values are derived?

Human values are associated with many theories. Humanism covers many such theories. Humanism places man at the centre of discussions in philosophy, morals and humanities. It focuses on human potentials, human concerns, and human happiness. It underlies the saying that man is the measure of all things. Man is the 'be-all and and-all' of all things. This idea is embedded in one of the versions of Kant's categorical imperative: Human beings have to be always treated as ends in themselves, and never as means to any end. Human rights and many such modern liberal ideas are based on Humanism.

One strand of Humanism is associated with Renaissance in Europe, that is, the revival (from fourteenth century) of ancient classical Greek and Roman culture. Renaissance scholars turned away from medieval Christian world views. They bemoaned the miserable lot humans in the earthly world which they regarded as a vale of tears. In contrast, Renaissance scholars celebrated human life, human, joys, and human dignity.

Many lists of human values are unmanageably long. Marshall Urban Wibur lists human values relevant to various aspects of human life. He classifies values as bodily values, economic values, values of recreation, values of association, character values, aesthetic values, intellectual values and religious values. This classification refers to values encompassing almost all human activities. The activities can be defined as bodily, social and those transcending these two.

The bodily, economic and recreation values involve the satisfaction of wants connected with man's bodily self. Values of character and values of association are connected with man's social self. They arise only in relations of the self to others. The aesthetic, intellectual and religious values while related to the bodily and social self and conditioned by them, arise only in functioning of the self that goes beyond them. These three categories are spiritual in two senses. They are spiritual in being hyper-organic. In addition, 'spiritual values' also mean objects of human interest which are of an ideal nature like truth, goodness and beauty. We call them things of the spirit.

The intellectual values of knowledge are highly prized. Knowledge has a highly instrumental value and is an indispensable means for acquisition of bodily and economic good. It helps in imbibing cultural, aesthetic and social values. Human beings have an urge to realise their innate potentials as part of self realisation. Education is needed for this purpose. Religious values concern divine things, but some people have little inclination towards them.

What people consider as human values can vary. Values are in one sense codes of internal conduct, the principles according to which men lead their lives and make decisions. We get the values first from our parents. To these are added the values from peers, teachers and religion. Human Values are also defined as those universal concepts found in all cultures and societies at all times and places. Five such human values are - truth, right conduct, love, peace and non-violence.

Many constitutional rights and entitlements which governments and courts recognize are derived from human values.

Humanism is often seen in opposition to religion. Religious doctrines contain various perspectives on God and divine purposes. They claim that the universe is moving inexorably towards divinely ordained purposes. In this process, man though important, has to follow divine will and divine prescriptions as revealed to holy men or prophets. Humanism rejects religious ideas, affirms autonomy of human reason and man's duty to chalk out independently the paths of self development and social progress. This approach will result in a different set of values, though generally not too different from those which religions uphold.

So far, we considered the meanings of human values. We have to examine the lives and doctrines of great leaders, reformers and administrators from this viewpoint. Religious discourse may often focus on spiritual exercises, theological or doctrinal questions and on external religious observances. Sometimes, religious leaders promote narrow outlook of bigotry and sectarian intolerance. We have to steer clear of such views. Religious approaches have to promote feelings of common humanity, human fraternity, social equality and mutual tolerance. Students, in their reading of famous historical personalities, should concentrate on this aspect.

Our selection of historical personalities has to be necessarily restricted. We have mainly included religious and social reformers. We tried to include the more well-known figures. But it does not mean that we regard the others as unimportant. India is a land of great saints and spiritual leaders. Only erudite and devoted scholars can do justice to the subject. Our limited purpose is to outline the inspiring lives and teachings of a few great spiritual thinkers. Students can follow this approach while reading about other leaders and administrators.

VIVEKANANDA

Swami Vivekananda was born in an affluent family in Kolkata in 1863. He possessed great intellect and innate spiritual powers. While studying in Calcutta University, he acquired deep mastery of Western philosophy and history. He used to practise meditation even from his boyhood, and was associated with Brahmo Movement for some time.

In his early youth, he experienced a spiritual crisis with his mind beset with doubts about the existence of God. Upon hearing about Sri Ramakrishna from one of his English professors, he met Sri Ramakrishna who was staying at the Kali Temple in Dakshineshwar. He straightaway asked the Master, "Sir, have you seen God?" Vivekananda put this question to many others but received no satisfactory answer. But Sri Ramakrishna, without a moment's hesitation, replied: "Yes, I have. I see Him as clearly as I see you, only in a much intenser sense." This was how a great Guru-disciple relationship of modern times began. Vivekananda made rapid spiritual progress under Sri Ramakrishna's guidance.

After sometime, Vivekananda had to cope with two misfortunes. His father died suddenly in 1884. Vivekananda had to bear the burden of supporting his mother, brothers and sisters. The second tragedy was the illness and death of Sri Ramakrishna. Vivekananda bore these troubles with fortitude. He also formed a monastic brotherhood with the other disciples of Ramakrishna, and set upon the mission of spreading the gospel of his master. So in the middle of 1890, Vivekananda set out on a long journey of exploration and discovery of India.

Discovery of Real India

During his travels all over India, Swami Vivekananda was deeply moved by the appalling poverty and backwardness of the masses. He was the first religious leader in India to understand and openly declare that the real cause of India's downfall was the neglect of the masses. The immediate need was to provide food and other bare necessities of life to them by spreading knowledge of improved methods of agriculture, by promoting village industries and through other similar activities.

Vivekananda saw the problem as two fold. Owing to centuries of oppression, the downtrodden masses had lost self-confidence. It had to be restored through a life-giving, inspiring message. Vivekananda found it in the principle of the Atman, the doctrine of the potential divinity of the soul, taught in Vedanta, the ancient system of religious philosophy of India. The masses had to be taught the life-giving, ennobling principles of Vedanta and the means of applying them in practical life. Besides, they needed worldly knowledge to improve their economic condition. Vivekananda thought that education is the means of providing both forms of knowledge.

Vivekananda also saw the need for an organization to spread education and to improve the condition of the poor and women. He wanted "to set in motion machinery which will bring noblest ideas to the doorstep of even the poorest and the meanest." It was with this end that he founded the Ramakrishna Mission.

During the course of his wanderings, Vivekananda heard about the World's Parliament of Religions to be held in Chicago in 1893. Prompted by friends and admirers, he decided to attend the Parliament to present his Master's message to the world. But he wanted a sense of inner certainty and of divine calling regarding his mission. He found these while in deep meditation on the rock-island at Kanyakumari. His speeches at the World's Parliament of Religions made him famous as an 'orator by divine right' and as a 'Messenger of Indian wisdom to the Western world'. After the Parliament, he spent nearly three and a half years mostly in the eastern parts of USA and in London spreading Vedanta as lived and taught by Sri Ramakrishna.

Awakening his Countrymen

He returned to India in January 1897. He delivered a series of lectures in different parts of India. In these lectures, Vivekananda attempted:

¤ to rouse the religious consciousness of the people and create in them pride in their cultural heritage;

¤ to bring about unification of Hinduism by pointing out the common bases of its sects;

¤ to focus the attention of educated people on the plight of the downtrodden masses; and

¤ to expound his plan for their amelioration by the application of the principles of Practical Vedanta.

Soon after his return to Kolkata, Swami Vivekananda founded (1897) Ramakrishna Mission. The Mission was to enable monks and lay people to jointly undertake propagation of Practical Vedanta, render various forms of social service, such as running hospitals, schools, colleges, hostels, rural development centres etc, and provide relief and rehabilitation to victims of natural calamities.

In early 1898, Swami Vivekananda set up at Belur on the banks of the Ganges the famous Ramakrishna Math.

His Spiritual Thoughts

New Understanding of Religion: Swami Vivekananda interpreted religion as a universal experience of transcendent reality common to all humanity. He denied any dichotomy between science and religion and described religion as the science of consciousness. This universal conception frees religion from the hold of superstitions, dogmatism, priest-craft and intolerance, and makes it the highest and noblest pursuit of freedom, knowledge and happiness.

New View of Man

Vivekananda's concept of 'potential divinity of the soul' is new and ennobles man. In the present age of humanism, scientific progress greatly improved human material wellbeing. The communications revolution made the world a 'global village'. But there has also been moral decay as evidenced in the great increase in broken homes, immorality, violence and crime. Vivekananda's concept of potential divinity of the soul prevents this degradation, divinizes human relationships, and makes life meaningful and worth living. He has laid the foundation for 'spiritual humanism'.

Principle of Morality and Ethics

The prevalent morality, in both individual life and social life, is mostly based on fear - fear of the police, fear of public ridicule, fear of God's punishment and fear of Karma. The current theories of ethics also do not explain why a person should be moral and be good to others. Vivekananda has given a new theory of ethics and new principle of morality based on the intrinsic purity and oneness of the Atman. We should be pure because purity is our real nature, our true divine Self or Atman. Similarly, we should love and serve our neighbours because we are all one in the Supreme Spirit known as Paramatman or Brahman

Bridge between East and West

Swami Vivekananda built a bridge between Indian and Western cultures. He did this by interpreting Hindu scriptures, philosophy, institutions and way of life to Westerners in easily intelligible terms. He made them realise that they could benefit greatly from Indian spirituality. He was instrumental in ending India's cultural isolation from the rest of the world. He was India's first great cultural ambassador to the West.

On the other hand, Vivekananda's interpretation of ancient Hindu scriptures, philosophy and institutions made Indians receptive to Western science, technology and humanism. He taught Indians how to master Western science and technology while retaining their religious and spiritual roots. He emphasised that Indians need to adapt Western humanism (especially the ideas of individual freedom, social equality and justice and respect for women) to Indian ethos.

His Contributions to India

In spite of her innumerable linguistic, ethnic, historical and regional diversities, India has had from time immemorial a strong sense of cultural unity. It was, however, Swami Vivekananda who revealed the true foundations of this culture and thus clearly defined and strengthened the sense of unity of Indians.

He reminded Indians of their great national spiritual heritage and revived their pride in their past. Furthermore, he showed the weaknesses of Western culture and how India could help in overcoming them.

Sense of unity, pride in the past and sense of mission - which Vivekananda proclaimed greatly strengthened India's nationalist movement. Jawaharlal Nehru wrote: "Rooted in the past, full of pride in India's prestige, Vivekananda was yet modern in his approach to life's problems, and was a kind of bridge between the past of India and her present ... he came as a tonic to the depressed and demoralized Hindu mind and gave it self-reliance and some roots in the past." Netaji Subhash Chandra Bose wrote: "Swamiji harmonized the East and the West, religion and science, past and present. And that is why he is great. Our countrymen have gained unprecedented self-respect, self-reliance and self-assertion from his teachings".

Swamiji's most unique contribution to the creation of new India was to open the minds of Indians to their duty to the downtrodden masses. Long before the ideas of Karl Marx were known in India, Swamiji spoke about the role of the labouring classes in the production of national wealth. Swamiji was the first religious leader in India to speak for the masses, formulate a definite philosophy of service, and organize large-scale social service.

His Contributions to Hinduism

Identity

Swami Vivekananda gave to Hinduism as a whole a clear-cut identity, a distinct profile. Although Hindus had a clear sense of their roots and identity, Hinduism was considered a loose confederation of many different sects. Speaking about Swamiji's role in giving Hinduism its distinct identity, Sister Nivedita wrote: "... it may be said that when he began to speak it was of 'the religious ideas of the Hindus', but when he ended, Hinduism had been created".

Unification

Before Swamiji's advent, discord and competition were common among the various sects of Hinduism. Similarly, the protagonists of different systems and schools of philosophy were claiming their views to be the only true and valid ones. By applying Sri Ramakrishna's doctrine of Harmony (Samanvaya) Swamiji brought about an overall unification of Hinduism on the basis of the principle of unity in diversity.

Defence

Vivekananda was foremost among those who raised their voice in defence of Hinduism. This was, in fact, his main accomplishment in the West. Christian missionary propaganda had created a false view of Hinduism and India in Western minds. Vivekananda had to face stiff opposition in his attempts to defend Hinduism.

New Ideal of Monasticism

A major contribution of Vivekananda to Hinduism is the rejuvenation and modernization of monasticism. In this new monastic ideal, followed in the Ramakrishna Order, the ancient principles of renunciation and God realisation are combined with service to God in man (*Shiva jnane jiva seva*). Vivekananda equated service to man with service to God.

Modern interpretation of Hindu Philosophy and religious doctrines: Vivekananda interpreted ancient Hindu scriptures and philosophical ideas in terms of modern thought. He also added several illuminating original concepts based on his own transcendental experiences and vision of the future.

Some Famous Sayings of Vivekananda

¤ So long as the millions live in hunger and ignorance, I hold every man a traitor who, having been educated at their expense pays not the least heed to them.

¤ Whatever you think, that you will be. If you think yourselves weak, weak you will be; if you think yourselves strong, strong you will be.

¤ If you have faith in all the three hundred and thirty millions of your mythological gods ... and still have no faith in yourselves, there is no salvation for you. Have faith in yourselves, and stand up on that faith and be strong; that is what we need.

¤ Strength, strength it is that we want so much in this life, for what we call sin and sorrow have all one cause, and that is our weakness. With weakness comes ignorance, and with ignorance comes misery.

- ¤ The older I grow, the more everything seems to me to lie in manliness. This is my new Gospel.
- ¤ Purity, patience, and perseverance are the three essentials to success, and above all, love.
- ¤ Religion is realisation; not talk, not doctrine, nor theories, however beautiful they may be. It is being and becoming, not hearing or acknowledging; it is the whole soul becoming changed into what it believes.
- ¤ Religion is the manifestation of the Divinity already in man.
- ¤ Teach yourselves, teach everyone his real nature, call upon the sleeping soul and see how it awakes. Power will come, glory will come, goodness will come, purity will come, and everything that is excellent will come when this sleeping soul is roused to self-conscious activity.
- ¤ They alone live who live for others, the rest are more dead than alive.
- ¤ This is the gist of all worship - to be pure and to do good to others.

Vivekananda is among the greatest Hindu saints. He fused Hindu Vedantic ideals with Western scientific and humanistic thought. He worked against the tendency of Hindus to devote themselves to exclusive sects and doctrines. He reminded Indians of their glorious traditions. He popularized Vedanta philosophy in the West. Above all, he reminded people of the need to help the masses submerged in poverty and ignorance.

RAMAKRISHNA PARAMAHAMSA

Sri Ramakrishna was born in 1836 in Kamarpukur village near Kolkata. His parents, Kshudiram Chattopadhyaya and Chandramani Devi, were poor but very pious and virtuous. From early days, Ramakrishna was disinclined towards formal education and worldly affairs. He was fond of serving holy men and listening to their discourses. He was also very often found absorbed in spiritual moods. At the age of six, he experienced the first ecstasy while watching a flight of white cranes moving against the background of black clouds. This tendency to enter into ecstasy intensified with age. His father's death when he was seven years old served only to deepen his introspection and increase his detachment from the world.

When Sri Ramakrishna was sixteen, his brother took him to Kolkata to assist him in his priestly profession. In 1855 the Kali Temple at Dakshineshwar built by Rani Rasmani was consecrated. When his brother died, Ramakrishna became its chief priest. Ramakrishna developed intense devotion to Mother Kali and spent hours in loving adoration of her image, forgetting the rituals of priestly duties. His intense longing culminated in the vision of Mother Kali as boundless effulgence engulfing everything around him.

Intense Spiritual Practices

Sri Ramakrishna's god-intoxicated state alarmed his relatives in Kamarpukur and they got him married to Saradamani. Unaffected by marriage, Sri Ramakrishna plunged into even more intense spiritual practices. Impelled by a strong inner urge to experience different aspects of God, he followed with the help of a series of Gurus, the various paths described in the Hindu scriptures, and realised God through each one of them. In this way, Sri Ramakrishna relived the entire range of spiritual experiences of more than three thousand years of Hindu religion.

With his unquenchable thirst for God, Sri Ramakrishna broke the frontiers of Hinduism, glided through the paths of Islam and Christianity, and attained the highest realisation through each of them in a short span of time. He looked upon Jesus and Buddha as incarnations of God, and venerated the ten Sikh Gurus. He expressed the quintessence of his twelve-year-long spiritual realisation in a simple dictum: "*Yato mat, tato path* - "As many faiths, so many paths." He now habitually lived in an exalted state of consciousness in which he saw God in all beings.

Sri Ramakrishna's name as a saint began to spread. He came into contact with several leaders and members of Brahmo Samaj and exerted great influence on them. His teaching on harmony of religions attracted people belonging to different denominations. Many householders and youth became his disciples.

The intensity of his spiritual life and untiring spiritual ministration to the endless stream of seekers told on Sri Ramakrishna's health. He developed cancer of the throat. Sri Ramakrishna gave up his physical body, uttering the name of the Divine Mother.

Contributions of Sri Ramakrishna to World Culture

Spiritual ideal: Sri Ramakrishna's life strengthened the ideal of God realisation in the modern world. Atheism, materialism and science have undermined people's faith in traditional religions. Sri Ramakrishna established the possibility of having direct experience of transcendent Reality. Mahatma Gandhi has said: "His (Ramakrishna's) life enables us to see God face to face. No one can read the story of his life without being convinced that God alone is real and that all else is an illusion."

Harmony of religions: Sri Ramakrishna was an advocate of harmony of religions. He did not regard all the religions as one. He recognised differences among religions but showed that, in spite of these differences, all religions lead to the same ultimate goal, and hence they are all valid and true.

Sri Ramakrishna expresses this idea in the following words: A lake has many ghats. From one ghat the Hindus take water in jars and call it 'jal'. From another ghat the Mussalmâns take water in leather bags and call it 'pani'. From a third the Christians take the same thing and call it 'water'. Suppose someone says that the thing is not 'jal' but 'pâni', or that it is not pâni but water, or that it is not 'water' but 'jal', it would indeed be ridiculous. But this very thing is at the root of the friction among sects, their misunderstandings and quarrels. This is why people injure and kill one another, and shed blood, in the name of religion. But this is not good. Everyone is going toward God. They will all realise Him if they have sincerity and longing of heart.

Thus Sri Ramakrishna anticipated the idea of pluralism. Sri Ramakrishna's view is singular in that it was based, not on speculation, but on direct religious experience. Since conflicts among religions and the rise of religious fundamentalism are threats to humanity, Sri Ramakrishna's doctrine of harmony of religions has great relevance to modern world. As the distinguished British historian Arnold Toynbee wrote: "... Mahatma Gandhi's principle of non-violence and Sri Ramakrishna's testimony to the harmony of religions: here we have the attitude and the spirit that can make it possible for the human race to grow together into a single family - and in the Atomic Age, this is the only alternative to destroying ourselves."

Divinization of love

Sri Ramakrishna elevated love from the level of emotions to the level of the spiritual unity of all beings in God. This principle of oneness of the Supreme Self and its immanence in all beings is a central tenet of the Upanishads. But it was hardly applied in practical life. Sri Ramakrishna saw the Divine in all, even in fallen women, and treated them all with respect. He embodied the famous dictum of the New Testament, "God is Love". This divinization of love and human relationships is a great contribution of Sri Ramakrishna to human welfare.

Sri Ramakrishna did not write any book, nor did he deliver public lectures. Instead, he chose to speak in simple language using parables and metaphors by way of illustration, drawn from the observation of nature and ordinary things of daily use. His conversations were charming and attracted the cultural elite of Bengal. Mahendranath Gupta, his disciple, noted down these conversations and published them under the title *Sri Ramakrishna Kathamrita* in Bengali. Its English rendering is *The Gospel of Sri Ramakrishna*.

Other Contributions

- Sri Ramakrishna bridged the gulf between the ancient and the modern by showing that the ancient ideals and experiences could be realised even while following the normal modern way of life.
- Sri Ramakrishna's emphasis on truthfulness and renunciation of lust and greed enhanced the moral life in modern times. He also cleansed religious life of immoral practices, external pomp, miracle mongering and the like.

The great contributions of Ramakrishna Paramahamsa are: establishing the possibility of directly experiencing God; preaching of harmony of religions; harmonizing ancient religious practices with modern secular life; discounting the abuses which have entered religions; and improving the tone of morality in social life. His thoughts were free from obscurantism.

SRI AUROBINDO

Aurobindo was a great scholar, litterateur, philosopher, patriot, social reformer and visionary. He was born in Calcutta in 1872. His father Dr K D Ghose was an anglophile (i.e. great admirer of English culture). When he was five years old, Aurobindo was admitted to the Loreto Convent School in Darjeeling. At the age of seven, he was sent to St. Paul's School in London and then to King's College, Cambridge. He mastered English, Greek, Latin and French and became familiar with major European languages. Being a brilliant scholar, he passed with record marks in the Classical Tripos examination. He qualified for the Indian Civil Service. However, he was dismissed from the service since he did not appear for horse riding test at the end of his training.

When he was 21, Aurobindo Ghose began working under the Maharaja of Baroda. He became a part-time lecturer in French at Baroda College. He later became a professor in English, and then the Vice-Principal of the college. He also became proficient in Sanskrit, Indian history and many Indian languages.

The Patriot

In 1906, Aurobindo resigned his position as the Principal of India's first national University in Calcutta to join active politics. He took part in freedom movement and became famous for his patriotic editorials in Bande Mataram. He was among the first of the Nationalist leaders to insist on full independence for India as the goal of the movement. He devoted all his great ability and energy to freedom struggle. C R Das described him as "the poet of patriotism, the prophet of nationalism and a lover of humanity". For Netaji Subhas Chandra Bose, he was "a name to conjure with". The Viceroy of India Lord Minto considered him "the most dangerous man we...have to reckon with".

Aurobindo espoused the idealism of the Leftist thinkers, and fearlessly pleaded for Indian independence. He awakened the national aspiration for freedom, and urged people to give up their languor and indifference. He was arrested and imprisoned from 1908 to 1909. During this year of seclusion, Aurobindo experienced a spiritual transformation. He realised that man should aspire and attain a New Being and try to create a divine life upon earth. His spiritual experience led him to believe that the route to this is the *Sanatana Dharma* - the ancient spiritual knowledge and practice of India.

A Divine Life

In 1910, obeying an inner call, he went to Pondicherry, then a French Indian territory, to evade police surveillance. He established the Auroville Ashram. The Mother was his spiritual collaborator. He totally abandoned politics, concentrating exclusively on a spiritual inner awakening. He was searching for a means of permanently elevating human spiritual state. He practised "Internal Yoga" for many years. It is the route to acquire spiritual elevation. It embraces various aspects such as the mind, will, heart, life and body.

Aurobindo also spoke of the conscious as well as the subconscious and the superconscious parts of human beings. His purpose was to reach a state which he termed the "Supramental Consciousness". With this aim, Sri Aurobindo struggled inwardly with the dark forces within man. He continually fought secret spiritual battles to establish truth, peace and perennial joy. He believed this to be the sole way of moving towards the divine.

Aurobindo did not want to establish a new religion or establish a new faith or an order. His focus was on an inner development of man. Man can use his will and intelligence to begin to participate consciously in this process of self-discovery and self-exploration. It will enable each human being to perceive the oneness in all. It will lead to an elevated consciousness in man. In the process, the god-like attributes in man's being will come to the surface and change his behaviour. Aurobindo's vision gives each individual a meaningful place in a progressive cosmic unfolding, and shapes his understanding of human endeavour, whether individual or collective, in a new and purposeful perspective.

A Great Litterateur

Aurobindo was a prolific writer. He wrote many works with a view to enlighten human souls. His major works include: *The Life Divine, The Synthesis of Yoga, Essays on the Gita, Commentaries on the Isha Upanishad, Powers Within* . They express the intense knowledge that he had gained in the practice of Yoga. He also wrote *The Foundations of Indian Culture, The Ideal of Human Unity, The Future Poetry, The Secret of the Veda* and *The Human Cycle.* His other famous work is *Savitri*, a great epic of 23,837 lines directing man towards the Supreme Being.

He died in 1950. He left behind a great heritage of spiritual glory which can free man from his troubles. His ultimate message to humanity was: *"A divine life in a divine body is the formula of the ideal that we envisage."*

Five Dreams

At the time of independence, people wanted his message. Aurobindo mentioned the following five dreams in his message:

- "... a revolutionary movement which would create a free and united India."
- "... the resurgence and liberation of the peoples of Asia and her return to her great role in the progress of human civilization."
- "... a world-union forming the outer basis of a fairer, brighter and nobler life for all mankind."
- "... the spiritual gift of India to the world."
- "... a step in evolution which would raise man to a higher and larger consciousness and begin the solution of the problems which have perplexed and vexed him since he first began to think and to dream of individual perfection and a perfect society."

Aurobindo is one of the most difficult writers to read. This is probably because it is hard to put into words the insights he gained through his long and arduous meditations. He is also a metaphysician whose thoughts are hard to fathom. Wading through his philosophical writings is like trying to climb towards remote peaks shrouded in mist. Clearly, his work is not amenable to common readers.

But even a cursory glance at some quotations which his admirers have put together, conveys deep insights into our ancient culture. There are three points to note. One is the deep reverence and love with which Aurobindo speaks about ancient Hindu religion, culture and the scriptures. The second point is the literary elegance of his language. The third is a strain of sadness which a sensitive person will feel while watching the slow decay of hallowed, venerable institutions and traditions. In the process, a sudden realisation dawns on us that we are letting our great culture go to seed.

Aurobindo says about Hindu religion: *"The Hindu religion appears ... as a cathedral temple, half in ruins, noble in the mass, often fantastic in detail but always fantastic with a significance - crumbling or badly outworn in places, but a cathedral temple in which service is still done to the Unseen and its real presence can be felt by those who enter with the right spirit ... That which we call the Hindu religion is really the Eternal religion because it embraces all others." (Aurobindo's Letters, Vol. II)*

Again: *"Hinduism ... gave itself no name, because it set itself no sectarian limits; it claimed no universal adhesion, asserted no sole infallible dogma, set up no single narrow path or gate of salvation; it was less a creed or cult than a continuously enlarging tradition of the God and endeavour of the human spirit. An immense many-sided and many staged provision for a spiritual self-building and self-finding, it had some right to speak of itself by the only name it knew, the eternal religion, Santana Dharma...". (India's Rebirth)*

Aurobindo makes the following interesting comments on Indian Culture: *"More high-reaching, subtle, many-sided, curious and profound than the Greek, more noble and humane than the Roman, more large and spiritual than the old Egyptian, more vast and original than any other Asiatic civilization, more intellectual than the European prior to the 18th century, possessing all that these had and more, it was the most powerful, self-possessed, stimulating and wide in influence of all past human cultures."* (*A Defence of Indian Culture*)

Here, Aurobindo rates Indian culture as greater than that of ancient Greece, Rome and of Europe before the eighteenth century.

He also speaks of the *Bhagavat Gita* as a timeless document amenable to renewed interpretations by succeeding civilizations and succeeding generations: "The Bhagavad-Gita is a true scripture of the human race a living creation rather than a book, with a new message for every age and a new meaning for every civilization." *(The Message of the Bhagavad Gita)*

We end with a quotation On Inner Strength: "The great are strongest when they stand alone, A God-given might of being is their force." (Savitri)

We may note that Aurobindo's writings would have boosted the morale of the nation still in bondage. They would have lifted the feeling of despondency, gloom and inferiority from the minds of people living in subjugation to a foreign power. The sense of the nation's glorious past would have stirred their hearts and minds. There is nothing narrow or chauvinistic in Aurobindo's thoughts. His message of spiritual self-enlightenment based on deep internal meditation is addressed to the whole humanity.

RAJA RAM MOHAN ROY

Ram Mohan Roy was a great religious, social, and educational reformer. He questioned orthodox Hindu practices. He is known as the 'Maker of Modern India', 'Father of Modern India' and the 'Father of the Bengal Renaissance'. He, along with Dwarkanath Tagore established the *Brahmo Sabha* in 1828, an influential Indian socio-religious reform movement. He worked tirelessly to abolish sati, the practice in which the widow immolated herself on her husband's funeral pyre. Child marriage was another social evil that he opposed.

Roy was born in a Bengali Hindu family in Visnagar, Hooghly, and West Bengal. His father was Ramkanto Roy and his mother was Tarinidevi. Ram Mohan Roy tried to revive the principles of the Vedanta school of philosophy contained in the Upanishads. He preached about the unity of God, made early translations of Vedic scriptures into English, co-founded the Calcutta Unitarian Society, founded the Brahmo Samaj, and campaigned against sati. He attempted to combine Western culture with Indian traditions. He established schools to modernize the system of education in India.

Ram Mohan Roy worked in the East India Company. He continued his activities as a traditional Brahmin. He also carried on with certain political activities. From 1803 to 1815, Ram Mohan Roy served the East India Company's "Writing Service". He formed *Atmiya Sabha in 1815.* Interestingly, Ram Mohan Roy estimated how much money was being drained out of India and where it was headed. He predicted that around half of the total revenue collected in India was sent out to England. Thus, he anticipated the 'drain of wealth theory' which later nationalists formulated. Ram Mohan Roy's tireless advocacy was important in William Bentinck's decision to abolish *Sati.*

In 1830, Ram Mohan Roy visited England. He was the first educated Indian to break the taboo on crossing the seas. Roy was an ambassador of the Mughal emperor Akbar II, who conferred on him the title of Raja to lobby the British government for the welfare of India. Roy also visited France. Roy died in Britain at Stapleton, Bristol, in September 1833.

Roy felt that social and religious reforms will politically strengthen Hinduism. He wrote: "The present system of Hindus is not well calculated to promote their political interests.... It is necessary that some change should take place in their religion, at least for the sake of their political advantage and social comfort." Ram Mohan Roy realised during his interactions with the British that Hindu traditions were often not respected or thought as credible by Western standards. He tried to justify traditions by showing that "superstitious practices which deform the Hindu religion have nothing to do with the pure spirit of its dictates" The "superstitious practices" Ram Mohan Roy objected included sati, caste rigidity and polygamy and child marriages.

Such practices gave British officials a sense of moral superiority over the Indian nation. Ram Mohan Roy's religious reforms aimed at creating a fair and just society by implementing humanitarian practices similar to Christian ideals. This process would enhance the prestige of Hinduism in the world.

Religious Reforms

The religious reforms of Roy form part of the tenets of the Brahmo Samaj. These basic ideas are found in every religion. Brahmos believe in the existence of One Supreme God, and worship Him alone. Brahmos believe that worship of Him needs no fixed place or time. Ram Mohan Roy declared the building housing Brahmo Samaj

"... as a place of public meeting of all sorts and descriptions of people without distinction, as shall behave and conduct themselves in an orderly, sober, religious and devout manner for the worship and adoration of the Eternal, Unsearchable and Immutable Being who is the author and preserver of the Universe, ..."

While proclaiming this Universalist religious principle, the declaration adds:

- Prayer should not invoke any name of individual or group.
- Images or idols should not be worshipped.
- No animals should be killed as scarifies.
- No rituals should be performed.
- Prayer should not ridicule forms of worship of other creeds.

"The discourses and songs should be such as have a tendency to the promotion of the contemplation of the Author and Preserver of the Universe to the promotion of charity, morality, piety, benevolence, virtue and the strengthening of the bonds of union between men of all religious persuasions and creeds."

The above ideas reflect the liberal religious views of Ram Mohan Roy.

Social Reforms

Roy demanded property inheritance rights for women. As we have mentioned, he set up the *Brahmo Sabha*. It is movement of reformist Bengalis to fight against social evils. Throughout his life, Ram Mohan Roy battled against ignorance, helplessness and oppression. He is among the first Indians who protested vehemently against the iniquitous treatment of women.

Education

Roy regarded educational reform as a supplement to social reform. In 1817, in collaboration with David Hare he set up the Hindu College. He founded the Anglo-Hindu school and later the Vedanta College. At his instance, his teachings of monotheistic doctrines were incorporated with 'modern, western curriculum'. Vedanta College's courses synthesized Western and Indian learning. Ram Mohan Roy supported inclusion of western learning into Indian education. He recommended the study of English, science, western medicine and technology. He spent his money to translate his ideas on education into practice.

Journalism

Ram Mohan Roy's journalistic activities spanned publication of magazines in English, Hindi, Persian, and Bengali. He published the popular magazine, the *Sambad Kaumudi*. He also published *Mirat-ul-Akbar* in Persian. *Sambad Kaumudi*, news weekly, covered topics such as freedom of press, induction of Indians into high ranks of service and separation of the executive and judiciary. Sambad Kaumudi continued for 33 years.

He registered strong protest against the introduction of Press Ordinance of 1823. The ordinance prescribed that a license from the Governor-General-in-council would be mandatory to publish any newspaper. When the English Company censored the press, Ram Mohan composed two memorials against this in 1829 and 1830. He strongly upheld the freedom of press and the right to individual expression of opinions.

Religious Catholicity

Ram Mohan Roy was by birth a kulin Brahmin, held high in social scale. But he wrote religious treatises in various languages including Persian. In his work, *The Principles of Jesus* he says:

"This simple code of religion and morality is so admirably calculated to elevate men's ideas to high and liberal notions of one God . . . and is also well-fitted to regulate the conduct of the human race in the discharge of their various duties to God, to themselves and to society, that I cannot but hope the best effects from its promulgation in the present form."

Ram Mohan Roy possessed an acute mind, broad religious sympathies, a very powerful personality and great drive for reforms. Both his range of interests and sphere of activities were wide. He fought relentlessly against the abuses and corrupt practices that crept into the once healthy body of Hindu doctrine. He looked beyond India's political downfall, loss of independence and humiliation. He looked towards a radiant future based on absorption of Western culture and democratic discipline. He was a true believer in the equality of sexes and toiled to raise the status of women.

DAYANANDA SARASWATI

Dayananda Saraswati was born in 1824, in Tankara town situated in the princely state of Morvi in Gujarat. His father, Amba Shankar, was a wealthy banker in the town and was also the hereditary jamaadar or headman of a small village. Amba Shankar grounded Mul Shankar - as Dayananda Saraswati was christened at birth - in the tenets of Saivism. By his fourteenth year, Dayananda Saraswati memorized the bulk of Vedas and mastered Sanskrit grammar.

Transformative Event

Dayananda Saraswati was an iconoclast who opposed the traditional rituals of Hinduism– idol worship, conventional priesthood and the caste barriers. His new vision of Hinduism appears to have arisen from an incident that occurred while he was keeping vigil (staying awake) during a Shivratri. He had great reverence for the Shiva lingam consecrated in the temple. But he noticed in the small hours of the morning a mouse creeping out of a hole; begin nibbling at the offerings to the god; and, still worse, run across the god's body as if in defiance of his presence and powers.

This trivial incident changed Mul Shankar's life. He lost faith in certain forms of worshipping divinity. The gods of Hindu pantheon fell from his esteem. It set him free from the trammels of tradition and parental control. After this incident, Mul Shankar became negligent towards customary religious practices. To escape from his father's insistence on his observing religious practices, he went away to his uncle's house. Unfortunately, two bereavements, of his uncle and later of his sister plunged Mul Shankar into deep gloom. He began to reflect on the mysteries of life and to search for Moksha, i.e. release from the continuous cycle of births and rebirths. Worried over the mental state of his son, Amba Shankar conceived, in the words of one writer, the idea "of marrying him off and thus killing his fine enthusiasms by the hum-drum routine which such a married life would impose on him". But unwilling to become a householder, Mul Shankar ran away from home.

Spiritual Search

During the next twenty-five years (1845-1870), which he spent on travels, he met many Sannyasis noted for their learning and piety. He studied their teachings intensely, but from a critical perspective. Dayananda Saraswati's religious views crystallized after he came under the influence of Swami Parmananda. Parmananda was a great advocate of Vedas as original springs of Hindu religious thought. It is from him that Dayananda Saraswati derived his battle cry "Back to the Vedas".

Basic Doctrine

To Dayananda Saraswati, the Vedas were the only revealed word of God; infallible, containing in them the secret not only of all religious truth, but also the promise and potentiality of all scientific discovery, of the latest philosophical view of life, of mechanical inventions and political theory. He was convinced that spiritual knowledge was to be found in its pristine purity in the Vedas. India's only hope was, according to him, to rediscover the faith that was once delivered to the Munis and Rishis as these were enwrapped in holy meditation, grappling with the ultimate mysteries of life. These views have not gone unchallenged. We will consider them shortly.

Dayananda Saraswati expressed his views forthrightly in a Hindu meet which Maharajah of Benares convened in 1879. These are:

¤ Polytheism was a monstrous fraud devised by priests who were blind leaders of the blind.

¤ Caste is an iniquitous system that has lain like an incubus on social relations in India.

¤ Caste was originally designed to be only a scientific division of labour on the basis of inherited and developed skills, and on the various aptitudes that people respectively acquired.

- Ancient Hindu women were free and equals of men, entitled to respect, honour and the fullest use of their opportunities.
- Only the pure, learned and industrious could be called priests.
- Social degradation was possible only by reason of wasted talent and atrophied powers. Social elevation to the highest caste was open, even according to Manu's Dharma Sastra, to persons of the meanest descent.
- India's downfall was owing to her disloyalty to her splendid heritage.
- The path of salvation lies through renewed loyalty to the priceless revelations of truth as embodied in the Vedas.

Practical Reformer

Dayananda Saraswati was basically a reformer, not an original religious thinker. He drew inspiration from a particular corpus of Hindu scriptures, Vedas. He realised that life in the modern world presupposes abandoning of certain pernicious customs and cultivation of progressive outlook. To this end, he thought it best to appeal to the nation's past as the means of weaning the masses from idol-worship, veneration of mere formalism and obscurantist practices.

Dayananda Saraswati as a practical reformer founded the Arya Samaj incorporating his views of Hinduism. Many educational, social and charitable activities were started under his inspiration. D.A.V. educational institutions bear a standing testimony to his constructive vision. Sidney Webb's introduction to Lala Lajpat Rai's book *The Arya Samaj* mentions the instance of a high caste Brahmin and his wife teaching scheduled caste children and living under the same roof with them. This reflects Dayananda Saraswati's progressive outlook and commitment to what is nowadays called 'social inclusion'. Remarkably, it is born out of his interpretation of ancient Hindu scriptures.

Opposition to Obscurantism

Dayananda Saraswati opposed many obscurantist Hindu religious practices. He decried religious self-torture as a degrading penance, that is gross superstition without religious value. Shraddhas or food-offerings for the souls of departed relatives are seen as mere animistic rites. Child-marriages are strictly forbidden. Many progressive Arya samajists followed the practice that men should marry after they are twenty-five and women after they are sixteen. An exchange of photographs between the contracting parties to a marriage was suggested by Dayananda as an improvement on the old-fashioned marriages, where the parties do not even see each other's faces until they are married.

Arya Samajists created new meanings for certain Hindu Puranic terms and practices. Lala Lajpat Rai's book, *The Arya Samaj: An Indian Movement* says:

"Devas (gods) are those who are wise and learned; asuras (demons) those who are foolish and ignorant;

Rakshas [are] those who are wicked and sin-loving; and pishachas, [are] those whose mode of life is filthy and debasing.

"Devapuja (or the worship of the gods) consists in showing honour and respect to the wise and learned, to one's father, mother, and preceptor, to the preachers of the true doctrine, to a just and impartial sovereign, to lovers of righteousness, to chaste men and women".

Some writers have questioned the ideas of Dayananda Saraswati. Many Indian philosophers like S. Radhakrishnan regard Upanishads as the source of sublime Hindu metaphysics and of Sankara's Advaita doctrine. The philosophy of Ramakrishna and Vivekananda is also based on Upanishads. In fact, Radhakrishnan considers the Vedas as the source of Hindu ritualism. This is more a theological than a practical question. It is, however, Dayananda Saraswati who broke the hold of ceremonials and caste barriers on Hinduism.

Assessment

Dayananda Saraswati, by holding that all human knowledge, including science and technology, is contained either explicitly or implicitly in Vedas, has overstated the case. Religious texts are documents frozen in time. Their moral and metaphysical insights are perennial. But where physical knowledge of world is concerned, they are overtaken by time.

Finally, Dayananda Saraswati's espousal of Hinduism is based on critical processes of self-cleansing. But in some quarters the religious hue of reformist ideas–even of Vivekananda, Tilak, and Bankim Chander Chaterjee and of Dayananda Saraswati occasions disquiet. They are seen as Hindu-centric, and not sufficiently inclusive. The religious reformers of Hinduism looked inwards for means of correcting the fault lines that developed in the system. They were searching for self-corrective processes. Their religious outlook remained essentially catholic and universal.

We may conclude with a few assessments of Dayananda Saraswati. According to D.N. Bannerjea, "Judged by any standards, however severe or exacting, Dayananda Saraswati, the founder of the Arya Samaj ... was indeed a great man, not only in the estimation of his friends and adherents, but what is still more striking in the judgment of his opponents as well".

In the words of Madame Blavatsky: "It is perfectly certain that India never saw a more learned Sanskrit scholar, a deeper metaphysician, a more wonderful orator and a more fearless denunciator of any evil than Dayananda, since the time of Shankaracharya."

NARAYANA GURU

Sree Narayana Guru was born in 1856 in Chempazhanthi village near Trivandrum. His parents were Madan Asan, a farmer, and Kutti Amma. His parents called him 'Nanu'. Nanu had three sisters. His family enjoyed social respectability and economic status. At the age of five, he began his education in the neighbouring school in the old 'Gurukula' model. But in those days, society was in the grip of a rigid caste system and untouchability was common. 'Madan Asan' was also a teacher ("Asan"), learned in Sanskrit and proficient in astrology and Ayurveda.

Education

Narayana Guru possessed a prodigious memory. He was also a quick learner. As a boy, Nanu would hear with keen interest stories from the *Ramayana* and the *Mahabharata* which his father narrated to the villagers. His education at home began under the supervision of his father and uncle Krishnan

Vaidyan. Vaidyan was an Ayurvedic physician and a Sanskrit scholar. Narayana Guru learnt the basics of Tamil and Sanskrit. He went through the traditional subjects like *Siddharupam, Balaprobhodhanam* and *Amarakosam*.

After this elementary grounding, he studied Sanskrit under the great Sanskrit scholar Raman Pillai. He learned poetry, drama, logic, poetics and grammar from another teacher. Narayana Guru loved solitude and contemplation. During his stay at Varanappally, he composed some hymns and devotional songs. He returned in 1881 from Varanappally and taught children for some time.

Marriage

According to the custom of the time a wedding could be solemnized in the absence of the bridegroom if the bridegroom's sister offered a *thali (mangalsutra)* to the bride. This was how his wedding was formally solemnized in 1882. But then he stopped going home, and soon left his native place forever.

Spiritual Wanderings

He became a *Parivrajaka* or one who wanders from place to place in quest of Truth. He spent his days in forests, caves, seashores, and in temples. When hungry, he would eat what was offered by strangers. Probably, he first met the Chattampi Swami here, and they became close friends. During this period, he met Thykkattu Ayyavu, a distinguished yoga guru of Trivandrum, and learnt yoga from him. His father died in 1884, and he had a vision of it before a messenger came bearing the news.

Narayana Guru observed *tapas* and meditation in Pillathadam cave at the top of the Maruthwamala, located near Kanyakumari. He found enlightenment here. Narayana Guru lived in this cave on a diet of berries and tubers, and water from mountain brooks. At that time, he prayed to God, conceiving him in the form of *Shiva*. Popular stories abound about his intimate communion with nature and animals. Soon people came to know about Narayana Guru's meditations and began flocking to Maruthwamala.

Religious Mission

Narayana Guru's mission was focused on not only promoting spiritual values and character ethics but also on social issues. He tried to redress bad social customs and to remove caste discriminations corroding the Indian society. He concentrated on ameliorating the conditions of castes at the bottom of the system. At that time, people in Kerala lacked social unity and tended to be superstitious.

During his period of wandering as a sanyasin, Narayana Guru spent his time mostly among the lower social groups. He told them about his life's mission. He lived among the poor and shared their food. At night he would sit on the seashore in deep meditation. Soon people thought of him as a great yogi with miraculous powers. People of all religions respected him.

He slept in inns, wayside rest-houses and on open grounds. In this wandering period of four to five years, he saw the inequalities, injustices and evil customs in society. They influenced his later activities. During his travels, he once reached Aruvippuram in Neyyattinkara – then within a dense forest.

Opposition to Old Customs

As many people flocked to him for healing or advice, he thought of building a Shiva temple. It was here that he built a temple in 1888. Tradition mentions that Narayana guru descended into the river and then re-emerged, holding an idol of Shiva. He stood beneath the canopy with it in his arms for three hours, totally lost in meditation, tears flowing down his cheeks. Finally, at three in the morning, he installed the idol on the pedestal. In those times, usually, only Brahmin priests used to install idols. After performing the sacred rite, he installed the idol on a small rock. It is said that when priests challenged his right to consecrate, he replied: "I installed my Siva; not a Brahmin Siva."

He instructed his disciples to place a plaque containing the following motto on the temple wall:

Devoid of dividing walls of Caste
Or hatred of rival faith,
We all live here
In Brotherhood,
Such, know this place to be!
This Model Foundation!

In 1904, Narayana Guru abandoned his wandering life and settled down in Sivagiri to continue his Sadhana. Goddess 'Amba' became his deity of worship. He started many schools and built many temples. He started a Sanskrit school in Varkala. Poor boys and orphans were taken under his care. They were given education regardless of caste distinctions. In 1913, he founded the *Advaita Ashram* at Aluva. This was an important event in his spiritual quest. This Ashram was dedicated to a great principle – *Om Sahodaryam Sarvatra* (*all men are equal in the eyes of God*). This became the motto of the new Ashram.

Commandments

Narayana Guru gave the following ten commandments of conduct.

1. Get enlightened with education.
2. Find strength through organization.
3. Attain progress through industry.
4. Don't speak caste, ask caste and think caste.
5. Think that there is only one caste, one religion and one God for mankind.
6. Whatever be the religion, it is sufficient if it is good for mankind.
7. Whatever be the difference in faith, dress or language, all humanity belongs to one caste; there is no harm in inter-caste marriage and inter-dining.
8. Do not make liquor, don't drink it and don't sell it.
9. Spend judiciously.
10. Man who knows dharma should work hard for the progress and well-being of his neighbour.

Tolerance and Catholicity

Narayana Guru believed that men should live in amity and harmony. He advocated religious tolerance and compassion. The following observations reflect his thinking in these matters.

¤ Religion of man will find its perfection only when the cult 'Ahimsa' preached by Lord Buddha, love by Jesus, fraternity among men by Mohammed Nabi and the philosophical thoughts of Rishis of India, find their confluence and consummation.

¤ Paganists and hot heads of multifarious religions plead for supremacy of their own religion as blind men tried to establish the identity of an elephant by touching a part of the body of the elephant. Men should study all religions with equanimity, serenity, wisdom and devotion.

¤ Let there be diversity of profession, nationality and language among men. But the Dharma that is inherent in the hearts of all men is 'humanism' and that is the caste of man.

¤ Man without compassion is tantamount to a lifeless mass of flesh emanating foul stink.

¤ Ahimsa is the greatest of all virtues. One who observes the Dharma of Ahimsa is the true manifestation of goodness. One who possesses all virtues except 'ahimsa' is none other than a brute.

Narayana Guru was a great spiritual master. He taught religious tolerance and social harmony. His teachings have a social orientation. He was concerned about the plight of the poor and the downtrodden and worked for their welfare. In his essential spiritual practices, he followed the hallowed, sacred traditions like other great saints.

SIR RABINDRANATH TAGORE

Rabindranath Tagore was a great poet, writer and philosopher. His works popularized Indian cultural thoughts in many parts of the world. He is the first Asian to win the Nobel Prize. Though famous as a poet, he also wrote novels, short stories, dramas, articles, essays and was a painter too. His songs, known as *Rabindrasangeet* are very popular in Bengal. He was a social reformer, patriot and humanitarian.

Tagore was born in 1861 into a wealthy family in Calcutta. He was the ninth son of Debenadranath and Sarada Devi. (Rajaji, it is said, used to cite this fact in jocular opposition to family planning!) Though he went to some schools, he never liked conventional methods of learning. After sometime, he went to the University College in England. His first book of poems was *Kabi Kahini* (tale of a poet) published in 1878. In 1882, he wrote *Sandhya Sangeet*. He married Bhabatarini Devi in 1883. *Chitrangada* was his famous dance drama. In 1901 he took the editorial charge of the magazine *Bangadarshan* and joined the freedom movement. He strongly protested Lord Curzon's decision to divide Bengal on the basis of religion. He wrote several national songs and joined protests. He introduced the *Rakhibandhan* ceremony, symbolizing the underlying unity of undivided Bengal.

Nobel Prize

In 1912, he went to Europe again. On way to London he translated some poems from *Gitanjali* into English. He gave them to William Rothenstein, a noted British painter, who showed them to Yeats and other English poets. India Society of London published *Gitanjali* (song offerings) containing 103 translated poems of Tagore. Yeats wrote the introduction for this book and Rothenstein did a pencil sketch for the cover page. The book created a sensation in English literary world. From England, Tagore went on a lecture tour of America. In November of 1913, the Nobel Prize for literature was awarded to Tagore for *Gitanjali*. He received Knighthood in 1915.

Tagore toured extensively in the country, delivering lectures and enthusing people. In 1919, in a historic letter he wrote to Lord Chelmsford repudiating his Knighthood in protest against the massacre at Jalianwalabag, Punjab. In 1920 he went to Gandhiji's Sabarmati Ashram. He again went on tour to Europe. In 1921, he established Vishwabharati University. He gave all his money from Nobel Prize and royalty money from his books to this University. In 1940 Oxford University arranged a special ceremony in Santiniketan to honour him with a Doctorate of Literature. Tagore passed away in August, 1941 in his ancestral home in Calcutta.

Rabindranath Tagore was essentially a poet and visionary with a cosmopolitan culture. His contributions to national life covered various aspects. Now, we will briefly outline the various facets of his work.

Poetic Vision of India

Tagore is the poet of modern India, conscious of her destiny and national culture. His poetry resonates with ideas of national regeneration and hope.

Give me the strength never to disown the poor
Or bend my knees before insolent might.

But his national philosophy is not sectarian or narrow-minded. He was aware of the insularity of the older phases of Indian tradition. He does not blow the national trumpet nor magnify the virtues of India and the vices of other countries, fearing that it will lead to jingoism.

The following long citation from his poem beautifully invokes his vision of independent India.

Where the mind is without fear and the head is held high,
Where knowledge is free,
Where the world has not been broken up by narrow domestic walls,
Where words come out from the depth of truth,
Where the clear stream of reason has not lost its way in the dreary desert sand of dead habit,
Where the mind is led forward by Thee into ever-widening thought and action —
Into that heaven of freedom, my Father, let my country awake!

Tagore's motto is: "*cultivate the spirit of invincible optimism; believe in life; live worthy of life.*"

Social Reform

Tagore was a social reformer. Having adopted the Brahmo Samaj, he and his family had broken away from caste, purdah and the spirit of religious insularity. He regards caste and nationality as incompatible with each other. While politics aims at national solidarity, caste creates endless distinctions. "*A great national unification implies, therefore, a great revolt against caste trammels, a strong impulse towards reconciliation of conflicting interests, the mutual composing of differences, rhythmic heart-beats as the result of engaging in common pursuits as brothers, co-equals. In India, caste is the greatest obstruction in the pathway of reform*".

Modernism

In his essays and his lectures, Tagore dwelt on a remarkably wide variety of subjects–on politics, on culture, on society, on education. In an essay written on the 150th anniversary of Tagore, Amartya Sen probes into the decline of interest in Tagore in the west, and Tagore's differences with Gandhiji. He traces the differences to Tagore's attachment to open-minded reasoning and to human freedom. Tagore admired Gandhi immensely, often praised his leadership, and insisted that he be called "Mahatma"–the great soul.

But Tagore frequently disagreed with Gandhi in matters over the need for adhering to logic and reason. Gandhi used the catastrophic Bihar earthquake of 1934 that killed many to further his fight against untouchability. He called the earthquake as "a divine chastisement sent by God for our sins," in particular the sin of untouchability. Tagore protested, insisting that "it is all the more unfortunate because this kind of unscientific view of phenomena is too readily accepted by a large section of our countrymen."

Gandhi advocated that everyone should use the charka–the primitive spinning wheel–thirty minutes a day. Tagore opposed this injunction. He disagreed with Gandhian economics. Tagore thought that in general modern technology reduced human drudgery and poverty. Nehru shared similar views. Tagore deprecated the spiritual argument for the spinning wheel: "The charka does not require anyone to think; one simply turns the wheel of the antiquated invention endlessly, using the minimum of judgment and stamina."

According to Amartya Sen, Gandhi advocated, in the words of Thomas Malthus, 'moral abstinence' as the right method of birth control. Tagore championed family planning through preventive methods. Tagore was also concerned that Gandhi had "a horror of sex as great as that of the author of "The Kreutzer Sonata"." And the two differed sharply on the role of modern medicine, which Gandhi distrusted. We should see such differences as arising from divergent world views.

Education

Tagore became famous in the West only as a romantic and a spiritualist. But his writings consistently emphasised the necessity of critical reasoning and of human freedom. These views guided Tagore's ideas on education, including his insistence that education is the most important element in the development of a country. In his assessment of Japan's economic development, he singled out the critical role of the advancement of school education. He observed that "the imposing tower of misery which today rests on the heart of India has its sole foundation in the absence of education." He considered the transformative role of education as the central story in the development process.

Tagore devoted much of his life to advancing education in India and spreading it everywhere. Nothing absorbed as much of his time as the school in Santiniketan that he established. He was constantly raising money for this unusually progressive co-educational school. In his distinctive view of education, Tagore particularly emphasised the need for gathering knowledge from everywhere in the world, and assessing it only by reasoned scrutiny. Students in Santiniketan were taught about Europe, Africa, the USA, and Latin America, and other countries in Asia. Santiniketan had the first institute of Chinese studies in India; Judo was taught there hundred years ago.

Communal Harmony

Tagore opposed the religious and communal thinking that was getting strong. He was shocked by the violence provoked by the championing of a singular identity of people as members of one religion or another. He believed that determined extremists sow seeds of discord among common people: "interested groups led by ambition and outside instigation are today using the communal motive for destructive political ends." Of course, some political scientists like Samuel Huntington now see the contemporary world as a "clash of civilizations" with "Muslim civilization," "Hindu civilization," and "Western civilization," defined largely on religious grounds, vehemently confronting each other. Tagore was born into a family of wide culture, and "his reliance on reasoning and his emphasis on human freedom militated against a separatist and parochial understanding of social divisions".

While he denied altogether the legitimacy of the Raj, Tagore was vocal in pointing out what Indians had gained from "discussions centred upon Shakespeare's drama and Byron's poetry and above all.... the large-hearted liberalism of nineteenth-century English politics." The tragedy, as Tagore saw it, came from the fact that what "was truly best in their own civilization, the upholding of dignity of human relationships, has no place in the British administration of this country."

Poetic Genius

Tagore is undoubtedly a great poetic genius. His thoughts and values greatly influenced national leaders. From his perspectives, he sometimes differed from them. There is certain sublimity and nobility about his thought. But this created a sense of remoteness from everyday realities, particularly in political and social sphere. The setting of his thoughts seems too idealistic and abstract. Bertrand Russell rather uncharitably wrote that he did not like Tagore's "mystic air," with an inclination to spout "vague nonsense," adding that the "sort of language that is admired by many Indians unfortunately does not, in fact, mean anything at all." Russell was a hard-nosed analytical philosopher. 'Nonsense' here is not too offensive; in philosophy, meaningless propositions are called nonsensical. As we saw, philosophers like Ayer consider literary propositions as meaningless in a logical sense.

Tagore was also at times criticized for underplaying the political aspects of independence struggle. For example, he commented that India's problems are social than political. His moderate approaches to patriotism and his cosmopolitanism were sometimes misunderstood. These in no way detract from the great beauty of his poetry and the charm of its ideas. We close with this poem about God with its undercurrent of humanism and compassion:

Leave this chanting and singing and
telling of beads!
Whom do you worship in this lonely
dark corner of a temple with doors
all shut?
Open your eyes and see your God
is not before you!
He is there where the tiller is tilling
the hard ground and where the
path maker is breaking stones.
He is with them in sun and in shower,
and his garment is covered with dust.

KAUTILYA

Kautilya also known as Vishnugupta or Chanakya was the Prime Minister of Chandragupta Maurya (345-300 B.C.), the founder of Mauryan dynasty. Chanakya is believed to have crowned Chandragupta Maurya as the ruler of Magadha. Chanakya established the Mauryan suzerainty over the whole of northern India. Kautilya or Chanakya is celebrated for his diplomacy and statesmanship. He is compared with Machiavelli for his political realism. Between 312 and 320 B.C. wrote Arthasastra, the oldest text on public administration in the world.

Arthasastra consists of the following three parts:

- Arthaniti (economic policies) to promote economic growth;
- Dandniti (administration of justice) to ensure judicial fairness; and
- Videshniti (foreign affairs policy) to maintain independence and to expand the kingdom.

Political Governance

Kautilya discussed State administration in detail in Arthasastra. Kautilya anticipated many modern administrative ideas such as organizational structure based on hierarchy and coordination between departments. Ancient Indian empires also had territorial divisions such as provinces, districts, villages and urban centres. Kautilya linked administration to the welfare of the people.

Kautilya exhaustively lists the duties and functions of the king, princes, ministers, and other state officials. The king and ministers have to observe strict discipline. Kautilya has prescribed strict code of conduct for ministers and administrators. In this regard, he anticipated modern ideas of codes of ethics and codes of conduct.

Kautilya believed in the adage "Yatha Raja Thatha Prajah" (As the King is, so will be the people"). Therefore, he laid down the condition that "an ideal King is one who has the highest qualities of leadership, intellect, energy and personal attributes". According to Kautilya, the King needs to check the integrity of those whom he wants to appoint as advisers. Ironically, Kautilya also points to the risks in serving kings. Nowadays, these are discussed under leadership qualities. Political leaders and public administrators need both skills and character in order to provide effective governance.

He discusses the defence of the state boundaries, protection of the forts, and the manner of repulsing external aggression. The *Arthasastra* classifies legal matters into civil and criminal. Kautilya outlines administration of justice with reference to evidence, procedures and witnesses. Kautilya strongly believed in *Dandniti* (punishment), but held that penalties must be fair and just, and proportionate to the seriousness of offence.

Kautilya believes that good governance is necessary for realizing the objectives of the state. This in turn needs proper administrative structures and processes. Kautilya suggests that governments should avoid extreme decisions and actions. Depending on exigencies, moderate or harsh actions should be taken. Moderate action relies on persuasion (*Sama*) and rewards (*Dana*). Harsh actions rely on punishments (*danda*) and on creating differences between one's enemies (*Bheda*). Kautilya recognises in true modern pragmatic style that: "Sovereignty is practicable only with the cooperation of others and all administrative measures are to be taken after proper deliberations." Here, Kautilya shows qualities of flexibility and realism.

Kautilya seriously addresses the problem of corruption. He lists nearly forty methods by which officials can swindle government funds. But he is sceptical of finding easy solutions. It is as difficult, he says, to discover the honesty or dishonesty in an officer as it is to discover whether or not it is the fish that drank the water. He adds: "It is possible to mark the movements of birds flying high up in the sky; but not so is it possible to ascertain the movement of government servants of hidden purpose." He recommends strictest deterrent punishment to offenders.

Kautilya proposed that the salaries of the King and his officials should not exceed more than a quarter of the revenue. This idea of containing administrative expenditure is again very modern. He also proposed that ministers, including the King, should be paid for the service they render and not for their ownership of any resources.

In Arthasastra, economic governance is the end, and political governance is its means. Good governance presupposes political stability. He makes a revolutionary observation that stability will prevail if rulers are responsive, accountable, removable and recallable. Otherwise, there will be instability. Kautilya shows great concern to the need for a responsible administration. However, the provisions for recall and removal can apply at best to state functionaries and not to the monarch.

The kingdom was of course a monarchy, but it was given well structured administrative machinery. It was divided both functionally and geographically. Functionally, it contained various departments and the heads of these departments were charged with clearly defined responsibilities. They had to run the department actively, efficiently, prudently and profitably. The king directed the administration with the help of a group of councillors, ministers and other high officials. They need to be carefully selected by the king after considering their character and background.

Economic Governance

Kautilya recommends penalties for officials of public enterprises which incur losses, and rewards for those who earn profits. This focus is on husbanding of resources both for efficiency and for meeting the costs of running a country's administration. In the economic sphere, the *Arthasastra* also proposes a wage policy based on economic, social and political conditions. It must be just, and promote state interests. Kautilya considers the State as a party along with farmers, merchants and industrialists to labour or wage legislation. Thus *Arthasastra* balances the interests of the concerned economic groups. Although government is seen as a monopolist, the need for evolving a reasonable solution for proper utilization of resources is recognised.

Kautilya also recognised that the State has to ensure that commercial activities do not violate laws or harm the consumer. The State would have to provide measurement and quality norms for sale of products. Absence of trust and guarantee of quality would reduce commerce, and increase search and verification costs of commercial transactions. Kautilya explicitly states that "Adulteration of grains, oils, alkalis, salts, scents, and medicinal articles with similar articles of no quality shall be punished with a fine." He provides punishments for selling inferior goods as of higher quality. He also fixes profit margins for home made and imported goods along with fines for exceeding the margins.

He also established explicit guidelines for the practice of the medical profession, incorporating ideas far in advance of his time.

Kautilya's treatise is remarkable for foreseeing many modern economic ideas. He tried to establish guidelines for professional service providers like weavers, washer men, boatmen and shipping agents. He accepts the role of markets and of demand and supply when he observes: "in case of failure to sell merchandise at the fixed rate, the rate shall be altered." Kautilya recommended that the State should reduce excessive price fluctuation detrimental to commercial activities. He considered that an interventionist policy is needed to counter a situation of glut in the market. Kautilya's Arthasastra is the first known treatise to discuss such concepts.

Agriculture dominated the economy in ancient times. Kautilya observes that cultivable land is better than mines because mines fill only the treasury while agricultural production fills both treasury and store houses. The *Arthasastra refers* to the functions of a Superintendent of Agriculture and says that the King should understand the intricacies of agriculture. *Arthasastra* recognises that taxes on agriculture and allied activities are necessary sources of State revenue. It advocates taxing the rich farmers. Kautilya also advocated proper systems of cropping pattern and of irrigation.

Kautilya discusses local and foreign trade which he considers the third pillar of economic activity. He emphasised that trade should be promoted by improving infrastructure. The state has to keep trade routes free of harassment by courtiers, state officials, thieves, and frontier guards. Kautilya distrusted traders believing them to be thieves, with a propensity to form cartels to fix prices, make excessive profits and deal in stolen property. He prescribed heavy fines for discouraging such offences by traders. He also recognised the usual trading arrangements and prescribed the methods of resolving commercial disputes. He recommended measures for safety of goods in transit. He made the villages responsible for loss of goods in their area.

Kautilya recommends that public servants while engaged in work, need to be closely supervised. Men are naturally fickle-minded and their temper keeps changing. Hence the agency and tools, which they make use of, the place and time of their work as well as the precise form of the work, the outlay, and the results shall always, be ascertained. Hence the chief officer of each department (adhikarana) shall thoroughly scrutinize the real amount of the work done, the receipts realised from, and the expenditure incurred in that departmental work both in detail and in the aggregate.

Arthasastra emphasises both on fraud prevention and fraud detection.

Arthasastra suggests that the King should appoint spies to secretly watch over the goings on in various departments. This suggestion will be regarded as rather unwholesome. Nowadays, we have systems of whistleblowers who expose frauds in the organizations they work. But setting spies on officers reminds one of a slogan from George Orwell's *1984*: *"The big brother is watching you"*.

The long list of areas of study which Kautilya gives reflects the progress being made at that time. Medicine, mathematics, military education, commercial education, statecraft, the arts, architecture are among the subjects for study. The eminent institutions of learning that flourished during the time included Nalanda and Takshila. In contemporary terms, this is the domain of human capital formation.

Main Themes

At this stage, we may note some interesting parallels between Kautilya's prescriptions and the principles of public administration and corporate management. We need to remember, however, that Kautilya wrote against the background of an ancient monarchy.

- Arthasastra lays emphasis on creating economic infrastructure.
- It indicates areas of economy which need state regulation.
- It broadly lays down the content, modalities and personnel for regulation.
- It shows remarkable perception of market forces.
- Kautilya recognises the significance of public finances.
- Kautilya describes elaborately the duties and functions of all the functionaries from top to bottom within the monarchy.
- The system relied on both penalties and rewards.
- Kautilya prescribes some rules governing private trade and commerce. But as the economy was primitive from a modern viewpoint, it did not have entities strictly comparable to modern corporates.

To sum up: the topics which Kautilya covers can be described in modern terms as - rule of law, judicial system, property rights, incentives for efficient and honest working of government officials, promoting moral and spiritual welfare, provision of infrastructure and capital formation. These are seen as means to strong nation building.

GURU RAVIDAS

We shall now briefly outline the life and teachings of Ravidas. Ravidas was born in a cobbler family. In those days, caste system was strong. People were bound by many social restrictions and taboos. Upper castes mainly pursued spiritual knowledge and avocations. The hereditary specialization virtually shut off others, especially the lower social strata from spiritual activities.

There have been saints who broke through such barriers. Ravidas was foremost among them. According to Dr. Vivek Bhattacharya, Ramananda initiated Ravidas into his religious order. Ramananda was an unorthodox Brahmin. Once he returned after a long pilgrimage. The orthodox Brahmins wanted him to undergo penance or *prayaschitta.* Ramananda abandoned the narrow caste concept, and allowed all to enter the temples and also allowed them to become Gurus. Ravidas was among his disciples.

Saintly Ways

Ravidas was a great devotee of Rama. He would spend his time in meditation and prayer. In the process, he neglected shoe-making. He would be absent minded, unable to concentrate on work and fall behind schedules. His father became exasperated and turned Ravidas out of home. However, Ravidas continued with his old ways.

He used to supply shoes free to saints and fakirs who happened to pass by his place. He had no interest in material possessions. He feared that they would divert his attention from God. He used to say, *"What shall I do with any other treasure? I want only my beloved God whom none would be able to steal. The name of god, simply by uttering, generates power in my mind. That bliss I can never get from anything else".*

Ravidas was initially opposed by Brahmins and other castes because of his low caste status. According to one legend, Brahmins once refused to join a feast in which Ravidas was expected to join. Ravidas did not attend it. But the Brahmins saw him sitting everywhere between them. Realizing their mistake, they apologized to him and paid him obeisance as to an acknowledged saint.

The story may lack historical authenticity. But it yields interesting insights. One is that Ravidas's saintly qualities triumphed over deep-seated social prejudices. Ramananda was considered a renegade by his fellow caste men. Still, he had the advantages of Brahminical birth and vast learning. In contrast, Ravidas despite his unquestioned piety and godliness had to overcome social barriers to receive his due (though he did not bother about worldly renown) from his coreligionists.

Ravidas is reputed to have miraculous healing powers. He liberally assisted whoever approached him.

He never accepted offerings of money. One of his devoted followers once presented him with money. On visiting Ravidas, he was surprised to find the money where he had placed it. When he asked Ravidas about it, Ravidas told him to spend the money on building an inn for pilgrims.

Religious Ideas

To Ravidas, God was all. He thought that men differed from God in having a body. According to *Bhaktamala*, Ravidas *"held that the soul differs from God in that it is encumbered with a body. God is everything, gracious to all passions, and should be worshipped with all the devotion that man is capable of. Ravidas selected virtue from vice, made choice of good acts and avoided things forbidden."* Ravidas used to compose songs in praise of God. They became very popular. Thirty have found a place in *Granth Sahib,* the sacred religious text of Sikhs. Attracted by his devotion to God and spiritual powers, many people used to visit him. People felt that "his conversation and poetry were like the suns to dispel the darkness of doubt and infidelity."

According to *The Cultural History of India:*

Ravidas was the worshipper of the one infinite God, who is above and beyond all religious sects and without beginning or end. He preached that the Lord resides in the hearts of His devotees, and cannot be known through the performance of rites and ceremonies. Only one who has felt the pangs of divine will alone find Him, and the highest expression of religion in life is the service of men.

Many other saints including Kabir respected him. The fame of Ravidas spread far and wide so much so that even the queen of Chittore touched his feet and had initiation done through him. Ravidas was also responsible for the initiation of Meerabai of Rajasthan, the great royal saint of divine music. Ravidas has a large following known as *Ravidasis* who subscribe to theistic form of *Vaishnavism*—which is a *Bhakti* cult.

Dr. Vivek Bhattacharya considers that the "appearance of Guru Ravidas in the spiritual arena of India in the fifteenth century was a turning point in Indian history". The acceptance by masses of the son of a cobbler as a spiritual guru represents the final culmination of the *Bhakti movement*. His elevation to the highest spiritual gallery of saints signals a great social and religious transformation.

GURU NANAK

Biographical sketch

Guru Nanak, a great spiritual leader and founder of Sikhism, was born on April 15, 1469, at Rai Bhoi di Talvandi, now known as Nankana Sahib, near Lahore. Nanak's father Mehta Kalu Chand was a farmer, and was the village accountant. Nanak's mother was Tripta. Even in his childhood, Nanak showed a mystic disposition. He was contemplative and pious. To the great surprise of his teachers, he would ask them questions on spiritual topics. His father tried hard to divert Nanak's mind towards worldly affairs. He entrusted Nanak with cultivation of the land. But Nanak paid little attention to his work. He meditated even in the fields. His father attempted to interest him with other avocations, but to no avail.

Guru Nanak had only one sister named Nanaki. She was married to Jai Ram, a Dewan in the service of Nawab Daulat Khan Lodi who had an extensive Jagir in Sultanpur near Kapurthala. Nanak also married soon after his sister's marriage. His wife was Sulakhani. But marriage and the birth of two children did not hinder Guru Nanak's spiritual pursuits. He would go even then to forests and lonely places for meditation.

Nanaki and Jai Ram had great love and respect for Nanak Rai Bular, the Zamindar of Talvandi, who respected Nanak greatly, secured for him a job in Sultanpur as in-charge of nawab's storehouse.

After some years, Nanak left the job and went on a spiritual search. In the manner of Indian saints, he went on a lengthy journey, travelling to various Muslim and Hindu religious centres of India. Nanak's quest perhaps led him to travels outside India. Nanak returned from his journeys in 1520.

The remaining years of his life were spent in Kartarpur, another village of central Punjab. It was most probably during this final period that the foundations of the new Sikh community were laid. Guru Nanak began to be revered as a spiritual master. Many people from different strata of society thronged to hear the message of Guru Nanak. They were greatly attracted to the moral teachings of Guru Nanak expressed in numerous devotional hymns sung by congregations of devotees. These continue to be a part of the vibrant Indian religious traditions.

Nanak spent the final years of his life with his family in Kartarpur. Guru Nanak died in the year 1538 A.D. at the age of sixty-nine. Guru Angad succeeded Guru Nanak. The other Gurus are: Guru Amardas, Guru Ramdas, Guru Arjan Dev, Guru Hargovind, Guru Har Rai, Guru Har Krishan, Guru Teg Bahadur and Guru Govind Singh.

Teachings

William Hewat McLeod (in an article in *Encyclopaedia Britannica*) observes that Sikhism is monotheistic and shows both Hindu and Islamic influences. It rejects idol worship and ritualism. But it shows deep influence of Hindu mystical and devotional beliefs. According to William McLeod, Nanak's message can be briefly summarized as a doctrine of salvation through disciplined meditation on the divine name. Salvation is understood in terms of escape from the transmigratory round of death and rebirth to a mystical union with God. The divine name signifies the total manifestation of God, who is a single Being, immanent both in the created world and within the human spirit. Meditation must be strictly inward, and all external aids such as idols, temples, mosques, scriptures, and set prayers are rejected.

Guru Nanak preached that not a single breath should be spent without *Nama Smarana* or remembering the Name of the Lord. For no one could tell whether the breath that had gone in would come out or not. Nanak says, "We are men of one breath. I know not a longer time-limit". According to Guru Nanak, he alone is a true saint who remembers the Name of the Lord with every incoming and outgoing breath. He tells people not to lose any time but to begin prayers at once.

Guru Nanak was a reformer who condemned the corruptions in society. He rejected formalism and ritualism in religion. He tried to infuse real spirit in the worship of God and true faith in religion and God. His outlook was liberal. He carried the message of peace and of love for everybody. Nanak opposed distinctions among men based on caste, creed, race or social hierarchy. To quote his words, "There is neither Hindu nor Mussulman (Muslim) so whose path shall I follow? I shall follow God's path. God is neither Hindu nor Mussulman and the path which I follow is God's."

He preached purity, justice, goodness and the love of God. He said, "Serve God. Serve humanity. Only service to humanity shall secure for us a place in heaven". Guru Nanak had great respect for women, allowed them to participate fully in all religious gatherings and accorded them full share in religious functions.

Guru Nanak clearly says: *"The road to the abode of God is long and arduous. There are no short cuts for rich people. Everyone must undergo the same discipline. Everyone must purify his mind through service of humanity and Nama Smarana. Everyone must live according to the will of the Lord without grumbling or murmuring. How to find Him? There is one way. Make His will your own. Be in tune with the Infinite. There is no other way"*.

The first stage in making the divine will one's own is attained through prayer for divine grace or favour–*Ardas* for *Guru Prasad.* He says that nothing can be achieved by man without divine favour. He says: *"Approach God with perfect humility. Throw yourself on His mercy. Give up pride, show and egoism. Beg for His kindness and favour. Do not think of your own merits, abilities, faculties and capacities. Be prepared to die in the pursuit of His love and union with Him. Love God as a woman loves her husband. Make absolute unreserved self-surrender. You can get divine favour and love"*.

Guru Nanak again and again insists thus: *"Realise your unity with all. Love God. Love God in man. Sing the love of God. Repeat God's Name. Sing His glory. Love God as the lotus loves water, as the bird Chatak loves rain, as the wife loves her husband. Make divine love thy pen and thy heart the writer. If you repeat the Name, you live; if you forget it, you die. Open your heart to Him. Enter into communion with Him. Sink into His arms and feel the divine embrace"*.

Guru Nanak has given a beautiful summary of his teachings in one of his hymns:

Love the saints of every faith:
Put away thy pride.
Remember the essence of religion
Is meekness and sympathy,
Not fine clothes,
Not the Yogi's garb and ashes,
Not the blowing of the horns,
Not the shaven head,
Not long prayers,
Not recitations and torturings,
Not the ascetic way,
But a life of goodness and purity,
Amid the world's temptations.

In Guru Nanak's conception, *"God is but one, His Name is true, He is the Creator, He pervades the whole universe, He is without fear, He is without enmity, He is immortal, He is birthless, He is self-born and self-existent, He is the remover of the darkness (of ignorance) and He is merciful"*. The Lord is eternal. He has no beginning and no end.

Guru Nanak created the *Gurumukhi* script by simplifying the Sanskrit characters. The holy *Granth* of the Sikhs is in *Gurumukhi*. Every Gurudwara has a *Granth Sahib.* The holy *Granth,* popularly known as *Adi Granth,* contains the hymns of the first five Gurus. They were all collected, arranged and formed into one volume called *Guru Granth Sahib* by the fifth Guru. It contains a few selections from the hymns of Kabir and other contemporary Vaishnavite saints. Later on, the hymns of the ninth Guru were incorporated in the holy *Granth* by the tenth Guru. The compositions of Guru Nanak are very extensive.

The *Granth Sahib* begins with the following: "There is but one God whose name is true–the Creator". It contains a code of high morals. Purity of life, obedience to Guru, mercy, charity, temperance, justice, straightforwardness, truthfulness, sacrifice, service, love and abstinence from animal food are among the virtues on which great emphasis is laid; while lust, anger, pride, hatred, egoism, greed, selfishness, cruelty, backbiting and falsehood are strongly condemned.

According to popular tradition, Nanak's teaching needs to be practised in three ways:

- Vag Chakk : Sharing with others, helping those with less who are in need
- Kirat Kar : Earning/making a living honestly, without exploitation or fraud
- Naam Japna : Meditating on God's name to control evil thoughts, to eliminate suffering and to live a happy life.

Besides moral earnestness and simplicity, syncretism, catholicism and liberalism are the other admirable attributes of Guru Nanak's teaching. These aspects of Guru Nanak's teaching have great contemporary relevance. They preach tolerance and amity between religions. Although persecution at one time in its history led Sikhism to acquire heroic military virtues, it has a strong mystical and devotional strain. In a historical period marked by political turmoil, Sikhism stood as a sentinel guarding the other faiths in India.

TIRUVALLUVAR

Tiruvalluvar was a great poet, preacher and thinker. The details of his life are not known with any great historical authenticity. Tiruvalluvar was born in Tamilnadu perhaps in Mylapore of present-day Chennai. Tiruvalluvar was a householder who probably worked under a king. According to some legends, he was a weaver. His wife's name is Vasuki.

Tiruvalluvar's fame rests on his great work *Thirukkural*. Scholars are divided on the period of its composition. The commonly accepted period of Tiruvalluvar is 2nd century AD. Thirukkural is assigned to this period because Tiruvalluvar seems to have borrowed ideas from Arthasastra (250 B.C. 150 A.D.) and because the two Tamil epics *Manimekhalai* and *Silappadikaram* (200-500AD) contain references to Tirukkural's couplets. However, 31 B.C. is the year of Tiruvalluvar's birth as accepted by the Tamil Academy of Madurai.

Despite its antiquity, Thirukkural reflects humane, refined and universal moral values. The following observations of Albert Schweitzer contained in his book '*Indian Thought and Its Development*' (1951) are worth recalling in this context:

"*With sure strokes the Kural draws the ideal of simple ethical humanity. On the most varied questions concerning the conduct of man to himself and to the world its utterances are characterised by nobility and good sense. There hardly exists in the literature of the world a collection of maxims in which we find so much lofty wisdom*".

Thirukkural consists of three parts covering:

(a) virtues;

(b) worldliness; and

(c) love.

Thirukkural contains 133 chapters, each with 10 couplets, thus making a total of 1330 couplets. Virtue is accorded the highest priority in Thirukkural. The chapters on virtue and love (*inbam*) deal with ethical living in private life. *Porul* or wealth deals with public affairs. Virtue is discussed in 380 verses, worldliness in 700 stanzas and love (*Inbam*) in 250 verses. A general idea of the contents of Thirukkural can be had by looking at the couplets and the topics they cover: 40 couplets are on God, Rain, Virtue and Ascetics, 200 couplets on Domestic Virtue, 140 couplets on Higher Virtue based on Grace, 250 couplets on Royalty, 100 couplets on Ministers of State, 220 couplets on the Essential requirements of Administration, 130 couples on Morality, both positive and negative, and 250 couplets on Human Love and Passion.

In what follows, we cite a few quotations from Thirukkural to convey the spirit of its moral sentiments. After paying homage to ascetics, Tiruvalluvar emphasises family and personal virtue.

On Virtue

"Rage, Envy, Greed and Harsh words Avoided is virtue."

He praises the qualities of affability, gratitude, self-control, right conduct and faithfulness in the first section of Virtue. Extolling the significance of vegetarianism he says:

"How can one be kindly? If he fattens on other's fat?"

He also expresses the Christian idea that one should forgive one's enemies, and return evil with good.

"Punish a sinner by paling him With a good deed, and forget."

On Love and family

Tiruvalluvar's idealism leads him to lavishly praise feminine virtue:

If woman might of chastity retain, What choicer treasure doth the world contain

Although Tiruvalluvar discusses romantic love, he preaches that it should culminate in married life. For it sets out the commitments and responsibilities of the couple towards each other and towards their families and society at large. Tiruvalluvar places high value on family life, and the joys of raising children. Professor C.R. Krishnamurti in *Thamizh Literature Through the Ages* observes, "These verses would be particularly relevant today when genuine commitment between married couples is gradually becoming conspicuous by its absence. One also wonders at what point in history the financial and religious inputs began to creep into the matrimonial relationships in the Thamizh social fabric!" As an aside, we may note that all over India religious inputs in matrimonial relationships are waning while financial inputs are growing.

On the Importance of Wealth

Tiruvalluvar recognises the supreme value of virtue, but thinks that without wealth it becomes impracticable. The following couplet shows how a poor man's thoughts will get fixated on the spectre of hunger.

"Will that hunger return? Which nearly killed me yesterday?"

Simultaneously, Tiruvalluvar finds fault with avarice and miserliness:

"He is poor though a millionaire Who neither gives nor spends."

Tiruvalluvar emphasises that worldly wisdom or prudence is necessary to live in harmony in society. One needs to get along well with fellow men.

On Politics & Governance

Tiruvalluvar has made many wise observations on statecraft. He discusses the relationship between the king, his ministers and subjects. He highlights the importance of learning, agriculture and social service. He denounces corruption and nepotism, the evils of current politics, as evil and unwise. His prescription for a thriving society is based on a blend of personal character, social conduct and state action.

On Moral Enforcement

Many moral thinkers advocate harsh morality and rigid enforcement of morals. Idealistic morals have to make allowance for common human weaknesses, and to the exigencies of real life. Tiruvalluvar takes this fact into account, and recognises the need for some exceptions from moral norms. He gives an instance where uttering a falsehood may be justified.

Falsehood may take the place of truthful word If blessing from fault it can afford

Literary aspects

We may note a few other significant points about Thirukkural. According to Tamil scholars, its composition is marked by great literary beauty. The expressions used for describing human emotions are very delicate. Various aspects of love are described in a subtle manner. Tiruvalluvar never misses an opportunity of cautioning people against unchaste behaviour.

"*Sacred Couplets is considered a masterpiece of human thought, compared in India and abroad to the Bible, John Milton's Paradise Lost, and the works of Plato. .... The Thirukkural is an all inclusive moral guide whose foremost moral imperatives are not to kill and to tell the truth*" (Webster's Encyclopaedia of Literature)

Tiruvalluvar's poetry reflects his moral seriousness, depth of conviction and his understanding of human psychology. His thinking is catholic and free from religious dogmatism. It is a matter of great wonder that Tiruvalluvar, who lived so long back in history, expressed such liberal and sublime thoughts. He was far, far ahead of his times.

In the end, we include a list of pithy sayings from Tiruvalluvar:

- Something may not be achievable even by God or through God's help. But the effort exerted to attain that non-achievable will yield its deserving result!
- Though the world goes round with many activities, it is dependent on agriculture. Hence, though laborious, farming is the foremost activity.
- As water changes its nature, from the nature of the soil in which it flows, so will the character of men resemble that of their associates.
- Friendship is not just a smile on the face; It is what is felt deep within a smiling heart.
- The stalks of water-flowers are proportionate to the depth of water; so is men's greatness proportionate to their minds (Knowledge).
- Avoid an act which you may repent later; if done by mistake, better not to repeat it.
- Whatever is thought to be done will be achieved as planned, if the planners possess firmness in execution.
- Excessive or deficient food or activity causes disorders in mobility, breathing and digestion.
- Agriculturists are the linchpin of the mankind since they support all others who cannot till the soil.
- The learned teacher makes you enjoy learning; on leaving, makes you to keep thinking of his teaching.
- Think and then undertake the work; to think after commencement will bring disgrace.
- Determined efforts result in prosperity; idleness will bring nothing.
- Defer not virtue to another day; receive her now; and at the dying hour she will be your undying friend.
- Water will flow from a water well in proportion to the depth to which it is dug, and knowledge will flow from a man in proportion to his learning.
- That which God gives, nobody can ban. That which God bans, nobody can give.
- If anyone does a wrong thing for you, do good thing for them.

We can discuss many other inspiring figures from our history. However, extending this account further will lead to repetition of the earlier pattern of discussions. Our purpose is to offer a model of analysis which students can apply to their readings on other leaders, rulers and reformers. Students need to learn about all such prominent figures and make short notes about them in the form of bullet points.

Summary

- This chapter is about lives of leaders, reformers and administrators.
- We interpret leaders to mean national leaders of freedom movement.
- Students would be reading about them while covering Independence movement and polity.
- We interpret administrators to mean able Indian rulers from ancient, medieval and modern times.

- We interpret reformers as social, moral and religious reformers. These are transformational figures that reshape the moral values and worldview of the society.
- As it is impossible to cover all important leaders, reformers and administrators, we have selected a few for discussion.
- Students need to take notes whenever they come across such personalities in their reading.
- Their lives have to be studied in the background of human values.
- Human values can be individual values – linked with man's bodily self, social self and spiritual self.
- Human values can also be interpreted as universal values found in all societies, religions and periods.
- Five such human values are - truth, right conduct, love, peace and non-violence.
- Human values can have another meaning as recognizing human rights. Humanism as a doctrine placed man at the centre of discussion in philosophy, morals and humanities. It focuses on human happiness, human concerns and human freedom and achievement.
- Human beings have to be always treated as ends in themselves and not as means to any putative higher end.
- Humanism rejects religious ideas, affirms autonomy of human reason and man's duty to chalk out independently the paths of self development and social progress.
- Religious discourse may often focus on spiritual exercises, theological or doctrinal questions and on external religious observances. Sometimes, religious leaders promote narrow outlook, bigotry and sectarian intolerance. We have to steer clear of such views. Religious approaches have to promote feelings of common humanity, human fraternity, social equality and mutual tolerance.
- Vivekananda fused Hindu Vedantic ideals with Western scientific and humanistic thought. He worked against the tendency of Hindus to devote themselves to exclusive sects and doctrines. He reminded Indians of their glorious traditions. He popularized Vedanta philosophy in the West. Above all, he reminded people of the need to help the masses submerged in poverty and ignorance.
- The great contributions of Ramakrishna Paramahamsa are: establishing the possibility of directly experiencing God; preaching of harmony of religions; harmonizing ancient religious practices with modern secular life; discounting the abuses which have entered religions; and improving the tone of morality in social life. His thoughts are free from obscurantism.
- Aurobindo's writings boosted the morale of the nation still in bondage. They lifted the feeling of despondency, gloom and inferiority from the minds of people living in subjugation to a foreign power. Aurobindo reminded people of the nation's glorious past. There is nothing narrow or chauvinistic in Aurobindo's thoughts. His message of spiritual self enlightenment based on deep internal meditation is addressed to the whole humanity.

¤ Ram Mohan Roy possessed an acute mind, broad religious sympathies, a very powerful personality and great drive for reforms. Both his range of interests and sphere of activities were wide. He fought relentlessly against the abuses and corrupt practices that crept into the once healthy body of Hindu doctrine. He looked beyond India's political downfall, loss of independence and humiliation. He looked towards a radiant future based on absorption of Western culture and democratic discipline. He was a true believer in the equality of sexes and toiled to raise the status of women.

¤ Dayananda Saraswati gave the slogan: "back to Vedas". He was an iconoclast who opposed the traditional rituals of Hinduism, idol worship, conventional priesthood and the caste barriers. He was a great practical reformer who built many institutions and promoted many constructive activities.

¤ Narayana Guru was a great spiritual master. He taught religious tolerance and social harmony. His teachings have a social orientation. He was concerned about the plight of the poor and the downtrodden and worked for their welfare. In his essential spiritual practices, he followed the hallowed, sacred traditions like other great saints.

¤ Rabindranath Tagore was a great poet, writer and philosopher. His works popularized Indian cultural thoughts in many parts of the world. He is the first Asian to win the Nobel Prize. Though famous as a poet, he also wrote novels, short stories, dramas, articles, essays and was a painter too. His songs, known as Rabindrasangeet are very popular in Bengal. He was a social reformer, patriot and humanitarian.

¤ The main themes in Arthasastra are:

It lays emphasis on creating economic infrastructure. It indicates areas of economy which need state regulation. It broadly lays down the content, modalities and personnel for regulation. It shows remarkable perception of market forces.

¤ Kautilya recognises the significance of public finances.

¤ Kautilya describes elaborately the duties and functions of all the functionaries from top to bottom within the monarchy.

¤ His system relied on both penalties and rewards.

¤ Kautilya prescribes some rules governing private trade and commerce. But as the economy was primitive from a modern viewpoint, it did not have entities strictly comparable to modern corporate entities.

¤ To sum up: the topics which Kautilya covers can be described in modern terms as -rule of law, judicial system, property rights, incentives for efficient and honest working of government officials, promoting moral and spiritual welfare, provision of infrastructure and capital formation. These are seen as means to strong nation building.

¤ The "appearance of Guru Ravidas in the spiritual arena of India in the fifteenth century was a turning point in Indian history". The acceptance by masses of the son of a cobbler as a spiritual guru represents the final culmination of the Bhakti movement. His elevation to the highest spiritual gallery of saints signals a great social and religious transformation.

- Sikhism is monotheistic and shows both Hindu and Islamic influences. It rejects idol worship and ritualism. But it shows deep influence of Hindu mystical and devotional beliefs.
- Guru Nanak preached that not a single breath should be spent without Nama Smarana or remembering the Name of the Lord.
- Guru Nanak was a reformer who condemned the corruptions in society. He rejected formalism and ritualism in religion. He tried to infuse real spirit in the worship of God and true faith in religion and God. His outlook was liberal. He carried the message of peace and of love for everybody. Nanak opposed distinctions among men based on caste, creed, race or social hierarchy.
- Nanak preached purity, justice, goodness and the love of God. Guru Nanak had great respect for women, allowed them to participate fully in all religious gatherings and accorded them full share in religious functions.
- Guru Nanak created the Gurumukhi script by simplifying the Sanskrit characters. The holy Granth of the Sikhs is in Gurumukhi.
- Granth Sahib contains a code of high morals. Purity of life, obedience to Guru, mercy, charity, temperance, justice, straightforwardness, truthfulness, sacrifice, service, love and abstinence from animal food are among the virtues on which great emphasis is laid; while lust, anger, pride, hatred, egoism, greed, selfishness, cruelty, backbiting and falsehood are strongly condemned.
- Besides moral earnestness and simplicity, syncretism, Catholicism and liberalism are the other admirable attributes of Guru Nanak's teaching.
- Tiruvalluvar was a great poet, preacher and thinker.
- Tiruvalluvar's fame rests on his great work Thirukkural. Scholars are divided on the period of its composition. The commonly accepted period of Tiruvalluvar is 2nd century AD.
- Thirukkural consists of three parts covering: a) virtues; b) worldliness; and c) love.
- Despite its antiquity, Thirukkural reflects humane, refined and universal moral values. It is considered a masterpiece of human thought, compared in India and abroad to the Bible, John Milton's Paradise Lost, and the works of Plato.
- Tiruvalluvar's poetry reflects his moral seriousness, depth of conviction and his understanding of human psychology. His thinking is catholic and free from religious dogmatism. It is a matter of great wonder that Tiruvalluvar, who lived so long back in history, expressed such liberal and sublime thoughts. He was far, far ahead of his times.

PRACTICE QUESTIONS

1. What do you understand by human values? Discuss three such values.
2. Name a national leader of your choice and discuss the values he represented.
3. Discuss any two saints who though untouched by Western ideas have shown a progressive modern outlook.

4. Do you think that the interest of Indian scholars in Kautilya's Arthasastra is a form of nostalgia for past?
5. "Indian saints have been too immersed in religious ceremonial and discourses to pay sufficient attention to social problems." Discuss.
6. Discuss the ideas of any Indian ruler who you think has contributed to welfare of people.
7. There have been many religious leaders who won great acclaim in spite of their humble birth. Discuss the teachings of any such saint.
8. What are the moral lessons one can learn from Gandhi and Netaji Subhas Chandra Bose?
9. "The lives of great reformers reflect ideals which though great are hard to follow". Discuss.
10. "Moral values and administrative realities are far apart." Discuss.

REFERENCES

- The Spirit of Indian Culture: Saints of India Dr.Vivek Bhattacharya
- Lecture (at British Museum) on Tagore's 150th birth centenary Amartya Sen
- India's Nation Builders D.N. Bannerjea
- Swami Vivekananda Ramakrishna matt and Ramakrishna Mission (web site)
- Sri Ramakrishna Ramakrishna matt and Ramakrishna Mission (web site)
- William Hewat McLeod Guru Nanak (Article from Encyclopedia Britannica)
- Sri Swami Sivananda Guru Nanak (From Lives of Saints)
- Manoj Sadasivan Thirukkural (About.com Hinduism)
- N.V.K. Ashraf An Introduction to Thirukkural and its author

CHAPTER

Sources of Ethical Guidance: Laws, Rules, Regulations And Conscience

INTRODUCTION

Ethics examines the criteria for judging human actions as right or wrong. From where do such standards come or what are their sources? Moral philosophers have identified **laws, rules, regulations** and **conscience** as important sources which guide human ethical conduct. In this chapter, we discuss the above four areas and how they influence ethical behaviour. The first three ideas have different meanings in Politics and jurisprudence on one side and in Ethics on the other.

Our discussion of law will cover two aspects. First, we look at modern conceptions of law. Thereafter, we consider it as it was viewed in medieval times, and especially the ideas of St. Thomas Aquinas. In earlier times, moral systems were designated as (moral) law. The earlier thoughts on law mixed up religious themes, social norms and law. The modern approaches (which arose in response to earlier thinking) seek to disentangle law from morality and religion. The advantage in starting with modern ideas on law is that it will help us in viewing medieval thoughts in proper perspective.

While discussing St. Thomas Aquinas, we avoid repetition of ideas on natural law ethics covered earlier in the chapter on Western Moral Thinkers. We discuss natural law based on the account which Patrick J. Sheraan gives in *Ethics in Public Administration: A Philosophical Approach*.

Ordinary Meaning of Law

By laws, we commonly understand the enactments of legislature. This is secular, as opposed to religious view of law. The concept of law historically arose from religion, philosophy and social norms. Gradually, the subject of jurisprudence evolved, and sharpened the notions of law used in courts to adjudicate property disputes and criminal offences.

There are many branches of law – criminal law, civil law and laws covering specific sectors like the Companies Act, the Indian Electricity Act and the Environment Protection Act. Laws are divided into two categories as substantive laws and procedural laws. Substantive laws define offences or crimes in terms of their ingredients and prescribe punishments. Procedural laws - like the Code of Criminal procedure or the Code of Civil Procedure – specify the modalities which courts have to follow while dispensing justice. The Indian Evidence Act mainly deals with the types of testimony and documents which are admissible as evidence and the nature of conclusions which courts can draw from evidence.

While considering the idea of law, we should not overlook the Constitution of India. Constitution of any nation is regarded as its fundamental law. All other laws have to be in consonance with the constitution. Besides delineating the framework of government of a nation, a Constitution also embodies the basic values and ethos of a nation. These are known as constitutional values. Broadly speaking, the Preamble to the Constitution and the Directive Principles of State Policy contain the constitutional values.

Austin's Positive Theory of Law

John Austin propounded a positive theory of law. Law in its essential nature differs from moral and religious principles. Austin's approach is based on analytical jurisprudence, and tries to remove evaluative or normative terms from discussion. Positivism in legal theory means that: (a) a law is a legal rule and that (b) if passed according to prescribed procedure, law is valid irrespective of its content. In other words, as long as an elected legislature (in modern democracy) debates and passes the law, everyone must follow it.

Austin's theory is also known as the command theory of law. *Its main features are the following*:

- Law is a command from a sovereign (legislature or king or ruler).
- The people are in the habit of obeying a ruler.
- Law is reinforced by sanction or punishment.
- Put simply, laws are orders backed by threats.
- A law, therefore, is the expressed wish of the sovereign and can be distinguished from other commands.
- The sovereign is the person or body whom others habitually obey, and who does not obey others.

The significance of the above theory lies in its exclusion of moral or normative elements from the conception of law. People speak about law as a duty or obligation placed on citizens. Austin tries to eliminate these ethical terms relying instead on the probability of punishment which criminals fear or the 'habit' of people to obey laws. He avoids any discussion on the merits of law.

Austin's positive view of law fails to explain some parts of law. For example, English "customary" laws or Common law includes decisions of judges made according to legal "principles" for which there is no written law. However, European nations which generally follow Roman law tradition have fewer such elements. Austin defends these by using the notion of tacit consent of the sovereign; since the king does not object, he must have consented. Some laws do not fit into Austin's theory. These are laws that repeal laws; laws with no penalties; laws merely creating rights like contract acts; and laws defining marriage. Austin calls them declaratory.

Other problems arise from international law and primitive law. There is no sovereign to enact international law. Most legal history recognizes unwritten tribal laws with no formal, legislated code. Austin's view denies that such law is law. Legal systems have "layers" of law. They treat the constitution and treaties as a "higher" law. Such a law "constrains" subsequent legislation. Austin's command theory cannot account for the higher laws.

HAL Hart's Views

Hart is a positivist though he raised some of the above mentioned objections against Austin. Hart mentions that two categories of rules, called primary and secondary rules, together form the basis of a functioning legal system. This is similar to the distinction between substantive laws and procedural laws we noted earlier. Students should carefully note that the term 'rule' sometimes as in this context is used as synonymous with law. Primary rules either impose legal obligations, as in criminal law, or they grant powers, as in the power to make a will in the law of succession, or the power to enter into a contract.

Secondary rules enable working of primary legal rules. Hart mentions three types of secondary rules. Rule of recognition gives criteria for identifying primary legal rules for example Acts of Parliament and judicial decisions. Rules of change identify how legal rules can be formed, amended or repealed. For example, an Act of Parliament goes through various readings in the Lok Sabha and Rajya Sabha and needs President's assent. Rules of adjudication enable the courts not only to settle disputes, but also to interpret the law.

Hart does not accept any necessary connection between law and morality. In other words, the validity of a law is not dependent upon its moral acceptability. Even a morally repugnant law may be legally valid. However, that does not mean one must obey laws that are morally repugnant. Obedience remains a matter of personal decision or conscience.

Both theories of positive law we discussed deny that law can be restrained by morality. It is a different matter that many laws rest on a society's moral and cultural consensus. Positive theories of law fail to capture the idea of moral ideal implicit in many views of law.

Lon Fuller's Views

Lon Fuller shares the view that there are necessary, substantive moral constraints on the content of law. But Fuller believes that law is necessarily subject to a procedural morality. Law subjects human conduct to various rules. According to Fuller, law seeks to achieve social "order through subjecting people's conduct to the guidance of general rules by which they may themselves orient their behavior".

Fuller's functionalist conception of law implies that nothing can count as law unless it is capable of performing law's essential function of guiding behaviour. In order to achieve this task, a system of rules must be:

(i) expressed in general terms;

(ii) publicly promulgated;

(iii) prospective in effect;

(iv) expressed in understandable terms;

(v) consistent with one another;

(vi) within the powers of the affected parties;

(vii) not subject to frequent changes so that people cannot rely on them; and

(viii) administered in a manner consistent with their wording.

On Fuller's view, no system of rules that fails minimally to satisfy these principles of legality can achieve law's essential purpose of securing social order through the use of rules that guide behaviour. If rules are not made known or are not clear, they cannot guide behaviour because people will not know what rules require.

According to Fuller, law is moral in two aspects: it promotes social order and it does this by respecting human autonomy because rules guide behaviour. Therefore the above principles of legality constitute a morality. Some writers argue that Fuller's rules ensure the efficacy of law or its proper implementation, and they are not moral ideas. However, most of Fuller's above mentioned eight principles stand for moral ideals of fairness. They do not however operate as moral constraints on the content of law.

Modern Normative Reaction to Positive Theories of Law

Austin's positive theory of law leads to odd consequences. As Hart pointed out, it could imply that rule of a mob of gangsters on a remote island is lawful. This is because Austin reduces legal obligations to habits and to calculation of probabilities of risk from disobeying laws. Hans Kelsen tries to resolve this problem. He argues that a law in order to be considered legitimate has to be prescribed by a body or institutions which is duly or properly constituted. He adopts the positive view, but regards law as socially constructed and as not derived from natural law or any higher source. Unlike natural law, it is dynamic and keeps changing.

As we mentioned earlier, Kelsen recognizes that law needs a normative base on which it can rest. He does not seek it in ordinary morals. He calls the basic norm as 'logical constitution'. Laws can be created but the basic norm states how they can be created and changed. Only those created in accordance with basic norm will be valid. He regards basic norm as an accepted custom: "when the custom through which the constitution has come into existence or the constitution-creating act consciously performed by certain human beings, is objectively interpreted as a norm-creating fact ..." then a basic norm exists. In way, Kelsen seems to regard constitution as providing the basic norms for laws.

Constitutional Values

The Indian constitution lays down the framework of norms and values to which Indian laws have to conform. As we mentioned before, these norms and values are found in the Preamble and the Directive Principles of State policy. We summarize them below.

Values included in the Preamble are:

- Socialism, secularism and democracy
- Social, economic and political justice
- Liberty of thought, expression, belief, faith and worship
- Equality of status and of opportunity
- Fraternity and dignity of the individual
- National unity and integrity

Directive Principles

The Directive Principles of State Policy are 'fundamental in governance of the country'. Government has to follow these principles while making laws.

1. Equitable distribution of wealth or the socialist pattern of society and equal pay for equal work for both men and women.
2. Provision of adequate means of livelihood to all citizens, men and women.
3. Provision of employment to all.
4. Free and compulsory education for children.
5. Living wage for workers.
6. Protection of childhood and youth against exploitation and against moral and material abandonment.
7. Organization of village panchayats as units of self-government.
8. Prohibition of the consumption, except for medical purposes, of intoxicating drinks and of drugs injurious to health.
9. Organization of agriculture and animal husbandry on modern and scientific lines.
10. Promotion of international peace and security and maintenance of just and honourable relations between the nations of the world.
11. Social welfare measures.

This does not mean that public servants can ignore ordinary moral rules applicable to all in personal and social life. The above values enshrined in the constitution will help them in many official situations which involve ethical questions.

Rules and Regulations

The terms 'rules' and 'regulations' have the same meaning in Ethics. However, the two terms are sometimes given different meanings in legal contexts. Every law contains a provision for making rules necessary for its implementation. The rule-making powers are with government's executive branch. Rules cannot go beyond the law and are subject to ratification of legislature. Rules are subordinate legislation.

However, Hart and Fuller use the term 'rule' in a sense equivalent to law. Naturally, students have to make out from the context of a question or discussion as to which meaning is appropriate.

The term 'regulation' refers nowadays to regulations which regulatory authorities - like Central Electricity Regulatory Commission - issue for regulating a particular sector like power, insurance or telecom. However, this is a current usage connected with regulating certain economic activities. But in Ethics, the terms 'rule' and 'regulation' have the same meaning.

Differences between Laws and Rules

Regulations focus on or relate to individual good whereas laws seek to increase public good. Laws can be enacted only by those who exercise sovereignty (or state power) or the lawfully constituted government (or its legislative wing). Regulations can be laid down by one's superiors, by organizations or by head of a family. Rules or regulations (in wider moral contexts) can be laid down by private persons and entities. Laws of a nation operate within its territorial boundaries. Citizens when abroad are not governed for most purposes by their national laws. Rules or regulations prescribed, for example, in official codes apply to government servants even when they are abroad. Similarly, rules which monks accept as part of their religious order, apply to them even outside the country. Students should note that the conception of rules or regulations we outlined is from Ethics and not from Law. But there could be commonalities between the ethical and legal conceptions.

Meaning of Law in Ethics

In the preceding sections, we discussed the positive theories of law and also covered rules. But the conception of law has much wider connotation and associations in Ethics. This view of moral law is the outcome of centuries of philosophical and ethical speculation. Moral law is defined in old Ethics books as a general rule of right living; especially such a rule or group of rules conceived as universal and unchanging and as having the sanction of God's will. We consider in this regard the views of St. Thomas Aquinas who was a great Roman Catholic theologian (i.e. one well versed in religious discourse) of the medieval times. He naturally subscribed to Christian doctrines which to their followers are truths revealed by God. They rest on faith and not on empirical ideas. Aquinas however used Aristotelian deductive logic to apply reason in the service of faith, that is to say, belief in God and associated religious ideas including morality. [We may note in passing that many 'rationalists' direct their fire at beliefs of Hindu religion. However, religious beliefs, especially belief in God's existence, of what Arnold Toynbee describes as 'higher religions' stand on very similar footing; if subjected to logical or scientific scrutiny, they disappear into thin air. Rationalists cannot pick and choose as between different religions; or accord especially favourable or unfavourable status to any religion.]

Types of Law according to Aquinas

Aquinas distinguishes four kinds of law: (1) eternal law; (2) natural law; (3) human law; and (4) divine law. **Eternal law** comprises laws that govern the nature of an eternal universe. Eternal law is derived from the idea of God as the ruler of the world. It can refer to all laws (including to laws of nature according to some writers) by which the universe is ordered.

Divine law is concerned with those standards that must be satisfied by a human being to achieve eternal salvation. One cannot discover divine law by reason; its principles can be known only through divine revelation. Aquinas cites as examples Old Testament of Bible (which Jews follow) and the New

Testament (which Christians follow) as divine laws.

The **natural law** consists of those principles of the eternal law that govern the behaviour of beings endowed with reason and free will. It is the 'participation of the eternal in the rational creature'. It is 'an imprint on us of the divine light'. According to St. Paul, the natural law is written in the hearts of men. We can understand natural law as divine moral ideas found in human heart.

How can we be sure of the existence of natural laws? One answer is that men, from ancient times, irrespective of the level of their civilization, distinguished between right and wrong actions. They also believed that men should pursue good and give up evil. As these ideas arose along with the emergence of mankind, they can be regarded as part of their mental makeup.

Human Law

Aquinas says that human law is made by men: it is an 'ordinance of reason for the common good, promulgated by him, who has the care of the community'. It is valid only insofar as it matches with the natural law; or in Augustine's famous remark, an unjust law is really no law at all. This is the defining characteristic of the natural law theory. According to Blackstone, in natural law theory: 1) there can be no legally valid standards that conflict with the natural law; and 2) all valid laws derive whatever force and authority they have from the natural law.

Parts of Natural Law

Aquinas mentions the primary, secondary and tertiary principles of natural law. Primary principles of natural law are universal rules of conduct and can be easily perceived by human reason. Examples of these principles are doing good, avoiding evil and following the dictates of reason. Human beings have a natural love of good and abhorrence of evil. All the remaining moral principles follow from the primary principles.

Secondary principles can be derived without much difficulty from the primary principles. A person of ordinary intelligence without 'invincible' ignorance can easily know them. Aquinas classifies ignorance as vincible and invincible. 'Vincible' ignorance, unlike invincible ignorance can be easily overcome with a little effort - which men need to make. From the primary principle of being good, it follows that one should respect elders and be considerate to others.

Tertiary principles of natural law cannot be easily derived from the primary principles. They often presuppose involved reasoning. People who are unaware of these principles incur no blame for it is a case of 'invincible ignorance'. An example is of a person who believes it right to cheat a rich man to help the poor. The three levels of natural law explain why people arrive at different moral conclusions on even similar matters. Aquinas says that in theoretical thinking while it is easy to see general principles or common notions, the conclusions which follow as their implications are hard to grasp. Similarly, while men subscribe to common principles of actions, their responses vary in similar particular instances.

Aquinas argues that natural law not only tells us what is good but also casts a moral duty on us to follow it. We are under a moral obligation to obey the commands of natural law. It is a universal law and applies to the entire humanity irrespective of race, nation, religion and sex. As we have noted, people may interpret or understand natural law in different ways. But they have to follow it according to their best reflective understanding. In practical terms, this means that people should think carefully about the moral aspects of their actions.

Infraction of laws entails sanctions and punishments. But the consequences of disobeying the natural law are unclear. This is true in case of all moral laws which lack the coercive power of legal enactments. For instance, if one violates the Indian Penal Code by committing theft, he will, upon conviction, be imprisoned. Normally, legal offences are a subset of moral lapses. To the extent a moral violation is also a legal offence, penal law will punish the offenders. But if one violates the command to love one's neighbour, secular law will not punish him. All religions mention that sinners will suffer in hell. But such concepts are non-empirical and fall outside the domain of logical discourse.

Civil Laws

Civil laws are different from canonical laws which applied to churches. We will now consider positive, manmade civil laws. Aquinas discusses the relation between positive civil laws and the natural law. Interestingly, he holds that positive civil laws partake of the character of law in so far as they are derived from the natural law. When they depart from the natural law, they are perversions of law. We can ignore his discussion on the ways in which civil laws can differ from the natural law. However, he makes a point that men are under no obligation to follow those parts of civil law which fail to conform to natural laws. The medieval theological context of the discussion is no longer relevant. But what is relevant is the revolutionary observation that under certain circumstances people will be justified in defying the law. In modern day language, this is an issue of legitimacy of laws.

According to Aquinas, laws have to meet the following conditions in order to qualify for people's obedience.

- Civil laws have to conform to the natural law. They should not prescribe what the natural law prohibits or forbid what the natural law prescribes.
- Civil laws have to be made by a lawful government with proper authority.
- They have to be reasonable and lie within the physical and mental capacities of men.
- They are not for individual but general social good.

If a law fails to meet any one of the above conditions, citizens need not obey it. This is the basic idea which underlies the concept of civil disobedience. In civil disobedience, people disobey unjust laws which though duly enacted, violate higher moral principles. Thus, during the Salt Satyagraha, Mahatma Gandhi violated the Salt laws then in force. Similarly, pro-life groups in many Western nations oppose laws which permit abortion.

We may note here the distinction between being above law and outside the law. A group of philosophers held that the sovereign or the law maker is above the law on the ground that there is no one to punish him. Aquinas argued that the sovereign is not above law since he can elect to obey it. Aquinas says, "whatever law a man makes for another, he should keep himself". The modern view is that no one is above law. 'Outside the law' can mean illegal actions and/or actions in locations where law does not apply. As we have already seen, laws only apply to those who live within the territorial jurisdiction to which they apply. Indian law will not apply to those in Sweden.

Relevance of the Ideas of Aquinas

Next, we will consider conscience as a source of ethical guidance. Before that, we need to make a few observations on the discussion so far. Readers may feel that we have discussed law mainly on the basis of Aquinas's account of Roman Catholic doctrines. However, the ideas of Aquinas can be seen more widely as indicating how moral laws can guide human action. His Roman Catholic theories can be replaced, for example, with Hindu or Buddhist ethical principles, without seriously affecting the validity of the argument. The central point is that laws derive their force not from the powers of the king or the legislature, but by reflecting moral principles dear to human heart. Many people believe that such principles have a divine origin.

Modern thinkers have abandoned the concept of natural law. It is considered a part of medieval metaphysics. Further, many people, especially in the west, have lost religious faith. Even otherwise, there is a tendency to replace religious morals with secular morals (in the sense of non religious) ethics). But many secular morals coincide with religious morals.

CONSCIENCE

Until now, we have discussed law as ethical guide to human action. Laws are external guides to men. In contrast, conscience acts as an internal moral guide to them. Conscience comes into play when mind passes a judgement on the rightness and wrongness of a particular act. Conscience can morally judge past actions, present action and those under contemplation. Conscience is different from moral laws. Moral laws are general and cover many actions. Conscience applies laws and rules to particular actions. Conscience complements human individuality or ego or selfhood. Both ego and conscience can think about actions, ascertain their meaning and evaluate their moral worth.

Historical Evolution of Ideas on Conscience

The concept of conscience used in moral philosophy has changed considerably over time. In fact, the earlier views on conscience have been discarded. Both Aristotle and Stoics described human consciousness (recognition) of moral value and of moral law simply as reason, or the ruling part of the soul. It is the scholastic writers who propounded the doctrine of conscience as a special form of knowledge of moral laws which God reveals to human soul. This theory of conscience or of moral knowledge is called intuitional. Its chief tenet is that the knowledge of good and bad is immediate or intuitive, and not as stated by the empirical view of conscience, the result of processes of association and reflection. That conscience is innate or inborn is also usually associated with this view.

Joseph Butler is the most prominent writer on the subject of conscience. According to Butler, God gives men conscience. It should be the final arbiter of human actions. This notion of conscience is problematical when considered from the methodological perspective of modern social sciences. Unlike other social science concepts, conscience cannot be operationised---there is no way of discovering it or knowing how it works in actual practice. For example, attitudes can be studied using methods of social science research. But we cannot study conscience that way.

Conceptions of Conscience

How is conscience conceptualized by different thinkers? We list a few views.

- **St Paul:** Conscience is a God-given ability in all human beings to know and choose the good.
- **Aquinas:** Conscience is knowledge of human nature and primary moral precepts or fundamental moral ideas.

- **Butler:** Conscience is a God-given ability to reason, our 'natural guide' with ultimate authority.
- **Newman:** Conscience is 'the voice of God' planted in us before we could reason. It is an intuition, the 'law of the mind'. Intuition is sixth sense, something we know without relying on logic or conceptual thinking.
- **Freud:** Conscience is the 'superego', and consists of moral ideas planted in us by authority figures like parents. It is part of the subconscious mind. The ego (conscious self awareness of oneself or personality) ordinarily guides human action.
- **Piaget:** Conscience develops over time. It is a part of a healthy human mind.

St Paul, Aquinas, Butler and Newman all agree that the conscience comes from God and should have ultimate authority over what we do. Aquinas and Butler see reason as an essential part of this, but Newman thinks it is intuitive. Freud and Piaget explain conscience without reference to God.

Conscience, moral reason and moral sense are often the same. These terms are used in this manner in old books on Ethics.

Ideas of Butler on Conscience

Conscience is a reflective principle. It judges morally what we did and want to do. All ordinary human beings have a sense of right. According to Butler, it is an aspect of human reason and of sentiments. Conscience has a unique authority among the principles belonging to human nature. It should direct other principles and not vice-versa.

Conscience is closely connected to autonomy of an individual's moral insight. It signifies being motivated by our inner sense of moral rightness and wrongness, and not by external considerations such as moral law, duty, obligation, or virtue. It is uninfluenced by fear of punishment or hope of reward.

Conscience is a principle superior to and governing particular passions, emotions, and instincts. There are various parts to human nature, and these are organised hierarchically. The part of human nature that is at the top of this hierarchy is conscience. The two principles of human nature at work are: self-love, that is, a desire for happiness in the self; and benevolence, that is, desire or hope for happiness in other people. Conscience adjudicates between these two principles. This is an intrinsic part of human nature. This guidance is intuitive. It is a gift from God, and as such, its guidance is not an option. It has universal authority in all moral judgments.

Objections to Butler's Views

There have been many objections to Butler's ideas. Some of these criticisms are essentially against the very concept of conscience. Sidgwick argues that conscience really is neither an independent nor a distinct moral principle. Briefly, his argument runs as follows. Suppose it is reasonable to obey conscience. Then "the rules prescribed by conscience" are either reasonable on their own or they are "the dictates of an arbitrary authority". If the latter, how can one justify the arbitrary authority? But if the former, there is no independent moral authority for conscience. Conscience becomes another name for reason.

It is difficult to justify conscience is a form of intuition. The appeal to intuitive conscience form the basis of a functioning legal system. He describes what they stand for.

- According to Fuller law seeks to achieve social "order through subjecting people's conduct to the guidance of general rules by which they may themselves orient their behavior". He lists such rules.
- Moral law is defined in old Ethics books as a general rule of right living; especially such a rule or group of rules conceived as universal and unchanging and as having the sanction of God's will.
- According to St. Thomas Aquinas, law imposes an obligation on people. It makes people act or desist from acting; or it prescribes some actions and prohibits some actions.
- The terms 'rules' and 'regulations' have the same meaning in Ethics.
- Regulations can be laid down by one's superiors, by organizations or by head of a family. Rules or regulations (in wider moral contexts) can be laid down by private persons and entities as well.
- Laws can only be made in exercise of sovereign power by legislature or in olden times by kings.
- Aquinas defines natural law in religious terms.
- Aquinas mentions the primary, secondary and tertiary principles of natural law.
- Natural law not only tells us what is good but also casts a moral duty on us to follow it.
- Primary principles of natural law are universal rules of conduct and can be easily perceived by human reason. Secondary principles can be derived without much difficulty from the primary principles. Tertiary principles of natural law cannot be easily derived from the primary principles. They often presuppose involved reasoning.
- According to Aquinas, laws have to meet certain conditions to qualify for people's obedience.
- According to modern jurists, no one is above law.
- Aquinas's analysis of law as a moral guide is still relevant if its religious ideas are replaced with contemporary secular ideas.
- Public servants should follow constitutional values while performing their official tasks.
- The concept of conscience has changed considerably over time.
- Modern writers consider conscience as a product of social evolution and of individual development. When our intelligence deals with the relations of persons and deeds we call it conscience.
- Conscience has three aspects - knowledge, authority and associated emotions.
- Our conscience or value commitments can be explained as resulting from our moral development, our education and our social environment.
- People generally remain loyal to the social morality imbibed in their formative years.
- Moral reformers seek changes even in social ideals and institutions esteemed as sacred.
- Moral relativism questions the validity of universal, objective moral values.
- It can be individual or cultural.
- The idea of individual conscience which each one has to exercise independently of historical

forms and contemporary ideals is misconceived.

- Reflective conscience has to find a mean between capricious self-conceit and dead conformity.
- Public servants cannot act mechanically in applying rules. They have to identify situations with moral implications and think through the possible alternatives.

PRACTICE QUESTIONS

1. What is the meaning attached to law in Ethics? How does it differ from the meaning attached to law in common usage?
2. *Mahabharata* contains moral discourses by one of the characters, Vidur. Will they qualify as law?
3. How are laws distinguished from rules or regulations in ethics?
4. What do you understand by moral law?
5. St. Thomas Aquinas argues that people can defy laws under certain circumstances. Do you agree?
6. What are the ethical values enshrined in the Indian constitution?
7. What is the difference between the intuitive and empirical conceptions of conscience?
8. What are the two different intuitive versions of conscience?
9. Explain the concept of moral relativism. Is it a suitable doctrine for adoption by civil servants?
10. According to the famous dictum of Nietzsche: "Nothing is true, all is allowed." Discuss.
11. "Nothing is good or bad, but our own thinking makes it so". Examine.
12. "To be moral is to live in accordance with the moral tradition of one's country". Discuss.
13. What is Austin's positive theory of law? What seems to be its main purpose? What are the main objections to it?
14. Discuss Butler's views on conscience. How can they be criticized?
15. What is Fuller's contribution to law? In what sense can it be said to contain moral elements?

REFERENCES

- Patrick J. Sheeran Ethics *in Public Administration: A Philosophical Approach*
- John Dewey *Outlines of a Critical Theory of Ethics*
- Wilbur Marshal Urban *Fundamentals of Ethics: Introduction to Moral Philosophy*

is seen as self-authenticating or self-certifying. It has its authority from within itself. However, conscience may not be infallible. It could turn out to be misinformed or wrong. Without checks from external, objective standards, Butler's idea of conscience could lead to moral anarchy. Some critics argue that people might end up intuiting what is in their interest as dictated by conscience. This criticism may be unjustified since Butler's notion of conscience does not sanction selfish or unethical actions for the supremacy of conscience.

Another problem connected with conscience arises from its individual nature. Each individual has a conscience. The actions sanctioned by consciences of different persons may vary sharply. Then there will be no way reaching agreement over the differences. This is a general problem which moral subjectivism, as we saw earlicr, creates.

EMPIRICAL CONCEPTION OF CONSCIENCE

Modern thinkers discarded former theories which regarded conscience as a divinely endowed quality, or as a special mental faculty, or as an infallible intuitive insight. They regard it as an empirical or historical category.

Conscience is considered simply as an act of consciousness dealing with a special class of objects and judgments. The objects are human conduct and character, the judgments value judgments. According to empiricists, our knowledge of what is right and wrong originates from individual and social experience. Conscience itself is, therefore, the product of social evolution and of individual development. Herbert Spencer and others suggested that conscience, or our elemental moral sentiments, while in some way innate in the individual, have emerged from the historical experience of the human race.

Modern thinkers do not regard conscience as a peculiar or separate mental or psychological faculty. It is simply an aspect of human intelligence and consciousness. Human intelligence when dealing with the nature and relations of things is called understanding. When our intelligence deals with the relations between human beings and relations of human deeds to their underlying motives or guiding moral norms we call it conscience. Our conscience or value commitments can be explained as resulting from our moral development, our education and our social environment.

The Customary or Conventional Conscience

Ethical thinkers also distinguish between customary or conventional conscience and reflective or independent conscience. Customary conscience represents traditional morality. Reflective conscience departs from conventional morality in an attempt to be more refined or in order to be more in line with changing social trends.

Human beings are born into an existing moral environment of a society which consists of various institutions and a dominant socially accepted moral code. This code and its components exert constant influence on the impressionable minds of children in their formative years. They make certain demands on them. These are enforced by such means as punishment, reward, blame, public-opinion, and the bestowal of social leadership. This is known as the process of socialization or acculturation.

John Dewey sums up the formation of the conventional conscience in the following passage:

These demands and expectations naturally give rise to certain convictions in the individual as to what he should or should not do. Such convictions are not the outcome of independent reflection, but of the moulding influence of social institutions. Moreover the morality of a time becomes consolidated into proverbs, maxims and law codes. It takes shape in certain habitual ways of looking at and judging matters. All these are instilled into the growing mind through language, literature, association and legal custom, until they leave in the mind a corresponding habit and attitude toward things to be done. The more important distinctions are fixed in language, and they find their way into the individual mind, giving it unconsciously a certain bent and colouring.

The Loyal Conscience

People seldom think about the social institutions and moral codes which shape their life and morality. They identify themselves with the social forms and their ideals. They do not consider the demands which the existing institutions make on them as burdens, but as reflecting their own will and deserving loyalty. However, people need to understand the grounds for belief in existing moral ideas. People who realise the significance of conventional morality become morally autonomous even when following it. But those who extend blind support to moral systems are not free.

The Independent or Reflective Conscience

Men not only follow the prevailing morality but may critically reflect upon it. They may feel that the current moral code of society no longer reflects the true needs of society or that it is an antiquated expression of bygone times. They may try to understand the true spirit of existing institutions and determine the sort of conduct it demands. Critical thinkers may criticize and seek reforms even in social ideals and institutions esteemed as sacred. This is the task which great moral reformers perform.

Conscience or moral sentiments can operate in situations of ordinary life also. Common people can reflect upon their immediate relationships in life to see if they are what they should be. These relationships may concern family, friends, neighbours and colleagues in office. They can regulate their own conduct not merely through customary habits and routines but by rationally re-examining the situations.

The idea of reflective conscience involves the 'right of free conscience'. This is the individual's right to discover the good or to determine the ends of action on his own. Its opposite is a situation in which some good, considered imposing or beneficent, is forced on him. According to Hegel, the right of free conscience is the principle of subjective freedom which marks off modern from ancient times.

Perils of Right to Independent Conscience

At this stage, students need to recall the doctrine of moral relativism. It denies the existence or validity of objective, universally valid moral standards. It is a commonly known fact that morals and social conventions vary both across societies and over historical time. This is called the relativity of morals. Or morals are relative to a particular society and a historical period. This relativity arises from the social function of morals – or their contribution to social stability and well-being. In this functional aspect, morals have to adjust to changes of society and to currents of time.

Because there appear to be no eternal or universal standards of morals and manners, many people wrongly conclude that there is no value in a local, temporary, and slowly changing ethics. Such views lead many into 'a *head-long jettisoning of their whole cargo of morals, manners and conventions, and the bringing about of a chaos which arouses mirth or terror according to the temperament of the social observer*'. It is expressed in extreme form in the famous dictum of Nietzsche: "Nothing is true, all is allowed."

According to Wilbur Marshall Urban, *"This philosophy of license, this idea that nothing is good or bad, but our own thinking makes it so, invariably appears in the first flush of realisation of historical relativity of morals and of the sense of freedom from external compulsion that comes with it. Yet it is based on such obvious fallacies that it persists only in the minds of the most unthinking."* Even if moral standards are changing and functional, they appear as practically absolute during the time they prevail. For individuals, they represent the "pragmatic absolute."

The idea of independence of conscience is often misinterpreted. There is no right of private judgment since moral standards and their sources have to be public. The right of private conscience means that the moral standard and its source are not the opinion of some other person, or group of persons. It is a common, objective standard expressed in social relationships themselves.

The idea of individual conscience which each one has to exercise independently of historical forms and contemporary ideals is misconceived. The feeling that one has to follow one's own notion of what is right becomes an excuse for all sorts of capricious, obstinate and sentimental actions. Hegel had such ideas in mind when he observed that: *"The striving for a morality of one's own is futile, and by its very nature impossible of attainment; in respect of morality the saying of the wisest men of antiquity is the only true one: To be moral is to live in accordance with the moral tradition of one's country"*.

PRESENT INDIAN CONTEXT

This raises the question: Does conscience, which is individual, override norms set up by society, law and religious teaching? Many writers believe that conscience should decide what is right or wrong. Individual conscience has the right of independently determining the criteria of good and evil and then acting accordingly. This results in an "individualistic ethic, wherein each individual is faced with his own truth, different from the truth of others." Fortunately, dictates of individual conscience and social ethics often coincide.

But nowadays we witness many situations where individuals and groups are aggressively voicing personal and maverick views which run counter to national ethos. They do so in the name of individual conscience and right of dissent. But dissent should not be irresponsible, or just a way of attracting attention by making shocking statements. Views should not override requirements of national security, social cohesion and our cultural ethos. One should avoid voicing fashionable and chic ideas in the name of individual conscience. These are often ways of sensationalizing things during TV appearances. One should not trivialize serious matters of conscience or apply them to inappropriate situations. Current examples include slogans of 'aazadi' in some universities (as if we are living under foreign rule), not getting up during national anthem or ridiculing national symbols. We have also discussed these issues in the chapter on political attitudes.

MORAL CHANGE

Conscience should not merely endorse the existing beliefs and opinions. Morality existing at any time is not likely to be perfect. One has to recognise both the possibility and the necessity of advance/ improvements in the prevailing morality. Reflective conscience has to find a mean between capricious self-conceit and dead conformity. It must be based on the moral consciousness expressed in existing institutions, manners and beliefs.

In John Dewey's words: "*Reflective intelligence cross-questions the existing morality; and extracts from it the ideal which it pretends to embody, and thus is able to criticize the existing morality in the light of its own ideal. It points out the inconsistencies, the incoherencies, the compromises, the failures, between the actual practice and the theory at the basis of this practice. And thus the new ideal proposed by the individual is not a product of his private opinions, but is the outcome of the ideal embodied in existing customs, ideas and institutions*".

Until now, we examined laws, rules, regulations and conscience as guides to ethical decision-making. Of course, they often provide a frame of reference for decision-making, and may not be amenable to direct application to a given situation. Further, there are innumerable laws, rules, regulations, opinions and court judgements on many subjects. Public administrators may not be able to internalize these in their thought. Besides while relying on rules, government servants have to understand the moral nature of decisions. We have noted elsewhere that morality (from another perspective) depends on the object of their action, circumstances of action and the purpose of the action. Public servants cannot act mechanically in applying rules. They have to identify situations with moral implications and think through the possible alternatives.

Summary

- We can seek ethical guidance (a) from moral criteria or standards; (b) from analysis of action in terms of its object, its surrounding circumstances and its purpose and; (c) from laws, rules, regulations and conscience.
- The ordinary meaning of law is that it is an enactment of legislature.
- The concept of law historically arose from religion, philosophy and social norms.
- There are many branches of law - criminal law, civil law and laws covering specific sectors.
- Laws are divided into two categories as substantive and procedural.
- Substantive laws define offences, rights and obligations.
- Procedural laws specify the modalities which courts have to follow while dispensing justice.
- Constitution of any nation is regarded as its fundamental law.
- It embodies the basic values and ethos of a nation. The Preamble to our Constitution and the directive principles of state policy contain the constitutional values.
- The concept of law has a much wider connotation and associations in Ethics. This view of moral law is the outcome of centuries of philosophical and ethical speculation.
- John Austin propounded a positive theory of law. Law in its essential nature differs from moral and religious principles.
- Positivism in legal theory means that: (a) a law is a legal rule and that (b) if passed according to prescribed procedure, law is valid irrespective of its content.
- Austin's theory is known as the command theory of law and we outlined its main features.
- Hart mentions that two categories of rules, called primary and secondary rules, together

ETHICAL QUALITIES THROUGH THE LENSES OF SAGES AND GREAT THINKERS

INTRODUCTION

The main theme of Ethics consists of virtues and vices. Virtue is any excellence of character. Virtue may be defined as the acquired power or capacity for moral action. This definition implies that virtue is cultivated through moral exertion. Virtue applies to qualities exhibited in right conduct, for example, courage. Virtues-such as 'just', 'liberal', 'brave', etc.-are applied to persons as well as to their acts. We do not regard these attributes as belonging to acts considered apart from their agents. Virtue is primarily a permanent attribute of the moral agent. It does not really belong to the transient acts and feelings which reflect it. Virtue is regarded as a possession worth aiming at for its own sake-to be indeed a part of the perfection of man that some regard as the sole ultimate good.

The synonyms of vice are fault, depravity, sin, iniquity, wickedness, and corruption. Vice is a practice, behaviour, or habit generally considered immoral, depraved, or degrading. Vice also refers to a fault, a negative character trait, a defect, or an infirmity. In common usage, vice may also refer to a bad or unhealthy habit such as smoking.

Ethical texts contain long lists of virtues and vices. But analysis shows that many of these are not separate and distinct. They stand for the same moral concept. If one eliminates such common virtues and vices, their number comes down. Thus, the ancient Greek philosopher Plato recognised only four cardinal virtues - wisdom, fortitude, temperance and justice. All other virtues can be reduced to these four or shown as equivalent to them. However, we will cover a wider range of virtues recognised separately in common parlance.

Moral philosophers have divided vices into major and minor categories. The major vices are called in religious language as deadly or mortal sins. These are anger, vanity, avarice, lust, sloth, envy and gluttony. Our discussion will cover these vices. They include virtually all the human frailties.

In this chapter, we adopted a particular style of presentation. Before starting discussion on any virtue or vice, we give a list of famous quotations on it. Each quotation expresses incisively some aspect of the virtue or the vice. Students can gain useful insights by reflecting on these quotations from great thinkers.

KINDNESS

"Be kind, for everyone you meet is fighting a harder battle." — *Plato*

"I would rather make mistakes in kindness and compassion than work miracles in unkindness and hardness." — *Mother Teresa*

"Allah is more loving and kinder than a mother to her dear child." — *The Holy Qur'an*

"My religion is very simple. My religion is kindness." — *Dalai Lama*

"If you want others to be happy, practice compassion. If you want to be happy, practice compassion." — *Dalai Lama*

"Kindness and love are the most curative herbs and agents in human intercourse"— *Friedrich Nietzsche*

"Compassion is that which makes the heart of the good move at the pain of others. It crushes and destroys the pain of others; thus, it is called compassion. It is called compassion because it shelters and embraces the distressed." —*Buddha*

"It would be true to say that the cultivation of loving kindness and compassion is all of our [Buddhist] practice" —*Buddha*

"Kindness is a language which the deaf can hear and the blind can see." —*Mark Twain*

"Do not injure, abuse, oppress, enslave, insult, torment, torture, or kill any creature or living being." —*Mahavira*

"Real kindness seeks no return; what return can the world make to rain clouds?" —*Tiruvalluvar*

These quotations touch upon various aspects of kindness. Aristotle defines kindness as helpfulness towards someone in need, not in return for anything, nor for the advantage of the helper himself, but for that of the person helped. Kindness is the quality of being friendly, generous, and considerate. It is the bedrock of humanist as well as religious ethics. As a virtue, kindness can be analysed in various ways.

What are the elements or ingredients of kindness?
What are the sources from which kindness springs?
What is the underlying rationale of kindness?
What is its moral significance?

Kindness is one of a cluster of closely related qualities. Love, mercy, benevolence, consideration for others, altruism and kindness are allied qualities. As a virtue, kindness is other-regarding. Those who perform kind deeds seek no return - a point mentioned in Tiruvalluvar's quote above. Dalai

Lama regards kindness as the essence of religion. This is virtually true of all religions. Charity or love towards fellow human beings is a core Christian principle. Hinduism emphasises on Daya or Anukampa - virtues very similar to kindness. Similarly, Karuna is a central Buddhist tenet. Islam has a similar concept of Reham or mercy. There is a similar sounding word with similar meaning in Jewish scriptures. Jainism preaches kindness towards all living creatures. Though all life is considered sacred, human life is deemed the highest form of earthly existence. Mahavira's quotation spells out one aspect of kindness in negative terms or as a prohibition–abjuring all forms of violence against living creatures. It sees nonviolence as the chief ingredient of kindness.

From a Christian point of view, all virtues of character directly spring from love, and are its manifestations. As St. Paul says, 'it is the bond of perfectness'. Kindness arises from human sentiments and feelings; men have a quality of empathy which enables them to experience by a kind of association or psychological simulation the emotions, pleasures and pains of others. Human beings share a sense of fellow feeling with others in virtue of their common humanity. Hence, they feel saddened by the sufferings of others and try to alleviate their pains. They participate in one another's sorrows and joys, 'weeping with those that weep, and rejoicing with those that rejoice'. Kindness can be regarded as the outcome of social conscience. Very often, men become hardened and coarse, and lose their delicacy of feeling. Religious texts and genuine literature seek to rekindle and keep alive such feelings in men.

Kindness cannot simply remain as an inactive sentiment. It has to become practical beneficence, of service and of deeds which help those in distress. Kindness is more than mere charity. Charity or generous contributions are necessary to provide for the physical necessities of the destitute and the needy. But the feelings of grief, anxiety and desolation which the sufferers feel can be partly relieved by extending to them emotional solidarity, support, and care. True service costs more than money. "No one can do a kindness who does not put something of himself into it."

Most religions regard forbearance and forgiveness as a special form of practical kindness. We can note the moral principles which fall within such practical kindness. One should not speak evil of others. One should be gentle and humble. One should live peaceably with all avoiding anything which may lead to strife. Even when there are differences and disputes, one should tolerate and forgive one another.

Plato's observation on kindness points out the need for other-regarding attitudes. Plato gives a reason why we should be considerate towards others. It is that they may be facing tougher situations or greater adversity than us. But this may not in fact be true. It is an empirical fact which needs verification. However, Plato urges the moral agent to make such an assumption, and adopt an appropriate moral stance towards others. In other words, given that assumption, one has to invariably act kindly towards others. Kindness becomes a permanent attribute of one's moral being.

Mother Teresa's observation means that we should be kind and compassionate even at the risk of mistakes. If we do so, we will never harm or hurt anyone. We may in the process be overindulgent towards some immoral or undeserving persons. But we will not injure them either physically or psychologically.

The expression "work miracles in unkindness and hardness" can be variously interpreted. Thus ambitious parents may put children through harsh educational grind damaging them psychologically in the process. Legal systems may impose harsh penalties on offenders – without tempering justice with mercy. It may refer to many means through which men try to achieve supposedly great or high ends. In this context, we may refer to the harsh and ruthless totalitarian regimes – as in Nazi Germany, Stalinist Russia or Communist China – which aimed at total social transformation. In the process, they killed, maimed, and ruined millions of people. Mother Teresa may be indirectly opposing radical social and political change or large scale experiments in social engineering which are invariably accompanied by great violence and human suffering. She may be highlighting the need for humane, incremental, gradual and peaceful social change.

Mark Twain means that kindness is a feeling which can be conveyed without using any words. People can readily see and sense kind words and deeds. Kindness is a sentiment which passes from one person to another without the need for an intervening medium. No special faculties or skills are needed for conveying or sensing kind sentiments. One need not be learned or tutored to experience kind sentiments or entertain kind thoughts. Even illiterate persons are capable of being kind. Kindness is part of man's original and natural emotional make up. Harsh circumstances may sometimes destroy this impulse. But with a little effort, they can be revived.

Kindness is an attribute of feelings, thoughts, words and deeds. It is a central moral tenet of all religious thought. In its absence, human beings become beastly, cruel, ruthless and pitiless. The need for kindness, tolerance and harmony can be seen from the violent conflicts which are currently tearing apart many nations of the world. As Goethe observed, "Kindness is the golden chain by which society is bound together".

FORGIVENESS

"One should never do wrong in return, nor mistreat any man, no matter how one has been mistreated by him."

—Plato's Socrates

"Forgiveness is the fragrance that the violet sheds on the heel that has crushed it." *—Mark Twain*

"He who is devoid of the power to forgive, is devoid of the power to love." *—Martin Luther King, Jr*

"To forgive all is as inhuman as to forgive none". *—Seneca*

"To forgive is human, to forget divine..." *—James Grand*

"Let us forgive each other-only then will we live in peace". *—Tolstoy*

'Forgiveness' means pardoning of an offence, wrongdoing, or obligation. The victim of the wrongdoing pardons the wrong doer. The phrase 'forgive and forget' sums up the idea. Forgiveness may extend to groups when the wronged group excuses the other. In recent times, governments have begun a practice of setting up commissions to establish truth and bring about reconciliation between perpetrators and victims of historical wrongs.

The benefits of forgiveness are the following:

- Continuing personal relationships.
- Getting rid of persistent negative emotions which could harm the wronged individual.
- Helping wrongdoers by releasing them from blame and hostility, and by enabling them to turn a new leaf.

Forgiveness involves the re-establishment or resumption of a relationship ruptured by wrongdoing. By forgiving, the victim gives up resentment or anger against the offender. The wrongdoer atones for his wrongs and seeks forgiveness.

However, Aristotle, Kant and Hume have pointed that forgiveness can be misdirected, and reflect an individual's weakness of character. Thus a woman in an abusive 'relationship' may go on forgiving the wrongdoer for no good reason. The repentance or apology of the wrongdoer may be pretence with no contrition. Here, forgiveness colludes with wrongdoing. Therefore, forgiveness has to be based on morally valid reasons. The wrong should be excusable and the wrongdoer should display guilt or remorse.

A tendency to too readily forgive may reflect lack of self-respect, or servility which is a vice. Aristotle mentions that any person who lacks appropriate anger is "unlikely to defend himself" and "endure being insulted" and is for this reason a "fool". Kant also says that a person who fails to become angry at injustices done to him lacks dignity and self-respect. According to Hume as anger and hatred are "inherent in our very frame and constitution", the lack of such feelings is sometimes evidence of "weakness and imbecility". This view implies that forgiveness is justified only under certain circumstances.

Forgiveness is a process of getting over resentment which is personal anger caused by an injury or wrong suffered at the hands of another. Resentment is anger that is felt on behalf of one's own self. Other forms of anger, such as indignation or scorn, may be aroused on behalf of oneself or for the sake of others. Anger may be sudden and instinctive or it may be deliberate and sustained over time. It is a "reactive attitude," provoked by beliefs about the intentions, attitudes, and actions of others towards us. Resentment involves taking offence, umbrage, or exception to the deeds and intentions of others.

Forgiveness has to be based on moral principles. They help an individual in overcoming resentment that he feels toward a person who has hurt him. The emphasis on moral principles in getting over resentment distinguishes it from other means of overcoming it. One may dissipate resentment by forgetting the wrong which occasioned it. One may also overcome resentment by will power so as to maintain relations with a wrongdoer. But these do not represent genuine forgiveness. Forgiveness involves overcoming other "retributive emotions" like indignation, contempt, or hatred. In religious traditions, forgiveness is seen as rooted in moral reasons.

Moral thinkers also discuss the question whether forgiveness should be unconditional or be based on the behaviour of the wrongdoer. It may be stipulated that that the wrongdoer should confess his wrong, apologize, show remorse or regret, or attempt to atone for it, or accept punishment. This type of behaviour from a wrongdoer, many would consider, is necessary for forgiving him. Religious ideas (especially Christian) hold that we should forgive others their wrongs as our own forgiveness by God depends only on it. True Christian compassion, say the Gospels, should extend to all, even to the extent of loving one's enemies.

The above account of forgiveness sees it as part of an individual's moral effort. But forgiveness is also linked to an individual's dispositions or character traits. In the Christian tradition, forgiveness is often aligned to such virtues as love and compassion, which are stable individual dispositions or traits. One is thus enjoined to abjure anger and resentment. In Greek philosophy, it is associated with magnanimity. Some writers regard forgiveness as a duty or what one ought to do. Other writers consider forgiveness as non-obligatory but desirable.

At times, an individual's resentment disappears not due to his efforts but just because he forgets about it. As the proverb says, time is a great healer and resentment also dissipates over time. In this mode of overcoming resentment, there is no effort or any examination of moral reasons for forgiving a wrongdoer. One may also note that there are many trivial offences and wrongs which people readily forgive or ignore in the ordinary course of business. Expressions or utterances like "don't mention it," or "forget about it," reflect the fact that injuries may be relatively trivial. In general, we should not take offence quickly for trivial reasons; nor should we bear grudges.

When we are wronged seriously, it is difficult to restrain our resentment or forgive the wrongdoer. Hence, forgiveness is a difficult virtue and involves mental struggle. Forgiveness calls for efforts of will; the victim has to overcome angry emotions caused by having been wronged, and has to refrain from chastising or punishing a wrongdoer. The victim has to let bygones be bygones. Self-control and strength of will are necessary in order to manage our temper and not hold grudges against those who wrong us.

SELF-CONTROL AND GOOD TEMPER (ANGER)

"Holding on to anger is like grasping a hot coal with the intent of throwing it at someone else; you are the one who gets burned."—Buddha.

"People who fly into a rage always make a bad landing." *—Will Rogers*

"Consider how much more you often suffer from your anger and grief, than from those very things for which you are angry and grieved." *—Marcus Antonius*

"Anger is the enemy of Ahimsa [nonviolence] and pride is a monster that swallows it [non violence] up." *—Gandhi*

"No man can think clearly when his fists are clenched." *—George Jean Nathan*

"Anger, if not restrained, is frequently more hurtful to us than the injury that provokes it." *—Seneca.*

"When you are offended at any man's fault, turn to yourself and study your own failings. Then you will forget your anger." *—Epictetus*

Anyone can become angry - that is easy, but to be angry with the right person at the right time, and for the right purpose and in the right way - that is not within everyone's power and that is not easy."—Aristotle

Plato mentions that display of anger reflects the vice of intemperance. Anger has to be rationally controlled since it overwhelms reason and self-control. Aristotle holds that "good temper" is the mean between the extremes of irascibility, an excess of anger, and inirascibility or total placidity. The good-tempered person "is not revengeful, but rather tends to forgive". Further, in Aristotle's view, morally appropriate anger is shown by the virtuous person. He is "angry at the right things and with the right people". He gets angry when he should, in right measure and for the right duration. For Plato and Aristotle, anger controlled by reason reflects virtue, whereas anger ungoverned by reason is a vice.

In Christianity anger is subordinated to forgiveness. This view differs from the Greek ideas of self-control and good temper. Christianity is based on an ethic of love. It focuses on the need to respond to wrongdoing by accepting it, turning the other cheek, and re-embracing the offender in an act of love or compassion. It is also not clear whether such forgiveness is conditional on the wrongdoer's remorse and acceptance of guilt. The Biblical injunction says: "Let all bitterness and wrath and anger and clamour and slander be put away from you, with all malice, and be kind to one another, tender-hearted, forgiving one another, as God in Christ forgave you".

We have noted two views on anger. One is that anger appropriately mediated by reason is a virtue. The other that is transcending anger in an act of love is a virtue. Uncontrolled anger is clearly a vice. One common instance of it nowadays is road rage in which motorists behave violently. Another example is of teachers who lose self-control and thrash children in a fit of rage. There are also instances in which bosses behave intemperately with their subordinates. Plutarch, a great Roman writer mentions that that anger is like a disease, and extreme or abiding anger such as rage or bitterness is an unnatural dispositional state. Such instances highlight the need for temperance or self-control.

We may note some more perspectives on anger. Anyone who is angrily obsessed by someone's wrongdoing may be harming himself since pent up anger produces adverse biochemical effects on the body. According to psychologists, it may be desirable to release anger into harmless channels. Uninhibited expression of anger and rage is desirable since venting is cathartic. Catharsis is similar to the process of incising a wound filled with puss; it cleanses the system.

However, considering its consequences, it is better to control intense anger rather than give free rein to it. It is true that anger may sometimes be the initial trigger for seeking constructive solutions to personal or political problems. But its indiscriminate expression is more likely to be harmful to those expressing it and to those around them. According to the Stoic Seneca, all forms of anger are inconsistent with moral life since they dispose us to cruelty and vengeance. These passions encourage us to see other people as less than fully human. Hence, the person of virtue is one who strives to extirpate anger in all its forms. This idealistic view has influenced many great moral leaders including Gandhi.

FORTITUDE

"Fortitude is the marshal of thought, the armour of the will, and the fort of reason." —*Francis Bacon*

"In struggling with misfortunes lies the true proof of virtue." —*Shakespeare.*

"Fortitude is the guard and support of the other virtues." —*Locke.*

"The gem cannot be polished without friction, nor man perfected without trials" —*Confucius*

These quotations and many similar ones express a common idea in different forms. They say that fortitude, courage, endurance or bravery acts as a guardian and protector of other human virtues. Aristotle mentions fortitude as the means by which men can control their fear of death. Soldiers often face threats to life in battle fields. As Archibald B.C. Alexander puts it: "Death is truly the limit to human existence: for, though the soul be immortal, the being of flesh and blood, that we call man, is dissolved in death, and, apart from supernatural hope of the resurrection, extinct forever." Fortitude enables one to contain this fear by the dictates of reason. Soldiers without fortitude will desert the battle field. In one sense, reason asserts that there are better things than life and things worse than death for men of honour. Fortitude is a mean between fear and rashness; cowardice leads one to fear, and daring to rashness. Fortitude moderates the two opposing tendencies.

Life is precious and should not be lightly thrown away or risked for trivial or ignoble ends. The courageous person is circumspect. It is not that the brave man fears no danger; he rather controls the fear in his mind through rational means. The recklessness of an angry man is not fortitude. It is also not fortitude to be brave from ignorance and folly. The brave man faces real danger in full consciousness of its gravity, but goes on in pursuit of duty or a noble cause. Older philosophers regarded magnificence, magnanimity and patience as parts of fortitude. Of these, patience can still be considered as part of endurance. But magnificence and magnanimity are seldom mentioned in modern discussions of fortitude.

Fortitude is not a virtue relevant only to warlike situations. Christian writers mention fortitude in the context of saints who have become martyrs defending their faith. In this regard, we should recall with reverence the martyrdom of some Sikh gurus. In modern times, voluntary workers sometimes perish while rushing to the aid of others in danger. In fact anyone risking life in line of duty or in order to relieve others from affliction shows fortitude. Fortitude can be shown by ordinary people in many situations of life. Many people - like sincere teachers, nurses and many others - serve society silently with little recognition and few rewards. Their services are also heroic. "Life is a battle, and there are other objects for which a man must contend than those peculiar to a military calling."

Fortitude is one of the four cardinal virtues which Plato and Aristotle identified – the others being wisdom, temperance (self-control) and justice. Plato identified three aspects of human nature and paired each, as shown below, with a particular cardinal virtue.

Aspect of human nature	Corresponding cardinal virtue
Cognitive or intellectual	Wisdom
Active power	Fortitude
Appetitive or pertaining to human impulses	Temperance

While the above virtues relate to an individual's own personality, the virtue of justice pertains to his interactions as a social being with others. These virtues are considered essential in any rational conception of human life. They are necessary for the goodness of human character.

Courage acts as shield of other virtues. In its absence, they are rendered nugatory or become nothing. Suppose an innocent passenger in a train is being harassed by some goons. One may want to rush to his support in a kindly spirit. But, then cowardice may intervene and urge against running any risk. These occurrences are not infrequent on the trains and streets of Indian cities. In such situations, the kindly sentiment simply gets stifled in the absence of courage or fortitude. Hence, Locke observes: "Fortitude is the guard and support of the other virtues". This is also the meaning of Bacon's observation that fortitude is the armour of the will. Although one may have noble intentions, one needs courage to act on them. Shakespeare's observation refers to the virtue of fortitude in its meaning as endurance. The true test of this virtue lies in bearing one's misfortunes without complaint and coping with them. Confucius says that an individual acquires strength of character by manfully facing difficulties and struggling against odds.

In administrative situations, civil servants need to have moral courage or the courage of conviction. They should display firm resolve, and adhere to rules, norms and follow courses of action that promote public welfare. They should not yield to illegal pressures or allow themselves to be won over by inducements. Nor should they yield to subtle threats or intimidation. This is easier said than done, especially since there are so many alluring prospects for civil servants. In the recent past, many instances have come to light in which the guardians of public welfare have decided to close their eyes to obvious wrongdoing. This shows that it is not enough to mouth high-minded moral sentiments; they have to be acted upon with necessary courage of conviction.

COWARDICE

Gandhi is wedded to ideals of truth and non-violence. He abhorred violence in all its forms. Gandhi however was concerned that non-violence or absence of anger may serve to hide cowardice. A cowardly person can never take up a cause and fight for it. As leader of a political movement, Gandhi knew that weak and cowardly people cannot fight battles. Gandhi has often condemned cowardice for this reason. The following quotations from Gandhi's writings illustrates this point.

Nonviolence and cowardice are contradictory terms. Nonviolence is the greatest virtue, cowardice the greatest vice. Nonviolence springs from love, cowardice from hate. Nonviolence always suffers, cowardice would always inflict suffering. Perfect nonviolence is the highest bravery. Nonviolent conduct is never demoralising; cowardice always is.

Better than cowardice is killing and being killed in battle.

Fear has its use but cowardice has none.

It is better to be violent, if there is violence in our hearts, than to put on the cloak of nonviolence to cover impotence.

It is any day better to stand erect with a broken and bandaged head than to crawl on one's belly, in order to be able to save one's head.

Incidentally, the last quotation from Gandhiji's thoughts reminds one of the following lines from William Henley's poem *Invictus*:

"Under the bludgeonings of chance
My head is bloody, but unbowed".

EMPATHY

"You can only understand people if you feel them in yourself" —*John Steinbeck, East of Eden*

"Yet, taught by time, my heart has learned to glow at other's good, and melt at another's woe". —*Homer*

"When a good man is hurt all who would be called good must suffer with him" —*Euripides*

"Seeing with the eyes of another, listening with the ears of another, and feeling with the heart of another".

—*Alfred Adler*

"I call him religious who understands the sufferings of others". —*Mahatma Gandhi*

"I do not ask the wounded person how he feels, I myself become the wounded person." —*Walt Whitman*

"As we have no immediate experience of what other men feel, we can form no idea of the manner in which they are affected, but by conceiving what we ourselves should feel in the like situation."—*Adam Smith*

"Self-absorption in all its forms kills empathy, let alone compassion. When we focus on ourselves, our world contracts as our problems and preoccupations loom large. But when we focus on others, our world expands. Our own problems drift to the periphery of the mind and so seem smaller, and we increase our capacity for connection - or compassionate action."
—*Daniel Goleman, Social Intelligence: The New Science of Human Relationships*

"If there is any one secret of success, it lies in the ability to get the other person's point of view and see things from his angle as well as your own." —*Henry Ford*

"A human being is a part of the whole called by us universe, a part limited in time and space. He experiences himself, his thoughts and feeling as something separated from the rest, a kind of optical delusion of his consciousness. This delusion is a kind of prison for us, restricting us to our personal desires and to affection for a few persons nearest to us. Our task must be to free ourselves from this prison by widening our circle of compassion to embrace all living creatures and the whole of nature in its beauty."—*Albert Einstein*

"Humankind seems to have an enormous capacity for savagery, for brutality, for lack of empathy, for lack of compassion." —*Annie Lennox*

Empathy is a quality which lies at the heart of our concern for others. It makes us feel keenly the sufferings, pain and torments of our fellow human beings. Empathy is fellow feeling and compassion and enables us to identify ourselves with the feelings, emotions and sentiments of others. There is a difference between sympathy and empathy. In simple terms, sympathy means that we feel *for* someone whereas empathy means that we feel *with* someone. Empathy implies emotional sharing with others. It is the first stage whenever anyone is moved to help others in distress.

A school of ethics, moral sentimentalism, considers that morality has its source in our emotions and desires rather than in our reason. Moral sentimentalism provides a plausible explanation of common aspects of morality. Empathy, a term is often used for a kind of concern for another, is considered as an important virtue. An empathetic point of view is achieved by setting aside our own interests, current disposition, and entering into the sufferer's mental state. For Adam Smith, the key mechanism of empathy is imaginatively placing oneself in another's position, or what would now be called simulation, rather than mere emotional contagion, association, or inference. Some other thinkers consider that empathy also has a rational element. As fairness, justice and interdependence are involved in empathy, it may be considered rational in nature and its application understood as an activity based on sound judgment.

As Annie Lennox observes, when the quality of empathy atrophies in men - driven by ideological or religious fanaticism or by xenophobia - they turn against one other with great ferocity. This explains the terrible massacres perpetrated in the twentieth century during wars and revolutions. Recognizing that empathy lies at the root humane virtues, philosophers, religious preachers and great writers have always urged men to cultivate this virtue.

The process through which empathy operates is often discussed in Ethics, and this can be shown in a few simple steps.

X notices that Y is injured and that he is in pain.

A mental state similar to that of Y arises in X.

He experiences the idea of pain, of Y.

This feeling arises from a kind of association (according to Hume) or due to psychological simulation of Y's pain in X's mind.

This feeling of empathy creates a motivational drive in X to rush to Y's help.

Some people may be cold, indifferent or unresponsive to the suffering of others. As it often happens with accidents, people just refuse to help the victims or just drive away leaving the victims to their fate. Their empathy is very weak and they fail to summon the necessary energy to assist those in trouble.

Empathy is considered an innate aspect of human nature. Like other aspects of human mental makeup, it might have arisen in the process of human biological evolution. As such, it has helped human beings to adapt to environment and to survive and reproduce. Of course, it also has a cultural component.

John Steinbeck mentions that to understand others we have to feel as they feel. Homer, the ancient Greek author of the epics *Iliad* and *Odyssey*, says that experiences teach us to share in the joys and sorrows of others. According to Euripides, virtuous people should experience the sorrows of other virtuous people. The observation of Alfred Adler (who along with Freud and Carl Jung pioneered early studies of psychoanalysis) is a pithy definition of empathy. Adam Smith's observation is a simple account of the mechanism of empathy. As mentioned, it consists in our placing ourselves in the shoes of others and imagining their plight.

Empathy comes into play in many situations - in personal life, social life, and professional life and in appreciating literary works like novels, dramas and poems. Empathy helps in breaking down the barriers which egoistic tendencies erect around men. Ordinarily, human beings are self-centred and self-absorbed - often preoccupied with domestic problems, petty rivalries and jealousies and frustrations over career and money. It is necessary to silence and calm the restless ego to strengthen the quality of empathy.

This can be done in many ways. One should listen carefully and attentively to others, and resist the temptation to switch off. While reading about literature and humanities, one should stay focused without getting distracted. One should take genuine interest in the problems which friends and relatives face, and extend a helping hand without getting intrusive. One should extend one's impersonal interests, and minimize self-preoccupation.

As Daniel Goleman points out, when people obsess over their problems, they seem huge and burdensome. They crowd out other matters from one's mind and create psychological stress. One's viewpoint becomes subjective and unbalanced. The best antidote to this problem is to widen the range of our interests, and to keenly pursue them. Albert Einstein suggests that our interests should not be limited to ourselves and our immediate family. Our interests should extend to the whole living world and to the beauty of nature. Einstein was particularly impressed by the mathematical simplicity and elegance of the natural laws of nature. In his words, "subtle is the Lord (God)". But Einstein does not believe in a personal God.

In the context of business, empathy is a chief ingredient of emotional intelligence which managers need. In modern day work environment, skilled teams work together. In this environment, empathetic understanding is necessary for effective work performance. In administrative situations, all relevant viewpoints have to be elicited and suitably accommodated. And administrators require this quality which depends on empathy..

ALTRUISM

Altruism or selflessness is the concern for the welfare of others. It is a traditional virtue in many cultures and a core aspect of various religious traditions and secular worldviews, though the concept of 'others' toward whom concern should be directed can vary among cultures and religions. Altruism or selflessness is the opposite of selfishness.

Altruism (also known as the ethic of altruism, moralistic altruism, and ethical altruism) is an ethical doctrine that holds that the moral value of an individual's actions depends solely on their impact on other individuals, regardless of the consequences on the individual himself. The altruist dictum can be stated as: "An action is morally right if the consequences of that action are more favourable than unfavourable to everyone except the agent." Auguste Comte's version of altruism calls for living for the sake of others.

Auguste Comte coined the word "altruism". He believed that individuals had a moral obligation to renounce self-interest and live for others. For Comte, the first principle of morality is the regulative supremacy of social sympathy over the self-regarding instincts." The law and duty of life in altruism can be summed up as: Live for others." There are other ways of defining altruism. But all these definitions generally mention a moral obligation to benefit others or the moral value of serving others rather than oneself. C. D. Broad defines altruism as "the doctrine that each of us has a special obligation to benefit others." W. G. Maclagan defines it as "a duty to relieve the distress and promote the happiness of our fellows...Altruism is to...maintain quite simply that a man may and should discount altogether his own pleasure or happiness as such when he is deciding what course of action to pursue."

In one way, utilitarianism can result in altruism. Utilitarianism recommends acts that maximise the good of society. As the rest of society will always outnumber the utilitarian, a utilitarian will practise some form of altruism. However, classical economic theory holds that if every economic agent pursues his self interest, social welfare will be maximised. This view works against altruism. As an ethical principle, altruism has been criticized. Friedrich Nietzsche held that the idea to treat others as more important than oneself is degrading and demeaning to the self. He also believed that the idea that others have a higher value than oneself hinders the individual's pursuit of self-development, excellence, and creativity. He however mentioned that one has a 'duty' to help those who are weaker than oneself. Many writers believe that sacrificing one's long term interests for the sake of others may be irrational. Psychological egoism, is the thesis that humans always act in their own interest and that true altruism is impossible. Rational egoism is the view that rationality consists in acting in one's self-interest (without specifying how this affects one's moral obligations).

Many writers question the possibility of 'true' altruism. According to the doctrine of psychological egoism, no act of sharing, helping or sacrificing can be described as truly altruistic. Although these seem as disinterested and self-denying, the moral agent may receive an intrinsic reward by way of psychological gratification. This may be stretching the idea of gratification too far since for example a soldier sacrificing his life receives no gratification in the normal sense.

TRUTHFULNESS

"Without truth social intercourse and conversation become valueless." —*Kant*

"It is said to God 'Your law is truth. And for this reason what is contrary to truth cannot be just. But who doubts that every lie is contrary to truth? Therefore no lie can be just." —*St. Augustine*

Lying lips are an abomination to the Lord: but is it a lie to put murderers off the scent of blood?

"The general rule is, that Truth should never be violated, because of its utmost importance to the comfort of life, that we should have a full security by mutual faith … There must, however, be some exceptions. If, for instance, a murderer should ask you which way a man is gone, you may tell him what is not true, because you are under a previous obligation not to betray a man to a murderer …. But I deny the lawfulness of telling a lie to a sick man for fear of alarming him. You have no business with consequences; you have to tell the truth." —*Johnson*

"Even if you are in a minority of one, the truth is truth". —*Gandhi*

"Truth is by nature self-evident. As soon as you remove the cobwebs of ignorance that surround it, it shines clear." —*Gandhi*

"Truth never damages a cause that is just." —*Gandhi*

"An error does not become truth by reason of multiplied propagation, nor does truth become error because nobody sees it." —*Gandhi*

"In matters of conscience, the law of the majority has no place." —*Gandhi*

"Even as wisdom often comes from the mouths of babes, so does it often come from the mouths of old people. The golden rule is to test everything in the light of reason and experience, no matter from where it comes." —*Gandhi*

"Abstract truth has no value unless it incarnates in human beings who represent it, by proving their readiness to die for it." —*Gandhi*

"He who trifles with truth cuts at the root of Ahimsa [nonviolence].He who is angry is guilty of Himsa." —*Gandhi*

"All the religions of the world, while they may differ in other respects, unitedly proclaim that nothing lives in this world but Truth." —*Gandhi*

"Morality is the basis of things and truth is the substance of all morality." —*Gandhi*

"Breach of promise is a base surrender of truth." —*Gandhi*

"Breach of promise is no less an act of insolvency than a refusal to pay one's debt." —*Gandhi*

"The pursuit of truth does not permit violence on one's opponent." —*Gandhi*

It is easier to perceive error than to find truth, for the former lies on the surface and is easily seen, while the latter lies in the depth, where few are willing to search for it . —*Johann Wolfgang Von Goethe*

"If you shut up truth and bury it under the ground, it will but grow, and gather to itself such explosive power that the day it bursts through it will blow up everything in its way." —*Emile Zola*

"From error to error, one discovers the entire truth." —*Sigmund Freud*

"For here we are not afraid to follow truth wherever it may lead." —*Thomas Jefferson*

"To announce truths is an infallible recipe for being persecuted." —*Voltaire*

"We swallow greedily any lie that flatters us, but we sip only little by little at a truth we find bitter."
—*Denis Diderot*

"Mental fight means thinking against the current, not with it. It is our business to puncture gas bags and discover the seeds of truth." —*Virginia Woolf*

"What is morality in any given time or place? It is what the majority then and there happen to like, and immorality is what they dislike." —*Alfred North Whitehead*

"There is no god higher than truth." —*Gandhi*

"If you are out to describe the truth, leave elegance to the tailor". —*Albert Einstein*

"What the imagination seizes as beauty must be the truth." —*John Keats*

"Everything you add to the truth subtracts from the truth." —*Alexander Solzhenitsyn*

"Man has always sacrificed truth to his vanity, comfort and advantage. He lives... by make-believe."
—*W. Somerset Maugham, The Summing Up, 1938*

"There is no truth. There is only perception." —*Gustave Flaubert*

Truthfulness is a vast theme with many ramifications. It figures in various discussions in philosophy, religion, morals and literature. Many political and social movements, their leaders claim, are grounded in truth. Gandhi, for example, placed the highest value on truth. It is a pre-eminent personal virtue. In discussing truth, we need to examine its various aspects. Briefly these are - 1) definition of truth 2) truth as a moral virtue 3) high value accorded to truth in the hierarchy of virtues 4) standards or criteria for calling something as true 5) social utility or function of truthfulness 6) socially sanctioned exceptions to truth telling and 7) other virtues allied to or included in truthfulness.

There are many synonyms of truth such as veracity, fact, reality, integrity, honesty, candour, fidelity and honesty. Keeping one's promise is also part of truthfulness. We may begin with early definitions of truth in ancient Greek philosophy. Aristotle says that: "to say of what is that it is, and of what is not that it is not, is true." He adds "he who thinks the separated to be separated and the combined to be combined has the truth, while he whose thought is in a state contrary to the objects is in error". In Greek philosophy, truth is seen as an accurate perspective on reality. Romans similarly spoke of *Veritas* as a factual representation of events.

There are three major theories of truth in modern philosophy. The correspondence theory states that what we believe or say is true if it corresponds to the way things are or to facts. When a proposition is true, it is identical to a fact, and belief in that proposition is true. This conception is similar to the Greek view. However, modern philosophers discuss the idea of truth with mind numbing logical rigour. In this context, we may mention the philosophical doctrine of objectivism. It is the belief that the world exists objectively, independent of the way we think about it or describe it. Our thoughts and claims are about that world. These two statements imply that our claims are objectively true or false, depending on how the world objectively is.

The second view on truth is known as coherence theory of truth. Those thinkers who subscribe to philosophical idealism tend to hold this view. Truth in its essential nature is that systematic coherence which is the character of a significant whole. In this view, one can speak meaningfully of truth about ideas or beliefs which are embodied in a system of ideas which form a whole. A belief is true if it is part of a coherent system of beliefs. Truth is a property of a whole system and not of isolated facts. This view is metaphysical, and many thinkers would naturally concede that individual facts are in a sense true. Idealist thinkers also speak in metaphysical terms of truth as a process of self-fulfilment.

Pragmatic philosophers such as William James proposed a theory of truth based on its social utility. Truth is something which we find useful or satisfactory to believe. This does not mean that we should permanently reside in a world of comfortable dreams. Truth of a (useful) belief is borne out by our later experience. It acts as a reliable guide to action. Some pragmatists associate truth with experimental or scientific truth. Truth is a settled position that emerges after a painstaking inquiry.

So far, we looked at truth from an epistemological point of view. Epistemology is a branch of philosophy which deals with theories of knowledge. This branch of philosophy logically scrutinizes the nature, scope, validity and limitations of human knowledge. In Ethics, truth is conceived very differently as an ideal to be pursued in our conduct or moral life. In this context, we have to understand truth either as religious truth or as moral truth.

Veracity or telling the truth is an intrinsic virtue, and is not based on rights of others or on any external circumstances. It is fit and proper that one should state facts, opinions and truths to the best of his knowledge without mixing any falsehoods. Social existence of human beings depends on truth telling. If truth is abandoned, accounts of human history become fictions. If witnesses habitually tell lies, judicial proceedings will end in mockery of justice. If people cannot trust one another, business and commerce will shrink drastically. In the absence of truth telling, the ordinary transactions of common life will be enmeshed in incessant doubt and suspicion. In short, human social life presupposes truth telling as a norm of behaviour. This is what is implied in Kant's quotation cited above.

Lay philosophers and religious teachers have always placed truth on a high pedestal. They hold that telling lies is wrong as such or inherently. Those who utter lies flout the basis of rational relationships between human beings. They also fail to respect themselves as rational beings. Falsehoods are uttered with a view to deceive others. People may not resort to wholesale lying. But they often distort truth partially and mislead others. That is why witnesses are asked to tell "the truth, the whole truth, and nothing but the truth". Another manner of deceiving others is "suppressio veri and suggestio falsi"—suppressing truth and suggesting falsehood.

A statement may have a double meaning, and in the given circumstances mislead people into accepting the false meaning. Only a part of the truth - half truth - may be told to misguide listeners. A truth may be told in such a manner as to falsify another fact. Gestures and intonations may be used to lead people astray. People may remain silent when lies are being told instead of rebutting them immediately. As Solzhenitsyn observes, truth has to be unvarnished; otherwise, it ceases to be truth. Similarly, Einstein mentions that truth has to be expressed plainly and simply without adornment.

There are many reasons for which people are reluctant to face the truth squarely. As Somerset Maugham points out, men pursue their comforts and advantage, and in the process abandon truth. Men shun harsh realities which shatter their cherished opinions, pet theories and comforting fantasies. Similarly, Diderot observes that men readily swallow flattering lies which bolster their egos, but avoid acknowledging unpalatable truths which undermine their self images.

People tell lies for various reasons. Sometimes religious and other groups who face persecution may tell lies to cover up their identity. Governments may not disclose (or dissimulate about) matters deemed vital for national defence. Often, people utter falsehood to damage the interests and reputation of others. Lies are essentially designed to deceive others and gain personal advantage. People may tell lies to flatter those in power, and thus get into their good books. People also seek to project themselves in an attractive but false light. Those wielding power may tell lies to mislead people and subvert public interest.

Are there any exceptions which justify departures from the duty to tell the truth? This question has divided philosophers and moral preachers. Socrates mentions that lies can be told to guard against enemies and to prevent harm to others. But many philosophers regard truth as a virtue to which there can be no exceptions. Thus, St. Augustine considers that no lie can ever be just since it is against divine dispensation. Immanuel Kant regards truth telling as a categorical imperative (absolute command or duty) which admits no exceptions. Many thinkers regard such views as too rigid and opposed to what commonsense prescribes in some situations of ordinary life.

Dr. Johnson's observations cover this issue. He says that lying for protecting an innocent man from killers is justified. However, he denies that lying to patients about their serious illness is justified. This raises the question of how to determine the circumstances which justify departures from truth. One can think of virtues as constituting a hierarchy, and that some virtues can at times override truth telling. In the example given by Dr. Johnson, protecting an innocent man takes precedence over truth telling. But telling lies to psychologically comfort a patient is unjustified. In these matters, it is impossible to exclude subjective considerations.

As we noted earlier, the purpose of falsehoods is to deceive others through misrepresentation and gain some advantage. Stringent moralists argue that falsehood – no matter whatever its motive or purpose – is inherently wrong. This is the view of St. Thomas Aquinas. He makes a distinction between 1) uttering a falsehood and 2) its intent to deceive. He holds that it is wrong to utter lies even if there is no loss or disadvantage to others or advantage to a liar. But others consider that the intention of deceit is an essential ingredient of falsehood, and without this ingredient a lie loses its sting.

Now, we turn to another aspect of truth. One may assert truth or say that X is true. One may also consider (a) the manner of arriving at truth X and (b) the standards or criteria used for judging that X is true. These two aspects are epistemological and are discussed in the theory of knowledge. But for a practical moralist these are of no great importance except in preventing him from falling into error. One of the quotations from Gandhi touches on this point. "Even as wisdom often comes from the mouths of babes, so does it often come from the mouths of old people. The golden rule is to test everything in the light of reason and experience, no matter from where it comes." The Bible says that wisdom (praise of God to be exact) comes out of the mouths of babes and sucklings. Gandhi observes that it also comes from the mouths of old people. Gandhi proceeds to lay down a test for examining claims to truth. Such claims can be logically analysed to see whether they conform to rules of logical validity or correct reasoning. Another way of testing is to see whether they are empirically borne out by human experience or the way things are in the natural world. Gandhi's comment shows his philosophical insight. Of course, Gandhi refers to truth as a practical moralist, as a reformer and as an ideologue.

Another point is how easy or hard it is to perceive truth. Gandhi says truth has a quality of self-evidence. Once we see it, we identify it without further intellectual effort. All that is required is to remove the veil of ignorance which surrounds it. Goethe puts this idea rather differently. For him error is visible on the surface whereas truth lies in buried structures. People are unwilling to undertake the labour of digging out truth.

Many writers mention the noble attributes of truth and the steadfast moral duty of pursuing truth. We consider in this context the quotations from Gandhi. Gandhi identifies truth with the highest form of divinity. For Gandhi, no higher God exists. He regards truth as the substance or essence of morality. It occupies Gandhi's highest position among virtues. Gandhi believes that though religions differ on various matters, they are united in proclaiming the perennial value of truth in this world. Gandhi also identifies truth with non-violence. In other words, even if one's ends are noble, violent means should not be used for achieving them.

The identification of truth with God or with non-violence is not free from obscurity. For example, truth and non-violence are two distinct concepts, and any claims of their identity or equivalence involves what is known as a 'category error'. Category error consists in comparing or identifying things which belong to distinct categories. However, we need only consider the moral spirit underlying the statements. One is that the nobility of ideals will not justify the use of violence for their attainment. This boils down to a question of ends and means. Both the ends we pursue and the means we employ for their realisation have to be good. This approach is critical to Gandhian thinking. Identification of truth with God implies that all believers in God have to follow the path of truth.

Pursuit of truth, whether in private or public life, is difficult. As a practical moralist Gandhi emphasised that mere theoretical discussions of truth or simply lavishing praise on truth as a virtue is of no use. People have to adopt truth as a practical virtue in their actual life. They should follow the narrow and straight path of truth and be ready to sacrifice life for it. In real life, few people are willing to go such heroic lengths, but usually seek compromises. However, there are many instances of both saints and even common people who laid down their lives for what they regarded as religious truth. Many individuals sacrifice themselves for movements and ideologies which they think embody truth.

As Voltaire says, those who propound unpopular truths invite risk of persecution. But as Virginia Woolf says, intellectuals have to puncture high sounding inanities in their search for truth. As Jefferson observes, one has to follow truth unmindful of wherever it may lead. Fear of bad consequences should not lead to abandonment of the quest for truth. It is of course not easy to bury truth and forget about it. It continues to live in the minds of people, gathers strength, and explodes with renewed vigour. In a way, this is what appears to have happened recently in Middle East.

John Keats, the English Romantic poet, identifies beauty and truth. According to him, "beauty is truth, and truth is beauty". The German poet Schiller mentions –

'When I dared question: "it is beautiful'

But is it true?" Thy answer was, "In truth lives beauty."

This identity may not hold entirely. Aesthetics is not concerned with what is morally beautiful, but with what is beautiful in itself irrespective of moral considerations. Ethics is concerned with man's moral worth as expressed in virtuous will and actions. Ethical judgements ignore mere beauty or utility of conduct. What is right may not be immediately beautiful, and can involve actions that are far from beautiful. Thus, the process of sanitizing an area stricken by a natural disaster will be far from aesthetic. However, both beauty and ethics involve pursuit of an ideal. In an ultimate sense, what is moral is beautiful and what is beautiful in an artistic sense may be moral. This idea is contained in the expression 'a beautiful soul' - the reference being to a moral soul.

According to Alfred North Whitehead, morality at any given place and time is what the majority then and there happen to like, and immorality is what they dislike. In other words, Whitehead believes that there is no universally applicable moral code but that morals are conditioned by time and place. This view is known as moral relativism. It is difficult to accept this view in toto. There are certain fundamental duties such as for one's family which are universal. There may be minor differences for example in the degree of freedom which parents in different societies allow for adolescent children. But no culture or society endorses murder, rape or dacoity. Moral codes may become lax in matters like severity of punishment. However, one can confidently assert that there are at least a few universal moral tenets.

Gustave Flaubert's view on truth reflects complete scepticism. He denies the possibility of knowing objective truth. He makes truth a matter of individual perception or viewpoint. Truth is what an individual thinks is true; it reduces to individual subjectivity. There is long tradition of philosophical scepticism or doubt going back to the Greek philosopher Sextus Empiricus. This is the view that true or objective knowledge is unattainable. This is in fact the core belief of the currently fashionable school of postmodernism. Any discussion on this subject will take us too far away from our main subject. It is enough to note that natural sciences contain objective knowledge which is vouchsafed by commonly accepted scientific procedures. However, ideological and other perceptions often create problems in modern social sciences. Those who are wedded to truth have to give truthful accounts of events. They have to avoid biased, ideological and self-serving interpretations. This is a fundamental aspect of truthfulness - though virtually abandoned in modern social science research. Some journalists and TV commentators are fond of saying that perception is more important than truth. This view may have some use in political propaganda and commercial advertising. But it is hogwash in any serious academic discussion.

Keeping Promises

Keeping promises, honesty and integrity are virtues which are part of veracity. Gandhiji regards breaking a promise as equivalent to abandoning truth. Inability or unwillingness to pay one's debts is an instance of insolvency. Failure to honour one's promises signals moral bankruptcy. One is under an obligation to keep promises made to others in all spheres of life. But acting according to one's promises is vital in the economic sphere. No economic transactions are possible in a situation in which no one is serious about keeping promises. The term 'contract' is the analogue of promise in business and commerce. Law of contracts is a major field of jurisprudence. However, contracts have to be routinely observed, and litigation should be the exception rather than the rule. In a capitalist economy valid contracts are considered sacred.

There are two parts to keeping promises. No one should light heartedly make a promise. Promise signifies a truthful intent of performing a stated act. There should be an honesty of purpose in making a promise. After making a promise, one has to take all possible steps within his power to deliver on it. One should not avoid the promised action because it may involve personal exertion, trouble, inconvenience and loss.

One should not enter into immoral or illegal promises. Such 'compacts with devil' are void from the outset. No one is under any obligation to deliver on such promises. If someone makes such a promise unknowingly, he should get out of it. If the person to whom the promise has been made was also innocent and is likely to suffer loss, he can be compensated in some measure.

In judicial proceedings, witnesses take an oath to tell the truth. Many constitutional functionaries also take oath to uphold the constitution and to perform their duties without getting influenced by personal or other extraneous considerations. Whoever takes an oath is duty bound to honour it.

Honesty

Honesty can be regarded as truthfulness in financial matters. In the modern world, there are many situations in which people handle money belonging to organizations and other individuals. Individuals who perform such functions–accountants, custodians of cash, wealth managers, and guardians of minors, trustees of charitable bodies, bankers and treasury officers–have to be scrupulously honest. They have to justify their positions in the offices of trust. Honesty in public administration implies that civil servants should discharge their duties in a bonafide manner without giving into monetary temptations or inducements. They should follow the adage that honesty is the best policy. Honesty is integral also to business transactions. Businessmen should avoid all forms of deception, cheating and fraud. They should also avoid sharp business practices. Their financial transactions have to be clean and above board. In fact, the present emphasis on corporate governance is designed to promote clean business practices.

Integrity

Integrity means that the moral agent acts according to his inner convictions. His conduct is free from hypocrisy and deception. His actions are in conformity with his stated values. But it is hard to follow the high morals which one proclaims. The British historian GM Trevelyan has commented on this aspect of Puritanism i.e. rigid pursuit of high morals: "by making a shibboleth of virtue, it (puritanical version of Christianity) bred notorious hypocrites". But it does not mean that one needs to abandon morals. One should be moral sincerely without making a show of it.

Public leaders who possess integrity create interpersonal trust. Integrity which refers to actions resulting from a set of well-ordered commitments and beliefs promotes trust. Trust implies the capacity to depend on and place confidence in the actions of others. All social interaction depends on integrity and trust. Integrity is especially relevant in public administration in which cooperative, corroborative and collective efforts are needed to solve interconnected problems. Hence, character, particularly integrity, is essential in public leaders.

In this context, public administration writers make a distinction between 'ethics of compliance' and 'ethics of integrity'. In ethics of compliance, public servants are trained or given detailed instructions on the various laws, rules, regulations and procedures which govern their working in an organization. After learning about these matters, public servants are expected to scrupulously follow them. In this process, public servants learn to follow a set of externally imposed commands. However, they may not do any moral thinking on their own.

Ethics of integrity in contrast tries to impart to civil servants the necessary skills to analyse moral problems on their own. They are trained in areas like public service ethos, ethical standards and values and in the processes of ethical reasoning. By using such skills public servants will follow ethical norms in their conduct. Ethics of integrity lead to development of moral character with self-responsibility and moral autonomy. It relies on internal, positive. proactive and voluntary efforts of public servants rather than on external commands and penalties.

Avoiding Breach of Trust

Another aspect of truthfulness implies that a moral agent should never betray trust placed in him. Some acts of betrayal are criminal offences. Cheating and criminal breach of trust are offences under the Indian Penal Code. There are many acts of breach of trust which though not illegal are morally reprehensible. These are matters that fall within human relations. Disloyalty towards family and friends or failure to perform duties implicit in human relations is the essence of breach of trust.

If someone claims to be in love with a girl and then ditches her later, he has betrayed her trust. Sometimes, people betray their friends. It may happen that X gets acquainted with rich or politically powerful individuals. He may then be tempted to forsake his old friends. Self interest or the excitement of rubbing shoulders with influential people makes X neglect his old friends. This type of behaviour reflects disloyalty. Another example of breach of trust involves refusal to help one's friends in difficulty. In such situations, one needs to extend material and moral help to friends within his means. The saying that a friend in need is a friend indeed emphasises the aspect of mutual support in friendship. There are many instances when people neglect their aged dependent parents or neglect their duty towards spouses who are chronically ill.

Many instances of disloyalty can be mentioned from other spheres of life. In politics, friends often become enemies; enemies may also become friends. This situation is summarized in the saying that there are no permanent friends or enemies in politics. Professional politicians are basically interested in advancing their careers and increasing their power. Hence, they change their stance towards others depending on calculations of political advantage. There are many instances in which the protege of a political leader works against him. Similarly, a leader may betray his friends or followers depending on how the political winds are blowing.

Instances of breach of trust are found also in administrative situations. The top level officials may evade responsibility or shift it towards their subordinates. When things go wrong, they may fasten blame wrongfully on junior officers. They may make scapegoats of their subordinates. Public servants have to uphold common interest. When they fail to do so, they betray the trust placed in them.

POWER AND MORALITY

"Power was my weakness and my temptation." —*J.K. Rowling*

"What is the cause of historical events? Power. What is power? Power is the sum total of wills transferred to one person. On what condition are the wills of the masses transferred to one person? On condition that the person express the will of the whole people. That is, power is power. That is, power is a word the meaning of which we do not understand." —*Leo Tolstoy, War and Peace*

"We know that no one ever seizes power with the intention of relinquishing it." —*George Orwell, 1984*

"The object of terrorism is terrorism. The object of oppression is oppression. The object of torture is torture. The object of murder is murder. The object of power is power. Now do you begin to understand me?" —*George Orwell, 1984*

"You can do anything and smash anything in the world with a kopeck." —*Nikolai Gogol*

"What power has law where only money rules?" —*Petronius*

"Everywhere the weak execrate the powerful, before whom they cringe; and the powerful beat them like sheep whose wool and flesh they sell." —*Voltaire*

"Power is not a means; it is an end." —*George Orwell*

"Power gradually extirpates from the mind every humane and gentle virtue." —*Edmund Burke*

"The greater the power, the more dangerous the abuse." —*Edmund Burke*

"Power has only one duty -- to secure the social welfare of the People." —*Benjamin Disraeli*

"Power, like a desolating pestilence,
Pollutes whate'er it touches". —*Shelley*

"It is excellent
To have a giant's strength
But it is tyrannous
To use it like a giant" —*William Shakespeare, Measure for Measure*

"Power lacks morals or principles. It only has interests." —*Horacio Castellanos Moya*

"Tyranny is a habit, it has its own organic life, it develops finally into a disease. The habit can kill and coarsen the very best man or woman to the level of a beast. Blood and power intoxicate ... the return of the human dignity, repentance and regeneraton becomes almost impossible." —*Fyodor Dostoyevsky*

"Therefore it is unnecessary for a prince to have all the good qualities I have enumerated, but it is very necessary to appear to have them. And I shall dare to say this also, that to have them and always to observe them is injurious, and that to appear to have them is useful; to appear merciful, faithful, humane, religious, upright, and to be so, but with a mind so framed that should you require not to be so, you may be able and know how to change to the opposite."
—*Niccolò Machiavelli, The Prince*

"The measure of a man is what he does with power." —*Plato*

We begin the discussion on power with definitions of a few important terms. The term 'political' refers to all those practices and institutions which are concerned with government. Power is the ability to get others to do what you want. Power can take many forms, from brute force to subtle persuasion. The term regime means any government. Authority refers to the ability of the government to exercise power without resorting to violence. A government which enjoys legitimacy tends to have a high level of authority. Its citizens usually obey the law because they think it is right to do so not because they are afraid of punishment. If people generally accept the political decisions taken by government, it is said to have legitimacy. A government is regarded as legitimate if the citizens think that it is right, lawful and proper for government to hold power. Loss of legitimacy seriously undermines the power of government.

In one way, the whole of political science can be said to be about political power. Bertrand Russell considers power as the fundamental concept of all social science. However, we need not concern ourselves with the whole subject of power. For our purposes, we need to briefly consider the relation between power and morality. Power takes many forms such as political, economic, social and religious. Most of political and economic power in modern nations is concentrated in governments. Governments are headed by political leaders who wield power and determine policies in various spheres.

The problem connected with political power is how to deploy or limit it to prevent or minimize oppression of people, how to secure the individual rights of people, and how to ensure their welfare. The exercise of arbitrary power by rulers against people has always troubled political thinkers and philosophers from ancient times. They advocated that kings or rulers should be virtuous, kind and considerate to people. But their pleas usually fell on deaf ears.

Plato, Aristotle, and Cicero were all political idealists who believed that there are some universal moral values on which political life could be based. This view received support later from Christianity. Till Machiavelli's times, political thinkers generally believed that politics, including the relations among states, should be grounded in morality, and that the methods of warfare should remain subordinated to ethical standards. Notwithstanding such advocacy from political thinkers, the actual conduct of rulers was generally immoral.

Later, Niccolo Machiavelli discarded political idealism in favour of political realism. Machiavelli has acquired an unsavory reputation as a cynical theorist of realpolitik who believes that the end always justifies the means. His ideas are to be found in *The Prince*, which is an advice to rulers on acquiring and retaining power. Machiavelli is the first modern political thinker. The medieval scholars tried to consider how politics and the State can be fitted into the divine scheme of things. Machiavelli examined the manner of organizing and preserving power.

Machiavelli is in fact a patriot and republican. He says: *"It cannot be called virtue to kill one's fellow citizens, betray one's friends, be without faith, without pity, and without religion; by these methods one may indeed gain power, but not glory*." He adds that "*it is necessary for a prince to possess the friendship of the people*." As regards power, he says that it is *"more proper to go to the real truth of the matter than to its imagination; and many have imagined republics and principalities which have never been seen or known to exist in reality; for how we live is so far removed from how we ought to live, that he who abandons what is done for what ought to be done, will rather learn to bring about his own ruin than his preservation*." He cautions against blind and imprudent pursuit of unrealistic ideals. Machiavelli mentions that good men will perish in a society full of evil doers. Later the German statesman Bismarck expressed similar sentiments: "*It is the destiny of the weak to be devoured by the strong*." Some things which seem virtues, if followed, will lead to one's ruin; and some things which seem vices, if followed, result in one's greater security and well-being. Machiavelli also says that princes need not necessarily keep their promises.

Such views ran counter to common moral prescriptions. Divergent views always prevailed on the question of acquiring and retaining power. Many thinkers believe that it is difficult to access and retain power without sacrificing moral principles. There are also other leaders like Gandhi, Lincoln and Nelson Mandela who emphasise that exercise of power has to be regulated by idealism. Going back to ancient Indian history, we may note that Kautilya's *Arthasastra* contains many prescriptions that sound Machiavellian. As a counter-example, we may recall that under the influence of the Buddhist concept of dharma, Asoka attempted moralization of political power.

Political theorists argued that kings or other rulers cannot exercise unchecked or absolute powers over people. Rulers should not become despotic and oppress people since their powers are derived from people. Hobbes, Rousseau and Locke developed the theory of social contract. These writers, notwithstanding the differences between their theories, mention that men lived in a state of nature before the emergence of government. In this state, they lacked security, civic facilities and means of developing trade and commerce. To secure these benefits, they seceded part of their rights and powers to the rulers through a social contract. Incidentally, social contract is one of the theories of origin of the State. Although social contract is an imaginary concept and a legal fiction, it became a strong argument for limiting State power and securing the rights of people.

The concept of rights which political writers developed acts as a check on unfettered exercise of powers. It was believed that men had certain natural and inalienable (which cannot be taken away) rights. The right to life, liberty and property were considered as such rights. Thomas Paine's *Rights of Man* is written in this vein. The French revolutionaries issued *the Declaration of the Rights of Man and the Citizen.* The American constitution also enumerates the rights of the citizen. It may seem that individual, political and other rights cannot be linked to morality. However, by incorporating such rights, national leaders impart a moral dimension to the framework of political governance. With the emergence of democracy, the processes of gaining and retaining power have become more orderly and peaceful; they have acquired legitimacy. We will discuss political power in democracies a little later.

Uptill now, we have discussed the checks that prevent governments from exercising powers dictatorially. Political thinkers and historians have noted a universal problem with power. The saying from Greek mythology from the story of Circe seems to apply to power: "*Those who drink of my cup become swine*". James Madison observes: "*The essence of government is power, and power, lodged as it must be in human hands, will ever be liable to abuse*". Ronald Regan expresses the same idea more crudely: *"Politics is supposed to be the second-oldest profession. I have come to realise that it bears a very close resemblance to the first [prostitution]."* Frank Herbert states: *"Power attracts the corruptible. Suspect any who seek it."* He adds: *"All governments suffer a recurring problem: Power attracts pathological personalities." "Power-lust"*, says Ayn Rand *"is a weed that grows only in the vacant lots of an abandoned mind."*

Power invariably leads to corruption, abuse and oppression. Anyone who acquires or is vested with power undergoes a psychological transformation. To use a familiar expression, power (like alcohol) quickly goes to one's head. People get drunk on power, and abandon the path of virtue and moderation. Unregulated power confers on an individual opportunities for money making, for heaping abuses on others and for subverting public interest. In the famous words of Lord Acton, "*Power tends to corrupt, and absolute power corrupts absolutely. Great men are almost always bad men.*"

Many writers argue, without going to the extremes of modern totalitarian ideologies, that politics regrettably but inevitably involve sacrifice of moral principles. They affirm this as a matter of fact. According to Bismarck, *"The great questions of the day will not be settled by means of speeches and majority decisions ... but by iron and blood*." He also says that politics is the art of the possible. Echoing Lord Acton's idea that great men are always bad men, a character in the novel *I, Claudius* of Robert Graves says, "*I have done many impious things–no great ruler can do otherwise. I have put the good of the Empire before all human considerations. To keep the Empire free from factions I have had to commit many crimes.*"

The above discussion on power and morality is based on the situation which prevails in a nation at normal times. In other words, there are no extraordinary circumstances like war, general turbulence, insurrection or revolution. In extraordinary times, the normal tenor of political life gets disturbed. The political system undergoes a sudden, drastic and violent change. Examples of such political contingencies include the French revolution, the Russian revolution of 1917, Nazi takeover in Germany and Communist revolution in China. In these instances, revolutionary groups overthrow government and seize power. Such seizure of power is invariably violent and bloody. Fascism and communism represent the two completely totalitarian ideologies of modern times. In such periods, the ordinary decencies of life are totally forgotten.

Both communists and fascists disregard traditional morals. Soviet communists created a new kind of "morality" in order to do things which common people abhor as immoral. According to Lenin, violence is essential for overthrowing capitalism. Both Lenin and Stalin considered that morality should be subordinated to the ideology of proletarian revolution. They rejected the morality based on traditional religions. For them, acts that advanced revolution are moral, and acts that hindered revolution are immoral. Party members were brainwashed into accepting this view which regards morality as a weapon in class struggle.

Communists justified their position on the ground that the world is full of injustice and immorality and they want to replace it by a just social structure in the form of communism. By this logic, whatever they did became right by definition. USSR denounced slave labour and killings in German camps (during Nazi regime) as immoral, but remained silent on slave labour and killings in Soviet Gulag camps. Stalin justified the gulag camps on the ground that they served the interests of revolution. (Based on *Communist Morality*, Ludwik Kowalski PhD)

Communist revolutions are violent. Communists believe that workers have to take up arms to destroy the capitalist state. Communists openly scoff at peaceful means of bringing about social change. They describe such views as "class collaboration". This is the view of the Naxal movement in India. Mao Tse-tung expressed these ideas with frank brutality: *"A revolution is not a dinner party, or writing an essay, or painting a picture, or doing embroidery. It cannot be so refined, so leisurely and gentle, so temperate, kind, courteous, restrained and magnanimous. A revolution is an insurrection, an act of violence by which one class overthrows another*". In another famous statement he says, "*Every Communist must grasp the truth: Political power grows out of the barrel of a gun*".

Like communists, Fascists have also discarded traditional morality. We need not get into the spurious arguments they used in justification. Both fascism and communism caused untold suffering and misery. In the holocaust, six million European Jews were killed. Many million people died in the war. Stalin's programme of collectivization of soviet agriculture led to death of millions of Kulaks or Russian peasants. The horrors of the Soviet regime are described in several books of dissidents, the most notable being Alexander Solzhenitsyn's *The Gulag Archipelago*.

Both communism and fascism are totalitarian systems which are marked by concentration of power in a single or few persons. Totalitarianism leads to control of all aspects of human life. No genuine participation of people or operation of rule of law is allowed. People are deprived of their fundamental and democratic rights. There is no free press. These circumstances create situations which permit governments to take violent and harsh measures against people. Such measures are justified in the name of historical necessity, revolutionary violence, proletarian justice, communist morality, need to fashion new type of human beings or exigencies of war and struggle. All these excuses repudiate conventional morality - which is mockingly called "bourgeois morality" - and lead to great violence.

In these collectivist systems, ends or the goals of State policy are seen as justifying means. As the end is supposedly noble, use of any means - good or bad - is seen as justified. The worth of the individual and sanctity of his life are totally ignored. People are seen as instruments of state policy instead of as its intended beneficiaries. Collectivist State rejects the humanist belief that no ideal however high can justify sacrifice of human beings.

Totalitarian systems aim at total and radical transformation of society. They seek to overturn the existing social arrangements and radically restructure society. Conservative thinkers and humanitarians have always argued that societies are bound by traditions and change slowly. Revolutionaries are in a hurry and want to bring about change instantaneously. In this process, they unleash forces of great violence. Many writers (for example Karl Popper and F.A. Hayek) have pointed out that measures which seek to radically and rapidly restructure societies are inherently dangerous. Societies have evolved gradually over centuries and embody wisdom accumulated over time. Social change should be allowed to occur spontaneously at its own pace and with the general consent of people. But totalitarian systems force the pace of change and attempt total social reengineering with disastrous consequences. (We may mention that students will benefit greatly from a study of two books: Karl Popper's *The Open Society and its Enemies* and Hayek's *The Road to Serfdom.* The former in particular is a source of invaluable insights for anyone who wants to study political and social problems.)

Gandhi strenuously opposed all forms of violence. Under his guidance, even the movement for national independence remained generally peaceful. However, the communal holocaust preceding Indian partition resulted in massacres on unprecedented scale. But it does not detract from the high moral ideals which Gandhi upheld. He always swore by truth, non-violence and dharma. This is his way of expressing the view that politics and power should be based on moral means. Gandhi's emphasis on non-violence reflects his commitment to morality in the exercise of power.

The following quotations from Gandhi's writings illustrate this point.

"What difference does it make to the dead, the orphans, and the homeless, whether the mad destruction is wrought under the name of totalitarianism or the holy name of liberty or democracy?"

"I object to violence because when it appears to do good, the good is only temporary; the evil it does is permanent."

"However much I may sympathise with and admire worthy motives, I am an uncompromising opponent of violent methods even to serve the noblest of causes."

"Victory attained by violence is tantamount to a defeat, for it is momentary."

"Non-violence is not a garment to be put on and off at will. Its seat is in the heart, and it must be an inseparable part of our being."

"The pursuit of truth does not permit violence on one's opponent."

"Experience convinces me that permanent good can never be the outcome of untruth and violence."

"Those who say religion has nothing to do with politics do not know what religion is."

"Power is of two kinds. One is obtained by the fear of punishment and the other by acts of love. Power based on love is a thousand times more effective and permanent than the one derived from fear of punishment."

Gandhi asserts that religion cannot be separated from politics. This does not imply that Gandhi repudiates the secular character of modern States. By religion Gandhi here means morality in a broad sense. Gandhi asserts the need to bind power and morality. Gandhi discounts the value of victory gained through violence. In fact, he equates it with defeat. Although his belief is rooted in morality, he also gives the rationale of his belief. Victory won through violence is temporary because the vanquished are unreconciled to their lot and will try to restore status quo ante. Gandhi believes that reformers should win the hearts and minds of people. From this perspective, no attempt should be made to impose views on people through force. Gandhi denies that worthy motives or noble causes justify violence. In this regard, his views are in sharp contrast to many other political and revolutionary leaders. On the relation between power and morality, Gandhi represents one extreme pole. The other pole is represented by those who argue that considerations of morality and the exigencies of power are irreconcilable. Thus, Adolf Hitler says: "*The very first essential for success is a perpetually constant and regular employment of violence.*"

Gandhi is not alone in advocating morality in politics. There are many thinkers who emphasise that political power has to be exercised morally and responsibly. James Madison comments that *"There is no power without justice."* In the words of the US author James Baldwin, "*... the relationship of morality and power is a very subtle one. Because ultimately power without morality is no longer power.*" The great Russian novelist Fyodor Dostoyevsky holds that "*the greater the power, the more terrible its responsibility.*"

Over the long course of human history, democratic forms of governments slowly emerged. Even today, many regimes in the world are non-democratic. However, democracy is the most preferred form of government. It has a mechanism for periodically changing governments peacefully through elections. It divides powers between legislative, executive and judicial branches of government. In this way, the chances of anyone exercising absolute or dictatorial powers and hanging on indefinitely to power are greatly reduced. Democracies protect the liberties and freedoms of people by enshrining them as rights in constitutions, and conferring power on an independent judiciary to guard against violation of such rights. Many mechanisms are now used to ensure that citizens are not harassed by officialdom. These include right to information, speedy provision of services through citizens charters and fight against corruption.

Misuse of power is not something that happens only at the higher echelons of power. Modern bureaucracies are full of minor officials who act as petty and troublesome tyrants. This explains the enormous interest now being shown in administrative ethics, in codes of conduct for public servants, in measures for checking corruption, and in the mechanisms for creating responsive and honest public service systems.

It is noteworthy that democracies control the likely dangers of misuse of power through institutional arrangements. It is hoped that politicians will become enlightened and pursue public interest. However, few people believe that such change of heart will remove the tension between exercise of power and practice of morality. The answer has to be found in distributing power and placing checks on it.

PRUDENCE

"The right measure [due proportion] is at the head of all." —*Ancient Greek poet Pindar*

The Greek hated a thing overdone, a gaudy ornament, a proud title, a fulsome compliment, a high-flown speech, a wordy peroration.

The golden mean is God's delight:
Extremes are hateful to his sight.
Hold by the mean, and glorify
Nor anarchy, nor slavery — *Aeschylus*

The dictionary meaning of prudence is discretion, cautiousness, care, forethought or good sense. Prudent individuals avoid rashness and recklessness and tend to be wary of needless risk taking. They tend to be conventional and stick to the well trodden path. They may not be adventurous, and instead seek safety and comfort. Prudence is an inappropriate basis of morality. Early Christianity called for purity of heart and rejected prudence, fear and desire for afterlife in paradise as grounds for piety or virtue. Mere calculating prudence or a desire for social conformity should not be the basis of morality. A prudent individual may simply observe the external forms of religion without putting his heart into it.

Aristotle, however, considered prudence as eminently desirable practical wisdom. It is a habit of intellectual perception that enables the virtuous man to discover the golden mean of moral virtue. For Aristotle, virtue is a mean between two other qualities which represent its two extremes - for example courage is a golden mean between timidity and rashness. Aristotle believed that no moral virtue comes into play without prudence. In any given situation, it is the judgement of the prudent man that hits upon the mean of virtue. For example, without prudence, fortitude becomes rashness, justice becomes vindictiveness, clemency becomes weakness and religion becomes superstition.

Aristotle regarded prudence as a skill which enables one to identify virtue and pursue it. The golden mean has to be defined by reason, according to the particular circumstances of each case. However, the actual pursuit or choice of right ends depends on the strength of one's moral will. Prudence identifies and shows the route for only virtuous actions. If the ends are impure, prudence will have nothing to do with them. In pursuing dubious ends, people are guided by other qualities like shrewdness or cunning.

Aristotle believed that virtuous conduct presupposes prudence. For prudence is the practical wisdom which enables one to steer between the two extremes within which lies virtue. To cite another example, in the absence of prudence in a judge, justice may end up in undue severity or in undue leniency. Since virtue for Aristotle is a mean, he values prudence as a method of discovering and pursuing virtue.

Prudence in the sense of moderation and practical wisdom is a highly desirable virtue in civil servants. In modern administrative contexts, prudence can be seen as consisting in avoiding extreme positions, and adopting moderate courses of action. People usually dislike one sided or unduly harsh actions. Policies which avoid extremes are likely to appeal to the majority of people.

TEMPERANCE

Temperance is a virtue which brings to bear the judgement of reason on human cravings for food, drink and sex. As we saw earlier, temperance promotes self control and checks other rash impulses like anger. But temperance stands for moderation in food and drink as opposed to gluttony, and for chastity as opposed to lust. Men naturally tend to overindulge in matters which delight them. By cultivating the habit of temperance, one can avoid the harm which excessive indulgence causes. Of course, in many matters, the same prescription will be inapplicable; it has to be relative. For example, temperance in food will be different for a saint and an athlete.

Temperance is said to be made up of abstinence, chastity and sobriety. In a secondary sense, temperance includes moderation and self control. Ancient moralists were concerned with which are the vices harder to avoid. Men in whom the rational nature is strong are able to overcome sensuality, but they succumb to temptations of ambition, power and glory. They have an exaggerated sense of self esteem and lack humility. Men in whom the animal nature dominates give in easily to sensual pleasures.

Modesty is reflected in an individual's outward demeanour, style of dress and carriage. It refers to an individual's comportment or manner of conduct. A modest individual's outward manner reflects his temperate habits. In Plato's phrase, modesty indicates the presence of temperance "set up on holy pedestal" within an individual's heart. A modest individual will avoid brash or impudent behaviour, and will show due courtesy and respect to others.

HUMILITY

"Humility and resignation are our prime virtues." —*John Dryden*

"It was pride that changed angels into devils; it is humility that makes men as angels.´ —*St. Augustine*

"Humility, that low, sweet root, from which all heavenly virtues shoot." —*Thomas Moore*

"We come nearest to the great when we are great in humility." —*Rabindranath Tagore*

"True humility – the basis of the Christian system – is the low but deep and firm foundation of all virtues." —*Edmund Burke*

"Blessed are the weak: for they shall inherit the earth." —*The Bible*

"In peace, there is nothing that befits a man so much as modest stillness and humility." —*Shakespeare*

"The first condition of humaneness is a little humility and a little diffidence about the correctness of one's conduct and a little receptiveness." —*Gandhi*

"I claim to be a simple individual liable to err like any other fellow mortal. I own, however, that I have humility enough to confess my errors and to retrace my steps." —*Gandhi.*

Humility is recognised as a virtue in all religions. Many other virtues spring from or gather lustre from it. Humility does not mean self debasement or denying one's merits, talents and accomplishments. It means that we should not place ourselves on a higher pedestal than others -even when we far exceed them in talents and achievements. Even if one is rich and powerful, one should not feel a sense of superiority over the poor and the weak. One should judge oneself in relation to one's abilities, and consider whether one has utilized them in full measure. One should, from a religious point of view, try to utilize one's abilities in performing duties towards God and fellow men. The fact that one has greater talents and means than others indicates that one has greater responsibilities towards them. Thinking about what we have done in relation to what we could have done serves as a corrective to pride and arrogance.

Traditionally vanity, pride and arrogance have been regarded as the vices opposed to humility. Vanity leads to ostentation or 'showing off', putting on airs and looking down upon others. It creates a superiority complex which others find insufferable. Especially those in power become self complacent and easily get addicted to flattery. Those who think well of themselves tend to think ill of others. Modesty and humility act as antidotes to ostentation and self righteousness.

Humility along with other similar virtues formed the basis of early Christianity. These are meekness, mercifulness and peaceableness. Love, goodness and gentleness go with humility. Historically, these were considered virtues of the masses or the poor and the wretched. The rulers and warriors of Roman times (towards the end of which Christianity arose) were full of martial pride and royal insolence. In those days, the rich nobles and royalty looked down upon people from lower social strata. Many commentators observe that early Christianity preached virtues which were diametrically opposed to the military traditions and virtues of Roman society. The famous saying that the meek shall inherit the earth (in a non theological sense) means that the poor will come to share in the power. In a way, it is a prophecy that the society will be eventually democratized. This is of course a secular, as opposed to a religious interpretation.

Things have changed with the advent of modern democratic spirit. Elected leaders go out of their way now to put on airs of humility. They are never tired of paying tribute to the wisdom of masses and to folk ways. Leaving aside the question of genuineness of the sympathy towards the poor which politicians express, there is little doubt that humility is especially a virtue in those vested with power. Humility will serve to ward off the insolence that usually goes with power. Humility will enable political leaders and administrators to approach ordinary people in a polite and courteous manner. Nothing is more galling to suffering citizens than to put up with the arrogant and patronizing ways of bureaucracy. Unless public servants cultivate humility, they will be unable to show concern and consideration towards the problems of common people. Public servants should regard their duty as service to people. They should not regard themselves as rulers or bosses. They are trustees of power which ultimately is derived from people.

GOLDEN RULE

"That which is hateful to you, do not do to your fellow. That is the whole Torah" —*Rabbi Hillel the Elder*

"Never impose on others what you would not choose for yourself". —*Confucius*

"Do not do to your neighbour what you would take ill from him." —*Pittacus*

"Avoid doing what you would blame others for doing." —*Thales*

"What you do not want to happen to you, do not do it yourself either." —*Sextus the Pythagorean*

"Do not do to others what would anger you if done to you by others." —*Socrates*

"One should never do that to another which one regards as injurious to one's own self. This, in brief, is the rule of dharma. Other behaviour is due to selfish desires." —*Brihaspati, Mahabharata*

"Hurt not others in ways that you yourself would find hurtful." —*Udanavarga*

"Do to others what you want them to do to you." —*Matthew*

Although golden rule is commonly associated with Christian ethics, many religions have preached similar principles. The quotation of Matthew is from the Bible; Udanavarga's observation is from Buddhism; and the statement attributed to Brihaspati is from Mahabharata. The first quotation is a statement of an ancient Jewish preacher. The other quotations are from ancient Greek philosophers and Confucius. The same idea runs through all these quotations.

Many writers assert that the golden rule forms the essence of any morality. It is an ethic of equity. If there are two individuals X and Y, their conduct towards each other should be governed by identical principles. Human beings like to be treated by others with kindness and consideration. Therefore, according to the golden rule, each will treat the other kindly. The golden rule will automatically lead to ethical behaviour. If people adopt the golden rule, they need not refer to any elaborate moral codes.

The golden has wide practical acceptance. The "Declaration Toward a Global Ethic" of the Parliament of the World's Religions (1993) proclaimed the Golden Rule ("We must treat others as we wish others to treat us") as the common principle of many religions. From a commonsense point of view, the golden rule is a most reasonable moral principle. Still, some eminent philosophers criticized it since it can lead to unintended consequences. The main objection is that one may not know how others would like to be treated. This is because the tastes, needs and attitudes of people differ. Thus Bernard Shaw proposed an alternative view: *"Do not do unto others as you would that they should do unto you. Their tastes may not be the same".* According to Karl Popper, *"The golden rule is a good standard which is further improved by doing unto others, wherever reasonable, as they want to be done by"*. In other words, one should act towards others appropriately after ascertaining their likes and dislikes. This may be difficult if they fail to reach a reasonable understanding.

Immanuel Kant argued that the golden rule overlooks the differences between particular situations. He gives an example of a situation of a prisoner duly convicted of a crime. The prisoner invokes the golden rule while asking the judge to release him, pointing out that the judge would not want anyone else to send him to prison, and that he should not therefore do so to others. Kant's counter example shows that the golden rule breaks down in certain situations. This only shows that the operation of the golden rule may not be universal and that some cases fall outside it. While this observation may be valid on grounds of logical consistency or rigour, the golden rule will cover substantial areas of ordinary life. Further, the prisoner's logic will apply only if the judge commits theft.

Vices

Uptill now, we considered various virtues. Now, we look at some common vices. Vices are the opposites of virtues. Obviously, we have to shun vices; otherwise, they harm us both physically and psychologically. Once, we get into the grip of a vice, it is hard to escape. It becomes a settled habit, and we can give up the habit, if at all, with great effort of will. Hence, it is best to watch our responses and nip in the bud any bad or immoral thoughts and responses that enter our mind. Like all other moral training, freeing ourselves from any vice needs arduous effort.

Moral and religious teachers have identified many vices. These are however, not separate and distinct. If we exclude the synonyms of the common vices, the list of vices becomes smaller. Moral philosophers have also made a distinction between grave and less serious vices. Grave vices are also known in theological terms as deadly sins. Although vices (like virtues) feature prominently in religious contexts, they are relevant to man's personal and social life. Vices harm not only an individual but also his family.

We reproduce a list of vices from an internet site. The list is neither too long nor too short. But it also lists separately some vices which are essentially the same. Thus anger and wrath are similar. Similarly, arrogance, bragging and vanity are similar. But the list is a useful reference for discussion. It covers the commonly recognised vices.

LIST OF VICES

(Alphabetical Order)	
Anger	Strong passion or emotion of displeasure or antagonism, excited by real or supposed injury or insult to one-self or others, or by the intent to do such injury.
Arrogance	Making undue claims in an overbearing manner; that species of pride which consists in exorbitant claims of rank, dignity, estimation, or power, or which exalts the worth or importance of the person to an undue degree; proud contempt of others; lordliness; haughtiness; self-assumption; presumption.
Bragging	Exhibiting self-importance, boastful talk.
Cowardice	Lack of courage to face danger; extreme timidity; base fear of danger or hurt; lack of spirit.
Disloyalty	Lack of loyalty; lack of fidelity; violation of allegiance.
Doubt	Lack of trust and confidence. To suspect; to fear; to be apprehensive.

Contd....

Envy	A feeling of discontent and resentment aroused by and in conjunction with desire for the possessions or qualities of another.
Greed	An excessive desire to acquire or possess more than what one needs or deserves, especially with respect to material wealth.
Injustice	The practice of being unjust or unfair.
Impatience	The quality of being impatient; want of endurance of pain, suffering, opposition, or delay; eagerness for change, or for something expected; restlessness; chafing of spirit; fretfulness; passion
Jealousy	The quality of being jealous; painful apprehension of rivalry in cases nearly affecting one's happiness; painful suspicion of the faithfulness of husband, wife, or lover.
Recklessness	Wild carelessness and disregard for consequences. Insufficient consideration.
Sloth	Aversion to work or exertion; laziness; indolence.
Untrustworthiness	The trait of not deserving trust or confidence
Vanity	Inflated pride in oneself or one's appearance.
Weakness	The quality or state of being weak; want of strength or firmness; lack of vigour; want of resolution or of moral strength; feebleness.
Wrath	Forceful, often vindictive anger.

PRIDE

We have discussed anger earlier, Gluttony needs no discussion. The seven deadly sins are pride, greed, lust, anger, gluttony, envy and sloth. Pride is excessive love of self so much so that one develops contempt for others. This goes against the brotherhood of humanity which all religions preach. As we discussed earlier, humility and modesty help in overcoming pride.

ENVY

"Resentment is like drinking poison and waiting for the other person to die." —Carrie Fisher

"It is in the character of very few men to honour without envy a friend who has prospered.'—Aeschylus

"A tranquil heart gives life to the flesh, but envy makes the bones rot." —The Bible

"There is no love; There are only the various envies, all of them sad." —W.H. Auden

"Envy lurks at the bottom of the human heart, like a viper in its hole." —Honore de Balzac

"How can we explain the perpetuity of envy, a vice which yields no return?" —Balzac

"As rust corrupts iron, so envy corrupts man." —Antisthenes

"The dullard's envy of brilliant men is always assuaged by the suspicion that they will come to bad end." —Max Beerbohm

"Envy is the deformed and distorted offspring of egotism; and when we reflect on the strange and disproportioned character of the parent, we cannot wonder at the perversity and waywardness of the child." —William Hazlitt

"Envy is blind, and has no other quality but that of detracting from virtue." —Titus Livy

"No man likes to be surpassed by those of his own level." —Titus Livy

"An envious man waxes lean with the fatness of his neighbours. Envy is the daughter of pride, the author of murder and revenge, the beginner of secret sedition and the perpetual tormentor of virtue. Envy is the filthy slime of the soul; a venom, a poison, or quicksilver which consumes the flesh and dries up the marrow of the bones." —Socrates

Envy is resentment of others for their wealth and success. Envy is a perversion in which desire for one's own good turns to a desire to deprive other people of their good. An envious person wishes ill of others. He is unable to bear their success and happiness. Often, he is unable to take active measures for harming others. But their very success and happiness become the source of his misery. Envy arises when another gets what one has unsuccessfully tried to acquire. People seek degrees, jobs, power and money. When they find that they have been unable to get such things, and that others have got them deservedly or otherwise, they become jealous.

Jealousy is a source of great unhappiness. It is a wholly negative emotion, and yields no advantage. In modern world people live in a highly competitive enviornment. Success in any field is highly valued. Even when people are otherwise well off with a comfortable job, they are in a rat race. This competitive environment creates situations in which rewards in professions and jobs are unevenly distributed. Competition and heartburn are especially high among individuals who are within similar groups. They compare themselves with others and feel envy whenever others seem to be going ahead of them. Competition extends to the education and career of children also. This attitude creates an unhealthy mental atmosphere.

Envy goes against the moral injunction that we should love our neighbours. Religions preach that one should love even one's enemies. Envy is basically irrational since the riches or poverty of another make no difference to our condition. We are in no way affected by what happens to others. It does not increase or diminish our wealth. Hence, many thinkers and writers advise that we should eschew envy.

SLOTH

Laziness is aversion to work or exertion. Indolent individuals can be effective in no field of human life. A lazy child can make no progress in studies. Fortunately, by and large, children are seldom lazy. Indolence is a vice which adults acquire. It may start as love of ease, the tendency to take things easy and avoid strenuous effort of any kind. Lazy people shun both physical and mental labour. After completing studies and joining a job with security, people may fall into easy ways. Hardwork may seem unnecessary since they may be under no great compulsion to perform and deliver results.

Falling into lazy ways is a great mistake. To be productive in any area, people have to be energetic and active. Physical and mental effort is the very basis of life. There is a common belief that one's education ends with getting a degree. In any subject area, one has to continue one's learning. It will increase one's depth of knowledge; and one will keep abreast of further advances in the subject. Such interested pursuit can be a great source satisfaction. By giving up such effort, one gets into a stagnant situation. It will reduce one's ability to assimilate and analyse information. One will gradually lose mental sharpness and the ability to study any subject in depth. These are qualities which are essential in any profession all through one's career.

Economists and sociologists assert that economic progress of any nation depends on energetic and industrious workers. In a famous book, the German sociologist Max Weber traced the origins of capitalism to Protestant work ethic. Protestants are a section of Christians. Protestant moral codes strongly emphasised that people should devote themselves wholeheartedly to work and that they should be punctual, frugal, and honest and that they should keep their promises. Max Weber argued that this work ethic created the attitudinal and institutional framework necessary for the emergence of capitalism.

To pursue any enterprise big or small, we need an energetic will. No one who is lazy can summon the mental energy and strength of will to undertake any tasks. Even small jobs will look like heavy burdens. Taking up and executing tasks is a habit. The more tasks one does, the more willing and ready he would be able to do things. If one shies away from one's functions and duties, one loses confidence and élan. One becomes hesitant and diffident. One is left with neither energy nor confidence for undertaking any jobs. Many people think that it is smart to duck work, and let others carry the burden. Such people get marginalized in the organization. They get stamped as idlers and non performers. It undermines their morale since they may be seen as parasites on the system. It is in one's own material and moral interest to lead an active and energetic life and resist temptations of shirking. Further, simply passing time without mental and physical exertion is unhealthy. It creates mental problems and leads one astray. As the saying goes, a lazy mind is a devil's workshop.

AVARICE

Avarice is covetousness or greed. It is a desire to possess more than one has need or use for or excessive love of money. Avarice may extend to power and to various material possessions. People desire wealth because it is a means of acquiring other material comforts. Avarice is a morbid excess of the propensity to seek wealth.

Desire for modest means of gratifying one's minimum needs and comforts is not a vice. Without minimum material means, no one can meet the physiological, social and cultural needs of his family. A householder is under an obligation to provide for the needs of his family. In Hindu philosophy, Artha in this sense is a dharma or a duty which a householder has to pursue. Without adequate savings, one cannot take care of himself and his wife in old age. Further, possession of wealth is a means of helping others. In the absence of money, many acts of beneficence and charity become impossible. This is the rationale of the Sanskrit saying: "*Dhanmulam idam jagat*" – money lies at the base of this world.

To start with, money is desired as a means of satisfying other desires. But as time goes on, money making becomes a habit by itself and gets detached from the original aim of seeking gratifications. Instead of being a means, it becomes an end in itself. This is the typical psychology of the miser depicted so often in literature. In a miser, money making becomes a compulsive obsession and gets separated from its instrumental use. It dominates one's whole character, becomes the sole aim of one's activity.

To begin with, an individual seeks wealth through legitimate means. No moral stigma attaches to even great wealth which is earned through business acumen or simple good fortune. However, more often than not, single minded pursuit of wealth deflects people from the virtuous path. People may want to get rich quickly by fair or foul means. They resort to fraud, extortion, deceit and injustice. The recent spate of scams can be traced to unscrupulous pursuit of wealth. Avaricious men become selfish, live only for themselves, and are always on the lookout for means of making money.

Moral teachers have consistently denounced greed. Wealth beyond what one needs for comfortable living is a superfluity. As Gandhi observes, wealth is trust which the rich hold on behalf of the poor. The rich are under a moral obligation to share with the poor. Such a view may seem too idealistic for any society. But it is one way of reducing social tensions. For great inequality of wealth has propelled many revolutions like the French and Russian revolutions. Much of socialist thought has its origins in excessive concentration of wealth and gross income inequalities in a society. RH Tawny, a noted socialist writer, described capitalism as "an acquisitive society".

In a discussion of greed as an individual vice, we cannot discuss the means a society should adopt for ensuring economic justice. For it is a matter of public policy. But at an individual level, charity, liberality and philanthropy are virtues which help in overcoming avarice. One of the main virtues of Aristotle's magnanimous man is liberality or generosity. Donating money to needy or to worthy causes is extolled as a virtue in many literary works. As an example, we may recall the characters Karna and King Bali from Indian mythology. To their credit, many industrialists and businessmen have contributed generously to charities.

LUST

Lust refers to excessive sexual desire. It takes many forms. All religions condemn sex outside marriage or adultery. Adultery involves disloyalty to one's spouse. It violates the vows taken at the time of marriage. Hence, it involves a type of untruthfulness or falsehood. Breaking the bonds of marriage affects family ties, damages children psychologically and hurts family interests. Adultery therefore hurts one's own long term interests and happiness.

Lustful men may sexually assault women. Such crimes are clearly violent. In addition, women also face sexual harassment in various forms. These incidents tend to remain under wraps. In cases of sexual harassment, men force their attentions on unwilling women. In this way, they violate the dignity and modesty of women. Responsible men have to cast themselves in the role of protectors of women. Social and official positions impose such roles on men. In many situations, women are entrusted to the care of men. Thus employed women have to be protected in work situations by their bosses. Their fellow workers have to maintain cordial but professional relations with them. Heads of office have to ensure that women employees are not subjected to unwelcome sexual attentions.

In recent times, many cases have surfaced in which young women have been sexually harassed or molested by those in authority above them. Such acts are reprehensible, and undermine the tender ties which should ideally exist between men and women. Further, they betray trust and are criminal acts. It is in this context that laws against sexual harassment at workplace have become necessary. Many feminists argue that men in positions regard exploiting women subordinates as an extension of their authority.

Such behaviour is a manifestation of power. Feminists also argue that men tend to regard women as sex objects rather than as fellow human beings who deserve respect. Victims of sexual harassment face social stigma, even when they are not to blame. If they show the courage to file complaints against the offenders, they have to go through traumatic court proceedings. Lawyers on behalf of the offenders, who generally are powerful individuals with political connections, attack the victim's character.

The problem can also be traced to the changing social situation. The number of women in the workplaces has increased. Certain culture of permissiveness has permeated the system. People have come under the influence of Western culture and its permissive morals. Movies, electronic media and internet have also contributed to this trend. People scoff at the traditional virtues of feminine chastity. Many young men and women lose their moorings in this unhealthy moral environment. They consider it fashionable and chic to enter into 'relationships' instead of getting properly married. It is invariably the young women who end up on the wrong side of these so called relationships.

Some groups of people who fancy themselves as artists and intellectuals feel that ordinary morality does not apply to them. They feel that such morality only applies to unenlightened and ignorant masses. Given this mindset, they are too ready to take advantage of the young women workers (who often take jobs from pressing economic need) in their midst. When they are caught in such acts, they tend to portray the victims as willing accomplices. In a commonly used expression, they pass off their crimes as 'consensual acts between consenting adults'.

No one however exalted or talented can claim exemption from ordinary morality. This point is brought out forcefully in George Orwell's essay 'The Benefit of Clergy'. Benefit of clergy refers to the special privileges and exemptions which Christian priests enjoyed in relation to their criminal offences sometime in the past. Salvador Dali, a famous Surrealist painter, has written in his autobiography about some obnoxious things he did as a boy. Either he or his admirers implied that Salvador Dali's artistic genius places him in a special category, and that those moral lapses, unlike those of ordinary people, do not count. Orwell demolishes this view, and rejects the argument that artistic genius or any similar trait exempts anyone from common morality.

When some well intended efforts are made by police and voluntary groups, they are attacked for moral policing. Many activists oppose regulation of bars and night clubs and late night entertainment in the name of personal freedom. At the same time, they become vociferous whenever women are sexually assaulted. Of course, men have to change their attitudes towards women. At the same time, young women need to take ordinary precautions. Sexual assault is a crime which depends on circumstances. It happens when the victim is alone with no one around to go to her help. Women need to scrupulously avoid such situations. There may be situations when economic or other circumstances make women helpless. These are likely to be exceptions. Barring exceptions, women can take reasonable precautions. They should also avoid late 'night outs' with men under the influence of alcohol. They should go out only with men with whom they have long acquaintance and whom they can trust.

We have discussed lust in relation to sexual harassment. Some readers may feel that we have departed from the topic. Obviously, lust is a topic which is rather remote from administrative situations. It becomes relevant mainly in relation to sexual harassment of women in workplaces whether in public or private sector. Lust in the form of sexual attacks on women is also a current issue. It is from these angles that we have briefly discussed the topic.

We have already discussed anger and vanity earlier. This completes our account of vices. Avoidance of vices is the negative aspect of morality. Often, avoiding evil is itself a virtue even if one makes no effort to help others. Eschewing vices generally prevents harm to others, and ennobles one's character.

Uptill Now, we have discussed ethical qualities based on the pithy observations of great sages and thinkers. Now, we outline a few cases to illustrate the situtations in which ethical qualities come into play.

Case Studies

CASE 1

Subodh Jha hails from an influential family of landlords. Tall and very handsome, he could well compete for a role in Bollywood. Being educated in Delhi in a top notch college he developed a preference for the civil services and got selected in the IRS and joined as an Income Tax Officer. During his college days he had been a cynosure of female eyes and had intimate relationship with a number of girls across the campuses in Delhi. He could not control his night life culture of visiting discotheque and night clubs with girl friends and getting inebriated even after joining this important branch of civil service.

Nowadays he is invariably out every weekend and can never come punctually to office on Mondays. On Fridays he loses concentration. Incidentally, his weekend begins on Thursday. Monday mornings are important in his office because the Commissioner takes a review of results achieved in the last week and plans for the ensuing week. Being late in office every time, he tries to fabricate a story and explain delay. His overall performance being good he has not attracted adverse notice of the bosses yet, but his immediate subordinates know why he is late on Mondays and smile while he narrates stories.

Question

What ethical problems do you see in his behaviour *from an official point of view*?

Envisage four alternatives and select the most appropriate one

1. Whatever Subodh is doing outside office hours is part of his personal life, and has no bearing on his official conduct.
2. The matter may concern Subodh's personal life, but it is likely to lower his official performance. It may be violative of official codes of conduct also.
3. It is for the income Tax Commissioner to discipline Subodh and ensure that he attends meetings on time.
4. The fact that Subodh is able to convincingly lie to explain delay so many times shows that he is smart.

Discussion

The first alternative cannot be supported. Fundamentally, he has not been able to make a transition from the lifestyle of a somewhat spoilt young man to that of a responsible public servant. What was nobody else's business when he was a student will soon become a matter of concern for his department and the sooner he realises this, the better for him. His lifestyle is indulgent and lacks prudence and temperance. One may recall here Aristotle's concept of golden mean and value of prudence. Even though Subodh can afford an extravagant life style because of inherited wealth, the habits he developed are fraught with problems. His delay in reaching office shows that his behaviour is affecting his official discipline.

The second alternative is the appropriate one. His life style has begun to undermine his official discipline. He is also cultivating the horrible habit of telling lies. Instead of addressing the cause of unpunctuality he is fabricating stories. This cannot work for long. His weakness cannot remain hidden for ever and when known to office he will lose credibility - which is already happening. When the burden of falsehood becomes heavy the moral agent no longer remains trustworthy and his esteem in the eyes of others melts away. When that happens the individual becomes unfit for any leadership role such as civil servants are expected to assume. Civil servants are expected to behave decently in personal life and philandering is not an acceptable quality. it can expose them to risks of blackmail and scandals thereby endangering public interest. His behaviour is a form of moral turpitude and violates the codes of public servants.

It is true that the Income Tax Commissioner has to enforce discipline. But then, Subodh is a senior officer and has to punctiliously observe official discipline and protocols on his own instead of waiting to be coerced into disciplined behaviour.

The fourth response is very inappropriate. A morally bad act or behaviour even if carried out with confidence and style is to be condemned. Smartness has to be admired or accepted only when displayed in moral conduct and actions.

CASE 2

Mr. Irfan Khan is a top level executive in an MNC in the IT sector. He hails from a cultured family and has a happy married life. His young kid Zafar, aged 7 is exhibiting some behaviour patterns that disturb Mrs. and Mr. Khan. Zafar has been taking pleasure in hurting and torturing creatures for the last two years. It all started when he would pick up some insects such as cockroaches and worms and take delight in cutting them to pieces with a blade. The family keeps some pets including rabbits and some days ago Mr. Khan detected the boy vivisecting a rabbit in a lonely corner of their garden. By the time Mr. Khan intervened it was all over and young Zafar was almost relishing the sight of his bloody hand. Mr. Khan, of course, scolded the kid but they are worried about the gruesome incidents likely to happen from this kind of perverse behaviour.

Question

What actions should the parents take? Select from the following options:

1. They should ignore the incidents as childish pranks.
2. They should explain to Zafar the need to behave kindly towards animals and to avoid violence in all forms.
3. They should take Zafar to a psychiatrist for counselling and treatment.
4. They should not let Zafar out of sight when he is alone.

Discussion

The first course of action will be unwise. The type of violent behaviour shown by Zafar is unnatural. It should not be left unattended since the tendency may grow strong and become ingrained.

The second course of action may not work. Parents can certainly inculcate non-violent thoughts and behaviour in Zafar. But it is a question as to what extent he would absorb such advice. As he is too young, he may not realise the danger of his behaviour trait.

The third option is the correct response. Normal children do not enjoy torturing and vivisecting insects. If Zafar has been doing this, there may be some underlying pathology. The last incident is definitely serious. More than adults, children generally get attracted to pets and start enjoying their company. Instead, if the boy is killing a pet which is as innocent as a rabbit, there may be a malady. This malady needs to be addressed or else it may spread and the boy may become more violent over time. Finally, he may end up even being a murderer. Early correction could circumvent many ugly situations in adulthood. Outbursts of violent episodes may originate from unpleasant events and a sense of frustration. This diagnosis is important and only after diagnosis a cure can be sought. Khan family would be well advised to consult a child psychologist for treatment of this pathological condition.

The last response will be impracticable. Parents cannot keep continuous watch over children. They may encourage Zafar to play with children of his age and promote his interest in group activities as a means of socialization.

CASE 3

Kalyanpur is a somewhat isolated headquarter of a block in a tribal district. Kalyanpur Primary Health Centre (PHC) has lots of vacancies and only one MBBS Doctor Kuldeep Goyal manages with a few core staff all the affairs of the PHC. About a year ago, the Pradhan of the Kalyanpur village had approached Dr. Goyal to issue a medical certificate for somebody who Dr. Goyal knew was not at all sick. So he had declined the request. Around same time, Dr. Goyal was planning to build his residential house in the same village. When the matter came up to the village panchayat for issuing a building permission for Dr. Goyal's plan, the panchayat adopted dilatory tactics in the sense that the panchayat neither gave the permission nor rejected the plan. Dr. Goyal had approached him twice requesting a decision yet there was no movement.

A few days ago in the early morning hours when only a cleaner, the staff nurse and Dr. Goyal were present in the PHC, the nurse received a call that the Pradhan's son and one of his friends had met with a car accident and that they were being brought to the PHC by the Pradhan and other local people. The nurse reported this call to Dr. Goyal.

Question

On hearing this news, Dr. Goyal thinks of the following responses : Which of those responses is appropriate?

1. Tell the nurse that when the patients arrive she may give them primary treatment and inform the Pradhan that the doctor is unwell and may come late. And then he should leave the PHC through the backdoor.

2. Since almost everyone carries mobile phones these days, he should tell the nurse to make a phone call to callers that as the PHC lacks critical medicines and equipment, they should remove the victims elsewhere.
3. Forget the bad treatment he received from the Pradhan and give the best possible medical attention to the accident victims.
4. Inform the Pradhan that because of the way he handled the house building application, he would find it psychologically difficult to attend to his son and that he should take him elsewhere.

Discussion

The correct course is fairly obvious. The first course is wrong because it would deprive the victims of the best possible treatment to which they are entitled. The main motive here is to teach the family of the Pradhan a lesson because the latter had not treated Dr. Goyal's legitimate request for building permission with fairness and had been unnecessarily obstructive. The Pradhan acted in this manner because Dr. Goyal did not agree to issue a false medical certificate. If the building plan had any deficiency, the Pradhan was duty bound to inform the applicant, and he had no business to sit over the application. Conduct of the Pradhan was definitely improper but Dr. Goyal should not imitate it. If the victims are serious, Dr.Goyal's action will endanger their life.

The second alternative is also a way of avoiding a doctor's primary duty. In this alternative, the doctor is instructing the nurse to tell a lie and divert the patients to another clinic.

The third alternative is the right course of action. Every public servant has to discharge his duties faithfully. He should not shirk his duty even towards those who may have wronged him in some way. This consideration applies with additional force in this situation since Dr. Goyal is bound by the Hippocratic Oath which governs all doctors. They have to do their best to help the patients, and should never harm them. He should not link his duty as a physician with other issues. He should not harm Pradhan's son for the wrong of his father.

The fourth alternative is also inappropriate. A doctor should not bring in issues of his psychological attitudes in these matters. He cannot choose patients based on his subjective feelings. He should treat all the patients irrespective of his attitude towards them.

CASE 4

Mr. X and Yashwant Mishra, sharing a room in Lal Bahadur Shastri National Academy of Administration (LBSNAA), became friendly very quickly. There were a few common threads that helped the bonding. They hailed from the same state and joined the same service through different career paths though, and they both got allotted to a state different from their home state.

Dissimilarities in their background are striking. Mr. X belongs to the reserved category and had humble schooling. While working as a railway clerk by dint of hard work and devotion he made it to the IAS. Mr. Mishra belonged to a rich family and had schooling in Doon School. He was focused on civil services right from school and easily walked into the LBSNAA after graduating from a well known college of Delhi.

These dissimilarities, did not come in way of their friendship. Mr. X was married at the time he joined the IAS. His wife Bhanumati joined Mr. X in the district posting as a probationary officer. Even Bhanumati was like her husband very affectionate to this 'young hero' from native state. On holidays Mishra would sometimes go to X's place of posting to enjoy meals and chitchat.

It was two and half years into the IAS, when Mr. Mishra married Sujata onetime beauty queen of his home state. She too was from an affluent background.

A few months into her new life, Sujata to the discomfort of Yashwant, showed early signs that his spouse's friendship with X's family did not mean much – is in fact an aberration. Initially she would join, Yashwant going to X's place, but her comments indirectly would, focus on her father's and in-laws' superior status. Once she even speculated that Yashwant will be the CS of the state if not the Cabinet Secretary to GOI.

Yashwant never relished this senseless chattering but remained silent as he did not want to bring discord in his family. To his utter dismay he slowly discovered that Mr. X's family was cooling off towards them. They would not invite Yashwant as frequently as before. Recently during the Holy festival, when Yashwant invited X with family, Mr. X gave an excuse of their school going son needing some attention. Yashwant is wondering how to bring back the same old warmth and cordiality in this friendship tie.

Question

What do you think is the root cause of the problem?

1. X and his wife may have started feeling jealous of Yashwant and Sujata.
2. Depending on paths of their life, individual interests diverge and this may lead to loss of ardour of friendship.
3. Modern work situations are characterised by intense competition and rat race among colleagues.
4. The problem appears to have started from Sujatha's arrogant behaviour and Yashwant should tell her to show modesty in her dealings with others.

Discussion

The answer choice (1) does not seem to be the case. X and his wife have been behaving in a friendly manner with Yashwant for quite a while. They have been affectionate towards Yashwant.

As for the second answer choice, it is true that friends can lose contact if they move away to different places due to professional and other reasons. Separation in terms of distance and time can lead to loss of friendship. But in this case, the friends have been in close proximity.

As mentioned in the third answer choice, sometimes, the desire to forge ahead of others in professional life creates rivalries. When rivalry develops between people, they cannot share genuine friendship. But at this stage of career, the two friends are not in a competitive situation.

The problem has been triggered most probably by the ego of Mrs. Mishra. This egoistic feeling has come about because she is pretty and has a 'star spouse' who has the great advantage of joining the service at a young age. Expression of this ego and pride must have surfaced in conversation and behaviour with Mr. X's family. That must be making them conscious about the difference in their endowments – mostly by birth. If individuals feel that they have different goals and have unequal 'status' in life, general reaction is one of avoidance. Avoidance is one way to express feeling of inadequacy or inferiority. This probably is the reason why X's family is cooling off towards Mishras.

Yashwant and Sujata must behave normally with X. Any talk about money, career and beauty of women should be strictly avoided. Discussion may focus on some activities they enjoyed together so that good memories are refreshed. It is not late yet but Yashwant must make some special efforts to restore the earlier level of friendship.

CASE 5

Ms. Vandana Subramaniam, IAS comes from a family with strong moral and religious inclinations. She is the DM of a Hindu majority district with substantial Christian population. There is only one good town-hall in the district headquarters controlled by the estate department under the DM. Every year Easter festival is celebrated in the Hall. This year Easter coincides with a well-known Hindu festival and both groups have asked for the same hall. Earlier Hindus used to celebrate this in the premises of a religious-social service institution but this year that hall is under renovation.

Question

What should be her decision from an administrative standpoint?

1. She should not rent the hall to either group
2. She should pass an order not to rent the hall to any religious group in future.
3. She should rent the hall to Hindus as they represent a far larger segment of the population of the district.
4. She should rent it for Easter as has been done in the past.

Discussion

In this context action as either at (1) or (2) will be over reaction. Just because on one particular day two festivals have coincided the DM need not be jittery, and ban future allotment.

Action as at (3) does not follow the principle of equity. Every year the Christians hold the cultural activities in the hall. The demand from Hindus has come because of a special situation. It would not be correct to accommodate that special situation and tell the Christians to go elsewhere. She should follow the well set precedent.

Action at (4) is correct. If the Hindus complain, they should be explained the reasons for favouring the trodden path. The DM may use her good offices to find a suitable venue for the Hindu congregation.

CASE 6

Lachhman Singh has recently purchased a costly wristwatch through an internet site. He was to send a cheque by post, but the wristwatch has been sent, even though he has genuinely forgotten to send the cheque. On top of it, he receives the wristwatch by courier with sticker 'paid' on the package.

Question

What are the options before Lachhman Singh in this case?

1. Make the payment immediately
2. Seek a clarification from the company as to whether he is getting the watch under some scheme and make payment when company asks for it.
3. Just ignore the matter.
4. Retain the 'paid' sticker with him and create a controversy on that basis when company seeks payment.

Discussion

Lachhman Singh need not make that payment immediately since there is no demand--due to an error--from the company.

The second alternative is the most appropriate one. Some employee of the company has for sure made a mistake. This has created some confusion. By writing to the company, Lachhman Singh can clear up the matter. He knows that he has to make a payment. He will be bringing the error to the company's notice.

Lachhman Singh can ignore the matter for the time being. But sooner or later the company will realise the mistake and ask him to pay. This is not a sensible choice.

The last alternative is totally unacceptable. Lachhman Singh should not take advantage of an error to deprive the company of payment. Although he may raise a dispute, he will not succeed in establishing that he had made the payment.

CASE 7

You are in a suburban overcrowded train station in Mumbai. While you are coming out from the ticket counter, rushing to the platform, one individual standing in queue of another ticket counter accidentally spits on your feet. You do not know this individual.

You immcdiatcly challenge him asking to know why he did this. This individual with folded hands begs pardon and says it happened without any intent on his part.

Question

What should you do?

1. Ask him to come to the Railway Police so that a formal complaint can be lodged.
2. Rush to the platform because your train must be arriving within a short while.
3. Spit on him.
4. Forgive him and caution him to take care in future.

Discussion

Notice that action choice (2) dodges the question. Rushing to catch the train may be necessary for you but such a response does not reveal your moral inclination at all and as such is an unsuitable answer.

Action choice (3) is both foolish and unethical. That individual has been careless. You were not the target of any vengeance. So you should avoid any 'tit for tat' response. Gandhiji insightfully observed that a policy of "an eye for an eye" would leave the world blind. Even if the whole world does not become blind, it will have many blind people. In fact, the moral offensiveness of your action would be much more serious than the careless action of that individual. Normal instinct triggers revenge but as Confucius had said, "Before you embark on a journey of revenge, dig two graves."

Forgiveness enables us to move forward without having to carry the ugly burden of bearing grudges. Forgiveness reduces the sum total of social costs that would otherwise accrue in its absence. No doubt that individual has been careless and uncultured. By forgiving you would encourage him to examine his own conduct. In a situation like this forgiving is the best thing to do.

In this case, there is no evil intent on the part of the individual and he has sought forgiveness. Therefore, action choice (4) is preferable to (1).

CASE 8

Your friend Umakant hails from a village whose surrounding areas were submerged due to floods during the monsoon last year. Government assisted the affected people by giving them cash doles to purchase household effects, seeds to replant crop and cash to compensate for loss of standing crop. Umakant had his house site on high ground and suffered no loss of personal effects. Luckily, his agricultural land being relatively far away from the flooded river escaped the ravages of the flood. Normally, government machinery is unable to thoroughly assess the damage suffered by each individual family. As a result, people take advantage by making extravagant and often fictitious claims. Umakant has made false claims like others in the village.

Question

What will be an appropriate response to Umakant's conduct?

1. Umakant should only have made genuine claims.
2. It is for the government agencies to ensure that no false claims are entertained.
3. When everyone is cheating the system, Umakant cannot do anything singly; he should join the crowd.
4. Governments provide relief whenever natural calamities occur for winning cheap popularity. They should scale down the benefits.

Discussion

The first choice is correct. Actually moral responsibility springs from within. One source of ethical values is conscience. Inside every sentient moral agent there is a voice which tells him/her what is right and what is wrong. An action is wrong, even when nobody else has observed it if it does not pass the test of morality. Umakant or for that matter anybody else deserves the benefit of flood relief only if he has suffered specific losses due to flood. If crop has been lost then for crop loss the claim is morally sound. If no loss has taken place, one cannot make a claim at all. Whether government sanctions a false claim or not is not relevant from his ethical perspective. It is with this deep sensibility that the great philosopher Immanuel Kant had written "Two things awe me most, the starry sky above me and the moral law within me". One has to remain sensitive to the promptings of conscience.

Knowingly or unknowingly, Umakant is harbouring a wrong belief that his moral responsibility does not arise because government functionaries are expected to verify details and only after verification pass a payment order. If the authorities have not taken care to do their job, it is they who are responsible and not he. But this answer choice, as explained above, is wrong.

Umakant is also wrong in justifying his improper conduct on the ground that everybody else in a similar situation in his village has done the same. This is a bandwagon impropriety as we may call it. Bandwagon behaviour is a conduct of imitating others - irrespective of whether the conduct in itself is right or wrong. Populism causes social aberration and this is common in our country - everybody wants to take the benefit of government schemes irrespective of whether the eligibility conditions apply to him or not. Other's conduct is good for imitation only to the extent it is worthy. Confucius put it very nicely: "If I am walking with two other men, each of them will serve as my teacher. I will pick out the good points of the one and imitate them and the bad points of the other and correct them in myself."

The fact that governments provide relief on a liberal scale is no argument for misusing such relief. Scale of benefits has no connection with morally desirable conduct in this case.

Ethical Reasoning and Moral Dilemmas

INTRODUCTION

Many decisions we take in personal, official and social life are relatively straightforward. They are based on routine and habitual responses and procedures. They may not involve questions of morals, but in case they do, the ethical criteria applicable to them are simple and clear. Ethical dilemmas, in contrast, are situations in which decisions involve conflicts between two or more moral principles. In these situations, moral agents (who have to make decisions) find themselves in a quandary since they have to choose between two ethical norms (N_1 and N_2) which have equal status. If the moral agent selects N_1, he has to give up N_2 and *vice versa*. In other words, the decision involves a trade-off between two moral criteria. This is the theme we discuss in this chapter. We cover this theme in four parts: definition of ethical situations; moral criteria which may clash; manner of resolving ethical conflicts; and the processes which clarify moral dilemmas.

Ethical Situations

Ethical dilemmas come up only in situations which have ethical or moral aspects or dimensions. Obviously, ordering paper, pencils or pens for office stores involves no moral questions. The criteria used for decision could be the requirements and the budget. Similarly, the design of a hostel or a bridge will have no moral aspects. These are non ethical contexts of decision-making.

What are the features which impart an ethical dimension to a situation? One general answer is that situations which involve issues of right and wrong are ethical situations. Moral philosophers have defined ethical situations more concretely. According to one such definition, ethical situation involves actions and decisions which are based on a moral agent's choice and volition and which significantly affect other individuals. In addition, ethical situations involve application of norms, standards, criteria or principles in decision-making. Moral criteria or standards include: fairness, honesty, justice, integrity, truthfulness and generosity. Some writers place emphasis on justice and rights. An ethical situation directly and explicitly involves considerations of moral standards or criteria. Dennis P. Wittmer defines an ethical situation essentially as one in which ethical dimensions are relevant and deserve consideration in making some choice that will have significant impact on others. According to Rest, ethical dimensions are those norms and principles that "provide the basic guidelines for determining how conflicts in human interests are to be settled and for optimizing mutual benefit of people living together in groups".

Process of Moral Decision-Making

After defining the ingredients that impart an ethical dimension to a situation, we need to consider three more aspects. First is the process of decision-making in ethical situations. Next, we look at moral criteria which come into play need consideration. Finally, we examine how civil servants and other decision makers can handle ethical dilemmas.

When administrators face uncertainty in ethical situations, they wonder what could be the morally correct and responsible decision. In this matter, they can get guidance from normative theories, decision-making models and decision processes. Normative or prescriptive principles help in determining what should be done and what is the correct course of action. Public servants are accountable and have to justify their decisions to the political executive and the public. Hence, they usually search for and base their decisions on reasons and principles. Ethical decision-making in public sphere requires detailed analysis of the situation and identification of the norms and criteria that apply to the situation. Standards and norms provide guidance to a decision and constitute its rationale. It is application of principles which makes decisions consistent, coherent and predictable. Decisions without the guidance of standards or principles will be arbitrary, capricious and unpredictable. Administrators can defend themselves against the charge that they used wrong principles in taking a decision. But they can never defend a decision which is not grounded in any principles.

There are many models of decision-making. These differ in their approach and the elements of the problem which they highlight. We will consider two important models. The processes or steps involved in taking decisions and the criteria that can guide decision-making tend to get mixed up in the models. But we should try, to the extent possible, to keep them apart.

Terry Cooper has reduced ethical decision making to a series to steps which begin with identifying the problem and end with its resolution. Although his schematized model may not be very realistic, it will enable practical administrators to place the situation within an easily intelligible analytical frame work. While going through the steps involved in taking the decision, the decision makers are free to select the appropriate moral standards. The procedure presupposes no fixed moral norms.

Perception or recognition of an ethical problem is the first step towards its resolution. Administrators can be morally insensitive or blind; they may just fail to notice the moral aspects of a problem. The failure may arise from their personality, inadequate moral development and a feeling that they are not in control and cannot influence the course of events.

Case Studies

CASE 1

We use a simple example to illustrate the steps involved in moral decision-making. In a district, the Panchayat has employed part time education assistants or *vidyasahayaks* to teach in primary schools. The District Development Officer (DDO) comes to know that many *vidyasahayaks* are not teaching for the prescribed number of hours. This is an ethical issue since the *vidyasahayaks* are in breach of the agreement or their promise. Another moral aspect is depriving rural children of their right to education. First, the moral aspect of the question has to be recognised.

The second stage consists in fully describing the situation. By description is meant not literary description, but a full recitation of the facts of the situation. Facts have to be objectively stated. The available facts may often be incomplete, and people may see them from multiple perspectives. In our example, facts can be the norms of teaching hours for *vidyasahayaks*, number of *vidyasahayaks* who teach below this norm, whether others are available for hire as *vidyasahayaks* and whether the functionaries at Tehsil level have noted the problem and tried to solve it.

In the next stage, decision makers have to spell out clearly the moral issues and moral norms involved in the situation. This is a rather difficult exercise since the officials usually have a non-ethical perspective on matters. Their normal response will be to view the problem from administrative or legal angles as a lapse of discipline, symptom of low morale or breach of employment contract. The moral aspects are the need to meet one's obligations, being fair to the children and being honest.

The next stage consists in visualizing the possible alternatives. Here, all possibilities should be considered without rejecting any solutions outright. The options should not be reduced to a simple either/or. In our example, an either/or approach will be either discharging the errant *vidyasahayaks* or just ignoring the problem. Some alternatives could be: altering the working hours, schedules or locations of *vidyasahayaks*, running quality improvement programmes, and holding a general meeting with them to remind them of their social duties of public service.

The next stage involves evaluating the alternatives. A simple procedure is to list the alternatives and show against each its merits and demerits. This requires a little imagination; it is a form of 'dramatic rehearsal'. In the example, the alternative of discharging may mean depriving children of teaching and parental dissatisfaction. If the existing practice continues, it may lead to slow deterioration of educational quality. We can list other advantages and disadvantages.

The process leading to the decision involves four steps which are interactive.

- Identifying the moral principles involved in each alternative
- Analyzing the extent to which each alternative can withstand criticism
- Considering to what extent higher moral principles apply to the situation
- Examining to what extent each alternative reflects on the decision maker's image

In the third step, one can consider what decision about *vidyasahayaks* will maximise the utility or good of all concerned. The last step does not imply that the decision maker's PR image has to be enhanced. But the decision has to reflect his moral approach.

Based on the above steps, a final decision is reached. In real life, one may not exactly follow the above sequence of steps. To put in general terms, public administrators especially in public policy making, have to make explicit the moral aspects of different policy alternatives. They also must bring to light the moral norms with which the policy alternatives are in accord or discord. Of course, in a democratic set up, the political executive takes the final call.

The final step is the resolution of the problem. But in practical situations the conclusion is hardly likely to be ideal. It will not represent a fine balance between duties and rights or lead to optimal consequences. It is likely to be a compromise on the whole more desirable than undesirable. In technical terms, such solutions are not 'optimizing' but 'satisficing'.

Method Based on Judicial Procedures: Outcome Justice

Gerald Pops and Thomas Pavlak, in *The Case for Justice: Strengthening Decision Making in Public Administration* have proposed another method based on procedures of justice which they regard as an integrative normative principle. Further, justice includes values like public interest, social equity and efficiency. They regard their approach as superior to other approaches which are based on technical rationality and efficiency (Max Weber's theory), social equity, ethics and virtuous character of public servants. The criteria which Pops and Pavlak suggest are outcome or distributive justice and process or procedural justice. They also suggest the conditions for outcome justice and procedural justice. Outcome justice has to satisfy the following conditions:

(i) Decisions should be based on the facts of the case. In evacuating people from a hazardous area, rescue workers should first remove women, children and the aged.

(ii) Decisions have to follow public policy. Decisions should seek to achieve the policy goals of the duly constituted political authority.

(iii) Decisions should not violate the formal canons of justice. Thus, no penalty should be imposed on anyone without giving him an opportunity of representing his case or allowing him to show why no penalty should be imposed on him.

(iv) Decisions need to strike a balance between strict adherence to rules and exercise of discretion. Rules try to ensure that decisions are taken objectively and avoid personal bias and partiality. As rules cannot cover all possible contingencies, administrative discretion has to be sometimes used.

(v) Decisions should serve the people or the 'clients' of the agency. If the interests of the agency or the service provider come first, then people will suffer injustice.

(vi) Decisions have to balance the interests of individuals and society at large. While taking care of individuals, organizations should not allow public resources to be wasted or dissipated.

CASE 2

Suman was a young, idealistic development officer in a district panchayat. After joining the district, he studied about its social and economic situation. He consulted various plan documents and looked at the social and economic parameters of the district. He found that the district is relatively better off than other districts in terms of irrigation, crop diversification and industry. But its social indicators were poor with high infant mortality rate, high maternal mortality rate and low literacy percentage among women. Based on his analysis, Suman thought that large investments in the social sector will be necessary in order to tackle these problems.

The panchayat was an elected body. It has decided to spend 40% of its budget on minor irrigation. Suman felt that the large allocation to minor irrigation will benefit land owning farmers and starve other social programmes.

Question

What should Suman do in these circumstances?

1. He should tell officers to surreptitiously divert money to social welfare programmes under some pretext.
2. He should follow the Panchayat's decision.
3. He should discuss matters with elected officials of the Panchayat and try to convince them of the need to accord greater priority to social sector.
4. He should reconcile himself to the economic inequalities and the power structure of the rural society.

Discussion

Suman should not adopt improper means in trying to achieve higher spending on social sector. In fact, he should not give any wrong or improper instructions to his subordinates. He will then be violating the principles of truthfulness and transparency. Suman is under an obligation to follow the public policy decision taken by the elected body. He can try to persuade them to his view. But he should not undermine their policy.

In the second alternative, Suman will be doing the right thing. But this is not enough in this case. Since he has studied the development problems of the district in detail, he should explain the position at length to non-officials in the panchayat. Young officers have to cultivate skills of communication, persuasion and negotiation. They should not give up on things without trying.

The third option gives the correct line of action. Here, Suman will be trying to persuade the non-officials of the need to give higher priority to social sector schemes. He should not assume, even before trying, that the non-officials will not take his advice. He would succeed partially even if they reduce some outlay on irrigation and divert it to education or health. In a democratic set up, one has to rely on discussions and negotiation. In any case, under the Panchayat system, as decision-making powers on policy matters rest with non-officials, he should not, as a disciplined officer, defy them in this matter.

The last option is a form of passive or fatalistic behaviour. Young officers should avoid such attitudes since they will undermine their initiative in other areas where they can act. One should not resort to abstract ideas as a means of avoiding constructive action.

Process Justice

Process justice has to meet the following requirements.

(i) **Equality of access:** All those concerned or affected by decisions have to be given equal access to decision makers, information and decision processes.

(ii) **Impartiality:** Public administrators should not be biased or swayed by extraneous considerations unconnected to the merits of the matter.

(iii) **Transparency:** Decisions have to be taken in an open manner after informing all the stakeholders and getting their inputs. Public participation in policy matters should be encouraged. Nowadays, proposed Government policies are first placed in draft form on websites and views of stakeholders are elicited. The policy is finalized after taking into account the views expressed by the stakeholders. For example, Planning Commission placed the draft approach to the Twelfth Plan on its website to obtain the views of the public. Similarly, telecom regulator places proposed changes in regulations on its website inviting the responses of the public.

(iv) **Efficiency:** The process should not be dilatory but should result in timely decisions. Undue delay detracts from the efficiency of process justice.

(v) **Participation and humaneness:** Those who participate in the process or who are likely to be affected have to be treated with dignity and courtesy.

(vi) **Right to appeal:** Avenues should be left open so that the affected persons can appeal to higher levels in decision-making. Without such process, people will have no way of seeking redressal of decisions which they consider as unjust.

In Indian administrative system, many decisions are based on quasi judicial procedures. These are not formal legal proceedings as in courts of law. However, they follow the principles of natural justice. The persons concerned are given a hearing so that they can explain their point of view before a decision is taken. In the process outlined by Pops and Pavlak, the moral aspect of situations and the applicable moral criteria will be urged before the decision makers by the interested participants. In this respect, they resemble court proceedings. Let us note further that both models we discussed are silent about the moral criteria which need to be applied in any particular situation. In this sense, they are formal procedural methodologies. It is for the decision makers to choose the relevant moral criteria or yardsticks in any given case. We have mentioned some of them earlier.

Ethical Dilemmas

The two methods of ethical decision-making we discussed will enable administrators to navigate through situations involving ethical dilemmas. As we saw, ethical dilemmas are situations which entail conflict between two or more equally cherished moral standards. In one of the steps in Terry Cooper's method of ethical decision making, the administrators have to carefully note the moral values relevant to the problem situation. Further, while considering the possible alternative solutions to the problem, their underlying moral standards have to be made explicit. This process will lead to conscious adoption of solutions which factor in the ethical dilemmas. In the procedure which Pop and Pavlak propose, the process of decision-making will enable the stakeholders to project the alternative moral viewpoints which administrators need to consider before taking decisions.

Ethical Dilemmas: Prima Facie Principles

W.D. Ross, a famous twentieth century moral philosopher, traces moral issues or dilemmas to conflicts between certain prima facie duties. Prima facie duties are commonly accepted moral principles. "Prima facie" is a Latin expression which means "on first view". These principles point to initial moral presumptions on how we should act as moral agents. Presumptions are presuppositions or conjectures which are made in any matter. Presumption is technical concept from rules of legal evidence. Courts consider a presumption as true unless there is evidence against it.

A moral presumption means that a moral agent should act in a particular way under any set of given circumstances. But if there are special reasons or justification opposing the presumption, the moral agent can ignore the presumption. Thus, if sufficient reason or justification exists, the presumption becomes inoperative or it becomes morally permissible for the moral agent not to act in accordance with the presumption. Ethical dilemmas arise in cases in which moral presumptions following from prima facie moral duties or standards come into conflict.

We have already mentioned various common values. We recapitulate below six prima facie principles to which most moral philosophers subscribe. (Students should note that the first and second prima facie principles are separated by cases 4, 5 and 6 in the exposition). It is conflicts between these which give rise to ethical dilemmas.

1. **Principle of Honesty:** Normally, we tell truth and expect others to do so. Apart from its intrinsic value, truth-telling serves a utilitarian function because exchange of accurate information is the basis for effective collective action in human society. If everyone in a group lies to everyone else in it, common action towards any goal is impossible.

CASE 3

Kailash and Chandan are friends. Both are working in the private sector. Kailash gained experience in marketing while working in garment manufacturing firms. With this experience, Kailash began making plans for setting up a big retail store for selling readymade garments of various brands. After setting up the first store in Bhubaneswar, he planned to expand his business to other centres. His plan, however, hit a snag. Although he tied up most of the finances, he fell short of some amount.

In the course of his conversations with Chandan, Kailash broached this topic with Chandan. He did not expect help from Chandan, but was rather sharing his problem with him. Chandan's imagination being hyperactive, he got carried away. On hearing Kailash's plan, he saw visions of instantaneous success with rapid growth of swanky shops all over India. He thought that marketing guys had a way of swinging things. He thought that he should join the venture, and not miss the opportunity.

But he had no money. He knew that it would be difficult to raise large cash from his family. His wife Rukmini was frugal, and wanted to save all they could for meeting the expenses on the education and marriage of their daughters. Nor were his parents or in-laws in a position to lend Chandan money. Still, Chandan rashly promised that he would become a partner, and would contribute the needed balance capital. Kailash was pleasantly surprised, but told Chandan that the cash would be needed in six weeks. Otherwise, it would be impossible to tie bank loans and other finances.

Unfortunately, Chandan failed to borrow the money to put into the venture. The banks refused to lend money to Chandan in the absence of any security by way of shares, deposits, gold or property. Kailash had to undergo great difficulty since Chandan failed to give him the promised money.

Question

In the situation narrated in the problem what should Chandan have done?

1. He should not have joined the venture.
2. He could have joined the venture, but told kailash that he may not eventually succeed in raising the cash.
3. If we let go opportunities that come our way in life, we will make no progress in any sphere.
4. There is no harm in hoping that somehow things will work themselves out.

Discussion

The first option is the best in this case. Chandan had no resources for ploughing into the venture. As his parents and in-laws also had no resources, there was no way he could have raised the money. In such situations, it is better to be realistic, and let go certain things beyond one's reach.

The second answer choice may seem reasonable, but it is not really so. There is no point in holding out even vague hope since it is pretty clear that Chandan could not raise the resources in any case.

The third alternative is hypothetical. In the absence of financial resources, Kailash's venture is not a genuine opportunity for Chandan. For instance, real opportunity for a student is an examination which can advance his career.

The last option is unrealistic. It is typical of Micawber, a character Charles Dickens created in one of his novels. Micawber always hoped for the best and believed that things would work out to his advantage. This may not happen often in life.

CASE 4

There are situations which seem too trivial to warrant invocation of any high moral standards. Suppose X invites Y to a function at his home. X is residing far away from the city in a suburb. Y is unable to summon the necessary energy to drive through the serpentine traffic to X's residence.

Question

What should Y do in this situation?

1. Pretend to be unwell or as tied up elsewhere.
2. Agree to attend but ring up X at the last minute and make an excuse.
3. Agree to attend if the function is important.
4. Try to induce some other guest to take his car and join him.

Discussion

In (1), in order not to hurt X's sentiments, Y pretends that he is unwell. From one point of view, Y's conduct may seem an innocuous attempt to avoid embarrassment in interpersonal relations. However, rigorous moralists will hold that Y should tell X the real reason for not attending the function and bear the likely discomfort or unpleasantness. They will add that convenient lies are habit forming and stepping stones for more serious moral transgressions. Incidentally, professional ethics or rules governing official conduct presuppose truth telling as an invariant norm. Exceptions, if any, can be condoned in non-official contexts.

The second alternative is worse than the first one. For in this case, X would have made arrangements and spent money in anticipation of Y's visit.

The third alternative is the best since one is expected not to skip major social functions. One has to undergo the necessary trouble which such attendance entails. If the function is minor, Y can frankly tell X of his difficulty in negotiating through heavy traffic.

The fourth option is undesirable. The other guest will also suffer the same irritation as X in driving through heavy traffic. X will be transferring his problem to someone else. It also shows an undesirable trait of freeloading or lack of self-reliance.

CASE 5

One textbook example of ethical dilemma is of a bystander who watches an innocent man trying to escape from thugs intent on killing him. On being questioned by the thugs about the whereabouts of the innocent man, the bystander misleads them by pointing towards a direction quite different from the actual as the route taken by the innocent man. Consider the following ways of looking at the bystander's conduct.

Question

What would be the most appropriate one?

1. The action of the bystander is correct.
2. The action of the bystander though appropriate from commonsense point of view violates a moral principle.
3. The action of the bystander is improper.
4. This is a moral quibble or puzzle not worth troubling about.

Discussion

The first response is correct. In our discussion of Kantianism, we mentioned that Kant would convict the bystander of a moral lapse. Ross takes a different view here. This example shows a conflict between two norms: truth telling and beneficence or in simpler terms avoiding harm to others. Ross would say that in this situation beneficence will trump truth- telling. In other words, the moral agent will correctly see beneficence as the overriding virtue in this case.

Very few philosophers will accept that the bystander's action violates any moral principle.

As we noted above, most thinkers will regard the third option as inappropriate. It is not in line with what philosophers call 'the commonsense of humanity'. Ross has provided the theoretical justification for adopting the higher moral value when two such values clash in any situation.

The fourth response is off the mark. We should not (at least in theoretical studies) ignore any problem even if it seems purely imaginary or even eccentric. Progress in Ethics or in any other subject happens as a result of examination of various problems from a logical point of view. Even problems that seem to be devoid of substance should be logically scrutinized.

2. **Principle of Promise-Keeping:** We have to keep our promises in official, social and family life. In official business or transactions, promises are embodied in contracts. Honouring legally made contracts is an ethical norm for public organizations. But contracts are difficult legal instruments, and often lead to litigation on grounds of breach of conditions. Of course, there are certain conditions which may prevent a contracting party from fulfilling his obligations. These are in the nature of 'Acts of God' over which one has no control. A contractor may enter into a contract to build within a specified period an aqueduct for a canal to cross a river. But if unexpected floods interrupt his work, he has to be given extra time, in view of this 'Act of God', to complete the work.

   ¤ In situations of ordinary life, two points concerning promise-keeping are relevant; one is what constitutes a promise; and the other is when a moral agent will be justified in breaking a promise. One clear form of promise is a direct statement by someone that he will do something. Suppose that X promises Y that he will pay his college fee for a year. If X later backs out, he will be clearly in breach. In commonsense terms, a promise made by one individual to another, induces the latter to embark on a course of action. If a promise is broken, the person who acts on that promise will suffer loss and embarrassment.

- 'Keeping promises' is a tenet which underlies the legal doctrine of estoppel. Suppose that in a matter B is led by A to believe that he will act in a particular way or will take a particular position. Based on it, B sets out on a course of action. Thereafter, looking only to his advantage, A takes a position different from the earlier position he communicated to B. A cannot do it because of the doctrine of estoppel. Or he is estopped from doing it.
- In human relationships, many promises are implied or understood. Parents can be said to have made a promise to look after their children. Similarly, husbands have made implicit promises to take care of their wives; in fact, Hindu marriage vows impose explicit duties on the husband. People have to keep promises unless they are physically or for other compelling reasons unable to do so.

3. **Principle of not harming others:** It is positively good if we help others. At a minimum, we should not harm others. Harm means both physical pain and mental trauma. The only exception to this rule is when harming others is the sole means of saving ourselves from danger. To put it differently, we can harm others while defending ourselves from their attacks.

4. **Principle of Beneficence:** This principle is another form of expressing the idea of altruism. 'Good' like 'harm' has both physical and psychological dimensions. The physical aspects of good include food, health and amenities of life. The psychological dimensions of good are security and happiness. There is one aspect which often causes confusion. Preventing others from coming to harm is an act of altruism. It does not fall under the principle which bars moral agents from harming others.

5. **Principle of Autonomy:** This is the freedom of individual human reason which Kant emphasized and which is part of Enlightenment movement. It means that men can lead their lives as they wish, provided that they do not in the process violate similar rights of others. This is another version of the democratic political value of individual freedom of action and speech. Further, as moral agents we have to permit people to make their own decisions and to live as they wish as long as they do not interfere with our exercise of our own rights.

   - This freedom has two sides to it. First, when our actions alone are enough to enable us to pursue our interests, others are precluded from interfering with our actions –a right of non-interference. Secondly, in situations in which we need the help of others, as in the case of a chronic patient who needs the help of a skilled physician, we have a right to control the actions that others take for our benefit. The patient, for example, has a right to control which procedures the physician follows to treat the ailments.

6. **Principle of Equality in Justice :** This principle is a form of the general principle that all are equal in the eye of the law. This follows also from Kant's dictum that moral rules should be universally applicable. Here, it means that the standard according to which we treat any person is the same standard that we use to treat all other people.

It does not mean that everyone should be equally treated. People enter into different types of relationships with concomitant responsibilities and duties. We recognize this and treat people differently depending on the nature of our relationship with them. We will not treat our children like acquaintances we meet on a journey.

What the principle means is that law will treat similarly placed individuals similarly. Everyone, irrespective of their background, should be treated according to the same legal standards. Of course, the police and the courts will not treat convicted criminals and ordinary citizens alike; but the same legal standards will be applied regardless of who they are.

Ethical Dilemmas and Prima Facie Principles

One can use the six prima facie principles as guides to decide moral questions. In addition, these principles can also used to explicitly define a moral dilemma in terms of conflicting principles.

CASE 6

Maria and Julie are friends who are working in a finance company. Julie comes to know that her boss Arunachalam is planning a fraud to dupe the depositors of their money. She tells Maria about it. Julie is loyal to Arunachalam, and is reluctant to make his plans public. Maria is alarmed that if Arunachalam goes through his plan, the company's financial stability will be threatened and will endanger the jobs of the employees besides ruining the depositors. She gathers courage and tips off the chief financial officer (CFO). Thereafter, the story ends happily with the CFO foiling the designs of Arunachalam.

Question

What could be the most appropriate reaction to what Maria did?

1. Maria should have kept quiet about the whole matter.
2. Maria's action is totally justified.
3. Maria has been disloyal to her friend.
4. Maria should not have become privy to the story or left it to Julie to act in whatever way she likes.

Discussion

If Maria kept quiet about the matters, CFO could not have taken the remedial actions. Many people would have been financially ruined. Hence, this alternative cannot be accepted.

Maria, as a friend of Julie, has a duty or is under an implicit promise to keep confidences or not to divulge the secrets which Julie tells her. But she is also under an obligation, according to the principle of beneficence, to prevent harm to depositors and fellow employees. So, her dilemma can be seen as a conflict between the principles of promise-keeping and beneficence. In such situations, the moral agent has to follow that moral principle which avoids or minimises possible harm. Hence, Maria's action is fully justified.

The view expressed in (3) cannot be justified. Maria had to sacrifice her obligation of keeping Julie's confidences to a higher obligation of avoiding harm to people.

Maria cannot possibly control the conversation or prevent Julie from saying whatever she wants. She can, of course, tell Julie to immediately apprise CFO about the matter. But we cannot predict what Julie would have done. Once Maria became aware of the risk, she has a responsibility to act, irrespective whatever Julie may do.

CASE 7

Vanajakshi, a police officer in control room, reaches a scene of a bad accident. Two young persons, a boy and a girl, are badly hurt. They need immediate first aid or their injuries will prove fatal. No other police patrol or ambulance can reach the site immediately. Vanajakshi has good paramedical training because of her background. She assesses that the condition of the girl is such that the probability of her singlehanded effort succeeding is slim. To whom should she attend first? This is an agonizing dilemma for her.

Question

How will you evaluate the problem?

1. Vanajakshi should toss a coin and decide whom to help.
2. Vanajakshi should help the boy first. .
3. Vanajakshi should help the boy as boys should always be given priority over girls.
4. There is no acceptable solution to the problem.

Discussion

In the first alternative, Vanajakshi is leaving the decision to the toss of a coin. In other words, no moral principle is being applied. We cannot endorse a decision which is not based on any moral criterion.

In this situation, the boy has to be helped first, because that choice is more likely to save at least one life. Should she start helping the girl first, it may so happen that both accident victims die. This kind of situation is called 'Triage' in which (as in war) wounded army men are often selected on the basis of productivity of resource and time.

In this choice, the reason given for the decision is incorrect. The reason relies on a perverse criterion of the sex of the accident victim. This perverse attitude accounts for the distortion of sex ratio now seen in many states.

It is true that in this case both accident victims deserve help. Ideally, Vanajakshi should try to help both of them. But only one victim is likely to survive with her help. She should save him. The problem has a solution.

Up till now, we have outlined prima facie moral principles, and given examples to show that moral dilemmas are situations involving conflicts of moral criteria. The next question is about the manner in which we can solve moral dilemmas. According to W.D. Ross, this can be done by looking at the morally relevant facts applicable to a situation, and then deciding which of the conflicting prima facie duties deserves priority. The prima facie duty to which the moral agent accords priority then overrides the others. It becomes the 'actual duty' of the moral agent in the situation. In many contexts, we select the appropriate moral standard unthinkingly, as in our earlier example of the bystander who lies to the thugs chasing the innocent man in order to save him.

There are, however, many situations which lead to rather intractable dilemmas in which it is hard to select one from among the competing moral standards. No simple intuitive judgments help in such cases. Moral philosophers have given ethical doctrines which can be used to resolve conflicts between moral criteria. They belong to the domain of theoretical normative ethics.

We have separately outlined two such doctrines: utilitarianism and deontological theories. We need not rehash these ideas here again. Briefly, utilitarianism recommends that course which maximizes social welfare or happiness. Rule utilitarianism is the preferred form of utilitarianism. Deontology recommends moral rules which can be applied across the board without exceptions and deviations. It replaces human inclinations with rigid adherence to duties which are universally applicable.

Frame Work for Analyzing Ethical Dilemmas

In our earlier discussion, we considered frameworks which public servants can use for taking decisions involving ethical situations. Those frameworks also cover ethical dilemmas. Now, we outline a framework from Harold Gortner's *Ethics for Public Managers.* It is from the chapter "Analyzing and Resolving Ethical Dilemmas".

Answers to the following questions will show whether or not the problem is an ethical dilemma.

(i) Is there a conflict between important moral standards in this case?

(ii) Can the values in conflict be identified straightaway or is it necessary to carry out further analysis to find them?

(iii) Is it necessary to analyze the matter further or to make a quantitative study to determine the values which need priority?

The following points need to be studied to arrive at a morally sound decision.

(i) The law. What is the direction of action which relevant laws indicate in this case?

(ii) The philosophical and cultural background. Philosophical and cultural ideas lead to ethical perceptions and what are regarded as appropriate responses. What light is thrown on this case by such philosophical and cultural ideas?

(iii) Professionalism. What are the inputs which are necessary in this case from specialists and general administrators? In government decisions, whether in moral or other contexts, the relevant professional inputs have to be brought in.

(iv) Organizational dynamics. Is the problem traceable in any way to the organization or its personnel? As we note in the chapters on corruption, many problems of citizens originate in the 'mindset' of Police Station house Officers, Village revenue officials and field level public works engineers.

(v) Personal aspects. This refers to introspection by decision makers. They have to ask themselves: "What do we need to know about ourselves to properly handle this moral dilemma?"

Summary

- Ethical dilemmas are situations in which decisions involve conflicts between two or more moral principles. In these situations, moral agents (who have to make decisions) find themselves in a quandary since they have to choose between two ethical norms ($N_1$and N_2) which have equal status.
- Situations which involve issues of right and wrong are ethical situations.
- Ethical situation involves actions and decisions which are based on a moral agent's choice and volition and which significantly affect other individuals. In addition, ethical situations involve application of norms, standards, criteria or principles in decision-making.
- Dennis P. Wittmer defines an ethical situation essentially as one in which ethical dimensions are relevant and deserve consideration in making some choice that will have significant impact on others.
- According to Rest, ethical dimensions are those norms and principles that "provide the basic guidelines for determining how conflicts in human interests are to be settled and for optimizing mutual benefit of people living together in groups".
- In addressing ethical dilemmas, government servants can be guided by normative theories, decision making models and decision processes. Normative principles help in determining what should be done and what is the correct course of action.
- Ethical decision making in public sphere requires detailed analysis of the situation and identification of the norms and criteria that apply to it. Standards and norms provide guidance to a decision and constitute its rationale. It is application of principles which makes decisions consistent, coherent and predictable.
- Terry Cooper has reduced ethical decision making to a series to steps which begin with identifying the problem and end with its resolution.
- These are:

  (i) perception or recognition of an ethical problem

  (ii) fully describing the situation

  (iii) spelling out clearly the moral issues and moral norms involved in the situation

  (iv) visualizing the possible alternatives

  (v) evaluating the alternatives

  This process involves four steps which are interactive.

  (a) Identifying the moral principles involved in each alternative

  (b) Analyzing the extent to which each alternative can withstand criticism

  (c) Considering to what extent higher moral principles apply to the situation

  (d) Examining to what extent each alternative reflects on the decision maker's image

  (vi) resolution of the problem

- The solution is likely to be a compromise on the whole more desirable than undesirable.
- Gerald pops and Thomas Pavlak, in The Case for Justice: Strengthening Decision Making in Public Administration have proposed another method based on procedures of justice.
- The criteria which Pops and Pavlak suggest are outcome or distributive justice and process or procedural justice.
- Outcome justice has to: follow facts of the case; follow public policy; comply with the formal canons of justice; strike a balance between strict adherence to rules and exercise of discretion; take decisions which serve the people; and balance the interests of individuals and society.
- Process justice involves: equality of access; impartiality; transparency; efficiency; participation and humaneness; and right to appeal.
- W.D. Ross traces moral issues or dilemmas to conflicts between certain prima facie duties. Prima facie duties are commonly accepted moral principles.
- A moral presumption means that a moral agent should act in a particular way under a set of given circumstances. But if there are special reasons or justification opposing the presumption, the moral agent can ignore the presumption.
- There are six prima facie principles to which most moral philosophers subscribe: honesty; promise-keeping; not harming others; beneficence; autonomy of reason (Moral agent has to think for himself); and equality before law.
- These principles can also be used to explicitly define a moral dilemma in terms of conflicting principles.
- A moral agent has to accord priority to one of the conflicting principles based on the specific circumstances of an ethical dilemma.
- Framework for analyzing ethical dilemmas: The following will show if there is an ethical dilemma.
- (a) Conflict between important moral standards; (b) Ease or difficulty in identifying values in conflict and (c) whether a quantitative study is necessary
- The other aspects which need consideration are: law; philosophical and cultural background; professionalism; organizational dynamics; and personal aspects.

PRACTICE QUESTIONS

1. How will you define an ethical dilemma?
2. What are the steps involved in resolving an ethical dilemma?
3. Give three examples of situations which involve ethical dilemmas.
4. What are the principles of substantial justice and procedural justice applicable to resolution of ethical problems?

5. How does W. D. Ross visualize the problem of moral dilemmas?
6. Describe the analytical framework which can help government servants in handling ethical questions?
7. Are ethical dilemmas which philosophers discuss too remote from administrative situations? Discuss.

REFERENCES

¤ John S. Mackenzie, M.A., A Manual of Ethics
¤ William Frankena, Ethics
¤ Terry l. Cooper, Handbook of Administrative Ethics (A collection of 34 essays by eminent public administration theorists) Consult relevant articles.

Codes of Ethics and Codes of Conduct

INTRODUCTION

We begin our discussion with codes of ethics. After outlining this concept, we explain the difference between codes of ethics and codes of conduct. We then examine two types of ethics: (i) ethics of professions and (ii) ethics of civil services. We outline the general principles of professional ethics and illustrate them with examples of codes of nursing and accounting professions. Thereafter, we consider general principles and approaches to public service ethics. We discuss civil service ethics using codes of conduct which govern All India Service officers. Finally, we consider the ethical codes recommended for government servants.

Ethical codes have been in existence since ancient times. They underpinned ancient religion and society. Ten Commandments, for example, belong to the religious code of Jews. Buddhism has ethical codes for householders, monks and nuns. The ancient Greek city state, Athens, had its code covering culture and politics. Ethical codes are systems of morals which cover many aspects of life. They usually consist of general obligations and admonitions, or what one should do and refrain from doing.

CODES OF ETHICS AND CODES OF CONDUCT

The Distinction between the Above

Let us examine the idea of an ethical code in a little detail, and differentiate it from a code of conduct. There is a tendency to use the two terms interchangeably. Codes of ethics usually contain general values while codes of conduct clearly spell out the principles which are derived from values. In the words of Jeremy Bentham, a principle is "a general law or rule that guides behaviour or decisions," whereas values articulate "an aspiration of an ideal moral state."

On the connection between values and principles in the domain of public administration, Terry Cooper says:

An ethical principle is a statement concerning the conduct or state of being that is required for the fulfilment of a value; it explicitly links a value with a general mode of action. For example, justice may be considered a significant value, but the term itself does not tell us what rule for conduct or state of society would follow if we include justice in our value system. We would need a principle of justice to show us what pattern of action would reflect justice as a value. A common form of the justice principle is "Treat equals equally and unequals unequally".

We might interpret this principle as meaning that all adult citizens have to be treated alike with the same political rights and obligations. If one is allowed to vote, then all must be allowed to vote.

Nowadays many companies post ethical codes on their websites. A code of ethics will first specify values that underlie the code and will describe a company's obligations to its stakeholders. It will describe how the company conducts its business. It will describe the manner in which the company proposes to implement its values and vision. It will guide the staff about the company's ethical standards and on how to achieve them. In contrast, a code of conduct is generally addressed to and meant for the use of employees alone. It usually lists unacceptable behaviours or actions; employees have to obey the code; and it may be silent on values.

Values are general moral obligations; principles are the expected ethical conditions or behaviours which follow from values. Values refer to political and social visions and exalted goals which societies seek to achieve. In contrast, codes of conduct have a narrow focus. Codes of conduct are particular rules of conduct either imposed from higher levels of an organization or voluntarily accepted as the requirements of a profession or occupation.

A code of ethics differs from a code of conduct in another way. A code of ethics or a code of morality has a wide canvas. It may virtually cover all aspects of a man's life. It will contain prescriptions and prohibitions which cover one's personal, social, economic, political and religious life. Codes of ethics apply to the culture, education, and religion of a whole society. Codes of conduct generally cover an individual's official or professional conduct.

CODES AND LAWS

The term 'code' is sometimes used to refer to a law. Thus we can speak of the Indian Penal Code, the Code of Criminal Procedure, or the Bombay Land Revenue Code. These are examples of laws. They are distinct from ethical codes and codes of conduct. In the ancient times, there was a famous Hammurabi Code. It was a collection of laws and edicts of the ancient Babylonian king Hammurabi. It contained legal procedure and penalties covering unjust accusations, false testimony, miscarriage of justice and other rules which sought to establish "stable government and good rule," so that "the strong may not oppress the weak". However, neither codes of ethics nor codes of conduct are normally considered as Code of conduct prescribed for All India Services officers is (legally speaking) a set of rules made under the All India Services Act.

To pursue the matter a little further, violation of a code of ethics involves no legal penalties. Of course, some acts (such as theft) are forbidden both by law and ethical codes. In that case one is liable to punishment. Further, violation of an official code of conduct is not a legal offence except in so far as it also violates a law. Violations of code of conduct constitute breaches of officially prescribed rules. In those cases, the concerned individual can be punished only under the provisions of conduct rules. In other words, he can be penalized by his employer, that is government in this case. Such offences are not criminal offences but are administrative lapses.

Codes of conduct broadly cover two areas: (i) public service and (ii) professions and occupations. Before examining these, let us note an ancient example of code of ethics. This is from the ancient city state of Athens, and its great ruler Pericles proclaimed it. Incidentally, Pericles created the first system of merit based public service with salary payments.

The Athenian Code

The Athenian Oath reads as follows:

- ¤ We will never bring disgrace on this our City by an act of dishonesty or cowardice.
- ¤ We will fight for the ideals and Sacred Things of the City both individually and collectively.
- ¤ We will revere and obey the City's laws, and will do our best to promote a like reverence and respect in those above us who are prone to annul them or set them at naught.
- ¤ We will strive increasingly to quicken the public's sense of civic duty.
- ¤ Thus in all these ways we will transmit this City, not only not less, but greater and more beautiful than it was transmitted to us.

This oath is a value system. It sets out a general vision and differs from a code of conduct. Thinking of Indian polity, we can regard the provisions included in the Directive Principles of the Constitution as forming an ethical political code.

Professional Codes of Conduct

Now, we will look at professional codes in general. These are often regulations which are voluntarily adopted by members of various professions and occupations. They define the standard practices which all members follow to ensure uniformity and acceptable quality of service in order to maintain their reputation and credibility. For example, various professionals such as nurses, doctors, engineers, accountants, auditors and lawyers have professional codes. Such standards, also known as professional standards, are sometimes prescribed by regulatory agencies for some professions.

One of the earliest professional codes is the Hippocratic Oath which physicians follow to this day. Hippocrates was a physician of ancient Greece, and prescribed rules which cover a physician's responsibilities towards patients and patient confidentiality. One part of the Oath says: "*Into whatever houses I enter, I will go into them for the benefit of the sick, and will abstain from every voluntary act of mischief and corruption*".

PROFESSIONAL ETHICS

Introduction

Professional ethics cover the personal and job-related standards of behaviour expected of professionals. Professionals possess and use specialized knowledge and skill. The manner of using such knowledge while providing a service to the public is considered a moral issue and is termed professional ethics. Professionals can make informed judgments in various situations based on their skills. The general public is unable to make such decisions for want of relevant training.

Many professional organizations define their ethical approach in terms of the following principles:

- Honesty
- Integrity
- Transparency
- Accountability
- Confidentiality
- Objectivity
- Respectfulness
- Obedience to the law

The International Federation of Accountants, in *International Good Practice Guidance, Defining and Developing an Effective Code of Conduct for Organizations*, defines a professional code as: "*Principles, values, standards, or rules of behaviour that guide the decisions, procedures and systems of an organization in a way that (a) contributes to the welfare of its key stakeholders, and (b) respects the rights of all constituents affected by its operations.*"

Implementation and Regulation

Implementation of Professional Ethics

Professional associations devise codes of practice which their members must follow. The purpose of the codes is to prevent exploitation of clients and to safeguard the integrity of the profession. The codes protect both the clients and the practitioners of the profession. Disciplinary codes enable the profession to prescribe standards of conduct and ensure that individual practitioners meet these standards. If individual practitioners fail to observe the standards, they face disciplinary action. Professionals who act conscientiously will feel reassured that they will not be undercut by less scrupulous colleagues. And the public will retain its faith in the profession and will continue to engage the professional practitioners.

Internal Regulation

There is a danger that self regulation in a profession can lead to self serving behaviour. The governing bodies can become lax in enforcing the codes. This can happen in professions where a small number of practitioners hold scarce knowledge. In such cases, government has to create non partisan public regulators. Many countries have provided for some statutory regulation of professional ethical standards in such areas like nursing and midwifery as in England and Wales. Failure to comply with standards can invite prosecution.

Two Examples of Professional Codes

We will now look briefly at two professional codes. It is pointless to get into details which are relevant only to the practitioners with relevant knowledge. The idea is to get a feel for what a professional code covers. The codes open with a preamble which sets out the values, mission and vision of the professional body. It is followed by sections which state the items of the code or the individual prescriptions and prohibitions. First, we briefly consider the international code of ethics for nurses.

An international code of ethics for nurses was first adopted by the International Council of Nurses (ICN) in 1953. It has been revised from time to time, the last being in 2012.

(i) Preamble of Nurses' Code

Nurses have four fundamental responsibilities: to promote health, to prevent illness, to restore health and to alleviate suffering. The need for nursing is universal. Inherent in nursing is a respect for human rights, including cultural rights, the right to life and choice, to dignity and to be treated with respect. Nursing care is respectful of and unrestricted by considerations of age, colour, creed, culture, disability or illness, gender, sexual orientation, nationality, politics, race or social status. Nurses render health services to the individual, the family and the community and coordinate their services with those of related groups.

The Code of Ethics for Nurses has four principal elements that outline the standards of ethical conduct. One deals with nurses and people. The second part deals with nurses and practice. The third deals with nurses and their professional knowledge. The final part deals with nurses and co-workers.

(ii) US Code of Accountants

Next, we look at the code of conduct which covers the profession of accountants in US. It requires members to comply with the following fundamental principles:

(a) Integrity

A member shall be straightforward and honest in all professional and business relationships.

(b) Objectivity

A member shall not allow bias, conflict of interest or undue influence of others to override professional or business judgments.

(c) Professional Competence and Due Care

A member shall maintain professional knowledge and skill at the level required to ensure that a client or employer receives competent professional service based on current developments in practice, legislation and techniques. A member shall act diligently and in accordance with applicable technical and professional standards when providing professional services.

(d) Confidentiality

A member shall respect the confidentiality of information acquired as a result of professional and business relationships and shall not disclose any such information to third parties without proper and specific authority, unless there is a legal or professional right or duty to disclose. Confidential information acquired as a result of professional and business relationships shall not be used for the personal advantage of the member or third parties.

(e) Professional Behaviour

A member shall comply with relevant laws and regulations and shall avoid any action that discredits the profession.

The Code recognises that circumstances may arise in which members face difficulties in complying with the fundamental principles. It is impossible to define every situation that creates difficulties for compliance with the fundamental principles and specify the necessary corrective measures. Further, as work assignments and the nature of difficulties vary, different safeguards may be needed. Therefore, the Code establishes a conceptual framework that requires a member to identify, evaluate, and address threats to compliance with the fundamental principles. The conceptual framework approach assists members in complying with the ethical requirements of the Code and in meeting their responsibility to act in the public interest. It accommodates many variations in circumstances that create threats to compliance with the fundamental principles and can deter a member from concluding that a situation is permitted if it is not specifically prohibited.

As we saw, a code of practice is adopted by a profession to regulate that profession. A code of practice can also be called a code of professional responsibility. It may discuss knotty questions and dilemmas that the professionals can face and throw light or give guidance on such matters. It can make clear what behaviour is considered 'ethical' or 'correct' or 'right' in the circumstances.

PROFESSIONAL RESPONSIBILITY

We will consider two examples to show how professional responsibilities far exceed those of lay men or general public. After a car accident, a passing pedestrian cannot be held responsible for saving the accident victim. He will be expected to call or inform the emergency service providers. An ordinary person has no medical knowledge to provide emergency treatment. But a trained doctor with necessary equipment is expected to correctly diagnose the victim's condition and carry out appropriate procedures. If a doctor fails to help in that situation, he would generally be regarded as negligent and unethical. An untrained person would not incur any blame for not acting. It is only the person with knowledge of professional skills who has to take responsibility.

Many technically qualified persons have to certify the quality and safety of equipment used in industry. Thus an environmental engineer has to certify that pollution control equipment installed in a plant will treat effluents to the standards prescribed by the pollution control board. If an environmental engineer falsely certifies that the equipment treats effluents to the required standards, he will be guilty of breach of professional code and worse. He has colluded with the owner of the industry.

Uptill now, we have looked at professional codes of conduct. They are the ground rules on which professions operate. They are the principles by which any profession swears. Code of conduct, together with possession of specific domain knowledge, is the basis of claims to professionalism. A professional code of conduct consists of both ethical principles and the best perceived ways of performing professional tasks.

CODES OF CONDUCT FOR CIVIL SERVANTS

General Principles and Approach

We will now consider codes of conduct in the sphere of public service. In recent times, with changing theoretical approaches to public administration and higher expectations from public servants, codes of conduct in public sphere assumed greater importance. Codes of conduct have existed in Indian administrative system since long. They serve the following purposes:

- Codes of Conduct increase the possibility that government servants will act in public interest and will avoid improper forms of behaviour.

- ¤ By continuously comparing their conduct against prescribed norms, civil servants get into the habit of doing the right things.
- ¤ Codes of conduct express the commitment of civil servants to certain moral standards.
- ¤ The codes set standards for public servants and express their special responsibility as members of civil administrative system.
- ¤ Codes of conduct can prove effective by appealing to one's pride and moral sense or by creating a sense of remorse for wrong doing.

International organizations have recognised the usefulness of codes of conduct in international anti-corruption agreements. The U.N. Convention against Corruption (2003) recognised a public service code as necessary for prevention of corruption:

States must endeavour to ensure that their public services are subject to safeguards that promote efficiency, transparency, and recruitment based on merit. Once recruited, public servants should be subject to codes of conduct, requirements for financial and other disclosures, and appropriate disciplinary measures. Transparency and accountability in matters of public finance must also be promoted, and specific requirements are established for the prevention of corruption, in the particularly critical areas of the public sector, such as the judiciary and public procurement. Those, who use public services, must expect a high standard of conduct from their public servants.

The motto that "public service is a public trust" recognises that compared to ordinary citizens, public servants enjoy many powers and privileges. Hence, codes of conduct for civil servants impose special obligations and restrictions on exercise of public power and authority. Codes of conduct are normally written documents. Besides the explicit codes, there are implicit unwritten norms too. Service or regimental traditions in the army fall in this category. They are found in expressions like 'not done' or 'not cricket'.

Seven Principles of Public life

The commonly stated principles of public service include: avoiding use of public office for private gain (integrity), displaying impartiality in performing duties (objectivity), and the concept of public service being a public trust (probity and effectiveness). Together these define a common mission for public servants. One famous example of an Ethics Code comprises the Seven Principles of Public Life which the Committee on Standards in Public Life in Great Britain formulated. Prime Minister John Major created the committee in 1994 with wide terms of reference: "*To examine current concerns about standards of conduct of all office holders of public office, including arrangements relating to financial and commercial activities, and make recommendations as to any changes in present arrangements which might be required to ensure the highest standards of propriety in public life.*" It defined office holders widely as including all elected officials and civil servants at the national and local levels.

The 'Seven Principles of Public Life' which the Committee recommended should apply to all in the public service consist of the following.

Selflessness

Holders of public office should act sohlely in terms of the public interest. They should not do so in order to gain financial or other benefits for themselves, their family or their friends.

Integrity

Holders of public office should not place themselves under any financial or other obligation to outside individuals or organisations that might seek to influence them in the performance of their official duties.

Objectivity

In carrying out public business, including making public appointments, awarding contracts, or recommending individuals for rewards and benefits, holders of public office should make choices on merit.

Accountability

Holders of public office are accountable for their decisions and actions to the public and must submit themselves to whatever scrutiny is appropriate to their office.

Openness

Holders of public office should be as open as possible about all the decisions and actions that they take. They should give reasons for their decisions and restrict information only when the wider public interest clearly demands.

Honesty

Holders of public office have a duty to declare any private interests relating to their public duties and to take steps to resolve any conflicts arising in a way that protects the public interest.

Leadership

Holders of public office should promote and support these principles by leadership and example.

Differences in Codes of Conduct

The purpose of codes of conduct is mainly to forestall undesirable conduct such as conflict of interest, self-dealing, bribery, and abuse of public office. Codes can be either short or long; but they tend to be quite detailed. Their emphasis is normally on prohibiting various types of undesirable conduct.

The types of civil service misconduct can change over time. The following "Duties of Public officials" which the US postmaster General Amos Kendall issued in 1829 (following major scandals) cover mainly office discipline. In contrast, modern codes of conduct are longer and contain many generic rules. Generic rules are general principles each of which covers many individual instances.

I. *Every clerk will be in his room, ready to commence business, at nine o'clock A.M., and will apply himself with diligence to the public service until Three o'clock P.M.*

II. *Every clerk will hold himself in readiness to discharge any duty which may be required of him in office hours or out, in no case where by labouring a short time after office hours an account can be closed or a citizen released from attendance at this city, must he refrain from continuing his labours after three o'clock.*

III. *Newspapers or books must not be read in the office unless connected directly with the business in hand, nor must conversation be held with visitors or loungers except upon business which they may have with the office.*

IV. *Gambling, drunkenness, and irregular and immoral habits will subject any clerk to instant removal.*

V. *The acceptance of any present or gratuity by any clerk from any person who has business with the office, or suffering such acceptance by any member of his family, will subject any clerk to instant removal.*

VI. *The disclosure to any person out of the office of any investigation going on, or any facts ascertained in the office, affecting the reputation of any citizen, is strictly prohibited without leave of the Auditor.*

VII. *No person will be employed as a clerk in this office who is engaged in other business. Except the attention which the families of clerks require, it is expected that all their time, thoughts, and energies will be devoted to the public service.*

VIII. *Strict economy will be required in the use of the public stationery or other property. No clerk will take paper, quills, or anything else belonging to the government from the office for use of himself, family, or friends.*

The points of this code of conduct are still valid today. Codes of conduct may range over a wide spectrum. At one extreme, are integrity based codes; at the other are compliance based codes. The integrity based codes merely outline the desired values. The civil servants are expected to imbibe the values and convert them into suitable behavioural principles of conduct. Some OECD nations and Australia follow this pattern.

Compliance based systems contain detailed rules of conduct, listing mainly the impermissible types of conduct. Those who infringe the rules invite disciplinary action. One criticism made against such rules is that they secure compliance at a minimal level. They generally do not inspire government servants to aim at higher standards.

Official codes of conduct in India have a long history. Without going too far back into it, we may note that in 1930s, a compendium of instructions containing 'do's and don'ts' was issued and collectively called 'Conduct Rules'. The compendium was given the shape of distinct rules in 1955. The Santhanam Committee recommended considerable enlargement of such rules. The Central Civil Services (Conduct) Rules (1964) and similar rules applicable to members of the All India Services and employees of various State Governments are based on them. These rules have been updated to include additional norms of behaviour which cover: courteous behavior towards people and their elected representatives eschewing dowry practice; avoiding any form of sexual harassment of women employees; and not employing children below 14 years of age as domestic help. These reflect the changing, often increasing expectations of society, from the civil services.

Specific Content of Codes of Conduct

Central Government has prescribed conduct rules for its officers and staff. Different conduct rules apply to different categories of officers belonging to All India Services (IAS/IFS/IPS/Indian Forest Service), Central Services (such as Indian Revenue Service and Indian Information Service) and to Central Secretariat Service. State governments have made conduct rules for those serving under them. However, the conduct rules for different services under the Centre and the States are similar.

The conduct rules are usually written in semi-legalistic bureaucratic language. They are laced with many explanations and clarifications. Many rules have been reformulated. We need not, however, concern ourselves with these minutiae. It is sufficient for our purpose to follow the nature of the conduct rules. For this purpose, we will consider the All India Services conduct rules. As mentioned earlier, conduct rules for other services are broadly similar.

Using the Best Judgement

While performing their official duties and exercising their powers, officers have to act in their best judgment. In other words, they have to do what they think is true and correct in any particular matter (or case in official parlance). They should act independently according to applicable rules and regulations, unmindful of any external influences. But if higher officers give them oral or written directions, they have to follow such orders.

Governments are hierarchical organizations. No government official acts singly - except when he/she is hearing matters in a quasi-judicial capacity. In many situations, administrative decision-making mimics (partly) judicial procedures. For example, while hearing an appeal from the order of an Income tax officer, Deputy Income tax commissioner decides on his own without inputs from others in his office. But many matters are processed from the lower levels of hierarchy and are decided at a higher level. Such decisions and the underlying reasons are recorded in writing in files.

Case Studies

CASE 1

Babu Rao is an officer on special duty in the project analysis wing of the Finance department. His job is to look at the financial and economic viability of projects. Given the available budget, the projects with higher returns are picked up for funding or seeking aid from external donors. Although the procedure is involved, its principles are simple. The analysts calculate for each year of the project's useful life, the expected expenditures and revenues. As these flows occur in different years, they have to be made comparable. For this purpose, the revenue and expenditure flows are discounted using a particular interest rate. Discounting means that their magnitudes are reduced by using a factor based on the interest rate. Due to discounting, the actual numbers of future streams of expenditure and income become smaller. The same numbers of expenditure and income of say year 5 will become smaller than those of year 3. The present values of future income and expenditure depend on two factors: interest rate and the future year in which they occur. In this process, the present value of the numbers of later years in future becomes less than that of earlier years in future. These income (benefit) and expenditure (cost) streams, which are reduced to their present values, are added and compared. In short, the projects which have higher benefit-cost ratios in terms of present values are selected for funding.

In this process, a pet project of a powerful minister is dropped. The incensed minister calls Babu Rao for discussion. Babu Rao tries to explain things. But the minister berates him for slashing the solid Rs 100 crore revenue of seventh year to almost Rs 15 crore. After some discussion, the minister realises that if the interest rate used for discounting expenditure and revenue flows is reduced, the project will become viable. He asks Babu Rao to cut that rate. Babu Rao refuses saying that the rate is prescribed by the Department of Economic Affairs. But the minister still insists that the discount rate should be reduced.

Question

What should Babu Rao do in the above circumstances?

1. Follow minister's orders.
2. Babu Rao should give up his narrow accounting perspective and adopt a wider social point of view.
3. He should politely express his inability to follow the minister's instructions.
4. He should tell the minister that he would write to the Department of Economic Affairs seeking a lowering of the rate of interest.

Discussion

Babu Rao is a professional in finance area. He has to follow the prescribed procedures of project analysis. Professionals like doctors and engineers have to follow the relevant technical codes in their work area. Babu Rao cannot be guided by the minister's unprofessional advice in this matter. So this option is wrong.

The second alternative confuses two distinct matters. Babu Rao, while discharging his functions as a finance professional, has to go by his professional training in accounting and related subjects. As a citizen, he can of course adopt whatever social philosophy appeals to him. His role as a finance specialist should not be confused with his role as a citizen. Hence this choice is inappropriate.

The third option is the correct one. Babu Rao has to provide professional inputs into decision making based on his knowledge and best judgement. He cannot substitute the minister's judgement in place of his judgement. The Department of Economic Affairs gave the discount rate which Babu Rao used. Incidentally, the rate measures the relative scarcity of capital in Indian economy and is a measure of the value or cost of capital. While evaluating projects, this uniform rate has to be used. It cannot be changed at the minister's bidding. Babu Rao should not quarrel with the minister, but simply indicate that he is bound to use that rate.

The last alternative is also inappropriate. He cannot write to the Department of Economic Affairs to change the rate. It is decided after detailed consultations with monetary and fiscal authorities and expert agencies. In addition, it is not within his province to make such proposals.

Written Orders

There is a rule which prescribes that when oral orders are given, they should soon thereafter be authenticated by the officer who issued them. This rule is a fall out of the Emergency period under Shrimati Indira Gandhi. Justice Shah Commission inquired into various controversial happenings during Emergency. Many officers then took the plea that they followed the orders of higher officers. The higher officials, as it usually happens in such contingencies, washed their hands of the matters.

To avoid this problem and fix accountability, Shah Commission recommended that officers who issue oral orders should confirm them later in writing. There is another rider to this rule which says that it should not be used to toss up matters which lie within one's assigned powers. The point here is that a civil servant should not evade responsibility.

CASE 2

Question

The State Civil Supplies Corporation has been entrusted with the task of moving kerosene needed for PDS system from district to tehsil and sub-tehsil towns. For this purpose, it had to finalize transport tenders for each district. In one of the districts, the tender rates received were very high and the managing director of the corporation decides to call fresh tenders. However, in tenders received initially which the managing director (MD) decides to reject as too high, the lowest rate is from the supporter of the cabinet minister for civil supplies. Citing the need of rushing supplies urgently to rural areas, the minister asks the managing director to accept the lowest tender. The minister further argues that it would be procedurally correct. Fearing likely audit objections and their fallout, the managing director refuses to do so. When the minister insists, the managing director asks him to send him written orders. The minister accuses the officer of being bureaucratic and sticky.

What can we say about the reaction of the MD in this case?

1. The MD's behaviour is bureaucratic and rule bound.
2. The MD's stand is justified.
3. The MD is ignoring the inconvenience his action will cause to public.
4. The MD has first delayed procurement, and is then creating further difficulties.

Discussion

The first view is unjustified. It just uses adjectives to criticise the MD's action without looking at all the circumstances. Many public systems are bureaucratic organisations, and there is no point in using the term in an abusive sense. It is also true that public systems are bound by rules. But they are necessary in order to secure financial propriety and to ensure equity.

The MD is justified in asking the minister for written orders. The minister is not supposed to interfere in the internal working of the corporation which is regulated by the Companies Act. Further, it is not necessary to accept the lowest rate if all the rates are high, and if the lowest rate is also above the market rate. The MD has to ascertain whether the rates received in response to the tender are reasonable. Acceptable rates have to be in line with market rates. In the absence of written orders from the minister, the MD will be held responsible for losses caused due to payment of higher than market rates. He will be left holding the can.

The third view is also unacceptable. The MD is not deliberately causing inconvenience to people. Because of the high rates received, he is forced by rules to retender. The decision was forced upon him. He cannot flout the prescribed rules.

The last view is irrelevant to the point at issue. The simple point is whether or not to accept the tenders which are above market rates. This view obfuscates the issue. Incidentally, it is a common weakness of our countrymen to ignore main issues in any debate and chase irrelevant or peripheral points. There is nothing in the narration to suggest that the MD delayed matters.

Integrity and Devotion

Officers have to ensure the integrity and devotion to duty of Government servants under their administrative control. Integrity mainly connotes honesty in a wide sense. A civil servant should not only refuse bribes (or illegal gratification in official parlance) but also display intellectual honesty. 'Lack of devotion to duty' has many manifestations. The conduct rules mention habitual failure to complete work with expected quality within prescribed time as one such manifestation. Here, the conduct rules indirectly refer to commitment to duty expected of a civil servant. There is also a reference to the high work standard and diligence expected from civil servants.

Reporting Details of Properties and Transactions

The conduct rules contain provisions which track the property and financial dealings of civil servants. Their purpose is to ensure that civil servants do not amass wealth (or acquire properties disproportionate to their known sources of income) by misusing their official position. A government servant cannot acquire any immovable property by any means (such as purchase, lease or gift) in his name or in that of any of his family members without government approval. Nor can he sell or dispose of any immovable property without similar approval. Civil servants are prohibited from speculating on stock markets and from undertaking investment and lending and similar financial operations. They are also prohibited from undertaking any private trade or business. They have to submit every year an annual property statement showing all their properties.

These are important provisions for ensuring the honesty of civil servants. These rules are like disclosure norms. Civil servants are under an obligation to intimate government of their property transactions and property holdings. This procedure also ensures transparency. It also acts as a deterrent to wrongdoing. For, under the Prevention of Corruption Act, civil servants are liable to prosecution if they own assets disproportionate to their known sources of income.

Bar on Influence Peddling

The conduct rules prohibit civil servants from using their influence to secure jobs for their family members in companies, firms or non government organizations. By doing so, a government servant places himself under an obligation to private persons or companies. This will jeopardize his independence and neutrality. Such practices can lead to 'crony capitalism' in which elites in government and individual entrepreneurs share cosy relationships. As a result, losses are caused to public exchequer through 'sweetheart deals' between government and industries it favours.

Avoiding Conflict of Interest

To avoid such perils, the conduct rules provide that civil servants should avoid getting into 'conflict of interest' situations. These are situations in which a civil servant dealing with a matter has a personal interest or stake in it. Thus, a civil servant should avoid dealing with any matter (including award of contract) relating to a private undertaking or non government organization in which a member of his family is employed or in which he has a financial interest. Similar situations arise when judges have to hear cases of individuals or firms whom they represented while practising at bar. Judges recuse themselves from such cases i.e. will not hear them.

CASE 3

Joginder served as DM in Amarpur district for quite a few years. He was an avid bridge player. He used to play bridge regularly in the Advocates' club. Many of his bridge partners were lawyers and became his close friends. Joginder later moved away from Amarpur, eventually joining the Board of Revenue as a member. As a member of the Board, Joginder had to hear appeals in land matters. It so happened that the sleepy Amarpur suddenly became an industrial hub. Its land values shot up. Joginder found to his discomfiture that his close lawyer friends from the bridge circle were appearing in the cases.

Question

What are Joginder's options in this case?

1. He should recuse himself from cases in which his close friends appear as pleaders.
2. He should simply hear the cases.
3. He should hear the cases and lean towards his friends if their cases and those of their opponents are on par in terms of merits.
4. He should seek a transfer to another job because of the conflict of interest situation.

Discussion

The first approach will be the correct one. This case involves a situation of conflict of interest. Officials have to act and decide matters in an objective manner. However, personal feelings of officers may come into play in matters in which their relatives or friends appear as parties. The concerned officials are said to have a conflict of interest in such cases. They should avoid taking decisions in such cases.

As discussed above, the second option is impermissible.

The third alternative is worse than the second one. A judicial or quasi-judicial decision should be based on objective considerations i.e. facts of the case and applicable law. No personal factors or any ideas of veering to one side--except on the basis of facts and law--are admissible. This option will count as favouritism.

It is not necessary for Joginder to seek a transfer. Cases involving conflict will not be many. He can stay out of such cases.

Financial Propriety

Conduct rules seek to ensure that civil servants observe other norms of financial propriety in their personal conduct. They are not allowed to organize subscriptions or donations in any manner for any cause or purpose. They can, however, seek contributions to official funds (e.g. CM's Relief Fund) and for assisting people hit by natural calamities or affected by other adverse circumstances.

To prevent conflict of interest situations and to avoid possibilities of money-making through indirect means, conduct rules prohibit civil servants from accepting lavish gifts or availing hospitality from private groups. There are some exceptions which allow civil servants to accept gifts up to certain limits from near relatives on religious or social events like marriages.

Civil servants have to arrange their private finances prudently. They should not get into a state of habitual indebtedness. They can take car loans or house loans if the Equated Monthly Instalments (EMIs) are affordable. The rationale of this rule is to ensure that difficult personal finances do not tempt civil servants into improprieties.

CASE 4

Badri Prasad is a young outgoing officer. He has a naturally care free temperament. He lived in the present, enjoyed himself with little thought of future. His wife Sarojini shared his temperament and life style. They were keen on owning a plush apartment and a glitzy car. Unmindful of the financial commitments, they borrow heavily and get into large EMI payments. Then, suddenly Sarojini loses her job because of industrial recession. They find it hard to handle their personal finances. Some of their business acquaintances offer to take care of the EMI payments temporarily till the young couple get out of their financial problems. Badri and Sarojini mull over things. They decide to sell the car and slash household expenditure at least till Sarojini can get another job.

Question

What will be your advice to them?

1. They should accept the offer to temporarily tide over the difficulties.
2. Officers should not feel that business friends when they help, they will always take advantage of them later in some way.
3. They should sell the car and slash household expenditure till Sarojini gets another job.
4. They should accept the offer but keep it completely secret.

Discussion

The first option is ill advised. This will place them under obligation to their business friends. Officials are expected to keep their finances in reasonable order, and relying on others to make their EMI payments means that their household finances are in a mess.

The second formulation can be accepted as a general statement. Rich businessmen can also be generous and may want to help their young friends in financial difficulty. This general principle has to give way before specific official codes of conduct which prohibit government servants from taking monetary assistance from private persons.

The third option is the most appropriate one. Badri should not become dependent on others in this way. His friends may be well intentioned. But by accepting such help, Badri will be placing himself in a false position. In any case, if he takes such help, he will be violating his official rules of conduct. It is incumbent upon Badri and Sarojini to immediately set their financial house in order.

In the last choice, Badri and Sarojini will be violating the official code of conduct but keeping it under wraps. They are in any case violating the code of conduct. Experience shows that such attempts at secrecy often fail. People have a tendency to talk, and somehow or the other matters will leak out.

Political Neutrality

Conduct rules expressly prohibit civil servants from taking part in political activities. The purpose of such rules is to ensure the political neutrality of civil servants. No government servant can join or otherwise associate himself with any political party or any political organization. Nor can he participate, aid or support any political movement or political activity. She cannot also canvass, interfere with, or use her influence in elections at central, state or local level. Civil servants should also try to prevent their family members from joining movements which directly or indirectly try to subvert lawfully constituted governments. Naxal or Maoist movement is a case in point.

CASE 5

Rajesh Chaudhary and Vaidehi Chauhan were university friends. After Rajesh Chaudhary got into the civil service, they got married. Vaidehi's father was a prominent politician who lived in the State capital. But the young couple did not publicise the fact and kept a low profile. Vaidehi's father did not want to entangle Rajesh Chaudhary in any political matters. After a few field postings, Rajesh was transferred to the State capital. The young couple moved into Vaidehi's parental home.

Being a politician's home, it had a stream of political visitors. Rajesh initially kept himself away from the political crowd. But then he slowly became interested in the political gossip. He began mixing with the more prominent and interesting politicians. He began telling some juicy bits of political news to his service colleagues in their tea club–the time civil servants take off for official gossip. He also helped out a few politicians in some minor cases. Some of them made frivolous comments about the 'synergy' which marriage ties between families of bureaucrats and politicians can create. Vaidehi was none too pleased. Being a politician's daughter, she had sharp antenna and did not want Rajesh to be identified with any political formation. She did not want him to land in any trouble. Her father was also wary of Rajesh getting mixed up with his political pals for many of them were dubious characters. But he was hesitant to say anything to his son-in-law.

Fortunately, the matter got naturally resolved. Rajesh Chadhary's younger sister got admission in a well known business school in the city. Vaidehi persuades Rajesh to move to their small official flat which is close to the school. She tells him that his sister can study peacefully in the flat. Her father also heaves a sigh of relief.

Question

What in your view can be an appropriate response to the situation depicted in the case?

1. Vaidehi is making a mountain of a molehill.
2. The couple should not have, in the first instance, moved into Vaidehi's parental home.
3. Vaidehi's concerns are valid.
4. Civil servants cannot avoid involvement in some measure with politicians and their activities.

Discussion

The first alternative is unacceptable. There is a problem since Rajesh is developing excessive proximity with political leaders. This can create problems for him in his career in future.

The second alternative is not relevant to the issue. The problem is not that they moved into the residence of Vaidehi's parents. It is that Rajesh is getting very close to politicians whereas civil servants need to maintain some distance from them.

The whole matter may seem innocuous. But the catch is that Rajesh is getting sucked into the political arena. We are fond of listening to political gossip as the popularity ratings of political news channels attest. But civil servants have to stay away from political matters. Rajesh is young and can be led astray by political operators. Though a politician, his father-in-law was aware of the danger. Vaidehi shrewdly realised that her husband's excessive political interests may undermine his neutral image. Her anxieties are well-founded.

The last alternative makes a misleading statement. It is true that politicians and civil servants interact constantly with one another. But this should not be seen as involvement of civil servants in political affairs. Their role is different from that of political leaders. In their interactions with political leaders, officials should be politically neutral and avoid getting into political matters of any sort.

Observing Social Laws and Cultural Norms

Civil servants should meticulously follow certain social laws which people seldom observe. They should neither accept nor offer dowry. Nor should they contract a bigamous marriage, even when permissible under a religious personal law, except with government's prior sanction. They should not engage persons below 14 years of age for household work.

Civil servants have to observe certain cultural norms in their personal capacity. These cover the existing policies regarding age of marriage; preservation of the environment, wild life and cultural heritage; prevention of crimes against women; and the two children family norm.

Civil servants should never be under influence of alcohol while on duty; nor should they allow or permit an addiction to drink and drugs to affect their work. They have to scrupulously observe prohibition laws that may be in force in any State.

CASE 6

Mallikarjunam was from Kurnool district in Andhra Pradesh. His father-in-law was a large farmer. Mallikarjunam's wife was used to having household workers around her. She found it hard to manage things at their home in Bengaluru without domestic help. Her father sends ten year old Balram to assist her at home. Balram's father is a farm-worker who has been living on their land for long. She treated Balram kindly, and also sent him to school. The boy helped her in small domestic chores. As it happened, Mallikarjunam had to discipline some employees in his office for neglecting their work and trying to fleece applicants visiting the office. The disgruntled employees made a complaint that Mallikarjunam was employing and exploiting child labour.

Question

How would you respond to the situation in this case?

1. Mallikarjunam should ignore the complaints as motivated.
2. Mallikarjunam should not have employed Balram.
3. Balram is much better off in Bengaluru than in his village.
4. Mallikarjunam should inflate Balram's age in school register to avoid any legal problems.

Discussion

The first alternative is not relevant because it is not for Mallikarjunam to ignore the complaints. They have been made by disgruntled staff. Nevertheless, the facts of the matter may come for investigation. This will embarrass Mallikarjunam.

This second option is the correct one. Government officials have to carefully follow the laws and social norms. Balram is clearly under aged. He cannot be employed for any kind of work in the household of Mallikarjunam. Government officers are constantly in public gaze. Interested persons will try to exploit even minor weaknesses and lapses of government servants. They should have no chinks in their armour. They need to, in their own interest, scrupulously follow all the rules and regulations.

The third point is irrelevant. The point is not whether Balram is more comfortable in Bengaluru or in his village. The issue revolves around whether he is being employed in child labour which is prohibited by law.

The fourth alternative contains an absolutely unacceptable suggestion. If that suggestion is followed, Mallikarjunam will be compounding his original error by trying to tinker with school records.

Other Norms

There are a few more conduct rules which have to do with the civil servants' official conduct in certain spheres. They should not try to use political influence to further their career or secure 'plum' jobs. At times, some civil servants with a view to self-publicity or self-promotion get functions organized in which they are praised sky high or conferred various 'awards'. The conduct rules frown upon such ego trips or scarcely disguised self-publicity. But it seems that after the recent spate of scams, government servants have become somewhat withdrawn and are trying to fly below the radar.

As is to be expected, no government servant should criticize government policies in public. However, they can use official channels to express and share their experiences in implementing policies and programmes. Further, government servants are prohibited from divulging information which they come to know from official documents. They can do so only in court proceedings or before official committees.

Even when government servants are subjected to defamatory attacks for any of their official acts, they cannot, without government's prior approval, take recourse to court proceedings or counterattacks in press.

There are a few aspects which find no mention in conduct rules. Civil servants have to conduct themselves with decency, decorum and dignity. They should be polite and courteous to Members of Parliament, Members of Legislative Assembly and to general public. They should always be cool and composed. They have to avoid boorish conduct, especially with women. They have to be soberly dressed and well groomed (should not look like hippies!).

Readers would have noticed that the code of conduct for officials consists mainly of prohibitions than prescriptions. The code is usually a list of inappropriate behaviours or of what officials should not do. It is understood (or goes without saying) that they should perform their duties faithfully, diligently and expeditiously in public interest, uninfluenced by extraneous considerations.

CODE OF ETHICS FOR CIVIL SERVANTS

The Santhanam Committee on Prevention of Corruption (1964) remarked:

"For a country like India, development of her material resources and raising the standards of life of all classes are indeed imperative. At the same time, the deterioration in the standards of public life has to be arrested. Ways and means have to be found to ensure that idealism and patriotism have the proper place in the ambition of our youth. The lack of moral earnestness, which has been a conspicuous feature of recent years, is perhaps the greatest single factor which hampers the growth of strong traditions of integrity and efficiency."

Values like altruism and empathy for poor are hard to imbibe after joining the civil services. They need to be instilled in childhood in family and school. The Indian Public Services have many established traditions. Many of these are in the form of conventions of propriety and acceptable behaviour without formal sanctions. However, there is also a need for a higher code of ethics. For the codes of conduct, while containing some general norms like 'maintaining integrity and absolute devotion to duty' and not indulging in 'conduct unbecoming of a government servant', are generally directed towards cataloguing specific activities deemed undesirable for government servants. There is no Code of Ethics prescribed for civil servants in India although such codes exist in other countries. What we have in India are several Conduct Rules, which prohibit a set of common activities. There is, of late, a concern that more 'generic norms' are needed in addition to the conduct rules.

Public Service Bill

A draft 'Public Service Bill', now under consideration of the Ministry of Personnel, Public Grievances and Pensions, seeks to lay down a number of generic expectations from civil servants, which are referred to as "values". The salient 'values' envisaged in the Bill are:

- Allegiance to the various ideals enshrined in the preamble to the Constitution
- Apolitical functioning
- Good governance for betterment of the people to be the primary goal of civil service
- Duty to act objectively and impartially

- Accountability and transparency in decision-making
- Maintenance of the highest ethical standards
- Merit to be the criteria in selection of civil servants consistent, however, with the cultural, ethnic and other diversities of the nation
- Ensuring economy and avoidance of wastage in expenditure
- Provision of healthy and congenial work environment
- Communication, consultation and cooperation in performance of functions i.e. participation of all levels of personnel in management.

The draft Bill also envisages a Public Service Code and a Public Service Management Code laying down more specific duties and responsibilities. Violation of the Code would invite punishments akin to the current major and minor penalties. A 'Public Service Authority' is also envisaged to oversee implementation of the Code and values indicated above and to tender advice in the matter of the values and the Code. The Second Administrative Refound Commission (SARC) has recommended that there should be a set of Public Service Values which should be stipulated by law. There should be a mechanism to ensure that civil servants constantly aspire towards these values.

Summary

- Codes of ethics apply to the culture, education, and religion of a whole society. The Athenian code is an example of an ancient ethical code.
- Thinking of Indian polity, we can regard the provisions included in the Directive Principles of the Constitution as forming an ethical political code.
- Codes of conduct generally cover an individual's official or professional conduct.
- Violation of a code of ethics involves no penalties; violations of code of conduct constitute breaches of officially prescribed rules. It is considered official misconduct.
- Official codes of conduct are not laws: their violations are not criminal offences but are administrative lapses. But some violations may be grave enough to amount to criminal offences.
- A professional code can be defined as a set of: "Principles, values, standards, or rules of behaviour that guide the decisions, procedures and systems of an organization in a way that (a) contributes to the welfare of its key stakeholders, and (b) respects the rights of all constituents affected by its operations."
- Professional ethics cover the personal and job-related standards of behaviour expected of professionals.
- The standards commonly mentioned in professional codes include: honesty, integrity, transparency, accountability, confidentiality, objectivity, respectfulness and obedience to the law.

- Because of their specialized knowledge and training, professionals have to bear higher responsibility in their work areas.
- The 'Seven Principles of Public Life' enunciated by the Nolan committee are - selflessness, integrity, objectivity, accountability, openness, honesty and leadership.
- Codes of conduct for officials vary in length and content. They can also be compliance-based or integrity-based.
- Compliance-based systems contain detailed rules of conduct listing mainly the impermissible types of conduct.
- The integrity based codes merely outline the desired values. The civil servants are expected to imbibe the values and convert them into suitable behavioural principles of conduct.
- Official codes of conduct covering officers of Central services, All India services and State services are similar. They are all compliance based.
- The aspects they cover include: using one's best judgement in official matters; reliance on written orders; integrity and devotion to duty; reporting details of properties and transactions; avoiding conflict of interest; financial propriety; political neutrality; observing social laws and cultural norms; and other miscellaneous provisions.
- There have been demands in recent past for including more 'generic norms' in the codes of conduct.
- Government is mulling over a draft 'Public Service Bill'.
- Its main ingredients are - commitment to ideals of the Preamble of the constitution; apolitical functioning; good governance; objectivity and impartiality; accountability and transparency in decision-making; following high ethical standards; observing economy in expenditure; creating healthy and congenial work environment; and participatory management.

PRACTICE QUESTIONS

1. How does a code of ethics differ from a code of conduct?
2. What are the financial norms which government servants have to observe? What is the rationale of the norms?
3. "Codes of conduct for civil servants which largely consist of prohibitions on undesirable actions represent the 'low road' to ethics". Discuss.
4. What are the purposes of professional codes? How do they differ from codes for government servants?
5. "An ethical code for government servants will be no more than an expression of pious intentions". Comment.
6. "Because of spiralling levels of corruption, the codes of conduct for civil servants have to be made very stringent." Examine critically.

7. What are the main ingredients which go into civil service codes of conduct?
8. What are the principal ethical norms which should guide public life?
9. Australia and many European countries have prescribed ethical codes for public servants whereas India has prescribed codes of conduct for them. What reasons can account for this difference of approach?

REFERENCES

- Jeremy F. Flant, *Codes of ethics*
- James S. Bowman, *From Codes of Conduct to Codes of Ethics: The ASPA case*
- All India Services Conduct Rules
- Terry l. Cooper *Handbook of Administrative Ethics* (A collection of 34 essays by eminent public administration theorists).

MECHANISMS FOR FIGHTING CORRUPTION

INTRODUCTION

Corruption in administration is a many-sided phenomenon. Naturally, it provokes popular anger and revulsion. Many think that it is retarding economic growth and compromising national security. It has become a deep-seated malaise eating into the vitals of the nation.

Although corruption evokes strong feelings, it requires objective study. People generally complain about corruption in administration and politics. One form of this corruption, at the interface between administration and common citizen, is what upsets people most. Government servants at the cutting edge of administration rarely provide timely and quality service that people need. Nor do they render such services without taking money. Besides administration and politics, corruption is prevalent in private trade, industry, professions and non-governmental organizations. Corruption in all these areas needs study.

For understanding corruption and its possible remedies, we have to look at it from various angles. Successive governments since Independence have tried to grapple with corruption. The existing laws and administrative arrangements resulted from steps which various governments took to check corruption. We will, however, examine the present laws and the administrative set up without entering into detailed historical discussions.

In this chapter, we will:

¤ Define 'corruption'

¤ Try to understand its sources or roots and

¤ Discuss the main institutions which deal with corruption.

There are some issues which are at the centre in current discussions on corruption. We will consider them in the next chapter.

DEFINING CORRUPTION

The Prevention of Corruption Act does not define corruption. It lists various offences which are acts of corruption. The Central Vigilance Commission (CVC) speaks of acts which have 'vigilance angle.' In other words, these are acts of corruption. CVC's list of such activities is reproduced below.

(i) Demanding and/or accepting [by any public servant] of gratification other than legal remuneration in respect of an official act or for using his influence with any other official.

(ii) Obtaining any valuable thing, without consideration or with inadequate consideration from a person with whom he has or is likely to have official dealings or with whom his subordinates have official dealings or where he can exert influence.

(iii) Obtaining for himself or for any other person any valuable thing or pecuniary advantage by corrupt or illegal means or by abusing his position as a public servant.

(iv) Possessing assets disproportionate to his known sources of income.

(v) Cases of misappropriation, forgery or cheating or other similar criminal offences.

The preceding paragraph defines corruption in simple terms. We have simplified the language which is used in The Prevention of Corruption Act 1988 (PC Act). This Act was amended in 2018. Although the acts which constitute corruption are the same as those mentioned in the preceding paragraph, the amended Act uses different expressions to describe them. We have summarized the relevant portion of the amended Act in Box 1.

Box 1 : Use of new wording to define acts of corruption

The PC Act amendment (2018) defines acts of corruption as at (a) to (e) below. The ingredients of the acts ofcorruption are the same as before except for criminal misconduct defined in (e) below. The amendment has introduced simplicity and clarity in the language used to define acts of corruption. For describing the illegitimate payments or gains that corrupt official receive, the unamended PC Act uses expressions such as 'illegal gratification', 'other than legal remuneration', and'receiving a valuable thing or pecuniary advantage without consideration or inadequate consideration'. The amended Act uses one phrase 'undue advantage' instead.

The wrong act a public servant does in return for getting an undue advantage is defined using three ingredients:(i) doing his public duty dishonestly or improperly (ii) prompting another official to do so and (iii) not performing his public duty or prompting another official not to do it.

(a) If any public servant gets or tries to get from any person, an undue advantage, with the intention of (i)doing his public duty dishonestly or improperly or causing it to be so done, or (ii) with the intention of (ii)not performing public duty or prompting another public servant not to do it.

(b) If any public servant gets or tries to get from any person an undue advantage as a reward for doing the things mentioned in (a) (i) and (ii); or

(c) If any public servant does the things mentioned in (a) (i) and (ii) in anticipation of or in consequence ofaccepting an undue advantage from any person.

The act of corruption may precede or follow the receipt of the undue advantage or may be performed in anticipation or as a consequence of it.

The very act of getting or trying to get an undue advantage is an offence even if public servant does his duty properly. It is immaterial and makes no difference whether a public servant gets an undue advantage through a third party or directly.

Illustration. –A public servant, 'S' asks a person, 'P' to give him an amount of five thousand rupees to process his routine ration card application on time. 'S' is guilty of an offence under this section.
In the three actions mentioned above, the public servant is the actor or takes the initiative. But there are instances when a public servant or someone else could take 'undue advantage' to influence other public servants.

(d) In this form of corruption, an individual gets or tries to get for himself or for another person any undue advantage as a motive or reward. Then, by corrupt or illegal means, or by exercise of his personal influence, he induces a public servant to do a wrong thing. This consists in a public servant performing a public duty improperly ordishonestly or making another public servant to do so; or not doing his public duty or prompting another public servant to refrain from doing public duty.

(e) A public servant is guilty of criminal misconduct if he dishonestly or fraudulently misappropriates or otherwise converts for his own use any property entrusted to him or under his control as a public servant or allows any other person so to do" or "before if he intentionally enriches himself illicitly during the period of his office".

Case Studies

CASE 1

Mohit has helped a businessman by quickly settling the bills for the supplies he had made to government. The amount was large and the payment relieved the businessman from the liquidity crunch he was facing. The businessman was overwhelmed and offers gifts to Mohit as goodwill gesture. Mohit refuses them. Shortly thereafter, Mohit goes with family to a hill station where the businessman has a hotel. He conveys in advance to the businessman that he would like to stay in his hotel and checks into that hotel. The hotel management, on instructions from the businessman, treats Mohit and his family as guests and refuses to accept payment from Mohit. Mohit does not insist on making payment.

Question

Which of the following will be an appropriate view in this matter?

1. Mohit did no wrong in accepting the hospitality of the businessman.
2. Mohit should not have accepted the hospitality.
3. This issue is rather minor and involves no major issues of administrative morality.
4. Mohit did not take any money but the hotel had unoccupied rooms.

Discussion

Official codes of conduct lay down that government servants should not accept gifts in cash or kind. Availing free hospitality in a hotel amounts to acceptance of a gift in kind. Hence, this alternative is incorrect.

The second option is correct. Mohit has to follow the official code of conduct. The code prohibits acceptance of valuable gifts. Further, Mohit had official dealings with the businessman who offered him the gift. Hence, he should not have accepted the offer. In fact, this is what he did on the first occasion.

It will be improper to take a lenient view of the matter. Mohit is clearly guilty of violating an official norm. No such violation can be treated as a minor matter.

Both the points made in the last option are unacceptable. Not only cash gifts but gifts in kind also cannot be accepted by civil servants. The question whether the hotel had vacant rooms is not relevant to the issue which is about violation of code of conduct. Hence (2)

CASE 2

Anand was approached by a trader with a request to settle his sales tax cases favourably. Anand told him that the case is being handled by Ramesh, an officer in another wing of the department. The trader refers to Anand's friendship with Ramesh and asks Anand to intercede with Ramesh. Anand speaks to Ramesh and the matter gets settled. Sometime thereafter, the trader presents Anand with a costly camera.

Question

How will you evaluate Anand's conduct in this case?

1. No fault can be found with Anand's conduct.
2. Anand is guilty of violating the official code of conduct.
3. As Anand did not directly help the trader, there is no harm in his taking the camera.
4. As the camera was presented after the trader's work was done, no mala fides can be attributed in the matter to Anand.

Discussion

Alternative (1) is incorrect. Anand is in fact guilty on two counts. First, he interfered in the official work of his colleague. He used his influence with Ramesh for helping the trader. Normally, officials are not supposed to do so. Thereafter, he accepted a gift from the trader. He is guilty of corrupt practice.

As explained above, the second option is correct. By accepting the costly gift, Anand has violated the code of conduct.

The third answer choice is incorrect. Although Anand did not directly help the trader, he has used his influence for helping the trader. Even otherwise, he cannot take expensive gifts from individuals other than close family members.

The fourth option is also incorrect. So long as an officer accepts a costly gift, it makes no difference whether he takes it before or after an official dealing.

CASE 3

Veerendranath is married into a wealthy family. His father-in-law keeps giving him lavish cash gifts on various occasions. He used to put them into bank deposits and the amount has grown steadily. Someone complains that Veerendranath has been quietly making money, and that his savings are very large compared to his pay.

Question

How will you respond?

Is Veerendranath to blame?

1. Veerendranath should not rely so much on his father-in-law's gifts.
2. Veerendranath may be taking dowry in a series of installments to avoid detection.
3. Veerendranath has not violated any codes since the gifts are from his father-in-law.
4. Veerendranath may be using his father-in-law as front for collecting bribes on his behalf.

Discussion

No judgement as in (1) can be made since this is a matter within a family. As it is personal matter, no official intervention or comment is warranted.

The second option is a wild surmise. There is nothing to suggest the possibility. In the absence of evidence, no such guess should be made.

The third answer choice is correct. As a result of the gifts he received, Veerendranath may have a sizeable bank balance. But it does not mean that he is holding assets much higher than can be justified by his income. He can legitimately account for his assets through his known sources of income including the gifts from his father-in law.

The fourth option is a wild speculation. There is no shred of evidence to support it. In fact, one should refrain from baseless speculations.

CASE 4

Surinder is the senior marketing manager in a public sector company. The company generally manufactures its products after getting a specific order. However, it keeps some stock of items in good demand. Surinder gets an order from London. But the buyer wants supplies urgently from ready stock of the company. He also wanted a confirmation immediately and asks for a discount. Surinder is unable to reach his boss, but accepts the order so as to sell the existing material. Later on, he is pulled up for irregularly accepting the order.

Question

How will you react to the action which Surinder took?

1. He should have somehow got in touch with his boss.
2. He should not have given the discount.
3. His action is justified.
4. He should have given greater importance to following the procedure than to securing the order.

Discussion

The first option is hypothetical. It is a fact that he could not reach his boss. So we cannot insist after the event that somehow he should have reached his boss. It may not have been possible for various reasons.

The whole aim in this case should be to sell the available stock. Giving some discount is a normal commercial procedure, especially when there is accumulation of stock. No fault can be found with such common business procedures.

Surinder is justified in what he did. His action is in organization's interest. He followed normal commercial procedures. In the absence of his boss, he had to use his best commercial judgement in the transaction. He also tried though unsuccessfully to contact his boss.

The fourth option is incorrect. In fact, this is the main problem with many of the operations of public agencies. Government officials give far more importance to following correct procedures than to attaining organizational goals. This approach leads to inefficiency and absence of dynamism.

Doubtful Conduct

An officer's integrity or honesty may come under cloud if he commits any irregularities. These are – gross or wilful negligence; recklessness in decision making; blatant violations of systems and procedures; exercise of discretion in excess where no ostensible public interest is evident; and failure to keep the controlling authority/superiors informed in time. In these cases, irregularities are studied in the light of their surrounding circumstances to see whether they raise reasonable doubt about an officer's integrity.

CVC recognises an important administrative problem in this context. There are situations in which corrupt conduct of officials is clearly evident. These are listed at (i) to (v) above while defining corruption. Now, it is common practice in any bureaucracy to lay down procedures for taking various decisions. If any officer violates these procedures, he commits an irregularity. An irregularity is only a *prima facie* indicator of possible dishonesty. There are situations in which officers may commit irregularities, as mentioned in the previous paragraph. But on that account, no officer can be dubbed corrupt without examining his decisions in detail. One point for consideration in such cases is whether his decision caused loss to the organization.

CVC has, however, recognised that loss by itself is insufficient to establish dishonesty. Managerial efficiency and effectiveness are hallmarks of commercial enterprises. Commercial risk-taking forms part of business. Therefore, every loss caused to the organization, either in pecuniary or non-pecuniary terms, need not necessarily become the subject matter of a vigilance inquiry i.e. an inquiry to determine whether there has been corruption. The test is whether a person of common prudence, working within the ambit of the prescribed rules, regulations and instructions, would have taken the decision in the prevailing circumstances in the commercial/operational interests of the organization. If so, the action is *bona fide* or well intentioned; otherwise, it is ill-intentioned or malafide.

At this point, we may note that corruption cases arise not only in Government but also in public sector enterprises. Cases involving senior officers of these enterprises fall within CVC's jurisdiction. We will consider them separately.

Widening the Definition of Corruption

Uptill now, we have considered the kinds of action which CVC regards as dishonest. The Second Administrative Reforms Commission (SARC) recommended that the definition of corruption should be widened. SARC considers that the CVC's definition is restrictive and excludes many official actions detrimental to public interest. SARC lists four types of official conduct which while outside the definition of corruption, cause immense damage to public interest.

The first type of such conduct involves gross perversion of the Constitution and democratic institutions, including, wilful violation of the oath of office. Constitutional functionaries act in this manner due to partisanship or animosity. No money-making or other forms of gratification may be involved in such actions. For such acts, the Supreme Court held individuals holding high office guilty of gross misconduct amounting to perversion of the Constitution. At present, no laws but only public opinion, political pressure and individual conscience can stop such behaviour.

The second category of these offences consists of abuse of authority by unduly favouring or harming someone, though without receiving any bribes or gratification. Here, the reasons underlying the action are often partisanship, kinship ties and prejudice. Though such acts are outside the purview of present legal definition of corruption, they undermine the moral basis of governance and rule of law.

The third such category of actions involves obstruction or perversion of justice by unduly influencing law enforcement agencies and prosecution. Here again, the actions are driven more by partisanship, kinship and prejudice than by monetary gain. Failure of justice which such acts cause has deleterious consequences.

The fourth type of action involves squandering of public money, including lavish official life-styles. These cause no financial gains or losses to individuals. However, they are a drain on public resources which have high opportunity value in other uses. They set a bad tone in the prevailing situation of general poverty.

These four types of conduct have to be checked to preserve democratic values and public trust in political system. They create a feeling among common people that government functionaries, instead of serving public interest, are busy in self aggrandizement. SARC has recommended that the following should be made offences under the Prevention of Corruption Act:

- Gross perversion of the Constitution and democratic institutions amounting to wilful violation of oath of office
- Abuse of authority by unduly favouring or harming someone
- Obstruction of justice
- Squandering public money

CASE 5

Hiren was a close aide of a minister in his constituency. He is known for his rough and tough methods of working. Once he got into a fracas in a mall and badly beat up a shop owner's son. Normally, Hiren had his way in such matters. However, the shop owner took a firm stand and registered a case against Hiren. The police officer in charge was new and was proceeding according to law. He refused to dilute the case against Hiren. He made frantic appeals to minister for help. The minister arranged for the transfer of the police officer, and his replacement by another officer close to him.

Question

How will you respond to the police officer's conduct in this case?

1. The police officer showed lack of realism and does not understand how things actually work out in criminal administration system at present.

2. He should have-in order not to draw the minister's ire-tactfully delayed the investigation.
3. The police officer acted correctly.
4. The police officer should have watered down the case, but at the same time advised the trader to approach the court for applying more stringent legal provisions.

Discussion

The first answer choice is incorrect. Police officers should scrupulously follow the law while conducting investigations into crimes. They should apply the legal provisions based on the facts of the case without getting influenced by extraneous factors. By acting according to the first answer choice, the police officer would be behaving prudently or opportunistically to stay in the minister's good books. He would be failing in his duty.

The second answer choice is also incorrect. The police officer has to act promptly and pursue the investigation. In such matters, the case gets weakened by the very process of delay. If the police officer follows this answer choice, he would be acting strategically in his self-interest, and not diligently in discharging his duty.

The third answer choice is correct. The course of action in this case is clear. A legal duty is cast upon an investigating officer in virtue of the official position he holds of duly taking cognizance of offences and pursuing them speedily and diligently. As this is his legal (and also moral) duty, he should not be distracted by other strategic or personal considerations.

Clearly, the minister is guilty of misusing his office. He has interfered in the investigative process. The new police officer may toe his line. But this should not worry the present incumbent officer. Each individual is responsible for following the official code irrespective of what other may do. As regards the minister's conduct, it is clear that he has tampered with the process of justice. The Second Administrative Reforms Commission has recommended that the definition of corruption should be widened to include such acts.

The fourth answer choice is inappropriate since it involves devious or deceitful conduct. By acting in this manner, the police officer would be transferring his job to the trader or the victim. Police have to perform their duty in a straightforward manner without resorting to stratagems or ruses. Police have to present the case before the courts through prosecutors without diluting or exaggerating it. As compared to police, the victims are in a weak position and can seldom take effective action on their own. They need full support from police.

ROOTS OF CORRUPTION

It is the individuals who are guilty of acts of corruption. In a way, corruption represents moral failure of individuals. They are unable to follow official rules, social norms or their own conscience. There is, however, more to acts of dishonesty than an individual's moral failings. Political, economic and social environment can create an atmosphere of permissiveness and laxity. Further, the gains from dishonesty may far outweigh the risks of detection, punishment or social opprobrium.

CAUSES OF CORRUPTION

Report of the Santhanam Committee is the basis for the existing administrative and legal structures and processes for combating corruption. Vigilance Manual (Part 1) mentions four major causes of corruption which the Santham committee identified. These are:

(i) administrative delays;
(ii) government overstretching its capacity and assuming too many regulatory functions;
(iii) scope for personal discretion in the exercise of powers vested in different categories of government servants; and
(iv) cumbersome procedures of dealing with various matters which are of importance to citizens in their day to day affairs.

These causal factors can also explain the various forms of corruption prevalent today. SARC has made an extended analysis of the sources or originating circumstances of corruption. We will presently outline SARC's ideas. But we will first note how these four factors increase scope for corruption. From the point of view of the businessman, delays postpone business operations, cash flows and profits. He would prefer to reduce these by bribing or paying 'speed money'. For him, it becomes a simple matter of calculating the loss due to delay against the illegal payment. As this payment is usually a small fraction of his likely losses due to delay, he will pay it.

Administrative decisions, as noted earlier, are taken after following the prescribed procedures. Further, there are criteria or rules for decision-making. But the situations which arise in any area of administration are too complex to be captured by invariant, iron clad rules. Hence, decision making which is rule bound, has to be supplemented by the discretion of individual officers. While exercising such discretion, government servants can ask for money; for the applicant knows that the decision depends on discretion and not on any fixed rule.

Governments regulate many activities in public interest. For example, governments regulate building construction or town development. Over years, the range of activities covered by regulations has increased. Increase of regulations brings more activities under control of governments and increases scope for corruption.

Ordinary citizens face the most vexing forms of corruption. A large lower bureaucracy extracts money from them for simple services like a ration card, driving license, birth certification or copies of their land holding. Such items, though seemingly trivial, often form part of the documentation for accessing other services like a gas connection or a bank loan. It may not be farfetched to describe these bureaucratic exactions, in a famous Marxian phrase, as "primitive accumulation".

Coercive and Collusive Corruption

SARC makes a distinction between two kinds of corruption which it calls coercive corruption and collusive corruption. An act of corruption has two players: the bribe-giver and the bribe-taker. In cases of coercive corruption, the bribe-giver is a victim of extortion. It is like a forcible payment at gun point. The bribe-giver is forced to pay for simple services like copy of his school certificate or entry in his land record. If he does not make the payment to the public servant, he loses far more than the bribe. He undergoes, to use a term from economics, psychological disutility on account of delays, harassment and uncertainty. The economic cost he pays consists of lost opportunity, loss of work and wages. Compulsions of earning daily bread force poor people into a vicious cycle of corruption.

Besides this coercive corruption, there is also collusive corruption in which the bribe-giver and bribe-taker act as partners and rob society. In this situation, the bribe-giver is as great an offender as the bribe-taker. The acts involved in these situations defraud public exchequer and also harm public welfare. Among such instances are - execution of substandard works, distortion of competition, depriving the public exchequer of due revenue, taking of kickbacks or commissions in public procurement, evasion of taxes by collusion with officials and causing direct harm to people by spurious drugs and violation of factory safety norms.

Public works such as roads, bridges, buildings, canals have to be built to the specifications mentioned in the tender documents. Tenders are the means by which contractors bid for government works. The lowest bidder is generally selected and does work according to standards mentioned in the tender documents. Of course, he can earn more profit by scaling down standards during execution with the connivance of project engineers.

The purpose of the tender procedure of executing public works is to encourage competition among contractors and to get reasonable prices. At times contractors form rings and collude with government servants to jack up prices. The tender bids are usually padded with amounts for paying bribes. In this way, competitive process is vitiated. It is believed that corruption payments get built into the tender costs of works. The risks of supplying substandard drugs into public health stores are too obvious to need any elaboration.

CURBING COLLUSIVE CORRUPTION

Systemic reforms can curb coercive corruption. For example, use of information and communications technology has reduced corruption in areas like railway reservation. Further, though corruption cases often fail in courts, there is greater success in cases of coercive corruption than in cases of collusive corruption. Here, the bribe-giver is the victim. He is willing to depose against the bribe-taker. Under the Prevention of Corruption Act, the bribe giver is also guilty. However, if he deposes against the bribe-taker, he gets immunity. Therefore, he often comes forward to depose against the bribe-taker. Besides, the 'trap cases' by the vigilance machinery are quite effective in such instances. Trap cases are those in which the government servant accepting bribe is caught red-handed. It is somewhat like a sting operation.

But the situation is different in cases of collusive corruption. As both the bribe-giver and the bribe-taker collude and are beneficiaries of the transaction, it is very hard to get evidence. The losses from collusive corruption to government and society are far greater than from coercive corruption.

SARC has recommended that the Prevention of Corruption Act should be amended to combat collusive corruption. It recommended that in collusive corruption, the 'burden of proof' should be shifted to the accused. In our criminal justice system, every person is presumed to be innocent till he/she is proved guilty. Accordingly, the burden of proving the charges lies totally on the prosecution. They have to produce evidence - witnesses and documents–to establish the case. There are certain situations where the burden of proof is placed on the accused. It means that he/she has to prove his/her innocence.

For example, the Prevention of Corruption Act stipulates that a public servant is said to commit the offence of criminal misconduct if he/she cannot satisfactorily account for the property in his/her possession, which is disproportionate to his/her known sources of income. In this case, the burden of proving his innocence, is on the accused public servant; he has to show that he acquired the property with his sources of income. The Prevention of Corruption Act also stipulates that when the accused public servant takes money, the court has to presume that it is a bribe; then the accused has to prove that the money is not a bribe.

SARC has recommended that the Prevention of Corruption Act should be amended to cover offences of 'collusive bribery'. An offence could be classified as 'collusive bribery' if the outcome or intended outcome of the transaction leads to a loss to the state, public or public interest. In all such cases if it is established that the interest of the state or public has suffered because of an act of a public servant, then the court shall presume that the public servant and the beneficiary of the decision committed an offence of 'collusive bribery'. The punishment for all such cases should be increased to 10 years of imprisonment.

ADMINISTRATIVE STRUCTURE AND PROCEDURES FOR CURBING CORRUPTION

Central Vigilance Commission

Before proceeding further, we need to understand the existing systems for checking corruption. In 1955, the Administrative Vigilance Division was set up in the Ministry of Home Affairs as central agency with overall responsibility for anti-corruption measures. Most of its functions were later transferred to the Central Vigilance Commission. The role of the Administrative Vigilance Division now is to formulate and implement policies of the Central Government - covering vigilance, integrity in public services, and anti-corruption measures.

Following the recommendations of the Committee on Prevention of Corruption [popularly known as Santhanam Committee], the Central Vigilance Commission was set up in 1964. It was created through a Government of India Resolution or as a result of an executive decision. After the Supreme Court judgement in *Vineet Narain vs. Union of India*, the Commission was accorded statutory status in 1998 through "The Central Vigilance Commission Ordinance, 1998". Subsequently in 2003, parliament passed the Central Vigilance Commission Act in 2003. An organization is said to have a statutory status if it is created as a result of legislation and not by a government resolution, that is to say, an executive order.

The Central Vigilance Commission consists of a Central Vigilance Commissioner [Chairperson] and not more than two Vigilance Commissioners [Members]. The Central Vigilance Commissioner and the Vigilance Commissioners are appointed by the President for four years or till they attain the age of sixty-five years, whichever is earlier.

According to the CVC Act, the functions and powers of the Commission are as under:

(a) CVC supervises the functioning of Delhi Special Police Establishment [DSPE] in its investigations of cases under the PC Act. The commission supervises cases involving All India Services officers working with the Central Government; Group 'A' officers of the Central Government; and officers of the Central Public Sector enterprises and of autonomous organization under it and similar others.

(b) The commission, in its supervisory capacity, can give directions to the DSPE. The Commission, however, cannot ask the DSPE to investigate or dispose of any case in a particular manner. This follows from a cardinal principle of criminal jurisprudence that the functions of investigating, prosecuting and judging an offence shall be performed by separate agencies absolutely free of one another.

(c) The Commission can investigate any matter which Central Government refers to it about the involvement of the categories of officers mentioned in (a) above in offences under the PC Act.

(d) The commission can order investigation into complaints it receives about the involvement in offences under the PC Act of the categories mentioned in (a) above.

(e) The commission reviews the progress of applications pending with the competent authorities for sanction of prosecution under the PC Act. As we shall see, the prosecuting agencies cannot start a prosecution without the prior approval of the Central Government. The Commission tries to speed up such sanctions.

(f) The Commission reviews the progress of investigations conducted by the DSPE into offences under the PC Act.

(g) The commission tenders advice on vigilance matters to Central Government, Central Public Sector Enterprises (CPSEs) and other Central agencies.

(h) The commission supervises the vigilance administration of various Ministries of the Central Government, CPSEs and other Central agencies.

In addition to the above functions mentioned in the CVC Act, the Vigilance Commission performs certain administrative functions. All Central ministries, CPSEs and other central agencies have vigilance or anti-corruption set ups usually under Chief Vigilance Officers (CVOs). The Vigilance commission approves the appointment of the CVOs. No one can be appointed as a CVO without the Commission's approval. If the CBI considers that a prosecution should be launched in any case and if the sanction for such prosecution is required under any law to be issued in the name of the President, the Commission will tender advice, after considering the comments received from the concerned Ministry/Department/Enterprise, as to whether or not prosecution should be sanctioned.

Students should note that the position on according sanction for prosecution of officials changed after enactment of Lokpal and Lokayuktas Act. Before this Act came into being, the powers for sanctioning prosecution of officials vested with the Central government. Now, if Lokpal takes cognizance of an offence under the PC Act committed by an official, Lokpal can also authorize necessary prosecution on its own.

Chief Vigilance Officers (CVO)

Basically, most of the personnel handling corruption issues are located in the Central Ministries, CPSEs, and other central agencies. Each of these organizations has a designated CVO who generally handles matters within that organization which raise doubts of corruptness. He functions under the head of the organization. CVO acts as a nodal point to CVC and CBI for all vigilance related matters. He is entirely guided by the directions he gets from the CVC.

Central Bureau of Investigation (CBI)

The Central Bureau of Investigation (CBI) was set up in 1963. The Special Police Establishment is a part of the CBI, and has two divisions: (i) Anticorruption division and (ii) Special Crimes Division. Anticorruption Division investigates following types of cases:

- Cases under the Prevention of Corruption Act, 1988
- Cases under the Indian Penal Code (IPC) or any other law which also involves bribery and corruption
- Cases pertaining to serious irregularities allegedly committed by public servants
- Cases against State government officials which State Governments entrust to the CBI

The Special Crime Division investigates both economic offences and conventional crimes. The latter include offences relating to internal security, espionage, sabotage, narcotics and psychotropic substances, antiquities, murders, dacoity/robberies, cheating, criminal breach of trust, forgeries, dowry deaths, suspicious deaths and other offences under IPC and other laws.

The investigation work is done through SPE wing of the CBI, which derives its police powers from the Delhi Special Police Establishment Act, 1946 to inquire and to investigate certain specified offences or classes of offences pertaining to corruption and other kinds of malpractices involving public servants. Arrangements have been evolved to avoid duplication between the investigations of State police and of CBI. Matters which involve mainly Central Government and its officers (even if some State officials are involved) are handled by CBI. State police handle matters falling mainly in the sphere of that particular state government. Army and CBI have also created coordination mechanisms.

The CVC supervises the Delhi Special Police Establishment in its investigation of offences under the Prevention of Corruption Act. Central Government supervises CBI in all other matters. The autonomy of CBI (from Central government) has become a contentious issue. We will discuss this separately.

A Collegium comprising the Prime Minister, Chief Justice of India and the leader of the largest opposition party in the Lok Sabha selects the CBI director. He holds office for two years.

The CBI cannot begin prosecution proceedings against officers of the rank of Joint Secretary and above without the approval of the Central Government. Similarly, CBI cannot prosecute officers of CSPEs and other central agencies without the approval of the Central Government.

CTE Organization

The Chief Technical Examiner's Organization (CTEO) functions under the administrative control of the CVC as its technical wing, carrying out inspection of civil, electrical and horticulture works of the Central Government departments, CSPEs and other central agencies. The works or contracts for intensive examination are selected from the details furnished by the CVO in the quarterly progress reports sent to the CTEO. The intensive examination helps in detecting cases of use of substandard materials, avoidable expenditure, and undue favours or overpayment to contractors.

Types of Vigilance

In this section, we look at how the CVOs go about their tasks or the three broad approaches which they can follow to reduce corruption. The three approaches are (i) Preventative vigilance; (ii) Punitive vigilance; and (iii) Surveillance and detection. Though 'surveillance' and 'punitive action' for commission of misconduct and other malpractices are certainly important, the 'preventive measures' to be taken by the CVO are comparatively more important as these are likely to reduce the number of vigilance cases considerably. Thus, the role of CVO should be predominantly preventive.

Preventive Vigilance

The CVO has to take following preventive vigilance measures:

(i) To study existing procedures and practices in his organization and modify those which allow scope for corruption

(ii) To find out the causes of delay, the points where it happens and devise steps to minimize delays at different stages

(iii) To review the regulatory functions, determine those which are unnecessary, improve the manner of handling regulations and of exercising powers of control

(iv) To improve control over exercise of discretionary powers so that they are not exercised arbitrarily but fairly and transparently

(v) To educate citizens about the procedures of dealing with various matters and also to simplify the cumbersome procedures to the degree possible

(vi) To identify the areas in the organization which are prone to corruption and to ensure that officers of proven integrity only are posted in those areas

(vii) To prepare a list of officers of doubtful integrity

(viii) To prepare the "agreed list" in consultation with the CBI. This list will include the names of officers whose integrity is in doubt or against whom there are complaints alleging corruption

(ix) To ensure that the officers appearing on the list of officers of doubtful integrity and the agreed list are not posted in the identified sensitive/corruption prone areas

(x) To ensure periodical rotations of staff

(xi) To ensure that the organization prepares manuals on important subjects such as purchases, contracts and the like and that these manuals are updated from time to time and conform to the guidelines issued by the Commission.

Punitive Vigilance

Punitive vigilance refers to actions which arise after commission of acts of corruption. Many such acts come to light from complaints which government organizations receive.

The CVO is expected to take following action on punitive vigilance aspects:

(i) To receive complaints from all sources and see if the allegations relate to corruption

(ii) To investigate specific and verifiable allegations involving corruption

(iii) To investigate personally or through others the allegations forwarded to him by the CVC or the CBI

(iv) To speedily process the investigation reports and get orders of the competent authorities on what to do about the reports and also obtain Commission's advice on the investigation reports

(v) To ensure that properly worded chargesheets are served on the accused officers

(vi) To ensure speedy appointment of authorities to inquire into charges

(vii) To examine the inquiry officer's report and take orders on it from the competent authority in consultation with CVC and UPSC (where necessary)

(viii) To ensure that the disciplinary authority issues a speaking order (i.e. one which states the reasons for the decision taken) while imposing a punishment on the delinquent officer

(ix) To ensure strict compliance with rules governing disciplinary proceedings at all stages so as to avoid legal challenges to their validity

(x) To ensure that the time limits prescribed for processing the vigilance cases at various stages are observed.

Surveillance Vigilance

This aspect refers to ongoing monitoring of vigilance cases. Often, in the process of other official work vigilance matters are neglected. CVO has to ensure that necessary actions are taken on time in vigilance cases. Surveillance vigilance involves the following steps:

- CVO should conduct regular and surprise inspections in the sensitive areas in order to detect if there have been instances of corrupt or improper practice by the public servants.
- He should also undertake prompt and adequate scrutiny of property returns and intimations given by the public servants under the conduct rules and take proper follow-up action where necessary.
- He should also gather intelligence from his own sources in whatever manner he deems appropriate about the misconduct/malpractices committed or likely to be committed.
- CVO should invariably review all pending matters, such as investigation reports, disciplinary cases and other vigilance complaints/cases every month and take necessary steps for expediting action on those matters.

HOW CORRUPTION COMES TO LIGHT

Information about corruption, malpractice or misconduct on the part of public servants may flow to the administrative authority/the CVC/the CBI/the police authorities from any of the following sources:

(a) Complaints received from employees of the organization or from the public;

(b) Departmental inspection reports and stock verification surveys;

(c) Scrutiny of annual property statements;

(d) Scrutiny of transactions reported under the Conduct Rules;

(e) Reports of irregularities in accounts detected in the routine audit of accounts, e.g. tampering with records, over-payments, misappropriation of money or materials etc.;

(f) Audit reports on Government accounts and on the accounts of public undertakings and other corporate bodies;

(g) Reports of Parliamentary Committees like the Estimates Committee, Public Accounts Committee and the Committee on Public Undertakings;

(h) Proceedings of the Houses of Parliament;

(i) Complaints and allegations appearing in the press and other media;

(j) Source information, if received verbally from an identifiable source, to be reduced to writing; and

(k) Intelligence gathered by agencies like CBI and local police.

In addition, the Chief Vigilance Officer concerned may also devise and adopt such methods, as considered appropriate and fruitful in the context of nature of work handled in the organization.

Up till now in the chapter, we discussed the notion of corruption based on the Indian law, the organizations government created for dealing with corruption, and the procedures they follow in dealing with it. Now, we discuss the administrative and legal hurdles that delay the processes of meting out justice to government servants charged with corruption. In this regard, we discuss how departmental proceedings and legal proceedings against delinquent officials get delayed.

Delays in Departmental Proceedings

Departmental or disciplinary proceedings can be broadly defined as structured processes to determine whether an employee is guilty of misconduct, and if so, the quantum of punishment he deserves. These proceedings have to go through a long process. A preliminary inquiry is held to determine if there is a prima facie case against the government. After that a charge sheet is issued to the officer. A hearing is held and the government servant is given an opportunity to defend his position or establish his innocence. Finally, based on the inquiry report, the competent authority imposes a punishment on him. CVC has identified 13 stages in inquiry process and fixed time limits for completing each stage. Students need not worry about the details of the stages. It is enough to know that the process results in considerable delays.

Disciplinary Rules envisage two kinds of penalties. Minor penalties consist of "Censure", "Withholding of promotion for a specified period", and "Withholding of increment and recovery from the salary of whole or part of pecuniary loss caused by the employee". Minor penalty can be imposed after calling for and considering the explanation of the accused employee. Major Penalties comprise reduction in rank through reversion to a lower scale of pay, compulsory retirement, and removal or dismissal from service. Such penalties can be imposed only after a detailed inquiry. With minor variations, the elaborate disciplinaty procedure also applies to group C and group D employees of central government, all state government employees and those working in central and state undertakings, in local self-government and cooperatives.

There is widespread dissatisfaction among all concerned about the way disciplinary proceedings are conducted. The time limits for various stages of departmental proceedings, which CVC prescribed, are rarely observed. Delays occur due to many reasons. The delinquent officers try to prolong the proceedings. They demand all sorts of documents both relevant and irrelevant. If the inquiring officer rules that any document is irrelevant, they challenge his order in a court. "Reasonable opportunity" clause opens the avenues to many opportunities to challenge the departmental proceedings. The proceedings often get bogged down in technical requirements. CATs and courts frequently intervene, even on interlocutory (interim) orders of the Inquiring officers. Lower courts have in many cases tied down the disciplinary authorities with technicalities by giving greater importance to procedure than to substance.

To get over these problems, many suggestions have been made. Some of these are:

- ¤ To rely more on minor than on major penalties
- ¤ To free inquiry officers of all other duties during the inquiry period
- ¤ Supplying the accused with documentary evidence against him along with the charge-sheet etc.

SARC has recommended the following steps to speed up departmental proceedings:

- ¤ Simplifying the procedure for completing proceedings quickly
- ¤ Relying mainly on documentary evidence to save time on calling and examining witnesses
- ¤ Creating an appellate mechanism within the department itself
- ¤ Imposing major penalties on the recommendation by a committee in order to ensure objectivity.

Speeding up Trials under the Prevention of Corruption Act

Speedy trials are essential for success of anti-corruption drives. For ensuring speedy trial of corruption cases, the Prevention of Corruption Act made the following provisions:

(a) All cases under the Act are to be tried only by a Special Judge.

(b) The proceedings of the court should be held on a day-to-day basis.

(c) No court shall stay the proceedings under the Act on the grounds of any error or irregularity in the sanction granted, unless in the opinion of the court it has led to failure of justice.

Unfortunately, despite these provisions, the experience with the trial of cases under the Act has been disappointing. The judges trying corruption cases have been declared as Special Judges; but they are loaded with many other non-corruption cases and are unable to complete trials quickly. The average time taken by trial courts for the disposal of cases has increased over the years.

SARC has made the following recommendations to speed up trial proceedings of corruption cases.

(a) Time limits should be fixed for various stages of a trial by amending the code of criminal procedure (CRPC).

(b) Judges declared as Special Judges under the provisions of the Prevention of Corruption Act should not be loaded with other work. Only if there is inadequate work of corruption cases should the Special Judges be entrusted with other responsibilities.

(c) Proceedings of courts trying cases under the Prevention of Corruption Act should be held on a day-to-day basis without any exceptions.

(d) The Supreme Court and the High Courts may lay down guidelines to preclude unwarranted adjournments and avoidable delays.

Sanction for Prosecution

Under the Prevention of Corruption Act, previous sanction of the competent authority is necessary before a court takes cognizance of the offences. Competent authority is one empowered to permit prosecution. This provision saves honest public servants from harassment they may face through malicious or vexatious complaints. The sanctioning authority, before according sanction, will see whether the available evidence shows that a prima facie case exists against the accused public servant. But opponents of this provision argue that it is often used by a sanctioning authority to shield dishonest officials. There are often inordinate delays in grant of such sanction. Further, unintentional defects in the grant of sanction have led to invalidation of the whole proceeding.

Many suggestions have been made to address these issues. One suggestion is that the requirement should be done away with in some cases. The provision of prior concurrence of the Central Government to prosecution applies to senior officers of the level of Joint Secretary and above and also to senior functionaries in CSPEs and other Central agencies. Some have argued that in the prevailing corruption ridden environment, there is danger of such a provision being misused to protect corrupt senior public servants, and if at all such a protection is to be given, the power should vest with an independent body like the CVC, which can take an objective stand. The flip side of this view is that officers at the level of Joint Secretary and above operate at important decision-making levels in the government and that in taking decisions or giving advice they have to act without fear or favour. If they are exposed to frequent enquiries, they will be demoralized. They will 'play safe' and just push files around without taking decisions. The current phrase 'policy paralysis' reflects this problem. This approach will slow down important economic decisions.

The provision seeks to protect public servants in the exercise of their legitimate duties, and need not extend to circumstances which show obvious misconduct. Hence, SARC recommended that the following categories of offences should be excluded from the requirement of sanction:

(i) Demand or/and acceptance of bribes,

(ii) Obtaining valuable things without or with inadequate consideration, and

(iii Cases of possession of assets disproportionate to the known source of income.

Sanction for investigation

Under the PC Act, police cannot start an investigation against a serving or retired public servant for actions/decisions taken by him in the course of his duty without the prior approval of the competent authority. No such permission shall be required for arrest of an officer on the spot for accepting or attempting to accept an undue advantage. These provisions protect honest officers who perform their duties in a bona fide manner from harassment. Courts have ruled that where government has to give sanction either for prosecution or investigation, it should be done within a reasonable time after duly considering the merits of the case.

Constitutional Protection to Civil Servants – Article 311

Part XIV of the Constitution deals with the regulation of service conditions of government servants. According to Article 309, Parliament can make laws dealing with the recruitment and conditions of service of its employees. State assemblies can pass similar laws for their State employees. Such laws have to be in line with the provisions of the Constitution. However, the provisions embodied in Article 311 confer extraordinary job security on government servants. Many writers argue that such excessive security emboldens government servants into various forms of misconduct.

We will now look at the service protection which government servants enjoy. Theoretically, Central Government employees hold office 'during the pleasure of the President'. State Government employees hold office 'during the pleasure of the Governor'. But the wording does not mean that government servants can be sacked at will. Far from it, the 'pleasure' is hemmed in by various conditions.

Article 311 of the Constitution enumerates these conditions. These conditions apply or 'kick in' when government wants to impose a major penalty on any government servant. Major penalty means dismissal, removal or reduction in rank of government servants. We briefly mention these conditions. First, no major punishment can be imposed on a government servant by an authority which is subordinate to an authority which appointed him. Secondly, no government servant can be awarded a major penalty unless an inquiry is held. These are the departmental or disciplinary proceedings we discussed earlier. In such an inquiry, he has to be informed of the charges ('the gravamen of the accusation' in the words of Jeeves in a novel of P.G. Wodehouse) against him. Thirdly, he has to be given a reasonable opportunity of being heard in respect of those charges. This means that he should be given a chance to rebut the charges. Earlier, government servants had to be also given an opportunity to represent against the quantum of punishment proposed to be inflicted on them. This protection was removed under the Forty Second Amendment to the Constitution.

There are certain circumstances under which it is not necessary to hold a departmental inquiry before awarding a penalty. These circumstances are (1) if the government servant is convicted on a criminal charge; (2) if it is not reasonably practicable to hold an inquiry; and (3) if the President or the Governor, as the case may be, is satisfied that in the interest of the security of the State, it is not expedient to hold such inquiry. These exceptions in practice apply to very few cases.

Article 311 gives job security to government servants. It provides procedural safeguards to them against arbitrary dismissal or removal or reduction to a lower rank. These provisions are enforceable in a court of law. Any order which a disciplinary authority passes in violation of Article 311 will be ab initio void or flawed or invalid from its very inception. The provisions of Articles 310 and 311 apply to all government servants.

There are arguments both supporting and opposing Article 311. Its opponents argue that it gives impregnable job security to civil servants. Those who support Article 311 trace the problems not to its provisions but to judicial interpretations and to the natural justice principle that civil servants facing major penalties have to be given reasonable opportunity of putting up their defence. However, Article 311 still stands as it is. SARC has made the following recommendations about it:

SARC's Recommendation on – Article 311

(a) Article 311 and Article 310 of the Constitution should be repealed.

(b) Suitable legislation to provide for all necessary terms and conditions of services should be provided under Article 309, to protect the bona fide actions of public servants taken in public interest; this should be made applicable to the States.

(c) Necessary protection to public servants against arbitrary action should be provided through legislation under Article 309.

Summary

- The Prevention of Corruption Act lists offences which are acts of corruption by government servants.
- These acts are: (i) asking or taking money by a government servant for performing official work or for using his influence with another official (ii) obtaining a valuable thing without payment or inadequate payment from a person with whom he or any of his subordinates has official dealings or where he can exert influence; (iii) abusing his position as a public servant for monetary gain or material advantage; (iv) having assets disproportionate to his known sources of income; (v) misappropriation, forgery or cheating or similar deeds.
- Some situations create doubts about an officer's integrity. These include cases involving gross or wilful negligence; recklessness in decision making; blatant violations of systems and procedures; exercise of discretion in excess where no ostensible public interest is evident; and failure to inform the controlling authority/superiors about his decisions in time.
- An irregularity is only a prima facie indicator of possible dishonesty. To come to any decision, the specific circumstances of the case have to be examined. One point for consideration in such cases is whether the decision caused loss to the organization.
- Commercial risk taking forms part of business. Even if reasonable commercial risk taking leads to loss, officers are not blamed.
- SARC has recommended that the following should be made offences under the Prevention of Corruption Act:
  - (i) Gross perversion of the Constitution and democratic institutions amounting to wilful violation of oath of office
  - (ii) Abuse of authority unduly favouring or harming someone
  - (iii) Obstruction of justice
  - (iv) Squandering public money
- Santhanam Committee identified four general causes of corruption. These are (i) administrative delays; (ii) Government overstretching its capacity by assuming too many regulatory functions; (iii) scope for personal discretion in the exercise of powers vested in different categories of government servants; and (iv) cumbersome procedures of dealing with various matters which are of importance to citizens in their day to day affairs.
- SARC makes a distinction between two kinds of corruption which it calls coercive corruption and collusive corruption.
- In cases of coercive corruption, the bribe-giver is a victim of extortion.
- In collusive corruption the bribe-giver and bribe-taker act as partners and rob society. The acts involved in these situations defraud public exchequer and also harm public welfare.

- Systemic reforms can curb coercive corruption. For example, use of information and communications technology has reduced corruption in areas like railway reservation.
- SARC has recommended that the Prevention of Corruption Act should be amended to combat collusive corruption. It recommended that in collusive corruption, the 'burden of proof' should be shifted to the accused.
- According to SARC, an offence could be classified as 'collusive bribery' if the outcome or intended outcome of the transaction leads to a loss to the state, public or public interest.
- The Central Vigilance Commission was set up in 1964.
- The Commission was accorded statutory status in 1998.
- The Central Vigilance Commission consists of a Central Vigilance Commissioner [Chairperson] and not more than two Vigilance Commissioners [Members]. The Central Vigilance Commissioner and the Vigilance Commissioners are appointed by the President for four years or till they attain the age of sixty-five years, whichever is earlier.
- In discharge of its functions the Commission:
  (i) Supervises the CBI in investigations of corruption cases;
  (ii) Supervises corruption complaints against All India Services officers working with the Central Government; Group 'A' officers of the Central Government; and officers of the Central Public Sector enterprises and of autonomous organization under it and similar others.
  (iii) Investigates complaints received from government;
  (iv) Orders investigation into complaints;
  (v) Advises Central Government and its agencies on corruption related matters;
  (vi) Oversees the work of CVOs; and
  (vii) Advises government departments and agencies on inquiry reports received against delinquent officers.
- Each department, public enterprise and agency has a CVO who is appointed in consultation with CVC.
- He acts as a staff officer to departmental head or head of the public enterprise. He coordinates with CVC and CBI.
- CBI was set up in 1963.
- CBI's Anticorruption Division investigates:
  (i) Cases under the Prevention of Corruption Act, 1988
  (ii) Cases under the Indian Penal Code (IPC) or any other law which also involve bribery and corruption
  (iii) Cases pertaining to serious irregularities allegedly committed by public servants
  (iv) Cases against State government officials which State Governments entrust to the CBI

- ¤ A collegium compresing the Prime Minister, Chief Justice of India, and the leader of the largest opposition party in the Lok Sabha selects the CBI Dreictor. He holds office for two years.
- ¤ The CBI cannot begin prosecution proceedings against officers of the rank of Joint Secretary and above without the approval of the Central Government. Similarly, CBI cannot prosecute officers of CSPEs and other central agencies without the approval of the Central Government.
- ¤ The Chief Technical Examiner's Organization (CTEO) functions under the administrative control of the CVC as its technical wing.
- ¤ The three approaches to reducing corruption are (i) Preventative vigilance; (ii) Punitive vigilance; and (iii) Surveillance and detection. Their components have been outlined above.
- ¤ Sources of information or the manner in which corruption cases come to light are – complaints, inspections, officers' property statements, their reported transactions, audits of accounts, parliament proceedings, parliament committee reports, press and media reports and routine intelligence gathering.
- ¤ The issues currently focus in fight against corruption include: (i) delays in departmental proceedings against erring officials (ii) delays in giving sanctions for prosecution of officials under the PC Act; and (iii) delays in conducting corruption cases in courts.
- ¤ Departmental proceedings are multi-stage quasi-judicial processes; CVC identified approximately 13 stages and prescribed time limits for each, but these are seldom observed.
- ¤ Departmental inquiries may end in imposition of major or minor penalties or acquittal
- ¤ There is wide spread dissatisfaction with delays in conducting departmental proceedings.
- ¤ Under the PC Act, the previous sanction of the competent authority is necessary for a court to take cognizance of the offence.
- ¤ This provision protects public servants from frivolous and vexatious prosecution, and ensures that senior officers act honestly and fearlessly in discharging their duties.
- ¤ However, it is believed that politically-connected dishonest officers in collusion with politicians arrange to inordinately delay sanctions
- ¤ Courts have laid down that sanctions for prosecution under the PC Act should be given by the competent authorities in reasonable time after duly considering the merits of the case.
- ¤ After the passing of the Lokpal and Lokayukta Act, Lok pal (Lokayukta) has the power to sanction prosecutions of cases on its own.
- ¤ Higher judiciary should consider ways of speeding up corruption cases in courts.
- ¤ Article 311 of the Constitution gives job security to government servants.
- ¤ Critics argue that the protection given by Art 311is excessive and emboldens government to become dishonest.
- ¤ SARC recommended that articles 310 and 311 should deleted, and that government arevants should be protected by passing laws under article 309.

PRACTICE QUESTIONS

1. Briefly outline the acts which fall within the legal definition of corruption.
2. What are the circumstances which create suspicions about an officer's integrity?
3. What is the recommendation of the Second Administrative Reforms Commission on widening the definition of corruption? Explain its rationale briefly.
4. What do you understand by coercive and collusive forms of corruption? In what category will you place Coalgate scam and why?
5. An overloaded truck is stopped by a traffic constable on the highway. He tells the driver that his number plates are covered with mud and have become unreadable. The driver tells the policeman that rain en route and certain muddy stretches caused the problem. The policeman wants to take him to the police station. The driver is worried that the delivery of the goods he is carrying will be delayed and that his boss will get angry. When he pleads with the policeman, the policeman asks for a gift to let him go. The driver pays him Rs 300 and drives away. Discuss this incident (100 words).
6. "Corruption is a problem not so much of individual character of officials as of the defects of government systems and procedures". Examine.
7. "Prevention is better than cure". How far does this apply to fight against corruption?
8. Write short notes on:
   (a) Illegal gratification
   (b) Abuse of authority
   (c) Assets disproportionate to known sources of income
   (d) Discretionary powers
   (e) Chief Vigilance Officers
   (f) Lack of integrity
   (g) Preventive vigilance.
9. What are the functions of the Central Vigilance Commission?
10. Suppose you are posted as CVO in an organization. How will you go about handling the likely corruption in the office? (300 words)
11. "The requirement of sanction for prosecuting dishonest officials is shield for corruption." Do you agree?
12. Explain why action to punish erring government officials gets delayed.
13. "Dishonest officials often escape punishment because of their secret partnership with political leaders." Do you agree with this popular conception?
14. One of the demands of Anna Hazare's movement was for dropping the provision in the PC Act for prior government sanction for prosecution of government officials. What are the difficulties with this demand?
15. Explain briefly the reasons which cause delays in court proceedings on corruption.

16. Write short notes (60-70 words) on:
    (i) Reasonable opportunity of being heard
    (ii) Departmental inquiry
    (iii) Major and minor punishments
    (iv) Protection given to government officials under article 311

REFERENCES

- Second Administrative Reforms Commission, Ethics in Governance (Fourth Report)
- The Prevention of Corruption Act 1988
- The Lokpal and Lokayuktas Act
- Advisory Panel on Strengthening of the Institutions of Parliamentary Democracy (Member-in-charge Justice Shri B.P. Jeevan Reddy, Chairperson Justice Shri H.R. Khanna, members Shri K. Parasaran, Dr. Jayaprakash Narayan and Dr. V.A. Pai Panandikar, member Secretary) Dr. Raghbir Singh, Probity in Public Life
- N. Vittal, Applying Zero Tolerance to Corruption

Multi-pronged Approach to Reducing Corruption

INTRODUCTION

In this chapter, we discuss the various means of reducing corruption that government has adopted. These include: enacting new laws; adopting systemic economic and administrative reforms; introducing modern technology; promoting transparency; entering into integrity pacts; clearly defining accountability; ensuring accessibility and responsiveness of officials to people; monitoring public complaints; watching over corruption-prone areas of administration and their personnel; and involving civil society in efforts to reduce corruption. We end the chapter with a brief account of political aspects of corruption.

Liability of Corrupt Public Servants to Pay Damages

For their corrupt acts, public servants are liable for punishment under the Prevention of Corruption Act (PC Act). But PC Act has no provision for civil liability of the wrong doer; nor does it have a provision for compensating the person/organization which has been wronged or has suffered damage because of the public servant's misconduct. The Constitutional Review Committee recommended the enactment of a comprehensive law to provide for the creation of liability in cases where public servants cause loss to the State by malafide actions or omissions.

SARC recommended that in cases where public servants cause loss to the State or citizens by their corrupt acts, they should be made liable to make good the loss and to pay damages. The circumstances of cases where such damages would be payable, the principles of assessing the damages and the criteria for awarding the damages to the persons who have been wronged should be clearly spelt out. Adequate safeguards should be provided so that *bona fide* mistakes do not lead to award of damages. Otherwise public servants would avoid fair and speedy decisions.

Confiscation of Properties Illegally Acquired by Corrupt Means

Prosecutions and convictions of dishonest public servants are too few in relation to deep public dissatisfaction over corruption. Many corrupt officials have escaped because of the high standard of proof needed to establish corruption charges and the legal obstacles to speedy trials. The guilty officials have often been enjoying their ill-gotten wealth.

The Supreme Court has observed that: "A law providing for forfeiture of properties acquired by holders of public offices by indulging in corrupt and illegal acts and deals is a crying necessity in the present state of our society". The Law Commission in its 166th Report (1999) observed as follows: "The Prevention of Corruption Act has totally failed in checking corruption. In spite of the fact that India is rated as one of the most corrupt countries in the world, the number of prosecutions and more so the number of convictions are ridiculously low. A corrupt Minister or a corrupt top civil servant is hardly ever prosecuted under the Act, and in the rare event of his/her being prosecuted, the prosecution hardly reaches conclusion. At every stage there will be revisions and writs to stall the process."

The amendments to the PC Act made in 2018 contain specific provisions for attachment and confiscation of property. These provisions make it difficult for corrupt officers to conceal or dispose of properties acquired through corrupt means. The amendment empowers the Special Judge conducting a trial under the PC Act to pass an order for attachment/confiscation of money or property procured by means of an offence under the PC Act. Earlier, powers to attach property derived from corruption were covered under the Prevention of Money Laundering Act, 2002. The PC Amendment Act specifically grants such powers to the Special Judge conducting trial under the PC Act.

Important Changes made in the PC Act in 2018

The Prevention of Corruption (Amendment) Act, 2018 (Amendment Act) came into force on 26 July 2018. It aims to bring the Indian anti-corruption legal framework in conformity with current international practices laid down by the United Nations Convention Against Corruption (UNCAC). The PC Act was considered restrictive in its scope and in comparison to the Foreign Corrupt Practice Act, 1977 of the United States of America and the UK Bribery Act, 2010 which are considered to be stringent anti-corruption laws. The Amendment in 2018 to the PC Act widens its scope and brings it on par with several aspects of these international anti-corruption laws. Some notable new provisions are outlined below. We have already noted in chapter 10 the new wording used in the amended Act for defining corruption.

(i) The PC Act did not have a specific provision for punishing the bribe-givers. Section 8 of the amended Act tackles the supply side of corruption. Any person who gives or promises to give undue advantage to another person to induce or reward a public servant for improper performance of public duty shall be punishable for imprisonment for up to 7 years or fine or with both. This provision will not apply where a person has been compelled to give undue advantage and has reported to law enforcement agencies within seven days from the date of giving such advantage. It is immaterial whether the undue advantage is received directly or through intermediaries. This provision aims at curbing collusive corruption by bribe-givers in taxation, regulatory matters and the like.

(ii) Section 9 of the amended Act introduces corporate liability of companies for indulging in corrupt activities. This section makes a company guilty and punishable with fine if any person associated with it gives or promises to give any undue advantage with the intent to (i) obtain/ retain any business or to (ii) obtain or retain an advantage in the conduct of its business. In this connection, a company cannot adopt a defence that such actions are individual decisions of persons associated with it unless it can show that it has instituted compliance mechanisms and safeguards against such actions. The amended Act has not laid down such procedures but left it to government to do so. However, in the mean while a company can rely upon provisions contained in Foreign Corrupt Practices Act Resource Guide (USA) and Six Principles of Adequate Procedures in the UK Bribery Act.

(iii) The amended Act also changes a provision which led to prosecution under the PC Act of honest public servants for their bona fide decisions which might have caused loss to public exchequer. Under an unamended section of the PC Act, civil servants became liable if their decisions caused loss to government. In such cases it was not necessary to show mens rea or the criminal or guilty intention of the public servant. The fact that his decision or action caused loss was sufficient to establish his/her guilt. This provision led many honest officials into problems

The unamended section reads –' 13(1) A public servant is said to commit the offence of criminal misconduct,–

if while holding office as a public servant, obtains for any person any valuable thing or pecuniary advantage without any public interest;

The new subsection reads:

'13. Criminal misconduct by a public servant.– (1) A public servant is said to commit the offence of criminal misconduct,–

(a) if he dishonestly or fraudulently misappropriates or otherwise converts for his own use any property entrusted to him or any property under his control as a public servant or allows any other person so to do; or

(b) if he intentionally enriches himself illicitly during the period of his office.'

The wording of the amended section introduces criminal intention or bad faith as a necessary ingredient for constituting an offence under the PC Act. It is hoped that the change will remove fears in the minds of civil servants and the policy-paralysis which they created.

Prohibition of 'Benami' Transactions

Corrupt public servants try to hide their illegitimate wealth through 'Benami' transactions. In these transactions, the government servant holds property in someone else's name. The Law Commission recommended enactment of a legislation prohibiting Benami transactions and acquiring properties held Benami. A law entitled The Benami Transactions (Prohibition) Act was passed in 1988. The Act precludes the person who acquired the property in the name of another person from claiming it as his own. The Act prohibits Benami transactions and prohibits the acquirer from recovering the property from the Benamidar. The Act permits acquisition of property held Benami: "All properties held Benami shall be subject to acquisition by such authority, in such manner and after following such procedure as may be prescribed". It makes it clear that no amount shall be payable for the acquisition of any property under the Act.

Even after many years, Government has not prescribed rules under the Act. The government is, therefore, not in a position to confiscate properties acquired by the real owner in the name of his benamidars. The wealth amassed by corrupt public servants is often kept in 'Benami' accounts or invested in properties in others' names. Strict enforcement of the Benami Transactions (Prohibition) Act, 1988, could unearth such properties and make property accumulation difficult for corrupt officers and also work as a deterrent for others.

Government notified the necessary rules for the implementation of the Act prohibiting 'benami' transactions with effect from 1 November 2016. The Act is now being implemented. The IT department has given advertisements warning people against entering into Benami transactions.

Protection to Whistleblowers

The term 'whistleblowing' is a newly coined expression. It refers to an individual who makes public the illegal or dark secrets carefully hidden within an organization. Daniel Ellsberg 'blew the whistle' on the so called 'Pentagon papers'. Pentagon is the headquarters of the US military, and the papers are classified military documents. He went through prolonged legal trials and troubles. Thereafter, whistleblowing has not only been protected by law but is encouraged as a moral duty of the citizens. One should note that whistleblowing means exposing illegally suppressed or hidden information about illegal actions. Organizations and individuals hide such information to escape from law.

Subsequent to the exposure of Pentagon papers, United States also witnessed corporate frauds on a massive scale. Chartered accounts colluded in falsification of accounts to hide losses and financial wrongdoing. As a result, two huge corporations, Enron and WorldCom, collapsed. The US Congress then passed laws giving sweeping protection to whistleblowers in publicly traded companies. Anyone retaliating against a corporate whistleblower can now be imprisoned for upto 10 years.

Whistleblowers help in providing information about corruption. Public servants in a department/ agency know the antecedents and activities of their colleagues, subordinates and bosses. They are naturally afraid of sharing such information for fear of reprisal. They are often willing 'to spill the beans' if their identity is kept secret and if they are assured of protection. If adequate statutory protection is granted to whistle blowers, Government can access substantial information about corruption.

There is some difference between whistleblowers and informers. Informers usually do not belong to the set up or organization about which they give information. They come to know of the information either accidentally or by 'keeping their eyes and ears open' or by just snooping around for information which can fetch some reward or money from the police. Whistleblowers are part of an organization whose members are involved in wrongdoing. They get to know things as insiders. When they leak information, they become vulnerable in various ways.

The vulnerability of those who expose hidden goings on in an organization is best shown by tragic death of two bright young Indians. One was Manjunath Shanmugam working with Indian Oil Corporation; he was a graduate of the Indian Institute of Management, Lucknow. He refused bribes and ignored threats to his life in his fight against adulteration by the petrol pump owners. He paid the price. He was shot dead on 19th November, 2005 allegedly at the behest of corrupt petrol pump owners. The other was Satyendra Dubey, working with the National Highways Authority of India. He exposed the rampant corruption in construction of roads. He was killed on 27th November, 2003.

UK, USA, Australia and New Zealand have laws which protect whistleblowers. The UK Public Interest Disclosure Act, 1998, the Public Interest Disclosure Act, 1994 of Australia, the Protected Disclosure Act, 2000 of New Zealand, and the Whistleblowers Protection Act, 1984 of USA afford protection to whistleblowers. They contain provisions which maintain the anonymity of the whistleblower and safeguard him/her against victimization within the organization.

The Whistle Blowers Protection Act, 2014 (referred to as the Act hereafter)

The preamble of the Act states that its purpose is to establish a mechanism to receive complaints relating to disclosure on any allegation of corruption or wilful misuse of power or wilful misuse of discretion against any public servant and to inquire or cause an inquiry into such disclosure and to provide adequate safeguards against victimisation of the person making such complaint.

The main provisions of the Act are listed below:

- The Act does not apply to the armed forces of the Union.
- Nor does it cover Supreme court and High court judges.
- Any public servant or any other person including any non-governmental organisation, may make a public interest disclosure before the Competent Authority.
- Any disclosure made under the Act will be considered as public interest disclosure.
- Every disclosure shall be made in good faith and the person making disclosure shall make a personal declaration stating that he reasonably believes that the information disclosed by him and allegation contained therein is substantially true.
- Every disclosure shall be made in writing or by electronic mail or electronic mail message and contain full particulars and be accompanied by supporting documents, or other materials, if any.
- Anonymous and pseudonymous applications will not be inquired into.

Competent authorities

Public servant complained against	Competent authority
Union minister	Prime minister
State minister	Concerned Chief minister
Lok Sabha member	Lok Sabha Speaker
Rajya Sabha member	Vice chairman Rajya Sabha
State assembly member	Speaker of concerned assembly
Central government/CPSE officials	Central vigilance Commission
State government/Sate PSE officials	State vigilance commission
Judicial officers (judges)	Concerned High court judges

- The identity of the complainant will not be revealed without his/her written consent.

- Any person who negligently or in a mala fide manner reveals the identity of the whistleblower may be sentenced up to three years in prison and also pay a fine upto Rs. 50,000.
- Knowingly making (or making mala fide) a false complaint will invite a two year prison term and a fine up to Rs. 30,000.
- The competent authority may make discreet inquires or open inquiry and also seek the explanation of the public servant complained against and within three months take any of the following steps:
  (i) Recommend that formal proceedings be initiated against the public servant complained against;
  (ii) Take appropriate steps to redress the loss caused to the Government;
  (iii) Recommend initiation of appropriate criminal proceedings against the person complained against;
  (iv) Recommend appropriate corrective measures;
  (v) Recommend any other necessary measure for the purpose of the law; or
  (vi) Close the case (after giving an opportunity to the complainant to object to the closure order.
- The public authority to whom the Competent Authority makes recommendation should act on it within three months of its receipt or within six months if the Competent Authority extends the time. In case the public authority does not agree with the recommendation of the Competent Authority, it shall record the reasons for such disagreement.
- The competent Authority shall not inquire into the following types of disclosure:
  (i) If it relates to a matter settled by a court or tribunal
  (ii) If it is subject of a proceeding under the Commissions of Inquiries Act or of under the Public Servants (Inquiries) Act
  (iii) If it relates to proceedings of union or State cabinet or of their committees
  (iv) If it relates to a complaint that is more than seven years old
- In any inquiry, the Competent Authority cannot question any bona fide action or bona fide discretion (including administrative or statutory discretion) exercised in discharge of duty by the employee.
- The Competent Authority shall not seek answers to such question or such document or information as is likely to prejudicially affect the interest of the sovereignty and integrity of India, the security of the State, friendly relations with foreign State, public order, decency or morality or in relation to contempt of court, defamation or incitement to an offence.
- The Competent Authority should not seek from anyone any evidence or any document which he could not be compelled to give or produce in proceedings before a court.
- The Central Government shall ensure that no person or a public servant who has made a disclosure under this Act is victimised by initiation of any proceedings or otherwise merely on the ground that such person or a public servant had made a disclosure or rendered assistance in inquiry under this Act.

- If any person is being victimised or likely to be victimised on the ground that he had filed a complaint or made disclosure or rendered assistance in inquiry under the Act, he may file an application before the Competent Authority seeking redress in the matter, and such authority shall take such action, as deemed fit and may give suitable directions to the concerned, to protect such person from being victimised or avoid his victimisation.
- The Act empowers the Competent Authority to direct the restoration of the public servant making the disclosure, to the status quo ante.
- The Competent Authority can take measures for the protection of witnesses and other persons helping in the inquiries under the Act.

False Claims Act

The existing provisions in the Indian Penal Code and other enactments are not adequate to enable interested citizens and civil society groups to approach the courts. The US Federal False Claims Act empowers any person who has knowledge about a fraud committed by another person or entity, to file a law suit on behalf of the Federal Government. And if the fraud is established in a court of law, the person committing the fraud is penalized and the plaintiff is rewarded with a percentage of recovery. The whole procedure is governed by rules of civil litigation and the standard of proof needs to meet civil court norms, and does not require proof beyond reasonable doubt, as in criminal cases.

As recommended by the SARC, a law on the model of the US False Claims Act should be passed in India with the following main provisions.

- Citizens and civil society groups can seek legal relief when people defraud governments by filing false claims against government.
- Any citizen can file a suit against any person or agency that makes a false claim against government.
- If the false claim is proved, then the person/agency responsible shall be liable for penalty equal to five times the loss sustained by the exchequer or society.
- The loss may be monetary or non-monetary such as pollution or other social costs. For non-monetary loss, the court would have the authority to compute the loss in monetary terms.
- The person who brought the suit shall be suitably compensated out of the damages recovered.

Systemic Reforms

According to IMF (Finance and Development; September 2005, Volume 42, Number 3): "A fallacy promoted by some in the field of anti-corruption and at times also by the international community is that one "fights corruption by fighting corruption" - through yet another anti-corruption campaign, the creation of more 'commissions' and ethics agencies, and the incessant drafting of new laws, decrees, and codes of conduct. Overall, such initiatives appear to have little impact, and are often politically expedient ways of reacting to pressures to do something about corruption, substituting for the need for fundamental and systemic governance reforms". These observations are similar to those of the British development economist Michael Lipton; legalistic solutions can seldom solve problems with deep social, economic and political roots. It is not possible to consign economic problems to oblivion through legislation. As an aside we may note that this warrants some scepticism about the many 'rights' and 'entitlements' now being created through various laws. Answers often lie in increasing savings, investment, productivity, output and employment.

As we saw earlier, one can view corruption as an individual moral failing and look for solutions in improving the moral conduct of individual government servants. One can impose strict codes of conduct and prescribe high ethical values for moral guidance. One may organize training programmes for instruction in ethical decision-making. All these approaches mainly target individual government servants without significantly altering their operating environment.

Another approach to tackling corruption places emphasis mainly on the government or public systems. In this approach, the focus is on structures and processes as also on operating rules governing decision making. We can, according to this view, attribute corruption not so much to human moral frailty as to inherent systemic weaknesses which create the opportunities for corruption.

Systemic Weaknesses Economic Sphere

We may consider the more commonly mentioned systemic weaknesses. One is monopoly which characterizes many government systems. In monopoly a single supplier provides or sells goods and services. Government provides many public services as a monopoly. As there is no competition, consumers have nowhere else to go. This enables government servants to act arbitrarily and exact illegal payments from people. From an economic point of view, such illegal extortions represent the monopolistic profits of a monopolist as opposed to normal profits under competition. The illegal payments can also be seen as monopoly rents.

In this connection, we may note that the elaborate system of economic controls which Pandit Jawaharlal Nehru created as part of the socialistic pattern of society proved to be a breeding ground for corruption. Entrepreneurs had to seek approval from government for virtually everything. C. Rajagopalachari, a brilliant thinker and leader of Independence movement, opposed the whole economic philosophy calling it "the license-quota-permit raj".

The economic logic here is simple. Those who secure licenses, quotas or permits virtually get hold of scarce economic resources at a price administratively determined by government. Now, this official price is less than the market price which is determined by actual demand and actual supply of the commodity. There is a 'premium' on the price of that commodity which is equal to the difference between the market price and the official price. The recipients of the scarce commodity are naturally willing to pay some amount from the profit they gain by securing the commodity at less than its market price. Many controlled industrial raw materials, cement, sugar, car and gas allotments and food grains supplied through public distribution system - all belonged to this category.

A similar situation prevailed in the foreign exchange market in which official exchange rate of rupee overvalued it in terms of hard currencies like dollar or yen. In other words, recipients of foreign exchange quotas got foreign currencies far below their market rates. Further, no industry could be started without a licence. This simply meant restricting competition and promoting monopolistic trends. Many economic reforms introduced deregulation of industry and trade and removed economic controls. This type of reform removes the incentive for giving bribes.

Administrative Sphere

The above mentioned two areas fall within economic sphere. We will now consider two areas which fall more directly within administrative sphere. One arises from an inherent feature of the modern administrative state. Its welfare orientation has created huge bureaucracies and vast public service delivery systems. These systems are riddled with financial and managerial problems. These have in turn led to serious complaints about service quality. The problem has become acute in almost all advanced countries including USA and UK. But political leaders are still luring voters with promises of more and more cheap services.

Besides the above syndrome, discretionary decision-making is seen as another major source of corruption. In theory, government decisions at various levels are objective in the sense that they rely on a set of impersonal rules and operate equally as between similarly situated individuals. However, in practice no set of rules no matter how exhaustive can cover all possible cases. Hence, rules cannot entirely guide decisions. There is a tendency for corruption to follow in the wake of discretion. Hence, suggestions are often made for reducing discretionary decision-making.

Lack of accountability is another frequently cited reason for corruption. As we know, the RTI Act, citizen's charters, bill on provision of services to people and redressal of their grievances are among the measures for promoting accountability of government servants. SARC gives an interesting formula (of American economist Robert Klitgaard) on corruption which links it to the operating environment of civil service:

Monopoly + Discretion - Accountability = Corruption

Case Study

There is a shortage of housing plots in the city. Government has released some vacant public land for construction of flats. The officials recommend that the flats after construction should be allotted at market prices. But as the demand is huge, they recommend a computerized draw for allotment. While accepting the proposal, the minister suggests that 20% of flats should be allotted from his discretionary quota.

Question

In this situation, what should the concerned officers do?

1. They should simply follow the orders of the minister.
2. They should tell the minister that the proposed discretionary allotments will lead to serious controversy.
3. They should delay the matters.
4. They should oppose the decision tooth and nail.

Discussion

The first alternative is inappropriate. The officers have to reiterate on file the risks involved in the process. They should cite examples from CAG's audits and reports of anti-corruption agencies showing how discretionary quotas are economically unjustified, and lead to abuses.

The second alternative is correct. The minister's proposal will lead to favouritism and corruption. This case shows a typical situation of extreme shortage of housing--a much desired item. There will be an inherent tendency for rich people to pay money to swing allotments in their favour. The houses will command a premium since the demand for them far exceeds supply. The shortage cannot be made up in the short run. This situation contains inherent possibilities for corruption.

There is another problem in this situation. Basically under law, any discretionary quota will be arbitrary. Even for making allotments from discretionary quota, criteria and procedures have to be laid down. There will be great pressure on the minister and the concerned officials to make exceptions to criteria and procedures. It is better not to create such situations. The best option will be to first lay down reasonable conditions for eligibility of flats and then allot them by randomised computer lottery. There can be some restrictions on transfer of the flats by allottes.

The third alternative is inappropriate. It will only postpone the implementation for some time. The problem will continue to linger. After some time, the minister will lose patience, and demand implementation of his decision.

Officers should not refuse to implement orders after a point. Once they again point out the problems which will arise from the decision, they should follow the minister's orders.

Recent Measures

Two Reforms

Corruption has to be tackled with both penal and preventive measures. Preventive steps reduce opportunities for corruption by creating transparent systems, by increasing accountability, by reducing discretion and by rationalizing procedures. Recent years have seen the introduction of many such systemic reforms which have improved systems and processes.

Two such reforms are:

Passenger Bookings on Indian Railways

Railway authorities have computerized passenger bookings and introduced 'on-line' booking and e-ticketing. This has eliminated the middlemen, decongested booking offices and made the Railway reservation process transparent.

Common Entrance Test (Karnataka)

This has made possible a timely and transparent merit-based selection in professional colleges.

Increasing Competition

We turn now to another approach which relies on reducing monopolistic elements in provision of goods and services. Government is the sole service provider in many sectors – a situation which breeds arbitrariness, complacency and corruption. Introducing competition in providing public services can reduce corruption. Telecom sector deregulation is usually cited as a case in point.

Till recently, telecommunication sector was a complete government monopoly. In telecom sphere, the Department of Telecommunication acted as the policy maker, service provider and the licensor. Telecom sector policy reforms introduced competition, allowed private players to provide international and national long distance services on land lines and on cellular devices. Policymaking has been separated from provision of services. The reforms led to sharp increase in teledensity, drastic reduction in the cost of services and major decline in corrupt practices.

While undoubtedly reducing 'retail' corruption at the interface between consumers and lower telecom bureaucracy, the policy reform also led to possibly the largest corruption scandal in post-independent India. We cannot discuss this matter in detail here. However, it relates to transfer of valuable public resources (spectrum in this instance) to private entities at throwaway prices. To this end, various stratagems were adopted. One was adoption of prices of a past period which were bound to be lower than the current market prices and the absence of a proper price discovery mechanism. The second device was the creation of dummy companies (by existing entities and others) for either circumventing tender conditions or for making a 'killing' through post acquisition sale. The principle of making spectrum allocation on first-come-first-served basis was changed. Finally, the owners of the dummy entities, who got the spectrum, transferred it indirectly in the guise of dilution of their shareholdings in the dummy companies rather than through direct sale of spectrum. Basically, they sold off the spectrum to other genuine telecom operators at a windfall gain. 2G scam is an instance of byzantine commercial intrigue. Of course, one has to await the outcome of judicial proceedings in the matter.

The process of breaking up monopolies and introducing competition often leads to introduction of private agencies as service providers or suppliers of commodities. To prevent malpractices by private agencies, regulatory agencies such as telecom regulatory authority are necessary. Regulatory agencies ensure that the private agencies meet the prescribed service standards. Further, if in any department, monopoly of service functions exists, the scope for introducing competition should be considered. This kind of exercise has to be undertaken at central, state and local levels. Competition need not be through introduction of private agencies; it can be between government departments. It is necessary to have multiple agencies for providing any services.

Streamlining Procedures

The complexity of official work methods also arises from the hierarchical structure of government organization and the multiple levels involved in decision making. Any matter is examined at many levels, leading to delay and diffusion of responsibility and accountability. This leads to a typical form of corruption known as 'speed money'. It means that the concerned official is paid money not for favouring any particular party but to quickly push a file on its onward journey to the next level in the hierarchy. One way of reducing delays and corruption will be to reduce the number of levels at which a matter is processed.

As we mentioned earlier, one way of simplifying procedures is to provide the common services which citizens require at one point and in a single stage. This is known as the system of single window clearance or one-stop service centre. A successful example is Andhra Pradesh's E-Seva model. E-Seva provides the services of 13 state and local government organisations, 3 central government organisations and 9 private sector organisations under one roof. The services that E-Seva offers include the payment of public service bills, provision of birth and death certificates, payment of property tax, train and bus reservations, private mobile phone bill payments, receipt of passport applications and, transfer of shares.

'Positive silence' sanctions represent another means of simplifying procedures from the citizen's point of view. These are also known as deemed approvals. Government regulations lay down many approvals which people have to take before starting any activity like opening a shop. In positive silence sanctions if the applicant does not receive a reply from the concerned departments by a stipulated time, he is deemed to have received the approval and can start with the work. Bureaucracies sometimes circumvent deemed approval procedures also. They refuse the application on the last date on flimsy grounds. Or they harass the individual who carries on with his work on the basis of the deemed approval. But deemed approvals certainly put pressure in most circumstances on government officials to decide a matter within a definite time period.

Official methods for processing licenses, permits and registrations were devised long ago. They are complex and involve documentation requirements which baffle common citizens. They create a system in which middlemen and the corrupt flourish. To reduce corruption, departments, should cut down procedural requirements to the minimum.

Using Information Technology

Information is a vital service which citizens need from government agencies. Information and Communication Technology (ICT) has transformed the traditional methods of storage, transmission and retrieval of information. Information can now be provided speedily and without human interactions. Notable progress has already made in providing access to information and data, in building management information systems and in electronic service delivery. Many transactions between government departments, between government and citizens and between government and business have been computerized.

ICT can reduce corruption by delivering information at great speed with almost no face to face contact. We have already seen how use of information technology can cleanse traditionally corruption prone areas of administration. We will consider one notable example. It is the Gyandoot project in Madhya Pradesh. It is based on a low cost intranet linking various market centres and villages. Local youth run kiosks on commercial lines charging a user fee. The kiosks render services such as – agricultural produce auction centre rates; copies of land records; online registration of applications; online public grievance redress; village auction site information; and updated information regarding beneficiaries of social security pension, rural development schemes and government grants of various kinds. The most sought after information (95%) was on agricultural produce rates, land records and grievance services. Gyandoot project empowered local communities and reduced corruption.

Promoting Transparency

'Transparency' signifies openness and accountability of administration. An organization is transparent when its decision-making and mode of working is open to public and media scrutiny and public discussion. A transparent system of administration encourages public participation in government's decision-making processes. It is especially useful in promoting grass root level democracy. RTI Act is the foremost measure that government took for promoting transparency in administration.

Integrity Pacts

'Integrity pacts' are added to public contracts to reduce scope for corruption. Governments are huge purchasers of goods and services. They make purchases by floating tenders which seek prices from sellers for supply of goods of given specifications. Ideally the tenders have to follow open competitive bidding process in which all qualified producers or sellers or suppliers can participate. The contract is awarded to the lowest responsive bidder. This simply means that the contract is given to the supplier who offers the lowest price and accepts all the conditions of the tender.

Contracts cover many areas – execution of works, supply of commodities and provision of services. Major contracts can be very complex involving intricate financial, commercial, technical, legal and managerial aspects. They often run into many volumes. We need not get into these complexities. The short point is that major contracts can be highly lucrative. The stakes are high, competition is cutthroat and the bidders are willing to pay kick backs to get the contract. In India, huge purchases are made by Ministries like Defence and Railways. In the recent 'railgate' scam, one officer wanted posting as a Member of Railway Board in a particular operational area or jurisdiction. This position as Member involves processing tenders running into tens of thousands of crores. Corruption in contracts is a 'big ticket item' and the means of draining huge amounts from public exchequer into illegitimate channels.

Integrity pact is an agreement between the public agency procuring goods and services and the bidder for a public contract. Through the pact the bidders give assurances that they have not paid and shall not pay any illegal gratification to secure the contract in question. From its side, the public agency calling for bids commits to ensuring a level playing field and fair play in the procurement process. Such pacts often involve supervision and scrutiny by independent, outside observers. Such pacts increase transparency and confidence in the processes through which Government and public sector units conclude major deals. Many national legal systems now recognise such pacts; ONGC signed a MoU with Transparency International India and the CVC in 2006. The revised Defence Procurement Procedure Manual, 2006 provides for adoption of an integrity pact in all defence contracts and procurements of more than Rs. 300 crores.

Government organizations are reluctant in adopting integrity pacts. Such pacts have an uncertain status in our legal framework. Government needs to clarify the legal status of the integrity pacts and build them into government transactions covering major tenders.

Accountability of Civil Servants

Lack of clear accountability of civil servants is often said to be a cause of corruption and misgovernance. The administrative system needs at every level of its structure a clear assignment of duties and responsibilities. Then only can a government servant be held accountable for the way he does his job. Duties have to be worded clearly and should also spell out the supervisory responsibilities of the controlling officers. The assignment of responsibility has to go up to the top of the hierarchy. This will create an interlocking accountability chain which forces government servants at every level to function efficiently.

The system needs an in-built system of rewards and punishments with objective criteria which can eliminate arbitrariness and subjectivity in granting rewards or awarding punishments. At present, incentives to diligence and efficiency are weak; shirkers, non-performers and the corrupt fear no adverse consequences. There is no performance audit of officials now; the old system of awareness in higher echelons of an officer's strengths, weaknesses and reputation is also missing. A robust performance audit to periodically monitor and objectively evaluate the performance of officers at various levels is needed.

Corruption Risk Management

Corruption risks in government revolve around various factors. First, an office with discretionary powers, public dealings and large project budgets offers scope for corruption. Offices without these features offer little scope for corruption. One may classify offices as susceptible to 'high risk of corruption', 'medium risk of corruption' and 'low risk of corruption'. For instance, the post of a tax assessing officer or an inspector at an inter-state border check-post could be classified as a 'high risk position', whereas the position of an official at an inquiry counter is a 'low risk position'. Government servants jocularly refer to these as 'wet' and 'dry' posts.

Secondly, levels of integrity of individual government servants can vary; some are absolutely upright; others are greedily grasping; and some others are opportunistic and succumb when the bait is attractive and the chances of detection seem remote. They resemble the wary transgressor of the Bible. They can be classified from corruption proneness as 'low risk', 'moderate risk' and 'high risk personnel'. To reduce possibilities of corruption, the 'low risk' personnel have to be posted to offices with 'high risk of corruption'.

Risk profiling of government officials is difficult because annual confidential reports seldom contain frank assessment about integrity. One suggestion is that a committee of 'eminent persons' can be entrusted with risk profiling officers after they have completed ten years of service, and then once in every five years. The committee can base its findings on the performance evaluation of the officers, their self-assessments, reports from the vigilance organization and confidential peer evaluation.

Some methods of risk profiling rely on integrity tests. Some developed countries apply these tests to identify suspected corrupt persons. As part of it, the candidate has to answer various questions. New York Police Department and London Police use such tests. Integrity tests, like all tests, are imperfect, and can lead to wrong conclusions and are thus not a foolproof method to evaluate integrity of a person. Therefore, these can be used as one of the inputs while risk profiling an officer.

Supervision

Governments have a hierarchical structure in which each functionary reports to one above him. Each officer has to supervise the working of his subordinates. Unfortunately, supervision in government is lax. Hardly any corruption cases arise from complaints of officers against their subordinates. Controlling corruption in an office or an organization should primarily be the responsibility of the head of the office. Supervisory officials should take preventive steps to minimize corruption among their subordinates. They should not regard it as the function of external vigilance agencies. Pro-active steps for controlling corruption consist of random inspections, surprise visits, confidential feedback from citizens or clients, putting procedures in place which make it difficult to seek bribes and use of decoy clients.

Government departments buy large quantities of various materials. These include: stationery, computer accessories and office equipment, consumables, lighting and sanitation items, drugs, pharmaceuticals, hospital requirements; clothing requirements of hospitals, uniformed services, educational institutions and hostels; books and other educational accessories and construction materials. These transactions create money making opportunities through price manipulations. Reviews or checks could be conducted internally to ascertain prices paid to different agencies to discover instances of suspiciously exorbitant payments. Similar comparative analysis could also be useful in revenue generating departments which obtain periodical returns from citizens, such as various tax departments.

Corruption occurs when a public servant commits illegal acts to benefit a citizen. Passing an illegal assessment order favouring a tax payer is an example. "Speed money" is a form of corruption for acting quickly in a matter. Corruption may also happen through deliberate negligence of a public servant - such as allowing an illegal consignment through customs. Supervisory officials should, after studying the patterns of corruption in their organizations, create an institutionalized system to prevent corruption.

Ensuring Accessibility and Responsiveness

Corruption can be reduced if government servants are accessible to applicants and promptly respond to their needs. Citizen's charters are one means to a responsive administration. Each department should prominently display the facilities, concessions and rights which it offers to public along with the details about authorities who are competent to grant them together with the procedure for securing them and getting their grievances redressed. Service standards need to be defined. Appeal procedures available to customers who want further redressal should also be specified.

Transparency in government offices can be improved in many ways. Some of these include: help desks at the cutting edge level, prominent display of names of officials, automatic call centres and simplified computerized systems of service delivery. Accessibility of government servants to the public should be so designed as to ensure regular, time bound and courteous interaction between the citizens and official functionaries. Public interaction should be limited to the head of office and some designated officers. This can be supported by a 'single window front office' for providing information.

Reducing Discretion

Discretionary powers of government, especially at lower levels, increase the scope for corruption. Opportunities for corruption can be reduced by; (i) reducing discretion; (ii) by maximizing transparency; and (iii) by introducing strict accountability for actions. Effective anti-corruption reforms have to reduce discretionary benefits which public officials control.

One instance of improved transparency is the new policy for transferring teachers in Karnataka. Every year nearly 15000 school teachers seek transfers to places of their choice. Applications are sent to multiple authorities necessitating action at many levels. The process of decision-making was non-transparent and riddled with corruption. In the new system, applicants have to give reasons for seeking transfer. Their applications are arranged in a priority list centrally. A computer-generated list containing the names of transfer seekers and their ranking (based on the reasons for transfer) is published. Objections are invited and considered. This scheme has considerably reduced corruption.

Following measures will help in reducing corruption which arises from discretionary use of authority.

- Discretion can be eliminated from many governmental activities. All such activities could be automated and supported by IT. Registration of births and deaths and recruitment of teachers based on marks secured in qualifying exams are examples of such activities.
- Where it is impossible to eliminate discretion, the exercise of powers should be regulated by guidelines to minimize discretion. Effective checks and balances should be built over exercise of discretion.
- Decision-making on important matters should be assigned to a committee rather than to an individual.

Involving Civil Society

From the early 1990s, many civil society groups in India have been active in trying to improve governance. They challenge current administrative models, test alternative approaches and share the learning from these experiences with others.

Citizen initiatives to fight corruption come from an active social consciousness. Governments can also promote an environment which enables citizens' groups to join in anti-corruption efforts. SARC has proposed the following measures to promote public participation in anti-corruption drives.

1. Inviting civil society groups to oversee government programmes
2. Establishing and disseminating service standards
3. Establishing credible complaints' redressal mechanisms
4. Assessing public confidence in anti-corruption institutions, judiciary and law enforcement for designing programmes to improve trust levels
5. Enforcing access to information
6. Educating society on the events of corruption and instilling moral commitment to integrity
7. Using public hearings in which audience learn about public work schemes of their local area and provide their own perceptions
8. Initiating media campaigns for public education and awareness on fighting corruption
9. Holding integrity workshops and public hearings to discuss problems of corruption and considering solutions
10. Periodically surveying and assessing public service delivery
11. Surveying corruption perceptions in general about government as also about its specific sectors
12. Incorporating corruption as a subject in the education curriculum and setting up websites on corruption for providing information, inviting suggestions and associating former public servants in lobbying against corruption.

Another way of involving citizens in reducing corruption is to give them cash rewards for reporting corruption. It is likely to bring to light many cases of corruption. In taxation departments, reward schemes already exist for paying complainants a percentage of the income unearthed based on the information. Similar rewards should be offered to providers of information on corrupt practices. Change will come when the incentives to throw out a corrupt system become stronger than the incentives to retain such a system. The need of the hour is to have zero tolerance towards corruption.

Social Audit

Comptroller and Auditor General (CAG) arranges for the audit of all government departments. CAG's audit looks at financial aspects of government transactions and dealings. Proper legislative authorization for expenditure, keeping of vouchers (signed receipts) for expenditure, maintenance of accounts in prescribed forms, following proper open tender processes before incurring expenditure and fully recovering all the government revenues – all these are financial aspects of audit. Audit frequently brings to light many financial irregularities.

Social audit, as separate from financial audit, is a concept which has evolved recently. While financial audit is conducted by qualified accountants and auditors, social audit is done through people's participation. It is particularly useful in ascertaining the true state of affairs about programmes which benefit large groups, such as local public works, distribution of welfare payments, and procurement of products and services for government and delivery of services to people. In social audit of these schemes, clients or beneficiary groups or civil society groups provide information on wrongdoing. Social audit helps in checking the attendance of teachers and students in schools and hostels, staff in the hospitals and other similar programmes which provide services to people. Provisions for social audit should be made a part of the operational guidelines of all such schemes. It has already been adopted in many schemes.

Building Societal Consensus

Many problems, according to political thinkers, can be solved only through consensus. Or people in general have to agree about the existence of the problem and the methods proposed for its solution. More importantly, political parties which are supposed to articulate pro people ideologies and which wield power (on winning popular mandate) have to actively fight against corruption. Political parties only pay lip sympathy to the need for eliminating corruption. Large scale corruption has a clearly political dimension. On hearing the ringing moral tones of speeches of some political leaders, one is reminded of the distinction which T S Eliot made (in an introduction to poems of John Dryden) between "pulpit pomposity and moral seriousness".

POLITICAL CORRUPTION

Elected leaders direct the legislative and executive wings of government. Hence, the standards which they adopt greatly influence governance. Our national leaders were motivated by political idealism during the independence movement. However, soon after independence, most of them abandoned the high moral ground.

The erosion of ethical values is manifested in various ways. Political parties raise money illegally for elections, use illegitimate money in elections and exceed the ceilings on election expenditure fixed by the Election Commission. During elections, political parties resort to unfair means such as impersonation, booth-capturing, violence, inducements and intimidation. Floor-crossing after elections (change of political affiliations by members to get into power) and abuse of power in public office have become common over time.

This process is known as criminalization of politics and 'participation of criminals in the electoral processes' has become widespread. Many reasons account for growth of crime, violence and of 'mafia' power in various sectors of economy. The main reasons are:

- Flagrant violation of laws.
- Poor quality of public services and the corruption in their delivery.
- Protection given to law-breakers based on their political, group, religious or caste affiliation.
- Partisan interference in investigation of crimes, poor prosecution of cases, inordinate delays lasting over years and high costs of judicial process.
- Mass withdrawal of cases, indiscriminate grant of parole, etc.

Given this abysmal state of affairs, some criminals have begun to dispense simple, speedy justice, wearing the mantle of Robin Hood. Based on this influence, they could enter politics and elections. This gave them (and the political parties they joined) the opportunity to influence crime investigations and prosecutions, to convert policemen into allies, and to secure votes by using money and muscle power. In this process, political parties and criminals who join them gain at the cost of public good and governance. This situation may not prevail everywhere. But it is significant that the Election Commission declared that one in six legislators in India faced grave criminal charges. Political parties are ready to go to any lengths in order to gain political advantage. For example, recently the Utter Pradesh Government withdrew cases of terrorism against some individuals. The High Court, however, reversed the order.

Huge illegal election expenditure also fuels corruption. Election Commission fixed ceilings for election expenditure and attempted to secure their enforcement, but with little effect. Donors who make contributions to political parties recoup them manifold through political favours. This process engenders a chain reaction in which illegal funding and corruption become the drivers of political process. It naturally erodes confidence in the political and administrative system and creates an atmosphere of pervasive cynicism. The recent '2G scam' and 'Coalgate scam' – though *sub judice* or pending in courts – are typical instances of political corruption. Of course, they also involve tripartite collusion between political leaders, civil servants and industrialists. The anti-corruption movement of Anna Hazare, though short lived, testifies to intense public revulsion towards corruption. The Second Administration Reforms Commission (SARC) observes, "Cleansing elections is the most important route to improve ethical standards in politics, to curb corruption and rectify maladministration."

Recent Improvements

Over past twenty years, many electoral reforms have been introduced. Some observers claim that in the past decade India has witnessed more political reform than any other large democracy since the Second World War. We will now briefly outline these reforms.

Improvement in Accuracy of Electoral Rolls

The Election Commission:

- Made voter registration very accessible to all eligible voters
- Printed electoral rolls and CDS and put them on sale.
- Completed computerization of electoral rolls in the country
- Issued photo identity cards to almost all the voters
- Improved electoral rolls by adding eligible voters who do not figure in it and by excluding bogus voters

Disclosure of Antecedents of Candidates

- The Supreme Court has directed that a candidate seeking election should declare if he has been convicted by a court and if any criminal case is pending against him.
- The court further directed that a candidate has to file a declaration of assets and liabilities, including those of his family members. This would serve as a check to his integrity at the time of the next elections.

Disqualification of Persons Convicted of Criminal Offence

- According to the Representation of the People Act, no one convicted in a criminal offence can contest elections. The Supreme Court clarified in 2005 that this provision will govern all candidates irrespective of their status as members of legislature or otherwise at the time of conviction.

Enforcement of the Code of Conduct

- During elections, political parties have to follow a code of conduct. Its purpose is to ensure free and fair elections. Earlier, it was mostly a voluntary code. The Election Commission has made the Code of Conduct for elections binding in all respects. It gave many directions regarding timings of campaigns, prohibition of festoons/cutouts, insistence on daily expenditure statements, appointment of a large number of observers, ordering of re-poll in specific polling booths and other such steps.

Reduction in Size of Council of Ministers

The first Administrative Reforms Commission recommended that the size of the council of ministers should be limited to 10% of the strength of the Lower House in Parliament/State legislature. The Constitution (Ninety-first Amendment) Act, 2003 increased this limit to 15%. The idea is to curb the normal tendency to have a jumbo sized ministry. It was a popular joke that the size of one AP cabinet was large enough to virtually fill up the then recently introduced Air Bus aircraft.

According to the SARC, these steps had no visible impact on criminalization of politics, on the illegal and excessive use of money in elections, on disguised forms of inducements and patronage like chairmanships and memberships of public undertakings and the anomaly of legislators functioning as executives. We will now turn towards other important measures proposed or taken to reduce political corruption.

Reform of Political Funding

Private donations are a major means of funding for political parties. There are three models of government funding for political parties and elections. In the minimalist model, followed in UK, Ireland, Australia, New Zealand and Canada, elections are partly subsidized usually through specific grants or state rendered services. Candidates are accountable to the public authority for reporting and full disclosure of expenditure for the limited election period. The second, maximalist model of government funding, as in Sweden and Germany, supports both elections and other party activities. It also enforces internal democracy and transparency. The third model is based on part-funding of party activities and elections with matching State contributions. France, Netherlands and South Korea follow this pattern. US is a variant of the same with election funding being largely private and subjected to strict reporting and disclosure requirements as well as limits on contributions.

Many writers keep making proposals for State funding of political parties in India. Such funding in India does not seem to lie in the realm of practical possibilities. In any case, the question falls more within a political than an ethical arena. We will restrict ourselves to a brief account of legal position that obtains in India in this regard.

Indian Context

Under the Representation of the people Act (RP Act), every political party may accept any amount of contribution voluntarily offered to it by any person or company other than a government company. However, no political party is permitted to accept any contribution from any foreign source as defined under the Foreign Contribution (Regulation) Act, 1976. Under RP Act, political parties are required to declare the details of contributions (from both private persons and companies) of more than

Rs. 20,000 and prepare a report for the same in each financial year. Political parties have to submit to the Election Commission a list of donations they receive of over Rs. 20,000, giving names and addresses of the donors. If they fail to do so, then they become ineligible for getting any tax relief under the RP Act.

As regards corporate funding to political parties, in the 1960s, the Congress party and the Swatantra Party (founded by C. Rajagopalachari with advocacy of free enterprise as its main policy plank) were the chief beneficiaries of donations from big groups like the Tatas and the Birlas. In 1969, government (led by Indira Gandhi) banned corporate funding to political parties. The ban ostensibly aimed at breaking the link between politics and businesses. To circumvent the prohibition, political parties resorted to fund-raising funds by publishing souvenirs which carried advertisements by the business houses. These times also witnessed "briefcase politics" through which sizeable amounts of black money was transferred to the ruling party. Later in 1985, Rajiv Gandhi government lifted the ban on company donations to political parties.

According to the Companies Act, a company which has been in existence for more than three years can contribute to political parties up to 7.5% of its average net profit earned during the three immediately preceding financial years. Such contributions have to be approved through a resolution passed at a meeting of the Board of Directors of the Company. A company can also make contributions within the above limits and restrictions to Electoral Trusts (discussed below).

Contributions made by companies and individuals to any political party or an electoral trust are deductible from income tax liability. However, no deduction is allowed for cash contributions.

Electoral Trusts Scheme, 2013

Electoral Trust is a Section 25 company under the Companies Act or a non-profit company. Their purpose is to ensure the transparency of corporate funding to the political parties' poll expenses. Electoral Trusts get tax benefits in proportion to the funds they provide to various political outfits. They have to distribute 95% of total contributions received by them in any financial year to the registered political parties within that year itself. They cannot accept contributions from foreign citizens or companies. They need to take the PAN number of all resident Indian contributors and passport number of NRI citizens while accepting the contribution. The objective of the Electoral Trust is not to earn any profit or pass any direct or indirect benefit to its members or contributors. The sole objective is to distribute the contributions received by it to the political party concerned. The Central Bureau of Direct Taxes (CBDT) follows a procedure notified for grant of approval to an electoral trust.

Electoral Bonds

An electoral bond is like a promissory note that can be bought by any Indian citizen or company incorporated in India from select branches of State Bank of India. The citizen or corporate can then donate the same to any eligible political party of his/her choice. The bonds are similar to bank notes that are payable to the bearer on demand and are free of interest.

Government notified the Electoral Bond Scheme in 2018. The bonds will be issued in multiples of Rs 1,000, Rs 10,000, Rs 100,000 and Rs 1 crore A donor with a KYC-compliant account can purchase the bonds and can then donate them to the party or individual of their choice. Now, the receiver can encash the bonds through the party's verified account. The electoral bond will be valid only for fifteen days.

Any party that is registered under section 29A of the Representation of the Peoples Act and has secured at least one per cent of the votes polled in the most recent General elections or Assembly elections is eligible to receive electoral bonds. The party will be allotted a verified account by the Election Commission of India (ECI) and the electoral bond transactions can be made only through this account.

The electoral bonds will not bear the name of the donor. Thus, the political party might not be aware of the donor's identity. A donor of electoral bond will get a deduction for it from his taxable income, and the recipient or political party, will get tax exemption, subject to filing tax returns.

Government claimed that electoral bonds will reduce use of black money in political funding. The donations made to a party would be accounted for in the balance sheets without exposing the donor details to the public. In the absence of electoral bonds, donors would have no option but to donate by cash after siphoning off money from their businesses

However, the scheme lacks transparency. Neither the purchaser of the bond nor the political party receiving the donation is required to disclose the donor's identity. Voters, too, will have no idea of how, and through whom, a political party has been funded.

Its critics allege that the scheme was designed to help big corporate houses donate money to political parties without their identity being revealed. The scheme short circuits three other prohibitions: ban on receiving donations from a foreign company; ceiling on a company's contribution at 7.5 per cent of its average three year net profit ; and requirement that companies should disclose details of their political donations in their annual statement of accounts.

Critics of the scheme have challenged it in the Supreme court. The Election Commission in its stand before the Supreme Court did not oppose the scheme but argued against the anonymity of donations made to political parties via electoral bonds.

State Funding to political Parties in India

At present, there is no direct state funding of political parties in India.

The Dinesh Goswami Committee on Electoral Reforms set up in 1990 recommended limited government support in kind, for vehicle fuel, hire charges of microphones, copies of electoral rolls etc. But it also recommended a ban on company donations to political parties. Later, the Supreme Court made it necessary for political parties to file returns under the Income Tax and Wealth Tax Acts. The Court also clubbed (in 1996) expenditure by third party(s) as well as by the political party under the expenditure ceiling limits prescribed under the Representation of People Act.

Parliament passed a law in 2003 on government funding of political parties based on the reports of Dinesh Goswami Committee, Indrajit Gupta Committee, 1999 and of the Law Commission of India (on Reform of Electoral Laws, 1999). Its main provisions are the following:

- ¤ Full tax exemption to individuals and corporates on all contributions to political parties.
- ¤ Exclusion of the travel expenditure of political party leaders from election expenditure.
- ¤ Disclosure of party finances and contributions over Rs.20,000.
- ¤ Indirect public funding to candidates of recognised parties - besides free supply of electoral rolls (already permissible and such items as the Election Commission may decide in consultation with the union government).
- ¤ Equitable sharing of time by the recognised political parties on the cable television network and other electronic media (public and private).

Tightening of Anti-defection Law

Summary of Anti-defection Law

Disqualification

If a member of a house belonging to a political party:

- ¤ Voluntarily gives up the membership and affiliation to a political party or
- ¤ Votes, or does not vote in the legislature in compliance to the direction of his political party he shall be liable to be disqualified from being a member of the House.

However, if the member has taken prior permission on the particular issue, or is condoned by the party within 15 days from such voting or abstention, the member shall not be disqualified. The other grounds for disqualification of a member are-

- ¤ If an independent candidate joins the party after the election.
- ¤ If a nominated member joins a party six months after he has become a member of the legislature.

Power to disqualify

(a) The Chairman or the Speaker of the House has been conferred with the power to take the decision to disqualify a member.

(b) If a complaint is made with respect to the defection of the Chairman or the Speaker, a member of the house elected by that House shall have the right to take the decision.

Exception

A person shall not be disqualified if his original political party merges with another, and he along with other members of the old party become the member of the new political party or he, and other members do not accept the merger and they opt out in order to function as a separate group. This exception shall only operate if not less than two-third members of the party in the house have agreed to the merger.

Decisions of the Supreme Court

The provisions under Schedule X do not violate Article 105 and Article 194 of the Constitution of India. They do not infringe the democratic rights of elected members of the Parliament or of the State Legislatures.

The phrase 'Voluntarily giving up of membership' has a wider meaning than simple resignation. Even the conduct of the member will be covered by the phrase. For example, a member's conduct against his party in the proceedings of the house could amount to his voluntarily giving up party membership.

An elected member would continue to belong to the political party that set him or her up as a candidate for the election as such member. This is notwithstanding the fact that he or she had been expelled from that party. (This view runs counter to commonsense, but is based on a legal interpretation too involved for a brief explanation here. Interested readers can look up Venu Sundaram's article,

'Amar Singh Expulsion Case: SC Misses Chance to Interpret Anti-Defection Law', The Wire, 05/Aug/2016.)

The Speaker can take a final decision on disqualification of a member of the House. However, the Supreme Court and the High Court have the power to review the Speaker's decision.

Speaker does not have the power to review his own decision on disqualification of a member.

Indian political system has been plagued by defections. Parties, in need of additional members, for securing or consolidating their majority try to win over members of other parties to their side. It is a mode of political manipulation to advance party or individual interest. Defections are secured by inducements, threats and cold cash payments. Defection is obviously a source of political corruption.

Government passed an anti-defection law in 1985 for disqualifying the defecting members of a party from holding their legislative membership. But this was linked to a threshold limit of defecting members. Disqualification operated only if the group of defecting members formed less than one third of the party's legislative strength. If the number exceeded this threshold, no disqualification was incurred. It was argued that defection, regardless of the number of defectors or the political context is inherently immoral.

The 91st Amendment to the Constitution made in 2003 remedied the situation by changing the provisions made in 1985.

As per the 1985 Act (Tenth Schedule to the constitution), a 'defection' by one-third of the elected members of a political party was considered a 'merger'. Such defections did not disqualify the defecting members. The Dinesh Goswami Committee on Electoral Reforms, the Law Commission in its report on "Reform of Electoral Laws", and the National Commission to Review the Working of the Constitution (NCRWC) all recommended the deletion of the Tenth Schedule provision regarding exemption from disqualification in case of a split.

Finally the 91st Constitutional Amendment Act, 2003, changed this. As a result, at least two-thirds of the members of a party have to be in favour of a "merger" for it to have validity in the eyes of the law. "The merger of the original political party or a member of a House shall be deemed to have taken place if, and only if, not less than two-thirds of the members of the legislature party concerned have agreed to such merger," states the Tenth Schedule. Hence, the process of defection has become very difficult

The Election Commission has recommended that the question of disqualification of members on the ground of defection should also be decided by the President/Governor on the advice of the Election Commission. Often, matters are deliberately delayed in legislative bodies even in cases of patent defections. SARC has endorsed this recommendation.

The moral base of a coalition government is lost when the coalition parties change partners before the full term and form new coalitions driven by opportunism and craving for power. The coalition's common programme adopted before the election or before forming government becomes a casualty. To maintain the will of the people, provision should be made to prevent opportunistic redrawing of coalitions between elections. A constitutional amendment should be made so that any change in the political composition through realignments of parties results in fresh elections.

Summary

¤ The issues currently in focus in fight against corruption are (i) delays in departmental (or disciplinary) proceedings against corrupt officials; (ii) the need for prior government sanction for prosecuting corrupt officials; (iii) speeding up trials of corruption cases; (iv) making corrupt public servants liable for damages for their actions; (v) confiscation of properties acquired through corruption; (vi) prohibition of 'Benami' Transactions; (vii) protection to Whistleblowers; and (viii) doing away with Article 311 of constitution which gives excessive job security to government servants.

¤ Departmental inquiries against dishonest officers are multi-stage quasi-judicial proceedings. CVC identified 13 steps of the process and fixed time limits for each. But these are seldom observed in practice.

¤ SARC recommended that the requirement of sanction should be deleted for cases involving: demand or acceptance of bribes; or obtaining valuable things without payment or inadequate payment; and possession of assets disproportionate to the known source of income.

¤ SARC recommended that the sanction for prosecution should be processed by an Empowered Committee, consisting of the CVC and the departmental secretary or cabinet secretary to Government.

¤ For securing speedy trials, the Prevention of Corruption Act provides for special Judges, day-to-day hearings, and restrictions on grant of stay on trials by other courts.

¤ The PC Act prior to its 2018 amendment had no provision of its own for attaching or confiscating the assets of public servants through corrupt means. Such action had to be taken under the Money laundering Act. The amendment to the PC Act introduced necessary provisions for this purpose.

¤ This amendment makes bribe-giving also an offence under the PC Act. Earlier, it was considered as abetment of an offence.

¤ This amendment bought companies within the purview of the PC Act.

¤ The amendment also makes changes so that honest officers are not penalized for their bon fide errors.

¤ Corrupt public servants try to hide their illegitimate wealth through 'Benami' transactions. In these transactions, they hold property in someone else's name.

¤ A law entitled The Benami Transactions (Prohibition) Act was passed in 1988.

¤ The Act precludes the person who acquired the property in the name of another person from claiming it as his own. The Act prohibits Benami transactions and prohibits the acquirer from recovering the property from the Benamidar. The Act permits acquisition of property held Benami.

¤ Even after many years, Government has not prescribed rules under the Act. The present government notified the rules and made the Act effective from 1st November 2016.

¤ Whistleblower is an individual who makes public the illegal or dark secrets carefully hidden within an organization. Whistleblowing means exposing illegally suppressed or hidden information about illegal actions. Organizations and individuals hide such information to escape from law.

¤ If adequate statutory protection is granted to whistleblowers, Government can access substantial information about corruption.

¤ There is some difference between whistleblowers and informers. Informers usually do not belong to the set up or organization about which they give information.

¤ The vulnerability of those who expose hidden goings on in an organization is shown by the tragic killing of two bright young Indians - Manjunath Shanmugam and Satyendra Dubey.

¤ Main features of the Whistle Blowers protection Act are given in the narrative portion of this chapter.

¤ Controlling corruption only through administrative vigilance is very difficult.

¤ It requires a multi-pronged approach - with public participation and systemic economic and administrative reforms.

¤ A law on the model of the US False Claims Act should be passed. Under this law, any citizen can file a case on behalf of the government if he comes to know that someone has defrauded the government. If he wins the case, he gets a part of the money returned to government.

¤ It is not possible to consign economic problems to oblivion through legislation. As an aside we may note that this warrants some scepticism about the many 'rights' and 'entitlements' now being created through various laws. Answers often lie in increasing savings, investment, productivity, output and employment.

¤ According to one view, corruption arises not so much from human moral weakness as from inherent systemic weaknesses which create the opportunities for corruption.

¤ One such problem is monopoly which characterizes many government systems. Government is the single supplier of many goods and services.

¤ As there is no competition, consumers have nowhere else to go. This enables government servants to act arbitrarily and exact illegal payments from people.

¤ Government is the sole service provider in many sectors – a situation which breeds arbitrariness, complacency and corruption. Introducing competition in providing public services can reduce corruption. Telecom sector deregulation is usually cited as a case in point.

¤ One way of reducing delays and corruption will be to reduce the number of levels at which a matter is processed.

¤ 'Positive silence' sanctions represent another means of simplifying procedures from the citizen's point of view. These are also known as deemed approvals. Basically, when an applicant's request is not decided within a specified time, it is deemed to be given.

¤ The modern administrative state's welfare orientation has created huge bureaucracies and vast public service delivery systems. These systems are riddled with financial and managerial problems. Corruption is a common problem in such systems.

¤ Discretionary decision-making is another source of corruption. Effective anti-corruption reforms have to reduce discretionary benefits which public officials control.

¤ Lack of accountability also leads to corruption.

- One way of simplifying procedures is to provide the common services which citizens require at one point and in a single stage. This is known as the system of single window clearance or one-stop service centre. A successful example is Andhra Pradesh's E-Seva model.
- ICT can reduce corruption by delivering information at great speed with almost no face to face contact.
- A transparent system of administration encourages public participation in government's decision-making processes. It also reduces corruption.
- Corruption in contracts is a 'big ticket item' and the means of draining huge amounts from public exchequer into illegitimate channels.
- Integrity pacts are added to public contracts to reduce scope for corruption.
- Integrity pact is an agreement between the public agency procuring goods and services and the bidder for a public contract. Through the pact the bidders give assurances that they have not paid and shall not pay any illegal gratification to secure the contract in question. From its side, the public agency calling for bids commits to ensuring a level playing field and fair play in the procurement process.
- It is necessary to create an interlocking accountability chain which forces government servants at every level from top to bottom to function effectively.
- Controlling corruption in an office or organization should primarily the responsibility of the head of office. Supervising officials should try to minimize corruption among their subordinates.
- Corruption can be reduced if officers are accessible to people and promptly respond to their needs.
- Offices with a large pubic interface should have an online complaint handling system.
- In order to reduce possibilities of corruption, honest officers have to be posted to 'corruption-prone' areas of administration.
- Governments buy large quantities of various materials. The purchases should be transparent, based on open competitive tenders, and at market rates.
- Civil society groups have been active in recent times in anti corruption movements.
- Some government departments provide services to large sections of population. Independent professional agencies should be used to contact these persons and get their responses. These can be used to rate the offices.
- Provisions for social audit should be introduced in all schemes which have many scattered beneficiaries. Social audit unlike CAG audit is based on information which beneficiaries provide.
- Political parties raise money illegally for elections, use illegitimate money in elections and exceed the ceilings on election expenditure fixed by the Election Commission. During elections, political parties resort to unfair means such as impersonation, booth-capturing, violence, inducements and intimidation. Floor-crossing after elections (change of political affiliations by members to get into power) and abuse of power in public office have become common over time. This process is known as criminalization of politics.

- Huge illegal election expenditure also fuels corruption. Donors who pay money to political parties recoup it manifold through political favours. This process engenders a chain reaction in which illegal funding and corruption become the drivers of political process.
- Over past twenty years, many electoral reforms have been introduced.
- The Supreme Court has directed that a candidate seeking election should declare if he has been convicted by a court and if any criminal case is pending against him.
- The narrative portion of this chapter has covered the legal provisions applicable to donations to political parties from the RP Act and the Company Law Act. It also discussed Electoral Trust and Electoral Bonds.
- The Box I of the Chapter summarizes the legal provisions on political defections.

PRACTICE QUESTIONS

1. What are the measures that government should take to enable civil society groups and the public to participate in anti corruption movements?
2. "Change will come when the incentives to throw out a corrupt system become stronger than the incentives to retain such a system. The need of the hour is to have zero tolerance towards corruption." Discuss.
3. What is a False Claims Act? What are the main provisions of such Acts?
4. Compare and contrast financial audit and social audit. What role can social audit play in reducing irregularities in government programmes?
5. "Corruption arises not so much from human moral frailty as from inherent systemic weaknesses which create the opportunities for corruption." Examine.
6. People feel that corrupt are sitting pretty on their ill gotten wealth. What can be done in this regard?
7. How can the Benami Transactions (Prohibition) Act help in the fight against corruption?
8. What is meant by whistleblowing?
9. Someone compared whistleblowing to ratting on onc's colleagues. Can we support this iew? Give reasons.
10. What are the ways of protecting whistleblowers?
11. Seetharam wanted to do some whistleblowing about the shady goings on in his office. His wife Rukmini dissuades him saying that there is no law or organization now for protecting whistleblowers. Is she correct? If so, to what extent?
12. Briefly explain how excessive economic controls which governments may impose create an environment that favours corruption. Give two examples.
13. How can information and communication technology (ICT) help in reducing corruption? Illustrate your answer with two examples.
14. A prominent view argued: "Introducing competition in providing public services can reduce corruption. Telecom sector deregulation is a good example." Is 2G scandal an argument against deregulation and introducing competition? What systemic failures led to 2-G scam?

15. What are the features of Coalgate as a corruption scandal?
16. What do you understand by discretionary decision making? Why is it considered undesirable? How can it be reduced?
17. Why is corruption in government contracts considered a serious problem? How can it be reduced? Mention two major examples of corruption in contracts.
18. What is meant by criminalization of politics? How is it connected with political corruption?
19. "Corruption is an inevitable concomitant of democratic electoral politics." Do you agree? Give reasons for your stand in the matter.
20. Write short notes on:
    (i) Government funding of political parties
    (ii) Integrity pacts
    (iii) Positive silence sanctions or deemed approvals
    (iv) False Claims Act
    (v) Accountability
    (vi) Simplification of procedures.

LOKPAL

HISTORICAL BACKGROUND OF LOKPAL

Although 'Lokpal' has shot into prominence recently due to Anna Hazare's anti-corruption crusade, the concept is quite old. Lokpal parallels the concept (which emerged globally and especially in the Scandinavian countries) of Ombudsman as a means of tackling corruption and/or of redressing public grievances. Late jurist L.M. Singhvi mentioned about this institution in the parliament and gave its rationale: "...an institution such as the Ombudsman must be brought into existence in our country. It is for the sake of securing justice and for cleansing the public life of the Augean stable of corruption, real and imaginary, that such an institution must be brought into existence..."

This is how the idea of Lokpal appeared on the national legislative agenda. Later, first Administrative Reforms Commission recommended appointing Lokpal at Centre and Lokayuktas in each State. Subsequently, to implement this recommendation eight Bills were introduced in the Lok Sabha from time to time. However, all these Bills, (except the 1985 bill) lapsed consequent upon the dissolution of the respective Lok Sabhas. The 1985 Bill was later withdrawn. The Bills had varied conceptions of the scope, structure and jurisdiction of the Lokpal. We will examine the matter based on The Lokpal and Lokayuktas Bill, 2011which Lok Sabha passed. Therein the institution of Lokpal appears with many changes which reflect the changing socio-economic conditions and the nature, level and pervasiveness of corruption in contemporary society.

RECENT DEVELOPMENTS

The proximate cause which pushed government into formulating the latest version of the Lokpal bill is Anna Hazare's anti corruption movement. Anna Hazare and his team demanded that government should pass their Jan Lokpal bill. After negotiations with Anna Hazare, government appointed a Joint Drafting Committee (which included Anna and four members of his team) for preparing the Lokpal bill. Its draft formed the basis (though it was not wholly adopted) for the government bill.

Based on the deliberations of the Committee and the inputs received from the chief ministers and political parties, government prepared a revised Lok Pal bill in 2011. This bill went through some more changes.

Later parliament passed the 'The Lokpal And Lokayuktas Act, 2013' it its final form. It received presidential consent on 1.1.2014 and came into force on the same day. The Act made a few changes in the earlier bill. Our discussion incorporates the changes, and gives the latest position.

MAIN PROVISIONS OF THE ACT

Composition

Now, we will outline the main provisions of the Act. The Lokpal will have a Chairperson and upto eight members. Four of these will be judicial members. The chairman can be i) a serving or retired chief justice of India; or ii) serving or retired Supreme Court judge or iii) an eminent person. A Judicial Member should be i) a serving or retired Judge of the Supreme Court or ii) a serving or retired Chief Justice of a High Court. A non-judicial member has to be a person of impeccable integrity and outstanding ability having special knowledge and expertise of not less than twenty-five years in the matters relating to anti-corruption policy, public administration, vigilance, finance including insurance and banking, law and management.

The Lokpal and Lokayuktas Act provides that not less than fifty per cent of the Members of the Lokpal shall be from amongst the persons belonging to Scheduled Castes, Scheduled Tribes, Other Backward Classes, Minorities and women.

The following categories of persons are ineligible for being chairman or members of the Lokpal

- Member of Parliament or a member of the Legislature
- Member of any Panchayat or Municipality
- A person convicted of any offence involving moral turpitude
- A person of less than forty-five years of age
- A person who has been removed or dismissed from the service of the Union or a State
- A person holding any office of trust or profit (other than his office as the Chairperson or a Member) or affiliated with any political party or carrying on any business or practising any profession. However, those holding any trust or office, those in business and profession can join Lokpal after giving up such vocations.

Manner of Appointment: Selection Committee

The President of India will appoint the Chairperson and Members of Lokpal based on the recommendations of a Selection Committee. The Selection committee will consist of-

(a) Prime Minister–chairperson;

(b) Speaker of the House of the People–member;

(c) Leader of Opposition in the House of the People–member;

(d) Chief Justice of India or a Judge of the Supreme Court nominated by him–member;

(e) One eminent jurist as recommended by committee members (a), (b), (c) to be nominated by the President–member.

Search Committee

The Selection Committee will have to constitute a Search Committee for preparing a panel of persons to be considered for appointment as the Chairperson and Members of the Lokpal. The Search Committee will have at least seven persons of standing. They should be experts in anti-corruption policy, public administration, vigilance, policy making, finance including insurance and banking, law and management or in any other matter which the Selection Committee considers relevant. Not less than fifty per cent of the members of the Search Committee have to be from Scheduled Castes, Scheduled Tribes, Other Backward Classes, minorities and women.

The Selection Committee may also consider any person other than the persons recommended by the Search Committee. The selection committee will devise its own procedures for carrying on its functions. The Chairperson and every Member of the Lokpal shall, on the recommendations of the Selection Committee, be appointed by the President.

The chairman and members of Lokpal can hold office for 5 years or until they attain the age of 70 years. The chairman and members are barred from holding any other offices in the Central or State governments. They cannot fight elections for parliament, assemblies or local bodies for a period of five years after completing their tenure in the Lokpal.

LOKPAL'S JURISDICTION

Lokpal represents a mechanism for dealing with complaints of corruption against public functionaries and public servants at all levels of government from top to the bottom. The term 'public functionaries' is often used to refer to persons other than civil servants holding public offices like ministers or other political persons. The complaint should contain allegations that a public servant has committed an offence punishable under the Prevention of Corruption Act. Lokpal has a wide jurisdiction of looking into complaints against public functionaries and public servants who may be serving or who may have retired. The Act mentions the following categories.

- Prime minister
- Ministers
- Members of parliament
- Group 'A' or Group 'B' officer or equivalent or above when serving or who has served in the Central government
- Any Group 'C' or Group 'D' official or equivalent rank holder when serving or who has served in the Central government
- Any person who is or has been a chairperson or member or officer or employee in any body or Board or corporation or authority or company or society or trust or autonomous body (by whatever name called) established by an Act of Parliament or wholly or partly financed by the Central Government or controlled by it. This covers the officials working in any Central government undertaking including banks and any other entity which receives Central government funds.

- Officials (such as directors, managers, secretaries or other officers) in bodies which are wholly or partly financed by the Government and the annual income of which exceeds such amount as may be specified by the Central Government.
- Officials of every other society or association of persons or trust which receives more than a specified amount or more than Rs 10 lakhs from any foreign donors.

Inquiry Wing and Prosecution Wing

The traditional practice is to place investigative and prosecution agencies under the executive wing of government. For example, State police, CBI and Enforcement directorate are investigative agencies. In recent years, to reduce political interference in corruption cases, CBI has been brought under the direction and superintendence of Central Vigilance Commission, with regard to corruption cases. Supreme Court is considering the question of making CBI autonomous from government, with a view to delink corruption case investigations from government influence.

Lokpal will have an in house Inquiry Wing headed by the Director of Inquiry for conducting preliminary inquiry into any allegations of corruption. Lokpal will also have a Prosecution Wing headed by the Director of Prosecution. This wing will prosecute public servants charged after investigation into complaints received by Lokpal. The Lokpal can independently constitute these Directorates.

Procedure for Complaint Handling

The Act lays down the procedure for handling the complaints. When Lokpal gets a complaint, they will first decide whether to proceed with the matter or to close it. Frivolous and unsubstantiated complaints will be closed. But if the Lokpal decides to proceed further, it shall order a preliminary inquiry against any public servant by its Inquiry Wing or any agency (including the CBI) to ascertain whether there exists a prima facie case for proceeding in the matter.

Lokpal can send complaints received by it about Group A or Group B or Group C or Group D government servants to the Central Vigilance Commission. The Central Vigilance Commission after making preliminary inquiry of the complaint shall submit its report to the Lokpal about public servants of Group A and Group B. As regards public servants belonging to Group C and Group D, it can decide the further course of action on its own.

During the preliminary inquiry, the Inquiry Wing or CBI also has to seek the comments on the allegations made in the complaint from the public servant and from the competent authority or his designated official superior. Thereafter, the report has to be submitted to Lokpal. A bench consisting of not less than three Members of the Lokpal will consider the report received from the Inquiry Wing or CBI. After giving an opportunity of being heard to the public servant, the bench will decide whether there exists a prima facie case and which course to adopt. There are three alternatives if a prima facie case is made out in the report: (a) investigation by any agency or the CBI; (b) initiation of the departmental proceedings or any other appropriate action against the concerned public servants by the competent authority; and (c) closure of the proceedings against the public servant. If the complaint is malicious or baseless, action can be taken against the complainant.

When Lokpal orders an investigation, CBI has to complete the investigation within six months and submit the investigation report containing its findings to the Lokpal. A bench consisting of three Members has to consider the investigation report. They may decide either to

(a) grant sanction to its Prosecution Wing or investigating agency to file charge-sheet or direct the closure of report before the Special Court against the public servant;

(b) initiate departmental proceedings or other appropriate action against the concerned public servant through the competent authority.

The Lokpal may, if it decides to file a chargesheet, direct its Prosecution Wing to initiate prosecution in the Special Court. Lokpal Act contains provisions for setting up special courts for the trial of cases filed by Lokpal.

No Prior Sanctions

Government has created safeguards to protect senior officers who participate in or take sensitive decisions. There are general legal clauses which protect actions which public servants take in good faith. In such cases, no action can be taken against them. In addition, there are provisions in relevant laws which lay down that investigations or prosecutions cannot be started against officers of certain seniority without the prior approval of government or other competent authority. These provisions are section 197 of the Code of Criminal Procedure, section 6A of the Delhi Special Police Establishment Act, and section 19 of the Prevention of Corruption Act.

These provisions have often become a means of delaying action against errant officials. They have also created avoidable legal complications in court proceedings. There have been persistent demands for removing these provisions. These requirements have been made inapplicable in the Lokpal Act. No sanction or approval of any authority is required when the Lokpal orders a preliminary inquiry or an investigation or prosecution.

The Act empowers the Lokpal to attach the proceeds of corruption (cash and other assets) in possession of a public servant. The attachment can be done for 90 days, and subject to the approval of the special court, for the duration of the prosecution against the public servant. If the charges are proved against the public servant, the attached proceeds can be confiscated by the central government. Otherwise, they are returned to the public servant.

CONTROVERSIAL ISSUES

As we noted earlier, Lokpal legislation emerged against the background of a popular anti-corruption agitation which Anna Hazare led. Creation of Lokpal was a main demand of the agitators. They also came up with their own conception of Lokpal, and proposed a Jan Lokpal bill. This was one of the inputs which went into the final bill that Lok Sabha Passed. There were also negotiations between government and Anna Hazare. A joint drafting committee with government members and the representatives of Anna team was formed. Now, we will turn to the issues which divided the groups seeking the Lokpal law.

Inclusion of Prime Minister in Lokpal's Purview

The Lokpal Act provides certain safeguards with regard to investigation of complaints against the prime minister. There were sharply divided views on whether the Lokpal bill should cover the prime minister. Without getting into too many details, the three principal positions can be summarized as follows.

(a) The Prime Minister should be altogether excluded, without exception and without qualification.

(b) The Prime Minister should be included, without exception and without qualification. Very few subscribed to this view.

(c) The Prime Minister should be included, with subject matter exclusions like national security, foreign affairs, atomic energy and space. Some variants and additions suggested the addition of 'national interest' and 'public order' to this list of subject matter exclusions.

The Act passed by parliament contains the following provisions.

¤ Lokpal shall not inquire into any allegation of corruption against the Prime Minister if it relates to international relations, external and internal security, public order, atomic energy and space. This is called the subject matter exclusion.

¤ Lokpal can inquire into allegations of corruption against prime minister if they refer to subjects other than the above. Further, even in these matters, the full bench of the Lokpal consisting of its Chairperson and all Members has to consider the initiation of inquiry and at least two-thirds of its Members have to approve such inquiry.

¤ There is another safeguard that any such inquiry shall be held in camera and that if the Lokpal concludes that the complaint deserves to be dismissed, the records of the inquiry shall not be published or made available to anyone.

Conduct of MPs inside Parliament

Opinion was also divided on whether the speeches, actions and conduct of members of parliament should come under Lokpal's purview. A concrete example is of a member of parliament taking a bribe to vote in a particular way. According to a long standing tradition, the activities of members of parliament within the House are regulated by the House itself or by the speaker. No outside influence from judiciary or elsewhere is countenanced in the matter. It is a question of supremacy of parliament in a democracy.

Actually, Constitution covers this point in article 105(2). MP's acts like speech or voting in the House cannot be inquired into by the Lokpal or by any other agency to the extent they are covered under Article 105(2) of the Constitution. But Anna Hazare's team contends that Article 105 of the Indian Constitution does not seek to immunize corrupt vote, corrupt speech and corrupt action within the House. Alternatively, they contend that if Article 105 is read as granting immunity to voting, speech or conduct involving corruption, then Article 105 must necessarily be amended.

The counter view is summarized in Report on The Lokpal Bill, 2011 of the Parliamentary Standing Committee on Personnel, Public Grievances, Law and Justice:

Vote, conduct or speech within the House is intended to promote independent thought and action, without fetters, within Parliament. Its origin, lineage and continuance are ancient and time-tested. Even an investigation as to whether vote, speech or conduct in a particular case involves or does not involve corrupt practices, would whittle such unfettered autonomy and independence within the Houses of Parliament down to vanishing point. Such immunity for vote, speech or conduct within the Houses of Parliament does not in any manner leave culpable MPs blameless or free from sanction. They are liable to and, have, in the recent past, suffered severe parliamentary punishment including expulsion from the Houses of Parliament, for alleged taking of bribes amounting to as little as Rs. 10,000/- for asking questions on the floor of the House. It is only external policing of speech, vote or conduct within the House that Article 105 frowns upon. It leaves such speech, vote and conduct not only subject to severe intra-parliamentary scrutiny and action, but also does not seek to affect corrupt practices or any other vote, speech.

In short, Article 105 does not provide MPs immunity or protection from disciplinary proceedings or sanctions initiated and conducted by the Parliament itself. The Committee cites the cash for questions scam which led to the expulsion of 11 Members from different political parties. Their appeal to the Supreme Court challenging their expulsion was also rejected by the Supreme Court. Lokpal Act excludes the conduct of members of parliament inside the house from Lokpal's scrutiny.

To quote the Act, "...the Lokpal shall not inquire into any matter involved in, or arising from, or connected with, any such allegation of corruption against any member of either House of Parliament in respect of anything said or a vote given by him in Parliament or any committee thereof covered under the provisions contained in clause (2) of article 105 of the Constitution."

Inclusion of Group C and D Employees in Lokpal's Purview

As members of armed forces - of army, navy and air force - are covered by separate laws, they are excluded from the purview of Lokpal. But this was not a point in dispute.

Another dispute about Lokpal centred on inclusion of Group C and D categories within Lokpal's jurisdiction. Anna Hazare sought their inclusion. Government functionaries like patwaris, other revenue officials, and police inspectors are seen as the exploiters of common people. Government pointed to the difficulties of including them because their sheer size can overwhelm the working of Lokpal. The total of Group A to D + Railways + Central PSUs + Post and Telegraph would be approximately 63 lakhs, or 65 lakhs at 2011 estimates. Of these, 57 to 58 lakh belong to Group C and D. (We can ignore the fact that after the Sixth Pay Commission, Groups C and D are getting merged for it makes no difference to the numbers.) On a conservative estimate of one policing officer per 200 employees (a ratio propounded by several witnesses including team Anna), approximately 35000 employees would be required in the Lokpal to police the Central Government employees. This policing is certainly not a practicable proposition for the Lokpal.

The Select Committee observes: *"Even after it is created, it may lead to a huge parallel bureaucracy which would set in train its own set of consequences, including arbitrariness, harassment and unfair and illegal action by the same bureaucracy which, in the ultimate analysis would be nothing but a set of similar employees cutting across the same A, B and C categories. As some of the Members of the Committee, in a lighter vein put it, one would then have to initiate a debate on creating a super Lokpal or a Dharampal for the policing of the new bureaucracy of the Lokpal institution itself".*

The Select Committee has therefore proposed that if from the total of 65 lakh government employees, C and D categories are excluded, the number of A and B categories employees would be approximately 7.75 lakhs. The Committee believes that this figure of 7.75 or 8 lakhs would be manageable figure for the Lokpal.

The Act passed by Lok sabha brings Group C and D employees under the purview of Lokpal. However, Lokpal can transmit complaints about them to the central vigilance commission. And the commission can take final decisions on those complaints. The Act has adopted a practical course in the matter.

Inclusion of Judiciary in Lokpal's Jurisdiction

Whether to include or exclude the judiciary from the ambit of the Lokpal was also a question on which opinion was divided. One side emphasised the judiciary as a separate organ of State distinct and independent of the executive. The Judiciary consists of about 31 judges of the Apex Court, 800 judges of the High Courts, and 20,000 judges of the subordinate judiciary. Separation of judicial power from executive is essential for an independent judiciary in a democracy and is recognised specifically in Article 50 of the Indian Constitution. The lower judiciary (below high courts) is under the disciplinary control of high courts as provided in Article 235 of the constitution. High court and Supreme Court judges can be removed only after impeachment proceeding in parliament which is virtually impossible. Further, conduct of higher judiciary cannot be discussed in parliament except in proceedings for their removal.

There has been public clamour for laying down standards for the Judiciary and creating a practicable mechanism for ensuring accountability of Judiciary, including effective mechanisms for criminal prosecution for corruption practiced by judicial officers and the higher judiciary.

The Anna Committee argued: "*.....The judiciary may be brought under the purview of anti-corruption system through a separate Bill, to be introduced simultaneously, provided the Judicial Conduct Commission so set up is also independent of the government as well as the judiciary and has the power of investigating and prosecuting judges for corruption. The Judicial Standards and Accountability bill of the government does not deal with criminal investigation of judges, nor does it set up an independent committee.....*"

However, the consensus was to keep the judiciary out of Lokpal's ambit. At the same time, there is an urgent need for a comprehensive law on judicial standards and accountability. A Bill has already been proposed on the subject. It provides a mechanism within judiciary itself for tackling errant judicial behaviour by taking disciplinary action such as censure, warning, suspension and removal. But the Judicial Standards and Accountability Bill, by conscious design, does not deal with issues of corruption.

There is a widely held view that self-disciplinary mechanisms within judiciary are no longer effective. Further, overtime, the role of executive in judicial appointments has reached a vanishing point. The collegium system of appointing judges is seen by many as opaque. The Select committee recommends: "*The appointment process cannot be allowed and should not be allowed to continue in the hands of a self-appointed common law mechanism created by judicial order operating since the early 1990s. A National Judicial Commission must be set up to create a broad-based and comprehensive model for judicial appointments, including, if necessary, by way of amendment of Articles 124 and 217 of the Indian Constitution.*"

Inclusion of Lokayuktas in The Law

Another issue which divided opinion is a constitutional point. Anna Hazare team wanted the bill to cover Lokpal at the Centre and Lokayuktas in States. Others argued that Central government cannot pass a law on Lokayuktas who have to function in States. The concerned States have to pass the necessary laws creating Lokayuktas.

There are two questions involved here. One is whether the centre has the constitutional power or legislative competence to pass a law creating Lokayuktas in States. India being a federal State, the subjects on which laws can be passed by the Centre and States are divided in the Constitution. There is a central list which enumerates the subjects on which the Centre alone can legislate. There is a State list which enumerates subjects on which States alone can legislate. Finally, a concurrent list contains items on which both can legislate. Some argued that Centre can pass, within the present scheme of things, a law on Lokayuktas relying on an Article of the constitution which permits Centre to enact laws to give effect to international treaties to which it is a signatory. They cited the instance of National and State Human Rights Commissions which were set up under this provision. Similarly, 'the Lokpal and Lokayuktas Bill' cites UN Convention against Corruption as the source of its legislative competence. In this connection, the Ministry of Law made an interesting observation that the requirement of following international treaties and conventions cannot override other constitutional provisions. Without intending to do so, Centre in the name of following international treaties can ride roughshod over rights of States.

The other question is that the procedure infringes the federal principle. In this case, it would be for the concerned State to create or not to create a Lokayukta. There are practical questions which are relevant here. For instance, it is necessary to ensure uniformity in such matters. Otherwise, government servants doing similar jobs will be governed by different laws in adjacent States. Further, the procedures for tackling corruption will vary as between States. The existing Lokayuktas clearly show the differences in their structure, functions and procedures. One suggestion was that the Central law can contain a chapter on Lokayuktas which States can adopt. The Act contains the following provision covering Lokayuktas: "*Every State shall establish a body to be known as the Lokayukta for the State, if not so established, constituted or appointed, by a law made by the State Legislature, to deal with complaints relating to corruption against certain public functionaries, within a period of one year from the date of commencement of this Act.*"

Other Important Provisions

- The Central Government shall constitute such number of Special Courts, as recommended by the Lokpal, to hear and decide the cases arising out of the Prevention of Corruption Act, 1988 or under the Lokpal Act.
- Every public servant shall make a declaration of his assets and liabilities in the manner as provided in the Act.
- If any public servant is convicted of an offence under the Prevention of Corruption Act, 1988 by the Special Court, it may make an assessment of loss, if any, caused to the public exchequer on account of the actions or decisions of such public servant not taken in good faith and for which he stands convicted, and may order recovery of such loss, if possible or quantifiable, from such public servant so convicted. Further, if the Special Court comes to the conclusion that the loss caused was pursuant to a conspiracy with the beneficiary or beneficiaries of actions or decisions of the public servant so convicted, then such loss may also be recovered from such beneficiary or beneficiaries proportionately. In this and other matters, the Act incorporates the recommendations which seek to deprive corrupt public servants of their ill gotten gains.

Conclusion

The Lokpal and Lokayuktas Act is a welcome addition to the mechanisms for fighting corruption. There is little doubt that Lokpal will have a salutary effect on improving the moral tone of the administration. It represents a consensus between government, civil society groups, political parties, experts and enlightened public. It gives legal backing to many recommendations made earlier for checking corruption. It will create a uniform system for fighting corruption in the country.

Summary

- Although 'Lokpal' has shot into prominence recently due to Anna Hazare's anti-corruption crusade, the concept is quite old.
- Lokpal parallels the concept (which emerged globally and especially in the Scandinavian countries) of Ombudsman as a means of tackling corruption and/or of redressing public grievances.
- The First Administrative Reforms Commission recommended appointing Lokpal at Centre and Lokayuktas in each State.
- For creating the Lokpal, eight Bills were introduced in the Lok Sabha from time to time. However, all these Bills (except the 1985 bill), lapsed consequent upon the dissolution of the respective Lok Sabhas. The 1985 Bill was later withdrawn. The Bills had varied conceptions of the scope, structure and jurisdiction of the Lokpal.
- The proximate cause which pushed government into formulating the latest version of the Lokpal bill is Anna Hazare's anti corruption movement. Anna Hazare and his team demanded that government should pass their Jan Lokpal bill.

- After negotiations with Anna Hazare, government appointed a Joint Drafting Committee (which included Anna and four members of his team) for preparing the Lokpal bill. Its draft formed the basis (though it was not wholly adopted) for the government bill.
- Lokpal and Lokayuktas Act, 2013 came into force on 1-1-2014.
- The Lokpal will have a Chairperson and up to eight members. Four of these will be judicial members.
- The President of India will appoint the Chairperson and Members of Lokpal based on the recommendations of a Selection Committee under the chairmanship of the Prime minister.
- The Selection Committee will have to constitute a Search Committee for preparing a panel of persons to be considered for appointment as the Chairperson and Members of the Lokpal. The Search Committee will have at least seven persons of standing.
- Lokpal will have a wide jurisdiction covering the prime minister, ministers, MPs, all categories of government and public sector employees and employees of entities receiving sizeable funding from government.
- Lokpal will have an in house Inquiry Wing headed by the Director of Inquiry for conducting preliminary inquiry into any allegations of corruption. Lokpal will also have a Prosecution Wing headed by the Director of Prosecution.
- The Act lays down the procedure for handling the complaints. This procedure was outlined earlier in the chapter.
- No sanction or approval of any authority is required when the Lokpal orders a preliminary inquiry or an investigation or prosecution.
- The following controversial issues arose during the consideration of the Lokpal legislation
    - (a) Inclusion of prime minister in Lokpal's purview
    - (b) Conduct of MPs inside parliament
    - (c) Inclusion of group C and D employees in Lokpal's purview
    - (d) Inclusion of judiciary in Lokpal's jurisdiction
    - (e) Inclusion of Lokayuktas in the law

PRACTICE QUESTIONS

1. What is the historical origin of the concept of Lokpal?
2. Briefly mention the history of Lokpal idea in India.
3. What is the rationale of the Lokpal institution?
4. What are the circumstances which led to the formulation of the Lokpal and Lokayuktas bill?
5. According to some critics, Anna's agitation for Lokpal was a damp squib. Do you agree? Give reasons in support of your view.
6. "The jurisdiction Anna demanded for Jan Lokpal was too wide to be practicable." Comment.
7. Briefly outline the procedure laid down in Lokpal and Lokayuktas Act for constituting the Lokpal.

8. What are the qualifications proposed in the Lokpal and Lokayuktas Act for the chairman and members of the Lokpal institution?
9. What are the arguments for and against bringing the prime minister under the jurisdiction of the Lokpal?
10. What are the practical problems in bringing group C and D employees under the purview of Lokpal?
11. What are the issues involved in bringing the conduct of MPs inside parliament within the ambit of Lokpal or other agencies?
12. What is the difference between Lokpal and Lokayukta? What is the problem in making a central law on Lokayukta?
13. Why is it necessary for Lokpal to have its own wings for investigation and prosecution?
14. Discuss the issue of judicial accountability in the context of the role of Lokpal.

REFERENCES

- The Lokpal and Lokayuktas Act 2014
- Parliamentary Standing Committee on Personnel, Public grievances, Law and Justice Report on the Lokpal Bill 2011

THE RIGHT TO INFORMATION ACT

BACKGROUND

The Right to Information Act (RTI Act) was enacted in 2005. Good governance, transparency and accountability are the three principles on which it rests. Our constitution implicitly guarantees the right of citizens to information. But parliament considered that it is also necessary to create a practical regime which will enable citizens to get information from public authorities and make such authorities transparent and accountable.

International experience also influenced Indian law makers in their efforts to create a framework for freedom of information. RTI Act represents a radical departure from the earlier bureaucratic practices. Formerly, government business was transacted in an atmosphere of secrecy. Government servants were expected not to divulge information to which they become privy in their official work. They had to be discreet, and share information on 'a need to know basis'. They could share information only with those who needed it for performing their official duties. Many files were routinely classified as 'confidential' and 'secret'. At one time, even the audit teams of Comptroller and Auditor General (CAG) were denied access to the 'noting section' of a government file. Incidentally, the noting section contains the analysis at various levels of government leading to decision on any matter. CAG had to comment on matters based on government's final order incorporating the decision, and the various letters and other correspondence on the file without knowing how government processed the matter.

Government also had the power of withholding secret documents and files from the courts. There is still an Official Secrets Act on the anvil. However, over a period of time courts whittled down the powers of government to withhold information from courts. Further, the emergence of 'investigative reporting' led to exposure of many matters formerly kept outside public view. Computers, internet and mobile telephony have eroded the traditional modes of secrecy. In this age of information explosion, few areas can remain in shades or shadows.

There was growing recognition that secrecy in government breeds misuse of power and corruption. Power wielders will be greatly encouraged if they know that their black deeds will never see the light of the day. Many examples such as Watergate scandal and Pentagon Papers have reinforced this consideration. Freedom of information and transparency were seen as important parameters of democratic governance.

Sweden enacted the first freedom of information law in 1766. But it was driven by parliament's desire to get the information with the King. USA passed its first freedom of information law in 1966. This law shifted the onus of justifying restriction of access to information on government. It placed time limit on public authorities for responding to requests for information. If secret information is mixed up in a file with other matters, all non-secret information is treated as disclosable through its 'severability'. The law provided for disciplinary action against officials for wrongful non-disclosure. Denmark and Norway passed right to information laws in 1970s and UK in 2000. In the wake of the Watergate scandal in 1974, USA passed a strong freedom of information law in 1976. Many other countries later followed suit. The number of national information laws increased from just 13 in 1990 to over 852 in 2011.

RTI laws seek to ensure that the government activities are transparent, fair and open. Except in matters of defence, atomic energy and national security, no secrecy is normally necessary in government affairs. For example, whether government takes a decision affecting the people or whether it enters into a transaction involving purchase or sale of government property or whether it enters into a contract – in all these matters, the government should act transparently. In other words, if a citizen wants any information on any of these matters, he should be entitled to receive it. Supreme Court Justice Mathew has observed: *"In a government of responsibility like ours, where all agents of the public must be responsible for their conduct, there can be but few secrets. The people of this country have a right to know every public act, everything that is done in a public way, by their public functionaries….to cover with veil of secrecy the common routine business, is not in the interest of public".*

As we noted before, the Official Secrets Act (1923) enacted during the British rule governed the disclosure of information held by public authorities in India. The Supreme Court of India had in several judgments prior to enactment of the RTI Act, construed the fundamental right to freedom of speech and expression and the 'right to life' as embodying also the right to information. The Supreme Court held: "*The freedom of speech and expression includes right to acquire information and to disseminate it. Freedom of speech and expression is necessary, for self-expression which is an important means of free conscience and self-fulfilment.*"

Side by side, the right to information became the focus of a protest movement. A group of poor wage workers in central Rajasthan demanded right to information (RTI) while protesting against ghost entries in muster rolls. False muster rolls show inflated attendance on works in order to siphon off public funds in the guise of wage payments. These muster rolls related to drought relief works which government opened to provide wage employment to drought affected villagers. To check this form of corruption, protesters demanded official information recorded in government rolls related to drought relief work. This would naturally help them to expose the malpractices. The movement spread to various parts of Rajasthan, leading to a nationwide movement for the RTI and related state legislations. It was, in fact, states like Tamil Nadu (1997), Goa (1997) and Rajasthan (2000) that first enacted RTI laws.

The demand for a national RTI law started under the leadership of National Campaign on People's Right to Information (NCPRI). The central government recognised the importance of this law. The Freedom of Information Bill (2000) was passed in the Parliament in 2002. But as government did not issue the necessary gazette notification, this law never came into effect. Later in 2005, the RTI Act was passed.

RTI ACT

Preamble

The preamble to the RTI Act that was passed in 2005 mentions the following reasons for its enactment:

- An informed citizenry and transparency of information are vital to the functioning of a democracy.
- They are also necessary to contain corruption and to hold Governments and their instrumentalities accountable to the governed (people).
- In actual practice, revelation of information is likely to conflict with other public interests including efficient operations of the Governments, optimum use of limited fiscal resources and the preservation of confidentiality of sensitive information.
- It is necessary to harmonise these conflicting interests while preserving the paramountcy of the democratic ideal.

We will now briefly outline the main provisions of the RTI Act.

Main Provisions

Information

RTI Act is all about providing information with public authorities to people. According to RTI Act, information means any material in any form including records, documents, memos, e-mails, opinions, advices, press releases, circulars, orders, logbooks, contracts, reports, papers, samples, models and data/material held in any electronic form. It also includes information relating to any privatc body which can be accessed by a public authority under any other law.

Key Concepts

The key concepts of the Act are the following:

- Transparency and accountability in the working of every public authority.
- The right of any Indian citizen to seek information and the corresponding duty of government to provide it except for the exempted information. As we shall see below, RTI Act permits certain information of a secret and sensitive nature to be kept outside the public domain. However, it casts a duty on the government to pro-actively make available key information to all.
- RTI Act places a responsibility for its implementation on all sections of society-citizenry, NGOs and Media.

RTI's Main Strategy

Disclosure

- The Act shifts the debate on governance from what should be revealed to public to what must be kept secret from it. The Act reflects the strength of Indian democracy.
- The Central Information Commission can require every public authority to "publish certain information or categories of information" under the Act. Should the public authority not comply, the Commission can use its power to impose any of the penalties provided under the Act.

Obligations

First, every public authority has to maintain all its records duly catalogued and indexed in a manner and form which facilitates the right to information. Secondly, it has to ensure that all records which can be computerized are put into electronic form within a reasonable time and subject to availability of resources. Thirdly, computerized information should be connected through a network all over the country on different systems to facilitate easy access.

Definition of Public Authority under RTI Act

Any law generally casts duties on certain officials and organizations and confers rights on individuals or classes of individuals. Both these groups have to be defined in the law. Otherwise, confusion can arise in courts which have to interpret the laws. We need not get into the legal technicalities of the matter. However, we need to know broadly: (a) who the information providers are; (b) what types of information they can provide; (c) what types of information they can withhold; and (d) how one can access information.

Under RTI Act, public authorities have to provide information. The term 'public authority' is given a wide connotation. 'Public authority' means any authority or body or institution of self-government established or constituted–

(a) by or under the Constitution;

(b) by any other law made by Parliament;

(c) by any other law made by State Legislature;

(d) by notification issued or order made by the appropriate Government, and includes any

  (i) body owned, controlled or substantially financed by the appropriate Government;

  (ii) non-Government organization substantially financed, directly or indirectly by funds provided by the appropriate Government.

In the above definition, (a) refers to constitutional bodies or institutions mentioned in the constitution. For instance, the Election commission is covered by (a). The statutory bodies set up under a central law are included in (b). For example, Central Electricity Regulatory Commission is covered in (b). Statutory bodies formed under State laws are covered in (c). For example, Gujarat Infrastructure Development Board will be covered in (c). All government departments and agencies are covered in (d) (i). Technically speaking, (d) covers agencies created under government's executive orders. These orders are printed in the official gazette – a process known as notification. Planning Commission is a textbook example of an institution created under an executive order. Finally, RTI Act covers non official agencies which receive substantial funding from government.

Central Information Commission (CIC)

RTI Act entrusts the Central Information Commission (CIC) with the responsibility of monitoring the implementation of the Act. CIC prepares a yearly report on the implementation of the RTI Act. State Information Commissions (SICs) perform similar functions at State level.

Content of Right to Information

As part of the right to information, one can

(i) inspect works, documents and records
(ii) take notes, extracts or certified copies of documents or records
(iii) take certified samples of material
(iv) obtain information in form of printouts, diskettes, floppies, tapes, video cassettes or in any other electronic mode.

Machinery of RTI

For supply of information, the Act creates elaborate machinery. It consists of Public Information Officers, Assistant Public Information Officers, Departmental Appellate Authorities, independent Central Information Commission (CIC) and independent State Information Commissions.

Processes

- Applications can be submitted in writing or electronically, with prescribed fee, to Public Information Officer (PIO) of a department or agency.
- PIO is authorized to receive requests and provide information. At sub-district level, Assistant PIO receives applications/appeals/ complaints. Where necessary, he sends them to the concerned PIOs. Serving departmental/agency officers are designated as PIOs/APIOs. They are not new appointees.
- The Act specifies time limits for furnishing information in different types of cases. The time limit for supplying information in ordinary cases is 30 days. Where matters of life or liberty are in question, information has to be given in 48 hours. The time limit is 35 days where request is made to APIO, 40 days where a third party is involved and 45 days for human rights violation information from specified security/ intelligence agencies.
- If no action is taken on an application for 30 days, it is deemed that the information has been refused.

Information Exempted from Disclosure

The following matters are exempt from disclosure:

- Information, disclosure of which would prejudicially affect the sovereignty and integrity of India, the security, strategic, scientific or economic interests of the State, relations with foreign States or lead to incitement of an offence.

- Information which has been expressly forbidden to be published by any court of law or tribunal or the disclosure of which may constitute contempt of court.
- Information, the disclosure of which would cause a breach of privilege of Parliament or the State Legislature.
- Information including commercial confidence, trade secrets or intellectual property, the disclosure of which would harm the competitive position of a third party, unless the competent authority is satisfied that larger public interest warrants the disclosure of such information.
- Information available to a person in his fiduciary relationship, unless the competent authority is satisfied that the larger public interest warrants the disclosure of such information.
- Information received in confidence from foreign Government.
- Information which would impede the process of investigation or apprehension or prosecution of offenders.
- Cabinet papers including records of deliberations of the Council of Ministers, Secretaries and other officers.
- Information which relates to personal information, the disclosure of which has no relationship to any public activity or interest, or which would cause unwarranted invasion of the privacy of the individual; or which infringes a copyright.
- Where practicable, part of the record can be released.
- Intelligence and security agencies are exempt from RTI Act except in cases involving corruption and human rights violation.
- Third party information can be released after giving notice to the concerned third party.
- Most exempt information (with some exceptions) can be released after 20 years.
- Information, which cannot be denied to the Parliament or a State Legislature, shall not be denied to any person.
- The Act contains an overriding provision that notwithstanding anything in the Official Secrets Act, 1923 or any of the above exemptions, a public authority may allow access to information, if public interest in disclosure outweighs the harm to the protected interests.

Complaints under RTI Act

Complaints can be made to the CIC which is an autonomous body set up to inquire into complaints received from citizens. The complaints can cover:

- Refusal of access to information.
- Improper handling by the public authority of request for information like failure to respond to request within the time limit or failure to explain reasons for extending the time limit or failure to give proper advice and help within the stipulated time.
- Failure to give information in the form or manner sought.
- Failure to properly explain reasons for refusing information.

Penalties

Information Commission can impose on a PIO or an officer asked to assist PIO a fine of Rs. 250 per day and up to Rs. 25,000 for unreasonable delay. It can impose fine up to Rs. 25,000 for illegitimate refusal to accept application, malafide denial, knowingly providing false information and destruction of information. The commission can recommend departmental action for persistent or serious violations. However, there is no criminal liability under RTI Act. It also provides immunity from legal action for action taken in good faith.

Access

The Act provides universal access, especially to the poor, with a low fee. There is no fee for people below the poverty line. APIOs at sub-district levels are to help people in filing of applications/ appeals. People will be helped in reducing their oral requests to writing. There is provision to provide all required assistance, including to disabled persons. The information is provided in local languages when necessary. There is no need to specify reasons for seeking information or to furnish personal details other than those necessary for correspondence.

Responsibilities of Public Authorities

Public authorities have to take the following actions.

- Appointing PIOs/Assistant PIOs within 100 days of enactment of the RTI legislation.
- Maintaining, cataloguing, indexing, computerising and networking records.
- Publishing within 120 days of enactment a whole set of information and updating it every year.
- Publishing all relevant facts while formulating important policies or announcing the decisions which affect public.
- Providing reasons for their administrative or quasi judicial decisions to affected persons.
- Providing information suo moto by placing it on internet.
- Providing information to Information Commission.
- Raising awareness, educating and training.
- Compiling in 18 months and updating regularly in local language guide to information.

Public Awareness and Educational Programmes

These seek to:

- Develop and organize educational programmes to advance the understanding of the public, particularly the disadvantaged, to exercise right to information.
- Encourage public authorities to participate in programmes; promote timely/ effective dissemination of accurate information on their activities.

LANDMARK JUDGMENTS BY CIC

The following are among the major decisions of the CIC:

- The CIC directed the Union Public Services Commission (UPSC) to declare individual marks scored by 2,400 candidates who appeared for the Civil Service Preliminary examinations in 2006 and ordered it to declare cut-off marks for each subject. (CIC/WB order, November 13, 2006)

- In the case of Paramveer Singh vs. Punjab University, the applicant applied for information regarding the merit list for selection of candidates to a particular post in the university. However, no proper information was provided. The Commission held that every public authority, must take all measures for efficient record management systems in their offices so that the requests for information can be dealt with promptly and accurately.
- In the case of Shyam Yadav vs. Department of Personnel and Training, the applicant had sought details of property statements filed by bureaucrats (CIC/WB/A/2009/000669, June 17, 2009).The Commission held that property statements filed by civil servants are not confidential and information can be disclosed after taking the views of concerned officials as per the provisions of the RTI Act.
- In case of Ram Bhaj vs. Delhi Government, the appellant has sought information about whether the guidelines which the Department of Personnel and Training issued regarding disposal of public grievances within a specific time frame have been notified by the Delhi Government (CIC/SG/A/2010/000537+000538/7492, April 19, 2010). CIC directed the Delhi Government to inform the common citizens about the timeframe required to redress their grievances.
- More recently, the CIC held that political parties are answerable under the Right to Information Act. It made RTI applicable to Congress, BJP, CPI-M, CPI, NCP and BSP. Some applicants sought information under RTI from these parties. The information related to their finances, the voluntary financial contributions they received, the names and addresses of the donors and some other details. The parties replied that they are not covered by RTI Act. CIC directed these political parties to appoint PIOs and respond to RTI questions. The CIC asked them to comply with the provisions of mandatory proactive disclosure clauses given under the RTI Act and show the information on their websites. The CIC took into account the fact that they have received substantial financial assistance from government by way of land, buildings and radio talk time. They come under the purview of the Election Commission. They affect the lives of people directly or indirectly. The concerned political parties opposed the Judgment. Government wanted to amend the RTI Act to exempt political parties from its purview but later dropped the move.

THE OFFICIAL SECRETS ACT

Many RTI activists have been asking for the abolition or drastic amendment of the Official Secrets Act (OSA). In 2006, the second Administrative Reforms Commission (ARC) recommended the repeal of the OSA and inclusion of a new chapter in the National Security Act to deal with espionage. A core group on administrative reforms subsequently studied the ARC recommendations, which were then forwarded to a Group of ministers headed by Pranab Mukherjee for a decision. The GOM accepted many recommendations of the ARC, but rejected the suggestion for repeal of the OSA. It instead sought amendments to the OSA to do away with ambiguity in defining the terms 'secret', 'espionage' and 'enemy state' and, thus, guard against use of the Act to block information. It seems that the Home Ministry is of the opinion that the 1923 anti-espionage law has stood the test of time and that there has been no significant misuse of its provisions to justify changes in its provisions.

RTI VICTIMS

- RTI activists face serious threats in certain situations. RTI activist Amit Jethwa was killed outside the Ahmedabad High Court in July 2010. Jethwa had named an MP while exposing illegal mining on the Gir forest periphery.
- Datta Patil, another activist, was found murdered in Ichalkaranji in May 2010. Patil had unearthed a corruption racket, leading to removal of a deputy superintendent of police and action against Ichalkaranji corporation officials.
- Vitthal Gite, an education activist, who had exposed irregularities in a village school in Beed, was killed in Aurangabad in April 2010.
- Shashidhar Mishra of Begusarai in Bihar, who had exposed corruption at the panchayat and block levels, was murdered by unknown assailants in February 2010.
- Arun Sawant, who filed many RTI applications about Badalpur Municipal Corporation, was shot dead on February 2010.
- Vishram Laxman Dodiya of Ahmedabad had filed an RTI application to get details about the illegal electricity connection of a private firm. He was murdered shortly after a meeting with the officials of the company in February 2010.
- Sola Ranga Rao of Andhra Pradesh had filed many applications seeking information from the Mandal Parishad Development Office on the funds sanctioned and utilized for the village's drainage system. He was murdered in April 2010.
- Ramdas Ghadegavkar, another RTI activist was found dead in August 2010 under mysterious circumstances after he exposed the sand mafia in Nanded.

PROTECTION FOR WHISTLEBLOWERS

The issue of protection for whistleblowers caught the attention of the entire nation when National Highways Authority of India engineer Satyendra Dubey was killed after he wrote a letter to the office of the then Prime Minister detailing corruption in the construction of highways. Dubey's murder led to a public outcry at the failure to protect him. As a result, in April 2004, the Supreme Court pressed the government into issuing an office order, the Public Interest Disclosures and Protection of Informers Resolution, 2004 designating Central Vigilance Commission (CVC) as the nodal agency to handle complaints on corruption. However, such unfortunate incidents kept increasing and brought renewed focus on the need for a law to protect whistleblowers. Necessary provisions for this purpose have since been made in the Whistle Blowers Protection Act 2014.

WORKING OF RTI ACT

All government departments, agencies and undertakings including banks have designated PIOs to handle RTI Act Requests. This openness of government has increased public awareness. But the RTI Act still faces many difficulties. Briefly, the problems are:

- Low awareness of the people about the Act.
- Inadequate skills of PIOs
- Inadequate strength of state information commissions.
- Absence of proactive disclosures by public authorities.
- Inadequate staffing and funding of PIOs.
- Lack of readily available computerized information.
- Threats which RTI activists face.

Overview of the Impact

The Act improved the quality of life of the poor and the marginalized. In all probability, it would have reduced corruption to some extent. It increased the accountability of government officials. In many cases, the CIC ordered disclosure of the decision-making processes. These included–file notings, cabinet papers, records of recruitment and promotion of staff and documents relating to tenders and procurement procedures.

Further, details of beneficiaries of government's subsidized schemes were made public. Among these schemes are–Public distribution system (PDS); connections for water, electricity and domestic gas; educational and health benefits; and muster rolls under MGNREGA. The disclosure of such vital information(s) resulted in checking corrupt practices in delivery of services and ensuring the reach of entitlements to the poor.

Concrete steps need to be taken to make the filing of RTI applications more convenient. Some of the recommendations regarding the role of the government as put forth by various studies are:

- Spell out specific responsibilities for implementation of specific provisions of the Act.
- Organize mass awareness campaigns both at Central and state levels. Their main objective should be to increase public awareness; encourage citizen involvement; and increase transparency within the government.
- Direct all public authorities and training institutions to incorporate training modules on RTI in all training programmes.
- Develop a consensus on a common set of minimum rules that would enable applicants residing in one state to apply for information from any other state, without first having to locate, study and understand the rules of each state and competent authority.

In conclusion, we may sound a note of caution about the RTI Act.

We don't want to question the popular enthusiasm for freedom of information. However, one should not be carried away by idealistic movements originating in the West. Westerners live in a different social and cultural milieu. It is often difficult to transplant Western ideas wholesale in Indian soil. Many activists and even government and judiciary tend to push such ideas to extreme limits. It seems as if we want to outdo the Western democracies in espousing so called liberal ideals. In fact, in USA information made public under the Freedom of Information Act is often highly redacted. This means that many portions deemed confidential are blacked out. But the average Indian perhaps thinks that public officials in USA readily part with information at the drop of a hat. There are big gaps between laws and their implementation. Our intention is not to question the usefulness or need for the RTI Act. But experience has shown that it needs to be implemented and interpreted with a sense of balance and due proportion.

Summary

- The Right to Information Act (RTI Act) was enacted in 2005.
- Formerly, government business was transacted in an atmosphere of secrecy. Government servants were expected not to divulge information to which they become privy in their official work.
- However, over a period of time courts whittled down the powers of government to withhold information from courts. Practices of investigative journalism, internet and international initiatives encouraged transparency.
- There was growing recognition that secrecy in government breeds misuse of power and corruption.
- The laws for freedom of information seek to ensure that government activities are transparent, fair and open. Except in matters of defence, atomic energy and national security, no secrecy is normally necessary in government affairs.
- The Supreme Court of India had in several judgments prior to enactment of the RTI Act, construed the fundamental right to freedom of speech and expression and the 'right to life' as embodying also the right to information.
- Side by side, the right to information became the focus of a protest movement in Rajasthan which later spread to other States.
- It was, in fact, states like Tamil Nadu (1997), Goa (1997) and Rajasthan (2000) that first enacted RTI laws.
- The preamble to the Act mentions the reasons for its enactment.
- RTI Act is all about providing information with public authorities to people. The term 'information' is given a wide meaning in the RTI Act.
- The definition of 'public authorities' who are placed under an obligation to provide information to citizens is also wide.
- RTI's main strategy is based on disclosure of information.
- RTI Act imposes extensive obligations on public authorities for disclosure of information.
- For an understanding of the RTI Act, we need to know broadly: (a) who the information providers are; (b) what types of information they can provide; (c) what types of information they can withhold; and (d) how one can access information.
- For supply of information, the Act creates an elaborate machinery. It consists of Public Information Officers, Assistant Public Information Officers, Departmental Appellate Authorities, independent Central Information Commission (CIC) and independent State Information Commissions.
- RTI Act entrusts the Central Information Commission (CIC) with the responsibility of monitoring the implementation of the Act. CIC prepares a yearly report on the implementation of the RTI Act. State Information Commissions (SICs) perform similar functions at State level.

- Complaints under RTI Act can be filed stage-wise before various authorities starting with the lowest designated level.
- The Act contains provision for imposing penalties on those who fail to provide information within the prescribed time limits.
- The RTI Act specifies the responsibilities of Public Authorities for maintaining information in computerized formats on interconnected networks.
- All government departments, agencies and undertakings, including banks, have designated PIOs to handle RTI requests. With this openness of the government processes before the public, awareness among the masses has increased. It increased government's accountability, and reduced corruption to some extent. The Act has improved the quality of the life of the poor and the marginalized. CIC has significantly increased the openness and transparency of the government.
- Many RTI activists have become victims of violence.
- Government has been considering whether to continue or repeal the Official Secrets Act. The current position of this matter has been indicated earlier.

PRACTICE QUESTIONS

1. What was the traditional view on how governments should handle information?
2. What are the circumstances which led to a change on how governments should handle information?
3. What are the main ideas on which the RTI Act rests?
4. Discuss the manner in which the RTI Act introduces transparency in government's working.
5. Write short notes on: (a) public authority; (b) information; (c) exempted information.
6. Discuss briefly the organizational set up which the RTI Act has created for supplying information to citizens.
7. Mention briefly the main achievements of the RTI Act.
8. What are the important judgements of the Chief Information Commission (CIC)?
9. State and discuss the recent judgement of CIC on disclosure of information by political parties.
10. Does the Official Secrets Act have any relevance now?
11. There is a view that the RTI Act can be used by anti-national forces to expose sensitive and strategic national secrets. Do you agree? What safeguards, if any, does the RTI Act provide in this regard?
12. Some critics argue that because of the RTI Act senior officers have stopped recording their views frankly on files. Discuss this view.

REFERENCES

- Shailesh Gandhi, The Right to Information Act 2005 (A power point presentation)
- Central Information Commission Presentation on RTI (Available on website)

CITIZEN'S CHARTER

INTRODUCTION

The functions of government fall into two broad heads: legal exercise of authority and provision of services. Modern states are welfare states and provide a wide range of public services to their citizens. The services cover areas such as education, health, housing and transport. Services also include such requirements as a driving license, telephone connection, gas connection, tax refund, Aadhaar card, passport, and extracts from public records of one's property, educational qualification and date of birth. Citizens often experience considerable difficulty in securing timely, reliable and quality services from government agencies. Citizen Charters are a means of solving the day to day problems which citizens experience while dealing with organisations providing public services.

The Conservative party government under John Major was the first to introduce the citizen's charter (1991). Citizen's Charters seek to continuously improve the quality of public services for the people so as to respond to their needs and wishes. Tony Blair's Labour government relaunched Citizen's Charters in 1998 under the name "Services First".

The six principles of the Citizen's Charter movement as originally framed were:

(i) **Quality:** Improving the quality of services;
(ii) **Choice:** provision wherever possible;
(iii) **Standards:** Specifying what to expect and how to act if standards are not met;
(iv) **Value:** For the taxpayers' money;
(v) **Accountability:** Of Individuals and Organisations; and
(vi) **Transparency:** Of Rules/Procedures/Schemes/Grievances.

The Labour Government later expanded them into the following nine principles of Service Delivery:

(i) Set standards of service;
(ii) Be open and provide full information;

(iii) Consult and involve;

(iv) Encourage access and promote choice;

(v) Treat all fairly;

(vi) Put things right when they go wrong;

(vii) Use resources effectively;

(viii) Innovate and improve;

(ix) Work with other service providers.

The UK's Citizen's Charter initiative was followed by similar programmes in other countries like Australia, Belgium, Canada, France, India, Jamaica, Malaysia, Portugal, and Spain. Some of these adopted the service quality model of the "Total Quality Management" (TQM) movement. For improving public services, some countries used methods such as the Business Excellence Model, Charter Mark and ISO 9000.

THE INDIAN SCENARIO

At a Conference of Chief Ministers held on 24 May, 1997 an "Action Plan for Effective and Responsive Government" at the Centre and State levels was adopted. It was decided that the Central and State Governments would formulate Citizen's Charters, starting with those sectors that have a large public interface (e.g., Railways, Telecom, Posts, Public Distribution Systems and the like).

The Charters have to cover various aspects of an organization. We discuss them below.

Vision and Mission Statements

The Citizen's Charter should begin with a clear statement of vision. Vision reflects the final objectives of an organization and the manner in which it seeks their achievement. A clear vision helps an organization to plan for and achieve its goals. The vision of an organization should be known to its personnel and the citizens it serves. Public bodies have to prepare their vision through a consultative process, involving multiple points in the organization as well as citizens, client groups or stakeholders. This will ensure the vision's wide acceptability.

Mission Statement

The 'mission' statement outlines the specific objectives which propel the organization in tune with its vision. An organization needs to think of the manner in which the vision is to be realised. This would help it in framing the mission in concrete rather than in vague terms.

Identification of Services

The Charter should clearly specify the services, which an organization would provide to attain its mission and vision. This should list all the services, which would be made available through its various agencies. Some Charters give information about 'details of business transacted by the organization'. An agency may use other expressions like 'Our Function', or 'Our Duties and Responsibilities'. But the main point is that all services should be clearly mentioned in the Charter.

Identification of Levels

Organizations operate at multiple levels; depending on the allocation of responsibilities and authority, particular levels deal with specific client groups/users/stakeholders. Irrespective of whether the organizations mention 'details of business', 'commitments', 'functions' or 'services' in their charters, they should clearly identify of the levels at which specific services would be provided. Citizens/ clients will know the levels at which they can access a specific service and not waste their time and energy in locating the service delivery point. The charter should make it clear whether it applies to all the agencies that come under the Ministry or Department or the agencies have their own specific Charters.

Identification of Client Groups/Stakeholders/Users

A citizen's charter has to clearly mention its client groups/stakeholders/users. This will lead to better service and greater interaction with them. One common weakness of citizen's charters is their failure to clearly spell out the services that will be provided to specific groups of clients, stakeholders and users. This deficiency needs to be remedied. Some organizations may not have regular customers. Some organizations have have paying customers. But others may have users who may access the service by virtue of being citizens. In some situations, even citizens or groups not using a service provided by an organization may be affected by its decisions. An example is an industrial or mining project which affects local people though they may not be its customers or clients. 'A public organization has to respond to all citizens even those who may not avail of its series'.

Big organizations with many client groups may have different services for different client groups. In such a situation, the Charter should list out the services for each client group and the 'commitments' for each of such services. This can be fine tuned further by listing out the specific 'commitments' at each level of the organization and the 'commitments' in terms of the special client groups like the Scheduled Castes, Scheduled Tribes, religious minorities and weaker sections.

Specification of Time-Frames for Each Service

The charter has to show the time by which a particular service will be provided. By mentioning the time, the organization will prevent undue public expectations and can work within reasonable schedules. Citizens can plan things from their end, and look for alternatives where available.

Specification of Time-Frames at Each Level

Time-frame for service delivery is required for each level at which specific services are delivered. They need to be observed. Ideally, organizations should publish information showing the extent of adherence to time-frames at each level. Public display of time within which services are provided by different levels/wings of an organization will introduce competition and improve performance.

Specification of Service Quality Standards

Organizations have to show the service quality standards in the charters. Based on this information, citizens can look for other available sources of service or may seek enhancement of the proposed standards. Organizations can also exercise internal controls based on their declared standards. While declaring standards, organizations have to follow both public policy requirements and clients' interests. For example, in passport delivery, clients prefer speed, but public policy interest requires proper scrutiny.

Specification of Service Delivery Standards

Citizen's charters need to include clear commitment on service delivery standards such as timeliness, access, accuracy, reliability, affordability, responsiveness, fairness, sensitivity, and courtesy. These standards should be stated in the form of commitments and not simply as targets. Standards have to be measurable so that the organization can concretely present its performance. Standards should be widely publicized and made known to people thorough suitable media advertisements.

Providing Information about the Public Grievance Redressal Procedures

Grievance redressal helps an organization in correcting its functioning. The charter should encourage the citizens/clients to ventilate their grievances. It should clearly lay down the grievance redressal procedures so that citizens/users/clients/stakeholders who have any grievances can seek redressal. This mechanism has to be taken seriously since unsolved citizen problems can damage an organization's image.

Providing Information about the Public Grievance Redressal Mechanisms

Citizens need to be informed about the grievance redressal mechanism available to them at various levels in the organization. A senior officer should be made responsible for inviting and processing 'grievances' for redressal. His/her name, designation, office room and telephone numbers and e-mail address should appear in the Charter. The officer in-charge of the grievances should ensure that they are received, diarized, acknowledged in a day or two and examined. Organizations should have mechanisms such as a committee for review, weekly or monthly meetings with concerned officers at various levels and reports on the number and type of grievances received.

Information about the Time-frame for the Public Grievance Redressal

Time limit for looking at complaints is an important item in the citizen's charter. The time-frame laid down for grievance redressal should be realistic and the organisation has to observe it. Otherwise, the system will lose credibility. A complaint may finally be accepted or rejected. If a complaint is rejected, the reasons for its rejection have to be clearly stated. A provision for appeal should be made for those citizens who still want to pursue their complaint after its rejection.

To summarize, a Citizen's Charter includes: vision and mission statements; identification of services; identification of levels; identification of client groups/ stakeholders/users; specification of time-frames for each service; specification of time-frames at each level/wing involved in service delivery; specification of service quality standards; specification of service delivery standards; and providing information about the grievance redressal procedures.

To be effective, citizen's charters need to give clear information on the following aspects:

¤ Processes/ Procedures for accessing services including about forms and charges
¤ Contact points for reaching service providers including addresses, telephones and e-mail
¤ Location and functions of Information Facilitation Counters (IFCs)
¤ Handbook on the scheme brought out under the RTI Act, 2005
¤ Monitoring mechanism for citizen's charter
¤ Procedure for receiving suggestions and comments from public

FEATURES OF A CITIZEN'S CHARTER

Rationale

A Citizen's Charter expresses the understanding between citizens and the provider of a public service. The service provider is usually the government department or the agency which provides the particular service. If the service is outsourced to a non government agency, that agency becomes the service provider. For example, a birth certificate may be provided by a village panchayat or a municipality or a city corporation. A citizen charter mentions the quality of service and the time for its delivery. It is a statement about the rights of the public and the obligations of the public servants.

Citizens have a right to a particular quality of service which meets their needs efficiently at a reasonable cost. The Citizen's Charter is a written, voluntary declaration by service providers. It specifies the level, quality or standard of the relevant services. It indicates the alternatives open to people or whether they can get similar services from other service providers. The charter indicates the procedure through which citizens can get the service from its provider. It assures that all eligible persons will be served in a non discriminatory manner. The relevant details about the service are made public and fully disclosed to ensure transparency. Its details are placed in the public domain so that all can know about it. Nothing about it is kept secret or hidden. Finally, a Citizen's Charter contains accountability clauses. It specifies the persons responsible for providing the services, and whom the citizens can approach for redressal if they fail to get the service as promised.

Citizen's charter borrows the idea of customer service from the private sector. No business can survive without a satisfied customer base. Successful businesses focus on product quality, after sales service and redressal of customer complaints. Citizen's Charters represent one application of the concept of reinventing government on the managerial model of successful private enterprises. In this model, the service providing department or its official is assigned the role of a manager. The citizens are treated as the customers of the department for that service. The service becomes the product which the department provides. The quality of service resembles the product standards of the business terminology.

This model of service delivery also seeks to change the attitudes of government servants. Traditionally, government servants in India have considered themselves as agents exercising government power. They like to lord it over people. The service delivery model casts government servants in a different role as providers of services to people. They have to render service with sympathy and ensure public satisfaction. People pay taxes and government servants, while providing services, have to ensure that people get value for their money.

The Citizen's Charter should not make promises which it cannot fulfil. It should offer services which are permissible according to the programme or policy guidelines and can be accommodated in its budget. It should not consist only of assurances or vague promises. It should adopt suitable procedures based on the nature of the service. The citizen's charter is a set of ideas to raise the level of standards and service delivery and increase public participation, in the most appropriate way. If properly implemented, the Charter will promote transparency and accountability.

A Citizen's Charter can lead to:

- Improved service delivery;
- Greater responsiveness of officials towards the public; and
- Greater public satisfaction with services.

Steps in formulation

Following steps are necessary for preparing a citizen's charter.

(i) Formation of Task Force consisting of the concerned officials for preparing the charter

(ii) Listing the major services which the Organization will provide and those who will be provided the services (clients or customers in business terminology)

(iii) Consultation with Clients/Stakeholders/Staff (primarily at cutting-edge level or implementation level) and their representative associations

(iv) Preparation of Draft Charter

- Circulating the draft charter to all concerned for getting their comments/ suggestions;
- Revising the Charter after considering the suggestions

(v) Consideration of the Charter by Core group (Core group is another group of officials which makes a peer review of the charter)

(vi) Modification of Charter by the Ministry/Department on the basis of suggestions/ observations of the Core Group

(vii) Approval by the Minister-in-charge

(viii) Submission of a copy of the charter to the Department of Administrative Reforms and Public Grievances (In State governments, the copy will be sent to the State Administrative Reforms department)

(ix) Formal issue/release of Charter and uploading it on website

(x) Sending copies to People's Representatives and all stakeholders

(xi) Appointment of a Nodal Officer to ensure effective implementation

Model Guidelines

The purpose of a Citizen's Charter is to reduce the dissatisfaction of the citizen/consumer/ customer with the quality of service which government departments and public sector entities provide. To serve this end, Citizen's Charter should adopt the following guidelines.

(i) The Charter must be simple.

(ii) While preparing the Citizen's Charter, senior officers or experts must consult both cutting edge staff who will implement it and the citizens (or their representative organisations) who will use it.

(iii) Merely pasting the Citizen's Charter on an office notice board or wall will not produce attitudinal change in the service staff. The necessary climate has to be generated through regular training and motivation of staff.

(iv) The Charter should clearly enumerate the services on offer.

(v) Against each available service, the Charter should mention the persons eligible for it, the entitlement of the user, service standards and remedies available to the user in case of breach of standards.

(vi) Procedures for availing the services and the payable charges should be shown on website/ display boards/ booklets/ inquiry counters.

(vii) It should be made clear that all attempts will be made to provide the services as indicated in the Charter, but that they are not justiciable (or cannot be enforced by courts).

(viii) The Charter should contain provisions for getting feedback (experiences of users), performance audit (which shows whether the services are being delivered as promised in the charter) and a schedule for reviewing the Charter every six months based on experience.

(ix) If an organization provides distinct services, the Charter may devote a separate section to each distinct service area.

General Structure

We have already mentioned the components of Citizen's Charters. More broadly, the Charter should begin with a brief statement about the services to be delivered. It has to mention the public interface of the service, for example, ticket reservation or passenger amenities in Railways, mail delivery, or premium services of postal department. The commitment to standards will specify the time limits and quality of service. The Charter will specify the staff or the service deliverers – where they can be found and what to expect of them. The Charters have to keep the people informed and especially consider the information they are likely to need for availing the service. The Charter has to consider any problem that may lead to failure of service delivery, and inform people about whom to contact in such contingencies and what help they can get from the personnel designated for this purpose. The Charter can mention how citizens can help the organization with their suggestions or in other ways.

Do's and Don'ts for Implementing the Charters

Based on its experience with the implementation of Citizen's Charters, the Administrative Reforms department has formulated the following positive and negative guidelines for their implementation.

1. Proceed steadily.
2. List areas of interface.
3. Introduce the Charter through small steps.
4. Involve customers and staff in formulating and implementing the Citizen's Charters.
5. Prepare a Master Plan for formulation and implementation of Charter over five years along with a budget for the period.
6. Win consumer confidence with small, highly visible measures.
7. Be ready to introduce changes in the Charter based on experience.
8. Inform people of the proposed commitments.
9. Use simple language.
10. Train the concerned staff.
11. Delegate powers.
12. Set up systems for feedback and independent scrutiny.

The following errors have to be avoided while preparing the Charters.

- Rushing with the Charters
- Being unrealistic
- Taking on excessive commitments
- Top-down formulation and implementation without inputs from operational levels
- Preparing a package for the whole Ministry/Department/Organization
- Promising more than what one can do
- Looking upon any Citizen's Charter as a one-time exercise, with a final outcome
- Informing the citizens before one is ready to deliver the service
- Centralization
- Continuing blindly without regular periodic reassessment of performance

Features of a Good Charter

The elements of a good Charter are:

(i) Focus on Customer Requirements;

(ii) Simple Language;

(iii) Service Standards;

(iv) Effective Remedies;

(v) Training;

(vi) Delegation;

(vii) Feedback Mechanism;

(viii) Close Monitoring;

(ix) Periodic Review.

Citizen's Expectations

Citizens have the following expectations from Government Departments/Service Providers:

(i) Reliability or consistency in performance;

(ii) Responsiveness or timely service;

(iii) Credibility or having customer interest at heart;

(iv) Empathy or attention to customer's needs;

(v) Courtesy and care or physical evidence of willingness to serve.

To sum up, the six principles of Citizen's Charters are: published standards; openness and clarity of information; choice and consultation; courtesy and helpfulness; redress when things go wrong; and value for money.

Working of Citizen's Charters

There have been various evaluations of Citizen's Charters. The findings have been generally negative. But there have been notable successes too. Among the successful examples which find mention in an official document of the Ministry of Personnel are: Regional Transport Office, Hyderabad; Jan Sewa Kendra, Ahmedabad; Chennai Metropolitan Water Supply and Sewerage Board, Chennai and Hyderabad Metropolitan Water Supply and Sewerage Board. However, there may be many other success stories. At least, the concept of a citizen's charter is now firmly lodged in the minds of governments and citizens. By January 2011, Central Government departments finalized 131 citizens charters and state government departments finalized 729 Citizen's Charters.

In an early study which the Ministry of Personnel commissioned, the following weaknesses were found. The impact of Citizen's Charters was reduced due to poor service delivery standards and under-performance. There was inadequate feedback from citizens about quality of service, limiting the impact of the Charter. The lack luster performance can be traced to various reasons such as:

- Absence of a planned approach to publicity
- Inadequate training and stakeholder involvement
- Preoccupation with programmes other than charters
- Bureaucratic style of functioning
- Lack of systematic identification of stakeholders
- Absence of citizen friendly approach and absence of avenues for the stakeholders to interact or give feedback

- Poor complaint redressal systems
- Outdated processes
- Inadequate staff training
- Centralization
- Lack of transparency
- Communication failure
- Lack of credibility and lack of confidence in the system.

Solutions

- A holistic approach to publicity through press, electronic media and user involvement
- 'Meet the citizen' programmes by the departments
- Changing the behaviour of the officers and staff through coaching, training and incentive systems
- Creating customer friendly environment in the offices
- Improving accessibility of officers and staff
- Training of staff at all levels
- Decentralization and delegation of authority
- Technology upgradation
- Process review and restructuring
- Customer confidence building measures, sharing information and reports with users of the service
- Setting up consultation committees welcoming negative feedback and removing fear from customers
- Assuring public that information from feedback will be used to improve services.

Bill on the Right of Citizens for Time Bound Delivery of Goods and Services and Redressal of Their Grievances.

Government has since decided to pass a law laying down obligations of every public authority towards citizens, specifying delivery of goods and services in a time-bound manner and providing for a grievance redressal mechanism for non-compliance of Citizen's Charter. A Bill was introduced in parliament in 2011 for this purpose.

Background

The Bill deals with two rights of citizens. One is time-bound delivery of goods and services. The other is redressal of grievances. The Bill mentions Citizen's Charter; it is the document that defines the standard of services which a public agency provides. It also gives the time limit for providing the goods and services.

In 2007, the Second Administrative Reforms Commission recommended that Citizen's Charters should stipulate penalties for non-compliance. In 2008, a parliamentary Standing Committee (on Personnel, Public Grievances, Law and Justice) recommended giving statutory status to grievance redressal mechanisms. The Central Information Commission also recommended that grievance redressal systems should be strengthened to reduce the public tendency to seek redressal of their grievances through use of the Right to Information Act. For applicants often resort to RTI Act not to get information but to have their problems resolved. The President, in her address to Parliament in June 2009, stated that the government would focus on ensuring effective delivery of public services. The Standing Committee that examined the Lokpal Bill, 2011 recommended the creation of a separate legislation to deal with Citizen's Charters and grievance redressal. The Parliament on August 27, 2011 while adopting the 'Sense of the House' Resolution on Lokpal, agreed in principle to the establishment of a Citizen's Charter. Currently, government departments deal with grievances internally. Persons may also approach the High Court through writ petitions. Further, as on March 2012, several states had enacted laws providing for grievance redressal mechanisms.

Main Provisions of the Bill

- The Bill requires public authorities to publish a Citizen's Charter within six months of enactment of the Bill.
- The charter should specify the services and the quality of services to be provided by the public authority.
- The heads of departments are responsible for disseminating and updating the Citizen's Charter.
- Public authorities include: (a) constitutional and statutory authorities; (b) entities established under any government notification; and (c) public-private partnerships. They also include NGOs that are substantially government funded, government companies, and companies that provide services under a licence or a statutory obligation.
- Public authorities are required to establish Information Facilitation Centres for efficient and effective delivery of services and redressal of grievances. Information Facilitation Centres may include customer care centres, call centres, help desks and people's support centres.

Public Grievance Redressal Commissions

- The Bill establishes Central and State Grievance Redressal Commissions. Each Commission would consist of a Chief Commissioner and upto 10 Commissioners. The Commissioners would be appointed by the President (Governor) on the recommendation of a selection committee.

- This committee would consist of the Prime Minister (Chief Minister), the Leader of the Opposition in the Lok Sabha (Legislative Assembly) and a sitting Supreme Court (High Court) judge.
- The Commissioners should be: (a) present or former Secretaries to the central (state) government; or (b) present or former Supreme Court judges or Chief Justices of a High Court (district court judges for 10 years, or High Court judges); or (c) eminent persons with at least 20 years (15 years) of experience in social sectors with a postgraduate degree in a relevant sector.
- The Commissioners may be removed by an order of the President (Governor) under certain conditions.

Complaint Mechanism

Complaint: Any citizen may file a complaint covering: (a) failure in delivery of goods or services listed in the Citizen's Charter; (b) the functioning of the public authority; and (c) any violation of a law, policy, programme, order or scheme. Complaints have to be redressed within 30 working days.

Complaints have to be made to the Grievance Redressal Officer (GRO). GROs are to be appointed by each public authority at the central, state, district, sub-district, municipality and panchayat levels.

- The GRO is required to: (a) ensure that grievances are redressed within 30 working days; (b) ensure that disciplinary action is taken against a defaulting officer if he has acted negligently; and (c) recommend penalties and compensation where an individual has wilfully neglected to deliver services or there is a prima facie ground for a case under the Prevention of Corruption Act, 1988. The GRO has to inform the complainant about the action taken on the complaint.
- Appeal: The orders of the GRO may be appealed before the Designated Authority (DA). The DA shall be an officer above the rank of the GRO and outside the concerned public authority.
- The DA shall dispose of appeals within 30 working days of their receipt. If a complaint with the GRO is not redressed within 30 working days, the GRO has to forward it as an appeal to the DA. The DA may penalize the defaulting officers.
- Second Appeal: The DA's orders may be appealed before the Central or State Public Grievance Redressal Commission within 30 working days. Appeals relating to complaints arising out of functioning of the central (state) departments would lie before the Central (State) Commission. The Commissions have to dispose of the appeal within 60 working days.
- Third Appeal: In relation to an offence under the Prevention of Corruption Act, 1988, an appeal against the decision of the Commissions shall lie with the Lokpal or the Lokayukta.

- Suo motu mechanism: The Central and State Commissions can suo motu refer matters related to non delivery of goods and services to the heads of government departments. The Commissions may also initiate suo motu inquiry if they believe that there are reasonable grounds to inquire into the matter.
- Complaints may also be made to the Commissions in certain cases. It is the duty of the Commissions to inquire into complaints by persons: (a) who are unable to file appeals before the DA; (b) who are refused redress of grievances; (c) whose complaints are not disposed of within 30 days; and (d) who are denied access to the citizen's charter because it has not been prepared or has not been widely disseminated.

Penalties

- GRO: The Bill requires the GRO to recommend penalties to the DA when: (a) he is convinced that the default was due to wilful neglect by an officer; or (b) when there is prima facie evidence of corruption.
- DA and Commissions: The Bill empowers the DA and the Commissions to impose a maximum penalty of Rs 50,000 upon the defaulting officer and the GRO. Penalties may be imposed upon the defaulting officer when he has acted in a malafide manner or has failed to discharge his responsibility in a proper manner. A portion of the penalty may be awarded as compensation to the complainant.
- If there is evidence of corruption against the defaulting officer, the DA and the Commissions would have to refer the matter to appropriate authorities. Additionally, the DA may initiate proceedings in such cases.
- Disciplinary proceedings may be initiated by the GRO, DA and the Commissions against the defaulting officer if there is evidence of malafide action.
- In any appeal proceeding, where it is alleged that the grievance has not been redressed by the GRO, the burden of proof shall be on the GRO.

Main Issues

Critics have pointed out certain legal and other difficulties involved in the provisions of the bill. These are briefly outlined below.

- Parliament may not have the jurisdiction to regulate the functioning of state public officials as state public services fall within the purview of state legislatures.
- This Bill may create a parallel grievance redressal mechanism as many central and state laws have established similar mechanisms.
- Companies that render services under a statutory obligation or a licence may be required to publish Citizen's Charters and provide a grievance redressal mechanism.
- The Commissioners may be removed without a judicial inquiry on an allegation of misbehaviour or incapacity. This differs from the procedure under other legislations.

- Appeals from the Commissions' decisions on matters of corruption will lie before the Lokpal or Lokayuktas. The Lokpal Act has come into force recently, and some Lokayuktas have not been established.

Summary

- The functions of government fall into two broad heads: legal exercise of authority and provision of services. Modern states are welfare States and provide a wide range of public services to their citizens.
- The services cover areas such as education, health, housing and transport. Services also include such requirements as a driving license, telephone connection, gas connection, tax refund, Aadhaar card, passport, and extracts from public records of one's property, educational qualification and date of birth.
- Citizens often experience considerable difficulty in securing timely, reliable and quality services from government agencies.
- Citizen's Charters are a means of solving the day to day problems which citizens experience while dealing with organisations providing public services.
- The Conservative party government under John Major was the first to introduce the Citizen's Charter (1991).
- Tony Blair's Labour government relaunched Citizen's Charters in 1998 under the name "Services First".
- The six principles of the Citizen's Charter movement as originally framed were - quality, choice, standards, value, accountability and transparency.
- A Citizen's Charter includes: vision and mission statements; identification of services; identification of levels; identification of client groups/stakeholders/users; specification of time-frames for each service; specification of time-frames at each level wing involved in service delivery; specification of service quality standards; specification of service delivery standards; and providing information about the grievance redressal procedures.
- Citizen's Charters represent one application of the concept of reinventing government on the managerial model of successful private enterprises. In this model, the service providing department or its official is assigned the role of a manager. The citizens are treated as the customers of the department for that service. The service becomes the product which the department provides. The quality of service resembles the product standards of the business terminology.
- The service delivery model casts government servants in a different role as providers of services to people. They have to render service with sympathy and ensure public satisfaction.

- The Citizen's Charter should not make promises which it cannot fulfill.
- Steps in formulation of a Citizen's Charter have been covered earlier.
- We have outlined the model guidelines for preparing the Citizen's Charters.
- We have detailed earlier the Do's and Don'ts for Implementing the Charters.
- There have been various evaluations of Citizen's Charters. The findings have been generally negative. As we have outlined the findings in the form of points, there is no need to repeat them here.
- Government introduced a Bill titled the Right of Citizens for Time Bound Delivery of Goods and Services and Redressal of Their Grievances.
- The main provisions of the Bill are:
  - (i) Public authorities should publish a Citizen's Charter
  - (ii) They have to specify the services and the quality of services to be provided.
  - (iii) The heads of department are responsible for disseminating and updating the citizen's charter.
  - (iv) 'Public authorities' have been defined widely covering all public or public sponsored service providers.
  - (v) Information Facilitation Centres have to be set up by each public authority.
  - (vi) The Bill establishes Central and State Grievance Redressal Commissions.
  - (vii) The Commissioners would be appointed by the President (or by Governors in States) on the recommendation of a selection committee.
  - (viii) The Bill contains a mechanism for dealing with complaints.
  - (ix) There is a provision for three appeals.
  - (x) There are provisions for penalties.
  - (xi) In relation to an offence under the Prevention of Corruption Act, 1988, an appeal against the decision of the Commissions shall lie with the Lokpal or the Lokayukta.
  - (xii) We have outlined some of the issues likely to arise from the system envisaged in the Bill.

PRACTICE QUESTIONS

1. What is a Citizen's Charter? How will it help people? What is the relation between citizen's charters and the idea of 'reinventing government'?
2. What are the six principles underlying the original Charter which John Major introduced?
3. What are the main components of a Citizen's Charter?
4. What are the steps involved in preparing a Citizen's Charter?

5. What do's and don'ts are important in preparing Citizen's Charters?
6. What are the main findings of the various evaluations of Citizen's Charters?
7. Outline the main provisions of the Right of Citizens for Time Bound Delivery of Goods and Services and Redressal of Their Grievances Bill.

REFERENCES

- Ministry of Personnel, Public Grievances, and Pensions Material on Citizen's Charter on the website
- Indian Institute of Public Administration Paper on citizen's charter

15

CHAPTER

CORPORATE GOVERNANCE

INTRODUCTION

According to a report prepared by Pune-based Indiaforensic Consultancy Services (ICS), at least 1,200 companies listed on domestic stock exchanges have forged their financial results. The figure included 20-25 firms on benchmark Sensex and Nifty indices. The study called 'Early Warning Signals of Corporate Frauds' had alleged that such improper accounting included deferring revenue and inflating expenses.

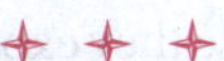

This was perhaps India's biggest corporate fraud case where M/s Satyam Computer Services Limited (M/s SCSL) caused loss to the investors to the tune of Rs.14,162 crore. The company head, Ramalinga Raju and members of his family secured illegal gains to the tune of about Rs.2,743 crore by various tricks. The fraud was perpetrated by inflating the revenue of the company through false sales invoices and showing corresponding gains by forging the bank statements with the connivance of the Statutory and Internal Auditors of the company. The annual financial statements of the company with inflated revenue were published for several years and this led to higher price of the scrip in the market. In the process, innocent investors were lured to invest in the company. Attempts were made to conceal the fraud by acquiring the companies of kith and kin – Central Bureau of Investigation.

After the mega corporate scam in Satyam Computer Services Limited, corporate governance, a rather arcane theme of ponderous reports with ringing moral tones, suddenly found itself in media glare. It became the subject of screaming headlines, high decibel TV debates and pontificating editorials. The scam unnerved not only the investors but also the government and the Indian corporates. Satyam, so to speak, was one of the poster boys of Indian software industry. Satyam fraud was among the propelling causes of the corporate governance reforms included in the revamped Companies Act which finally saw the light of the day after long wait.

The introductory quotes to the chapter refer to the type of shenanigans which corporate governance seeks to forestall. The quotes mention the perpetrators of the fraud, their corroborators, the custodians who slept on their watch, the modalities of the fraud and its victims. Frauds are usually financial and involve cooking of accounts or 'creative accounting'. It is for this reason that accountants and watchdog auditors are so important in corporate governance. To understand these matters, we need a little background on the structure and processes of corporates. Therefore we begin with these preliminaries.

STRUCTURE AND PROCESSES OF COMPANIES

Companies are bodies incorporated under the Companies Act. Registrar of companies registers them after putting them through the prescribed processes. Companies are regulated under the Companies Act, and also by their articles of association and memorandum of objects/purposes. If they are listed on the stock exchange, Securities and Exchange of Board of India (SEBI) watches over certain operations especially to protect the interests of small shareholders (who it is believed are often taken for a ride by the companies).

Companies are owned by shareholders. Companies need money to create the initial capital facilities for starting operations and then running them. Companies operate in various sectors of the economy such as infrastructure, manufacturing, finance, banking, trade and services. The type of equipment, machinery, factory site, offices and other facilities they require depend on the nature of their activity. Companies have to incur capital expenditure upfront for creating these facilities. Companies generate revenue or cash by selling whatever they produce or by rendering services. Companies have to incur capital expenditure before they start receiving cash from their operations.

Companies are set up by entrepreneurs or promoters. They put some money of their own and collect the balance from others. This is called share capital or equity. The amount is divided into units (normally each with a value of Rs 10 or Rs 100). Each contributor or shareholder receives shares in proportion to his equity. If X has contributed Rs 10,000 and if each share has a value of Rs 10, he will get 1000 shares. People invest in shares because they expect returns in the form of annual dividends and also because they expect the value of share to go up. The value of Rs 10 on our example is the initial book value of the share. If the company does well and makes profit, the share value will increase. If the company is listed in stock exchange, the share may, for example, sell for Rs 50. This is its market value.

Normally, a major part of share capital comes from promoters and the institutional investors. These are Life Insurance Corporation of India, general insurance companies, provident funds, Trusts (to the extent permitted), pension funds, investment funds and hedge funds. No project is funded wholly by equity. The promoters borrow money from banks and other institutions. Normally, projects are financed with 30% of share capital and 70% of loans or debt. Loans are repaid over a time with the revenue generated from the operations of the company.

Companies run on the basis of corporate democracy. In a democracy, each adult has one vote. But in a company the 'voting power' depends on share capital holding. If an individual or institution owns 10% of share capital, it commands 10% of votes. The promoter and his partners generally hold the required percentage of shares for management control and for taking necessary decisions. We can straightway note a problem here. As promoters have a controlling ownership of shares, they (along with institutional investors) 'call the shots'. In the process, the interests of small investors get neglected.

The affairs of the company are managed by a board of directors. This is what 'board room' means. It is the dream of MBAs and other professionals to make it to this sanctum sanctorum. The managing director is the chief executive who runs the day to day operations of the company. He is responsible to the board. The directors are classified into three groups: (i) those representing the promoters, (ii) nominee directors who represent the financial institutions and (iii) independent directors. The independent directors are selected on the basis of their expertise, experience, proven track record and impeccable integrity. Independent directors have a special role as custodians of corporate ethics. We will consider this aspect later in greater detail.

One writer has described the board of directors as the epicentre of the company's operations. The board is actually more of a policy making body. It does not handle the company's daily operations. The board devises the company's long term strategy, creates the organizational structure, lays down broad policy, prescribes necessary processes, and works out suitable mechanisms of external and internal control. Normally, it meets every month to review performance and take necessary policy decisions.

The operations of the company are divided into different areas depending on the nature of its activities. The normal divisions are production, purchase, marketing, finance, logistics, human relations (HR), communications and company law. The structure consists of managers at senior, middle and junior level. The managers carry out the operations in the different areas. Three areas are of particular importance for corporate governance – finance, audit and corporate law (which ensures compliance with regulations). Chief financial officer and company secretary play critical parts in corporate governance.

The results of a company's operations over the financial year are placed for approval before the general body of the shareholders. The results are reflected in the profit and loss account for the year and the balance sheet (as on 31st March of the financial year ended). Profit and loss account shows all the revenues and expenditures and any resulting profit. The accounts are audited by both internal and external auditors.

Before concluding this preliminary account, we may note that many malpractices involve the manipulation of accounts. Accounts have to convey a fair and accurate picture of the company's financial position. The Institute of Chartered Accounts has prescribed the 'accounting standards' or the correct ways of writing accounts. To put it simply, a company's profit is a resultant figure derived from calculations of thousands of revenue and expenditure elements (or pluses and minuses). Since the way accounts are prepared has a bearing on profits, there is a temptation to fiddle with accounts to inflate profits.

The profit can be increased or decreased, only within a narrow range, by tweaking the numbers. The auditors may not accept such procedures if they deviate too far from normal accounting conventions. We need not get into the details which involve intricacies of accounting. But we may note that accounts can be slightly manipulated to show higher profits. Nowadays, a whole bunch of financial analysts track the performance of companies, and project estimated profits. If a company's profits fall below these estimates, its stock takes a beating on the stock market thereby eroding some of its shareholders' wealth. This is one reason why accounts are to some extent manipulated.

This is obviously wrong. There can be more sinister motives such as increasing share price for selling it on market to unsuspecting small investors. They will suffer losses when in due course the stock value dips to its realistic level. There can be various other irregularities like embezzlement, diverting Company's money to personal uses and taking money in purchases and sales. Incidentally, the Companies Act prescribes the procedure for calculating net profit. The method of calculating profits also follows from accounting standards.

Before proceeding further, let us consider some examples which illustrate financial wrong doing.

Case Studies

CASE 1

Janakiraman's company routinely purchases lot of consumables for use in Headquarter and other offices. Janakiraman looks after this function in the company and reports to the General Manager. Janakiraman has a brother-in-law Varadarajan who has a business of office stationery and consumables. Janakiraman's wife requests him to place the order on her brother's firm (X). The company has a policy which specifies that purchases have to be made after getting offers in closed covers from four bidders and by selecting the best offer looking to quality and prices. In case of purchases above a certain limit, open tender is required to be invited through newspaper advertisement. At this time, purchase of a lot is being considered for which Janakiraman is required to initiate purchase process.

Question

The following courses of action come to his mind. What should he do?

1. Anyway he is likely to get a much better job offer compared to his present job in a large multinational company (MNC). The offer has been negotiated and is close to finalisation. He might just place the order directly to firm X.
2. If the policy does not dictate invitation of open tender because of the likely value of order, he might as well directly give the order to firm X.
3. The order quantity is such that there is no need to invite tender through newspaper. He should ask three known dealers to make offers above the range of market prices and ask firm X to submit offer in line with market prices. The desired result will follow.
4. He should not mix up private and official life and advise his brother-in-law to participate in normal course of competition.

Discussion

1. A professional career is a serious pursuit. This is very different in nature compared to say selling vegetables in urban streets. Vegetables sold today to a consumer may not be remembered by the customer tomorrow. Irrespective of whether tendering in newspaper is required or not, he has to invite at least four genuine offers, compare the offers, negotiate if necessary and then select vendors for supply. If he directly gives order to firm X, that will be a serious violation of Company's policy. Suppliers working with the company may complain or even whisper in the ears of Janakiraman's superiors. Then a controversy may arise. MNCs before giving final offer often confidentially verify the background of the candidate. If verification reveals such negligent act, the potential offer could even be in jeopardy. He must resist this temptation.
2. In this choice also, there is a violation of company policy. The policy is easy to understand and no senior manager will be unfamiliar with this kind of purchase process. This violation would definitely, be noticed by his direct subordinates (juniors in department). If known to superiors, this will lower his image of competence if nothing more. Hence an unacceptable choice.
3. The general principle is that what is a wrong action ethically cannot be corrected by manipulative behaviour of making it appear right. A manager is required to act in the best interest of the company. So he should accept only offers that result from competition in marketplace. That is the substance of the policy. Any violation would be unethical.

Moreover, he can never be sure that vendors willing to oblige will not become loud mouthed later. They may pass on the message or curiously enquire about whom he is trying to favour. Should the facts somehow come out the façade of propriety that he is trying to create will fall in pieces. He should not think of this manipulation.

4. The lesson is that managerial career and private life should not be mixed up. He should tell his wife that Varadarajan is welcome to compete like any other vendor. We are presuming that this is a routine kind of decision where the relationship will not be a liability for Janakiraman. If that happens and he has to make sharp evaluation of offers, he should give such task to next level in management so that "Not before Me" principle (i.e. not deciding a case which involves conflict of interest) can be followed.

CASE 2

Vishnu Mohan is the dynamic, pushy managing director of a fast growing retail sales chain. He has struck a deal with the board of directors for receiving a part of his pay as a percentage of the company's net profits. Although the company is doing well, the growth of sales and profits has been modest. Vishnu Mohan realised that his pay has become less compared to that of his peers drawing pay but without profit sharing. It was then that he called the chief finance officer Sarita Gohil. He told her that the chairman had expressed anxiety about profitability levels of the company in view of the need to raise funds from banks for the proposed expansion plans. He wondered how they could reach a more attractive profit figure.

Sarita knew that pushing up profits will be an artificial move. But she joined the firm recently and wanted to make a good impression on the boss. She also thought that the feelings of the chairman can be hardly ignored considering his interest in the expansion plans. She also knew that an increase in the company's turnover will help her in eventually migrating to a blue chip company.

Question

How should Sarita deal with the situation?

1. Sarita should recognize that she is playing with fire and politely explain to the MD that all significant manipulations are expressly barred by Accounting Standards prescribed by ICAI. Banks will definitely see through such gimmicks when they do due diligence before making fresh advances.
2. Sarita knows there are ways to increase profitability such as lowering depreciation, refusing to write off bad receivables, and reducing payables under pretext of fresh negotiation etc. Such adjustments, she thinks, will meet the urgent need of enhanced profits and advance her career prospects.
3. Sarita thinks that manipulations described above will not be easily detectable by shareholders and as such would not invite any problem.
4. Sarita may actually suggest these steps to the MD and seek his informal clearance.

Discussion

1. This is the only right course of action. A sensible MD would understand. Anyway, MD cannot compel CFO to massage the accounts. CFO has to sign the accounting statements first, before they go to MD.

2. Remember that ethics is a beautiful discipline that operates right from the stage of contemplation of an action. Mere thought about a course of action attracts ethical principles. Sarita should be clear that such profit enhancement works against the interest of shareholders because it colours the true and fair picture of the operations. Shareholders cannot take correct decision based on such accounts. Also MD walks away with increased incentives without increased profitability thus hurting the shareholders.

   It is legitimate to pursue career goals but not at the price of befooling stakeholders such as shareholders and lenders. That is bad corporate governance.
3. Sarita is living in a make believe world if she thinks that such manipulation will not be recognised by shareholders. Auditors, especially external auditors, would definitely detect some of this window dressing. That will reflect in audit report and shareholders particularly the smarter lot will smell a rat. This is 'Dumb World' hypothesis (belief that people are foolish) and no mature manager should proceed on that basis.
4. In this choice, the evil thought expresses itself. Once proposed, the MD will quickly agree in self-interest and then Sarita will lose the path to the fire exit so to say. She cannot then extricate herself from the ensuing complications. Even if in one year she can get away with this, the next year also MD may like to walk farther down the same road thus aggravating her problem. Remember, MD has strong incentive to do so.

CORPORATE GOVERNANCE

With the above background, we can look at the concept of corporate governance. First, we will discuss corporate governance in general terms and will then consider how it is being implemented in India.

Corporate governance refers to the processes, and the related organisational structures, by which organisations are directed, controlled and held to account. It "involves a set of relationships between an organisation's management, its board, its shareholders and other stakeholders. Corporate governance also provides the structure through which the objectives of the organisation are set, and the means of attaining those objectives and monitoring performance are determined". It can also be viewed as the laws, rules, regulations, systems, principles, and processes which regulate companies.

Corporate governance is also intimately connected with the following:

- Bringing the interests of shareholders and investors to the forefront
- Linking the company's governance mechanisms to society's conception of corporate accountability
- Commitment to values, ethical business conduct and strictly observing the distinction between personal and corporate funds
- Promoting fairness, transparency and accountability in company policies
- Observing principles of corporate social responsibility (CSR).

Corporate governance can help companies financially in the following ways:

- Improving corporate performance
- Attracting financial and human resources
- Tapping international financial markets
- Managing risks
- Avoiding corporate failure.

Ideas of corporate governance emerged in late 1980's and early 1990's. In this regard, the National Commission on Fraudulent Financial Reporting (Treadway Commission) in the United States, and the Committee on the Financial Aspects of Corporate Governance (Cadbury Committee) in the United Kingdom did pioneering work. OECD Principles of Corporate Governance came out in April 2004.

Cadbury Committee

The 'Cadbury Committee' was set up in May 1991 with a view to overcome the huge problems of scams and failures in the corporate sector worldwide in the late 1980s and the early 1990s. Cadbury Committee based its recommendations on three principles: transparency, integrity and accountability. Openness (transparency) of companies in disclosing of information, within the limits set by their competitive position, is "the basis for the confidence which needs to exist between business and all those who have a stake in its success".

Integrity was defined as meaning "both straightforward dealing and completeness". The Report stated that financial reporting should be "honest and ... should present a balanced picture of the state of the company's affairs". As regards accountability, Cadbury committee held: "Boards of directors are accountable to their shareholders and both have to play their part in making accountability effective", the former through the quality of information they provide and the latter through a willingness to exercise their responsibilities.

The Committee formulated a Code of Best Practice in four parts for compliance by the boards of all the listed companies.

(i) Board of Directors: The board should meet regularly, retain full and effective control over the company and monitor the executive management. There should be division of responsibilities so that no one individual has unfettered powers of decision. Where the chairman is also the chief executive, there should be a strong and independent member on the board. All directors should have access to the company secretary, who is responsible to the Board for ensuring that proper procedures are followed and that applicable rules and regulations are complied with.

(ii) Non-Executive Directors: The non-executive directors should bring an independent judgement to bear on issues of strategy, performance, resources, including key appointments, and standards of conduct. The majority of non-executive directors should be independent of management and free from any business or other relationship which could materially interfere with the exercise of their independent judgment, apart from their fees and shareholding. There should be full and clear disclosure of total emoluments of directors paid in any form.

(iii) Financial Reporting and Controls: The board should present a balanced and understandable assessment of the company's position. The financial reporting should give a true and fair picture.

(iv) Dealing with the Rights and Responsibilities of Shareholders: The shareholders, as owners of the company, elect the directors to run the business on their behalf and hold them accountable for its progress. They appoint the auditors to provide an external check on the directors' financial statements. The Committee's report particularly emphasises that the board should fairly and accurately report company's progress to shareholders. Institutional investors/shareholders should make greater use of their voting rights and take positive interest in the board's functioning. Both shareholders and boards of directors should consider how to strengthen the accountability of board of directors to shareholders.

Role of Auditors

The annual audit is one of the cornerstones of corporate governance. It provides an external and objective check on the way in which the financial statements have been prepared and presented by the directors of the company. The Cadbury Committee recommended that a professional and objective relationship between the board of directors and auditors should be maintained, so as to provide to all a true and fair view of company's financial statements. Auditors' role is to design audit in such a manner that it provides a reasonable assurance that the financial statements are free of material misstatements. Secondly, every listed company should form an audit committee which gives the auditors direct access to the non-executive members of the board. The Cadbury Committee further recommended regular rotation of audit partners to prevent unhealthy relationship between auditors and the management. It also recommended disclosure of payments to the auditors for non-audit services they render to the company.

Risk Management

Corporate governance in developed economies was also seen from the perspective of risk management. The collapse of Lehman brothers, the huge losses which banks suffered and instances of reckless risk trading by mangers in search of profits and bonuses made it necessary for boards to ensure better risk management. The Turnbull committee provided guidance to companies in UK in this matter. In September 2011, Financial Reporting Council, UK examined this question further. Its main conclusions on how boards should handle risk are listed below.

- The Board should determine the company's approach to risk, covering risk identification, oversight of risk management, and crisis management.
- Boards have to concentrate on those risks capable of undermining the strategy or long-term viability of the company or of damaging its reputation.
- Shareholders should be given meaningful reports on risk through an integrated account of the company's business model, strategy, key risks and their mitigation.
- Good corporate culture is essential to good risk management.
- The board should link up risk management and internal audit functions.
- Transparency and clear lines of accountability in the organisation are essential for effective risk management.
- The Board should spell out its appetite or tolerance for key individual risks.
- The exact dividing lines between the Audit Committee and the Board and between the Audit and Risk Committees need to be defined.

Evolution of Corporate Governance in India

Policies on corporate governance in India followed a path similar to one taken in the West. The emphasis in Indian policies can be said to be more on protecting small shareholders, preventing frauds and malpractices and promoting corporate social responsibility. The components of corporate governance are embodied in the recently passed Companies Act. Many of the individual elements of corporate governance which figured earlier in separate regulations and voluntary codes have now become part of the Companies Act.

PROVISIONS CONTAINED IN THE COMPANIES ACT

We will now outline the different points covering corporate governance which were included recently in the Companies Act.

1. National Financial Reporting Authority

National Financial Reporting Authority will be set up. Institute of Chartered Accountants of India earlier had many of the powers vested in the Financial Reporting Authority. This authority will formulate the accounting and auditing standards. It will monitor and enforce compliance of these standards. To this end, it will oversee the quality of the professions like accountancy, auditing and financial analysis connected with these matters. The authority will investigate professional and other misconduct of chartered accountants or their firms.

2. Audits and Auditors

Every company has to appoint an auditor. Listed and other specified companies can appoint an individual auditor for a five year term and a firm for two consecutive terms of five years each. Any firm having a same partner or partners shall not be appointed in its place. The remuneration of auditors shall be fixed by the company in its general meeting. It means that the decision can be taken neither by the management nor by the board but only by the general body of shareholders. This removes chances of collusion between management and the auditors.

Every auditor of a company shall have a right of access at all times to the books of account and vouchers (signed receipts for payments made) of the company. An auditor can demand (as a matter of right) from the company officials such information and explanation as he may consider necessary for the performance of his duties as auditor. The law enjoins upon the auditors some matters on which they must conduct a special inquiry and include in their report.

The Companies Act imposes a special obligation on auditors, company secretaries in practice and cost accountants of a company. If during the course of the performance of their duties they notice that an offence involving fraud is being or has been committed against the company by its officers or employees, they have to report the matter to the Central Government. The government will prescribe the time limit and method for making such reports. The law prohibits the auditors from providing banking, financial and similar services to the company. This is intended to avoid conflict of interest and to preserve the auditor's independence. Otherwise, the company may entice auditors with alluring financial assignments.

CASE 3

Nikunj is auditing the accounts of a firm owned by a few partners. The accounts showed investments of Rs 2 crore in time deposits of banks. He wants to see these fixed deposit receipts. But the managing partner has pledged them in Labhada Bank without telling his partners and took a loan. Nandita, the chief accountant, goes to the managing partner and tells him about Nikunj's demand. He is in a fix and wonders what to do. Nandita volunteers that she knows the manager of Labhada Bank well, and will get photocopies of the fixed deposit receipts. She gets the copies and shows them to Nikunj pretending that the originals are in a safe deposit vault in a faraway suburb. Nikunj unsuspectingly accepts her story.

Question

To which of the following comments you would agree?

1. Nikunj must be either incompetent or corrupt.
2. Managing partner has committed a breach of trust by securing a personal loan on the support of fixed deposits belonging to the partnership firm.
3. Manager of the Labhada Bank must be corrupt.
4. Only (1) and (2)

Discussion

Regarding (1) we have no evidence to come to the conclusion that Nikunj is corrupt. He should have asked Nandita why she is showing photocopies of fixed deposit receipts. What is the compulsion or requirement to keep FDs in a safe vault in a faraway place? He could have given some time to Nandita to bring the original receipts and show him. Nandita could not have then tricked him because the Labhada Bank or for that matter any bank would not part with the receipts on which loan has been taken.

Managing partner has committed a breach of trust. There is no doubt about that. He is in a position of trust with respect to other partners. They have entrusted the management of the firm to him. He cannot use property of the partnership as security to get a loan for himself. The partnership firm is an entity separate from the managing partner. Somebody may incorrectly argue that no loss has been caused to the firm because the bank had no occasion to realise the value of the deposits. Nor that the firm has been deprived of the use of the money. However, ethically we do not need to see the result of the action. Mere possibility of doing harm is sufficient for ethical evaluation.

We have no basis to conclude that manager of Labhada Bank is corrupt. Giving a photocopy to the owners or their representative is a permissible action. The manager who sanctioned personal loan to managing partner committed an error. However, there is no statement that the same manger allowed the copies of the FD receipts to be taken. Hence (3) is not a correct statement. Hence (4)

3. Directors

Every listed company and companies of prescribed classes shall have at least one-third of total number of directors as independent directors. For the first time, the Companies Act has defined the term 'independent director'. An independent director has to give an annual declaration of independence to Board. He is not entitled to receive stock option (i.e. the benefit or right to purchase or to subscribe for, the shares of the company at a future date at a pre-determined price) but may receive remuneration and reimbursement of expenses. An independent director can hold office for a term of five consecutive years. However, he cannot hold office for more than two consecutive terms. But he will be eligible for appointment after a break of three years. Independent directors shall not be subject to the provision of retirement by rotation.

The Companies Act has prescribed the qualifications of independent directors and the procedure for their appointment. Their appointment has to be approved in general body meeting. To help companies in selecting independent directors, a data bank will be maintained containing names, addresses and qualifications of eligible and willing persons.

The independent directors are the custodians of corporate governance and the conscience keepers of the board. The Companies Act includes a code as a guide to professional conduct for independent directors. Independent directors should adhere to the standards laid down in this code and guide. By doing so, they will enhance the confidence of investors (particularly small investors), financial institutions, regulators and companies in the institution of the independent director.

The qualities expected of an independent director include: integrity and probity; objective and constructive approach; bonafides of action; banishing extraneous considerations that threaten his objective, independent judgment; refraining from abuse of his office and from any action that would lead to loss of his independence.

A listed company may have one director elected by small shareholders. A small shareholder holds shares worth up to Rs 20000. There shall be at least one woman director in companies of prescribed class or classes.

The articles of a company may provide for the appointment of not less than two-thirds of the total number of the directors of a company based on proportional representation.The duties of directors mentioned in the Companies Act include good faith, due and reasonable care, skill and diligence, independent judgment, and no direct or indirect conflict of interest. Any violation of duties is punishable with a fine from one lakh to five lakh rupees.

CASE 4

Munnalal started a business from scratch, and ended up as substantial owner of a midsized engineering company. The position of technical director in the company fell vacant when its incumbent resigned to take up another assignment. To the surprise of the board, Munnalal proposed that his young son Kishorilal should be made the technical director. One director openly expressed his opposition to the proposal and doubted Kishorilal's credentials. Munnalal replied that his son has studied engineering in Remote Westbrook Technical University. In reply to the member's question, he added that Remote Westbrook Technical University is an accredited University in New Mexico. Kishorilal, he added also took training in some workshops near Detroit. When there was further opposition, he pleaded that his health was poor and that he would like someone from his family to take reins if he were to become too ill. Kishorilal, he added, would be elected a member on the strength of his shareholding.

Question

Assume that you have been the Secretary of the company for many years and have the ear of Munnalal. What would be your advice to Munnalal?

1. You would advise Munnalal that such opposition from Independent Directors is routine in corporate life. Munnalal should not change his position.
2. Your advice would be that Kishorilal should start at the shop floor and then gradually take up higher responsibility.
3. Company should appoint an elderly technocrat with management experience who is nearing retirement and he should be appointed with specific mission to groom Kishorilal.
4. You should stay away because in family matters people do not pay heed to reason.

Discussion

1. As a Secretary you are required to act in the interest of the company. Keeping Munnalal happy may be important for your career advancement, but obviously ignoring the opinion of Independent Director as routine is not a sensible approach. Independent Directors are required precisely for such purpose of balancing the interest of the promoter and the interest of other shareholders who are not controlling the affairs of the company. Secretary needs to pay heed to valuable opinion of Independent Directors(s). Clearly, Kishorilal does not have the requisite experience and even education to start from that level of management. That precisely is the issue here.
2. Munnalal would want to see tangible result in a time frame because he may not be keeping good health and is anxious to have a successor from family. This option is somewhat vague as Kishorilal may take long time to move up the ladder. This option does not meet with the demand of the situation.
3. This is the right option. When the company brings in an executive with sound experience and maturity, its current operations will not suffer. Since the incumbent is near retirement he would not try to extend his career horizon but instead sincerely groom Kishorilal. In about two years, it should be possible to groom Kishorilal. After that Kishorilal may take over substantial responsibility. If the incumbent still wants to continue for some more time he may be given some advisory position wherefrom also he can support Kishorilal. This is the pragmatic course of action.
4. No doubt Munnalal is personally concerned about this issue. However, the matter affects the whole company. Since Munnalal has controlling interest in the company and he is not keeping good health, the succession anxiety is understandable. In that situation good advice surely has value. If the Secretary shies away from tendering that advice, he would be failing in his duty. He is no stranger either to the company or to Munnalal. He cannot afford to remain a mute spectator.

4. Committees of the Board of Directors

Every listed company and some other specified companies have to constitute an audit committee. Audit committee shall have not less than three independent directors; at least two of them should be able to understand financial statements like balance sheets, profit and loss accounts, cash flow statements and statements of changes in equity. The chairperson should have this ability. The terms of reference or jurisdiction of an audit committee shall include all matters relating to finance, accounts, commercial transactions, investments and audit.

The audit committee shall have power to investigate into all these matters. The auditors and key managerial personnel have a right to be heard in the meetings of audit committee. Where Board does not accept any recommendation of the audit committee, it has to be disclosed.

The Act provides a vigilance mechanism so that directors and employees can report their genuine concerns or apprehensions about things happening in the company. Any person who uses such mechanism shall have direct access to chairperson of the audit committee. This is a kind of whistleblower provision.

5. Nomination and Remuneration Committee, Stakeholders Relationship Committee

The Act has made provision for a Nomination and Remuneration Committee and a Stakeholders Relationship Committee. The Nomination and Remuneration Committee will identify persons who are qualified to become directors and who may be appointed in senior management. The Board of Directors of a company which consists of more than one thousand shareholders, debenture-holders, deposit-holders and any other security holders at any time during a financial year will have to constitute a Stakeholders Relationship Committee.

6. Related Party Transactions

Related party transactions are those in which board directors or their immediate family members have a personal financial interest. They place them in conflict of interest situations. Their gain may depend on company's loss. It is a cardinal principle that they should keep a safe distance from such transactions. Or they have to deal with them 'at arm's length'.

The Companies Act includes safeguards in this matter. No company can enter into any contract or arrangement with a related party without consent of board of directors given by a resolution. If the transaction exceeds certain limit, it needs the prior approval of the company in general meeting by a special resolution. Any member who is interested in the transaction can vote on such special resolution. However, no approval is needed if the transaction is on an arm's length price i.e. at full market price. The Board has to disclose every related party transaction in its report to shareholders. The company has to maintain a register showing the contracts and arrangements in which directors are interested.

7. Secretarial Audit

Every listed company and or specified company has to attach to its Board's report to shareholders a secretarial audit report given by a company secretary in practice. The task of a company secretary who heads its secretariat is to ensure that the company duly complies with all the legal requirements as specified in the Companies Act and other relevant laws. The secretarial auditor will audit the working of the company's law division whose task it is to ensure that the company conforms to all the applicable rules and regulations. Secretarial auditor will report on (a) whether the company has complied with the Companies Act and other laws applicable to it and (b) whether the company's law division or secretariat is maintaining the proper professional standards.

8. Class Action

The Companies Act has introduced the concept of class action for the first time in India. Class action is different from legal action which individual litigants take. An individual litigant or a group fights a case on its own behalf. For example, suppose that twenty farmers suffer losses when industrial effluents flow into their fields. One of the farmers files a case in a court and gets compensation. This is an individual legal action. The judgement will not apply to other farmers, though they belong to the class or group who suffered loss. However, there is a provision in countries such as USA for filing class action suits. In such suits, the judgement will apply to all similarly placed persons even if they do not join the suit.

The Companies Act has introduced a similar provision. Where members, depositors or any class of them are of the opinion that affairs of company are being conducted in a manner prejudicial to the interest of company, its members or depositors, they may file an application before tribunal. The class action can also cover the auditors.

9. Corporate Social Responsibility (CSR)

(i) If a company (a) has a net worth of rupees five hundred crore or more, or (b) turnover of rupees one thousand crore or more, or (c) a net profit of rupees five crore or more in a financial year, then it has to constitute a Corporate Social Responsibility Committee of the Board. The committee should have three or more directors, with at least one independent director. The Board's report to share holders should disclose the composition of the Corporate Social Responsibility Committee.

(ii) The Corporate Social Responsibility Committee has to perform the following functions: (a) Formulate and recommend to the Board, a Corporate Social Responsibility Policy for taking up the activities specified in the Companies Act. (b) Recommend the amount of expenditure to be incurred on the CSR and (c) monitor the Corporate Social Responsibility Policy of the company

(iii) The company's board has to approve, after considering the CSR committee's recommendations, the Corporate Social Responsibility Policy. The policy has to be included in its report to shareholders and also has to be placed on the company's website. The board has to ensure the implementation of the activities included in its CSR policy.

(iv) A company to which CSR applies has to spend on it every financial year, at least two per cent of the average net profits made during the three immediately preceding financial years. The company shall give preference in its CSR policy to the local area where it operates. If the company is unable to spend the CSR money, it should explain the reasons in its report to share holders.

(v) CSR can cover programmes for:

(a) eradicating extreme hunger and poverty;

(b) promotion of education;

(c) promoting gender equality and empowering women;

(d) reducing child mortality and improving maternal health;

(e) combating human immunodeficiency virus, acquired immune deficiency syndrome, malaria and other diseases;

(f) ensuring environmental sustainability;

(g) employment enhancing vocational skills;

(h) social business projects;

(i) contribution to PM's National Relief Fund or fund set up by the Central Government or the State Governments for socio-economic development and relief and funds for helping vulnerable groups.

To sum up, the new Companies Act includes various aspects of good corporate governance such as independent directors on boards; enhanced disclosure norms; enhanced accountability of management; stricter enforcement; audit accountability; protection for minority shareholders; investor protection and activism; and CSR.

UNGC: A Modern Cornerstone of Corporate Governance

Recognizing that solutions to the most fundamental challenges facing society require extraordinary collaboration, the UN entered the corporate sustainability realm in 2000 with the Secretary-General's launch of the United Nations Global Compact (UNGC).

The UNGC is a United Nation's initiative to encourage businesses worldwide to adopt sustainable and socially responsible policies, and to report on their implementation. The UN Global Compact is a principle-based framework for businesses, covering ten principles in the areas of human rights, labour, the environment and anti-corruption. Under the Global Compact, companies are encouraged to work along with UN agencies, labour groups and civil society.

The UNGC is the world's largest corporate citizenship initiative with 10000 corporate participants and other stakeholders over 130 countries with two objectives: "Mainstream the ten principles in business activities around the world" and "Catalyse actions in support of broader UN goals, such as the Millennium Development Goals (MDGs)."

The precursor to the launch of UNGC was in an announcement of the UN Secretary-General Kofi Annan in an address to the World Economic Forum on January 31, 1999, and UNGC was officially launched at UN Headquarters in New York on July 26, 2000.

The Global Compact Office is supported by seven UN agencies: the United Nations Framework Convention on Climate Change; the United Nations High Commissioner for Human Rights; the United Nations Environment Programme; the International Labour Organization; the United Nations Development Programme; the United Nations Industrial Development Organization; and the United Nations Office on Drugs and Crime.

The UN Global Compact is a call to companies everywhere to:

1. Voluntarily align their operations and strategies with ten universally accepted principles in the areas of human rights, labour, environment and anti-corruption and
2. Take actions in support of UN goals, including the Millennium Development Goals.

By doing so, business can help ensure that markets advance in ways that benefit economies and societies everywhere. The UN Global Compact is a leadership platform endorsed by chief executives of global companies for the development, implementation, and disclosure of responsible corporate policies and practices. The initiative brings companies together with key stakeholder groups including: Government, civil society, labour, investors, educators and the United Nations.The Global Compact asks companies to embrace, support and enact, within their sphere of influence, a set of core values in the areas of human rights, labour standards, the environment and anti-corruption. The Ten Principles enjoy universal consensus and are derived from the Universal Declaration of Human Rights, the International Labour Organization's Declaration on Fundamental Principles and Rights at Work, the Rio Declaration on Environment and Development, and the United Nations Convention against Corruption.

Human Rights

Businesses should

Principle 1: support and respect the protection of internationally proclaimed human rights; and

Principle 2: make sure that they are not complicit in human rights abuses.

Labour

Businesses should

Principle 3: uphold the freedom of association and the effective recognition of the right to collective bargaining;

Principle 4: eliminate all forms of forced and compulsory labour;

Principle 5: ensure effective abolition of child labour; and

Principle 6: eliminate discrimination in respect of employment and occupation.

Environment

Businesses should

Principle 7: support a precautionary approach to environmental challenges;

Principle 8: undertake initiatives to promote greater environmental responsibility; and

Principle 9: encourage the development and diffusion of environmentally friendly technologies.

Anti-Corruption

Businesses should

Principle 10: work against corruption in all its forms, including extortion and bribery.

CASE 5

Stylemakers plc.in UK is a rising star in garment manufacturing and retailing business in UK, Europe and North America. The company supplies design and gets garments stitched in a number of developing countries including India and Bangladesh. A Bangladeshi firm X takes orders from Stylemakers and supplies garments to Stylemakers as per their order and schedule.

The firm X also does not on its own account manufacture garments but gets this done from a number of other parties. One of the contract manufacturers had been doing this job in a large multistoreyed building 'Golden plaza' which collapsed due to structural failure. The catastrophe resulted in more than a thousand fatalities and even larger number of grievous injuries. The workers were mostly poor and their families depended on the income from this contract job. In Golden Plaza the workers were stitching garments not only for Stylemakers plc. but also for many other multinational corporations who have an interest in garment selling.

Mr. Alex Bradford is the CEO of the company. He knew quite a bit about the condition of workers in outsourced countries especially Bangladesh. He had also travelled to that country for the same business as Bangladesh is the major supplier to Stylemakers plc. When the news of this major accident flashed in global media and he could see the footage, the following courses of action occurred to him. Which course of action would you recommend to him?

Course of Action

1. Stylemakers plc. is not directly employing any workers in Bangladesh. Even firm X is employing contractor to get the job done. So, Stylemakers plc. need not take any action with the matter.
2. Stylemakers plc. though not directly connected with the workers have a humanitarian duty and need to express sympathy and concern for the deceased and the injured.
3. Stylemakers plc. in view of its commitment to UNGC principles, needs to support firm X to give immediate succor to the families as per the policy of Bangladesh Government.
4. Stylemakers plc. should give the same scale of benefits to the families of the deceased and the injured as if the accident occurred in UK or USA.

Discussion

The answer choice (1) is not correct. Stylemakers plc. cannot escape responsibility on the pretext that the labourers were not in its direct employment. The principal who is getting job done as per their design and schedule does have responsibility in Corporate Governance framework. The accident was the outcome of shoddy construction and overcrowding of machines and workers in a weak structure and hence responsibility attaches to Stylemakers plc.

The answer choice (2) is an inadequate response. Expression of grief and sympathy is absolutely necessary but not enough. The accident victims or their families need to be compensated so that they could restart their shattered lives.

Obviously, the answer choice (3) is appropriate. It is possible that Bangladesh Government will have a scale of benefits for victims of such calamities. The company needs to follow that policy prescription in the minimum and compensate the victims.

Answer choice (4) is strictly speaking not necessary. First of all, such an accident is unlikely in a developed country. Secondly, the cost of living in a developed country is very different from that in Bangladesh. So it is not pragmatic to try and give compensation on the scale of UK or USA. The CEO is not required to go that far though his heart may suggest so.

Summary

- Companies are bodies incorporated under the Companies Act. They are regulated under this Act and also by SEBI.
- Companies are owned by shareholders. Companies are set up by entrepreneurs or promoters. They put some money of their own and collect the balance from others. This is called share capital or equity.
- Normally, a major part of share capital comes from promoters; institutional investors also contribute to equity.
- In a company the 'voting power'- which ultimately confers management control - depends on share capital holding.
- The promoter and his partners generally hold the required percentage of shares for management control and for taking necessary decisions. They may ignore or neglect the interests of small investors.

- The affairs of the company are managed by a board of directors. They are classified into three groups: (i) those representing the promoters, (ii) nominee directors who represent the financial institutions and (iii) independent directors.
- The results of a company's operations over the financial year are placed for approval before the general body of the shareholders popularly known as annual general meeting.
- Profit and loss account shows all the revenues and expenditures and any resulting profit. The balance sheet reflects the assets and liabilities of the company as on March 31 of the financial year. The accounts are audited by both internal and external auditors.
- Accounts have to convey a fair and accurate picture of the company's financial position. The Institute of Chartered Accounts has prescribed the 'accounting standards' or the correct ways of writing accounts.
- The profit can be increased or decreased, only within a narrow range, by tweaking the numbers.
- Many malpractices involve the manipulation of accounts – ranging from misrepresentation of finances to fraud.
- The essence of corporate governance consists in observing ethical norms.
- It connotes commitment to values, ethical business conduct, adherence to law and CSR. Cadbury committee observed that corporate governance is based on promoting fairness, transparency and accountability in company policies.
- Corporate governance can improve a company's efficiency and financial performance.
- Cadbury committee defined openness or transparency as disclosing of information, within the limits set by the competitive position of a company to its stakeholders.
- Integrity is defined as meaning both straightforward behaviour and presenting a balanced picture of the company's affairs.
- Boards of directors are accountable to their shareholders and both have to play their part in making accountability effective.
- Cadbury committee highlighted the role of board of directors, auditors and share holders in promoting corporates governance.
- Corporate governance in developed economies is also seen from the perspective of risk management. The collapse of Lehman brothers, the huge losses which banks suffered and instances of reckless risk trading by mangers in search of profits and bonuses made it necessary for boards to ensure better risk management. Financial Reporting Council, UK examined this question and gave guidelines to boards on handling business risks.
- The emphasis in Indian policies on corporate governance can be said to be more on protecting small shareholders, preventing frauds and malpractices and promoting corporate social responsibility. The components of corporate governance are embodied in the recently passed amendments to Companies Act.
- The new Companies Act includes various aspects of good corporate governance such as independent directors on boards; enhanced disclosure norms; enhanced accountability of management; stricter enforcement; audit accountability; protection for minority shareholders; investor protection and activism; and CSR.

- It has created a National Financial Reporting Authority for prescribing and enforcing accounting standards.
- It has strengthened audits and independence of auditors.
- If a chartered accountant, company secretary in practice or cost accountant during the course of work notices that an offence involving fraud is being or has been committed against the company by its officers or employees, they have to report the matter to the Central Government.
- The independent directors are the custodians of corporate governance and the conscience keepers of the board. The Companies Act includes a code as a guide to professional conduct for independent directors.Independent directors should adhere to the standards laid down in this code and guide. By doing so, they will enhance the confidence of investors (particularly small investors), financial institutions, regulators and companies in the institution of the independent director.
- The qualities expected of an independent director include: integrity and probity; objective and constructive approach; bonafides of action; banishing extraneous considerations that threaten his objective, independent judgment; refraining from abuse of his office or from any action that would lead to loss of his independence.
- The audit committee is an important body which watches over the propriety of the company's financial dealings.
- There is a kind of whistleblower provision under which directors and employees can express their concerns to the chairman of the audit committee.
- Related Party Transactions are strictly controlled.
- Secretarial audit ensures the company's compliance with rules and regulations.
- The Companies Act has introduced the concept of class action for the first time in India.
- A company to which CSR applies has to spend on it every financial year, at least two per cent of the average net profits made during the three immediately preceding financial years.
- CSR policy has to be formulated and monitored by the board's CSR committee.
- CSR can cover health, education, anti poverty, skill development and other similar programmes which help the poor and needy.
- UNGC's appraoch can serve as an important guide for corporate governance.

PRACTICE QUESTIONS

1. Elucidate the concept of corporate governance.
2. "Corporate governance is only a public relations gimmick to polish the image of corporate bosses or honchos". Comment.
3. What are the ingredients of corporate governance? What is their rationale?
4. What is the importance of audit committee in ensuring corporate governance?

5. "The independent directors have to do moral policing in a company." Discuss.
6. Write short notes on - (a) National Financial Reporting Authority (b) related party transactions (c) arm's length dealings (d) class action suits and (e) Secretarial audit.
7. "Corporate social responsibility is a camouflage for pursuing populist political agendas, depriving corporates of investible resources and hurting share holder interests." State your view with supporting reasons.
8. After the recent financial crisis, regulators in developed economies have come out with many prescriptions on how boards of companies should handle risks involved in their operations. Do you think that it is like shutting the stable door after the horse has bolted?
9. Briefly outline the main features of corporate social responsibility policy applicable in India.
10. What qualities of head and heart should an independent director have?
11. List briefly (in a sentence or two) the main ways or means which can promote corporate governance in companies.

REFERENCES

- The Companies Act.
- Corporate Governance in India: A legal Analysis - Prabhash Dalei, Paridhi Tulsyan and Shikhar Maravi.
- Corporate Governance of Public Bodies: Hong Kong Institute of Certified Accountants.
- The Cadbury Committee Report, 1992.

ATTITUDES

ATTITUDE

Definition and Elaboration

Psychologists define attitude as a learned – as opposed to an in-born-tendency to evaluate things in a certain way. This can include evaluations of people, issues, objects or events. Such evaluations are often favourable or unfavourable but they can also be uncertain at times. Thus we often speak of 'mixed feelings'about an individual or an event. An attitude is an expression of favour or disfavour toward a person, place, thing, or event (or the attitude object). Attitude object is an entity towards which an individual's attitudes are directed.

Gordon Allport once described attitudes as "the most distinctive and indispensable concept in contemporary social psychology".

Psychologists have also fine tuned this definition. According to Eagly and Chaiken, an attitude is "a psychological tendency that is expressed by evaluating a particular entity with some degree of favour or disfavour." The evaluations which people make can range from the extremely unfavourable to the extremely favourable, or can be more moderate. Attitudes can be mixed, and with regard to thc same object, may vary from time to time.

Attitudes are classified as explicit and implicit. If a person is aware of his attitudes, and they influence his behaviour and beliefs, his attitudes are explicit. Explicit attitudes are formed consciously. A person may be unaware of his implicit beliefs though these still have some influence on his conduct and behaviour. Implicit attitudes are subconscious attitudes.

Carl Jung, one of the founders of psychoanalysis, defines attitude as a "readiness of the psyche to act or react in a certain way". According to Jung, attitudes occur in pairs out of which one is conscious and the other unconscious. Within this broad definition, Jung defines several attitudes. He identifies the following pairs of attitudes:

Conscious	Unconscious
Extroversion	Introversion
Rational	Irrational
Individual	Social
Abstract	Creative

Structure

Modern psychologists regard attitude as a complex, multidimensional construct. Construct means a theoretical concept. In this context, the term 'construct' means that it has been created by the practitioners of a discipline. A construct can also result from social practice or the manner in which people use common language. A construct is not a simple (natural or social) occurrence or event or observation; it is something which is theoretically formulated. Thus, sociologists formulate social constructs for analyzing social phenomena. The constructs mediate between the observations sociologists make and the way they interpret them. Multidimensional means that the theoretical concept consists of more than one component or ingredient.

Attitude has three components. These components are cognitive, affective and conative. Cognitive part consists of a person's thoughts and beliefs about the attitude object. 'Cognitive' means 'relating to the process of acquiring knowledge through reason, intuition and perception'. The emotional (or affective) part consists of the feeling which the object, person, issue or event evokes. 'Affective' means emotional. The behavioural part consists of the manner in which the attitude influences a person's behaviour. 'Conative' in psychology means a mental process involving the will-impulse, desire or resolve. In simple terms, it means 'behavioural'. William J. McGuire proposed this classic, tripartite view of attitudes.

Researchers who made empirical studies could not, however, clearly isolate the thoughts, emotions, and behavioural intentions associated with a particular attitude. There is often no consistency, as required by the tripartite view of attitudes, between cognitive, affective, and behavioural associations of an attitude. Some psychologists think that in attitude structure, the cognitive and behavioural components are products of the emotional component, and that behaviour is driven by underlying beliefs.

Although there is disagreement on the particular structure of attitudes, evidence shows that they reflect more than the positive and negative evaluations of a particular object. Attitudes have other features - like importance, certainty, or strength and associated knowledge. Further, inter-attitudinal structure connects different attitudes to one another and to deeper psychological structures, such as values or ideology.

Functions

In psychology (and in sociology), functionalism means a particular approach which theorists adopt for understanding social or psychological phenomena. In simple terms, they try to understand the purpose which the phenomenon under study serves in the society or in the personality of the individual. For example, sociologists do not study religion in the manner in which theologians study it. Theologians may study the details of the religious doctrine, its evolution, and how it can contribute to the spiritual progress of its followers. Sociologists will study it differently. They will examine how religion contributes to social stability. That is the function of religion in society.

Psychologists study attitudes similarly considering how attitudes contribute to the overall well being of the individual. Attitudes perform various functions for the psychological and mental benefit of the individual. An individual's attitudes often satisfy his particular psychological needs. Men have not only physical but also psychological needs. Thus, men need a sense of self-esteem. Otherwise, they will be demoralized. This is called the functional aspect of an attitude since it performs a psychological function for the individual. Psychologists explore the general and particular attitudes of individuals by considering the manner in which an individual's attitudes affect him. They ask, 'what purposes in a psychological sense are served by the attitudes which an individual holds?'

According to functional theories of attitude, attitudes are important to human psychological functioning. Attitudes are constructs that people create in order to meet their physical, social, and emotional needs.

In Daniel Katz's view, attitudes perform various functions. First, attitudes have a knowledge function, which enables individuals to understand their environment and to be consistent in their ideas and thinking. Most attitudes serve this basic function in some measure.

Secondly, many attitudes have a utilitarian function. They help individuals in maximizing benefits and minimizing disadvantages while interacting with individuals, groups and situations in their environment. Utilitarian attitudes lead to behaviour that optimizes one's interests.

Thirdly, attitudes perform a social role, helping in an individual's self-expression and social interaction. Subscribing to a given set of attitudes signals one's identification with important reference groups to express one's core values, and to establish one's identity. This social role of attitudes is known as social identity function; it underlies an individual's desire to establish his individual and social identity.

Fourthly, attitudes promote and maintain an individual's self-esteem. As we shall shortly see, psychologists have identified the psychodynamic mechanisms by which attitudes support self-esteem. This aspect suggests that attitudes can serve as defence mechanisms for handling an individual's internal mental conflicts. These conflicts reflect tensions within the individual psyche. The defence mechanisms hide an individual's true motives from himself or psychologically isolate him from groups perceived as hostile or threatening.

Attitudes maintain self-esteem in other ways also. An individual's attitudes toward many things are influenced by his view on how they affect his own self-assessment. For instance, our attitudes toward our friends and social acquaintances depend on whether we regard such association as enhancing or lowering our social standing. Attitudes which lead individuals to associate with successful groups (such as a winning cricket team) may be motivated by an unconscious desire for boosting their self-esteem by "basking in reflected glory".

(Based on The Role of Attitude Functions in *Persuasion and Social Judgment* Sharon Shavitt Michelle R. Nelson)

Case Studies

CASE 1

In one particular backward caste, the practice of girl child marriage is prevalent. Government finds that the custom is very deep rooted. The members of the group are reluctant to give up the practice. Government engages a social psychologist to formulate a strategy and campaign for convincing the caste members to change the old custom. He suggests that the message should be framed in such a manner that it triggers the ego defence mechanisms of the fathers of the child brides.

Question

Which of the following messages will be in line with the social psychologist's advice?

1. Highlighting that child marriages are out of place in progressive modern societies.
2. Highlighting old practices like *Swayamvaram* which allowed girls to choose their husbands.
3. Engaging NGOs to propagate the message.
4. Highlighting the evil effects of early marriage of girls and appealing that as loving fathers they should not expose their daughters to such consequences.

Discussion

The first alternative points to an important fact, but is unlikely to touch any chords in the hearts of the parents. As they are backward and uneducated, pointing to the feature of another society outside their experience will not have much impact.

The second alternative links the message to a social practice prevalent earlier and which finds mention in traditional narratives. But these traditions have lost their strength and relevance to the situation narrated in the case.

The third alternative suggests that the message should be conveyed through NGOs. It is not about linking the message to ego-defence mechanisms but about the messenger.

The last alternative connects the message to the psychological feelings of fathers. It appeals to the "ego-defensive" mechanisms of the fathers to overcome their prejudice in favour of girl child marriage. Ego means selfhood, and everyone has a sense of decency. Ego-defence attitudes help him to preserve this sense of his own decency. Fathers see themselves as deeply affectionate to daughters and concerned with their welfare. If the harm which marriage brings to a girl child (by depriving her of many opportunities of life) is highlighted, it is possible that those who regard themselves as loving fathers will change their views. By appealing to an individual's self image as a loving father, it may be possible to change his attitude more in conformity with his self image.

CASE 2

Prices of sugar in international markets have gone up. Export traders see an opportunity of making profits. There are restrictions on exports of sugar. They approach government seeking relaxation of the export restrictions.

Question

How can the psychological attitude of the exporters be characterised in this case?

1. It is cognitive since it is based on the knowledge that exports will increase country's foreign exchange reserves.
2. It is based on ego-defence mechanism since it promotes their self-interest.
3. It is based on perception that circumstances afford an opportunity of entering into and stabilizing their position in foreign markets.
4. Their attitude is utilitarian since they are essentially trying to maximise their profits.

Discussion

The first alternative is correct in noting that the exporters' request is based on their knowledge of market conditions. But their attitude cannot be characterised in terms of increasing country's forex reserves.

Answer choice (2) is incorrect. As we discussed in case 1, ego-defence mechanisms of an individual are connected with his self-image and not directly with promoting his self-interest.

The third alternative suggests one of the economic motives of the exporters. But it does not point to the immediate aim underlying their attitude.

Answer choice (4) is the correct one. As we have mentioned earlier, attitudes can be categorized, based on their functions, into four groups: utilitarian, cognitive, ego-defensive, and value-expressive. Broadly, utilitarian attitudes help people materially or in making gains and avoiding losses. They are based on self-interest.

CASE 3

In olden days, people believed that diseases like chicken pox are visitations of goddesses. They would perform various ceremonies to propitiate the deities. They used to resist inoculation measures organized by government.

Question

What approach could government adopt in order to persuade parents to inoculate their children?

1. Spread modern knowledge among villagers by arranging lecture tours of professors of medicine in rural areas.
2. Show audio clips of celebrities recommending inoculation of children.
3. Persuade some parents first to inoculate their children and employ them to spread the message to other parents.
4. Arrange discourses by well-known religious preachers.

Discussion

The first alternative is unsuitable because the villagers will not be able to understand what the professors are saying. Professors are used to addressing medical students and not villagers.

The second answer choice is incorrect. Since the reluctance to inoculation is a superstition, appeals of celebrities may not work.

The third option is the most appropriate one. Once a few villagers are persuaded to have their children inoculated, and as the benefits are seen, other villagers will be convinced. Word of mouth from fellow villagers will carry great weight. This approach depends on actually demonstrating the benefits of inoculation. Villagers tend to relate to others in the rural community as their reference group.

The fourth alternative may not work by itself. The preachers are used to giving religious discourses. Explaining the mechanisms of infectious diseases and the needed preventive measures are not in their line.

CASE 4

Priyamvada's husband Prabhu is unfaithful to her. Somehow he could never keep his marriage vows and be constant to his wife. He had a string of relationships with various women. He would explain away matters to Priyamvada through flimsy excuses. One day Priamvada's friend Jalaja sees Prabhu with his lady colleague late at night in a restaurant. She alerts Priyamvada and tells her to rein in Prabhu. Priyamvada gets angry and stoutly defends Prabhu.

Question

What do you make of Priyamvada's conduct?

1. She is trying to play the role of loyal and trusting wife.
2. Like some women, Priyamvada has a tendency to act like a doormat in relation to her husband.
3. She genuinely believes that Prabhu's affairs are Platonic relationships.
4. She is psychologically in a state of denial.

Discussion

The first answer choice may be partly true. But Priyamvada is refusing to look at facts. Loyalty and trust are two way relationships. Displaying loyalty or trust in the absence of reciprocity is dysfunctional behaviour.

The second choice points to a tendency which some women have due to various experiences they undergo. They lose their sense of self-respect. They readily accept and put up with unacceptable behaviour from others. This is a weakness. But in this case, we need to specifically consider Priyamvada's response to her husband's infidelity.

The third answer choice could be a possibility. But she really has no reason to regard the affairs as innocent friendships. Prabhu has been having the affairs, and she readily accepted his airy-fairy explanations without showing any critical attitude.

The fourth answer choice is the most appropriate one. Priyamvada's response seems to indicate the working of the ego-defence mechanism called denial. As we saw earlier, ego-defence mechanisms are psychological devices which people use to avoid psychological harm. In other words, they do not want to go down in their own eyes. Typically, these mechanisms come into play in situations in which individuals feel a sense of humiliation, shame, indignity and loss of self-respect. This is the situation that Priyamvada faces. But instead of facing the reality of Prabhu's infidelity and squarely dealing with it, she has gone into denial. She refuses to look at the reality of Prabhu's betrayal and takes shelter in illusions.

CASE 5

X has a strong dislike for Y. As Y is an influential and rich local politician, X is unable to express his true feelings. Gradually, he convinces himself on flimsy grounds that Y does not like him.

Question

How will you account for X's feeling that Y does not like him.

1. Y must have through his behaviour led X to this feeling.
2. X may have misread Y's behaviour towards him or misinterpreted his body language.
3. X seems to have come to a random conclusion.
4. This feeling could be a psychological projection on X's part.

Discussion

The firsts answer choice is incorrect since X has come to this conclusion on flimsy grounds.

For the same reason, the second option can also be ruled out.

The third choice does not contain any clue to explain the feeling which X has formed. It gives no reason or suggestion for the feeling that X has formed.

The fourth answer choice is the appropriate one. X has transferred his feelings to Y. That is to say he converted his dislike for Y into an unfounded feeling that Y does not like him. Projection allows the expression of one's desire or impulse, but in a way that the ego cannot recognise. It hides one's real feelings from one's self. It thus reduces anxiety.

CASE 6

In one of Aesop's fables, a fox is attracted by lovely bunches of grapes hanging from a tree. It makes several jumps to reach them but they are hanging high beyond its reach. Upon failing to reach the grapes, the fox consoles itself with the thought that they are sour.

Question

How can we interpret the story in psychological terms?

1. It is a story for entertaining children and has no hidden psychological insights.
2. When we are unable to attain an object of our desire, we should take comfort in the thought that its achievement would have made no great difference to us.
3. One should not unrealistically pursue unattainable goals.
4. The fox's reaction is a form of rationalization.

Discussion

The first answer choice is incorrect. The story contains an important insight. It points ironically that when we fail to reach a desired goal, we often depreciate its worth. Thus an individual who fails in his efforts to acquire wealth may end up with the view that the advantages of wealth are highly exaggerated.

The second option is also wrong. It may enable us to reconcile to failure but in a manner which is intellectually dishonest.

The third answer choice is prudent advice to reduce chances of frustration. But in life we should not give up any worthwhile goal because the attempt to attain it may carry risk of failure. Success and failure have to be taken in one's stride. Otherwise, we will be unable to attempt anything.

The fourth answer choice is correct. The fox naturally feels frustrated. To get over this frustration, it makes an unfounded conjecture that the grapes are sour. It is taking comfort from an illusory idea. In this way, it feels that it has not lost anything and that there is no cause for regret. It derives psychological solace from this process of rationalizing. The term "rationalizing" despite its verbal similarity to 'rational' (which means based on reason) has an opposite meaning. Rationalizing means that we are giving a false explanation to an event, an explanation which satisfies our need for emotional comfort but ignores facts. As it ignores reality, rationalizing is an unhealthy trend.

Cases 4-6 illustrate respectively the ego-defense mechanism's denial, projection and rationalisation.

LEARNING THEORY OF ATTITUDE CHANGE

Classical Conditioning

Psychologists mention three learning theories of attitude change: classical conditioning; operant conditioning; and observational learning. Ivan Pavlov, a Russian biologist, discovered classical conditioning. In an experiment with feeding a dog, he noticed an interesting fact. Whenever food was brought to a dog, its smell made the dog salivate. Here, the smell of the food is called an unconditioned stimulus. It naturally and automatically triggers salivating, and this is known as unconditioned response. Pavlov then began ringing a bell whenever the food was brought to the dog. The sound of the bell is known as the neutral stimulus. In this way, Pavlov associated a neutral stimulus with the unconditioned stimulus (smell of food). Pavlov found that the dog began to salivate at the sound of the bell even in the absence of food. Conditioning involves pairing a previously neutral stimulus (such as the sound of a bell) with an unconditioned stimulus (the taste of food). The sound of the bell is now known as the conditioned stimulus and salivating in response to the bell is known as the conditioned response.

Classical conditioning can be used to create positive emotional reactions to a person, object or event by associating positive feelings with the target object. Commercial advertisements use classical conditioning to create a favourable impression about a product in the minds of readers or viewers. For example, it will show popular cricket stars consuming a particular brand of soda while having fun. It influences the audience by carrying over their favourable feelings about their cricketers to the particular soda brand.

Operant Conditioning

Operant conditioning is another mechanism which leads to attitude formation. Operant conditioning is also known as **instrumental conditioning**. B.F. Skinner coined the term operant conditioning; it means changing of behaviour by the use of reinforcement which is given after the desired response. **Positive reinforcers** are favourable events or outcomes that are presented after the behaviour like praise or reward. **Negative reinforcers** involve the removal of an unfavourable event or outcome after the display of desired behaviour. In these situations, a response is strengthened by the removal of something considered unpleasant. Both these strengthen the likelihood of behaviour in future. **Punishment**, on the other hand, is the presentation of an adverse event or outcome after behaviour that causes a decrease in that behaviour.

In this method, learning occurs through rewards and punishments for behaviour. Through operant conditioning, an association is established between behaviour and a consequence of that behaviour. Behaviour which is reinforced tends to be repeated (i.e. strengthened); behaviour which is not reinforced tends to die out or be extinguished (i.e. weakened). Skinner's theory explains how we acquire learned behaviours.

CASE 7

(a) The small children in the class became noisy. The teacher tried to silence them. But they were too excited to listen to her. Then, she promises to give chocolates to students if they remain silent. They soon became silent.

(b) A dog trainer was throwing a ball and asking the dog to retrieve it. Whenever it ran promptly and retrieved the ball, he was patting it affectionately. When it was slack, he gave it cold looks and ignored it. After a long training session, the dog began to sprint immediately as soon as he threw the ball.

Question

What according to you is the method of teaching (or learning) employed in the above examples?

1. These are common practices which teachers and trainers use based on their practical experience.
2. The examples illustrate how rewards can be used as a means of persuading trainees to change their behaviour.
3. The examples show how operant conditioning is used in training.
4. The examples illustrate how classical conditioning is used in training.

Discussion

The first answer choice generally refers to common practices without identifying the actual methods which underlie such practices. It is not a specific answer.

The second choice is nearer to the answer, but it also fails to make a specific mention of the method.

The third answer choice is the correct one. Teachers, parents, psychologists, animal trainers and others use operant conditioning for many purposes. In this method, learning occurs through rewards and punishments for behaviour. Through operant conditioning, an association is established between behaviour and a consequence of that behaviour. Behavior which is reinforced tends to be repeated (i.e. strengthened); behavior which is not reinforced tends to die out or be extinguished (i.e. weakened).

The fourth answer choice is incorrect. As we saw earlier, in classical conditioning, the behaviour is involuntary. Classical conditioning creates an association between an involuntary response and a stimulus, while operant conditioning is about making an association between a voluntary behavior and a consequence. In operant conditioning, the learner is rewarded with incentives. In classical conditioning, there are no rewards. In classical conditioning, the learner is passive. In operant conditioning, the learner is active and is rewarded or punished.

Observational Learning

People form attitudes by observing people around them. People are particularly influenced by the attitudes of those whom they admire. Children observe the attitudes of their parents and imitate their ways including attitudes. Some psychologists believe that observational learning is the source of most of our attitudes.

Theory of Persuasion

In many commercial and administrative situations, we want to persuade people to change their attitudes, beliefs and habits. A firm which introduces a new brand of hair highlights would try to wean women away from other brands. A new Australian university may try to persuade students to join it. Governments may try to induce parents in rural areas to enrol their children in primary schools. Theories of persuasion describe the ideal means of persuading people to change their beliefs, attitudes and habits. Theory of persuasion is also known as **Elaboration Likelihood** theory of attitude.

This theory posits that attitudes of people on any subject can be changed by suitably communicating appropriate information to them. Many aspects are relevant in trying to persuade people to change their attitude on any subject. These are:

(i) object of the attitude i.e. thing, person, group or idea towards which an attitude is directed;

(ii) the message or information;

(iii) the manner in which it is delivered;

(iv) the messenger; and

(v) the target audience i.e. individuals whose attitudes are to be changed.

An advertisement is a simple example of an attempt to persuade consumers to buy a particular brand of product like jeans. It shows all the above mentioned aspects of persuasion. We will now discuss the elaboration likelihood theory in detail.

Success in persuading people depends on the interplay of various aspects we mentioned above. These are:

(i) characteristics of target audience;

(ii) characteristics of the messenger or the source of the message;

(iii) characteristics of the message; and

(iv) cognitive routes.

Audience Characteristics

To change the attitude of people on any object, they have to be provided with information which they may not possess. In other words, they have to be given a message. Success of a message – which is designed to change attitudes – first of all depends on audience characteristics. It is the audience who has to receive and process the information. Their ability to do this depends on their intelligence. Researchers have studied various characteristics of audience to determine how they influence audience response to the message.

Experiments show that people with higher intelligence are unlikely to be persuaded by one-sided messages. Researchers have also studied the correlation between self-esteem of individuals and their willingness to be persuaded. The conventional view is that it is hard to persuade people with high self-esteem to accept new attitudes. But the relationship between self-esteem and willingness to change one's attitude seems to be curvilinear, meaning thereby that individuals with average level of self-esteem are more ready to change their attitudes than those with either high self-esteem or low self-esteem. The state of mind and mood of the target audience also influence the manner in which they respond to the message.

Source Characteristics

These refer to the person who is delivering the message. The variables which determine how effective a person will be in delivering the message are his expertise, trustworthiness and attractiveness to audience. The audience, in order to be convinced, have to be assured that the message is authoritative and authentic. One will be more inclined to trust information on any scientific topic if it is found in an article in *Nature* than if it is aired on a TV talk show. Although this trend generally holds, there can be exceptions. In this connection, psychologists mention the "the sleeper effect", according to which the effect of telling people about the credible source of information disappears after some time. It is likely that if people know of the source of a message before hearing it, they will not overlook the fact. But "sleeper effect" may operate if they are first given the message and then informed about its source.

Impressionable audiences are also swayed by the personality or attractiveness of the messenger.

CASE 8

A company is working on an advertisement campaign for launching a new liquid soap for washing clothes. The advertising consultant suggests that the message (advertisement) should be delivered by a female character likely to appeal to the audience consisting of the consumers (target audience). The choice is between a home maker, a nurse, a popular lady film star and a finance executive.

Question

Select the appropriate character and give reasons for your choice.

1. Nurse
2. Popular film star
3. Finance executive
4. Home maker

Discussion

The first choice is inappropriate. Nurses, though often seen in white dress, are associated in popular mind with hospitals, injections or other medical contexts. The message will not register strongly with the target audience.

For similar reasons, the second answer choice can be excluded. Popular film stars are mentally associated in the minds of audience with romance, adventure, drama, dance and music. A glamorous filmy character appearing in a domestic scene showing washing of dirty clothes will create dissonance in the minds of audience. They will find it hard to imagine her washing clothes. Her role will lack credibility and will be ineffective.

The finance executive will also fail to create the necessary mental responses in the target audience. They will associate her with accounts, investments, taxes and the like.

The last answer choice is the most appropriate. A home maker will fit the role for people can imagine her washing the clothes as part of her daily chores. She will be seen as knowledgeable about the message. She will carry conviction with the target audience.

Cognitive Routes

A message seeking to change an attitude can appeal to an individual's intellect or logical faculty. This appeal can be either through the central route or the peripheral route. In the *central route* to persuasion, the individual is presented with the data and motivated to evaluate the data and arrive at an attitude-changing conclusion. In the *peripheral route* to attitude change, the individual is encouraged to not look at the content but at the source. This is commonly seen in modern advertisements that feature celebrities. You are asked to buy a sports shoe because Virat Kohli is wearing it. In some cases, physicians, doctors or experts are used. In other cases film stars are used for their attractiveness.

Uptill now, we have briefly outlined a theory of persuasion. In actual practice, it can be elaborated and refined in many ways. But even in its simple form, it has several applications in many administrative situations. In the 1950s, government launched a community development programme all over the country. Its aim was to change the attitudes of villagers in many areas ranging from agricultural practices to family planning. Its method was called 'extension'. It tried to persuade people to change their traditional attitudes to things.

At present, government is running numerous economic and social programmes for the poor and the needy. Examples of such programmes are : Construction of private toilets under Swachh Bharat programme, enrolling girls in schools, and recently, taking Covid-19 vaccines. In implementing such programmes, their intended beneficiaries have to be involved. It is necessary to secure their participation by persuading them of the advantages of the programmes. The various aspects mentioned above in the theory of persuasion will have to be taken into account while organizing campaigns to secure peoples' participation.

Attitudes, Beliefs and Actions

Social psychologists study the relation between an individual's attitudes, beliefs (or views) and actions. Earlier, social psychologists thought that attitudes of an individual result in compatible beliefs and actions.

CASE 9

Revathi keeps telling her friends that she is fond of classical music. Her friends notice that she, however, does not attend classical music concerts. One of her friends is associated with a musical group, and frequently orgnises classical concerts. He offers her tickets on a few occasions for the concerts but she shows no interest.

Question

What probable explanations can be given for her conduct?

1. She may be a hypocrite pretending to be an art lover.
2. She may be lazy.
3. This type of inconsistency is common since individuals lack the necessary energy and drive to pursue their interests.
4. Revathi may be too busy with her other tasks to find time for attending classical music concerts.

Discussion

The first answer choice could be a possibility. But there is no reason to assume that she will gain anything by her pretence. Hence, this can be ruled out.

The second answer may be true but it is too general and can apply to many situations. It is an insufficient explanation of her conduct in this case.

The third and fourth answer choices can be selected as probable explanations. The third option mentions a commonly observed lack of correlation between people's beliefs, attitudes and interests and their behaviour. Revathi's behaviour shows this lack of correspondence between her avowed interest and behaviour. The third reason is psychological. The fourth reason links her behaviour to her other preoccupations and can be a plausible explanation.

Cognitive Consistency

Normally, we expect an individual to hold views which are consistent with his attitudes. We believe that an individual's thinking will be marked by cognitive consistency. This is the theory that people try to be consistent in their attitudes, views and in their behaviour.

CASE 10

Suppose that X supports foreign direct investment in retail trade and relaxation of labour laws. One day he is discussing India's balance of payments situation with his friends. It is showing a large deficit in the current account. Analysis shows that large gold imports are a reason for the large deficit. They note that government is considering a proposal to restrict import of gold except for its use in making ornaments for exports.

Question

What can one say would be a consistent stand for X to take in the discussion and why?

1. X should support restrictions on gold imports as a means of reducing current account deficit in the balance of payments.
2. X should oppose any restrictions on imports of gold.
3. X though he may subscribe to economic reforms need not support all its elements.
4. X should not comment on the matter unless he has an interest in it.

Discussion

The first answer choice will be inconsistent with X's economic ideology. The first sentence of the case indicates that X supports reformist economic agenda. In this instance, one does not expect X to recommend that government should impose direct import controls to cut down gold imports. For that will be inconsistent with the logic or values underlying his other beliefs which together make up economic reform agenda. Economic reforms oppose direct intervention of government in economic sphere. They argue that market forces should have free play in the economy.

The second answer choice is correct since it is consistent with X's ideology. It will be logically consistent with his belief system.

The third option is correct in one sense. Though one may adopt an ideology, he may not agree with all its tenets. But in this case, the question is about one's consistent stand. Hence, the second answer choice has to be preferred.

The fourth option does not answer the question. It goes off the tangent and proposes an irrelevant answer. The answer has to be in the terms of the question which is about what would be X's consistent stand.

CASE 11

Nakul Patel is keen to study in USA. Unfortunately, he has a poor academic record. He has not appeared in GRE and TOFEL. His uncle Kushal Patel while on a visit to India advises Nakul to visit USA on a tourist visa. Kushal runs a few grocery stores in Alabama. He assures Nakul that he will secure him admission in a university and that any Indian student reaching America will do well. Nakul finds that his problems do not interest Kushal because of his own business preoccupations. He finds Kushal's uncle becomes too busy with his business to pay much attention to Kushal's problems.

Question

How can we evaluate the position in which Nakul landed?

1. Things do not always happen in accordance with one's plans.
2. Kushal Patel's advice to Nakul was improper.
3. Nakul did not carefully plan his strategy and work towards his goal.
4. Luck did not favour Nakul.

Discussion

The first answer choice is a general observation which though true fails to address the specific ingredients of the case. As we shall see, Nakul did not have a proper plan for reaching his chosen goal.

The second answer choice is partially true, but really does not explain the predicament of Nakul. Kushal being a grocery store owner lacks the necessary background to advise Nakul about studies in USA. Kushal rightly observed that Indian students in USA do well, but had no idea of the preparatory work they do before they go to USA, and the efforts they make thereafter. It was for Nakul to plan and get ready for the academic career in USA.

The third option is the correct one. It zeros in on the mistakes Nakul made. As Nakul did not have a good academic record, he should have worked to improve his skills and knowledge. He should have taken the necessary tests before going to USA. He could have consulted his teachers and friends. In short, he did not prepare himself adequately for pursuing studies in USA. He allowed his thinking to be taken over by his dreams. Both rationalization and wishful thinking are irrational ways of acting on the basis of our attitudes. Hence, his chances of success were bleak from the start.

Luck or fortune is the final or residuary factor in success. It is not in our hands. If after making earnest efforts one does not succeed, then he can ascribe failure to fortuitous factors. But Nakul did not make the necessary efforts. Here, we may recall the famous saying that fortune favours the prepared mind.

Cognitive Dissonance Theory

Uptill now, we have looked at beliefs (or views) and actions (or behaviours) as flowing consistently from attitudes. Leon Festinger showed that the relation can operate also from the opposite direction. That is to say, just as attitudes can affect behaviour, behaviour can affect attitudes. This is called the theory of cognitive dissonance. Dissonance means disharmony or inconsistency. When an individual's beliefs and attitudes oppose each other or the behaviour, he experiences psychological tension or discomfort. He is then motivated to reduce the dissonance through changes in behaviour or cognition.

CASE 12

Vaishali is keen on learning classical music. But her teacher lives far from where Vaishali lives. Her father is also making her work in the family business. He is also insisting that she should continue with her post graduation. Vaishali is caught in the conflict between her love for classical music and her other engagements. She decides to reduce her attendance in music lessons by half.

Question

What is the psychological concept which Vaishali's behaviour illustrates?

1. She is showing excessive dependence on her father and is allowing herself to be dictated by him.
2. She has no genuine interest in classical music.
3. She has too many irons in the fire.
4. Through her action, Vaishali has reduced the cognitive dissonance she was experiencing.

Discussion

The first answer choice is inappropriate. There is no reason to believe that she is over-dependent on her father. His advice to her on pursuing post graduation and learning about family business is sensible.

The second answer choice can be rejected since Vaishali has not given up learning classical music in spite of her other pressing commitments.

The third alternative is a general observation. In fact, we have to pursue several tasks and perform many roles simultaneously in life. This is a common situation. Multitasking skills are needed in life and in professions.

The fourth answer choice correctly explains the psychological rationale of Vaishali's decision. She is pursuing divergent tasks demanding her time and effort. All the tasks are important. But the pull of tasks in different directions and time pressure are creating a situation of cognitive dissonance for her. This leads to mental tension. She has overcome the cognitive tension by striking a balance between the time allotted for different tasks. Her decision can be conceptualized in non-psychological terms also. In that case, one speaks of the relative priorities she should attach to the different tasks she is pursuing.

Attitude-behaviour mismatch

As mentioned earlier, governments sometimes want to change the traditional beliefs and attitudes of people. This is connected with efforts towards modernization. Conservative beliefs and behaviour could hinder development and social change. Thus people may resist family planning, refuse to send their girls to school or fail to adopt new agricultural technologies. Then how can government induce people to adopt new attitudes and undertake actions that promote economic development? The emphasis on attitudes often arises from the view that they lead to concomitant actions.

Two Crucial Studies

Surprisingly, this common sense view received no support from empirical studies. In fact, early psychologists took it for granted that attitudes of people govern their behaviour. This view appeared doubtful as a result of two famous studies. The first study showed that people do not behave according to their stated attitudes. In the early 1930s, LaPiere accompanied a young Chinese couple during their travel in USA, and observed whether they faced any racial prejudice in motels, restaurants or hotels. It may be noted that Chinese faced discrimination in USA at that time. He found that they were well-treated. Later he sent a questionnaire to these very establishments asking whether they would welcome Chinese guests. Surprisingly, most of the respondents said that Chinese are unwelcome. Thus, though the establishments treated the Chinese well, they expressed a different attitude in the questionnaire. In other words, people did not behave according to their stated attitudes.

The second study was made by Corey. At the start of the semester, Corey devised a measure of the attitude of students towards cheating in the examination. The measure indicated that the students were inclined to copy in the examinations. During the semester, he took many tests, and allowed ample scope for students to cheat in the tests. Here again, the conclusion was negative. Although the students said that they were willing to cheat in examinations, they did not in fact do so. Subsequent empirical studies confirmed that attitudes did not result in behaviour consonant with them. One social psychologist Wicker in fact suggested that the concept or construct attitude is a worthless research tool and should be abandoned.

In the meanwhile, social psychologists began developing reliable measures to study attitudes. Researchers also started studying the processes of attitude formation and attitude change. We discussed these two topics in the previous sections. Further, American army's use of films and mass media during the Second World War, spurred interest in communication and persuasion. Notwithstanding findings to the contrary, the users of communication theories relied on the assumption that change in attitudes would alter behaviour.

Explaining Inconsistency

Faced with the evidence about the attitude–behaviour inconsistency, some researchers doubted the validity of survey procedures and the suitability of the samples. Some scholars argued that the persons included in the sample and covered in the survey were unrepresentative of the general population. Doubts were expressed about the verbal attitude measures (or what the people surveyed said). The individuals covered in the survey showed a response bias; to questionnaires which tried to discover their attitudes and personality traits, they gave replies which carry social approval. (They tried to be goody-goody.) They concealed their true feelings. Nobody wants to give the impression of being nasty!

To get over such problems, researchers adopted disguised verbal procedures camouflaging the true purpose of the instrument or the questionnaire. Another procedure relied on physiological reactions like heart rate, palmar sweat and galvanic skin response. However, both the procedures proved unsatisfactory.

Researchers also tried another approach. Attitudes measurement techniques then in use, generated a single score representing the respondent's overall positive or negative reaction to the attitude object. Many theorists felt that attitude measures reflected only one of the three components of behaviour. Most of the time, the attitude measure was based only on the affective or emotional component and left out the cognitive and conative or behavioural components. Attempts were then made to build measures covering the three components. However, the three-component approach failed to explain the attitude-behaviour inconsistencies.

Two Kinds of Inconsistency

In their studies, investigators examined two kinds of inconsistency and explored various possibilities One approach relied on refining surveys and investigative procedures. Another approach looked at reasons which prevented people from acting fully in line with their attitudes. Social psychologists also explored situations which showed a better fit between attitudes and behaviours. They propounded theories incorporating additional explanatory variables. We will briefly outline these approaches. One type of inconsistency consists in people failing to act (in psychological terminology) according to their declared behavioural intentions. In simple language, during a survey, they would tell the investigator that they would do X (general symbol for act or behaviour) or not do X. But in practice, they would do its opposite (or not do anything).

Psychologists use questionnaires or surveys to discover the general (evaluative) attitudes of people toward any chosen object of their behaviour. They believe that favourable attitudes will elicit positive responses to the object and unfavourable attitudes will elicit negative responses. Inconsistency arises when the general attitude fails to correlate with the specific behaviour under investigation. This is called evaluative inconsistency because the evaluation expressed in verbal attitudes (or what is said) does not match with actual behaviour.

Most instances of attitude behaviour inconsistency fall into this category. To visualize the problem, we need to think of: (a) the general attitude; (b) the person, group, thing or event towards which attitude is directed i.e. object of the attitude; and (c) a specific behaviour towards the object of attitude. The inconsistency is that (a) does not lead to (c). An example can be of a person who says that he is deeply religious, but does not visit temples.

Moderating Factors

Evaluative inconsistency arises from the complexity of relation between general attitude and individual behaviour.

Attitude and behaviour, according to some researchers, diverge due to certain moderating factors. These are connected with (a) traits of the individual performing the behaviour, (b) the situation in which it is performed; and (c) the characteristics of the attitude itself. As regards differences between individuals, researchers refer to three individual difference variables: self-monitoring tendency, self-consciousness or self-awareness, and the need for cognition.

(a) Individuals high in self-monitoring speak or act appropriately depending on the social or interpersonal context of a situation. They tailor their true attitudes to situational requirements. They hide their true feelings. But individuals who are not very self-conscious say or do things that truly reflect their own attitudes, traits, feelings, and other current inner states. They show greater attitude-behaviour consistency. Further, people are likely to act according to their attitudes if they have vested interest in a topic or if they are confident of their attitudes or if they regard the attitude object as important.

(b) The situational moderators of the attitude-behaviour relation include time pressure and presence or absence of a mirror in the behavioural situation. Time pressure forces one to think quickly. Introduction of a mirror increases the subject's self-awareness. Both the factors lead to greater correspondence between general attitude and specific behaviour.

(c) As for qualities of the attitude that may moderate the strength of the attitude-behaviour relation, investigators examined three aspects. First aspect is the degree of consistency between the cognitive and affective components of the attitude. If the two are correlated, behaviour tends to follow attitude. Secondly, behaviour tends to follow attitudes when they are based on direct experience as opposed to second-hand information. Attitude formed as a result of central processing [route] is more likely to lead to corresponding behaviour than if it is formed through peripheral processing. As we saw before, in central processing, information is closely scrutinized for its logical validity and factual veracity. In peripheral processing, the participant does not subject the information to rigorous scrutiny.

Domain of Interest and Set of Behaviour

Above mentioned moderators partly explain attitude-behaviour divergence. However, social psychologists would like to predict accurately from an individual's general attitude his individual behaviours or actions. On one side is an individual's attitude; on the other are his individual behaviours expected to flow from his attitude. The latter sometimes do not materialise because general attitudes can manifest in numerous ways. While some may result from it, others do not follow as anticipated

For example, 'religiosity' is a general attitude. A specific, single behaviour may not follow from it. An avowedly religious person may not regularly visit temples. However, he may be attending bhajans, listening to religious discourses on TV, reading religious treatises and practising meditation. We can list several similar religious activities. It will be found that a set or group of individual religious acts will together reflect his religiosity.

What this shows is that if we exhaustively enumerate all the individual behaviours which flow from an attitude, we can predict that an individual with that attitude will display some of the associated individual behaviours. However, we are often interested not in a broad multiple-act complex of behaviour, but with predicting when specific individual behaviours occur. We want to know the factors which lead to the individual behaviours of interest to us.

Hypothetical Example of Swachh Bharat in Rural Saurashtra

Let us consider Swachh Bharat programme in a village in Saurashtra. How can we predict the response of a poor village household to it? Now, women in rural Saurastra have very positive attitude to cleanliness. Even in small houses, the single living room is kept clean; the meagre furniture and articles are kept in neat and tidy order. The kitchen is spic and span with a row of gleaming copper vessels.

However, this general attitude towards cleanliness could be insufficient to elicit the individual behaviours needed for Swachh Bharat programme. While the interior of the house is spotlessly clean, its surrounding public area is neglected. People may prefer to continue with the old habit of answering nature calls in public. They may be reluctant for want of resources to invest in private toilets. At the same time, before visiting officers canvassing the programme, they will welcome it.

The challenge is how to convert the attitude into appropriate individual behaviours. Similarly, people may express general concern for environment. But often this is not followed by individual behaviours such as conserving water, reducing electricity consumption or recycling wastes.

The problem for administrators is often to induce people to act in particular desirable ways based on general attitudes. Another way of looking at the problem is: When are people likely to act according to their attitude? Social psychologists give partly theoretical answers. We try to express them in practical terms.

A single behaviour consists of an action directed against a target, performed in a context, and at a certain point of time. An officer may be interested in knowing why villagers may or may not join (action) Swachh Bharat programme (target) in their village (context) at a point of time (non agricultural season). Here, we explicitly stated the four elements. If one wants to ensure compatibility between attitude and individual behaviour, both should contain the same action, target, context and time elements. In this example, the context has to be widely understood including provision of financial assistance, technical advice and supervision for toilet construction and other factors affecting the willingness to join the programme. If the four elements likely to translate attitude into individual behaviour are satisfied, then the programme will get off the ground. In plain language, the constraints acting on people and impeding the desired action have to be removed.

The Mode (Motivation and Opportunity as Determinants) Model

In this model, Fabio explains how people's attitudes influence their evaluation of people and events. Attitudes bias the manner in which people view and judge information about other people and events. Bias depends on the strength of people's attitudes.

This model outlines how bias is triggered, and how it operates in two groups of people. The first group consists of intelligent and motivated individuals; the second one consists of less intelligent and motivated individuals. In both the groups, unless the attitude is activated, bias will not occur.

The attitude can be activated in two ways: in a controlled or deliberative manner and in an automatic or spontaneous manner. Intelligent and motivated individuals process information deliberately; less intelligent and less motivated individuals process information spontaneously.

Attitudes have to be readily available in the memory of the second group for bias to arise. When motivation and ability to carefully process information are high in individuals, attitudes need not be readily available from memory. They can recall them through mental effort. For other individuals, attitudes have to be present in memory so that they can be activated automatically. In whichever way the general attitude is activated, it can introduce bias.

Individuals with favourable attitudes are likely to take into account and process the object's positive attributes. Individuals with unfavourable attitudes toward the object are likely to concentrate on its negative aspects. Although one may harbour prejudice against a caste, he may hide it if the group in which he is placed in a situation opposes casteism. Though perceptions tend to guide behaviour, people will also factor in the likely consequences of acting in line with such perceptions.

Activation of an attitude is more difficult when an individual's motivation or cognitive capacity is low than when it is high because the individual cannot retrieve or construct it easily. However, attitudes will be available if they are automatically activated. In the spontaneous processing mode, weak attitudes will not be activated and will, thus, not be available to bias the definition of the event or guide behaviour.

Thus, automatic or spontaneous activation takes place when attitudes are strong. Attitude is defined in this context as a learned association in memory, between an object and a positive or negative evaluation of that object, and attitude strength is equivalent to the strength of this association. Automatic attitude activation occurs when a strong link has been established in memory between the attitude-object and a positive or negative evaluation. The stronger the attitude, the more likely it is that it will be automatically activated and, hence, be chronically accessible from memory. Further, due to a biased perception/interpretation of information, strong attitudes are more likely to be resistant to change than weak attitudes. This is consistent with the general view that strong attitudes involve issues of personal relevance and are held with great conviction or certainty. As a result, they are assumed to be persistent over time and be resistant to attack, to influence perceptions and judgments, and to guide overt behaviour.

If one is a right wing thinker but is working in civil service, his prejudices may get pushed back due to work pressure and the time he spends with colleagues. But if he happens to read an article written with a leftist slant or a policy proposal with mild leftist flavour, he will not overlook the leftist overtones of the two. His intelligence and motivation will operate to trigger his ideological attitude. But a less intelligent or motivated individual will miss out ideological nuances in the two.

Intention and Behaviour

Many theorists regard that the nearest cognitive antecedent of actual behavioural performance is the agent's intention than his attitude. It means that one can accurately predict specific behaviours from the intentions of their performers. Many studies have substantiated the predictive validity of behavioural intentions.

There is an important difference between performing behaviour and attaining a goal. Behaviour is within one's control. But goal achievement depends also on extraneous factors. One may exercise and regulate diet (behaviour) to lose weight (goal). But weight loss also depends on physiological conditions beyond one's control. Intentions are immediate antecedents of behaviour. When people feel that a goal depends on many factors beyond their control, they may refuse to act. Or the intention fails to produce the expected behaviour.

We may note two other aspects concerning intentions and behaviour. One is that intentions have to remain stable if they are to produce the expected behaviour. The intentions which investigators record tend to change with passage of time. Secondly, there has to be compatibility between the measures of intention and of behaviour. For instance, a question whether X intends to exercise in future does not have a compatible behaviour measure. But the question whether X will walk four times a week in the coming eight weeks will elicit an answer which is likely to match X's exercise behaviour.

Models of Reasoned Action

We will now discuss the theory of reasoned action. These theories go beyond prediction of likely behaviour; they discuss factors that lead to formation of intentions.

The decision to adopt a particular behaviour will be determined by:

(i) positive or negative consequences of behaviour;

(ii) approval or disapproval of behaviour by respected individuals or groups; and

(iii) factors that may facilitate or impede behaviour.

Positive or negative consequences of behaviour are also known as behavioural beliefs, or outcome expectations, and costs and benefits. An individual will have a favourable attitude towards a particular behaviour if its perceived benefits outweigh its costs. If the perceived benefits are less than the costs, he will have an unfavourable attitude.

Normative beliefs refer to the likely approval or disapproval of a particular behaviour by family, friends, colleagues and such others. They create a social pressure or norm to engage in or to avoid the behaviour. When respected persons or groups expect a particular behaviour or disapprove of it, the pressure influences behaviour either positively or negatively. Similar social pressures operate when respected individuals or groups (nowadays called 'role models') adopt a particular behaviour or shun it.

Control beliefs are determined by perceived factors which help or hinder the performance of behaviour. They lead to the belief that one has or does not have the capacity to perform the behaviour. Control beliefs denote self-efficacy and personal agency or perceived behaviour control. Self-efficacy arises from feeling that one has the skills and resources needed for completing a task. Behavioural control means the factors within his/her control which determine success or failure.

The reasoned action model is schematically depicted in the diagram below.

It will help students follow the terms used in the theory and their connections. Obviously, there will be not time or space for reproducing it (even if a question on it appears) in the answer. But the diagram shows how behaviour can be traced back to intention immediately preceding it. Intention is worked backwards to three components of attitude which in turn are linked to belief. Finally, many background factors influence these intervening variables leading to behaviour. Students can use this broad perspective in many contexts.

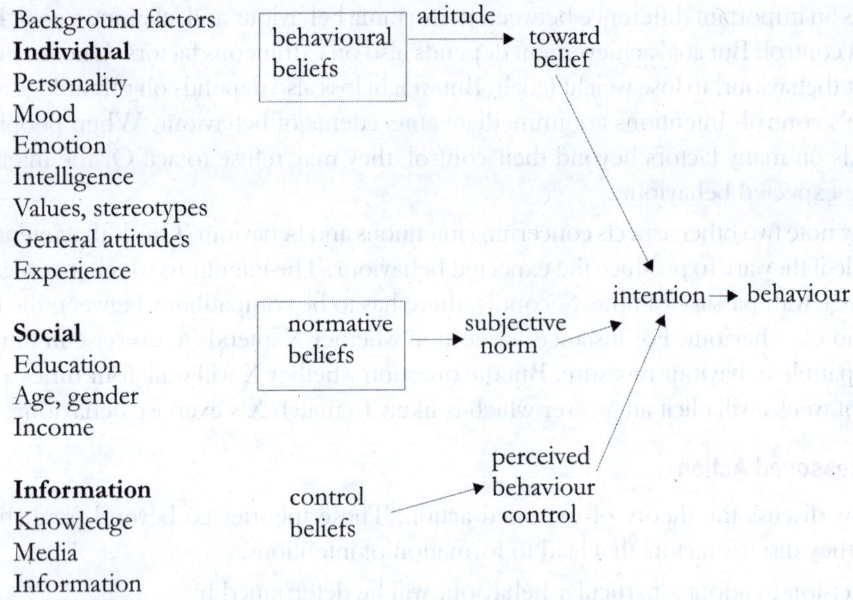

The background factors are individual, social and informative. They lead to formation of beliefs covering behaviour, norms and control. These create attitudes toward belief, norms and perceived behaviour control. These in turn lead to intention and action.

This model assumes:

1. Intention is the immediate antecedent of actual behaviour.
2. Intention, in turn, is determined by attitude toward the behaviour, subjective norm, and perceived behavioural control.
3. These determinants are themselves a function, respectively, of underlying behavioural, normative, and control beliefs.
4. Behavioural, normative, and control beliefs can vary as a function of a wide range of background factors.

These beliefs need not be true; may be inaccurate, biased, or even irrational. However, once a set of beliefs is formed, it provides the cognitive foundation from which attitudes, perceived social norms, and perceptions of control and ultimately intentions are assumed to follow in a reasonable and consistent fashion.

The behavioural, normative, and control beliefs people hold about performance of a given behaviour are influenced by a wide variety of cultural, personal, and situational factors. Thus, we may find differences in beliefs between men and women, young and old, Black and White, educated and uneducated, rich and poor, dominant and submissive, shy and outgoing, and between individuals who have an individualistic orientation and those who have a collectivistic orientation. In addition, they may be affected by the physical environment, the social environment, exposure to information, as well as such broad dispositions as values and prejudices.

SOCIAL INFLUENCE AND PERSUASION

(This section is based on Lisa Rashotte's article on Social influence, in Blackwell Encyclopaedia of Sociology.)

If someone changes his ideas, feelings, attitudes, or behaviours due to interaction with another person or group, he has been socially influenced. Social influence can be distinguished from conformity, power, and authority. Conformity connotes that an individual voices the opinions of others or follows in their footsteps because they expect him to do so and not out of genuine conviction. Power signifies that one has the means to force or coerce others to act in a given manner against their wishes. Authority is power, but those subject to it, regard it as legitimate and not coercive. Unlike conformity, power and authority, social influence genuinely changes the feelings and behaviours of people as a result of their interaction with others. This change comes about because people feel a sense of solidarity with others (consider them a referent social group) or because they think such others as more knowledgeable (as experts) or virtuous.

According to French and Raven, social influence operates via five sources of social power. The following table shows the five sources of social power and the manner in which they bring about change.

Name of social power	Manner in which it brings about change
Reward power	Benefiting individuals changing their views
Coercive power	Forcing individuals to change their views
Legitimate power	Making people feel that they are following just and fair rules/orders
Expert power	Promoting regard for scholarship, professional knowledge and skills
Referent power	Creating a sense of solidarity with his peer social group and desire for changing opinion in line with a majority of that group

As against common usage, French and Raven considered a change in opinion or attitude (conformity) as an instance of social influence although it may not be a true change of heart. The settings of French and Raven's original research were situations in which a supervisor influences a worker in a work situation. Later studies covered many other social interactions such as families, classrooms, doctors and their patients, salespeople and customers and political figures.

Subsequent research distinguished changes caused by true social influence from those due to forced public acceptance (conformity) or due to conferring rewards or exercising coercive power. An individual's outward public compliance arising from conformity, reward power, and coercive power are, though still studied, differentiated from social influence.

Social influence is presently studied with reference to five main areas: (1) research on persuasion; (2) dynamic social impact theory; (3) structural approach to social influence; (4) minority influence in group settings; and (5) social influence in expectation states theory. Although we have discussed a few aspects of these topics earlier, we will recall them briefly in the context of social influence.

Two Theories of Persuasion

Persuasion means change in attitudes or beliefs based on information received from others; its study, as we saw earlier, mainly revolves around written or spoken messages sent from source to recipient. The two main theories of persuasion are the elaboration likelihood model (ELM) and heuristic-systemic model (HSM). They discuss how the recipients of messages process them. Messages are processed in two ways according to these two theories, and hence they are called dual-process models. The two processing routes are central and peripheral.

In the central route to persuasion, recipients process the message attentively and diligently, thoughtfully considering its arguments, ideas and content. In central processing mode, the recipient acts as an active partner in the process of persuasion. Central processing can only occur when the receiver has both the motivation and the ability to think about the message and its topic.

In the heuristic processing route, recipients do not pay much attention to the information content or logic of the message. Then what do they do? They are likely to agree with messages delivered by experts, or messages endorsed by celebrities. These factors influence them more than the content and logic of the message.

As compared to peripheral or heuristic processing, central route processing leads to more permanent attitude changes; such changes lead to corresponding changes in behaviour; and the changes are also more resistant to counter persuasion.

Both HSM and ELM were propounded in the early 1980's and share many of the concepts and ideas. It is difficult to clearly distinguish between the two theories also since both are based on dual information processing models. However, the heuristic-systemic theory sets greater store on peripheral processing route. This theory holds that individuals tend to minimize their use of cognitive resources, and this tendency affects how they receive and process messages. In plain language, people tend to be lazy-minded. They tend to receive messages casually paying little attention. Of course, whether this is actually so depends on individuals and the circumstances in which they operate. HSM tries to examine what motivates people in any social environment to regard some messages as being more valid than others.

Normally, the degree and type of thinking a person devotes to a message will affect its power of persuasion. As we saw earlier, other parameters important for messaging models include source, message, and recipient, affect (emotion), channel, and context. The personal relevance of the message to the recipient is critical.

Social Impact Theory

Social impact refers to changes an individual experiences (physiological, cognitive, emotional, or behavioural) due to the presence or action of others, who are real, imagined, or implied. According to social impact theory, three factors determine the impact of any information source: number of others in the source; their nearness; and their strength or, salience or power. Hindrances to the influence of any of the three factors will reduce impact.

Social impact theory helps in describing and predicting the diffusion of beliefs in society. This theory regards social structure as the result of individuals influencing each other in a dynamic and iterative way. The likelihood of being influenced by someone nearby, rather than far away, (the nearness factor mentioned above) produces localized cultures of belief within communication networks. In this way, attitudes and beliefs, which are to begin with scattered, can become clustered or correlated. The less popular beliefs become consolidated into minority subcultures. Dynamic social impact theory looks upon society as a self-organizing system in which individuals interact and influence beliefs of one another.

Structural Approach to Social Influence

The structural approach also studies how people influence one another within a larger social network. In this network, attitudes and opinions of individuals mirror the attitudes and opinions of their 'referent others' with whom they have a sense of belonging. An individual's socialization (i.e. getting attuned to social norms and mores) and identity (i.e. sense of belonging or feeling of solidarity) depends on interpersonal influence. Social influence is seen as the process by which a group of actors will assess and accept the opinions of leading members of their referent group while staying within the social structural framework. The structure creates the initial set of ideas of group members and strength of interpersonal influences within the group. In a nut shell, it states that individuals combine their originally held beliefs with influential opinions of larger social structures. They reach a set of new opinions blending their initial opinions and the network norms.

Minority Influence

Minority influence operates when a minority subgroup attempts to change the majority. For example, teachers often influence their students' beliefs, and political and religious leaders frequently influence the behaviour of their followers. Earlier, the process of social influence was seen as the majority weighing down on the minority. But now many writers believe that every member of a group can influence others in some measure. This appears to be particularly true when the minority group is consistent in what it presents to the majority. In addition, it is believed that the presence of minority groups within a larger group often leads to more creative thinking and better overall solutions on group tasks.

Expectation States Theory

Expectation states theory of social influence deals with the relative influence of individuals within groups, and is based on the study of Bales (1950). Bales observed that even when group members had equal status at the beginning of the group session, some members would become more influential than others later. Based on the behaviour of group members, a hierarchy would emerge. If group members are initially unequal in status, this inequality would reflect that of the larger society (to which group members belong) based on age or sex or race.

Berger and others proposed the Expectation states theory in 1980 to explain Bales's finding that groups with members of equal status would develop inequalities in influence. According to this theory, group members have expectations about how all group members, including themselves, are likely to perform, and these expectations guide group interactions. In fact, expectations both guide and are maintained by the interaction. Those group members for whom the highest expectations are held will be the most influential in the group's interactions.

Expectation states approaches to social influence have been studied in settings such as classrooms, jury rooms, and the workplace. Status characteristics that produce influence have been identified and extensively studied, including sex, race, and physical attractiveness.

Summary

- An attitude is a psychological tendency that is expressed by evaluating a particular entity with some degree of favour or disfavour.
- Carl Jung, one of the founders of psychoanalysis, defines attitude as a "readiness of the psyche to act or react in a certain way". According to Jung, attitudes occur in pairs out of which one is conscious and the other unconscious.
- Attitude has three components: cognitive, affective and conative or behavioural.
- Cognitive part consists of a person's thoughts and beliefs about the object.
- The emotional (or affective) part consists of the feelings which the object, person, issue or event evoke.
- The behavioural part consists of the manner in which the attitude influences a person's behaviour.
- Attitudes perform various functions for the psychological and mental benefit of the individual.
- Psychologists ask, 'what purposes in a psychological sense are served by the attitudes which an individual holds?'
- According to Daniel Katz, a famous psychologist, attitudes can serve utilitarian, ego-defensive, value-expressive, or cognitive functions.
- Knowledge enables us to understand the world, and respond suitably to the things and happenings around us.
- Ego-Defensive attitudes, as the name shows, refer to psychological responses involving use of defence mechanisms.
- Ego-defence mechanisms are psychological devices which people use to avoid psychological harm. Typically, they come into play in situations in which individuals feel a sense of humiliation, shame, indignity and loss of self-respect.
- Among these mechanisms are: denial, repression, projection and rationalization.
- Denial simply means that one refuses to see the manifest reality.
- Basically, these mechanisms enable an individual to deny the harsh reality, and seek refuge in illusions. Use of these mechanisms is a symptom of mental maladjustments.
- Repression means that an individual who suffers a traumatic experience completely forgets about it. He removes it from his conscious memory so that it lies buried even unknown to him in his subconscious mind.
- Projection is a defence mechanism in which one ascribes his own unacceptable qualities or feelings to other people.
- Rationalization is a form of self-deception. It allows one to adjust to it an unwelcome situation or outcome by falsely seeing it as to one's benefit or otherwise misinterpreting it.
- Value-expressive attitudes articulate an individual's core values and self-image. Core attitudes serve two purposes: (i) establish an individual's identity, showing who he is or what he stands for; and (ii) secure social approval for him.

- Our attitudes arise from our experience: (i) from direct personal experience, or (ii) from observation.
- Psychologists mention three learning theories of attitude change: classical conditioning; operant conditioning; and observational learning.
- Classical conditioning can be used to create positive emotional reactions to a person, object or event by associating positive feelings with the target object.
- Operant conditioning means changing of behaviour by the use of reinforcement which is given after the desired response. In this method, learning occurs through rewards and punishments for behaviour.
- In classical conditioning, the behaviour is involuntary.
- In operant conditioning, the learner is active and is rewarded or punished.
- People also form attitudes by observing people around them.
- Theory of persuasion posits that attitudes of people on any subject can be changed by suitably communicating appropriate information to them. Many aspects are relevant in trying to persuade people to change their attitude on any subject. These are:
  - (i) object of the attitude i.e. thing, person, group or idea towards which an attitude is directed;
  - (ii) the message or information;
  - (iii) the manner in which it is delivered;
  - (iv) the messenger; and
  - (v) the target audience i.e. individuals whose attitudes are to be changed.
- This attempt at persuasion can be either through the central route or the peripheral route. In the *central route* to persuasion, the individual is presented with data and motivated to evaluate the data and arrive at an attitude changing conclusion. In the *peripheral route* to attitude change, the individual is encouraged to not look at the content but at the source.
- The various aspects mentioned above in the theory of persuasion will have to be taken into account while organizing campaigns to secure people's participation.
- Social psychologists study the relation between an individual's attitudes, beliefs (or views) and actions. Earlier, social psychologists thought that attitudes of an individual result in compatible beliefs and actions.
- Cognitive consistency is the theory that people try to be consistent in their attitudes, views and in their behaviour.
- In theory, consistency between one's beliefs and behaviour is derived from a feeling for logical consistency.
- Wishful thinking means that our thinking, instead of being grounded in reality and logic, is guided by our desires.
- When an individual's beliefs and attitudes oppose each other or the behaviour, he experiences psychological tension or discomfort. He is then motivated to reduce the dissonance through changes in behaviour or cognition. This is called the theory of cognitive dissonance.
- For the early social psychologists, it was almost an article of faith that human behaviour is guided by people's attitudes.

- Later research has led to considerable modification in the simple relation posited between attitudes and resultant behaviour.
- In trying to explain the attitude-behaviour connection, social psychologists proposed new theories and conducted studies to empirically validate such theories.
- Social psychologists divide attitudes into two categories. The first category consists of general attitudes toward physical objects, linguistic, ethnic, or other social groups, institutions, policies or similar general targets.
- The second category comprises attitudes toward performing specific action or behaviours with respect to an object or target.
- Psychologists also distinguish between broad behavioural categories or multiple-act aggregates and single behaviours. Broad behaviour is made up of many individual components which are its discrete manifestations.
- Psychologists tend to analyse attitude-behaviour relation in two ways: (i) connection between general behaviour and multiple-act aggregates; and (ii) connection between behaviour-specific attitudes and single behaviour.
- As we mentioned earlier, early psychologists took it for granted that attitudes of people govern their behaviour. This view appeared doubtful as a result of two famous studies.
- Faced with the evidence about the attitude-behaviour inconsistency, some researchers doubted the validity of survey procedures and the suitability of the samples.
- There are two kinds of attitude-behaviour inconsistency. When someone fails to act according to his declared *behavioural intention*, we have literal inconsistency. Evaluative inconsistency occurs when the *evaluation expressed* in verbal attitudes (or what is said) does not match with actual behaviour.
- Attitude and behaviour, according to some researchers, diverge due to moderating effect of factors related to the person performing the behaviour, the situation in which it is performed, or the characteristics of the attitude itself.
- Better results in terms of attitude-behaviour consistency were obtained when investigators selected a domain of interest and identified a set of behaviours broadly representative of the same behavioural domain. This procedure is an example of the principle of aggregation.
- According to the principle of compatibility, measures of attitude and behaviour should contain exactly the same action, target, context, and time elements. Then attitude and behaviour will show consistency.
- The MODE Model looks at how attitudes influence perceptions and judgments. It looks at two types of individuals and two modes of activation of general attitudes which result in favourable or unfavourable bias.
- Many theorists regard that the nearest cognitive antecedent of actual behavioural performance is the agent's intention than his attitude. It means that one can accurately predict specific behaviours from the intentions of their performers.
- Models of Reasoned Action go beyond prediction of likely behaviour; they discuss factors that lead to formation of intentions.

- They assume:
    - Intention is the immediate antecedent of actual behaviour.
    - Intention, in turn, is determined by attitude toward the behaviour, subjective norm, and perceived behavioural control.
    - These determinants are themselves a function, respectively, of underlying behavioural, normative, and control beliefs.
    - Behavioural, normative, and control beliefs can vary as a function of a wide range of background factors.
    - Government servants should avoid the risks of stereotyping individuals and harbouring prejudices.
    - Social influence and persuasion need to be distinguished from social conformity, power, and authority as causes that change attitudes.
    - Social power can operate through the mechanisms of rewards, coercion, authority, expertise, and authority-groups in changing attitudes.
    - We have also mentioned five areas with reference to which social influence is now studied.

PRACTICE QUESTIONS

1. Define attitude. What is the process through which attitudes are formed?
2. What do you understand by the structure of attitudes?
3. Outline briefly the psychological functions of attitudes.
4. Write short notes on the following: (i) rationalization (ii) denial (iii) repression (iv) projection (v) Ego defence mechanisms (vi) wishful thinking (vii) cognitive dissonance (viii) stereotyping.
5. What do you understand by (a) classical conditioning and (b) operant conditioning? How will you distinguish between them? Which of the two is more relevant to administrative situations?
6. Outline the main features of the theory of persuasion. Is it of any practical use to government servants? How?
7. What is cognitive consistency?
8. What are the two famous studies which showed the mismatch between the professed attitudes of people and their actual behaviour?
9. What are the reasons which prevent people from acting in any matter in accordance with their attitudes?
10. How did social psychologists modify the methodological procedures of their studies to produce greater convergence between attitudes and behaviours?
11. Discuss the MODE model. What does it seek to explain?
12. Outline the theory of reasoned action (also called the theory of planned behaviour). In what way does it advance beyond the earlier theories in explaining the connection between attitude and behaviour?

REFERENCES

- Charles Stangor, Introduction to Psychology
- Saylor URL: http://www.saylor.org/books Principles of Social psychology
- NCERT classes XI and XII texts on psychology (The above references are available on internet)
- Articles from Wikipedia, the free encyclopedia on the following topics:
  - Attitude (psychology)
  - Cognitive dissonance
  - Elaboration likelihood model
  - Persuasion
  - Theory of reasoned action
  - Theory of planned behavior
  - Behavioural change theories
  - Expectancy-value theory
  - Social psychology
- Kendra Cherry, About.com Attitudes - How Attitudes Form, Change and Shape Our Behavior
- J. Cooper and K. M. Carlsmith, Cognitive Dissonance
- Lisa Rashotte Social influence Blackwell Encyclopaedia of Sociology
- Sharon Shavitt & Michelle R. Nelson The Role of Attitude Functions in Persuasion and Social Judgment

CHAPTER 17

POLITICAL ATTITUDES

INTRODUCTION

People hold divergent opinions on public issues. For example, they may support or oppose practices and policies such as (a) Jallikattu, (b) women's entry to the hill temple Sabarimala in Kerala, (c) triple talaq, (d) FDI in retail trade, (e) death sentence, and (f) confidence-building measures with Pakistan. One way people form opinions is by judging each issue separately and on a 'stand-alone' basis. Or they may look at them through their political or party or ideological prisms, and form opinions. Thus, those who regard themselves as 'left, democratic, progressive and secular' will oppose (a), (d) and (e), remain silent on (c), and support (b) and (f). Those who are right leaning will support (a), (d), (e), oppose (c) and (f) and could be ambivalent on (b).

For our purposes, we need not judge such opinions. But what is important is to recognise that such opinions rest on political attitudes. People do not judge issues just on their merits. People's political attitudes and ideological orientations influence their way of thinking on issues. People examine issues with a particular slant derived from their ideological predispositions. This is why political attitudes are important; they predispose people to view matters from a definite angle. Students would have observed this while listening to debates in Parliament or on TV.

In this chapter, we discuss political attitudes and ideology. These are studied in economics, political science, sociology, psychology and philosophy. But strands of such studies intersect, and no single factor explanation is adequate. We outline political attitudes and ideologies relying on simple ideas from political science.

THE POLITICAL SPECTRUM

Political attitudes are best understood based on the idea of political spectrum. Students would be familiar with the concept of spectrum of colours into which white light is divided when passed through a prism. Political spectrum is a graphic, or more specifically, a straight line along which political positions are shown from left to right. These positions are radical, liberal, moderate, conservative and reactionary. These terms are generic descriptions of political attitudes. They also refer to specific ideologies.

The spectrum of political attitudes can be shown as below:

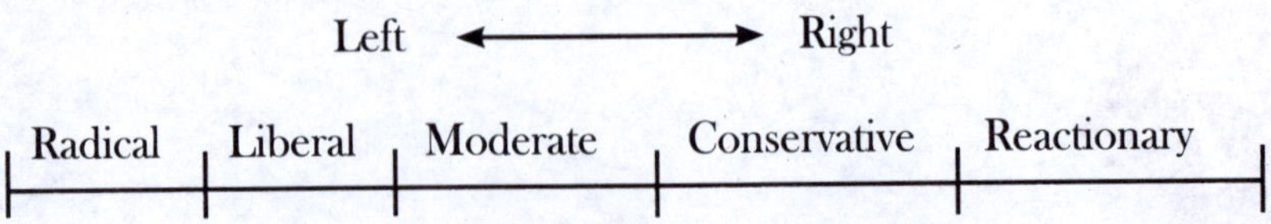

Figure 1: The Political Spectrum

The terms *left* and *right* are of French origin. Supporters of the emperor's policies were seated to his right, and their opponents who proposed changes in the prevailing system were seated to his left. Before looking at the meanings of the above five terms, we should note a few important points. The five terms designate political attitudes which (a) seek changes in the existing political set up and (b) which uphold certain political values. Another noteworthy point is that these terms have meanings specific to a given society. Thus they stand for different ideas in USA, Saudi Arabia and India. But within these countries, the five terms can be applied to characterise particular sets of political views. Further, what we commonly understand as ideologies such as communism, socialism and liberalism can be fitted into these five terms. On the spectrum, radicals are at the extreme left and reactionaries at the extreme right with others in intermediate positions. In political science, a radical means an individual on the extreme left of the political spectrum.

POLITICAL CHANGE

Radicals, liberals, moderates, conservatives and reactionaries (we will call them 'the five groups' hereafter) have differing attitudes on whether and /or how far the existing political system or the status quo should be changed. They differ also on policies or courses of action needed for changing the system. Status quo means the existing social, economic and political set up. Disturbing the status quo does not mean tinkering with it, but refers to fundamental changes in deep-rooted beliefs or in foundational institutions. We have to separate ordinary changes from fundamental social transformations. When one ruling party is displaced during elections in a democracy, the new government still represents status quo. There will be cosmetic changes; some old wine will be poured into new bottles. This is the likely scenario, despite the cacophony in main stream Western media, after the election of Donald Trump to US Presidency.

Direction of Political Change

Political thinkers use four dimensions to explain the differences between the five groups to political change. The first aspect is the **direction of change**, or whether the proposed change will take society forward or backward. A forward change is progressive and a backward change is retrogressive. However, we need to be on guard here, for these terms are value-loaded. 'Forward' and 'progressive' are, to borrow an expression from George Sabine, 'honorific' or in plain language, smell of roses. 'Backward' and 'retrogressive' remind us of the smelly things of life. But we should attach no intrinsic value to these terms. We should think of progressive change simply as a change from the status quo to something new and different in that society. Likewise, we should understand retrogressive change as return to a policy or institution that existed in the past in that society.

The demarcation line between progressive and retrogressive change lies between the conservative and reactionary segments on the spectrum. The line between these two segments represents absence of any significant change or continuation of the status quo. Everyone to the left of the reactionary segment is progressive. Students may wonder whether conservatives can be called progressive in any sense. Even conservatives are progressive to some extent; though they dislike too much tinkering with the status quo, they allow a few institutional innovations. Only reactionaries want a change from the status quo to something that existed earlier.

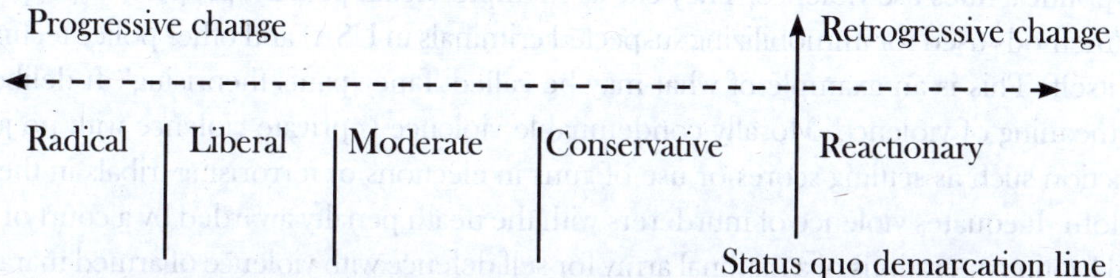

Figure 2: The position of status quo on the political spectrum

Most people cannot be placed exclusively in any single group because their attitudes on issues will range over two or more segments on the spectrum. Even ardent conservatives may have some liberal views. Thus conservatives may agree on the need to cleaning up temple surroundings, and on entry of women into temples on the same footing as men. But we can observe a general tendency; some people more often support conservative policies than any other policies; consequently, we might call them conservatives though their opinions on some questions may not be conservative. Only doctrinaire individuals and party spokespersons may be highly consistent in their political attitudes.

Depth of Political Change

The five groups as outlined in figure 2 above also differ on the **depth of political changes** they seek. Some would be satisfied with incremental changes or minor social adjustments. These will cause no ripples. Others want fundamental alterations in society or root and branch reforms. They would like to overturn many basic political institutions and create new ones. Such changes will bring in their wake unforeseeable and uncontrollable consequences. To cite an example, many educational reforms can be accommodated in the present system without overturning it. However, measures such as abridging fundamental rights or the powers of judiciary will be drastic systemic changes.

As with the direction of change, so with the depth of change, the demarcation line is that which lies between conservative and reactionary positions, or at the status quo point on the spectrum. The farther people are from the status quo, the greater is their dissatisfaction with the existing order and more drastic the changes they want.

Speed of Political Change

Uptill now, we considered the attitudes of the five groups towards direction and the depth of political change. The third dimension refers to how eager are people for change or how soon they want to see the change. Clearly, the more unhappy people are with the status quo, the more impatient they would be. Therefore, they would like the changes to be ushered in fast.

Methods of effecting political change

The five groups differ lastly on the appropriate methods for effecting political change. Political change can occur in many ways: officially or unofficially; legally or illegally/ extra legally; gradually or abruptly; and peacefully or violently. We tend to associate use of violence with extremist political groups.

Here, we make a small detour to alert students to some misinterpretations which are based on shuffling or playing with meanings of common words. Some leftist political thinkers point out that people of all political hues use violence. They cite as examples death penalty, property expropriation, chokeholds (methods used for immobilizing suspected criminals in USA) and other police techniques, and warfare itself. This is an example of what may be called 'fancy pants theorising'. It deliberately changes the meaning of violence. Morally condemnable violence is private violence with no judicial or moral sanction such as settling scores or use of guns in elections or terrorising tribals in the name of their freedom. It equates violence of murderers with the death penalty awarded by a court of law. It puts on equal footing operations of a national army for self defence with violence of armed marauders. A different example is of a feminist writer who declared that all sex is rape. Though provocative, this statement is ridiculous: how can forcible sexual attack be compared with union of happy married couples? Sadly, many agitations such as for for *aazadi* which seduce students use similar perversions in the garb of logic and democratic ideals.

Those on either extreme of the status quo on the political spectrum are likely to be at odds with the laws of the society. This is because laws stand for the purposes, goals, and structures of the society. They broadly embody the current social ethos. Opponents of the values, goals, or structures of society will also oppose its laws. On the contrary, conservatives in tune with social values tend to be law-abiding and patriotic, since they are satisfied with the system. Radicals and reactionaries, and liberals to lesser degree, may not endorse the laws or the prevailing judicial system. However, conservatives may also violate the law to gain their political objectives. It is possible that even the conservative rich may be hurt by laws. Then they could violate laws. Examples include corporations ignoring health and safety requirements or stock market manipulators cheating small investors.

We now turn to the values, programme world views of the five groups mentioned in figure 1, their conceptions of desirable societies and their methods for attaining their goals.

RADICALISM

"Radical" refers to individuals, parties, and movements that seek to drastically alter any existing practice, institution, or social system. As radicals are highly dissatisfied with the society, they want immediate and revolutionary changes. Extreme leftists challenge the most cherished values and assumptions of society. They reject the institutions of the establishment, and seek a more humane, egalitarian, and idealistic social and political system. Many people may share such ideals. But they lack the idealism, are too selfish or suffer from inertia and so remain passive.

Many radicals espouse violence. Some writers consider pacificists also as radicals. Pacifists totally reject violence as a means to achieve justice. They uphold human rights and believe that no one has the right to injure or kill another in pursuit of any goal. Some writers cite Gandhiji and Dr. Martin Luther King as radicals wedded to non violence. Although Gandhiji aimed at profound political and social changes, he was also conservative in many ways.

The causes and aims of Radicalism and its forms have been changing in recent times. Earlier on, Radicalism was associated with anarchism and opposition to the very existence of governments. In India, we tend to associate Radicalism with ultra left movements. In the west, radicalism stood for various movements in recent past.

- During the Cold War, Radicalism was associated with proposals to fundamentally alter the capitalist economic and social system.
- During the 1960s, the civil rights movement in USA and the beat cultural movement created, in C. Wright Mills's words, a New Left.
- Student movements of the west in 1960s advocated an activist participatory democracy and a radical restructuring of society, either through social revolution, or by 'tuning in, turning on, and dropping out'. The beat movement developed into the mass "hippie" counterculture, which championed "alternative" living arrangements and philosophies of life.
- Feminists opposed denial of work opportunities to women and advocated change in women's status in homes. They also fought for abortion rights and for equal rights as with men.
- The social radicalism of the 1960s also created consumer and environmental movements. Ralph Nader encouraged activist researchers and lawyers to expose and challenge the abuses of corporate power.
- In the 1980s, alliances of radicals and liberals challenged and slowed down nuclear power industry, demanded a nuclear freeze and defended reservations for minorities and women and opposed President Ronald Reagan's "Star Wars" proposal.

Many of these programmes have become part of the liberal democratic agenda in the West. These forms of radicalism are reactions to elite hegemony. One writer observes, "*They [radicals] protest against the gap between democratic rhetoric and real life realities. They challenge complacency, think the previously unthinkable, and induce society's mainstream to mend its ways.*" These ideas also inspire Indian protest movements like for women's entry into temples on equal footing with men.

LIBERALISM

Unlike radicals, liberals subscribe to the core values of society. But liberals are open to reform for correcting the defects of society. Historically, liberals pioneered political, social and economic reforms in England, America and Europe. Liberals also differ from radicals in upholding laws. Radicals see laws as instruments which elites use to ensure their hegemony. Liberals regard laws as essential to protect individual liberty and orderly social life. While they may try to change some laws, they value legal system as a whole. Liberalism, like other doctrines, changed over time.
We briefly outline these changes.

Liberalism aims primarily at protecting and increasing an individual's freedom. Liberals believe that government is necessary to protect individuals from being harmed by others; but they also fear that government itself, by usurping excessive power, can threaten individual liberty. Over time, liberalism got divided into *classical liberalism* and *modern liberalism*. Classical liberalism argues that government should merely protect individual liberty. Modern liberalism believes that government should enhance individual freedom by promoting conditions for its enjoyment by the poor. Classical liberalism is said to be based on negative freedom, or liberty and modern liberalism on positive freedom.

Classical liberalism

Political foundations

John Locke, the founder of classical liberalism, argued that absolute monarchical rule negates the very basis and justification of political authority. Its *raison d'être* is to protect the life and property of individuals and to guarantee their natural rights to freedom of thought, speech, and worship. The early liberals aimed to free individuals from two kinds of social constraint–religious conformity and aristocratic privilege–both enforced by state power. While trying to limit state power over the individual, early liberals wanted government to be accountable to people. This required a system of government by majority rule in which government implements the expressed will of a majority of the electorate. This would imply periodic election of government by popular vote. Thus, liberalism is the progenitor of democracy.

Early liberals feared popular sovereignty or what they considered mob rule. They preferred that power should rest with property owners and other natural elites. As they saw the likely ascendancy of masses, they devised mechanisms for protecting individual liberties. They advocated separation of powers or dividing governmental power between three wings: legislature, executive, and judiciary. Next, they wanted periodic elections. The third safeguard was creation of individual rights of three sorts. One set of rights confers freedom to speak and write freely, freedom to associate and organize and, above all, freedom from fear of reprisal. But the individual also has rights, apart from his role as a citizen. These rights secure his personal safety and hence his protection from arbitrary arrest and punishment. The third type of rights preserve large areas of individual privacy. In a liberal democracy, these are affairs that do not concern the state such as the practice of religion, creation of art and the raising of children by their parents.

Economic foundations

Economic policy at the start of industrial revolution was driven by mercantilism which strictly regulated the economy internally and externally. Mercantilism regarded international trade as a zero-sum game–in which gain for one country meant loss for another. National governments intervened to determine prices, protect their industries from foreign competition, and avoid the sharing of economic information. Liberals challenged these policies. The French thinkers known as physiocrats argued that the best way to increase wealth is to allow unrestrained economic competition. Their advice to government was "laissez faire, laissez passer" ("let it be, leave it alone").

Adam Smith expounded this laissez-faire doctrine in *The Wealth of Nations* (1776). He favoured free trade and markets. If economic agents are allowed to pursue their self-interest in a market economy, the welfare of all will be optimized. The self-seeking individual promotes public good because in a market economy he must serve others in order to serve himself. Adam Smith spoke of 'an invisible hand' transforming private interest into public good. However, only a truly free market can ensure this happy outcome; other arrangements, whether state control or monopoly, sap initiative and cause inefficiency and economic stagnation.

The task of any economic system is to produce and distribute goods and services people. This process also leads to a particular distribution of wealth and income. In a market economy, the price mechanism governs production and distribution. Well functioning markets generate the best outcomes in terms of production, prices and distribution. Markets are self adjusting or cybernetic systems. They factor in consumer choices. Markets create wealth patterns which assure reward in proportion to merit. Economic agents rationally and self-interestedly minimize costs and maximize gains. As each one knows what is best for him, government interference in his economic activities will only hinder and never enhance his interests.

Thus both from political and economic perspectives, liberals wanted to limit government activity. Jeremy Bentham's sole advice to the state was: "Be quiet." Classical liberals however acknowledged that government must provide education, sanitation, law enforcement, a postal system, and other public services that were beyond the capacity of any private agency. But apart from these functions, government must not try to do for the individual what he is able to do for himself.

Modern Liberalism

Problems of market economies

People became disenchanted with classical liberalism by the end of the 19th century because of serious unforeseen consequences of the Industrial Revolution. A few became enormously wealthy, many became abjectly poor, and sprawling slums sprang up in industrial towns. Trade cycles appeared with alternating booms and busts---the latter throwing people en masse into unemployment. The rich corrupted and controlled governments.

T.H. Green argued that excessive government powers which hindered freedom earlier shrank by mid 19th century. But other hindrances such as poverty, disease, discrimination, and ignorance have emerged. Governments should positively help needy individuals to overcome these problems and enjoy freedom. Modern liberalism enlists government to establish public schools and hospitals, to help the needy, and regulate working conditions to promote workers' health and well-being. It is only through public support that the poor and powerless can truly become free. This is the logic which supports the pro-poor and inclusive growth strategies. Modern liberalism has borrowed many elements from socialism. Its approach is more socialist than conservative.

Liberalism in twentieth century

The First World War and its turbulent aftermath shattered many liberal illusions. Between the two Great Wars, people turned to anti-democratic and to anti-liberal alternatives on the extremes of the political spectrum. Germany, Italy and Spain became fascist dictatorships. Russia took to communism. In the 1930s, the Great depression hit the world economy. US president Roosevelt introduced the New Deal (1933–39) involving massive government interventions to tackle depression. British economist JM Keynes propounded an economic doctrine that government management of the economy could smooth out the highs and lows of the business cycle in order to produce more or less consistent growth with minimal unemployment.

Liberal policies in post War era brought about phenomenal growth in Western Europe, North America, and Japan. Western industrialized nations pursued full employment, maximum use of industrial capacity, and greatly increased peoples' purchasing power. Instead of the old policy of "sharing the wealth", liberals used the government's power to borrow, tax, and spend not merely to counter contractions of the business cycle but to encourage expansion of the economy. It appeared to create class harmony and the basic consensus essential to a democracy.

Limited intervention in the market

Modern liberals recognize the achievements of the market system. They want to modify and control the system rather than abolish it. Regimentation in centrally planned Soviet style economies and bureaucratization even in mixed economies deterred them from giving up on the market for an omnipotent state. *But in contrast to classical liberalism, modern liberalism intervenes in the market for following reasons:*

- The rewards market fail to correctly measure contributions of most people to society.
- Market ignores the needs of those who lack opportunity or who are economically exploited.
- The enormous social costs incurred in production are not reflected in market prices and resources are often wasted.
- Market allocates human and physical resources toward satisfaction of consumer appetites–e.g., for automobiles, home appliances, or fashionable clothing. It often ignores basic needs such as schools, housing, public transit, and sewage systems.
- Although prices, wages, and profits should be based on negotiation among the interested parties and market trends, those affecting the economy as a whole must be reconciled with public policy.

Greater equality of wealth and income

Liberals usually rely on following approaches for mitigating inequality:

- Organization of workers into trade unions for increasing their power to bargain with employers
- Undertaking variety of government-funded social services for helping the poor
- Progressive taxation
- Employment and income generating programmes and provision of minimum needs of housing, health, sanitation and education as in India.

Contemporary Liberalism

The revival of classical liberalism

Modern liberalism faced problems with declining economic growth from the mid-1970s in western economies. Economic stagnation and high costs of social benefits of the welfare state forced governments into unsustainable levels of taxation and debt. The Keynesian prescriptions lost their efficacy.

These led to a revival of classical liberalism notably through efforts of Friedrich von Hayek and Milton Friedman. Hayek argued that interventionist measures aimed at the redistribution of wealth lead inevitably to totalitarianism. Friedman, a founder of the modern monetarist school of economics, held that the business cycle is determined mainly by the supply of money and by interest rates, rather than by government fiscal policy–contrary to the long-prevailing view of Keynes and his followers. Students should note that these are actually conservative arguments extolling the ideal of markets and sharply limited governments. Prime Minister Margaret Thatcher (1979-90) in Britain and President Ronald Reagan in USA (1981-89) embraced these ideas. These ideas represent neo-liberalism which is a form of conservatism. Incidentally, our economic reforms of 1991 are based on neo-liberalism and on Washington Consensus, though 'with a human face' in the words of P. V. Narsimha Rao.

Students should understand the connotation of terms which have changed in confusing ways. Classical liberalism is equivalent to modern conservatism and neo-liberalism. Modern liberalism has become socialism with heavy emphasis on welfare state. Further, many radical ideas migrated into socialism and into modern liberalism. The scope of the terms has become ambiguous. As we shall see, these ideological orientations explain the positions which academics and journalists take on current controversies in India. Modern liberalism has become the dominant academic orthodoxy.

Civil rights and social issues

Contemporary liberalism tried to extend individual rights in new directions. Liberals see rights as bulwark against tyranny and oppression; in late 20th century claims to rights are used as tools in struggles for social justice. Thus the American civil rights movement of the 1950s and '60s led to laws forbidding discrimination against African Americans; and movements for equal rights for women, gays and lesbians, the physically or mentally disabled, and other minorities or disadvantaged social groups. Liberalism historically has sought to foster a plurality of different ways of life, or different conceptions of the 'good life', by protecting the rights and interests of first the middle class and religious minorities, then the working class and the poor, and finally of racial minorities, women, gays and lesbians, and the physically or mentally disabled.

Liberalism has altered the Western society in other ways as well. It removed restrictions on contraception, divorce, abortion, and homosexuality based on the right of individual choice. Emphasis on right to freedom of speech reduced restrictions on depicting sexual content in works of art and culture. Students should connect frequent public debates on censorship of films and homosexuality with liberal thoughts imported from west.

MODERATES

It is difficult to characterize moderate political positions or to identify political groups allied with them. Long ago, Aristotle spoke of the virtue of moderation or of the golden mean. But it refers to human temperament than to political creeds. Still, the label 'moderate' often appears in political discussions. Moderates may belong to groups who combine elements from two rigid systems or doctrines. Thus, socialism borrows elements from communism and capitalism. It takes democracy and individual freedom from capitalism, and collective ownership of means of production, public sector and planning from communism. It is a via media. Moderates are reluctant to introduce major changes. They are not too worked up about the state of society.

There can be hardliners and soft peddlers within the same party or organization. For example, in the US Democratic Party, Bernie Sanders is to the extreme left of the party. Journalists speak about hawks and doves in foreign policy establishments of USA or Russia. Analysts also speak about hard line and gentle Islamists. At times, such distinctions may exist only in the minds of writers.

Moderates, though not enthusiastic for change, allow for greater innovations than conservatives. They live in an uncomfortable half way house and draw flak from committed party ideologues. They are derided as vacillating and feeble minded. Margaret Thatcher used to refer to her less firebrand supporters as 'wets'. However, moderates often oppose the harsh and rigid versions of doctrines. They are more humane, and oppose pushing policy measures in violation of human considerations. Their approach can be summed up in the saying, "politics is the art of the possible".

We can think of two examples from Stalinist Russia of how moderation could have prevented great harm. If collectivization of agriculture had been implemented less ruthlessly, it would have saved millions of lives. Soviet state would not have suppressed dissent by lining up political opponents before firing squads or by exiling them to forced labour camps in Siberia. Our regrets over such past tragedies are unavailing since history is irreversible, and has no room for might-have-beens. One has to be cautious and wake up in time.

CONSERVATISM

Conservatism is a political doctrine that emphasizes the value of traditional institutions and practices. It regards society as a living organism with organically interlinked parts. Conservatives value institutions which evolved slowly, for they promote social stability and continuity. Government should guard existing ways of life and not attempt to transform society rapidly. Suspicion of government activism separates conservatism from liberalism and radicalism.

Conservatism was first propounded as a systematic doctrine in late eighteenth century largely as a reaction to French revolution. Two famous thinkers associated with conservatism are Chateaubriand in France and Edmund Burke in England. According to them violent, non-traditional and disruptive methods polluted the liberal principles of French Revolution.

General characteristics of conservatives

Conservatives reject the optimistic Enlightenment belief in human perfectibility. They deny that human beings can be morally improved through political and social change. They point out that human history under most political and social circumstances witnessed great evils. Men are neither good nor rational. On the contrary, they are driven by passions and desires, and are naturally selfish, disorderly, irrational, and violent. Traditional political and cultural institutions are needed to curb men's base and destructive instincts. Burke says that men need "a sufficient restraint upon their passions," and it is government's function "to bridle and subdue." Families, churches, and schools must teach the value of self-discipline. Governments and laws must punish moral defaulters. Without the curbs of such institutions, conservatives believe, there can be no ethical behaviour and no responsible use of liberty.

Conservatism is not only a political creed but also a temperament. First, conservatives distrust human nature, rootless individuals disconnected with traditional social values, and untested innovations. They trust unbroken historical continuity and believe that human affairs should be conducted within traditional structures. These could be political, cultural, or religious. Secondly, conservative temperament abhors abstract argument and theorizing. They argue that efforts by philosophers and revolutionaries to plan society in advance, using political principles derived from reason alone, are misguided and likely to end in disaster.

Conservatives and liberals differ sharply on this matter. Whereas liberals like abstract theories, conservatives instinctively prefer concrete traditions. Conservatives therefore oppose government's interference with social or economic realities and believe that social engineering is futile and dangerous. To understand society, one has to learn its history and tradition since people follow inherited manners, morality, and culture. Political leaders should immerse themselves in the traditions of the society they want to govern.

Historical Trends

A few historical milestones will provide a thumb sketch of conservatism. The massive dislocations and turmoil of the French Revolution led to a strong conservative reaction. The Congress of Vienna was convened towards the close of Napoleonic wars. It was based on conservative principles of traditionalism and legitimism (hereditary monarchy as the only lawful rule and restoration of kings deposed during French Revolution). The political settlement soon proved untenable due to unrest among liberal urban population. There were many revolutionary outbreaks from 1830 to 1848.

The population of conservative social groups like peasantry began to dwindle. Urban dwellers grew in number because of industrial revolution. Conservatives found it difficult to win majorities in legislatures. In this situation, conservatives allied with forces of growing patriotism. While this helped them in gaining power, it also led, according to some writers, to the First World War.

World War I resulted in the downfall of four great imperial dynasties in Russia, Austria-Hungary, Germany, and Ottoman Turkey. These were the last strongholds of conservatism resting on monarchy, landed aristocracy, and church/institutional religion. After the war, conservative parties espoused frustrated nationalism in Germany, Italy and other countries. Starting from the 1930s, conservative parties across central and Eastern Europe were destroyed or co-opted by the Nazis.

After World War II, many Europeans turned once more to conservative policies, which seemed to promise both economic growth and democratic freedoms. This revived conservatism gave up its old aristocratic associations. Instead, it emphasized the raising of living standards through a market economy and the provision of a wide array of social services by the state. In fact, the ideological divide between liberalism and conservatism reduced greatly.

In the 1970s, however, the post war economic growth that the United States and other Western countries had relied on to finance social welfare programmes began to slacken. At this point, a new group of mainly American conservatives, neoconservatives, arose. They identified high taxation and government's intrusive regulation of private enterprise as hurdles to economic growth. Social welfare policies were making their recipients increasingly dependent upon government. Neoconservatives defended middle-class virtues such as thrift, hard work, and self-reliance, which declined due to sexual freedom and lax life styles of 1960s. They prefer US intervention in global arena and holding up American democracy as model which others should adopt.

REACTIONARIES

Reactionary outlook favours restoration of a previous, and usually outmoded, political or social order. Reactionaries hanker after a society whose days are over. It is a form of nostalgia for the past. Political and social changes occur due to various forces. Once some institutions and ideas are dethroned, they cannot be restored.

Marxists use 'reactionary' as a term of abuse. Reactionaries are seen as fighting a rear guard action against advancing, dynamic forces propelling new classes to power. Reactionaries may be on the losing side of the battle between the old and the new social orders. They may be the beneficiaries of the old order. During the period of *jagir* abolition, Zamindars and jagirdars had to make way for the emerging peasant proprietors who supported Congress during the Independence movement. At the time of integration of native states into India, a few rulers held out. In a way, they were trying to protect their vested interests in the Pre-Independence dispensation. After World War I, monarchical groups, aristocracy, church and military classes lost power in Europe. They attempted hard to restore their lost social position. Their approach is reactionary.

We can look at two examples of reactionary thinking from European history. The French writer Joseph de Maistre advocated extreme conservatism in early 19th century. Maistre rejected revolution in favour of traditional authority–especially the authority of monarch and church. Maistre rejected the entire heritage of the Enlightenment, attributing the revolutionary disorders of Europe to pernicious Enlightenment ideas. Against the French Revolutionary slogan "Liberty, equality, fraternity," Maistre proclaimed the value of "Throne and altar." (kings and priests). Maistre, since he stressed the authority of the traditional elite, is not conservative but reactionary.

The peace settlement of the Congress of Vienna (1815) which ended Napoleonic wars was reactionary because it aimed at reinstating the political and social order that existed before the French Revolution. Nevertheless, the restored monarchies in France, Austria, and Spain thought it prudent to create parliamentary institutions in order to mollify liberal sentiment.

IDEOLOGY

So far, we discussed positions on political spectrum besides liberal and conservative ideologies. Now, we consider the concept of ideology and cognate issues. Ideologies provide insights into many current public debates in India.

Definition

Political Ideology is a form of social or political philosophy which combines theory and practice. It is a system of ideas that seeks both to explain the world and to change it. Particular categories of ideology are socialism, communism, anarchism, fascism, nationalism, liberalism, and conservatism. Destutt de Tracy coined the term ideology during the French Revolution. Ideologies evoke both strong attachment and revulsion.

Ideology may be loosely defined as any kind of action-oriented theory or approach to politics based on a system of ideas. Ideology, in Destutt de Tracy's original conception, has five characteristics:

- It contains a comprehensive explanatory theory about human experience and the external world.
- It proposes a general programme for social and political organization.
- It believes that the programme can only be realized through a struggle.
- It seeks not merely to persuade but to recruit loyal adherents with commitment.
- It addresses a wide public but assigns special leadership role to intellectuals.

Ideology and sociology of knowledge

Surprising as it may sound, Hegel and Marx use 'ideology' in a pejorative sense. Ideology in this sense is a set of beliefs with which people deceive themselves; it is theory that expresses what they are led to think, as opposed to that which is true; it is false consciousness. Ideology is used in this disparaging way also by exponents of the sociology of knowledge, including Max Weber and Karl Mannheim.

They regard idea systems as the outcome or expression of certain interests. The true nature of ideologies is hidden from their followers; Mannheim proposed that sociological research should unveil the "life conditions which produce ideologies." An example will help us understand the deceptive nature of ideologies and the need to unmask them. Thus, Adam Smith's economic theory should not be taken as an independent intellectual construction or be judged in terms of its truth, consistency, or clarity; rather, it is to be seen as the expression of bourgeois interests, as part of the ideology of capitalism. The sociology of knowledge later sought support from Freudian psychology (notably the concepts of the unconscious and of rationalization) in order to suggest that ideologies are unconscious rationalizations of class interests.

Neither Weber nor Mannheim used 'ideology 'consistently. Weber opposed Marx's theory that all idea systems are products of economic structures. He argued that some economic structures are produced by idea systems. In this vein, he argued that Protestantism (by promoting appropriate entrepreneurial mind sets) generated capitalism; and not capitalism Protestantism. Mannheim, on the other hand, tried to restore Marx's view that ideologies spring from the social structure. However, Mannheim suggested that the word 'ideology' should be reserved for conservative idea systems and the word utopia for revolutionary or millenarian idea systems.

But this sort of approach which attributes doctrines or ideologies to a believer's unconscious mind runs into a contradiction. For, the doctrine of sociology of knowledge itself becomes an unconscious rationalization. Mannheim tries to overcome this difficulty by postulating somewhat unconvincingly a classless class of intellectuals, a "socially unattached intelligentsia," capable of thinking independently by virtue of its independence from any class interest or affiliation. Rival contenders in Indian public debates show no awareness of this problem. Each side, no less than the other, is often hostage to its unconscious ideological predilections.

Are ideologies rational or irrational?

Political theorists are divided on whether ideologies are rational or irrational. Some discount efforts to understand politics through abstract ideas rather than lived experience. They distrust political punditry based on bookish learning. Michael Oakeshott, however, thinks that ideologies could be rational. As an example, he cites Locke's theory of political liberty as an "abridgment" of the Englishman's traditional understanding of liberty. If such a conception is abstracted from its originating tradition, it becomes a rationalistic doctrine or metaphysical abstraction, like liberties contained in the Declaration of the Rights of Man.

On the other hand, Edward Shils regards ideology as irrational with its roots in extreme romanticism. Romanticism repudiated the faith of the Enlightenment in reason as the foundation of all knowledge. Romantics emphasized the importance of emotional sensitivity and individual subjectivity and imagination. It represented a reaction against the order and restraint of classicism and neoclassicism. It rejected the rationalism which characterized the Enlightenment. Shils says that romanticism, by its cult of the ideal and by its scorn for the actual, influences ideological politics. It holds in contempt actions based on political calculation and compromise. As politics demands compromise, prudent self-restraint and responsible caution, ideologies driven by romanticism are contemptuous of civil politics.

Ideology and Violence

Many critics notably Hannah Arendent and Karl Popper analysed the 'total' character of ideology, its extremism and violence. Opposing revolutionary violence, Camus believes that a true rebel (or dissenter) does not conform to the orthodoxy of some revolutionary ideology but says 'no' to injustice. The true rebel would prefer the politics of reform, such as trade-union socialism to the totalitarian politics of Marxism or similar movements. He condemned the systematic violence of ideology or the crimes of logic committed in its name. He believed that the rise of ideologies in the modern world increased human suffering greatly.

Karl Popper advocated "piecemeal social engineering" instead of total ideologies. Popper argued that ideology rests on a logical mistake which believes that history can be transformed into science. Ideology seeks certainty in history and aims at historical predictions similar to scientific predictions. As ideologies misconceive the nature of science, they produce only prophecies which are neither scientific predictions and nor have any scientific validity.

Not all ideologies support violence. However, ideological writings are replete with military and warlike language. Words like struggle, resist, march, victory, and overcome are often used. The terminology suggests that commitment to an ideology is akin to enlisting in army or to become the adherent of an ideology is to become a combatant or partisan.

Many ideological writers go beyond language use and frankly approve violence. George Sorel, for example, had done so before World War I in his book *Reflections on Violence.* Sorel used the word violence, according to some writers, as passion, not as throwing of bombs and the burning of buildings. Black militant writers of the 1960s like Frantz Fanon advocated violence. Jean-Paul Sartre's dramatic writings highlight that 'dirty hands' are necessary in politics and that a person with so-called bourgeois inhibitions about bloodshed cannot usefully serve a revolutionary cause. Sartre's attachment to the ideal of revolution tended to increase as he grew older, and in some of his later writings he suggested that violence might even be a good thing in itself.

Ideology and Pragmatism

Many writers distinguish between ideological and pragmatic approach to politics. Pragmatism examines problems purely on their merits without attempting to apply doctrinal, preconceived remedies. Some thinkers believe that politics has become less ideological and speak of the end of ideology. They think that pragmatism is better than ideology. There was decline in the hold of ideologies on people in the fifties. But many leftist groups sprang up in the sixties world over.

It is hard to get rid of ideologies. Almost any approach to politics consists of a system of beliefs. Some of these are more systematic than others. Though an ideology is a type of belief system, not all belief systems are ideologies. Ideology in loose form is Weltanschauung or a "view of the world".

Ideology and International Relations

Political thinkers believe that in the 20th century ideology has begun to influence diplomacy. World War I led to huge casualties and needed justification. Earlier, soldiers fought for the crown and nation. The Allied side fought the war to make the world safe for democracy, and Germany as struggle of civilization against barbarism. Emergence of communism and fascism made world politics ideologically more competitive. The Cold War was a conflict between the free world and the communist bloc. Most of 20th century was dominated by '-isms'. Wars were fought, alliances were forged, and treaties were made on ideological grounds. But in recent times, nations have reverted to relations based on pragmatic economic interests.

COMMUNISM

Introduction

Communism lies to the extreme left of the political spectrum. The term communism was coined around in the 1840s. It is derived from the Latin communis, meaning 'shared' or 'common'–visions of a society. Communism is a political and economic doctrine which seeks to replace private property and a profit-based economy with public ownership and control of the major means of production (e.g., mines, mills, and factories) and the natural resources of a society.

Karl Marx is the chief theorist of communism. His theory covers three main aspects: (1) materialist conception of history; (2) critique of capitalism and its workings; and (3) revolutionary overthrow of capitalism and its eventual replacement by communism.

Historical materialism

Materialist theory characterizes history as a series of class struggles and revolutionary upheavals, leading ultimately to freedom for all. Earlier, Hegel regarded history as the dialectical (logical or rational) self-development of "spirit". Marx replaced it with a materialistic interpretation. According to Marx, material production depends on (i) "material forces of production"–tools, technology and raw materials---and (ii) and "social relations of production"–organization of production in an economy. Growth of knowledge and technology revolutionize material forces of production. But the social and economic structures in the absence of concomitant change act as drags on dynamic technologies. This contradiction is overcome when society undergoes a revolution as from feudalism to capitalism.

Industrial capitalism is an economic system in which one class– ruling bourgeoisie–owns the means of production. The working class or proletariat effectively loses its independence. The worker becomes part of the means of production, a mere "appendage of the machine."

Marxist Critique of Capitalism

Marx held that human history went through several stages, from ancient slave society through feudalism to capitalism. In each stage, a dominant class uses its control of the means of production to exploit the labour of a larger class of workers. But internal tensions or "contradictions" in each stage eventually lead to the overthrow and replacement of the ruling class by its successor. Thus, the bourgeoisie overthrew the aristocracy and replaced feudalism with capitalism. Similarly, Marx predicted, proletariat will overthrow the bourgeoisie and replace capitalism with communism.

Capitalism was a historically necessary stage of development. It led to remarkable scientific and technological changes and greatly increased wealth. But this wealth–and the political power and economic opportunities that went with it–was unfairly distributed. The capitalists reap the profits while paying the workers a pittance for long hours of hard labour. This wealth also enables the bourgeoisie to control the government or state, which does the bidding of the wealthy and the powerful to the detriment of the poor and the powerless. But the dominant thinking of society hides these facts. Religion, which Marx called "the opium of the people" causes ideological obfuscation. It dulls the critical faculties and leads workers to accept their wretched condition as part of God's plan. Besides inequality, poverty, and false consciousness, capitalism also produces a feeling of alienation among workers.

Revolution and Communism

Marx believed that capitalism is a volatile economic system that will suffer a series of ever-worsening crises–recessions and depressions–that will produce greater unemployment, lower wages, and increasing misery among the industrial proletariat. These crises will convince the proletariat that its interests as a class are implacably opposed to those of the ruling bourgeoisie. Armed with revolutionary class consciousness, the proletariat will seize the major means of production along with the institutions of state power–police, courts, prisons, and so on–and establish a socialist state that Marx called "the revolutionary dictatorship of the proletariat." The proletariat will thus rule in its own class interest, as the bourgeoisie did before, in order to prevent a counterrevolution by the displaced bourgeoisie. Once this threat disappears, however, the need for the state will also disappear. Thus, the interim state will wither away and be replaced by a classless communist society.

Marx's vision of communist society is remarkably (and perhaps intentionally) vague. Unlike earlier "utopian socialists," whom Marx and Engels derided as unscientific and impractical, Marx did not produce detailed blueprints for a future society. It was not his task, he said, to "write recipes for the kitchens of the future."

We need not follow the twists and turns which communism later took. One group led by Bernstein, the first revisionist, advocated that communism should take parliamentary route of trade unionism. Lenin adapted Marxism to the needs of revolution. Marxism-Leninism propounded that

(i) Society needs a centralized, vanguard party and does not need multiparty competition through peaceful, lawful political participation.

(ii) Imperialism has shaped the development of capitalism and altered the terms of revolutionary struggle from those outlined by Marx; namely, revolutions are more likely in less developed capitalist economies, contrary to Marx's theory.

MARXISM IN TWENTIETH CENTURY

In twentieth-century, Marxist thought deviated substantially from Classical Marxism. This new form of Marxism is known by different names such as Cultural Marxism, Neo-Marxism, Libertarian Marxism, Existential Marxism, or Western Marxism. It has influenced the now dominant leftist liberal radical Western thought. Cultural Marxism originated in the writings of Anthony Gramsci and the Frankfurt School.

Gramsci, in *The Prison Notebooks*, answers why revolutionary communist doctrines failed to take root in Western Europe. This is due to persistence of capitalist ideas embedded in the institutions of "Civil society" such as family, church, trade unions, and education system. They create consensus in society. They are independent of "political society" made up of institution like police, army, and legal system. Whereas Marx believed that the material conditions of economic existence ("the base") determine all other aspects of society ("the superstructure") including its culture, Gramsci argued that it is culture that determines a society's economic structures. It therefore follows that a change in the economic structure will depend on prior change in the cultural institutions that implant capitalist ideas in people. The only way to do this is by cutting the roots of Western civilization – in particular, its Judeo-Christian religious values. Gramsci says, "In the new order, Socialism will triumph by first capturing the culture via infiltration of schools, universities, churches and the media by transforming the consciousness of society."

Theodore Adorno and Herbert Marcuse of The Frankfurt School infused Freudian psychology into Marxism and tried make Western culture hospitable to communism. This School also formulated Critical Theory, an incisive social critique, aimed at undermining the status quo. Critical Theory trenchantly and unrelentingly attacks all aspects of Western culture considered to be oppressive or dehumanizing. It holds Western civilization responsible for the aggression, oppression, racism, slavery, classism and sexism that mark post-industrial society. Some writers think that it has given rise to ideas and practices of extreme left-wing liberalism in the West such as 'political correctness, free speech crackdowns, no-plat forming [or cancel culture which consists in removing unpalatable views from social platforms and media sites], and the epidemic of boorish and thuggish university "protests," Antifa intimidation and violence. directed against illusory "fascists"'. It is from such trends that Indian leftist narratives and argumentative positions draw inspiration.

SOCIALISM

The word 'socialism' was coined in the early 1800s. It advocated policies which meet the basic needs of the entire society instead of policies that serve needs of individuals. Socialism opposed competing ideologies (such as classical liberalism) that rank in their political priorities, individualism above the common good. Saint-Simon (1760-1825), Robert Owen (1771-1859), and Charles Fourier (1772-1837) were early socialists. They argued that competitive individualist societies destroyed the possibility of collective harmony. Individuals are capable of living cooperatively, they insisted, and the socialist society would prove it. Saint-Simon envisioned socialism as a large, complex social system. In it, scientific planners would coordinate economic activity in order to produce goods in exactly the proper quantity and distribute it evenly throughout society without waste or shortages. Owen and Fourier believed in small self-sufficient cooperative societies. In these societies, all community members share both labour and the wealth it produces.

Later, socialists were called social democrats or democratic socialists. They reject Marxism-Leninism. They see its advocacy of a vanguard party as authoritarian. Social democrats believe in integrating socialism and democracy. Unlike Marxist-Leninists, social democrats support peaceful, legal efforts to work toward socialism, and they believe in multiparty competition and civil liberties. They view socialism as a way of organizing society so that all groups are guaranteed some level of social well-being and economic security. They propose to distribute society's riches among all sectors of the population by enacting public policies very similar to those advocated by modern liberalism. In fact, social democrats support extensive welfare programmes, which they believe, promote economic self-determination, just as democracy promotes political self-determination. As we mentioned earlier, socialist and liberal policies have come closer in Europe and USA.

Elements of socialism have been embedded in modern capitalism as welfare measures. Thus, western societies, though market-oriented, are welfare states. They make budgetary provisions for free school education, health care, unemployment benefits, old age pensions, child care support, subsidized public transport and the like. These nations (other than USA) are often described as social democracies. Social welfare programmes are funded in USA, and to a lesser extent in Europe, by running huge programmes of public borrowings. Many economists argue that this model is unsustainable.

ANARCHISM

Anarchism, or anarcho-communism advocates not only communal ownership of property but also the abolition of the state. The important anarcho-communists were William Godwin in England, Mikhail Bakunin and Peter Kropotkin in Russia (though both became exiles), and Emma Goldman in the United States.

They argued that the state and private property are interdependent institutions. The state exists to protect private property, and the owners of private property protect the state. If property is to be owned communally and distributed equally, the state must be smashed once and for all. In *Statism and Anarchy*, Bakunin attacked Marx's view that the transitional state–the dictatorship of the proletariat–would simply wither away after preventing a bourgeois counterrevolution. He argued that no state has ever withered away, and no state ever will. On the other hand, the very nature of the state is to extend its control over its subjects, limiting and finally eliminating whatever liberty they once had over their lives. Marx's interim state would in fact be a dictatorship "over" the proletariat. Thus, in this regard, Bakunin proved more prescient than Marx.

FASCISM

Fascism is a totalitarian ideology. It opposes liberalism, conservatism, and socialism. Fascism claims to be an elitist response to modern social and political problems which other ideologies are unable to resolve. Mussolini and Hitler are well known fascist dictators.

The main attributes of Fascism are:

(i) Need for a totalitarian state that regulates all parts of life deemed relevant to politics

(ii) Belief that the state is more important than the individual

(iii) Rejection of the view that civil institutions are necessary for limiting state power and criticizing state laws

(iv) Assertion that individuals gain a sense of purpose by psychologically identifying with a totalistic state and devoting themselves to its service

(v) Rejection of equality principle

(vi) Advocacy of nationalism and/or racism.

Fascism is a dangerous creed, but its trivialization by dubbing one's opponents as fascists should be avoided.

HOW DO PEOPLE CHOOSE IDEOLOGIES?

Many factors determine the political attitudes and ideological allegiance of people.

Values

A few examples will show how values predispose people towards certain ideological preferences. Belief in an individual's right to privacy and woman's personal liberty leads Liberals to support abortion without restrictions. Belief in sanctity of life underlies the conservative view that pregnant women are morally obliged to bear their children, and have no right to abort except in extreme circumstances. Liberals again invoke individual liberty to support homosexuality. Conservatives oppose because it negates natural processes and family values.

There is no need to multiply examples. We have already discussed various ideologies and the principles on which they rest. Each ideology takes stand on a whole range of social, political and economic and cultural issues. Each ideology is like a packet with attitude objects and appropriate attitudes towards each such object. Ideologues are therefore unable to get over their predetermined attitude sets towards issues.

Personality traits

An individual's psychological traits also influence his ideological orientation. Individual personality is moulded by family, education, culture and work. Psychologists claim that five individual personality traits influence his/her ideological preferences.

Extraversion signifies an active and energetic approach to social world. It includes traits such as sociability, activeness, assertiveness, positive emotionality or cheerful, optimistic outlook. **Agreeableness** implies a pro-social and community orientation (as opposed to antagonism) and includes traits such as modesty, altruism, tender mindedness and trustworthiness. **Conscientiousness** refers to socially prescribed impulse control that facilitates goal-directed behaviour. Its attributes are thinking before acting, delaying gratification, following norms and rules, and planning, organizing and prioritizing tasks. **Emotional stability** stands for equanimity and is the opposite of negative emotionality. Negative emotions which it avoids include feeling anxious, nervous, sad or tense or angry. **Openness to experience**, as opposed to close-mindedness, signifies breadth, depth, originality and complexity of an individual's experienced moral life.

Political attitudes are typical adaptations that result from interactions between essential dispositional traits and environment. Individuals observe political issues and ideological labels in the social environment. The big five dispositional traits shape the response to such issues, and lead to formation of political attitudes. US political scientists made studies showing connections between these dispositional traits and political attitudes. Conscientiousness is seen to promote a conservative outlook. People with pronounced openness to experience prefer liberalism and leftist views. Those who tend to be anxious opt for authoritarian views. However, many writers still think that political attitudes spring from economic roots.

Psychological Reason

Besides dispositional traits, some people are more psychologically attuned to liberalism or conservatism than others. A liberal has to be fairly tolerant to disorder. Many people are not so inclined; therefore, though they may have no great stake in the system, they resist change because they fear disorder. Yet, some people crave for almost constant change; the status quo never satisfies them.

Age

Age is important in determining political attitudes. Ordinarily, the young are more likely to be liberal than the elderly. One reason could be that older people have a vested interest in the status quo whereas the young would not have yet acquired it. Young people may have weaker sense of commitment and belonging. The elderly feel a stake in society, partly because they have created it, and partly because they have become used to it. Neither of these reasons operates strongly with the young.

View of Human Nature

One crucial determinant of whether someone will be leftist or rightist is how he she views human nature. If one believes that people are bad, selfish, and aggressive, then one is likely to be conservative. Anyone who thinks that people are inherently evil will tend to rely on strict laws and punishment for violators to control errant behavior. On the other hand, people who believe that human beings are well meaning and rational will lean toward the left. They will try to avoid reducing human liberty by "unnecessarily" severe laws, and they will try to reason with offenders. The difference lies in assumptions about human nature on whether people are good or bad.

Economic Determinism

Traditionally, economic factors were seen as the main determinants of political attitudes. More specifically, it was thought that a person's economic class determined his political beliefs. It was argued that people from different economic classes generally had different economic interests and these translated into different political viewpoints. Karl Marx was the most prominent proponent of this view. One's class position and class interest determine one's political attitudes. Max Weber, while conceding the role of economic interests in determining political viewpoints, was of the view that Marx had over-emphasised the relationship between individuals and the means of production. Weber argued that a well-paid worker may have more in common with capitalists than with other lower paid workers. It was not the bond between workers that creates a shared set of preferences, but the bond between similar levels of wealth and consumption.

After the Second World War, many features of the classical description of industrial societies became outdated. Increasing mass prosperity created new well off classes and increased the bourgeoisie character of society. The simple distinction between workers and owners of capital or between the wealthy and the poor broke down. New theories emerged based on a sophisticated understanding of the interaction of economics and social structure, and the increased complexity of post-industrial advanced democracies. A new middle class emerged with the fragmentation of society and this group sometimes sided with the traditional workers and at other times with elites.

In Indian politics, caste, religion and regional attitudes also determine political identities. These are important factors in political mobilisation process, as these factors reflect economic interests. Indian Marxists often identify class with caste. This leads to odd conclusions as when a poor Brahmin priest is seen as embodiment of dominant bourgeoisie ideology in a village. Students can reflect on their own as how the other two factors influence political attitudes.

CONNECTING POLITICAL ATTITUDES TO INDIAN CONTEXTS

In this section, we try to link the preceding theoretical account of political attitudes and ideologies to Indian situation. Basically, these matters fall within political science. But UPSC papers contain questions that involve application of theory portions of syllabus to current Indian problems. In order to help students with such questions, we make a few observations, more by way of illustration than detailed exposition. We explain how best to deal with questions on current controversies.

Indian Political Context

Going back to Indian Independence movement, we note that it is neither radical nor revolutionary. It was avowedly peaceful. There were a few outbursts of revolutionary violence led by Bhagat Singh, Raj Guru and Bengali revolutionaries. Netaji Subhash Chandra Bose also represents the radical strain of our Independence movement though he took help from Hitler. It no way detracts from Bose's greatness. After all, the arch conservative Churchill said that he would be ready to shake hands with the devil to defend Britain.

Independence movement inaugurated democratic protest politics based on British model. The movement was largely middle class and urban centred. Gandhi, however, introduced elements of mass politics into it. It remained largely peaceful, operated within law, and used tactics covered by norms which democracy sanctions. (While appreciating the peaceful nature of Independence movement, we should not forget the partition which witnessed one of the greatest massacres in human history.) The Indian Independence movement occupies the middle segments of the political spectrum.

Indian politics are essentially centrist or moderate. There were unsuccessful attempts at communist insurrections in Telangana and Andhra soon after independence. But Naxals still represent this strain of radicalism seeking violent and extensive overhaul of society. Naxals have so far been contained by the Indian state. No political party is ready to give them free rein.

The moderate nature of Indian politics derives from the parliamentary democratic model which all parties including communists have adopted. Communists try to make the best of a bad bargain. As they cannot hope to seize state power, they settle for power sharing. They use rationalizations like 'alliances with progressive, democratic, and secular forces' for taking piggy-rides on the backs of stronger parties. As parties depend on numerous groups with diverse interests, they have to find compromise solutions. They cannot offend or ignore any sizeable group. Some people observe that diversity is an existential feature of Indian society.

Democracy is based on rule of law and is unfavourable to extreme or sudden changes. In a more self congratulatory note, we observe that Indian people, barring occasional emotional outbursts, shun extremes and are peace-loving. On the flip side, they may seem passive and lacking in spirit.

Indian Economic Context

The economic policies of Indian state steered the middle course. Pandit Nehru was a socialist, and was influenced by the Soviet model of growth. He induced Congress to pass a resolution in favour of the socialistic pattern of society. This concept, like so many other thoughts of Nehru, remained vague and dreamy. However, government adopted certain socialist principles and polices such as planning, state capitalism with large public sector, economic regulations, self-reliant industrialization, and strict controls on foreign trade, progressive taxes and the like. These might have retarded India's growth. But we need to give due credit to Nehru for his pioneering efforts, for his emphasis on science and technology, and for creating top class institutions like IITs, IIMs, and research bodies. It will not be too farfetched to attribute ISRO's recent successes to his vision.

Nehruvian economic policies were to the left of the centre. But they did evoke opposition. Rajaji founded the *Swatantra Party* which was conservative. Rajaji opposed the Soviet style of planning and favoured free enterprise. He opposed economic controls describing them as 'licence, quota permit Raj'. Chaudhury Charan Singh, a peasant leader, can be cited as another example of conservative opposition. He objected in particular to ideas like state farming, collectivist farming and cooperative farming. He belongs to the conservative spectrum, and represents the ideal of independent peasant farmers.

Government let go of the old economic model in the nineties. Again, it was not any ideological fervour which prompted this switch into a new economic lane. The economy got into dire straits and ran out of foreign exchange needed even for essential imports. Government had to introduce economic reforms which can be summarized as liberalization, privatisation and globalisation. It adopted the pragmatic alternative. Cynics comment that it made a virtue of necessity.

There is consensus in India around current economic policies. Leftists oppose reforms but not too vehemently. The main political parties broadly agree on reforms. The passage and implementation of GST (notwithstanding the hype and hoopla in Parliament) represents a triumph of political accommodation over contention. It points towards paths to our future national progress.

SOME CONTROVERSIES

Introduction

In the previous section, we very briefly traced the ideological strands that run through Indian political and economic setup. Ideologies also drive many debates on current controversies. These debates are held on TV; articles also appear in press in support of rival positions. We have no desire to wade into these controversies. It may seem like rushing into areas where angels fear to tread.

Still, a few reasons led us to briefly touch upon these controversies. Questions on current controversies may be asked in UPSC examinations or in interviews. Students need to acquire balanced perspectives on questions like entry of women into Sabarimala temple. We suggest a procedure for a balanced understanding of such matters.

Before doing so, we indicate, by giving a few examples, how the controversies are ideologically driven. Western liberalism is now the dominant orthodoxy in universities and in media. As we saw, the western liberal ideologies favour among others sexual freedom, dilution of traditional marriage ties, alternative living styles, and abortion without restrictions. They oppose censorship or any restrictions on uninhibited depiction of sexuality in art, literature, and cinema. Many Indian commentators of this ilk reflect these views.

Both electronic and print media present tendentious and ideologically coloured accounts of such issues. By critically reflecting on media versions, students can easily see that many writings mechanically and mindlessly mimic western liberal attitudes with little concern towards national perspectives and social ethos. We look at three examples in order to show how the ideological mind-sets play out in such matters.

Vulgarity in Cinema

Debates on TV often revolve around censorship of some vulgar movies. The director will paint the movie as delicate, sensitive and artistic portrayal of love or joy of life or diversity in human sexuality. Lurid sexual depictions in movies may be defended in the name of artistic creativity and freedom. Some sexual radicals attack the Film Censor Board and the moderate elements. The debates ridicule anyone who speaks for refined treatment of sexual themes. Hysterical statements are made that the lights of freedom are being put out or that the barbarians are at the gate.

Censorship involves *inter alia* definition of art and obscenity. Literature is hard to define. It is an authentic, refined depiction of life. Literature is idealistic and attempts 'a criticism of life and manners'. Literature operates on a high aesthetic plane. For example, many novels and movies depict adultery. But they do not scale artistic heights like Tolstoy's *Anna Karenina* or Gustave Flaubert's *Madam Bovary*. A.C. Bradley, in *Oxford Lectures on Poetry* says that true works of art should help readers to get rid of crude emotions like "cheap pathos, rancid sentiment, vulgar humour, bare lust, ravenous vanity". This sets the bar too high for common readers. But we just want to convey what art stands for.

Invoking art and literature is common in disputes with censors. Often movies in whose defence artistic freedom is invoked are not even remotely artistic by the criteria we mentioned. But there is no bar on producing and showing trashy films. The point is different. Censor Board has to follow some norms so that movies for public exhibition do not flout common decencies or injure sentiments of any section of the population. The standards of what constitutes obscenity have been considerably diluted over time. But even so, a line has to be drawn about depictions and language in movies. These are reasonable restrictions over which there should be no hue and cry. In this matter, western liberal ideologies are unsuited to our still conservative Indian society.

Runaway Girls

When an impressionable girl elopes with her boy friend, her parents are placed in a terrible quandary. But often on TV shows, these episodes become occasions for celebration. These misguided girls are eulogised (for a day or two) as exemplars or role models bravely exercising personal freedom and rebelling against oppressive social conventions. Any participant in the debate who advises that girls should be circumspect is accused of gender bias, hidebound thinking and patriarchal mind-set.

Many such girls are imprudent and end up ruining their lives. They need parental counselling for constructively resolving the problem. Ideological celebration or disapproval of their silly actions just does not help. If a bonded labourer is released, he becomes free, and this is commendable from any ideological angle. But the girl acting foolishly in the first flush of love is not exercising her liberty, but being imprudent in all probability.

'Live-in Relations'

Similar debates take place when a 'live-in' relationship goes go sour. But this practice is strongly defended by liberal ideologues. Often 'live-in' relations create problems for girls. When things sour, they end up holding the dirty end of the stick. They gain nothing in that predicament by denouncing the gender bias of the society. Notwithstanding some judicial pronouncements, their status in no way equals that of a legally wedded woman. If girls are so enamoured of their boyfriends, all they have to do is to go to the nearest marriage registrar's office. If nothing else, they will have rights and protections under law.

Again in debates on this issue, anyone pointing out the risks to girls from these alternative living styles is pilloried as antediluvian and as a throwback to medieval ages. At times, some girls accuse their partners, after long periods of cohabitation, with rape. These unfortunate modern girls, pitiable though their plight might be, hardly stand a chance of any legal redress. Laws are administered coldly according to strict rules of evidence in courts. Despite such obvious disadvantages to girls, liberals continue to support such 'live-in' practices in the name of freedom.

Restrictions on Entry of Women to Some Temples

Students are advised to study this issue on their own. We confine ourselves to a few observations. The Kerala Hindu Places of Public Worship (Authorisation of Entry) Rules, 1965 banned women between the ages of 10 and 50 from entering the Sabarimala temple. This practice has been going on for centuries and is based on certain religious beliefs about Lord Ayyappa. Some activists challenged this practice on the ground that it deprives women of their religious freedom. A five-member constitution bench struck down provisions of The Kerala Hindu Places of Public Worship (Authorisation of Entry) Rules, 1965 as unconstitutional. Some review petitions were filed challenging the Supreme Court's decision. These were referred to a larger bench. The then Chief Justice of India Ranjan Gogoi reportedly observed that the question whether a court can intervene in matters that are essential to a religion is yet to be decided. He is also reported to have said, "In a legal framework, when a court does not have apostolical jurisdiction, (that is to say, authority to adjudicate on religious tenets and practices) it should tread cautiously," This is how the matter now rests.

Till the matter is finally decided by the larger bench of the Supreme Court, as law abiding citizens, we have to follow the order of the five-member constitution Bench of the Supreme Court. Without questioning this order of the Supreme Court, we want to make a few observations on the question of women's entry into Sabarimala temple with a view to illustrate how ideologically driven individuals (secular liberals in this instance) get into positions that are logically inconsistent and contrary to their professed ideology.

Religions at times need reform. Religions have harboured harmful beliefs and practices like *Sati* or human sacrifices or dangerous ceremonies. These violate human rights. Religions have promoted undesirable practices like child marriage and obscurantist/superstitious beliefs. These need to be discouraged. Religious laws which deny equal share to women in family property need to be changed. Much of Indian awakening in later nineteenth century owes to religious reformers. But religious beliefs with no direct bearing on individual welfare (like *Kavadiyas* walking from Allahabad to Varanasi carrying water) should be left alone.

Liberal activist groups are behind the women's temple entry agitation. There is an obvious anomaly and irony in their enterprise. But they seem to be blissfully unaware of it. It does not fit into the framework of their ideology. Unlike conservatives, liberals set no great store on religion. Most liberals and activists are rationalists and atheists. To use a court room expression, it does not lie in their mouth to raise the issue. What does the liberal position on religion imply?

Faith in God was once a main plank of philosophy. St. Thomas Aquinas gave many logical arguments to prove the existence of God. However, Immanuel Kant (*A Critique of Pure Reason)* demolished all philosophical arguments for theism once and for all. Modern science makes no mention of God. Many earlier beliefs in God arose from the problems men faced in their speculations about universe. They felt that existence of universe, natural phenomena like motions of planets and origin of men including biota can be explained only by postulating an actor or divine agency. As science began to explain such phenomena through natural laws, the need for God as the creator and regulator of universe and natural phenomena disappeared. This led to loss of religious faith in the west. Few scientists now are theists. Even in 18th century, one astronomer told an emperor that God is a gratuitous or superfluous hypothesis for astronomy.

On a strictly a rationalist view, therefore, all religions are false belief systems. Their internal practices and procedures lie outside rationalist spheres of action. If there is no God (as most liberals think), how does it matter where a woman offers her prayers from? In any case, she no less than her male counterparts, is only harbouring illusions. Logical consistency demands that rationalists should focus not on conferring illusory rights of equal worship on women but rather on removing the illogical clutter from their mind.

There is even a stranger aspect. Suppose that one is an atheist. Then it would be very strange if he were to advise the priests in Badrinath or Tirupati on how to conduct religious services. Stranger still is the touching concern of Indian liberals for the *moksha* of the Hindu women. They are applying secular concepts of rights and equality rooted in political sphere to ceremonial religious practices.

Religious practices are traceable to myths, legends and stories. They never fit into frameworks of logical thought. One can trace their historical origins. Religious practices have traditional but not logical rationale. Trying to decide them by modern views or standards by disassociating them from the traditions in which they arose is a unhistorical procedure. It is to judge past by present standards and values. Either we are willing to tolerate the tradition or discard it. Conservatives would continue with it. Liberals oppose it in the name of equality. But unless the traditions are sources of intolerable injustice, the state should leave them alone.

One such totally unacceptable injustice (linked to untouchability) is objection to entry of scheduled castes into temples. These two practices (now on wane) are a blemish on Hindu society and culture.

Religious leaders were always a little wary of female influence on men. They feared women as temptresses who could wean men away from spiritual pursuits. Ramakrishna Krishna Paramhamsa used to tell his devotees to be wary of *kamini* (woman) and *kanchana* (wealth). This may raise hackles among feminists who would argue that it is men who drag women into sin. Be that as it may, we note that historians identify mixed hostels for monks and nuns as one of the reasons for the decline of Buddhism.

One last point is that issues of this type should be left to legislators. They represent people. If they want to change the tradition, they will pressurize politicians. Judicial intervention on this tradition could be an example of judicial overreach. Judiciary sometimes allows itself to be dragged into pseudo-issues. There is a risk of their getting embroiled in questions like religious ceremonials and the content of *bhajans*. *Laissez faire* could be at times a virtue in judiciary no less than in government.

Our brief observations aim to bring out the anomalies involved in the temple entry debate. This practice is confined to a few temples and is connected to certain legends. Women are generally allowed to go freely to temples. Female devotees usually outnumber men. The few remaining restrictions are quaint survivals and can be done away with. Let us hope that the debate will create greater enthusiasm in young Hindu women to visit temples in colourful traditional or ethnic costumes sporting bindi on their foreheads.

PROBLEMS OF AN IDEOLOGICAL APPROACH

These examples point to the difficulties with ideological thinking. Ideologues tend to apply general principles across the board and often to inapplicable situations. For example, they fail to see that a young girl's freedom has to be regulated by her parents for her own safety and well-being. Liberty is crucial in many situations. Obviously, one should vote as one wants. But individual liberty may not be an unmitigated virtue for adolescent girls making life choices. Parental guidance and supervision are indispensable for protecting them from hasty moves and evil doers. Grown up girls can go to bars. But they need to exercise this freedom cautiously without getting into harm's way. These are matters of ordinary prudence and common-sense. Upholders of liberal principles are willing to expose girls to risks in the name of liberty. Any attempts to impose some checks on such risky behaviour immediately raise howls of moral policing.

Stock Responses

Ideologues have pre-determined responses to many issues. Ideology is applied to many policies, actions and behaviours. Ideology is like a big package with many items each with approval or disapproval markings. Its faithful followers have to respond according to the markings. *Let us look at how a set of ideas and actions elicit unthinking approval (A) or disapproval (D) from leftists and liberals:*

Shouting of anti-national slogans (A); police operations against terrorists (D); alleged police violations of rights of criminals (D); reports of foreign agencies about human rights violations in India (A);

and standing up for national anthem (D). On all these questions, Indian leftists/liberals have stock responses which resemble conditioned reflexes. Their views flow from their ideological predilections such as aversion to nationalism, opposition to state/police powers, devotion to human rights and fear of symbols of patriotism. Commitment to these general principles prevents them from objectively evaluating individual events or situations.

Group Thinking

As Weber and Mannheim recognized, ideological thinking is self-deceiving and self-serving. As self-deception, it helps one to live out his illusions in a personal or group bubble. These bubbles have become large in academia and media in USA and west. Similar bubbles have also formed in India. Some of them represent current ideological academic fashions and fads.

This has led to creation of likeminded groups of ideologues in universities. They resemble street gangs with fierce codes of loyalty. They are in violent opposition with those who think differently. But within the group, minor variations on the principal doctrinal positions are allowed to create cosmetic atmosphere of academic discussion and dissent. Otherwise, ideological purity is preserved within the group in Stalinist style. Real dissent is treated like betrayal, and dissenters like traitors. In this milieu, most social science departments seem to have become echo chambers which reproduce similar noise.

The principal ideology sweeping across US and other western universities is described as 'liberal, democratic, humanist, secular, tolerant, and multi-cultural'. Similar trends are also in evidence in India. The tolerance however does not extend to rival ideological views. Thus, Harvard University seems to have terminated Dr Subramaian Swami's teaching contract because of some views he expressed. We are neither competent to judge Dr Swami's academic standing nor are cognizant of his views which provoked the Harvard establishment. Our limited point is that their action negates academic freedom in what is unquestionably among the top few academic centres of the world. It might not be free from self-interest and designed not to offend prospective donors. The liberal ideology received a temporary setback with Brexit and Trump's election, but is likely to ride out this hurdle. It may be symptomatic of the end of US exceptionalism and its approaching decline.

We do not suggest for a moment that Indian students should turn away from US universities. In spite of the ideologically induced aberrations especially in social sciences, Ivy League US universities are still the best in the world. Indian students should also bear in mind that our national commitment to knowledge pursuits goes back to our ancient history. However, they should not join hypocritical choruses.

Vulnerability of Students to Ideologies

Students are especially vulnerable to snares of ideological thought. Idealistic students are enraptured by their first exposure to leftist grand theories like Marxism. It is like falling in love. The ideology seems to hold the master key to set at rest all the perplexities and doubts of students about social and economic problems. It does away with need for troublesome collection of facts or analysis. They feel a sense of enlightenment or religious awakening. In fact, many writers like Schumpeter have pointed that Marxism is not only an intellectual doctrine but also a millenarian religion promising a paradise on earth for its followers.

Ideologies proved to be collections of mostly wrong ideas. For example, most of Marx's predictions proved incorrect. Individual ideas of any ideology hardly ever stand up to scientific verification. Ideologies also contain many value judgements. These are neither true nor false; some people adopt them; and others reject them. But many academics preach them as gospel truths.

Getting Hooked to Political Positions

Programmes of political parties include ideological elements. This leads to affinity between political parties and academics espousing similar ideological views. These academics lose their neutrality and objectivity. They become interested advocates of political positions. It is quite common to see academics appearing on TV and supporting party positions in awkward academic and political *Jugalbandi*. Their views have to be duly discounted.

Hasty Application of Theories to Social Issues

American scholars pioneered in their studies of social problems an empirical, practical, and statistical and factually grounded approach. This stands in contrast to theoretical approaches based more on pure logic and speculation. This practical application of knowledge and dislike of theories and ideologies partly explains the great American achievements in science and technology---which still continue.

But this approach of rapidly mixing theory and practice also creates difficulties in social studies. It works best in experimental and application-based knowledge. Its real life, case study methods also work well perhaps in management studies and teaching. But unlike in medicine or pharmacy or management, theories cannot be readily applied to social problems. The complexity of social problems precludes such ready application.

This can be illustrated with a simple example. People complain that hostile acts against foreigners in England have increased after Brexit. They attribute it to hate speeches of Brexit advocates like Nigel Farage. Incidentally, he is no fire breathing xenophobe. As many Indian origin people stay in UK, we should be grateful to the tolerant Brits for their concerns. But here we consider not their laudable sentiments but a methodological point.

We can assess such statements by forming a rough idea about such increase of 'hate crimes' by comparing crimes against foreigners in any town over comparable periods before and after Brexit. The difficulty is that even if there is an increase, it cannot be readily ascribed to hate speeches. There are far too many intervening variables such as circumstances of individual crime, criminal's motivation and social ambience of the crime scene. Students will easily understand this problem by browsing through chapters on hypothesis testing in any elementary Statistics book. But even academics (who are supposed to know better) glibly link events to their supposed causes.

Orchestrating Agendas through Ideologies

Many genuine but misguided people espouse unpopular agendas or causes due to ideological obsessions. But often the events especially those into which students are enticed are not innocent. There is more than meets the eye. Interested and malicious groups use these seemingly high minded movements for ulterior ends. They find it easy to target idealistic youth and misguided ideologues. These manipulators pulling the levers from behind have no interest in students or in democracy or in rights. They use these platforms and occasions for harming the nation Students should be on guard against such forces. They should focus on studies. They should look at issues dispassionately and objectively, and in Janet Yellen's words, adopt 'a data dependent approach'.

Some students may feel that we have been harsh on the left without mentioning the conservative right. Others may remind us of Madonna's song 'Papa don't preach'. We concede that we have been more critical of the left mainly because it has become the orthodox ideology. People tend to accept it uncritically as they accept current fashions. Somehow left wing radicalism has got into anti national stances on many matters. It is shy of any form of patriotism and promotes self-loathing. All these are unhealthy attitudes.

At the same time, we readily concede that right wing ideologies are often socially regressive, irrational and hark back to 'golden days gone by'. They create a halo over obscurantist religious and social practices.

HOW TO ANALYSE CONTROVERSIAL ISSUES?

But we have not delivered any sermons. We alert students to some pitfalls. We do not want tell students *what* they should think. It is their job. We focus rather on *how* they should think about issues. In conclusion, we explain how to deal with questions on current controversies.

Students are advised to carefully consider the approach we adopted in the next chapter in dealing with modern ethical conundrums. *Following the pattern we used in that chapter, students should consider the following five aspects of any burning issue:*

- Facts and issues involved
- Relevant theories bearing on it
- Stands which main ideologies take on the issue
- Supreme court/High court decisions, if any, on it
- Government's stand on the issue.

After reading about the first three dimensions, they should form their views based on the last two aspects.

As we have already mentioned, students should think logically and objectively about issues without succumbing to momentary passions or herd mentality or group think. Nor should they see such controversies as opportunities for airing unfounded personal opinions or slogan shouting. That is not the vocation of would be scholars, managers or civil servants. It is rather to patiently think through and analyse issues. It is in this spirit that we mentioned a few current controversies and traced certain views on them to their ideological roots.

Summary

- Political attitudes are best understood based on the idea of political spectrum.
- Political spectrum is depiction of radical, liberal, moderate, conservative and reactionary views from left to right along a line.

- The five terms designate political attitudes which (a) seek changes in the existing political set up and (b) which uphold certain political values.
- The five groups differ represent different views on political change, direction of change, depth of political changes they seek, speed of political change and methods of effecting change.
- "Radical" refers to individuals, parties, and movements that seek to drastically alter any existing practice, institution, or social system. As radicals are highly dissatisfied with the society, they want immediate and revolutionary changes, and espouse violence.
- The causes and aims of Radicalism and its forms have been changing in recent times. Many of these programmes have become part of the liberal democratic agenda in the West.
- Liberalism aims primarily at protecting and increasing an individual's freedom, and fearing government overreach, seeks to restrict government power.
- Over time, liberalism got divided into classical liberalism and modern liberalism. Classical liberalism argues that government should merely protect individual liberty. Modern liberalism believes that government should enhance individual freedom by promoting conditions for its enjoyment by the poor.
- To ensure government's accountability, liberals advocate government by majority rule through periodic election of government by popular vote.
- To reduce state power and protect individual freedom, liberals advocate separation of powers, periodic elections and creation of individual rights.
- Liberals generally disfavour state intervention in markets.
- They believe that free markets produce optimum results by maximizing production and ensuring due rewards to economic agents.
- Liberalism was questioned because unregulated industrialism created income inequalities, poverty and slums.
- The First World War and its turbulent aftermath shattered many liberal illusions. Between the two Great Wars, people turned to anti-democratic and to anti-liberal alternatives.
- JM Keynes propounded an economic doctrine that government management of the economy could smooth out the highs and lows of the business cycle and produce more or less consistent growth with minimal unemployment.
- Liberal policies in post War era brought about phenomenal growth in developed market economies. But growth slowed from 1970's.
- Liberals favour limited intervention in the market for correcting its weaknesses.
- They use progressive taxes for bringing greater equality of wealth and income.
- Contemporary liberalism tried to extend individual rights in new directions.
- It led to laws forbidding discrimination against African Americans; and movements for equal rights for women, gays and lesbians, the physically or mentally disabled, and other minorities or disadvantaged social groups. Liberalism historically has sought to foster a plurality of different ways of life, or different conceptions of the "good life,"

- Based on the right of individual choice, liberalism promoted contraception, divorce, abortion, and homosexuality. Emphasis on right to freedom of speech reduced restrictions on depicting sexual content in works of art and culture.
- Moderates may belong to groups who combine elements from two rigid systems or doctrines.
- It is difficult to characterise moderate political positions or to identify political groups allied with them.
- They live in an uncomfortable half way house and draw flak from committed party ideologues.
- Suspicion of government activism separates conservatism from liberalism and radicalism.
- Two famous thinkers associated with conservatism are Chateaubriand in France and Edmund Burke in England.
- According to conservatives, men are neither good nor rational. On the contrary, they are driven by passions and desires, and are naturally selfish, disorderly, irrational, and violent
- Conservatives distrust human nature, rootless individuals disconnected with traditional social values, and untested innovations
- Traditional political and cultural institutions are needed to curb men's base and destructive instincts.
- Conservative temperament abhors abstract argument and theorizing.
- Neoconservatives defended of middle-class virtues such as thrift, hard work, and self-restraint, which declined due to sexual freedom and lax life styles of 1960s.
- They identified high taxation and government's intrusive regulation of private enterprise as hurdles to economic growth.
- Social welfare policies, they feel, are making their recipients increasingly dependent upon government.
- Reactionary outlook favours restoration of a previous, and usually outmoded, political or social order. Reactionaries hanker after a society whose days are over. It is a form of nostalgia for the past.
- Political Ideology is a form of social or political philosophy which combines theory and practice. It is a system of ideas that seeks both to explain the world and to change it.
- In Destutt de Tracy's original conception, ideology has five characteristics. Particular categories of ideology are socialism, communism, anarchism, fascism, nationalism, liberalism, and conservatism.
- In one conception of Hegel and Marx, ideology is a set of beliefs with which people deceive themselves; it is false consciousness.
- Sociology of knowledge (exemplified by Weber and Mannheim) regards idea systems as the outcome or expression of certain interests. The true nature of ideologies is hidden from their followers.
- But this sort of approach which attributes doctrines or ideologies to a believer's unconscious mind runs into a contradiction. For the doctrine of sociology of knowledge itself becomes an unconscious rationalization. Mannerheim tries to overcome this difficult by postulating somewhat unconvincingly a classless class of intellectuals, a "socially unattached intelligentsia".

- Political theorists are divided on whether ideologies are rational or irrational.
- Many critics notably Albert Camus and Karl Popper analyzed the "total" character of ideology, and opposed its extremism and violence. Arendent condemned the systematic violence of ideology or the crimes of logic committed in its name.
- Ideological writings are replete with military and warlike language.
- Many ideological writers go beyond language use and frankly approve violence.
- Many writers distinguish between ideological and pragmatic approaches to politics. They think that pragmatism is better than ideology.
- Most of 20th century was dominated by "-isms". International diplomacy revolved around ideologies.
- Communism is a political and economic doctrine which seeks to replace private property and a profit-based economy with public ownership and control of the major means of production and the natural resources of a society.
- Marx is the chief theorist on Marxism. His theory covers three main aspects: (i) materialist conception of history; (2) critique of capitalism and its workings; and (3) revolutionary overthrow of capitalism and its eventual replacement by communism. Marxian ideas have been revised by later thinkers.
- Socialists advocate policies which meet the basic needs of the entire society instead of policies that serve needs of individuals.
- Later, socialists were called social democrats or democratic socialists. They reject Marxism Leninism.
- Social democrats support peaceful, legal efforts to work toward socialism, and they believe in multiparty competition and civil liberties.
- Anarcho-communists argue that the state and private property are interdependent institutions. The state exists to protect private property, and the owners of private property protect the state. If property is to be owned communally and distributed equally, the state must be smashed once and for all.
- Fascism is a totalitarian ideology. It opposes liberalism, conservatism, and socialism. Fascism claims to be an elitist response to modern social and political problems which other ideologies are unable to resolve.
- Many factors influence people's choices of political ideologies. They include: values, psychological traits, age, psychological reasons, and their view of human nature, their social milieu and economic interests.
- We tried to link various ideologies to Indian political and economic currents and contexts.
- We gave examples to show how ideological thinking influences debates on current issues.
- We mentioned that liberal western ideologies distort perceptions on current issues.
- Students should analyze burning issues based on facts and logic, relevant theories, positions of main ideologies on the issue, Supreme court/High court decisions, if any bearing on the issue, and government's stand on the issue. After reading about the first three dimensions, they should form their views based on the last two aspects.
- Students should think on the basis of facts and logic and not rely on spurious ideologies.

PRACTICE QUESTIONS

(Answer each question inclusive of parts in around 150 words.)

(1) What is meant by the spectrum of political attitudes? What are the five main categories of political attitude? What are the two aspects over which they differ?

(2) What is status quo? What is establishment?

(3) How are political attitudes and ideologies related? What are the main features of radicalism? Name radical Indian groups and their agendas.

(4) How will you define liberalism, classical liberalism and modern liberalism?

(5) What is neo-liberalism? Does it differ, and if so in what manner, from modern liberalism and conservatism?

(6) What are the main tenets of conservatism? What will you regard as conservative values in Indian social context? Do they have any relevance?

(7) 'Modern liberals make use of rights and entitlements as tools for fighting social justice.' Discuss. Explain how MGNREGA and recent initiatives on school education reflect this approach.

(8) Recently a social worker approached Supreme Court seeking a ban on pornographic internet sites. Analyze this issue from liberal and conservative perspectives.

(9) One recent newspaper editorial proposed that the Film Censor Board should be abolished. Discuss the proposal from the angle of principal ideologies and of Indian policy makers.

(10) List themes which were once considered as radical but have now become part of liberal agenda in the West. Illustrate with examples how this trend is influencing for good and bad attitudes to some social issues in India.

(11) How will you define ideology? Name some important ideologies and their position on the spectrum of political attitudes.

(12) Are ideologies reflections of false consciousness? What is the stand of sociology of knowledge on this question? Is it logically acceptable?

(13) Write short notes (50 words each) on: (i) ideology and rationality (ii) ideology and violence (iii) ideology and pragmatism and (iv) ideology and 20th century diplomacy.

(14) What are the main strands of Marx's theory of communism? What are the changes that Lenin introduced in it?

(15) How will you distinguish communism from social democracy? List the socialist components of Indian economic policies. Name those still in place after economic reforms.

(16) What are the main features of fascism? Why is it considered a dangerous doctrine?

(17) What are the factors which influence an individual's political attitudes? What weight will you assign to economic and psychological factors?

(18) What are the relevant aspects for analysing controversial issues? Should civil servants be guided by personal convictions or dominant ideologies or laws and court decisions?

(19) Discuss with examples the manner in which liberal western ideologies influence our thinking

on national and social problems. Point out the relevance and limitations of these ideologies to Indian political and social situations.

(20) Chinese communists and media proudly display their patriotic and national fervour and celebrate their global status and dominance. In India, communists and leftists are apologetic and diffident about nationalism. What could be the explanation of the opposing attitudes generated by the same ideology in the two countries?

REFERENCES

The Spectrum of Political Attitudes (Chapter 2): available on internet but with no mention of the book's title or the author.

Analysing Politics: An Introduction to Political Science Ellen Grigsby (available on internet)

Ideology Maurice Cranston Encyclopaedia Britannica

Radicals and Radicalism Dictionary of American History

Liberalism Terence Ball, Harry K. Girvetz, Kenneth Minogue, Richard Dagger Encyclopaedia Britannica

Conservatism Peter Vivereck, Terence Ball, Kenneth Minogue, Richard Dagger Encyclopaedia Britannica

MODERN ETHICAL CONUNDRUMS

Introduction

In this chapter, we discuss moral problems which have become prominent in recent times. They can be traced to two main sources: changes in social attitudes or mindsets towards human sexuality; and repercussions of advances in genetics and molecular biology. New problems that follow in the wake of these changes have important moral and legal dimensions. Another area we discuss is terrorism. We cover the doctrines, ideologies and worldviews influencing current thinking on terrorism, human rights and state integrity. We have outlined the Indian laws bearing on all these problems. Many problems covered in this chapter (and similar others) are discussed in US textbooks under the rubric 'applied ethics' because ethical theories and principles are used to analyse such problems.

HOMOSEXUALITY

Introduction

Human beings feel a natural sexual attraction for members of their opposite sex. This is commonly taken as a universal norm. But some men (called homosexual or gay) are sexually attracted towards other men. Similarly, some women (known as lesbians) are sexually attracted not to men but to women.

Religious and social customs have generally condemned homosexuality. For example, the Bible enjoins upon men and women, "Be fruitful and multiply". Obviously, no conception results from homosexuality, unlike in heterosexuality-union between persons of opposite sexes. The Bible denounces homosexuality as 'an abomination'. Hinduism and other religions regard marriage and procreation as essential stages of human life.

Although homosexuality was known from early human history, it carried strong social stigma. Many societies consider it a crime. Homosexuals used to inhabit a dark, shadowy world. In earlier times, if homosexuality of an individual became known, he was publicly denounced. Oscar Wilde, a famous literary figure, was imprisoned for his homosexuality. Others such as E.M. Forester and Andre Gide had to hide their homosexuality. In western society, homosexuality is no longer a taboo.

To a great extent, prejudices against homosexuals, lesbians, bisexuals and transgender (neither male nor female) are waning. Many states in USA allow same sex marriages.

In spite of such changing attitudes, homosexuals still face many problems. In India, homosexuality is a crime, though prosecutions of homosexuals are negligible. Many groups who consider themselves as liberal, secular, progressive and modern, advocate decriminalization of homosexuality. In this context, animated debates are held on the morality of homosexuality. In what follows, we discuss (i) the arguments in favour of and against homosexuality, (ii) its position under Indian law, and (iii) a possible stance towards it.

Arguments Against Homosexuality

Homosexuality is unnatural and perverse. It violates the natural mode of propagation of human species. Therefore, homosexuality is against the laws of nature; it militates against the morals of Nature.

Homosexuality is against divine commands. Even if we question the divine origin of moral commands, homosexuality still violates moral principles which most religions uphold. Marriage between sexes and rearing of children within families are important institutions. They not only regulate sexual behaviour but also ensure rearing of children in congenial and moral home environment. Homosexuality will destroy these anchors of stable social life.

Homosexuality sets a bad example for children by undermining conventional family and cultural values. If homosexual behaviour is instilled in children, and if it becomes widespread, humanity will not survive. Even if this fear may seem farfetched, there are real dangers of homosexuals assaulting children.

Many people believe that homosexual practices have led to rapid spread of HIV and AIDs. Homosexuals are officially recognised as high risk groups in spreading HIV and AIDs. Hence, homosexuality is not merely a private but also a public health risk.

We all live in societies which are predominantly heterosexual. To be honest, most people react to homosexuality with revulsion and distaste. Homosexuality is confined to a miniscule minority. There is no warrant to treat it as a main stream phenomenon.

On these grounds, it is argued that homosexuality should be prohibited in order to protect children and families, cultural and moral values and in order to ensure human survival.

Arguments in Favour of Homosexuality

Homosexuality is neither unnatural nor immoral. It is how some persons are sexually endowed by nature. It should not be considered as aberrant or deviant behaviour. Psychologists are not agreed on whether homosexuality is abnormal or normal in some circumstances. American Psychological Association has removed homosexuality from its list of mental diseases.

Just because a society is predominantly heterosexual, homosexuals cannot be labelled as immoral. No such conclusion can be validly drawn. No divine commands can be actually proved for there can never be any empirical evidence for them. They are matters of religious faith. They may be accepted by believers of a particular religion, but do not bind followers of other religions or agnostics or atheists.

It is true that prudent rules of behaviour or of husbanding resources can be drawn from Nature. But they carry no compelling force of logical demonstration. Further, it is impermissible to derive moral principles from facts of nature. This is known as the error of trying to draw moral conclusions from factual premises or values from facts.

Homosexuality is practised between consenting adults who are supposed to know what is good for them. As long as such behaviour does not harm others, no objections can be made against it. The spread of HIV and AIDS through homosexual contacts was due to ignorance of the homosexuals about risks of such contacts. Thereafter, homosexuals have adopted protective practices and have greatly reduced risk of spreading HIV and Aids. They acted far more responsibly than drug addicts in this regard.

Acceptance of homosexuality does not imply condoning sexual assaults on children. In fact, most child sex predators are heterosexuals. This is a matter of moral depravity which is unconnected with homosexuality.

Homosexuality is not a threat to family values. Many gay and lesbian couples in USA are adopting children. They are raising them in healthy home environment. Many US States have legalized such marriages.

Homosexuals are human beings, and part of our moral community. The fact that their sexual orientation or behaviour differs from that of others should be no bar to their right of humane treatment.

Homosexuality in the Indian Penal Code

Section 377 of the Indian Penal Code (IPC) makes homosexual sex punishable with life imprisonment. In September 2006, Amartya Sen, Vikram Seth and others demanded 'In the name of humanity and of our Constitution, abolition of this cruel and discriminatory law'. The Law Commission recommended retention of Section 377 in its 42nd and 156th report, but recommended its repeal in its 172nd report. The then health minister (2009) favoured abolition of Section 377. But the Home ministry opined that the abolition would increase criminal incidents of sodomy or offences involving sexual abuse of boys.

The United Nations urged India to decriminalise homosexuality. It would strengthen anti-HIV/AIDS drive by extending its benefits to homosexuals. As homosexuality is criminal, homosexuals cannot be given essential HIV, health and social services.

Court proceedings

In December 2002, Naz Foundation filed a Public Interest Litigation in the Delhi High Court challenging Section 377. On July 2, 2009, the High Court of Delhi struck down most of Section 377 as being unconstitutional. On December 11, 2013, in an appeal filed by Suresh Kumar Koushal and others, the Supreme Court upheld the constitutionality of Section 377 of the IPC. Supreme Court however declared that Section 377, to the extent it criminalises consensual sexual acts of adults in private, violates Articles 21, 14 and 15 of the Constitution. But it upheld the provisions of Section 377 covering non-consensual homosexuality and homosexual acts involving minors. Supreme Court also suggested that Parliament should suitably amend Section 377.

This judgment upholding Section 377 was met with opposition from some religious leaders. However, some religious leaders like Sri Sri Ravihsnaker opined that consensual sex between adults should be tolerated. Bills introduced by private members (as distinct from bills introduced by government) for decriminalising homosexuality were defeated in parliament. In August 2016, Cabinet approved the draft law on ban of commercial surrogacy (discussed later). The bill denied homosexuals from having surrogate children. Ms Sushma Swaraj said in this context: "*We do not recognise live-in and homosexual relationships….this is against our ethos*".

On 24 August 2017, the Supreme Court agreed to reconsider its 2013 judgment; it said it would refer petitions to scrap Section 377 to a five-member constitutional bench.

On 24 August 2017, the Supreme Court The judgement noted, "Discrimination against an individual on the basis of sexual orientation is deeply offensive to the dignity and self-worth of the individual. Equality demands that the sexual orientation of each individual in society must be protected on an even platform. The right to privacy and the protection of sexual orientation lie at the core of the fundamental rights guaranteed by Articles 14, 15 and 21 of the Constitution."

On 10 July 2018, the Supreme Court upheld the importance of the rights of the LGBT community. The court further decided that choosing a partner was every person's fundamental right.

On 6 September 2018, the Supreme Court struck down the part of section 377, criminalizing consensual homosexual activities. The court upheld other aspects of section 377 criminalizing unnatural sex with minors and animals.

ABORTION

A Cursory Review of Reproductive Biology

This background will help in understanding the debates not only on abortion but also on embryonic stem cell research.

Conception or fertilization takes place when a female germ cell or ovum is penetrated by a male germ cell or spermatozoon. The result is a single cell containing a full genetic code of forty-six chromosomes known as zygote. In ordinary course, in 2-3 days the zygote moves down the fallopian tube which carries ova (plural of ovum) from the ovary to the uterus. After reaching the uterus, the multi cell zygote floats in the fluid inside uterus, and develops into a blastocyst. The blastocysts are microscopic balls of undifferentiated cells. At the end of the second week, the blastocyst gets attached to the uterine wall. From the end of the second week until the end of the eighth week, the unborn entity) is called embryo (or as conceptus). During the period from 4th to 5th weeks, organ systems start developing, and embryo shows the outlines of external human form.

In the 8th week, brain activity becomes detectable. From this stage, the conceptus is known as foetus though in common language the term is used from the beginning of inception. Two other terms are important in designating the development of foetus. One is 'quickening' which refers to the point when the mother is able to feel the movements of the foetus. The second term is viability which designates the point at which the foetus is able to survive independently outside uterus.

The main stages of pregnancy and their time lines are shown in the following table.

Developmental time table

Stage	Time
Zygote	1-3 days
Blastocyst	From 2nd day to end of 2nd week
Embryo	3rd week to 8th
Foetus	9th week until birth
Quickening	13th to 20th week
Viability	From 24th week

Abortion refers to the termination of the unborn entity (or termination of pregnancy) at any of the above stages. Abortions at times occur due to internal biochemical processes of the pregnant woman or due to injuries suffered by her. These are known as miscarriages and create no moral issues. Debates on abortion centre on induced abortions which are brought about by human action.

Procedures for abortion

A brief outline on medical procedures for abortion will help in understanding why it creates a sense of unease in some circumstances.

In very early stages, abortion can be induced by 'morning-after-pill'. It prevents the blastocyst from attaching to the uterine wall.

Vacuum aspiration is used for abortion until the 12th week (first trimester). In this method, the narrow opening of uterus, cervix, is dilated; a small vacuum tube is inserted in uterus; and its contents are removed through suction.

Dilation and extraction (D&E) procedure is commonly used for abortion after the 12th week of pregnancy. In D&E also, the cervix is dilated; but doctors have to use surgical instruments, instead of a suction tube to empty the uterus. Until the 15th week of pregnancy, the tissues of foetus can be easily broken; and a spoon-shaped instrument (curette) is used to scrape uterus walls in order to ensure that no foetal issue remains. Thereafter, the foetus becomes too large to pass through cervix; the bones harden and are difficult to break. Evacuation requires that foetus be dismembered after it is partially pulled through cervix. A little later, the procedure becomes more cumbersome with need to collapse the skull.

Before D&E became popular, abortions were induced by saline injection i.e. introducing salt water into uterus. This went out of use because it is unsafe for mothers.

Another method of abortion is mifepristone or RU-486, the abortion pill. This works by blocking the action of progesterone which is a steroid hormone needed to maintain pregnancy. Incidentally, this pill cannot be used after the 7th week following the woman's previous menstrual period.

Moral issues surrounding abortion

For long time in history, women hardly had a safe medical option for ending an unwanted pregnancy. But with the discovery of safe abortion procedures, it became possible for women to decide whether or not to terminate an unwanted pregnancy. Many countries have legalized abortion, and created clinics for abortion. Abortion debate has therefore lost some of its earlier intensity. However, anti-abortionists (described as prolife) still attempt through laws and court cases to restrict the rights of women for abortion. And pro-abortionist groups (known as prochoice) attempt to remove all restrictions on abortion and to provide full public funding for it.

Abortion debates involve two broad issues: (i) the value of life, both of mother and foetus; and (ii) individual freedom and rights of women over their bodies. These debates also cover the rights of foetus or unborn baby, definitions of human life and the point at which life begins.

Arguments against abortion

(1) The genetic make-up of a human being is constituted as soon as the chromosomes of male sperm and female ova are united. Once this union is established, it leads to creation of a unique individual. Therefore, the conceptus has full human status.

(2) Every unborn, innocent child has full human rights from the time of conception. Its life is as sacrosanct as that of any other human being. Its right to life is absolute i.e. it overrides the rights of the pregnant woman.

(3) Respect for human life in its every state and stage is a cardinal principle. Once disregard is shown to early human life, it will in principle get extended to human life in general. The value and worth of human life will get degraded. This can lead to ruthless and cruel measures as the experience of Nazi Germany shows.

(4) Abortion procedures are hazardous for a woman's physical and psychological health. As we noted earlier, abortion procedure after the 12th week can harm a woman's reproductive system. It makes women vulnerable to future miscarriages. Some women may feel that abortion involves killing a 'would-be-baby'. Abortion may create feelings of guilt in a woman's mind and create psychological stress.

(5) Nowadays, many simple contraceptives are available for preventing pregnancy. An unwanted pregnancy often results from a woman's carelessness or irresponsibility. Once pregnancy occurs, parents should accept their responsibility, and should not victimize innocent life.

(6) There are alternatives for abortion. Many childless couples are willing to adopt babies. They would happily welcome the unwanted babies into their homes. Further, many public institutions are available for housing unwanted babies. These two alternatives are open to poor parents who cannot afford to have another child.

(7) Most religions oppose abortion in all its forms. Since most people have religious beliefs, they may not like abortion. Parents, who feel compelled by economic circumstances to resort to abortion, may experience cognitive dissonance.

Arguments in favour of abortion

(1) Women have absolute rights over their bodies, including procreative rights. If they become pregnant accidentally, they can undergo abortion. It is just another method of birth control which can be used if others fail. Conceptus, in this view, is another part of a woman's body until it is born. She has absolute right to decide whether or not to continue pregnancy. Further, pregnant woman alone should be allowed to decide whether or not to undergo abortion.

(2) Strict abortion laws arose from a patriarchal mindset. Since men never experience the troubles and travails of pregnancy, they can afford to show phony feelings of reverence for unborn life. Unwanted pregnancies can completely disrupt a woman's plans and dreams for her future. She can therefore decide whether or not to have an abortion.

(3) Foetus is not a 'person' and hence not a being to whom human rights apply. Here, we have to distinguish biological or genetic concept of humanity from psychological or moral concept of humanity. The idea that whoever is conceived by human beings becomes human immediately upon conception is untenable. It is quite a while before a conceptus even acquires a semblance of human form. In very early stages, it has no brain architecture, and hence no sensations or feelings.

(4) The concept of psychological humanity or personhood involves the following traits:

- Consciousness of external world and the capacity to feel pain
- Reasoning ability
- Self-motivated activity independent of genetic or external control
- Capacity to communicate
- Presence of self-concept and self-awareness

None of these traits constituting psychological or moral humanity is found in conceptus. Hence, it has no quality of humanity.

(5) If abortions are prohibited or severely restricted, women rely on illegal and dangerous 'back alley abortions'. Further, poor women, who can ill afford high end abortion facilities, bear the brunt of the risks and hazards of illegal abortions.

(6) Any serious birth defects or dangerous medical conditions in foetus can be usually detected after 9th week of pregnancy. In this situation, abortion is the only way to prevent birth of a human being condemned by nature to debilitating or dangerous hereditary diseases.

(7) Neither handing over new born babies for adoption nor placing them in public charitable orphanages is an attractive alternative. To argue that a woman should carry her pregnancy to term for these purposes is unconvincing. First, they cause much greater stress to a woman than early stage abortion. Secondly, public homes for orphans lack personal and humane touch and are inhospitable locales for growing children. Adoption has its own problems with chances of foster parents losing interest in their adopted children.

(8) In some situations, abortion is virtually the only way out: pregnancy resulting from rape; pregnancy which endangers a mother's life; and incurable birth defects in a foetus.

(9) In modern times, abortion is very safe, and unlikely to cause any mental traumas especially in early stages of pregnancy. It is one of the methods included in programmes for Planned Parenthood. We may conclude that couples should follow preventive methods to avoid unwanted pregnancies. If abortion becomes necessary, it should be undertaken in early pregnancy. Well off couples should accept accidental pregnancies.

Indian law on abortion

Before 1971

Under the Indian Penal Code, induced abortion was illegal. Both abortion practitioners and the woman undergoing abortions were liable to prison and/or a fine. The only exception was when abortion was induced in order to save the life of the woman. Widespread incidence of illegal abortions, and the view that abortion could be a means of birth control led government to reconsider the law.

Post 1971 situation

Abortion in India is now covered under the Medical Termination of Pregnancy (MTP) Act 1971. According to MTP Act, Pregnancies not exceeding 12 weeks may be terminated based on a single doctor's opinion formed in good faith. In case of pregnancies exceeding 12 weeks but less than 20 weeks, termination needs opinion of two doctors. Abortion is legal only up to twenty weeks of pregnancy.

The MTP Act specifies the persons qualified to conduct the abortion and the places where abortions can be done. It permits abortions in the following circumstances:

- When physical and/or mental health of the woman are endangered by the pregnancy
- When pregnancy is likely to result into the birth of a potentially handicapped or malformed child
- Pregnancy resulting from rape
- Pregnancy in unmarried girls under the age of eighteen with the consent of a guardian
- Pregnancy in 'lunatics' with the consent of a guardian
- Pregnancy due to failure in sterilization

An adult woman requires no other person's consent except her own. Recently, Supreme Court permitted a rape survivor to terminate her pregnancy at 24 weeks, which is beyond the permissible 20 weeks limit under the MTP Act.

Sex selective abortions

Indian couples have a strong preference for a male child. This led to misuse of the provisions of MTP Act for conducting abortions of female foetuses. Subsequently, new technologies such as sonography made sex detection easier, and increased sex-selective abortions. To control these abortions, the Pre-natal Diagnostic Techniques (PNDT) Act, was passed in 1994.

PNDT Act

The PNDT Act provides for the following:

- Prohibition of sex selection, before and after conception
- Regulation of prenatal diagnostic techniques (e.g., amniocentesis and ultrasonography) for the detection of genetic abnormalities, by restricting their use to registered institutions
- Use of these techniques only at a registered place, for a specified purpose, and by a qualified person registered for the purpose
- Prevention of misuse of such techniques for sex selection, before or after conception
- Prohibition of advertisements of any techniques used for sex selection and for sex determination
- Prohibition on sale of ultrasound machines to persons not registered under the Act
- Violations of the Act are cognizable, non-bailable and non-compoundable and carry stiff prison terms and fines.

CLONING

We now turn to moral problems which recent advances in genetic engineering have thrown into sharp relief. We consider such issues from three domains of advancing technology: cloning, stem cell research and surrogate motherhood. Some moral problems emanating from cloning, stem cell research and abortion overlap. But cloning and stem cell research also give rise to more complex theological and metaphysical questions. *A brief biological background on cloning and stem cell research helps in understanding these issues.*

Biological Background

A clone is an exact genetic copy of a molecule, cell, plant, or animal. It is no novel phenomenon but common in nature. Whenever single cell organisms like bacteria reproduce by cell division, the resultant cells are clones of the original cells. Similarly, when a worm is divided into two parts, each part will regenerate into a full genetic duplicate of the original worm. Identical twins resulting from separated embryos in uterus are natural clones.

Cloning refers to various processes used to produce genetically identical copies of a biological entity. A clone is the copied material, which has the same genetic makeup as the original. Scientists have cloned a variety of biological materials like cells, tissues and even whole organisms, such as a sheep.

There are three different types of artificial cloning: gene cloning, reproductive cloning and therapeutic cloning. Gene cloning produces copies of genes or segments of DNA. Gene cloning is also known as DNA cloning. Reproductive cloning produces copies of whole animals. Therapeutic cloning produces embryonic stem cells for experiments aimed at creating tissues to replace injured or diseased tissues. Gene cloning denotes a very different process from reproductive and therapeutic cloning. Reproductive and therapeutic cloning share same techniques, but for different purposes.

Gene cloning

Scientists use gene cloning in order to generate copies of genes that they select for study. In this procedure, a gene from one organism, (called foreign DNA) is inserted into the genetic material of a carrier called a vector. Vectors include bacteria, yeast cells, viruses or plasmids, which are small DNA circles carried by bacteria. After inserting the gene, the vector is multiplied in a laboratory so that the gene is replicated on a large scale.

Reproductive cloning

In reproductive cloning, researchers remove a mature somatic cell from an animal that they wish to copy. Somatic cells are all the cells that make up an organism, other than sperm or egg cells. Researchers then transfer the DNA of the donor animal's somatic cell into an egg cell, or oocyte, that has had its own DNA-containing nucleus removed. Thus, to make a clone, scientists transfer the DNA from an animal's somatic cell into an egg cell after removing its nucleus and DNA. The egg develops into an embryo that contains the same genes as the cell donor. Then the embryo is implanted into an adult female's uterus to grow. In due course, the adult female gives birth to an animal that has the same genetic makeup (clone) as the animal that donated the somatic cell. Reproductive cloning may require the use of a surrogate mother to allow development of the cloned embryo. This was how the most famous cloned organism, Dolly the sheep, came into being. Clones contain identical sets of genetic material in the nucleus–the compartment that contains the chromosomes–of every cell in their bodies. Thus, cells from two clones have the same DNA and the same genes in their nuclei.

Therapeutic cloning

In therapeutic cloning, cloned embryos are made solely for producing embryonic stem cells with the same DNA as the donor cell. Stem cells have the ability to divide repeatedly and give rise to both specialized cells and more stem cells. Stem cells derived from embryos are called embryonic stem cells. Embryonic stem cells (ES cells) are also called pluripotent stem cells because their progeny include all cell types that can be found in a post-implantation embryo, a fetus, and a fully developed organism. They are derived from the inner cell mass of early embryos (blastocysts). These stem cells can be used in experiments aimed at understanding diseases and developing new treatments for diseases. The richest source of embryonic stem cells is tissue formed during the first five days after the egg has started to divide. At this stage of development, called the blastocyst, the embryo consists of a cluster of about 100 cells that can become any cell type. Stem cells are harvested from cloned embryos at this stage of development, and result in destruction of the embryo while it is still in the test tube

Potential applications of therapeutic cloning

Researchers hope to use embryonic stem cells, which have the unique ability to generate virtually all types of cells in an organism, to grow healthy tissues in the laboratory that can be used replace injured or diseased tissues. In addition, it may be possible to learn more about the molecular causes of disease by studying embryonic stem cell lines from cloned embryos derived from the cells of animals or humans with different diseases. Finally, differentiated tissues derived from ES cells are excellent tools to test new therapeutic drugs.

Risks of therapeutic cloning

Stem cells have a striking resemblance to cancer cells. Both cell types have the ability to proliferate indefinitely and some studies show that after 60 cycles of cell division, stem cells can accumulate mutations that could lead to cancer. Therefore, the relationship between stem cells and cancer cells needs to be more clearly understood if stem cells are to be used to treat human disease.

As for human beings, no cloning is allowed. Human cloning is as yet only a theoretical possibility. Moral discussions on human cloning are based on futuristic scenarios.

Arguments in favour of cloning

(1) An important unresolved problem in psychology is how human beings acquire their traits of character. Are such traits derived mainly from one's biological make-up or are the outcomes of the environment in which one is raised or the result of chance factors? This knowledge will help in formulating appropriate approaches to child development. Children will grow into healthy, happy adults and be able to realize their potentials.

(2) Cloning can benefit society by creating clones of great scientists, artists, and sportsmen/women. It is simplistic to assume that great scientists or mathematicians such as Max Planck or Carl Gauss can be reproduced through cloning. Besides native intelligence, other factors like unique early life environment and interest in fruitful research areas explain great scientific achievement. Obviously, these are not replicable. However, factors which contribute to creativity such as tenacity, concentration, determination and self-belief can be created to some extent through a right combination of heredity and environment.

(3) Healthy and happy life of an individual greatly depends on his heredity. It can endow him with a long, disease-free life and cheerful temper; or it can render one's life short and troublesome physically and psychologically. By cloning an individual who has no major debilitating or psychological problems like depression, healthy and happy individuals can be produced.

(4) Many parents desire that their children should have specific talents or traits. They may want their children to have specific scientific or artistic talents. In some measure, cloning can produce such offspring.

(5) In future, cloning can be a solution to infertile couples. But as we noted, at present cloning is prohibited for such reproductive purposes. It raises many intriguing ethical issues.

(6) Though reproductive cloning is illegal, therapeutic cloning for creating replacement tissues or 'body spare parts' holds great promise. An embryo can be created for generating an organ for transplant.

Arguments against cloning

(1) Cloning deprives the clone of the right to be a genetically a unique individual. It impairs the uniqueness of on individual, and is intrinsically immoral. However, philosophers disagree on this point. Mere presence of an identical being---in a distant land or planet---in no way affects an individual. Even if an individual knows about the existence of his double or genetic copy, it makes no difference to him. Further, cloning does not produce another individual biologically indistinguishable from the original. This can be seen from the following table.

Relationship	Correlation of traits in %
Identical twins*	50
Fraternal twins*	25
Non-twin siblings	11
Strangers	Close to zero

***Fraternal twins** are "dizygotic," meaning that they developed from two different eggs fertilized by two different sperm cells, while **identical** twins are "monozygotic" i.e. they developed from a single fertilized egg that split.

(2) Another objection to cloning relies on what may be called 'an open future argument' or 'right to ignorance of a certain sort'. According to this argument, the future of a clone appears to him or her like a rerun of an earlier life. It resembles a refurbished model. The clone may lose feelings of novelty or miss elements of surprise which are part of normal life. He may have a sense of following a well-worn path in life. Knowledge of the life experience of the original person, his successes and failures in life, will constrain the clone's future; it will shut out many experimental life moves he could have made. In reply, it is argued that such fears are exaggerated. Besides one's genetic make-up, external circumstances will affect his/her course of life. The life histories of identical twins---natural clones---are often very different.

(3) It is further claimed that even if we discount the arguments based on need for individual identity or for open future, the clone nevertheless experiences psychological distress. He may regard himself as no more than a duplicate or a photocopy without individuality and deprived of prospects of open life horizons. This point has been answered earlier. We may note further that since these feelings are irrational and incorrect, they merit no consideration.

(4) Although reproductive cloning is prohibited, many writers point to alarmist future possibilities. They can be termed as 'brave new world' anxieties. Aldous Huxley, in his novel *Brave New World*, envisaged a future society in which different social categories such as proletarians, clerks, intellectual workers and political leaders are genetically created as test-tube babies. They are pre-programmed, and each fits snugly into his social station, experiencing no discontents or grievances. Cloning can theoretically be used to similar sinister purposes. One may Xerox many Hitlers or murderous soldiers for savage regimes. These fears belong more to science fiction than to any possible reality.

(5) Human beings have to be considered as ends in themselves and not as instruments for achieving some other goals which transcend intrinsic human worth. This view is widely accepted among philosophers. While it may apply to reproductive cloning, its force is greatly reduced in settings of gene therapy.

(6) Cloning may appear to violate the principle of individual personal autonomy. Once a clone is created with various predispositions, he will no longer develop into a free, spontaneous being. This point is partly valid. But all said and done, cloning only creates certain attributes and dispositions in individuals. These are potentialities and can be used in diverse ways by an individual.

(7) Writers also point to some other risks of cloning. It can reduce diversity among human beings which nature has created, and lead to some form of human monocultures. Cloning is tantamount not to exercising procreation rights but to manufacturing human beings which can never be justified. Cloning is open to danger that people may be cloned without their knowledge or consent. Cloning messes up family relationships. If a woman bears her husband's clone, is he the father to the son she bears or its twin brother?

(8) According to Micahel J. Sandel, cloning alters our perspective on nature and undermines important human values. Human beings are children of nature and have no role in creating their biological make-up. Whatever natural talents or traits or abilities they have are gifts of nature. We attribute these aspects of being to God, nature or chance. This creates in us a sense of humility and reverence towards nature. If we control this function of nature, we take our biological destiny into our hands.

This may not be an unmixed blessing. At present, we accept our biological endowments in a spirit of resignation. New technologies can make parents responsible at least partly for the traits of their offspring, and thus create moral dilemmas for them. They may be blamed for their choices or inaction. Cloning may reduce our sense of solidarity with our less fortunate fellow human beings. Often we attribute their misfortunes or failures to luck and chance. Once character and success become matters within our volition, we may blame the failures of others on their own incapacity. In this way, we lose empathy for them. In short, there may be grave dangers in tinkering with the tried and tested ways of wise nature.

In conclusion, we may note that cloning is in experimental stage yet. The first law regulating cloning is UK's Human Fertilisation Embryology Act (1990). It permits licensed research using human embryos only for very limited purposes involving studies into infertility treatment, congenital diseases, and causes of miscarriages, contraception techniques and the detection of genetic abnormalities.

GENE THERAPY

Brief Biological background

- **Genes** consist of deoxyribonucleic acid (**DNA**) as well as protein.
- DNA contains the code, or blueprint, used to synthesize a specific protein that functions in one or more types of cells in the body.
- Genes vary in size, depending on the sizes of the proteins whose code they contain.
- Each DNA molecule is a long double helix that resembles a spiral staircase containing millions of steps. The steps of the staircase consist of pairs of four types of molecules called bases (nucleotides).
- **Chromosomes** are structures within cells that contain a person's **genes**.
- **Chromosomes** are in the cell's nucleus.
- A chromosome contains hundreds to thousands of genes.
- Every normal human cell contains 23 pairs of chromosomes, or a total of 46 chromosomes.
- A trait is any gene-determined characteristic and is often determined by more than one gene.
- As the single cell divides, all **genes are** copied so that every new cell possesses a full set of **genetic** material: the **genome**.
- The human genome contains 20,687 protein-coding **genes**.
- In a non-dividing cell, each **chromosome** consists of one **DNA** molecule.
- Visualize the above information this way: **DNA** is in **genes**; **genes** are on chromosomes. When "mapping" all **genes** on all human chromosomes was first thought of, it was called the Human Genome Project - a combination of **gene** and chromosome.
- **DNA** is vital for all living beings: for inheritance, for coding for proteins and as the genetic instruction guide for life and its processes. **DNA** holds the instructions for an organism's or each cell's development and reproduction and ultimately death.
- Functionally, **DNA** maintains the **protein**-encoding information, whereas RNA uses the information to enable the cell to synthesize the particular **protein**.
- Gene therapy can be said to consist in removing mutated DNA and replacing it with its correct sequence or adding missing DNA.

(Students should note that the above information only provides minimal background for following ethical discussions on gene therapy. As genes/DNA/RNA etc. are important topics in general studies, they should master it fully from a standard NCERT text.)

Genes and diseases

Defects in genes present within cells can cause inherited diseases like cystic fibrosis, sickle-cell anaemia, and haemophilia. If some chromosomes are missing in a cell, diseases like Down syndrome are caused. A change in proper sequence of genes can cause diseases like atherosclerosis and cancer.

Gene therapy replaces missing genes or provides copies of functioning genes to replace defective ones. The inserted genes can be naturally-occurring genes that produce the desired effect or may be genetically engineered (or altered) genes.

Scientists have been manipulating a gene's structure since early 1970s through a process called gene splicing. The process involves removing a fragment of DNA which holds the needed specific genetic sequence, and inserting it into the DNA of another gene. The resultant product is called recombinant DNA, and the process genetic engineering.

Gene therapy introduces genes into the body to treat diseases. It corrects or replaces the genes which are defective and unable to perform the disease-controlling functions of cells. Somatic gene therapy introduces therapeutic genes at the tissue or cellular level to treat individual patients. Germ-line gene therapy inserts genes into reproductive cells or possibly into embryos so as to prevent children from inheriting the genetic defects of parents. Gene therapy was used first to treat inherited diseases like cystic fibrosis and Huntington's disease, and later to treat cancers, arthritis, and infectious diseases.

Viral vectors

Most gene therapy at present is somatic gene therapy in which therapeutic genes are inserted into tissue or cells to produce a naturally occurring protein or substance that is lacking or malfunctioning in a patient. Such insertion needs a means of transporting either the entire gene or a recombinant DNA to the cell's nucleus, where the chromosomes and DNA reside. Scientists use vectors or viruses as molecular delivery vans. The earliest common transport vectors were viruses. They were chosen because they invade cells as part of the natural infection process. They have a specific relationship with the host, which consists in their colonization of certain cell types and tissues in specific organs. As a result, vectors are chosen according to their attraction to certain cells and areas of the body.

First, the cells are removed from the patient's body, and the virus, or vector, carrying the correct gene is inserted into them. Next, the cells are placed into a nutrient culture where they grow and replicate. Once enough cells are gathered, they are returned to the body, usually by injection into the blood stream. Theoretically, as long as these cells survive, they will provide the desired therapy.

Problems in Gene Therapy

The potential scope of gene therapy is enormous. More than 4,200 diseases result directly from abnormal genes, and many others are partially influenced by a person's genetic makeup. *But many problems outlined below confront gene therapy*.

(i) Viral vectors must be carefully controlled; otherwise, they infect the patient with a viral disease.

(ii) Some vectors, like retroviruses can enter normal cells, interfere with natural biological processes, and possibly cause other diseases.

(iii) The immune system recognises and destroys other viral vectors, such as adenoviruses, reducing their therapeutic life.

(iv) It is difficult to maintain gene expression so that it performs its role properly after vector delivery. As a result, some therapies need to be repeated often to provide long-lasting benefits.

(v) Gene regulation is very difficult since they work together for turning other genes on and off. For example, certain genes work together to stimulate cell division and growth, but if these are not regulated, the inserted genes could cause tumour formation and cancer. Scientists yet have no idea on how to make the gene go into action only when needed. For safe and effective treatment, a specific gene should turn on, for example, when certain levels of a protein or enzyme are low and must be replaced. But the gene also should remain dormant when not needed to ensure it doesn't oversupply a substance and disturb the body's delicate chemical makeup.

Stem cells

Before considering the ethical issues involved in gene therapy, we need to consider the working of stem cells. A stem cell is a unique type of cell with remarkable qualities. It can differentiate into other types of functional cells like nerve cells or skin cells. It can renew itself, and also form, as mentioned, other cells. However, most stem cells reside in particular organs and tissues, and produce a limited range of cells. Thus, bone marrow cells only produce blood cells. These are known as adult stem cells.

Embryonic Stem (ES) cells are vastly more potent. They can produce any other type of cell--blood, brain, intestine, muscles, bone and skin. Hence, they are known as pluripotent. They can be isolated from embryo, and grown in Petri dishes in laboratory. They can grow continuously in culture. ES cells are taken from the pith of inner cell mass of embryo after six days of its growth. The genetic modification of cell in the dish becomes the genetic modification of organism in the uterus.

Human ES cells are obtained from in vitro fertilization clinics. By 1990s, in vitro fertilization has become a way of treating various forms of human infertility. IVF is performed by taking eggs from a woman after ovulation. Typically around 10-12 are obtained and fertilized with male sperm in Petri dishes. The embryos are briefly grown in incubators and implanted in uterus. Not all embryos are implanted. It is unsafe to implant more than three embryos. The other embryos are discarded. It is these embryos which are the source of ES cells.

Moral issues in Stem Cell Research

Some moral issues involved in stem cell research and abortion are similar. Essentially these revolve on when an embryo acquires life and about the sanctity of human life. We have discussed these earlier. Further, use of ES cells, if ever permitted in future in cloning, raises moral questions similar to cloning we discussed earlier. But human cloning is strictly prohibited. No genetically modified embryo is allowed in uterus. Gene therapy is also strictly regulated by governments.

(i) Although gene therapy is a very promising approach to treatment of disease, ethical concerns over its use and ramifications are often voiced. As present knowledge about gene manipulation and editing is limited and the long term effects of gene therapies are not fully known, testing these therapies on humans could have disastrous unknown results.

(ii) As with most clinical trials involving new therapies, including many drugs, the patients participating in these studies are those who have not responded to more established therapies and often are so ill that the novel therapy is their only hope for long-term survival. Their choices are born of desperation and wild hope.

(iii) Another questionable outgrowth of gene therapy is that scientists could possibly manipulate genes to genetically control traits in human offspring that are not health related. For example, if a gene is found that can enhance intelligence of children who are not yet born, will everyone in society, the rich and the poor, have access to the technology or will it be so expensive that only the elite can afford it?

(iv) The Human Genome Project, which is integral for future of gene therapy also has social repercussions. Genetic information about individuals when available can be used against them. Insurance companies will demand higher premium from disease-prone people. Employers could discriminate between two potential employees, one with a "healthy" genome and the other with genetic abnormalities.

Genetics embodies both the immense promise and the worst fears associated with modern biomedicine. The prospect of altering what many viewed as the blueprint of human life raised questions about 'playing God.' While some had hopes of eliminating virtually all disease, others saw the spectre of designer babies and catastrophic unintended consequences.

Stem Cell Guidelines in the Indian Context

ICMR and Department of Biotechnology issued National Guidelines (Guidelines) for Stem Cell Research. According to the guidelines, "*There is no conclusive proof of safety or therapeutic efficacy of stem cells in any condition yet. Unfortunately, some clinicians have started exploiting hapless patients by offering unproven stem cell treatments prematurely. Such fraudulent practices need to be stopped urgently, while ensuring that scientifically designed and responsible research on stem cells is not hindered.*"

The guidelines cover individual researchers, organizations, sponsors, oversight/regulatory committees and any others associated with both basic and clinical research on all types of human stem cells and their derivatives. The guidelines classify stem cell research into three categories, namely Permitted, Restricted and Prohibited categories. All institutions and investigators, both public and private, carrying out research on human stem cells should be registered with the NAC-SCRT through IC-SCR. All institutes engaged in stem cell research must establish an Institutional Committee for Stem Cell Research. A National Apex Committee for Stem Cell Research and Therapy (NAC-SCRT) will monitor and oversee activities at national level and Institutional Committee for Stem Cell Research (IC-SCR) at institutional level. These oversight committees shall ensure that review, approval and monitoring of all research projects in the field of stem cell research are done rigorously and effectively as per the national guidelines. Research using human stem cells shall have prior approval of IC-SCR for permitted research and of the NAC-SCRT for restricted research.

Research on human subjects involving cells and tissues derived from human embryos and foetuses must safeguard human rights, dignity, and fundamental freedom. This includes processes related to obtaining human tissues and cells for research, diagnosis and therapy. The fundamental tenets of beneficence, non-malfeasance, justice and autonomy should be adhered to in all research involving human subjects.

The guidelines make the following observation on status of gene therapy: "*Accordingly, any stem cell use in patients must only be done within the purview of an approved and monitored clinical trial with the intent to advance science and medicine, and not offering it as therapy. In accordance with this stringent definition, every use of stem cells in patients outside an approved clinical trial shall be considered as malpractice.*"

SURROGACY

Surrogacy means a practice whereby one woman bears and gives birth to a child for an intending (mainly infertile) couple with the intention of handing over such child to the intending couple after the birth. The Surrogacy (Regulation) Bill distinguishes between altruistic and commercial surrogacy. In altruistic surrogacy, no monetary incentives of any kind are given to the surrogate mother or her dependents or her representative. However, she can be paid for medical expenses incurred on surrogacy and insurance coverage. Commercial surrogacy refers to commercialisation either in whole or part of surrogacy services or procedures. Commercialisation may cover selling or buying of human embryo or trading in the sale or purchase of human embryo or gametes or selling or buying or trading the services of surrogate motherhood by giving incentives in cash or kind, to the surrogate mother or her dependents or her representative. Medical expenses incurred on the surrogate mother and on her insurance are excluded from incentives.

The Union Cabinet approved The Assisted Reproductive Technology (Regulation) Bill, 2020 (ART Bill). The purposes of the ART Bill are "the regulation and supervision of the assisted reproductive technology clinics and the assisted reproductive technology banks, prevention of misuse, safe and ethical practice of assisted reproductive technology services" and prescribing other connected provisions. The ART Bill was introduced in the Lok Sabha on September 20, 2020. India has emerged as a surrogacy hub for couples from different countries for the past few years. There have been reported incidents of unethical practices, exploitation of surrogate mothers, abandonment of children born out of surrogacy and import of human embryos and gametes. Widespread condemnation of commercial surrogacy in India has been regularly reflected in different print and electronic media for last few years. The Law Commission of India has, in its 228th Report, also recommended that commercial surrogacy should be prohibited by enacting a law. Due to lack of legislation to regulate surrogacy, the practice of surrogacy has been misused by the surrogacy clinics leading to rampant commercial surrogacy and unethical practices.

Assisted Reproductive Technology (ART)

The Bill defines ART to include all techniques that seek to obtain a pregnancy by handling the sperm or the oocyte (immature egg cell) outside the human body and transferring the gamete or the embryo into the reproductive system of a woman. Examples of ART services include gamete (sperm or oocyte) donation, in-vitro-fertilisation (fertilising an egg in a laboratory), and gestational surrogacy (in which the child is biologically unrelated to surrogate mother). ART services will be provided through: (i) ART clinics, which offer ART related treatments and procedures, and (ii) ART banks, which store and supply gametes.

The National Board

The National Board to be set up under the ART Act will have following powers and functions:

(a) to advise the Central Government on policy matters relating to the assisted reproductive technology;

(b) to review and monitor the implementation of the Act, rules and regulations made thereunder and recommend to the Central Government, any suitable changes therein;

(c) to lay down code of conduct to be observed by persons working at clinics, to set the minimum standards of physical infrastructure, laboratory and diagnostic equipment and expert manpower to be employed by clinics and banks;

(d) to oversee the performance of various bodies constituted under this Act and take appropriate steps to ensure their effective performance;

(e) to supervise the functioning of the National Registry and liaison with the State Boards; and

(f) to pass orders as per the provisions made under this Act;

The State Boards:

The powers and functions of the State Boards under the ART Act are:

- To follow the policies and plans laid by the National Board for clinics and banks in the State
- Co-ordinate the enforcement and implementation of the policies and guidelines for assisted reproduction based on the recommendations, policies and regulations of the National Board
- Exercise such other powers and functions as may be prescribed
- Give such directions or pass such orders as directed by the National Board

Regulation of ART clinics and banks

The Bill provides that every ART clinic and bank must be registered under the National Registry of Banks and Clinics of India. The National Registry will be established under the Bill. It will maintain a central database with details of all ART clinics and banks in the country. State governments will appoint registration authorities for facilitating the registration process. Clinics and banks will be registered only if they adhere to specified standards on specialised manpower, physical infrastructure, and diagnostic facilities. The registration will be valid for five years and can be renewed for a further five years. Registration may be cancelled or suspended if the concerned entity violates the provisions of the ART Act.

Conditions for gamete donation and supply

Only registered ART banks are authorized to screen gamete donors, collect and store semen, and arrange for oocyte donors. A bank can obtain semen from males between 21 and 55 years of age, and oocytes from females between 23 and 35 years of age. An oocyte donor should be an ever-married woman having at least one child alive of her own (minimum three years of age). The woman can donate oocyte only once in her life. A bank cannot supply gamete of a single donor to more than one commissioning couple (i.e., couple seeking services).

Conditions for offering ART services

ART procedures can only be carried out with the written informed consent of both the party seeking ART services and the donor. The party seeking ART services will be required to provide insurance coverage to the oocyte donor (for any loss, damage, or death of the donor). A clinic is prohibited from offering to provide a child of pre-determined sex. The Bill also requires checking for genetic diseases before the Embryo implantation.

Rights of a child born through ART

A child born through ART will be deemed to be a biological child of the commissioning couple and will be entitled to the rights and privileges available to a natural child of the commissioning couple. A donor will not have any parental rights over the child.

Offences and penalties

Offences under the Bill include:

(i) abandoning, or exploiting children born through ART,

(ii) selling, purchasing, trading, or importing human embryos or gametes,

(iii) using intermediates to obtain donors,

(iv) exploiting commissioning couple, woman, or the gamete donor in any form, and

(v) transferring the human embryo into a male or an animal.

These offences will be punishable with a fine between five and ten lakh rupees for the first contravention. For subsequent contraventions, these offences will be punishable with imprisonment for a term between eight and 12 years, and a fine between 10 and 20 lakh rupees.

Any clinic or bank advertising or offering sex-selective ART will be punishable with imprisonment between five and ten years, or fine between Rs 10 lakh and Rs 25 lakh, or both.

No court will take cognizance of offences under the Bill, except on a complaint made by the National or State Board or any officer authorised by the Boards.

CAPITAL PUNISHMENT

Introduction

As far back as in 1868, one Mr. Gilpin introduced a bill in British Parliament for abolishing capital punishment or death penalty. The liberal philosopher JS Mill opposed such abolition. Mill argued that the passage of the bill for abolition would be a 'fatal victory', and reflect 'an enervation, effeminacy, in the general mind of the country'. Immanuel Kant was harsher in his support of capital punishment:

The penal law is a Categorical Imperative; and woe to him who creeps through the serpentine –windings of Utilitarianism to discover some advantage that may discharge him from the Justice of Punishment, or even from the due measure of it. ... For if Justice and righteousness perish, human life would no longer have any value in the world. ... Whoever has committed a murder must **die.** *...*

Our purpose in beginning with citations from these two great philosophers is to dispel the notion that the case for abolition of capital punishment is obvious and straightforward. Opponents of death penalty often display nauseating moral smugness, and portray supporters of death penalty as blood-thirsty barbarians favouring an outmoded, savage practice. Capital penalty needs a balanced and sober approach.

Nature and definition of punishment

Moral philosophers consider punishment as made up of five elements. A punishment must (i) involve some pain or unpleasantness; (ii) must be administered under an existing law or rule; (iii) must be administered to someone who has been adjudged guilty of an offence; (iv) must be imposed by a person other than the offender; and (v) the punishment must be imposed by a rightful authority. These aspects of punishment are too well known to need any elaboration. By combining these five ingredients, we can formulate a definition of punishment. Punishment is harm inflicted by a rightful authority on a person who has been adjudged to have violated a law or rule. This definition sums up the legal conception of punishment. There can be other types of punishment as in parental discipline or in monastic orders.

Goals of punishment

We need to briefly consider theories of punishment since they underlie many arguments for and against death penalty.

Retribution

'**Retribution**' is punishment awarded for a wrong done. It is the view that any offence merits punishment, and the offender deserves it. Conventional theorists consider retribution as a principle of justice or retributive justice. In this view, offenders should be made to suffer in kind for the harm they caused to others.

There is another dimension to retributive justice. In any society, restrictions are placed on freedoms of people. Thus, one cannot steal someone else's car. If the thief is not suitably punished, it constitutes a form of injustice against law abiding citizens. Leaving crimes unpunished will disturb the social balance of fair arrangements, and will harm society. Hence, it is essential to impose just and proportionate punishments on those who break laws enacted by society.

Prevention

According to **preventive** theory of punishment, criminals should be penalised so that they do not commit the offences again. If a robber is locked up, he will be unable to steal while in prison. The punishment will make him realize that stealing is not a costless or painless operation.

Deterrence

The **deterrence** theory argues that criminals should be punished so as to dissuade or discourage others from committing crimes. It serves as a kind of warning to law breakers. It will thus help in lowering crime rate. Further, in order to be efficacious, punishment has to be severe enough and known to all concerned. Its visitation on criminals caught and charged should be certain.

Reform

The **reform** theory holds that punishment should induce criminals to realise their error in violating legal codes, and dispose them to follow law in future. Reforming criminals and their rehabilitation usually go hand in hand. But they are conceptually different. Reform seeks to change a criminal's attitudes, and wean him away from anti-social behaviour. Rehabilitation seeks to enable a criminal to become a useful and productive member of society.

The above four theories of punishment are not mutually exclusive. They overlap, and their elements have to be combined in order to make punishments morally legitimate. We may note that preventive, deterrent and retributive theories of punishment can justify death penalty. With this background, we can consider the arguments in support of and opposed to death penalty. Shorthand expressions are often used to refer to protagonists of the two rival positions. Those who support reinstituting or retaining capital punishment are called retentionists. They believe that capital punishment is justified in heinous crimes like premeditated or cold blooded murder. Abolitionists believe that capital punishment is never morally justified. We will now consider these opposing viewpoints.

Arguments 'against' and 'for' death penalty

The following account first gives arguments opposing death penalty and then the arguments supporting death penalty.

(i) **Against :** The most common argument against capital punishment is based on the sanctity of human life. Death penalty, according to critics, is legal murder. The crime committed by a criminal does not detract from the inherent value of his life. Citizens can be protected by imprisoning murderers without parole. Death penalty like legal torture and mutilation should have been abolished long ago.

For : Supporters of death penalty argue that it actually upholds the value of life by punishing depraved murderers. In this way, it shows respect for the life of the murder victim. Further, the logic based on value of life argument is false. If we extend this logic, then legal fines would imply lack of respect to property rights, and imprisonment would negate the principle of freedom. Premeditated or cold blooded murder is the gravest crime, and those who commit it should pay the maximum price with their own life. Moreover, death penalty cannot be placed among, to use phrases from US Constitution, 'cruel and unusual' punishments. Whether a punishment can be so characterized depends on contemporary moral standards, and by these standards, death penalty is neither cruel nor strange.

(ii) **Against :** Abolitionists observe that capital punishment is imposed with class bias. It operates against the poor, the uneducated, and the minorities. First, the poor and the underprivileged are more likely to be hanged than the rich and the privileged. Secondly, the death penalty is more likely to be imposed when the victim is poor than when he is rich.

For : Retentionists argue that this objection is not against death penalty per se, but the manner it operates at present in the judicial system. The class bias argument can be applied to other punishments, and in fact---as Marxists do---to the entire group of judges. The answer lies in reforming the judicial system and not in doing away with capital punishment.

(iii) **Against :** Abolitionists make another point based on risk of loss of innocent lives if there is any miscarriage of justice. Since death penalty is irrevocable, there no way of compensating wrongly executed persons. They suffer irremediable loss.

For : Retentionists point out that the chances of execution of innocent individuals are extremely low. The judges bend over backwards to exclude even a shadow of doubt about the guilt of the accused. Besides the intense judicial scrutiny, the accused are allowed to file mercy petitions to constitutional heads. The chances of convicting innocent people have greatly reduced with advances like DNA evidence.

(iv) **Against :** Contrary to common sense, death sentence has, as statistical evidence shows, no deterrent effect. Most murders happen on the spur of the moment due to uncontrolled passions arising from sudden provocation. As murderers seldom think beforehand about the crime, death penalty has no deterrence.

For : Statistical evidence is unreliable in matters of this sort. Normally, the risk which criminals perceive in any crime depends on the scale of the punishment. It stands to reason that death penalty carries the highest risk and deterrent effect.

(v) **Against :** Death penalty is a form of blood thirsty revenge. Law does not sanction torture of murderers who torture their victims; nor does it permit rape of rapists. In this way, penalties have become refined and humane. Hence, murder should not lead to death penalty.

For : Notwithstanding the high sounding humanism of this view, it fails to recognize that capital punishment alone balances the scales of justice in some cases. The purpose of punishment is not only preventive or reformative but also retributive. In crimes like coldblooded murder, proportionate justice has to be rendered through moral retribution. Society has the right and duty to express its moral outrage over heinous crimes committed against it.

(vi) **Against :** Another argument against death penalty is that murder convicts hardly commit murder again either when in prison or when on parole. Hence, executing them serves no preventive purpose.

For : In answer to this, retentionists argue that executions certainly prevent murderers from committing any more murders. If sentenced to prison, they can still be a threat to fellow inmates and prison guards. In any case there are other strong arguments in favour of death penalty.

(vii) **Against :** There are two other arguments sometimes used in the debate on capital penalty. One is that it compromises the judicial system. Since judges are reluctant to impose death sentences, they play down or undervalue even the sound evidence which the police produce. Even other authorities find excuses for condoning the offence.

For : The retentionists rebut the argument by observing that the problem is not with death penalty, but the way judges and others handle it. The remedy lies in correcting the procedures than in abolishing death sentence.

(viii) **Against :** Finally, it is argued based on US experience that executions are more expensive than life sentences. This counterintuitive fact is derived by calculating the time costs and legal expenses which death penalty cases entail.

For : The retentionists argue that the matter is not about costs but about principles of justice.

The Indian Context

IPC prescribes death penalty for grave crimes such as murder, rape resulting in victim's death, and waging war against the State. Similarly, The Arms Act, The Narcotic Drugs and Psychotropic Substances Act, The Scheduled Caste and Scheduled Tribes (Prevention of Atrocities) Act, The Commission of Sati (Prevention) Act, The Army/Air Force/navy Acts, contain capital punishment for serious offences.

Article 21 of the Indian Constitution guarantees the Fundamental Right to life and liberty for all persons. No person, it says, shall be deprived of his life or personal liberty except according to procedure established by law. Courts interpreted this to mean that that state can deprive a person of his life subject to fair and valid procedure under law. The central government has consistently maintained that it would retain death penalty to act as a deterrent, especially for those who are a threat to society.

The Supreme Court upheld the constitutional validity of capital punishment in "rarest of rare" cases. It ruled that if capital punishment is provided in the law and if the procedure is fair, just and reasonable, death sentence is constitutional. "Rarest of rare" cases imply that courts should specify "special reasons" while awarding death penalty. It should be given only when the option of awarding life imprisonment is "unquestionably foreclosed". Courts have to balance aggravating and mitigating circumstances in individual cases to ascertain whether ends of justice can be met by any punishment less than the death sentence. This will depend on two factors. First judges have to see if there is something uncommon about the crime which makes life imprisonment inadequate and calls for death sentence. Secondly, the circumstances of the crime should be such that even after according maximum weightage to the mitigating circumstances in favour of the offenders, there is no alternative except to impose the death sentence.

In some laws, punishments include compulsory death penalties. The Supreme Court ruled that such mandatory death penalty is unconstitutional. But some laws still have mandatory death penalties, and a few of them are before the Supreme Court.

ANIMAL RIGHTS

Introduction

Traditionally, moral philosophers discussed ethical issues in terms of human relationships. Individuals have moral rights (to human dignity) which others have to honour. In their turn, individuals should discharge similar obligations they owe to others. Philosophers excluded animal kingdom and Nature from moral discourse. According to conventional thinking, the terminology of Ethics or its categories are inapplicable to non-human entities. As we shall see, this view is derived from Western religious and philosophical traditions.

Traditional Western View

This approach towards animal rights is partly based on Judaeo-Christian religious ideas. In support of this view, authors usually cite Genesis, the part of the Bible which deals with God's creation of the world. In it, men are exhorted, *"to fill the earth and subdue it; and have dominion over the fish of the sea and over the birds of the air and every living thing that moves upon earth."* Another portion later says, *"Every moving thing that lives shall be food for you; and as I gave you the green plants, I give you everything."* This may seem to give unfettered licence to man to exploit other animals. But it was greatly diluted by preachers like St. Francis of Assisi, famous for his love of animals. However, the injunctions of the Bible promoted a tendency to regard animals as resources for human use.

Early philosophical thought reinforced this attitude. Rene Descartes, the founder of modern philosophy, regarded animals as biological automata. He believed (wrongly) that human reason is located in a non-material mind; animals lacked mind, and could have no feelings and pains. Immanuel Kant gave other grounds for excluding animals from moral considerations. As we saw, Kant urged that human beings should be treated as ends in themselves and not as means or instruments for achieving any other objectives, no matter however noble. He grounded this moral status of men in their ability to reason or to think conceptually. In modern terms, the sacredness of human life arises because men possess intelligence, reason and autonomy. This view automatically excludes animals, from moral consideration. Incidentally, Kant opposed cruel treatment of animals because it would make men coarse and cruel.

Another way of expressing this idea is that concepts of morality have application only within human society, and applying them to non-human context involves a 'category error'. In the words of Carl Cohen, *"The misapplication of concepts leads to error and, sometimes, to nonsense. So it is with rights also. To say that rats have rights is to apply to the world of rats a concept that makes good sense when applied to humans, but which makes no sense at all when applied to rats'*. Similarly, no arguments can ever be made in support of emotions of oak trees or criminality of snakes.

A stream of social thought known as 'contractarianism' implies that morality is exclusively a human institution. Morality consists of mutually agreed rules of behaviour whose purpose is to ensure smooth and harmonious working of social arrangements. As morality is viewed as a contract, it becomes applicable to only those members who participate in it. This idea of a kind of social contract is a legal fiction. It is a way of visualizing how social norms come into being and why they command wide acceptance. One problem with this view is that morality becomes inapplicable to those, who in some sense are excluded from the imaginary contract. This can give rise to discriminatory behaviour even within human societies. In any case, it will automatically exclude animals which cannot even notionally be parties to any contract.

New Approach

From early 1970s, environmental issues and animal rights became popular topics of discussion both among philosophers and lay public. (Recently in our country, public interest in *Jallikattu* and other animal sports has reignited the debate on animal rights.) In 1975, Peter Singer published his work *Animal Liberation*. Its basic message is---'All animals are equal'. It implies that human beings are also (biologically speaking) animals, and should not ill-treat or abuse other animals. Singer argues that men treat animals as a resource for human uses without bothering about the suffering and pain inflicted in the process on animals. He opposes any use of animals---whether for food, or for scientific experiments, or hunting and sport, or for making articles.

These views have led to lot of argumentation in support of and against animal rights. Few thinkers support callous or cruel treatment of animals. Disagreements revolve around two issues: the degree to which men should give up activities that involve cruel use of animals; and whether and how animal rights can be irrefutably established on logical grounds.

Case for Animal Rights-'Ethical Approach'

Notwithstanding conventional religious and philosophical ideas to the contrary, many writers have argued in recent times for animal rights. In support of their position, they rely on doctrines from ethics and rights theory. In one way, utilitarianism can support animal rights. Utilitarianism advocates that among possible courses of action open to moral agents, they should select that which maximizes net utility after considering both its advantages and disadvantages. While applying the utilitarian criterion, the benefits and harms resulting from actions should not be restricted to human beings but also be extended to animals. Bentham, who founded utilitarianism, had anticipated modern sensitivities on this question: "*The day* **may** *come when the rest of the animal creation may acquire those rights which never could have been withholden from them but by the hand of tyranny*". He also foresaw what could be a reasonable basis for animal rights: "*The question is not, can they* **reason**? **Nor**, *can they* **talk?** *But, can they suffer?*"

No clear conclusion in favour of animal rights can be, however, drawn from utilitarianism. Though animals do suffer in many ways from human actions, total ban on animal use for certain purposes leads to unacceptable consequences. Important medical discoveries like vaccines for polio, diphtheria, hepatitis, measles, rabies, rubella and tetanus, could never have been found without experimentation on animals. Extreme advocates urge a total ban on medical testing on animals irrespective of consequences. This view based on animal rights has few takers.

Right-Based View

The second strand of reasoning for animal rights is based on the view that animals are entitled to rights similar to those which human beings enjoy. As we saw earlier, many philosophers argue that the concept of rights makes sense only within a human community. The unique moral status of human beings arises from their abilities of conceptual thinking, speaking and independent decision-making. Further, men are sentient, self-conscious, with desires, hopes, and plans for future. Unlike animals, they can think of the future which holds out both hopes and anxieties. In this way, men have interests while animals lack ability to formulate or express their interests. As animals lack these human characteristics, they cannot be regarded as members of human moral community.

Animal rights protagonists challenge this view on various grounds. First, they question the appropriateness of the demarcation line drawn between human beings and animals. The relevant distinction, they claim, is not reason but capacity for suffering. This can be more fully described as capacity for suffering and/or ability for enjoyment or happiness. Animals have consciousness and feelings. They experience fear, anxiety, and joy. They are sensitive to pain. There is sufficient scientific evidence to show that animals can suffer pain. Although they cannot formulate their interests, men should take into account such interests. If we adopt this criterion, we can see that animals, no less than human beings, have rights.

Animal rights groups also accuse human beings of *speciesism*, that is, systematic discrimination based on species membership. Men are prejudiced in favour of fellow members of *Homo sapiens* and biased against other species. Advocates of animal rights bracket speciesism with sexism---prejudice against women---and racism----dislike of certain racial groups like blacks. In doing so, they may be stretching the point a bit far.

Animal rights activists also point to an inconsistency in applying the criterion of human dignity based on human intelligence and rationality. If this criterion is applied, then extremely retarded people and those in a vegetative comatose state should not be entitled to human rights. For example, they can be subjected to medical experiments and even put to death to end their misery. But no such acts are permissible, and the concerned individuals are treated humanely.

How should we evaluate these arguments? We are of the view that the case for animal rights is *logically* and *philosophically* unsustainable. To quote Carl Cohen again, "*Rights are universally human; they arise in a human world, in a moral sphere. In the human world, moral judgements are pervasive; it is the fact that all human beings including infants and the senile are members of that moral community---not the fact that as individuals they have or do not have certain special capacities, or merits---that makes humans bearers of rights.*" Therefore, even if animals possess certain attributes and abilities, these cannot confer rights on them in a human moral community. Of course, this is not to say that animals do not deserve care and concern. However, it is better to approach the question from the point of view of humane treatment of animals rather than from a rights perspective.

Way Forward

Many laws have already been passed for preventing wanton and needless cruelty to animals, and to ensure their humane treatment. Hence, we look at the human activities in which animals are abused, and consider the ways of reducing unnecessary suffering.

Use of animals for food

Human beings in primitive state were carnivores or meat eaters. Cave men hunted wild animals for food, clothing and for making primitive tools. Later, men began domesticating animals such as cows, pigs, sheep and poultry. Animals were grown and reared both for food and as a source of power in pre mechanical age.

Animals were raised in a 'free range system'. They were left free in fields with their mothers or in groups. They were, of course, killed but swiftly and without needless pain. But the methods of animal rearing changed with 'factory farming'. Animals are now often cooped up in dark, narrow pens with little moving space, and are injected with chemicals and hormones which ensure rapid growth. Other horrible practices are followed in order to make their meat palatable to consumer tastes. For example, deer calves (source of veal meat), are kept thirsty and forced into narrow dungeons so that veal meat looks pale and becomes soft.

Quite obviously, it is futile to hope that the world would adopt vegetarianism overnight. However, many people in the world are taking to vegetarian diet, or at least cutting down on meat consumption. The 'vegan' group in USA does not consume even animal products like milk. The moderate position in use of animals would consist of gradually reducing meat eating, raising animals in humane conditions, and killing them as painlessly as possible.

Medical experimentation on animals

There are scientific grounds which indicate that higher mammals feel physical pain as acutely as human beings. Even so, it may be impossible to altogether do away with medical experiments on animals. New drugs have to be tested on living organisms, and in the first stage, drug testing cannot be done on human volunteers. If medical experiments on animals are given up, the consequences will be catastrophic for medical progress and human well-being. Hence, drug testing on animals has to be allowed. But, strict guidelines have to be followed for medical experiments on animals. Gratuitous and pointless experiments on animals have to be prohibited. Books pleading for animal rights often contain blood curdling accounts of cruel animal experiments. It is essential to provide safeguards for minimizing pain to experimental animals.

Killing of animals for sport

Hunting has long been a royal sport. It was a considered a warrior sport which would promote courage. The flesh of many hunted animals was eaten. The body parts and skins of animals were used for various purposes. The heads of hunted animals were displayed as trophies. But in modern times, almost all these activities have been legally banned. But there is still considerable poaching and many animal parts (like ivory) are used for decorative purposes and under false beliefs as sources of male potency. Of course, hunting has to be strictly regulated as a sport; it can be allowed only for a few animals which tend to multiply too fast.

As regards, animal sports the position is more complicated. It shot into prominence with the recent controversy over *Jallikattu*. One may have to take a more nuanced view on traditional animal sports. Some of them like cock-fights (in Andhra), can be quite bloody. But other sports (for example bull or buffalo racing), do not aim at or result in animal deaths. These traditional sports have long ancestry. They should be allowed with suitable safeguards which minimize dangers to animal and human life.

With all the sympathy in the world for animals, one cannot help noticing the hypocrisy and selective opportunism of animal group activists. To put the matter plainly, most animals are killed for food, and not for sport. But animal activists usually raise a hue and cry over traditional sports like *Jallikattu.* In reality, the amount of violence involved in such sports is insignificant compared to slaughter of animals for food. The self-styled activists jump into the fray in practices such as *Ganesh Visarjan*, kite festivals, and use of Diwali crackers but remain discreetly silent in similar other matters. Be that as it may, any moves which make these traditional festive occasions less dangerous are welcome.

TERRORISM, STATE ACTION AND HUMAN RIGHTS

Introduction

Terrorism in its various hues is a serious problem plaguing the world now. India has also been in the cross hairs of terrorists since long. We need to separate terrorism form force and violence with which it is associated. Force involving elements of compulsion or coercion is socially acceptable as when a judge awards a prison sentence to a criminal. Violence which involves force and physical injury is justified in individual self-defence and/or when a nation fights its invaders. But few countenance violence for achieving political and social ends.

Notwithstanding the general loathing for terrorism, it occasionally evokes mixed feelings. Defence of terrorism has become fashionable in some quarters. Many citizens are disturbed when they sometimes come across open or thinly disguised defence of terrorism in public discourse and in television channels.

Defence of terrorism in such discussions wears a mantle of high morality, sublime and beyond the reach of smelly masses. Such defences of terrorism appear in the garb of high minded battles for intellectual liberty, academic objectivity, individual freedom and human rights. These defenders claim to uphold the democratic right of dissent and represent the worldviews of the oppressed. These defences obfuscate and cloud the moral issues which terrorism creates. This sows confusion and weakens the will to fight terrorism. It may seem that we are taking a militarist or anti-humanitarian stand and swimming against some streams of popular opinion. But our intention is simply to correct the one-sided view which students may gather from current discussions. This is particularly important since many defenders of terrorism are established academics, commentators and celebrities.

We will discuss the issues involved in terrorism from the perspective of moral philosophy. We will also trace the roots of what we regard as wrong perspectives on the challenges which terrorism poses.

Definition of Terrorism

Terrorism is defined in many ways. Its main attributes are the following:

- A type of violence harming people and damaging property
- Specific use of violence for achieving social and political ends
- Creating great fear, alarm and a sense of panic among people
- Reliance on random or arbitrary use of violence
- Targeting innocent people or non-combatants

Another definition of terrorism which Caleb Carr gave is: *"... the contemporary name given to, and the modern permutation of, warfare deliberately waged against civilians with the purpose of destroying their will to support either leaders or policies that agents of such violence find objectionable."* It is noteworthy that terrorism is warfare and aims at undermining peoples' will and belief in their way of living.

Ordinary people usually condemn terrorism. This attitude is part of common-sense. But what are the possible attitudes of ethical theories towards terrorism? As may be imagined, virtually no ethical theory supports terrorism. This may prove helpful since, as we have seen, ingenious explanations and defences of terrorism are sometimes offered.

Terrorism and Moral Theories

Consequentialism

Consequentialism may possibly condone some terrorist acts if their benefits or welfare effects far exceed the harm they cause. But this is only a theoretical possibility. Terrorism promotes the agenda of small groups at great cost to large populations. It imposes terrible costs on the targeted groups for questionable ends. Terrorist acts create backlash and stiffen opposition to terrorist aims. Terrorist groups often claim to be fighting for justice or for removal of injustice. Very few people subscribe to the justice of terrorist causes. It is, therefore, most unlikely that the net gains from terrorist acts can ever exceed the losses.

Consequentialist theory will also question the efficiency and efficacy of terrorist means. There are other means such as peaceful non-cooperation and civil disobedience for achieving political ends. Democracy allows other means of advancing one's agenda, and these conform to political morality.

Consequentialist thinkers point out that what counts as doing justice in a given situation is often unclear. For example, in the Arab-Israeli conflict, is it possible to remove grievances of one side without adding to the grievances of the other? If we take into account the above considerations, few real life terrorists will be able to measure up to the requirements imposed by consequentialism.

Kantian and natural law approaches

Two other moral traditions---Kantian and natural law---are directly opposed to random violence which terrorism causes. They impose an indefeasible prohibition on the killing of the innocent. 'Indefeasible' here means that killing of innocents is never permissible in any circumstances whatsoever. Sometimes this prohibition is expressed as the right of innocents not be killed or as our duty not to kill innocents. Thus, these traditions will never permit killing of innocents in malls, restaurants or on railway platforms. This is of course absolutely in line with common-sense.

Terrorists therefore portray the victims as far from innocent. They may claim that the targets belong to national groups which sanctioned injustice and oppression, and are therefore, complicit in evil deeds. The term 'innocent' usually designates an individual who is not guilty of moral or legal wrong doing. Terrorist groups tend to attribute remote and farfetched constructive liability to innocent people. For example, Emile Henry, after exploding a bomb in 1894 in a Paris cafe said, "There are no innocents". This statement is, of course, a fig leaf to cover the crime.

Contractarian view

How will contractarianism react to terrorism? This tradition conceives justice as a system of principles and dispositions which bind a group of people in so far as they mutually abide by that system. To use a phrase from John Rawls, justice is a sort of "cooperative venture for mutual advantage". According to this view, justice is not binding under certain conditions, as for example, in the absence of cooperative behaviour and dispositions from others. Thus, terrorists place themselves outside the justice system by violating common (moral) principles and dispositions. In this view of the matter, the terrorist acts are ab initio unjust and indefensible, and deserve to be put down.

Up till now, we considered how different moral approaches are likely to view terrorism. Naturally, these approaches lead to conclusions similar to common sense ideas. Terrorists are misguided, ferocious fanatics who have no regard for human life or common decencies. Still, some writers seek to create a false, revolutionary, romantic halo (a la Che Guevara) around terrorists. Impressionable, idealistic young men and women have to guard themselves against this tendency.

Terrorism in India and State Responses

In India, terrorism has diverse origins and aims. Whatever its form, terrorism questions the legitimacy of the state and its instrumentalities. It regards security forces and law and order machinery as oppressors and enemies. Terrorists engage security forces in war-like operations. Naxalites espouse what they consider as economic justice agenda. Terrorism in J&K is externally sponsored. In the north-east, it is linked to local identities. We have characterized these movements in single sentences since our aim is only to outline the moral issues they create.

In early years after our Independence, government measures to tackle terrorism and secessionist movements enjoyed almost universal support. There were occasional reports about the excesses of army and/or paramilitary forces in North-East. But gradually disquiet arose in some quarters over the means being used for handling terrorists. We need to consider the roots of such disquiet and the groups which articulate it. As we shall see, some people feel that anti-terrorist operations violate liberal, democratic, humanist and legal norms. However, as there is a trade-off between these norms and the requirements of national security, a balance has to be struck between them.

Administrative and Legal Fallout of Encounters

Operations of security forces against terrorists lead to varied outcomes. A terrorist may be captured during surveillance or investigations. He may be charged for serious offences. Then he becomes entitled to fair trial, due process of law and all the judicial safeguards available to ordinary criminals. The standard of evidence for proving guilt is as high as in ordinary crimes. It is but natural that few witnesses would like to risk their lives by deposing against the accused.

Terrorists are not treated as enemy agents. Although, according to Caleb Carr, terrorism is a form of warfare, terrorists are covered (asymmetrically) under ordinary law like other criminals. US security missions against hard-core terrorists are often based on the principle, 'Take no prisoners'. The purpose is either to avoid ordinary trials of such terrorists or to avoid the inherent risk in trying to capture terrorists alive.

Often, encounters take place between security personnel and terrorists with casualties on both sides. In these encounters, lives of soldiers are greatly imperilled. They have to observe prescribed rules of engagement while fighting terrorists in encounters. If terrorists die, they cannot be tried. But at times, relatives of deceased terrorists and activists file criminal charges like murder against men conducting operations. Existing laws partly insulate government servants, including security personnel, from culpability for acts done in good faith in line of duty. As such general law protection is inadequate the Armed Forces Special Powers Act (AFSPA) is enforced in disturbed areas. The provisions of this Act are outlined later in the chapter.

Terrorist deaths in encounters create uproar in media and activist community. Encounters are often depicted as brutal suppressions of human rights, security forces as cold blooded killers, and terrorists as innocent, harmless individuals or martyrs fighting for a cause. Soldiers sometimes err and deplorably kill innocents. Army should do its best to avoid such lapses. But critics also need to place themselves in the shoes of soldiers. In the fire and smoke of battle, in the heat of the moment, while staring death in face, and remembering loved ones back home, soldiers may overreact. Only better training and experience in handling such situations can improve their responses.

But many well-meaning individuals overlook the grave risks which soldiers face. They have a right to self-defence even under strict moral codes. They cannot be expected to fight with hands tied behind their back. They face real time situations whose essence can be summed up as "Kill or be killed". They are tackling battle hardened terrorists, and not pickpockets or fellows whistling at girls walking on the street. They have to act fast, and cannot calculate carefully 'the quantum of appropriate force'. In such situations, soldiers are likely to keep firing till guns on the other side become silent.

Nowadays, many activists and academics argue for abolition of AFSPA. But its abolition will expose soldiers to a dual risk: the risks in armed encounters; and prosecutions and imprisonment. Withdrawing protection to soldiers fighting arduous battles will be most unjust. It will prevent them from acting fearlessly. Of course no disciplined soldier will 'take it easy', and let terrorist-driven events run their course. However, withdrawal of legal cover will definitely undermine his/her morale.

Tender Hearted Reactions to Terrorism

Why is it that intelligent and reasonable people of good will argue in favour of excessive legal safeguards for terrorists? Why is it that they are willing to expose security forces battling terrorists to legal hazards in addition to battle risks? Diverse ideologies, doctrines and worldviews singly and jointly feed into this approach. These need earnest consideration.

Our views differ to an extent from some current opinions. However, we feel that serving and those who want to join civil service have to adopt a hard-nosed, realistic approach in these matters. They cannot be soft headed or get carried away by stars-in-the-eyes romanticism. This does not involve dumping civil liberties or human values. The issues merit consideration since the stakes involved are very high---the very survival of our nation.

Human Rights

There is a tendency to regard human rights and civil liberties as absolute, unabridgeable and inviolable. This amounts to impracticable moral or legal absolutism. Rights and liberties have to be balanced against equally valued national objectives. Our Constitution permits reasonable restrictions on fundamental rights. Accordingly, courts watered down the right to property. The right to equality is diluted for accommodating policies providing reservations and other benefits to groups considered as victims of past injustice or prejudice. Similar logic would allow reasonable restrictions on civil liberties for fighting terrorism.

Moral Standing of Terrorists

Opposition of human rights groups to cruel treatment of terrorists is valid though by any moral criteria terrorists stand condemned. They nevertheless have moral status or moral standing. According to Kantianism and natural law ethics, the human rights of terrorists have to be respected. Human rights are rights we possess simply by virtue of our nature or humanity, and we retain them throughout our lives. A killer acts wrongly without thereby losing his moral standing. He should not be tortured or mutilated. This applies to terrorists who are captured and tried in courts. However, if they are awarded death penalty after due legal process, there should be no uproar about it.

Paradox of Freedom/Tolerance

Liberal advocates of civil liberties overlook another important issue. This point is made by Karl Popper in his book *Open Society and its Enemies*. He speaks of 'paradox of tolerance' and 'paradox of freedom'. He highlights a dilemma which liberal, humane and democratic societies face. These societies are grounded in principles of tolerance and liberty. But can these be extended to those individuals or groups who oppose such principles? According to Popper, if unfettered liberties are granted to groups who believe neither in liberties or nor in tolerance, it will sound the death knell of free, open democratic societies. Some writers think that Western Europe is already facing such threats to its way of life.

Equity and Reciprocity

Principles of equity and reciprocity are also relevant to this discussion. As we noted earlier, John Rawls characterized justice as a cooperative venture for mutual benefit. All members of society which adopts a system of justice should abide by its rules. Otherwise, besides being iniquitous, it will break down. If any individuals or groups are disinclined to abide by constitutional arrangement, they cannot still claim its benefits. They automatically forfeit such rights. Giving full benefits of such rights to them is injustice to other law abiding citizens.

Protecting the Nation

Obviously, no one will deny the need for individual liberties to protect law-abiding citizens against governmental overreach. However, this principle works ideally in a normally functioning democracy in ordinary times. But when the even tenor of ordinary life is disturbed and when armed groups intent on insurrection challenge the state, restrictions on individual liberties become unavoidable. There are many historical examples which show that even established democratic states had to restrict individual liberties during wars and similar emergencies. The first duty of the state is protect a nation's integrity, and to this end, it has to take all necessary measures. If a state loses to its armed enemies, there will be nothing left---neither constitution, nor order nor citizenry. This is not an alarmist view. Contemporary world has seen the disappearance of many states. And complete anarchy and total civil disorder now prevail in many other nations.

Misapplication of Concepts

People often make 'category errors' i.e. apply principles applicable in one context to inapplicable situations. They show lack of due proportion in applying general principles to practical life. Ludwig Wittgenstein's phrase 'language game' helps to explain such errors of activists. Wittgenstein uses characteristic situations of life as examples to illustrate certain philosophical ideas. Any language is governed by its rules (or grammar).

As it happens, rules are not easily transferable from one sphere of life to another. Often, we fail to recognize this point. For example, a seminar in a university is an academic game. Its rules may have no ready application to family dispute between parents and their kids. Pleading cases in favour of one accused of rape is a legal game. Its rules will hardly be applicable to preaching religious sermons. Similarly, a police encounter with terrorists is a different game whose rules arise in warfare. In these games, the bloodless categories of Ethics or philosophy have limited application. (However, some conventions of fair conduct of war may apply.) The phrase, "It is a different ball game" recognizes such difference between situations of life. This fact is overlooked in the heated debates on terrorism and human rights. Battle ground is not a seminar hall or a court room.

Role of NGOs

A characteristic feature of modern world prevents dispassionate and objective discussion on human rights and allied issues. Modern society has a mind boggling number of NGOs and activist groups. Rich donors set up agencies and NGOs for single minded pursuit of specific agendas such as women's rights, civil liberties, animal rights, and minority rights.

Although such pursuits are unexceptionable in themselves, they generate many attendant problems. One problem is their single-pointed, obsessive, compulsive pursuit of their aims to the exclusion of everything else. These groups are implacable and never satisfied unless their demands are met in toto. In anything and everything, they see violation of their cherished principles. In the process, their advocacy loses moderation and perspective. For example, they will cry hoarse over violation of civil liberties in a country while remaining absolutely silent on its originating cause like violence of disgruntled armed groups often supported by enemy nations. They behave like brief-holding lawyers arguing for only one client. NGOs are sometimes misused by nation states as stalking horses to run their agendas or to muddy political waters in foreign nations to which they are inimical.

Another problem is that these groups are most active in open and democratic nations. Since they have to ply a trade, they select the most hospitable locations. These are of course the diverse democratic nations like India. Unlike in olden days, individuals who manage these bodies are neither philanthropic nor charitable. They are 'professionals' with fat salaries. They are always on the lookout for spots where they can produce the maximum 'bang for the buck'.

Many of these groups have tie ups with UN and other international agencies. Now, we have to show due respect to UN since it is the pillar of the post Second World War global order. But it is also part of the international diplomatic system. It is an international political chess board on which national interests dictate the moves. These are accompanied by postures of moral high mindedness and concern for human values. Without being overly cynical, one has to take such moves and postures with due realism. It is a matter of no small irony that such moral posturing often comes from nations running the most autocratic and despotic regimes. As some of these nations are powerful militarily or economically, smaller nations and even activists and think tanks maintain a studious diplomatic silence. They find it more advantageous and politically convenient to attack soft democratic regimes by weaponizing concepts like human rights and civil liberties.

Readers may feel that we have been harsh on the NGOs. We have no intention of running down NGOs. Our comments are directed mostly against 'activist' NGOs. There are many others such as Bill Gates and Melissa Foundation and Aga Khan Foundation which render yeoman service to poor and suffering humanity. We hold such bodies in high esteem.

Climate of Current Opinion in Media and Academia

Media

Finally, the current climate of opinion both in media and social science academia fuels the false narrative on terrorism. Their opinion is anti-establishment, that is, against the existing political set-up. The political wing of media is hostile to governments of the day. There are exceptions. The US mainstream media was completely in sync with Obama and Hillary, and now with President Biden. They were (and continue to be) highly hostile to Trump who is a somewhat highly polarizing and maverick political personality. The media is ever ready to pounce on what it regards as the misdeeds of government and its agencies. They are ready to attack government with any available means even those that may harm national interest. We refer to general trends without meaning to paint all with the same brush.

Media houses are involved in cut throat competition for audience and advertising revenues. In order to attract audience attention, they resort to sensationalism and hype. Once again our intention is not to place all media persona in the same bracket. Many of them are learned, enlightened and perceptive. But media enterprises seem to have got trapped in a dynamic which modern technology and the need for gaining commercial traction have created. Given this background, media frequently highlight stories of alleged human rights violations of security personnel and other stories which grab immediate interest in viewers.

Negative Academic Currents

Critical outlook

Many currents feed into the negativity of academic comment on our national affairs. Academic activity in its very nature aims at questioning prevailing opinions, practices and world views. As Herbert Marcuse remarked, the function of reason is negative and critical. Seeing philosophers as social critics, Karl Marx urged them to submit existing public institutions, and available alternatives, to *"ruthless criticism"... "ruthless in two senses: the criticism must not be afraid of its own conclusions, nor of conflict with the powers that be"*. They have to consider with detachment and impartiality whether political institutions and practices are justified.

Many writers such as Foucault have argued that institutions of modern society are oppressive, hierarchical, and dehumanizing. Many social theorists argue that deep conflict and dissonance simmer beneath the surface of liberal democracies. But these are effectively masked from us because we are conditioned by falsifying forms of social consciousness. To quote Karl Marx again, critical reflection consists in *"enabling the world to clarify its consciousness, in waking it from its dream about itself, in explaining to it the meaning of its own actions."* From such perspectives, it is possible to argue that liberal democracies are charades which hide social inequities, and use sophisticated means for pacifying oppressed groups.

Identity groups

Modern political thinkers often adopt in their writing the point of view of specific identity groups as distinct from that of the larger polity. The groups identify themselves with their race, religion, and gender or minority status. They regard themselves as victims of society and as excluded from its privileges. 'Multiculturalism' advocates that dominant groups openly embrace the socially excluded and the marginalized and celebrate social diversities. Many social thinkers sympathise with these groups, and regard them as victims of social injustice. In this vein, scholars expose the ways in which what may appear to be impartial operation of rule of law in fact disguises various unacknowledged political agendas. Similarly, feminists highlight 'gendered' practices which are tacit forms patriarchal oppression.

How do these ideas feed into the current criticism of state operations against terrorist groups? Many terrorist groups are portrayed as victims of oppression and social marginalization. Their alienation is the result of ill treatment they suffer at the hands of the state. Their terrorism, according to some people, is a justified response to the highhanded actions of the state. One may concede that some terrorist groups such as Naxalites and others in North-East have justifiable grievances. Enlightened economic, social and political policies are needed to remove those grievances and set right past wrongs. But some terrorist groups may be absolutely implacable in their attitudes and just refuse compromise and accommodation. In that case, the state may have few options for pursuing peaceful approaches. In any event, no state can unravel itself.

Irrational fear of nationalism

Occasionally, we come across situations in which students (and some teachers) express anti-national sentiments. Fortunately, student responses are one-off, not deeply thought out actions. But how do we explain such responses from teachers? Their reactions are part of a modern trend which sees nationalism as a danger. Modern thinkers equate genuine nationalism with jingoism, associated among others, with Rudyard Kipling. Fascism is seen as a consequence of unbridled nationalism. Nationalism is also feared since it creates xenophobia or hatred for foreigners. Many writers mistakenly associate anti-terrorist operations with violent assertion of nationalist feelings, state authority and elite hegemony. But such views are mistaken, and have no support among masses.

Many academics have a self-image of being anti-establishment dissenters. They tend to identify with other dissenters even if they resort to violence and terrorism. Some self-styled intellectuals consider themselves as keepers of a nation's conscience, and try to hold it to unattainable and impracticable moral standards. Some frustrated people also join with any group which opposes government in any manner.

In the preceding paragraphs, we explained why some influential individuals and sections express views out of line with broad national sentiments. In conclusion, we would urge that due consideration should be shown to those who battle for our safety and freedom. We cannot claim unfettered rights of expression to ourselves, or cleanse our consciences by mouthing high moral platitudes while discounting or downplaying the sacrifices of those who safeguard our freedom. We should not place the moral, psychological and emotional burden of fighting terror only on soldiers. It will be a moral double standard if we preserve all of these privileges of unfettered liberty of expression for ourselves. and expect our soldiers to follow the motto (in Tennyson's words):

Not for us to reason why

But to do and die

Indian Context and AFSA

AFSPA empowers army officers operating in "disturbed" areas with following powers.

- After due warning, resort to fire or other force, even if it causes death, against those disturbing law or order, for maintaining public order
- To destroy arms dumps, hide-outs, fortified positions/shelters/training camps used for launching armed attacks
- To arrest without a warrant anyone who has committed or suspected to have committed cognizable offences and use needed force for arrest.
- To enter and search any premise for making arrests, or to rescuing wrongfully restrained persons or for seizing arms, ammunition or explosives
- Stop and search any vehicle or vessel carrying suspects or weapons
- Any one arrested should be handed over to the nearest police station at the earliest along with a report on the circumstances of the arrest.
- Army officers have legal immunity for their actions. No prosecution, suit or other legal proceeding can be launched against anyone acting under that law.
- Judiciary cannot review government's judgment on why an area is disturbed.
- No person can be prosecuted for acting in good faith under AFSPA except with the sanction of the Central Government.

On July 8, 2016, The Supreme Court of India ended the immunity of the armed forces from prosecution under AFSPA, saying, "It does not matter whether the victim was a common person or a militant or a terrorist, nor does it matter whether the aggressor was a common person or the state. The law is the same for both and is equally applicable to both... This is the requirement of a democracy and the requirement of preservation of the rule of law and the preservation of individual liberties."

Summary

On Homosexuality

- Religious and social customs oppose homosexuality.
- It carries social stigma.
- In western society, homosexuality is no longer a taboo.
- Opponents of homosexuality argue that it is unnatural and perverse; violates laws of nature and divine commands, and will destroy anchors of stable social life such as marriage and family. It is a threat to human survival.
- Supporters of homosexuality argue that it is neither unnatural nor immoral, and is not a mental disease according to American Psychological Association.
- Further, it is impermissible to derive moral principles from facts of nature.
- Homosexuality is practised between consenting adults who are supposed to know what is good for them. It harms no one.
- The uncommon sexual orientation of homosexuals should be no bar to their humane treatment.
- Section 377 of IPC makes homosexual sex punishable with life imprisonment.
- Law commission recommended its repeal in its 172nd report.
- Delhi High Court struck down most of Section 377 of IPC as unconstitutional.
- Supreme Court however declared that Section 377, to the extent it criminalizes consensual sexual acts of adults in private, violates Articles 21, 14 and 15 of the Constitution. But it upheld the provisions of Section 377 covering non-consensual homosexuality and homosexual acts involving minors.
- Supreme Court observed, 'Discrimination against an individual on the basis of sexual orientation is deeply offensive to the dignity and self-worth of the individual. Equality demands that the sexual orientation of each individual in society must be protected on an even platform.

On Abortion

- **Abortion** refers to the termination of the unborn entity (or termination of pregnancy) at any stage.
- Abortion debates involve: (i) the value of life, both of mother and foetus; and (ii) individual freedom and rights of women over their bodies. These debates also cover the rights of foetus, definitions of human life and the point of origin of life.

Prolife arguments against abortion

- Human being is constituted as soon as the chromosomes of male sperm and female ova are united.
- Its life is as sacrosanct as that of any other human being. Its right to life is absolute i.e. it overrides the rights of the pregnant woman.
- We should value human life in all its stages.
- Abortion procedures are hazardous for a woman's physical and psychological health.
- There are alternatives for abortion.
- Most religions oppose abortion.

Prochoice arguments in favour of abortion

- Strict abortion laws arose from a patriarchal mindset.
- Foetus is not a 'person' and hence not a being to whom human rights apply.
- The concept of psychological humanity or personhood, and not biological humanity, really matters.
- If abortions are prohibited, women rely on illegal and dangerous 'back alley abortions'.
- There is no option to abortion for serious birth defects or dangerous medical conditions in foetus.
- To argue that a woman should carry her pregnancy to term to give baby for adoption or for placing it in orphanages is unconvincing.
- In modern times, abortion is very safe, and unlikely to cause any mental traumas.
- The MTP Act specifies the persons qualified to conduct the abortion and the places where abortions can be done. It permits abortions in specific circumstances.
- PNDT Act prohibits sex selection, before and after conception and misuse of modern technologies for sex selective abortions. It contains necessary provisions for this purpose.

On Cloning

- A clone is an exact genetic copy of a molecule, cell, plant, or animal.
- Scientists extract DNA from the cell of an adult mammal and insert it into a hollowed out donor egg. By stimulating the egg with a mild current of electricity, they can create an embryo that would become, if implanted into a surrogate mother, the patient's identical twin.
- Dolly, a female domestic sheep is the first mammal cloned from an adult somatic cell.
- As for human beings, no cloning is allowed.

Arguments in favour of cloning

- Will help in understanding how human beings acquire their traits of character.
- Cloning can benefit society by creating clones of creative scientists, artists, and sportsmen/women.
- Cloning can promote healthy and happy life of an individual.
- Cloning can produce offspring with traits parents want.
- Cloning can help in saving lives.
- Though human reproductive cloning is illegal, therapeutic cloning for creating replacement tissues or 'body spare parts' holds great promise.

Arguments against cloning

- Cloning deprives the clone of the right to be a genetically a unique individual.
- The future of a clone appears to him or her like a rerun of an earlier life or a refurbished model.
- A clone may regard himself as no more than a duplicate or a photocopy without individuality and deprived of prospects of open life horizons.
- Cloning can in theory lead to sinister outcomes as envisaged in the novel *Brave New World.*

- Human beings have to be considered as ends in themselves and not as instruments for those who want to clone.
- It can reduce natural diversity among human beings, and lead to standardized human forms.
- Cloning alters our perspective on nature and undermines important human values.
- In a sense, men become responsible for their biological endowments.

On Gene therapy

- Defects in genes present within cells can cause inherited diseases.
- Gene therapy replaces missing genes or provides copies of functioning genes to replace defective ones.
- Scientists use vectors or viruses as molecular delivery vans for introducing modified genes.
- More than 4,200 diseases result directly from abnormal genes, and many others are partially influenced by a person's genetic makeup.
- There are many technical problems associated with gene therapy.

Stem cells

- Embryonic Stem cells are taken from the pith of inner cell mass of embryo after 6 days of its growth. The genetic modification of cell in the dish becomes the genetic modification of organism in the uterus.
- Human ES cells are obtained from discarded embryos of in-vitro fertilization clinics.

Moral issues

- As gene therapy is still in clinical trial stage, its testing on humans could have disastrous unknown results.
- Patients participating in these studies usually have not responded to more established therapies. Their choices are born of desperation and wild hope.
- Unscrupulous doctors can manipulate genes to genetically control traits in human offspring that are not health related.
- Gene therapy also has social repercussions since knowledge of genetic codes of individuals may lead to preferential job selection or favourable insurance rates.

On Surrogacy

- Surrogacy means a practice whereby one woman bears and gives birth to a child for an intending (mainly infertile) couple with the intention of handing over such child to the intending couple after the birth.
- India has emerged as a surrogacy hub for couples from different countries for the past few years.
- There have been reported incidents of unethical practices, exploitation of surrogate mothers, abandonment of children born out of surrogacy and import of human embryos and gametes.

- Due to lack of legislation to regulate surrogacy, the practice of surrogacy has been misused by the surrogacy clinics leading to rampant commercial surrogacy and unethical practices.
- Surrogacy Bill seeks to end these abuses.
- The provisions of the bill have been summarized in the narrative portion of this chapter.

On Capital Punishment

- Punishment is harm inflicted by a rightful authority on a person who has been adjudged to have violated a law or rule. Many people want abolition of death penalty.
- The four goals of punishment are retribution, prevention, deterrence and reform.
- Four theories of punishment also carry above names.

Arguments *against* and *for* death penalty

- Capital punishment violates the sanctity of human life. Supporters of death penalty argue that it actually upholds the value of life by punishing depraved murderers.
- Abolitionists observe that capital punishment is imposed with class bias. Retentionists argue that this objection is not against death penalty, but against the way the judicial system functions.
- Abolitionists refer to risk of loss of innocent lives if there is miscarriage of justice. Retentionists point out that the chances of execution of innocent individuals are extremely low.
- Death sentence has, as statistical evidence shows, no deterrent effect. The counter point is that statistical evidence is unreliable in these matters.
- Death penalty is a form of blood thirsty revenge. Capital punishment alone balances the scales of justice in some cases.
- The Indian Penal Code (IPC) prescribes death penalty for grave crimes such as murder, rape resulting in victim's death, waging war against the State. Other laws also have death sentence.
- The Supreme Court upheld the constitutional validity of capital punishment in "rarest of rare" cases. It ruled that if capital punishment is provided in the law and if the procedure is fair, just and reasonable, death sentence is constitutional.
- Supreme Court indicated how the "rarest of rarc" cases should be identified.

On Animal Rights

- Traditional Western view based on Judaeo-Christian religious ideas promoted a tendency to regard animals as resources for human use.
- Early philosophical thought reinforced this attitude since animals lack reasoning ability.
- In modern terms, the sacredness of human life is attributed to the fact that men possess intelligence, reason and autonomy. This view automatically excludes non-human animals, which lack these traits, from moral consideration.
- Contractarianism leads to similar views.
- In 1975, Peter Singer published his work *Animal Liberation*. Its basic message is—'All animals are equal'. It implies that human beings are also (biologically speaking) animals, and should not ill-treat or abuse other animals.

- Animal rights activists argue that the relevant distinction is not reason but capacity for suffering.
- If we adopt this criterion, we can see that animals, no less than human beings, have rights.
- Animal rights activists also point to an inconsistency in applying the criterion of human dignity based on human intelligence and rationality. They accuse men of speciesism.
- The case for animal rights is *logically* and *philosophically* unsustainable.
- But the approach to animals should be humanitarian.
- The moderate position in use of animals would consist of gradually reducing meat eating, raising animals in humane conditions, and killing them as painlessly as possible.
- Strict guidelines have to be followed for medical experiments on animals.
- Hunting has to be prohibited as a sport; it can be allowed for a few animals which tend to multiply too fast.
- Traditional animal sports on festivals have long ancestry.
- They should be allowed with suitable safeguards which minimize dangers to animal and human life.

Terrorism, state action and human rights

- Caleb Carr defines terrorism as: *"... the contemporary name given to, and the modern permutation of, warfare deliberately waged against civilians with the purpose of destroying their will to support either leaders or policies that agents of such violence find objectionable."*
- Terrorism is warfare and aims at undermining peoples' will and belief in their way of living.
- Moral theories such as Consequentialism, Kantian and natural law approaches and Contractarianism oppose terrorism.
- In early years after our Independence, government measures to tackle terrorism and secessionist movements enjoyed almost universal support.
- Some people now feel that anti-terrorist operations violate liberal, democratic, humanist and legal norms.
- These considerations have to be balanced against national security needs.
- Tender hearted reactions to terrorism and excessive emphasis on their rights at the cost of security needs can undermine security operations.
- Anti-terrorist operations are usually confined to encounters.
- If terrorists are captured, they have to be tried according to law.
- In public discussions and TV debates, the slant appears to favour terrorist groups.
- This can create confusion in the minds of the public.
- We have traced the various doctrines, ideologies and worldviews that converge towards critiques of anti terrorist operations.
- While human rights and civil liberties are important, a hard headed approach is essential for fighting terrorism.
- We have discussed the topic at some length since students may be get influenced by one-sided and untenable views.
- The issue is important since it has a bearing on the morale of security agencies and also on national security.

PRACTICE QUESTIONS

(1) What are the two extreme positions on abortion? What do you think is a moderate stand? Do you think that MTP Act takes a centrist position on abortion?

(2) Distinguish between the following: life, human life, human person, potential life, actual life.

(3) Under what conditions would you consider abortion moral? When do you consider it immoral? Why?

(4) Instead of passing the law banning pre-natal sex determination tests, government should have concentrated on changing the underlying social attitudes. Do you agree? Give reasons.

(5) Do you think that homosexuality is immoral and unnatural? Explain.

(6) Discuss the likely impact of homosexuality on family and social values.

(7) Briefly outline the present legal position on homosexuality in India.

(8) In Hindu mythology, Brahma is the creator of the world (*srushti karta*). Mairavan wanted to rival Brahma and do *prati srushti* or counter creation. Do you think that cloning reflects a similar mindset of 'playing God'?

(9) To what extent should genetic experimentation and development be permitted? Discuss with reference to (i) experiments that involve creation of human life in laboratory (ii) stem cell research and (iii) and human cloning.

(10) Discuss the arguments *for* and *against* human cloning.

(11) Briefly outline how stem cell research is regulated in India.

(12) Newspapers sometimes carry advertisements about surefire gene therapy for debilitating diseases. One of your close relatives wants to try one such cure. What will be your advice to him? Give reasons.

(13) What is surrogacy? How can it be misused? What are the measures proposed in ART Bill to prevent its misuse?

(14) John Locke wrote that a murderer " by the unjust Violence and Slaughter he hath [has] committed upon one, declared War against all Mankind, and may therefore be destroyed as a *Lyon* or *Tyger* [spellings are obsolete], one of those Savage Beasts, with whom Men can have no Society or Security." Discuss whether and to what extent this view is acceptable in modern times.

(15) In the debates on murder and other heinous crimes, the hearts of some participants seem to bleed more for perpetrators of crimes than for their victims. What reasons could account for this attitude?

(16) "We do not outlaw swimming even though some swimmers will drown. Similarly, we do not execute all murderers even though some will murder again. In both cases, we allow some risk to the innocent in order to protect our freedoms." Do you agree with this analogy (of Bedau)? Why or why not?"

(17) What is the view which Supreme Court took on death penalty? When can courts impose death penalty in the light of this view?

(18) Define terrorism. Discuss the pros and cons of treating terrorists under ordinary criminal law or under tougher anti-terrorist legislation.

(19) Two US Supreme Court justices, Robert Jackson and Arthur Goldberg, facing a plethora of petitions in favour of civil liberties after 9/11 terrorist attacks, observed: "The Constitution is not a suicide pact." How will you interpret this observation in the context of dilemmas in tackling terrorism?

(20) "We might think we're only hurting the terrorists and other criminals when we chip away at civil liberties, but we're putting ourselves at risk too." Evaluate.

(21) "And were a civilized nation engaged with barbarians, who observed no rules even of war, the former must also suspend their observance of them, where they no longer to any purpose; and must render every action or encounter as bloody and pernicious as possible to the first aggressors." Discuss this view of philosopher David Hume.

(22) Some intellectuals regard that the recent Supreme Court judgement on playing the national anthem in cinema theatres panders to jingoist sentiments? How will you defend the judgement?

(23) Discuss Dr. Johnson's quip that 'Patriotism is the last refuge of a scoundrel'.

(24) Examine rival views on whether animals can have rights.

(25) What could be a reasonable view on how animals should be used for human ends? Do you think that animal sports like *Jallikattu* should be continued?

REFERENCES

1. Jacques P. Thiroust with Kenneth W. Krasemann
Ethics Theory and Practice (Tenth Edition) Prentice Hall

2. Julie C. Vancamp, Jeffery Olen, Vincent Barry
Applying Ethics A text with Readings (Tenth Edition) Wodsworth

19

CHAPTER

Emotional Intelligence

Data is a character from *Star Trek: the Next generation*. He resembles a super smart computer without any feelings. "*Data seeks to feel, knowing that something essential is missing. He wants friendship, loyalty; like the Tin Man in the Wizard of Oz, he lacks a heart. Lacking the lyrical sense that feeling brings, Data can play music or write poetry, with technical virtuosity, but not feel its passion. The lesson of Data's yearning for yearning itself is that the higher values of the human heart—faith, hope, devotion, love—are missing entirely from the cognitive [purely intellectual] view. Emotions enrich; a model of mind that leaves them out is impoverished.*" -Daniel Goleman

INTRODUCTION

The expression 'emotional intelligence' may itself seem to be a contradiction. In the history of philosophy, the terms 'appetites', 'passions' and 'emotions' are used as opposites of 'reason', 'intellect' and 'understanding'. Philosophers saw a sharp dichotomy between the two sides - emotional and intellectual - of human mental life. They felt that emotions cloud human understanding and lead men astray. For them, as for saints, moral endeavour was a never-ending effort to bring momentary emotions and passions, often selfish, under the control of reason. This strain of thought continues to be a perennial theme in practical ethics.

However, philosophers have also recognised that a strong character grounded in sound ethics is necessary for pursuit of good. Otherwise, good people with weak minds and convictions will succumb to the forces of evil. Modern thinkers proceeded further and recognised many emotions as good *per se*. Thus, a mother's love for her children, a soldier's heroism, and a scholar's commitment to his vocation - all these are intrinsically good emotions. These emotions are spontaneous and have no other motives underlying them.

Even other emotions, though not as noble as the previously mentioned ones, can prove effective in daily personal life, social relations, and business management and in public administration. For these functional purposes, we have to change our normal emotional responses and mind-set or mental makeup.

Intellectual Abilities

Before beginning our discussion on emotional intelligence, we may note that the skill sets which public servants require fall into three distinct, though not watertight, categories. The first set consists of intellectual abilities. These are subdivided into mathematical, logical, and verbal skills. Mathematical and logical strands are more or less identical. They are essential for analyzing problems, understanding their quantitative dimensions and for structured thinking. These are the intellectual qualities which computer programmers, mathematicians and statisticians are likely to possess.

Verbal skills denote the ability to speak and write clearly and lucidly. They are the skills of oral and written communication. Literary writers and critics - such as Tolstoy, Thomas Hardy, TS Eliot and Samuel Johnson - possess them in abundant measure. But hardly anyone can match the standards of these writers. However, we can try to express our thoughts simply, directly and clearly without pretentiousness and artificial props. These skills are extremely important for civil servants since government business is transacted on files in the form of letters and notes. Furthermore, civil servants nowadays have to make computer-aided oral 'presentations' on various subjects.

Moral Qualities

The second type of skill set consists of moral qualities suited for government servants. These are the core virtues which should form part of the moral outlook of an ideal civil servant. Codes of ethics and codes of conduct embody such desired moral behaviour. Of course, it will be more appropriate to describe these as morals than skills.

Emotional Intelligence

The third skill set in the repertoire of civil servants can be called 'emotional intelligence'. This is a term coined by American scholars. These are the qualities which influence an officer's personal behaviour and his interactions in the course of his official work with people, both within and outside his organization. Many management theorists emphasise that these personal and social skills of officers contribute to increased organizational effectiveness. Empirical research studies have shown that emotional intelligence contributes far more than academic intelligence to an individual's success in management, profession and administration.

BRIEF HISTORICAL BACKGROUND

Intelligence Quotient (IQ)

The term IQ, or Intelligence Quotient, is a score on a test that measures an individual's cognitive ability in comparison to the general population. IQ tests use a standardized scale with 100 as the median score. The following table shows roughly how the scores reflect intelligence.

Score in the test	Level of intelligence
90-100	Average or normal
>130	Exceptionally high
<70	Very poor or retarded

When children are given the test, their age and background is taken into account. IQ scores tend to remain stable. Repeated practice makes no significant difference to scores.

IQ tests are designed to measure general ability to solve problems and understand concepts. These in turn include reasoning ability, problem-solving ability, and ability to perceive relationships between things and ability to store and retrieve information. IQ tests measure various aspects of general intellectual ability from diverse angles. They usually focus on:

Ability	Main component
Spatial	Visualize/ manipulate shapes
Mathematical	Solve problems and use logic
Language or linguistic	Complete sentences or recognise words in which letters are removed or rearranged
Memory	Recall visuals shown or things spoken

Questions in each of these categories measure a specific cognitive ability. Some psychologists believe that each category also reflects general intellectual ability.

For over hundred years, intelligence meant only the scores of intelligence tests. They were considered adequate measures of human intelligence. Intelligence meaning cognitive skills as shown by IQ was considered an innate unalterable natural endowment. Being naturally given, it is a fixed quality; study and industry may increase the absorption of information, but make no difference to one's native intelligence. Practice at best may increase the speed of acquisition and manipulation of information.

During World War I, the intelligence tests which the Stanford psychologist Lewis Terman developed were extensively used in army recruitment. They created the IQ way of thinking. Intelligence was seen as one dimensional or as a monolithic quality. Even now, Scholastic Aptitude Test used to admit students to prestigious or Ivy League American universities, is a test of intellectual skills. This is also true of other educational tests like GRE and GMAT.

Seven Varieties of Intelligence

Howard Gardner, a famous educational psychologist working at Harvard University, questioned the conventional method of measuring intelligence as a single, one-dimensional skill and as the only golden key to success in life. He spoke of multiple intelligences, and included emotional qualities which lead to success in professions and life as among the components of 'intelligence'. This is a radical departure from earlier approaches which conceived intelligence (comprising mathematical, logical and linguistic skills) as a purely cerebral quality.

Howard Gardener outlined his views in *Frames of Mind*. He mentions that a single type of intelligence is inadequate for success in life. He goes on to identify seven varieties of intelligence including the usually recognised intellectual skills. We show them in the following table.

Type of intelligence	Related activity	Great practitioners
Mathematical/logical	Solving structured problems	Newton, Gauss, Russell, Einstein, Riemann
Linguistic	Literature	Milton, James Joyce, Goethe, Tagore
Spatial visualization	Painting, architecture and artistic design	Raphael, Michelangelo, Louis Corbusier
Kinaesthetic genius	Physical fluidity and grace as in classical dance and Olympic gymnastics	Larisa Latynina, Anna Pavlova, Birju Maharaj
Musical	Great classical musical compositions of West and East	Mozart, Beethoven, Tansen, Thyagaraja
Interpersonal intelligence	Interpersonal skills of great leaders	Mahatma Gandhi, Abraham Lincoln
Intrapersonal intelligence	Great insights into human psyche; and finding inner peace through adapting oneself to one's true feelings	Sigmund Freud, Aurobindo, Buddha

Emotional Intelligence

We have deliberately cited men of great eminence to give striking examples and fix the ideas in the minds of students. There are many common people who embody similar skills starting from humble teachers to struggling but dutiful housewives. The main point to note is the way in which Howard Gardener expands the concept of intelligence. He includes in intelligence talents that lead to cultural activities such as literature, art, music, painting and architectural design. He also includes talents involved in sports and games. Finally, he adds interpersonal skills or social skills and the insights men gain by looking into themselves and the mental feelings of others. Emotional intelligence refers mainly to "personal intelligences" that help in getting along well with people and in prudently ordering one's life.

We will now further elaborate the concepts used in explaining emotional intelligence. Daniel Goleman explains emotional intelligence as consisting of "*abilities such as being able to motivate oneself and persist in the face of frustrations; to control impulse and delay gratification; to regulate one's moods and keep distress from swamping the ability to think; to empathize and hope.*" We can regard these as positive qualities which help us in steadfastly pursuing goals which ultimately lead to success and happiness. Except empathy, the other qualities are directed towards one's own self. Before proceeding further, we will illustrate these ideas with simple examples.

Case Studies

CASE 1

Shekhar is doing a BBA program in a middle-tier management school in the USA, and has aspirations to do an MBA from a top 10 level Business School and to eventually join the management consulting profession. He is in the last but one semester and so far his grades have been in line with his expectation. In the present semester, he has two marketing courses and he could not do well in the first term paper of both the courses, in particular, he has got poor grades from an Indian origin professor. The professors while evaluating the term papers have given extensive comments and listed suggested readings.

Shekhar is feeling nervous about the next term papers. The topics are already selected by him and now he has to research and write. He is not able to concentrate as he is anticipating failure in getting admission to a management school of his choice set for MBA programme. Whenever he starts reading fresh material from new resources as suggested by the professors, the 'spectre of imagined rejection letter' from Graduate School comes to his mind.

Question

Imagine you are one of Shekhar's close friends. What do you think is Shekhar's problem and what would be your advice to him?

1. Marketing is perhaps not a subject in which Shekhar could be good at. In the next semester, he should not take any of that stuff.
2. Indian origin professors in USA think too high of themselves and are an alienated class and Shekhar should avoid doing courses with Indian origin professors.
3. Shekhar should absolutely focus on the current semester, act on the advice coming from professors, and not worry about eventual rejection from Graduate Schools.
4. Shekhar should realise that even without going to a select set of Graduate Schools, he could do well in life.

Discussion

The answer choice (1) reflects a hasty conclusion. Shekhar is in the last leg of the BBA programme and must have done marketing courses earlier. At that time he got good grades. So there is no problem with his aptitude for the subject. Moreover, the present anxiety results from one term paper in each of the two courses. One should not read too much into this initial hiccup.

The second answer choice is obviously wrong based as it is on illicit generalisation of a class of eminent people. Moreover, Shekhar has not got good evaluation from the other professor who surely is not of Indian origin. Shekhar should not try to find malice in others but reflect on the real weakness of the papers he has produced. Such fault finding is always self-defeating.

The answer choice (3) is appropriate. Anxiety functions in two ways. A mild anxiety to do well on a task enables one to summon all the physical and mental energy towards doing that task well. An overdose of anxiety however, has a damaging effect in so far as it creates fear of failure thus depriving the individual of the necessary power of concentration to do the task in a superb or even orderly manner. Shekhar obviously has a surfeit of anxiety which he needs to control.

Shekhar's second problem is that that he has started thinking of failure and its eventual consequences. He should live in the present time, keeping his goal in view though. Present time demands that he concentrates on the necessary readings and follows the advice of the professors in letter and spirit. He should not worry about graduate school admission at this time.

The answer choice (4) is a correct observation about life and its infinite possibilities. But the observation does not tell what Shekhar should and should not do. Hence, this is an inappropriate answer choice.

CASE 2

Pavitran is reading about the Indian economy. His teacher told him that the falling rupee is a most likely question either in the 'Civil Services Mains Examination' or in interview if he makes to it. Pavitran was wrestling with CAD, FII sell off, RBI's squeeze on money supply, rising yields on government securities, mounting losses to banks and other arcane details of the monetary economy. He was struggling to grasp the concepts and understand the links between them which he was told explain the rupee's downward journey. But his mind kept moving off to a far more enchanting scene. Pavitran is a great fan of the Southern movie queen Sunita. He always watched her movies on a 'first-day-first-show-basis'. But this time around, he was forced to accord higher priority to stories of rupee's travails. While he was settling down to his study, his friend Armugam who watched the newly released Sunita starrer *Trichy Junction* told him that that her item number in it was simply mind blowing. Pavitran found Sunita's imagined dance postures and gyrations floating alongside the CAD numbers and the bond yield curves. He wondered whether it would be best to watch the movie or at least the dance number to get the whole distracting business out of his head.

Question

Assume that you are Pavitran's elder brother with whom he shares intimate thoughts and concerns. At this time what would be your advice to Pavitran?

1. Knowing that Sunita's curvaceous figure keeps Pavitran obsessed for days after he has seen the movie, he should altogether avoid thinking about Sunita and not allow Armugam to discuss this film and its details.
2. This being one time distraction, Pavitran might well watchthe movie and leave it at that.
3. Pavitran should focus on studies as the mains examination is near and it is a very important examination.
4. Both (1) and (3)

Discussion

There is nothing very unique or perverse in Pavitran's mental state. Many young men (women) develop fascination about heroines (heroes) popular in the celluloid. It is acceptable if there is an artistic appreciation and strong liking of the role played by some actress or actor. But the trouble starts when one falls in morbid love with lights and shadows on the screen. Since Pavitran has such a condition and since the mains examination is not far it is good for him if he can avoid the distraction. He can see the movie after the examination gets over if not in a cinema hall but certainly on TV screen.

It is also necessary that he learns to discipline himself from the temptations of instantaneous self-gratification. Emotionally mature individuals are able to postpone gratification of desire and concentrate on the immediate challenges.

Such distractions sometimes have an infectious quality. One friend starts a discussion about heroines and this or that dance sequence, sexual appeal etc. and everybody joins the rally. It is also good to cut oneself off from such company at least till the time exam is over - without being unpleasant or rude.

Thus answer choice (1) is appropriate.

One might think that no great a loss would follow if Pavitran just spends three hours for Trichy Junction. The issue is not that. The issue is whether Pavitran is able to set his priority right looking to his tasks at hand. The issue is also whether he has the emotional capability to delay gratification whatever it is worth. Today it is Trichy Junction and Sunita, tomorrow there could be something else. To be a winner in such a difficult examination, he has to cultivate the right temperament or aptitude. From that perspective answer choice (2) is not acceptable.

Answer choice (3) is based on pure rationality. Powerful emotions or urges need moderation by reason. That is the essence of suggestion in (3). It is appropriate.

Hence (4) is the right answer choice.

CASE 3

Akshay Pande is preparing to take the State Level Forest Services examination. He had a background of physics and chemistry in graduation but now for this examination he has to be proficient in ecology. He is trying hard to understand the legal framework which governs management of biosphere reserves and national parks and other contemporary issues. The examination is three months away and before two weeks his mother has developed some health problems for which the consulting physician has advised Catscan to be sure about whether there is a cancerous growth causing the present problem. In the family, she is the only lady managing household affairs. So, Akshay is not able to concentrate on his studies all the time thinking whether his mother has got cancer and if so what will be the consequences as the disease unfolds. He has started feeling that there is no hope for success in the examination this time.

Question

What is your assessment of Akshay's emotional problem?

1. It does not make sense to talk about his emotional problem. His apprehensiveness is understandable as cancer, after all, is a deadly disease and most of the time incurable.
2. Akshay does not need to presume at this time that his mom has got cancer. If that is something going to happen worrying will not prevent its occurrence.
3. Losing hope is the worst thing that can happen to an aspirant in a competitive examination. Hope is a strong motivator. By losing hope one invites failure.
4. Both (2) and (3)

Discussion

The fact that cancer is a deadly disease is well-known. Some anxiety therefore, is not out of place or context. However, this anxiety should not get out of control and pervade Akshay's mind. At this time, at worst that is a possibility but diagnosis is yet to come. He should not think it is given and sure. One outstanding Guru of positive thinking, Norman Vincent Peale, used to pray that God give us the capacity to distinguish between situations where our actions matter and where they do not. We need to focus all our energy on the first set of conditions and accept the second. Calm acceptance is the first step necessary before looking for solution. Worrying about cancer at this time cannot change the diagnosis and therefore, not much thought should be given to the possibility except trying to get the tests done from the right place and getting the right medical advice. Thus answer choice (1) is not correct but (2) is appropriate.

The point made in (3) is apt. In the west, scholars have made many studies about the temperament and behavior of Olympic winners and great sports stars. Great champions share a common mindset in that they have high hopes about eventual success. That goes to explain how great sports persons come back to win even after initial setback in a competitive event. They quickly analyse the causes of setback, make immediate adjustment and start the next round with renewed vigour never ever losing hope. Akshay is losing hope for no good reason. He must not allow that to happen. Hence answer choice (3) makes a valid point.

Thus (4) is the right answer choice.

Gardener's Summary

After these illustrations, we give two brief summaries which Howard Gardener gave of his thoughts on emotional intelligence.

Interpersonal intelligence is the ability to understand other people: what motivates them, how they work, how to work cooperatively with them. Successful sales people, politicians, teachers, clinicians, and religious leaders are all likely to be individuals with high degrees of interpersonal intelligence. Intrapersonal intelligence … is a correlative ability, turned inward. It is a capacity to form an accurate, veridical [true] model of oneself and to be able to use that model to operate effectively in life.

In another formulation, Howard Gardener mentions that the core of interpersonal intelligence includes "the capacities to discern and respond appropriately to the moods, temperaments, motivations, and desires of other people". In intrapersonal intelligence, the key to self-knowledge, he included, "access to one's own feelings and the ability to discriminate among them and draw upon them to guide behaviour."

Howard Gardener's approach to intelligence has remained cognitive. He emphasises that one should understand the motives and habits of work of others so that one can get along better with them. His focus is also on self-understanding so that one can live a productive and happy life. This approach is based partly on the doctrine of behaviourism - first propounded by Watson and made popular in 1960s by B.F. Skinner. They argued that only behaviour which is observable can be a subject of scientific study. As we know, science deals with matters which are observable, measurable and verifiable. Human behaviour, such as blushing, can be studied by observing physiological changes i.e. change of skin colour of cheeks. However, we cannot observe feelings and things going on in the minds of people. Hence, behaviourists banished study of mental life from science. However, Howard Gardener included them in his studies.

Some psychologists like Thorndike recognised the concept of social intelligence. He regarded social intelligence as one aspect of emotional intelligence. Social intelligence is the ability to understand others and to act wisely in human relations. However, in the 1960s, the mainstream psychologists were sceptical of the concept of social intelligence and thought it useless. As we saw, the tide turned with the advent of Gardener's ideas. Changes in business environment, as we shall see, also brought emotional intelligence to the fore.

Emotional Intelligence Theory

Two psychologists, Peter Salovey and John Mayer, proposed a comprehensive theory of emotional intelligence in 1990. Daniel Goleman has also written extensively on emotional intelligence. Daniel Goleman has conceptualized emotional intelligence on the basis of five main aspects.

Self-awareness

This is the ability to accurately assess our feelings at any given time, and to take decisions according to our preferences. Another dimension of self-awareness consists in making a realistic assessment of our capabilities and acquiring an adequate degree of self confidence.

Self-regulation

This aspect implies control over emotions so that they help and do not hinder the task at hand; it also implies sincerity of purpose and the willingness to delay gratification of tempting immediate pleasures; finally it means that one is able to bounce back quickly from emotional stresses.

Motivation

This involves relying on our strongest preferences to guide and move us towards our cherished goals; it strengthens and encourages our drives towards self-improvement; and it makes us persevere even when faced with heavy odds and grim prospects.

Empathy

This is the ability to sense what others are feeling; it enables one to look at things from the perspective of others; it implies readiness to have rapport and adapt to diverse groups of people.

Social skills

These consist in the ability to handle emotions in relationships; accurately understanding social situations and networks; behaving smoothly with people; using these skills to lead and persuade; to negotiate and resolve disputes; and to promote cooperation and team work.

The above aspects of emotional intelligence virtually cover the whole of one's personal, social and official life. They apply to children, youth and the aged. An enormous literature has developed covering emotional competencies and their applications in different contexts of life. But for our purposes it is sufficient to consider the essential points and their applications especially in work situations. We present cases to show how aspects of emotional intelligence or competence come into play in work situations. These are also known as soft skills. Students should learn the process of analyzing situations using concepts of emotional intelligence.

Changes in Business Environment and Emotional Intelligence

In recent years, emotional intelligence has become a major topic in management studies. Its emergence marks a major shift in thinking. Earlier managerial models, based on hierarchical systems, placed senior executives on a high pedestal. The boss used to keep his distance from his subordinates fearing that familiarity would breed contempt and lower discipline. Sensing the emotions of the subordinates was considered dysfunctional. For generally organizational goals differed from personal goals, and trying to satisfy individual aspirations or needs interfered with realisation of an organization's objectives. The personal feelings of employees did not matter. Top managers were reluctant to lend their ears to "sob stories".

We live in a different business world now. The twin forces of globalization and information technology have radically transformed the operating environment of businesses. This transformation also altered the emotional environment within organizations. Corporate heads are no longer the 'manipulative, jungle fighter' stereotypes. They can no longer produce results by dominating or ordering subordinates around. They have to be virtuosos in interpersonal skills. Senior managers have to understand the feelings of their subordinates who are to be treated as fellow workers. They have to prevent differences from escalating and enable people to comfortably 'move with the flow' in organizations.

In any organization, work is done cooperatively in a team. Nowadays, the teams are made up of knowledge workers with specialized skills. In these situations, managers have to evaluate the work done by others and offer constructive criticism for its improvement. This is an everyday activity in any organization at almost all levels. But managerial behaviour here is marked by common dysfunctionalities. Managers fail to clearly indicate specifically how to improve any piece of work produced by subordinates. They criticise the work in general terms without indicating any line of improvement and launch personal attacks on subordinates, laced with malicious comments. Such behaviour creates among subordinates confusion, resentment and a tendency to avoid work and contact with the manager.

CASE 4

After completing post graduation in economics and statistics, Ramana Rao was compelled by family circumstances to join a periodical as assistant to a sub-editor. The periodical specialised in doing racy stories on politics, social scandals, and film stars, with occasional pieces on the economic misery sweeping the society. Ramana Rao carefully studied books on economic journalism and on current state of Indian economy as background knowledge needed for his job. He was conscientious and worked hard on the economic news items. Having studied in Telugu medium, he found it hard to get rid of certain mannerisms which crept into his writing. Further, his math background made it hard for him to handle woolly generalities and gushy emotions.

His boss Velayudham was from a brash, investigative news background. He scoffed at Ramana Rao's factual writing referring to it as watery tea or Sambar without masala. Ramana Rao pleaded that it is hard to wring emotion out of economic news. Velayudham dismissed the pieces as lacking in punch and kick. Ramana Rao's occasional 'Telugish' bits, he said, were screamingly hilarious. He often taunted Ramana Rao for his humble origin and rural background. Ramana Rao was miserable and would have quit but for economic compulsions. But his luck changed. Vasanthi, the owner's niece, returned after graduating from London School of Economics, and became the subeditor. She discussed matters with her uncle and changed the tone of the stories. Though a hard taskmaster, she clearly told Ramana Rao about the slant and the main content of the stories. She made some changes, but after consulting him. She liked the stories loaded with facts and figures which Ramana Rao wrote.

Question

In contrast to the style of well-educated Vasanthi, what intellectual shortcoming and emotional pathology do you notice in Velayudham as supervisor of Ramana Rao?

1. No deficiency or pathology is evident, Velayudham is only trying to supply what the Indian market with poor taste (generally speaking) wants.
2. Velayudham has no grasp of the fact that economic journalism cannot be given the robe and trappings of masala stories about socialites or film stars.
3. As a supervisor he is failing to provide workable guidance. Moreover, oblique reference to one's family background in business or official environment is crude and distasteful.
4. Both (2) and (3)

Discussion

As regards answer choice (1) there is substance in the statement that a substantial segment of our readers indeed have poor taste and they are interested in inane and juicy stories. However, economics and the study of an economy are analytical subjects. These matters cannot be put in the same style of narration as done in gossip market – except in certain contexts such as investigation of financial fraud or scandals. But that is a small part of the whole ambit of economic analysis. Velayudham is failing to understand this essential distinction of themes: film story vs. economic analysis. Not only that, he is stepping into the forbidden territory of social and economic background of an employee. This kind of behavior assumes the hue of discrimination and in worst cases will be regarded as human rights violation. All managers need to be careful about these implications of behaviour more so because they occupy positions of authority. Thus answer choice (1) is not acceptable.

From the previous discussion, you can easily appreciate that observations in (2) and (3) are valid. It is also the duty of Velayudham to direct efforts of Ramana along the lines that market demands. There may be less scope of doing that in economic journalism, but some avenues do exist. For example, interesting and readable stories can be written on the theme of farmers' suicide due to distress in agrarian economy. Aligning efforts of staff towards the goal of the business is a key responsibility which Velayudham is failing to discharge.

Therefore, (4) is the correct answer choice.

Art of Criticism

Harry Levinson mentions that the work of employees working under a manager should be criticised in the following way:

Specificity

As we noted earlier, a critic has to be specific. He can use an example or cite an incident to show the area in which the work falls short or the pattern of its deficiency. He should point to the areas which need reworking and the way of going about it. He should not be indirect or delicate, but should call a spade a spade so that others get the message.

Providing solutions

If possible, the group leader should offer a solution. This is the usual counter to critics: If you think that things are in a mess, tell us how to set them right. When subordinates are merely criticised without being told how to mend their work, they get frustrated, disheartened and demotivated. One need not give them a fully worked out solution; they can be told of the other possibilities, alternatives or ways of advance. One may pinpoint the areas of deficiency or the manner of addressing errors.

Face to face contact

Though some people revel in running down others to their face, many others tend to avoid such unpleasant encounters. But it is best to criticise and praise people in their presence. Sending a long note of criticism or praise will not have the same impact as a one to one talk. It promotes dialogue, reduces distance and forces managers to squarely face up to their responsibilities.

Empathy

As we have noted, managers have to avoid a carping or belly-aching note in criticism. Criticism should be based on empathy or on understanding sympathetically the viewpoint of others. Otherwise, it will breed ill-will. Daniel Goleman says of destructive criticism: "instead of opening a way for a corrective, it creates an emotional backlash of resentment, bitterness, defensiveness, and distance."

Levinson also gives the following advice to those at the receiving end of the criticism:

- Look upon it as a means of improvement, and not as a personal attack.
- Avoid the tendency to defensiveness, cool down for a few days and discuss matters again with your manager.
- Consider criticism as an opportunity of working with your critic.

Knowledge Workers and Work Teams

We now consider another feature of modern organizations which makes emotional intelligence vital to their working. Emotional intelligence enhances the group IQ of an organization. Any organization represents a pool of talent covering various subject areas like finance, marketing, quantitative analysis and creative design. Group IQ can be thought of as a summation of the IQs of individual workers. Lack of emotional intelligence can bring down the group IQ. Prof MGK Menon used to say that a single Indian worker matches or exceeds the skills of his Japanese counterpart; but two Indians working together are far less productive than their Japanese counterparts. This shows the importance of emotional intelligence in working together in groups.

Peter Drucker, the doyen among management theorists, coined the term 'knowledge worker' and predicted that more than a third of the American work force would soon consist of knowledge workers. He mentions that their productivity consists in adding value to information. Knowledge workers are people such as financial analysts, writers and computer programmers. Their knowledge is highly specialized and their productivity depends on their individual work getting integrated into the work of a work team. For example, novelists are not publishers; and nor are hardware designers sellers of computer parts. With knowledge work, team replaces the individual as the work unit. As a result, emotional intelligence which comprises skills that promote harmonious group working has become important. Studies have shown that efficiency of work teams is highly correlated with their internal social harmony. Let us look at a case which shows how mutual rivalry and envy can derail projects.

CASE 5

Prajapati is a Finance member in a team commissioned to prepare a project for seeking aid from a foreign philanthropic fund. The project leader Mallick is an egoistic self-seeker who belittled other team members, created an impression of being the sole driver of the project, and generally hogged the limelight. He never allowed anyone else from the team to visit abroad for discussions or to talk to foreign donors. Being a smooth talker, he impressed people. Prajapati was a rank holder in CA examination and resented Mallick's ways of ignoring other team members. Often, he differed from Mallick. Mallick bypassed Prajapati and consulted his subordinates on how best to make the project look attractive. In due course, the visit of the fund's appraisal team was fixed. While studying the financials of the project, Prajapati realised that the calculations underlying its financial viability were flawed. He felt that Mallick would lose face when the appraisal team spots the errors. He thought that it would be a fitting lesson to Mallick.

Question

In the office drama narrated, what dysfunctional behaviour do you observe here? Point out at least three significant remediable dysfunctionalities.

Discussion

The following style and/or conduct of Mallick and Prajapati are dysfunctional for their managerial roles.

1. Mallick's egocentric conduct is problematic. Apparently he has no real grasp of the intricacies of project preparation and evaluation. Yet he wanted to demonstrate that he is leading from the front. That too may be tolerated but he must keep some specialist on his side so that mistakes are avoided. This he failed to do.
2. Mallick's second problem is his manipulative behaviour. He wanted to make the project appear better than what it really was. Painting a project white is a common practice but it should be done this with great moderation. If many wrong assumptions are made and revenues are over exaggerated, trained evaluators will be able to see through the deficiencies and the project proponents will lose credibility. Then no foreign donor will be enthusiastic to provide aid. This Mallick should have listened to and not pushed malleable subordinates to window dress the project.
3. Prajapati should have been candid with Mallick and pointed out the flaws in the project proposal. Whether Mallick would have listened to him or not, we cannot say. He should have pointed out the deficiencies upfront; that action would have been in the interest of the organisation. Instead Prajapati wished humiliation of Mr. Mallick in due course when the proposal gets rejected. This approach is a deviation from team work and cohesive working in an organisation. Prajapati would not at the end of the day gain anything from eventual rejection of the project. This is somewhat akin to shooting at one's own feet.

New Management Tools

As we noted earlier, modern organisations can no longer be managed through handing down commands. Management has to rely more on persuasion than on ordering people around. In this situation, use of social skills for gaining influence and communicating ideas has become important. The following are vital for this purpose:

- Influence: Deploying suitable means of effective persuasion
- Communication: Putting across messages clearly and convincingly
- Conflict management: Holding discussions and settling disputes amicably
- Leadership: Creating enthusiasm and giving direction to subordinates
- Acting as catalysts for change: Introducing, sustaining and managing change

Influencing People

Influence involves winning over others to support our point of view. It may be hard to influence people who have closed minds or absolutely rigid views. Sometimes, the differences are irreconcilable. However, in many situations the aim is to persuade people to adopt one view instead of another. In such situations, one has to present facts and arguments in a manner which will appeal to the listeners. The matter has to be explained from their perspective, highlighting the advantages they will gain. Open advocacy of a particular line, ignoring other alternatives, often leaves people unconvinced. People have to be influenced indirectly. To gain influence, it is necessary to build coalitions and create support. People are receptive to ideas conveyed through dramatic incidents and telling examples.

CASE 6

Manjit was asked to make a presentation to wholesale agents about the company's new product. The communications team asked him to restrict the presentation to 20 minutes and 20 slides. They added that no slide should have more than 5 lines. Manjit ignored the advice. He felt that under these constraints no informative presentation could be made. As the Head of the communications was away, Manjit had his way. But his presentation did not go well. He had 50 slides, each cluttered with data in small font and with no graphics. He droned on giving details on each slide. The wholesalers began yawning. Many told him to keep it short and give them brochures on the product.

Question

What fault lines do you see in the emotional competence of Manjit? Point out at least three important concerns.

Discussion

1. Manjit failed to assess the taste, temperament and motivation of the wholesalers. The wholesalers were having short attention span and were unable to absorb lots of information in one session. As they were not interested in minor details, they started yawning. Manjit did not adapt the presentation to the taste and requirement of his audience.
2. His presentation lacked focus. The wholesalers are primarily interested in marketability of the product, its price and their commission. These core concerns of wholesalers should have been addressed. Major product features could have been narrated, but there is no need to drown them in information. More the information presented, more likely the focus would get lost.
3. Manjit should have listened to the advice of the communication team. They specialise in this subject and know how to make an effective presentation. In his enthusiasm and over confidence, Manjit ignored their advice and ended up making ineffective presentation.

Communicating

Communication is a two way process. One has to take in the views of others attentively and sincerely. One has to put across one's views clearly and unambiguously. In many situations, the mood of the audience has to be accurately sensed, generally through their non verbal behaviour, and the message has to be suitably worded. If any difficult questions crop up, they should not be avoided, but should be addressed directly and honestly. It is essential to hear people and register what they are saying. One should not mentally 'switch off' when others are speaking. Communication should aim at mutual understanding. One-sided harangues have no communication value. In communications, both sides should fully share the available information with each other.

CASE 7

Probir is the regional manager of the marketing department of a thriving business. The business has been growing and the regional marketing office has recruited quite a few specialists recently. The functional heads in the company have to meet their staff in an open meeting every two months. Probir detested these meetings. It was open to everyone in the office. The staff came up with a long list of trivial and tiresome complaints and grievances. They repeated the same things and spoke at length. Even when the staff knew of the constraints, they went on with their complaints. They wanted more space for lounge, for bathrooms and crèche. Probir pointed to lack of space, and yet the staff continued to complain. Probir cultivated a habit of sitting through the meeting with a cheerful face, but with his mind switched off from the proceedings. The meeting became a tiresome ritual he had to get through.

Question

In Probir's situation what action would you have taken and why?

Discussion

Probir needs to do the following gracefully:

1. Since the business is thriving and more specialist staffers have been recruited, Probir should expand office facilities quickly say within six months.
2. Till such time that office expansion takes place relieving the pressure on facilities, he should seek a moratorium on discussion of the same old topic.
3. He need not switch off in the meeting. These meetings serve a purpose. If he ignores all that the staff members have to say, demotivation may set in.

The question focuses on understanding the needs of a team and the leader's role in resolution of mundane problems of the team members. The source of the problem in this case is perhaps rooted in the fact that success of the regional marketing function has brought forth induction of new team members and the present accommodation has thereby become inadequate. This condition should not be allowed to linger. If it does, dissatisfaction will surely result. He has to get rid of this core problem. For this, he needs to develop a concrete plan of action and follow it up. After he reveals the plan of action, team members will know that the problem will hopefully get resolved soon and they would be willing to accept the moratorium.

Probir's boredom or frustration in listening to the same set of problems time and again is understandable. He should have been proactive and anticipated the problem. However, problems need resolution. Till the problems are resolved, the affected staff will keep raising them in meetings. That means status quo. He has to break it. He has also to be attentive to what staff members say. Carefully listening to a person and then solving his or her problem are marks of sincere concern for that individual. Leaders in office need to show this quality. So he has to be attentive however much he dislikes the grievances or narration thereof in the meetings.

Conflict Management

Conflict management is another skill that managers need. The conflicts here mean the quarrels and disputes which frequently arise in organizations. They are not international or political conflicts. Tact and diplomacy are the two means of handling such organisational issues. The quarrels usually involve people with difficult temperament and/or problematic situations. Auditors, Police and mediators often face such situations.

It is useful to identify potential areas of conflict and the points of dispute. In any organization, there are areas where functions overlap between two divisions. If the work is interesting, people will try to grab it from others. [This is a form of turf war.] If it is tedious, they will try to dump it on others. People get into bad moods and begin to have personal quarrels. Some mangers are antipathetic to one another and there are cliques and groups. These problems afflict most organizations in some measure.

The best way of addressing these problems is to bring them into open and arrange discussions between the concerned people to iron out differences. Open and frank debate is the simple means of settling such differences. Solutions have to be so devised as to satisfy all the parties to the dispute. Managers have to scale down such disputes. Turning a blind eye or sweeping problems under the carpet will allow them to fester.

CASE 8

Priya and Pinky are working in the finance wing. At one time, they were fast friends. But over a small matter they quarrelled and fell apart. Their relationship turned hostile. Arun was their immediate supervisor. He tried to patch things up but failed. Pinky and Priya did not hide their feelings even before customers. As they dealt with two vital finance areas, they could not be kept away from customer meetings. Arun met his boss and told him that the 'daggers drawn' situation between the two ladies was creating problems. His boss responded by saying that he had no stomach for mediating in a women's quarrel.

Question

From the standpoint of organisational behaviour and emotional intelligence what deficiencies do you notice in the conduct of Arun's boss?

Discussion

First and foremost, Arun's boss (X in short) is ducking the issue. He cannot evade the issue, because the quarrel is creating an embarrassment to the organisation. When customers get different vibes or feel from different individuals in the organisation they lose trust and confidence in the organisation. The result can be only one: loss of business. Both the employees Priya and Pinky need to be firmly told about this organisational imperative. They should know that any such ugly show in future will invite disciplinary action against both.

Second, X needs to delve deeper to know the root cause of the problem. Such conflicts may arise from multiple reasons. The job description and duty assignment of two individuals may come in conflict. Partiality shown by the immediate boss to one employee may be another trigger and so forth. Talking to Priya, Pinky, Arun and others in confidence, X should be able to find the true reason for this conflict. Sometimes it may be easy to resolve such conflict by purely organisational measures such as defining job of individuals well so that no one treads into another's work domain.

Third, his comment shows sexist bias. His language presumes that women are prone to fighting in this manner. That is an illicit generalisation. Sometimes men also fight in exactly the same way. Managers or officers should clear their mind of such prejudice and refrain from using such language.

Leadership

Leadership in organisations involves inspiring and guiding individuals and groups. Leaders have to formulate a shared vision and mission for the organisation. In working out the vision, they have to involve others to create a sense of participation. Otherwise, the vision will fail to command allegiance. Vision gives a sense of purpose which is a spur to human effort. People will not work if there is a feeling of drift or aimlessness. Visions do not have to be grandiose. Small organisations and groups can keep their sights lower. But some kind of vision gives direction to one's efforts.

Leadership naturally implies taking lead in doing things. Journalists often advise politicians to assume leadership and get a grip on things. One cannot impose himself on others in the organization in the name of leadership – nor would others countenance such moves. Leadership is not merely an attribute of one's position in an organisation. No one becomes a leader only by virtue of occupying the top slot in the organisation. One has to show leadership qualities particularly by acting in difficult times and by assuming responsibility for decisions that go wrong. Passing the buck to others in troubled times is indefensible in any leader. Leaders have to decide matters democratically, not in the sense of taking votes, but in the sense of consulting all concerned and examining all the relevant technical inputs.

Most positions in an organisation involve leadership in greater or lesser measure. Except at the lowest level, all positions involve supervision. Naturally, at the lower level, decisions will be simpler, and involve fewer individuals. However, managers have to take initiative and be proactive in handling problems. At any level, leaders should not play favourites. They need to evaluate performance of everyone on the same criteria, avoiding subjectivity and personal likes and dislikes. They have to be accessible equally to all subordinates and avoid creating any charmed circle of intimates.

Leaders have to act as catalysts for change. This is particularly critical now when many new programmes and policies are being put on ground. New or innovative work methods change old procedures and settled routines. They create unease since people in organisations are used to the old ways. New processes involve what are known as learning curves which people have to traverse.

The process requires learning, effort, and "getting used to". Thus, computerising any office creates tensions. Unlike the young who have learnt how to operate computers, many middle-aged employees find the process troublesome. This explains the inertia of organisations in adopting to change. For organisational leaders, this is a major challenge especially since the world and the workplaces are being swept by rapid changes.

Leaders can manage change in the following ways:

- They have to recognise the need for change and remove obstacles from its path.
- They have to explain to others why the status quo is no longer viable.
- They have to be vocal and open in pursuing change and form a group to drive the change.
- They should adopt the new processes in their working and set an example to others.

CASE 9

Vishvambar was the transport commissioner in a progressive, happening State. Responding to audit comments about loss of revenue and irregularities in vehicle registration centres and at toll points, Government has introduced computer systems and CCTV cameras. A control centre was created at State headquarters with real time data and image transfer. The new system evoked strong opposition from vested interests within and outside government. Vishvambar studied English literature in his college days. He had no background of computers. The whole process, he confided to his close aides, went over his head. Fortunately, he had some officers who studied in IITs. He left the whole matter to them. When asked to visit and supervise the control room operations, he joked that the new fangled ideas are for the young and that it is difficult to teach new tricks to an old dog.

Question

Select one of the following answer choices and give reasons why you accept or reject an answer choice.

1. Vishvambar is over delegating. Technicalities need to be managed by specialist professionals but he should know what's and why's of every important step or decision related to the project from management perspective.
2. In a responsible position such as Vishvambar is holding, the leader has a duty to be passionate about major projects going on in the Department. By that test he is failing.
3. Government has made a blunder in posting an officer with academic background in literature into such technically intensive job as that of the transport commissioner.
4. Only (1) and (2)

Discussion

Answer choice (1) is correct, because it is clear from the behaviour of Vishvambar that he has adopted hands off approach towards this project. Senior managers too need to 'make their hands dirty' – struggling with the problems and the challenges. This process includes learning new subjects (at least at the basic level) and acquiring new skill set. Apparently Vishvambar is unwilling to do that for IT application in his department.

Obviously the project is an important one which is expected to bring transparency in functioning of the department, reduce corruption and enhance state's revenue. He cannot avoid thinking about the problems involved in IT applications in his department because there are a few IITian employees working for him. A project like this needs consideration not only of technical dimensions but also others such as convenience of public in general in transacting business in the new format or system and elimination of touts from the department. These matters concern general administration and IT interface with people will be guided by these considerations. Vishvambar is failing to appreciate how much a person who has eyes and ears open and acquaintance with affairs of common man's life can contribute to the development of a good web based platform. He can make that contribution only when he appreciates how the technology works. He does not have to become a designer or software code writer for that purpose. In the context, therefore, his hands off approach is far from being responsible.

In view of the discussion in the previous two paragraphs the answer choice (2) is also correct.

Answer choice (3) is definitely wrong. Academic background should not be the dominant consideration in appointment of senior executives in Government. Yes, extraordinary achievement in some field of relevance can and should be taken into account. There is no principle that a person with literature or liberal arts background in University cannot be placed in a department which has an IT intensive project. There have been many distinguished civil servants who have done exceptionally well in a field in which she or he did not have previous exposure. It all depends on motivation and passionate application. Background is never an insurmountable barrier for achievers in management or civil services. Thus answer choice (3) is incorrect.

Hence (4)

Programmes for Poor

We have so far discussed how emotional intelligence is necessary for increasing organisational efficiency in the new knowledge-based global business environment. There is, however, another aspect which is relevant to organizing and implementing welfare programmes for the deprived groups. Government servants implement such programmes according to the prescribed guidelines. But mere mechanical efficiency is inadequate for successful implementation of these programmes. They need to show personal commitment to ensure that such programmes succeed. They have to put their heart and soul into the effort. Programmes for scheduled castes, scheduled tribes, women and children fall into this category.

These programmes are hard to design and execute. Unlike other sectoral programmes, these lack adequate infrastructure, committed and knowledgeable staff and suffer from low visibility. They lack glamour. Government servants find it much harder to implement these programmes than those in infrastructure or industry. This is true of all social welfare and poverty alleviation programmes. Their client groups are poor, illiterate and unorganized. Unlike industrialists or project developers, they have neither initiative nor drive. They can confer no benefits of any sort on government servants. Government servants often view them as a troublesome burden, and seek transfers to other departments. This is where young officers have to display idealism and compassion even at the cost of undergoing some personal inconveniences.

CASE 10

Sen Gupta is working as a Sub divisional officer in Visakhapatnam. He married his childhood friend Poornima Chaterjee. Poornima studied fine arts in college. They live in the city outskirts near the beach. Poornima was delighted to find a cultural forum which organised cultural events and concerts regularly. She attended all the programmes. The organisers were delighted at the interest she showed and lavished attention on her. Meanwhile, government asked for volunteers to serve in a remote, backward, tribal area. Sen Gupta, along with some others, volunteered, and was transferred. Poornima was terribly upset that she would have to leave Visakhapatnam. She would especially miss the cultural programmes. She chides Sen Gupta for his folly.

Question

From the standpoint of intimate interpersonal relationships examine each of the following answer choices and give reasons why you accept or reject an answer choice. More than one choice may be valid.

1. Poornima is right; there is no point in volunteering for posting in a tribal area. Governments are very poor in appreciating good work done in the face of challenges and hardships. Then why to dive into such a situation knowing well that Poornima is enjoying stay in Visakhapatnam?
2. There is an idealist streak in Sen Gupta's personality or else why would he opt for such posting? Poornima, being a friend of Sen Gupta from childhood days should have appreciated this.
3. Sen Gupta is selfish and is a careerist. He is trying to get attention of Government unmindful of suffering of his spouse.
4. Poornima's disappointment is understandable. However, she is taking a somewhat myopic view of life. In this type of career, such inconvenience and loss of community contact is very common. She needs to accept that gracefully.

Discussion

Answer choicc (1) looks at things from Poornima's perspective.It argues that as Governments are generally slow to appreciate an officer's commitment and contribution, there is no point in Sen Gupta making such a choice. He will be better off, if he does not volunteer.

This view of human motivation is superficial at best. Career choices cannot mirror commercial transaction. Sometimes officers make choices that reflect their world view and their sense of purpose in life. Don't we know that there are many eminent individuals who left civil services and took different paths to serve the community? Some of them acquired name and fame after long years of effort. The concept of self-actualisation captures such motivation well. Sen Gupta possibly has a genuine desire to serve the poor tribal community with full knowledge that his contribution may not earn any special recognition. Thus answer choice (1) does not express an objective view of human motivation and hence it is incorrect.

(2) This action of Sen Gupta suggests that he at least for some time wants to serve in tribal area. Those areas may not offer urban facilities and social interaction with elites in the ordinary sense we understand the term. However, they offer rich potential to do good for a section of disadvantaged Indians. No doubt, it is a worthy cause that Sen Gupta has espoused. An element of idealism in his personality may be inferred from this choice. It is also true that Poornima should have known him better and should have been prepared to live for some time in tribal area. Thus, this statement is correct.

(3) There is no substance in the argument that Sen Gupta is trying to capture Government's attention by making this choice. Government memory is known to be too short to register such quality of an individual officer. For Government it is a routine. If nobody indicated preference they would select some officer in their best judgement and post him in that place. Hence this statement is incorrect.

(4) It is true that Poornima has to have a holistic appreciation of facts and their family life. Government servants do not stay long in one place except when they become senior and gravitate towards state and/or national capital. Anyway, she should have realised that stay in Vishakhapatnam cannot be for too long. While transferring government officers, Governments seldom take their preferences into account. That is the way it works, and officers know this as soon as they join civil services.

She is a bit myopic too. As an educated person she would have known that tribal areas offer different kinds of avenues for culture related pursuits. With time and open mind she would perhaps discover one or two such avenues and then put her drive and energy into them. She should not allow disappointment to weigh heavily on her mind. Hence this statement is also correct.

Empathy

This brings us to empathy which is a most important aspect of emotional intelligence. It is the quality which enables government servants to address the problems of the poor, deprived and the vulnerable sections of the population. It lies at the root of human altruism and concern for others. Its total absence leads to criminal psychopathic behaviour as in killers, rapists and child molesters.

Self-awareness opens the gates to empathy. If one cannot gauge one's emotions, he will hardly know how others feel. The inability to observe the feelings of others is a notable failing of emotional intelligence. It means that one misses out on what it is to be human. For building rapport with others and concern for fellow human beings arise from attuning oneself to the emotions of others or from capacity for empathy. Empathy or the ability to read the emotions of others is critical for many tasks – whether it is parenting, teaching, negotiating or explaining government policy to villagers.

Deep attentive interest in fellow human beings is a mark of empathy. This does not mean unwholesome curiosity about the personal life of others or maliciously gossiping about them. At the same time, we should not be indifferent to others or ignore their existences and well being. But it means that we should observe them and guess at their moods and feelings. Emotional states of people are usually revealed through bodily clues, facial expressions and general movements, gestures and postures. By paying attention to these, we can interact with them better in various situations. The purpose is not take advantage of their emotionally vulnerable states but to help them better.

Empathy is the basis of considerate behaviour towards others. A famous line of John Donne runs: "Never send to know for whom the bell tolls; it tolls for thee." In simple terms, it means that we should consider the troubles of others as our own. Empathy is feeling one with another; its opposite is antipathy. This feeling and concern for others frequently crops up in ethical dilemmas. Should X share the difficult office situation with his pregnant wife or spare her the anxiety?

In empathy we are moved by the pain of others. When a bystander meets with an accident, we rush to his aid. Empathy also leads to higher principles of conduct and justice. In this situation, we put ourselves in the place of the other and view things from his perspective. The idea of punishment for a crime originates in this manner. We feel one with the victim and feel from his point of view that his pain should be assuaged at least partly through the punishment meted out to the criminal.

Empathy is a first step in cultivating social skills needed in an organization. Empathy enables us to observe the feelings and perspectives of others and actively follow their interests. In this process, we understand others. This makes us recognise their needs and offer them help. In a business context, this translates to anticipating, recognizing and meeting customer needs. As we noted earlier, this service orientation will be of great use in social and economic development programmes focused on the poor and the weak.

Managers have to attend to and foster the development needs of those working with them. Empathy is essential for performing this task. One part of this task is to recognise the good performance of subordinates and reward them suitably. Second is to see their likely career growth path in the organization and help them along the way. Finally, subordinates have to be supported with advice, feedback and through assignment of challenging tasks.

Though it may seem surprising, empathy helps managers to follow the political dynamics within an organization. The politics within an organization are not part of national politics. It refers to the way senior managers combine forces to exert influence in organizational decision making. It may also mean recognition of the prominent social networks in the organization and the manner in which they operate. This awareness will also promote understanding of the forces that shape the views and actions of clients, customers and competitors. It will help in accurately reading the actual situations within and outside the organization. These insights are important in devising and implementing corporate policies and programmes.

Conclusion

In one sense, the components of emotional intelligence we discussed can be called character. It is a term which moral philosophers used since ancient times. One writer described character as the psychological muscle needed for moral conduct. We conclude with the following passage from Daniel Goleman which can serve as a summation of this chapter. "*The bedrock of character is self discipline; the virtuous life, as philosophers since Aristotle have observed, is based on self control. A related key-stone of character is being able to motivate and guide oneself, whether in doing homework, finishing a job, or getting up in the morning. And, as we have seen, the ability to defer gratification and control and channel one's urges to act is a basic emotional skill, one that in a former day was called will. ... Being able to put away one's self-centered focus and impulses has social benefits. It opens the way to empathy, to real listening, to taking another person's perspective. Empathy, as we have seen, leads to caring, altruism, and compassion."*

CASE 11

Rohini is the marketing chief of a globally reputed multinational corporation. This evening the Board of the corporation decided that she is to be appointed as the Chief Executive and President of the Board of the corporation for a term of three years. Obviously, she was overjoyed with the recognition and honour bestowed upon her – though she had migrated to USA only 18 years ago. After exchanging pleasantries with all the senior colleagues who had come to greet her in her chamber, she was late reaching home. When she just parked the car in her garage, on the spacious balcony, she saw her well-educated mom Malathi waiting for her. Seeing her, Rohini spoke in a cheerful tone "Mom, today I have great news to share with you." Malathi's response was instantaneous, "Rohini, there is no milk in the house. At least for tomorrow, why don't you go and pick up some packets rightaway?"

Rohini was a bit surprised because her husband Ashwath should have reached home much earlier. When she asked what prevented Ashwath from doing this as she was already late, Malathi coldly told that Ashwath was tired and resting.

Rohini was already at a high position in corporate ladder in USA and they were staying in an exclusive area. So she had to go to the nearby town to pick up milk and she took another 45 minutes to come home. Once in home she shared the good news with Malathi. Malathi however, in a sober tone told her that a woman has to look after husband, children and parents and that that is inevitable. So, Rohini would do well to leave her 'crown' in office and remain the good daughter she is.

Question

Review each of the following statements from the standpoint of emotional intelligence and state with reasons whether you agree with the statement or not. There may be more than one valid statement.

1. Rohini did not expect this treatment from her mom. Before asking her to get milk right way Malathi should have at least shown curiosity about the good news that Rohini hinted at.
2. Malathi is right. An individual owes his/ her first duty to family members.
3. Malathi has shown poor emotional competence. Even after knowing the good news instead of complimenting Rohini, she preferred to give a lecture like a wise person.
4. With too little expression of positive emotions and obsessive focus on performance and duty, Indian parenting acquires a robotic quality. Malathi is a victim of that type of culture.

Discussion

The statement (1) is definitely valid. Rohini was late from office, and she had mentioned that she had good news to share. Any sensible family member at that time would want to know what the good news is. That is applied emotional intelligence - plain and simple. Procuring milk is not such a big issue. It would have been understandable if somebody had fallen seriously ill and shifting him/her to hospital was required. Then that activity would have overriding preference and sharing of good news could wait. That was not the situation.

The second statement has got the first part wrong. Yes, there is a primary duty to family members, but that duty must be a sensible call. Trivia like buying milk cannot be elevated to the level of duty to keep in abeyance the joy of life and make it mechanical.

The third statement is correct. After hearing the news the educated lady that Malathi is, she should have appreciated the implication. It is no ordinary achievement for a woman executive to break the glass ceilings in American society. The achievement is especially remarkable because the executive is an immigrant and carries an unspoken burden of being non-native. Once that appreciation is in place she should have felt proud that her daughter has accomplished this feat and should have profusely congratulated her. There was no need to talk about duties - much less about the office 'crown'. That sarcasm was completely out of place.

There is substance in the fourth statement. Emphasis on performance and duty is fine. At the same time positive emotions - support, friendliness, empathy and sharing of joy in achievement - are equally important. The scale should be balanced in the middle and be not tilted on either side. Indian parenting may indeed have a bias and this bias might have found expression in the behaviour of Malathi.

Summary

- The expression 'emotional intelligence' may seem a contradiction in terms.
- Philosophers saw a sharp dichotomy between the two sides - emotional and intellectual-of human mental life.
- The skill sets which public servants require fall into three distinct, though not watertight, categories.
- These are intellectual abilities (comprising mathematical and verbal skills), moral qualities and emotional intelligence.
- The term IQ, or Intelligence Quotient, is a score on a test that measures an individual's cognitive ability in comparison to the general population.
- IQ tests are designed to measure general ability to solve problems and understand concepts.
- These in turn include - reasoning ability, problem-solving ability, and ability to perceive relationships between things and ability to store and retrieve information.

- For over hundred years, intelligence meant only the scores of intelligence tests. They were considered adequate measures of human intelligence.
- Intelligence meaning cognitive skills as shown by IQ was considered an innate, unalterable natural endowment.
- Howard Gardener questioned the conventional method of measuring intelligence as a single, one-dimensional skill and as the only golden key to success in life.
- Howard Gardener identified seven varieties of intelligence including the usually recognised intellectual skills.
- These skills are - mathematical/logical, linguistic, spatial visualization, kinaesthetic genius, musical, inter-personal intelligence and intrapersonal intelligence.
- Emotional intelligence refers mainly to'personal intelligence' that help in getting along well with people and in prudently ordering one's life.
- Two psychologists, Peter Salovey and John Mayer, proposed a comprehensive theory of emotional intelligence in 1990.
- Daniel Goleman conceptualized emotional intelligence on the basis of five main aspects: self-awareness; self-regulation; motivation; empathy; and social skills.
- In recent years, emotional intelligence has become an important topic in management studies. Its emergence marks a major shift in thinking. It arose from radical changes in the operating environment of businesses.
- The twin forces of globalization and information technology radically transformed the operating environment of businesses. This transformation also altered the emotional environment within organizations.
- Managers can no longer produce results by dominating or ordering subordinates around. They have to be virtuosos in interpersonal skills.
- In any organization, work is done cooperatively in teams. Nowadays, the teams are made up of knowledge workers with specialized skills. In these situations, managers have to rely on social skills.
- Critical review of work is a common activity in any organization.
- But managerial behaviour in supervising subordinates' work is marked by common dysfunctionalities.
- Harry Levinson mentions that the work done by subordinates should be criticised constructively based on the factors of specificity, providing solutions, face to face contact and empathy.
- In knowledge based work, team replaces the individual as the work unit. As a result, emotional intelligence, which comprises skills that promote harmonious group-working, has become important.

- The following skills are vital in such organizations: influence, communication, conflict management, leadership and acting as catalysts for change.
- We have given the gist of these skills in the narration. Students can refer to it.
- Government servants need to show personal commitment in implementing welfare programmes for the deprived groups.
- Empathy is a fundamental aspect of emotional intelligence. It is the quality which enables government servants to address the problems of the poor, deprived and the vulnerable sections of the population.
- Empathy or the ability to read the emotions of others is critical for many tasks - whether it is parenting, teaching, negotiating or explaining government policy to villagers.
- Empathy is the basis of other-regarding behaviour.
- Empathy is a first step in cultivating social skills needed in an organization.

PRACTICE QUESTIONS

1. "The expression 'emotional intelligence' is a contradiction in terms." Comment.
2. Define emotional intelligence.
3. What are the broad ingredients of emotional intelligence?
4. Distinguish between the concepts of 'intelligence' as used in IQ approach and in emotional intelligence approach.
5. What are the seven varieties of intelligence which Howard Gardener included in emotional intelligence?
6. What are the three types of skill set which civil servants need?
7. Discuss briefly the five components which Daniel Goleman included in his theory of emotional intelligence.
8. Why have social skills assumed new significance in the workplace?
9. "Emotional intelligence comprises many interesting ideas which however have little practical utility." Discuss.
10. How can emotional intelligence help government servants in India?
11. Briefly discuss two family situations in which emotional intelligence can be of help.
12. What is the role of empathy in emotional intelligence?
13. "Stress makes people stupid." Examine critically.
14. "Leadership is not domination, but the art of persuading people to work toward a common goal." Comment.
15. Briefly explain how the predominance of knowledge workers in industry has increased the need for using emotional intelligence.

16. What are the main qualities of an organizational leader?
17. How does empathy of government servants help in the implementation of welfare programmes for the poor and the needy?
18. Write short notes on: (i) interpersonal intelligence; (ii) intrapersonal intelligence; (iii) motivation; (iv) self-awareness; (v) self-regulation; (vi) empathy; (vii) soft skills; (viii) group IQ; (ix) knowledge worker; (x) conflict management; (xi) social skills; (xii) personal skills; (xiii) IQ; and (xiv) work teams.

REFERENCES

- Daniel Goleman *Emotional Intelligence*.
- Daniel Goleman *Working with Emotional Intelligence*.
- Howard Gardner *Frames of Mind*
- Peter Salovey and John D Mayer, *Emotional Intelligence* (article available on internet)

INTERNATIONAL MORALITY

INTRODUCTION

International morality refers to morals or codes of conduct governing relations between nations. The present day world is divided into many independent territorial political communities. They constitute the international political order, sometimes called international legal order. The basic feature of this order is the 'sovereign equality' of states. The present conception of sovereign equality is derived mainly from the United Nations Charter.

SOVEREIGNTY

'Sovereignty' is a term from political theory. It is the ultimate authority or power possessed by a state as an embodiment of its political community. Sovereignty represents the will of the people, which is theoretically absolute and unfettered. It is the supreme political authority which a state exercises within its territory. States exercise these powers without any restrictions from other states. This is the meaning of political independence.

State, in this sense, needs to be distinguished from government. Governments are temporary and hold office for certain specified periods; and in democracies, they may be replaced by other governments after elections. However, a state is permanent, and lives as long as the political community which it represents.

Political theorists commonly use the term sovereignty in three contexts. From an international legal perspective, it refers to the terms of the reciprocal recognition that states accord one another in the international political order. In its reference to domestic polity of a state, it means the ultimate source of legal or constitutional authority. Empirically, it means effective capacity to exercise unilateral control over various fields of activity and to formulate policies unilaterally.

NATION AND STATE

Political theorists make a distinction between 'nation' and 'state'. A nation is a group which thinks of itself as 'a people,' usually because they share many things in common. These consist of a common territory, history, culture, language, religion and way of life. The state has a narrower meaning referring to the constitutional arrangements which determine how a nation is governed. Or 'state' refers to the machinery of government which organizes life in a given territory. Thus, we can distinguish between the Austrian state and the Austrian people or between the Thailand state and the Thailand people.

Modern nations are largely nation states. States have been in existence since ancient times. However, before the modern period in history, countries were mostly monarchies and empires, held together by loyalty to a ruling dynasty rather than by any sense of nationalism. Historians trace the origins of nation states, if not of nationalism, to eighteenth century. The first movements for nation states arose in Italy and Germany and spread later to other parts of world. Political thinkers distinguish between the terms 'nation', 'country' and 'State'. In speaking of a nation, the emphasis is on the common heritage which the people of a country share, and which underlies their sense of nationhood or nationality.

Some writers argue that in some countries, such as America, Australia and Canada, the state comprises many nations, and that they are 'multi-national societies.' Societies with heavy immigration are seen as multi-national. Multi-national countries are sometimes prone to civil wars between the different groups. This has been especially true of central Africa in recent years, where different peoples fight to gain control of the state, or try to secede from the existing state. As we shall see, this question can lead to issues of international morality. 'Nation' and 'country' are used as synonyms in common parlance. In this chapter, we will use the three terms - nation, state and country - interchangeably. However, we need to bear in mind the conceptual differences between nation and state.

Irrespective of the nature of any state, it generally has relations with other states; these are known as foreign relations or international relations. A country's relations with other countries are determined by its foreign policy. Foreign policy is also closely allied to a country's diplomacy. A country's foreign policy is seen as distinct from its domestic or internal policy. Thus, a country's policy towards health or primary education is a part of its internal or domestic policy. But whether a country will join in a military arrangement with other countries will be determined by its foreign policy. However, there is always some interdependence between a country's domestic and foreign policies. After these preliminaries, we will discuss the main questions connected with international morality.

INTERNATIONAL MORALITY

International morality is a topic which philosophers, historians and political thinkers have discussed since ancient times. Human history has been bloody - marked by wars, invasions, massacres and plunder. Wars are brutal and ugly, often horrid spectacles of barbaric slaughter. They have been central to human history and wrought forcible social change in the vanquished countries. They have moved humane and thoughtful scholars from ancient times into reflections about the morality which ideally should guide the relations between nations.

International morality as a subject falls in the domain of international relations (IR), which is a study of the forces which shape the conduct of nations towards one another. International relations can be studied as part of history or more theoretically as part of political science. Many writers combine the theoretical and historical approaches in their studies. Insights from the discipline of Ethics are also used in studying international morality.

International relations can be studied from three points of view. One perspective focuses on simple factual aspects – how nations actually behave towards one another and the reasons or motivations behind their behaviour. Secondly, one may study international relations normatively to prescribe desirable kinds of behaviour to nations. Finally, international relations can be studied for advising governments on how best to conduct foreign relations in national interests. In one way or another, moral aspects enter into these different approaches. Further, in all these studies, writers use various theories.

Topics Covered in this Chapter

In this chapter, we will discuss the following topics:

- Theories of international relations and their relation to international morality
- Ingredients of international morality
- Morality in relation to war
- Moral aspects of some major international problems
- Moral dimensions of international economic problems
- Moral roots of India's foreign policy

THEORIES OF IR

The main theories of IR are – realism, idealism, their variants and a collection of views drawn from other schools of thought. The most prominent theories are realism and idealism, both of which have a long history. Neorealism and neoliberalism have become popular in the twentieth century. Doctrines of postmodernism and feminism have also influenced some IR theories.

Realism and Critique of the Moral Tradition

Realism is an old doctrine; its lineage is traced to Thucydides, Machiavelli and Hobbes. Thucydides (460–411 B.C.) wrote *History of the Peloponnesian War* – a war that Athens and Sparta fought from 431 to 404 B.C. Thucydides touches upon the usual themes of realism. Athenians affirm the priority of self-interest over morality. They say that considerations of right and wrong have "never turned people aside from the opportunities of aggrandizement offered by superior strength". *The History of the Peloponnesim war* contains dialogues between protagonists of realism and idealism. Thucydides supports neither side unreservedly. He cautions both against "naïve-dreaming on international politics" and against "the other pernicious extreme: unrestrained cynicism". A ruler should make a realistic assessment of the dangers from external enemies, and take defensive measures. He should not merely place faith in the good intentions of other rulers. At the same time, a ruler should abide by rules of good behaviour. He should not attack and annexe weaker kingdoms.

Critique of the Moral Tradition

Plato, Aristotle, and Cicero were all political idealists who believed that there are some universal moral values on which political life could be based. This view received support later from Christianity. Till Machiavelli's times, political thinkers generally believed that politics, including the relations among states, should be virtuous, and that the methods of warfare should remain subordinated to ethical standards.

In *The Prince*, Machiavelli seeks "the effectual truth of the matter rather than the imagined one." In modern terms, rulers have to face up to harsh realities and avoid chasing illusions. He outlines practical prescriptions for making both individuals and countries prosperous and strong. Machiavellianism is a radical type of political realism. It denies the relevance of morality in politics, and claims that all means (moral and immoral) are justified to achieve certain political ends. This is the doctrine of *raison d'état* which implies that rulers should follow whatever is good for the state and not ethical scruples or norms.

In the nineteenth-century, Hegel and Treitschke, pushed Machiavellian realism to even further extremes, and applied it to international relations. Hegel's statement that "the state has no higher duty than that of maintaining itself," gave an ethical sanction to the state's promotion of its own interest and advantage against other states. For Treitschke the state was power; it has to assert itself against other equally independent powers; and its supreme moral duty is to maintain its power. States need to follow international agreements only if it is expedient to do so. These views are part of realpolitik or a ruthlessly realistic and opportunist, as opposed to a moralistic, approach to statesmanship. Realpolitik is a national policy which regards advancement of national interest as its sole aim. Power politics rejects traditional ethics and invokes a 'higher' or different type of morality.

According to modern realist thinkers, in the absence of a common rule-making and enforcing authority, the international arena is essentially a self-help system. Each state has to ensure its survival, define its interests and pursue power. Anarchy (which here means absence of an effective international body which can regulate the conduct of sovereign nations) creates a situation in which power primarily shapes inter-state relations.

For realists, the world of (nation) states is anarchic, and security is the overriding goal of any state. To this end, states try to increase their power and engage in power-balancing for the purpose of deterring potential aggressors. Wars are fought to prevent competing nations from becoming militarily stronger. This is the famous concept of balance of power.

Realists doubt the relevance of morality to international politics. This usually leads them to the following conclusions: there is no place for morality in international relations; morality and successful conduct of international relations of a nation are incompatible; morality of States is different from customary morality; and morality, if any in international arena, is merely used instrumentally to justify states' conduct. The doctrine of realism can also be applied to domestic politics. In the domestic sphere, realism sees politics in general as a conflict of interests and a struggle for power, and seeks peace by trying to recognise common group and individual interests, rather than by moralizing.

Political thinkers distinguish between descriptive and prescriptive realism. Descriptive realism claims that in real world states do not behave morally. Either they lack the moral motivation, or are unable to act morally due to competitive struggles. Moral talk centering on interstate conflict is vacuous. States do not value morality and justice; they value power, security and national interest. States cannot afford to be moral if they want to survive in the violent international arena, and if they want to serve and protect their citizens. "Morality is simply not on the radar screen for states, given their defensive function and the brutal environment in which they subsist."

Descriptive Realism and Prescriptive Realism

Some writers oppose extreme realism and argue that states value morals, though they may often violate them. Two reasons are advanced to support this view. Individuals create states, and also desire that states should act decently. This is part of a deeper sense of community and justice. The "necessity" of state conduct in terms of pursuing power is exaggerated and rhetorical; it ignores the facts of foreign policy choice which states have in the international sphere. In normal times, states are not trapped into desperate do-or-die struggles. Many international problems can be sorted out through calm and reasoned discussions.

Prescriptive realism advocates that states should be prudent in their international conduct. States should be amoral – wedded neither to rigid moral or immoral conduct. Prudence requires that a state should adhere to a policy of smart self-regard in international affairs. A smart state will ignore morality when considering what to do on the international stage. If it is too moral, other ruthless states will exploit it. (Nice guys finish last.) A holier-than-thou state will offend other communities with different values. The approach can be summed up as: "Better to stick to the sober calculus of national interests and leave ethics out of it."

Idealism

Idealism may be defined as the spirit which leads an individual or group to adopt loftier moral standards than those which prevail around them. Idealism in international relations can be traced back to the practices which governed relations between rulers in olden times. One area in which the practices operated was war. Over time, norms arose which regulated conduct of war, treatment of prisoners and of the vanquished who surrendered. As wars were led by nobles who often had family ties, they tended to be merciful. Moral thinkers condemned wanton cruelty in wars.

Idealism in the sense of adherence to moral principles also became relevant to treaties which ended wars or laid down agreements between rulers. Treaties involved principles of good faith, reciprocity and honouring agreements in letter and spirit. Honouring international agreements and observing conventions of warfare became moral principles. It was commonly agreed that nations should not violate these to secure any undue advantage.

Immanuel Kant is among those who anticipated many modern themes of idealism in international morals. The following observations of Kant illustrate this point.

- No state shall by force interfere with the internal affairs of another state.
- It would be fatal to divide the states according to the principle of feudal lord and vassal.

- No state shall, during war, permit such acts of hostility which would make mutual confidence in the subsequent peace impossible.
- Governments need to reduce military spending and armaments. Standing armies shall in time be totally abolished. (*Immanuel Kant and International Relations of Modern Times* by Dr Habil Vyacheslav Dashichev)

Notwithstanding such sentiments expressed by philosophers, European diplomatic practices by and large ignored idealist considerations. The great powers pursued politics of naked power. The major European powers such as Austria, France, Germany, Russia and England were involved in a complicated game of maintaining balance of power in Europe. The idea was not to let any nation become the dominant power. This policy led to frequent wars.

We need not trace the twists and turns of nineteenth century European history. But it is this lack of idealism which led to the outbreak of the First World War (1914-1918). The war wreaked great havoc and shattered the belief in Western moral and cultural ideals. It also brought idealism to the fore of international diplomacy under the leadership of the US president Woodrow Wilson. As we shall see, realism reemerged after the failure of Woodrow Wilson's efforts during the period between the two world wars.

Liberal Internationalism (Utopians Idealism)

The idealists of the 1920s and 1930s are also known as liberal internationalists or utopians. The main ideas of idealists were:

- Ensuring peace and avoiding another world conflict
- Creating a system of international law, backed by international organizations
- Viewing wars as results of imperfect social conditions and political arrangements, and not of egoistic human nature
- Focusing on the common interests that could unite humanity and rejecting any inevitability of conflict between states and peoples
- Appealing to human rationality and morality.

Efforts of idealists resulted in founding of the League of Nations in 1920; and to the Kellogg-Briand Pact of 1928, outlawing war and providing for the peaceful settlements of disputes. U.S. President Woodrow Wilson was a prominent idealist of that period. He propounded a liberal programme of Fourteen Points during World War I.

But US finally did not join the League of Nations; Japan and Germany left it; and it could not prevent the outbreak of the Second World War. These events led to loss of faith in idealism both among academic thinkers and practical diplomats. However, United Nations, founded in 1945 after the Second World War, is an outcome of idealism. But thereafter, because of cold war between USA and USSR, realism became influential in the political thinking in the initial years of the post-war period. The famous 'classical' realists of this time included Hans Morgenthau and George Kennan. However, we will first consider the realist reaction to idealism during the interwar period.

E. H. CARR'S CHALLENGE TO UTOPIAN IDEALISM

In his *The Twenty Years' Crisis,* E. H. Carr attacks idealism. He lists, the main tenets of idealism as: faith in reason, confidence in progress, a sense of moral rectitude, and a belief in an underlying harmony of interests. Carr disputes the belief of idealism in moral universalism and harmony of interests.

1. Carr argues that standards used to judge policies are the products of circumstances and interests. What a nation regards as moral principles is always determined by its interests. Hence, these principles are not universal. Policies are not, as the idealists claim, based on some universal norms, independent of interests of the parties involved.
2. Carr adds that interests underlie the supposedly absolute principles or universal moral values. There are neither universal values nor universal interests. Those who refer to universal interests are in fact acting in their own interests. They think that what is best for them is best for everyone, and identify their own interests with the universal interest of the world at large.
3. Carr says that the idealist concept of the harmony of interests presupposes that human beings can rationally recognise that they have some interests in common, and that cooperation is therefore possible. Carr calls attention to the reality of conflict of interests. The world is torn apart by the particular interests of different individuals and groups. In this environment, order is based on power, not on morality. Further, morality itself is the product of power, and is embedded in the legal system which a coercive power enforces. Dominant nations claiming to represent the international community impose international moral norms on other countries.
4. Carr considers peace, social justice, prosperity, and international order, and similar universal values which idealists advocate as status quo notions. The powers that are satisfied with the status quo regard the arrangement in place as just and therefore preach peace. On the other hand, the unsatisfied powers consider the same arrangement as unjust, and so prepare for war. Hence, the way to obtain peace, if it cannot be simply enforced, is to satisfy the unsatisfied powers.

However, Carr recognises that "pure realism can offer nothing but a naked struggle for power which makes any kind of international society impossible". There is a deep yearning in many human beings, both privileged and unprivileged, for peace, order, prosperity, and justice. Idealists fail if in their attempt they do not pay enough attention to the reality of power. But in the world of pure realism, in which all values are made relative to interests, life turns into nothing more than a powergame and is unbearable.

Hans Morgenthau's Realist Principles

Hans J. Morgenthau is another famous writer who formulated an international relations theory based on realism. He identifies unquenchable human lust for power, the desire to dominate, as the main cause of conflict. He states in his *Politics among Nations: The Struggle for Power and Peace*, that "international politics, like all politics, is a struggle for power"

Morgenthau uses six principles to show how realism underlies international relations. First, realism is based on objective laws of unchanging human nature. He adopts realism into a theory of international politics and also into a political art or tool of foreign policy.

The second principle of his realist theory is the concept of power or "of interest defined in terms of power"; political leaders "think and act in terms of interest defined as power". It provides rational perspective on international politics. It serves as a basis for objective analysis delinked from motives, preferences, and intellectual and moral qualities of individual politicians.

In the third principle, Morgenthau explains that though interest defined as power is the operating principle of politics, it can assume various forms depending on times and circumstances. Political and cultural circumstances determine its substance and how it is used.

The fourth principle is about the relationship particularly the conflict between realism and ethics. Morgenthau says, "Universal moral principles cannot be applied to the actions of states in their abstract universal formulation, but ...they must be filtered through the concrete circumstances of time and place". These principles have to be prudential: "there can be no political morality without prudence; that is, without consideration of the political consequences of seemingly moral action".

The fifth principle is that prudence, and not conviction of one's own moral or ideological superiority, should guide political action. All state actors, including our own, must be seen as political entities pursuing their respective interests defined in terms of power. A state which views other nations in this light will avoid ideological confrontation, and be able to pursue policies that suitably factor in the interests of other states, while protecting and promoting its own.

Finally, Morgenthau says that power or national interest cannot be subordinated to ethics. However, ethics is still relevant to politics. "A man who was nothing but 'political man' would be a beast, for he would be completely lacking in moral restraints. A man who was nothing but 'moral man' would be a fool, for he would be completely lacking in prudence" Political art needs a fine balancing of power and morality.

To summarize: Power or interest makes politics an independent field of study. Rational state actors pursue their national interests. This premise can be the basis for a rational theory of international politics. Such a theory ignores as irrelevant the morality, religious beliefs, motives or ideological preferences of individual political leaders. It implies that states should avoid moral crusades or ideological confrontations, and look for compromise on the basis of satisfaction of their mutual interests alone. This is how conflicts can be prevented.

Criticism of Morgenthau's Views

Following criticisms are usually made against Morgenthau's realism.

1. Considering every individual as driven by a perpetual quest for power is questionable. Human beings are seldom in a single-minded pursuit of power. They are influenced by many goals and beliefs imbibed through family traditions and education.
2. Morgenthau introduces a normative (or ethical) principle of rationality into his theory. He considers a rational foreign policy "to be a good foreign policy". For him, rationality consists in calculating the costs and benefits of all alternative policies and selecting that which maximises

national power. Foreign policy failures occur when statesmen depart from a rational course aimed at minimizing risks and maximizing benefits. His critics say that all this is theorizing quite at variance with the real state of human affairs. It may be true that even statesmen act irrationally at times; but we cannot deny that foreign policy should be invariably based on cool, rational calculation.

3. The fundamental concept of Morgenthau's realism, power, is ambiguous. It can be either a means or an end in politics. But if power is only a means for gaining something else, it does not define the nature of international politics in the way Morgenthau claims. It does not allow us to understand the actions of states independently from the motives and ideological preferences of their political leaders. It cannot serve as the basis for defining politics as an autonomous sphere. Morgenthau's principles of realism are thus open to doubt. International politics cannot be studied independently of the wider historical and cultural context.

Neo-realism: Kenneth Waltz's International System

Kenneth N. Waltz reformulated realism in international relations in his book *Theory of International Politics.* His version is called structural realism or neorealism. Waltz abandoned Morgenthau's speculations on human nature and the struggle for power. He argues that states in the international system, like firms in a domestic economy, seek survival. "Internationally, the environment of states' actions, or the structure of their system, is set by the fact that some states prefer survival over other ends obtainable in the short run and act with relative efficiency to achieve that end"

According to Waltz, classical realists and idealists err alike in focusing on the individual state, and on ideological, moral and economic issues. They are unable to see the international system in isolation by separating it from the associated socio-political domain which obscures it. One can understand the primary determinants of international politics only by viewing it without the distracting background.

Waltz's neorealist theory serves a limited purpose. It cannot help in formulating domestic or international policies. His theory helps only to explain why states behave in similar ways despite their different forms of government and diverse political ideologies, and why, despite their growing interdependence, the overall picture of international relations is unlikely to change.

Waltz explains that states continue to behave uniformly over long periods because of the constraints which the structure of the international system imposes on them. Anarchy, or the absence of central authority, is the ordering principle of the international system. The units of the international system are states. Waltz considers non-state actors as relatively unimportant. Since all states want to survive, and anarchy presupposes that each state has to take care of itself, no cooperative mechanisms like division of labor or functional differentiation exist among them. Nations perform similar functions, but have differential capabilities due to differences of their strengths.

Consequently, Waltz sees power and state behaviour in a different way from the classical realists. Morgenthau claimed that states seek to rationally maximise their power. In contrast, Waltz assumes that each state seeks security and would therefore concentrate on the distribution of power in the international system.

No matter what may be the distribution of power among states, anarchy continues to be the ordering principle of international relations. This forces states to adopt the logic of self-help. In this connection, Waltz gives two reasons for rejecting the neoliberal idea that interdependence even in the anarchic international system leads to cooperation. The reasons are insecurity and unequal gains. In the context of anarchy, each state is uncertain about the intentions of others. It is afraid that the possible gains which accrue to it from cooperation may be less than those to others and thus lead it to depend on others. "States do not willingly place themselves in situations of increased dependence. In a self-help system, considerations of security subordinate economic gain to political interest."

NEOLIBERALISM

We discussed the economic doctrines of neoliberalism in the chapter on political Attitudes. Neoliberal ideas on international morality and relations are more positive and constructive than those of realists and neorealists. According to these two groups, the behaviour of nation states in international arena is wholly self-centred and offers little scope for cooperative endeavours. Neoliberals, on the other hand, see multilateral institutions and agreements as offering a route for international cooperation. Liberal institutionalists (another name for neoliberal thinkers) believe that states can seek security through construction of international agreements, regimes and structures such as arms control agreements (like START I and START II) and multilateral economic institutions like the WTO. States can engage each other through these structures, learning norms of peaceful cooperation and developing a common interest in the status quo. Liberalism is most closely associated with the work of Immanuel Kant who argued that peace is achieved through international institutions and the spread of democracy.

Realists considered states as the main players in international politics and their relations as the substance of international affairs. However, the Cold War between USA and USSR ebbed in the 1970s, and new actors became important. These are: international agencies, non-governmental organizations, and multinational corporations (MNCs). In fact, these developments led to doctrines of neoliberalism and pluralism. The concept of complex interdependence is used to describe this emerging state of global politics. They argued that there can be progress in international relations and that the future does not need to look like the past.

Objections to Neorealism

For some time, neorealism became influential in international relations – at the expense of realism. But major international developments weakened it greatly. To Waltz it seemed that in the nuclear age the international bipolar system, based on two superpowers–the United States and the Soviet Union–was not only stable but likely to persist. The fall of the Berlin Wall and the subsequent disintegration of the USSR disproved this belief. The end of the bipolar world ushered in new opportunities and challenges connected with globalization. Many critics began to argue that neorealism, like classical realism, cannot adequately account for changes in world politics.

Questions of human nature and morality disappeared from the debates between international (neo) realists and (neo) liberals. However, there are some writers who still cling stubbornly to the belief that nations of the world will learn to abide by moral principles in their mutual dealings This can at best be regarded as triumph of hope over experience. Neorealists and nediberals now discuss two main issues. Are states influenced in their international policies mainly by the anarchic structure of the international system? Or are they influenced by institutions, learning, and other factors that are conductive to cooperation? Robert Keohane, in his book *International Institutions and State Power*, accepts Waltz's emphasis on system-level theory and his general assumption that states are self-interested actors that rationally pursue their goals. However, by employing game theory he shows that states can widen the perception of their self-interest through economic cooperation and involvement in international institutions. Patterns of interdependence can thus affect world politics. Keohane calls for systemic theories that would be able to deal better with factors affecting state interaction, and with change.

POSTMODERNISM

Some writers believe that three schools of thought – critical theory, postmodernism and feminism – have also influenced thinking on international relations morality. Feminist agendas are often articulated in many UN forums. Many themes of gender equity and justice have been accepted in western and other nations. These nations try to propagate feminist agendas in other nations and in UN institutions, policies and programmes. However, it is difficult to imagine what real role can be played by doctrines like critical theory or postmodernism in diplomatic practice.

We have briefly discussed critical theory in the chapter on Political Attitudes in the context of twentieth century developments in Marxism. Critical theory, as the name implies, is an attack on the basic values of traditional Western Societies and their culture. It argues that government and dominant institutions like media, academia, research agencies and thinktanks represent the views of hegemonistic elites. It has turned large groups against their own nation and society. It is therefore unlikely to influence a nation's diplomacy or international stance.

Postmodernism is a movement in Western philosophy which arose in late 20th century. It rejects the values and worldview derived from modern Western philosophical theories grounded in rational scientific outlook. It has little faith in human reason and denies the possibility of objective knowledge, especially in social sciences. Postmodernism regards the conclusions of social science, art and literature as based on an individual's subjectivity. It views mainstream social values and institutions with scepticism and suspicion. It regards that the political and social power of dominant sections of society, based on overt or covert ideology, permeates social sciences and humanities. It is doubtful whether post modernism can significantly influence international relations or morality.

FEMINISM

Feminism is the belief that men and women should have equal rights and opportunities; it is organized activity in support of women's rights and interests. The movement witnessed three waves. In the first, women sought full legal equality with men, including full educational opportunity, equal compensation and the right to vote. In 1950s, a second wave of feminism arose challenging the restricted role assigned to women in the workplace and the tendency to confine women to the household arena. A third wave of feminism arose in the late 20th century and was notable for challenging middle-class white feminists and for broadening feminism's goals to encompass equal rights for all people, regardless of race, creed, economic or educational status, physical appearance or ability, or sexual orientation. Students will find a more detailed account on feminist ethics in the chapter glossary of terms.

TENETS OF INTERNATIONAL MORALITY: UN CHARTER

With the above background, we can now consider the tenets of international morality. We have already listed above while discussing idealism one set of maxims of international morality. Any list of international morals will include these general maxims. We, need to consider two more formulations. We adapt one list from the famous liberal thinker John Rawls. The other formulation or listing is from the UN Charter to which we made a passing reference earlier while discussing sovereign-equality of states in international legal order.

In one sense, the UN Charter (adopted in San Francisco in 1945) represents the set of moral principles which its member-states promise to follow in their international dealings. Of course, cynics may argue that nations subscribing to UN Charter are making moral gestures and virtue-signaling with no intent of observing them in practice. Nevertheless, the UN Charter represents the solemn commitments of its member-states. The moral ideas of the UN Charter are partly obscured by its ponderous, legalistic, and grandiloquent language. It includes matters like social development which seldom feature in core discussions on international relations. Its content also includes matters of procedure and affirmations of commitment. Leaving aside these issues, we abstract and express the Charter's maxims of international morality in simple terms.

The portions directly bearing on international morality consist of three parts: Preamble, Purposes of the UN, and the principles which member-nations agree to follow.

The Preamble

- The Preamble refers to the great human misery which the First World War and the Second World War caused and affirms its determination to save future generations from the scourge of war.
- It reaffirms faith (i) in fundamental human rights (ii) in the dignity and worth of the human person (iii) in the equal rights of men and women and (iv)in the equal rights of big and small nations.
- It seeks to establish conditions for maintaining [international] justice and for respecting obligation arising from treaties and other sources of international law.
- It seeks to promote social progress and better standards of life in larger freedom.

For achieving the above ends, the members express their determination:

- To practice tolerance and live together in peace with one another as good neighbours
- To unite our strength to maintain international peace and security
- To ensure, by accepting principles and by instituting necessary methods, that armed force shall not be used except in the common interest
- To employ international machinery for promoting economic and social advancement of all people

The Charter mentions the following as requirements for achieving the aims set out in the preamble.

- An environment of peace, tolerance and good neighbourly relations
- A commitment to act together for collective or international security
- Adoption of principles and institutions for avoiding use of armed forces

Purposes of the UN

The main purpose of UN is to maintain international peace and security. From this two instrumental objectives follow: to act collectively to prevent and remove threats to peace; and to suppress acts of aggression or other breaches of peace. An allied purpose is to settle peacefully, and in accordance with the principles of justice and international law, international disputes or situations which can disrupt peace.

As we noted, UN has created a new international political order of independent and sovereign states. It seeks to develop friendly relations among nations based on respect for the principle of equal rights and self-determination of peoples. It commits to take suitable measures to strengthen universal peace.

It emphasises the need for international co-operation for solving international problems of an economic, social, cultural, or humanitarian character. It gives high priority to respecting human rights. It strongly advocates granting of fundamental freedoms to all without distinction of race, sex, language, or religion.

Principles of Conduct Adopted by UN Members

- Sovereign equality of all Members
- Fulfilling in good faith the obligations assumed by Members in accordance with the Charter
- Settling by members of their international disputes by peaceful means so as not to endanger international peace and security, and justice
- Avoidance by Members of the threat or use of force against the territorial integrity or political independence of any state, or in any other manner inconsistent with the Purposes of the United Nations
- Assisting UN in its actions under the present Charter, and refraining from assisting any state against which the UN is taking preventive or enforcement action

- ¤ Ensuring by UN that non UN member states comply with these Principles to the extent necessary for the maintenance of international peace and security.
- ¤ Non intervention by UN in internal affairs of members nor requiring them to submit such matters for settlement under the Charter.

From the above paraphrase, it is clear that the UN Charter is mainly focused on world peace, amity among nations, peaceful resolution of disputes and international cooperation. Its themes are derived from idealism. Its emphasis on international cooperation is also in line with neoliberalism. There is no place for radical realism within this framework. However, in actual practice, nations while subscribing to the UN Charter, have followed diluted realist approaches in their actual diplomatic practices. Even after the UN came into being, there have been numerous wars, though of course not on significant global level. But for our purposes, it is sufficient to note that the principles embodied in UN Charter form the norms or maxims of currently accepted international morality. There have been attempts to widen and modify these principles. We will consider them later in the chapter.

John Rawls's List of International Morals

John Rawls discusses the morality of international politics in his book *The Law of Peoples*. His list of international moral norms is based on his version of political liberalism. States have to comply with these norms (code of conduct) to qualify as members of good standing in the international political community. The code is minimalist or represents the lowest common denominator of international morality.

The code of conduct which John Rawls gives is outlined below. John Rawls uses the term 'peoples' while referring to states or nations. We have replaced it (in the following list) with 'state' which accords more with common usage.

1. States are free and independent, and their freedom and independence are to be respected by other states.
2. States should observe treaties and undertakings.
3. States are equal and are parties to the agreements that bind them.
4. States have to observe a duty of non-intervention 'in the domestic affairs of other nations'.
5. States have the right of self-defence but no rights to instigate war for reasons other than self-defence.
6. States should honour human rights.
7. States should observe certain specified restrictions in the conduct of war.
8. States have a duty to assist other peoples living under unfavorable conditions that prevent their having a just or decent political and social regime.

We need to consider briefly the implications of the preceding list of international morals. John Rawls's code for guiding the international action of states includes the rights of each state to independence and non-intervention by others in its domestic affairs. The code also contains traditional norms which outlaw war as an instrument of policy and which prescribe that treaties and agreements should be observed. However, the human rights which Rawls identifies in this context do not include democratic rule or the freedoms which go with it. Of course, within a state wedded to liberalism, democracy and liberties are cardinal values. But Rawls is concerned here with proposing an international framework in which states with different internal political regimes (i.e. liberal and non liberal) can live in peace and harmony. In this framework, liberal states will not insist that all states should follow full blown liberalism; and illiberal regimes will adopt some watered down principles of liberalism.

The illiberal states will have to accept two fundamental limitations on their policies. They will not try to expand their territorial boundaries, or use war as an instrument of their policy. They will adopt legal systems which prescribe some moral duties on their citizens. Rawls formulates in this context the concept of illiberal but decent societies. Such illiberal societies usually ignore equality of individuals before law and liberal rights such as freedom of speech. Still, public officials in such societies sincerely work towards common welfare. If government actions harm the interests of any individuals, they are allowed to represent their point of view at some stage in the political process. It is of course possible that their views may be suppressed thereafter. Illiberal states who observe the fundamental limitations on their powers will be accorded legitimacy in the comity of nations.

States which do not meet the minimum requirements are termed outlaw regimes. Rawls regards their existence as an unfortunate fact. One can easily think of many contemporary examples. But Rawls cites examples of societies which recognise no limits on the applicability of their philosophical or cultural views and impose them on all people. For this purpose, he goes into past history. The examples he gives (during certain periods in history) are of Spain, France, and the Hapsburg Empire. Rawls condemns such societies for refusing to tolerate other reasonable ways of organizing political life. We may note that Rawls is hesitant to give contemporary examples. Rawls is a very eminent writer, but his avoidance of contemporary examples appears to be an instance of academic diplomacy.

Rawls's framework implies that states should avoid ideological crusades and struggles against other nations with divergent regimes. During the years of cold war, the liberal western democracies and Soviet bloc were engaged in an ideological struggle which threatened world peace. Many nations in UN are autocracies of various hues which do not respect civil rights. But so long as they observe minimum levels of decency in governance, they have to be left alone according to the norm of non intervention.

Rawls also mentions that some countries face extremely unfavorable circumstances like famine and immiseration. Rawls urges that well-ordered societies should help these countries. Well-ordered societies can be liberal or illiberal states. They are able to effectively organize their collective political life and maintain minimally decent political institutions and morally acceptable relations with outside nations. The well-ordered societies should help other societies in reaching a similar state of governance. But Rawls does not advocate distributive justice between nations. The rich nations are under no moral obligation to transfer their wealth and resources to poor nations for promoting economic equality between nations. For Rawls, the international community is a well-ordered society of well-ordered societies, in which each state should respect and tolerate the different methods of governance of other states.

JUST WAR THEORIES

As we noted before, conduct of war according to accepted conventions is an important aspect of international morality. There are three main schools of thought on the ethics of war and peace-Realism; Just War Theory and Pacifism.

Realism

We have already discussed realism. Realism denies the applicability of moral concepts like justice to foreign policy. Power and national security guide states in wartime; talk of the morality of warfare is fictitious. Ethics have no role in the harsh domain of global politics. Nations pursue their vital interests in security, dominion over others, and economic growth, unmindful of moral ideals.

Just war theory

Aristotle, Cicero and Augustine are regarded as the founders of Just war theory. Hugo Grotius is a great thinker of this tradition. Many tenets of the just war tradition have been included in current international laws - such as The United Nations Charter and The Hague and Geneva Conventions – which govern armed conflict.

Just war theory is divided into three parts which have Latin names. These parts are: 1) jus ad bellum, which is about the justice of resorting to war in the first place; 2) jus in bello, which is about justice of conduct within war; and 3) jus post bellum, which is about the justice of peace agreements and the termination phase of war.

Jus AD Bellum

Just war theory maintains that recourse to war is justified only if a state fulfils all the following six requirements:

- A state may launch a war for right reasons. Just causes of war are: self-defence from external attack; defending others from such attack; protecting innocents from brutal regimes; and punishment for an uncorrected grievous wrong.
- Just war should have right intention and not ulterior motives like seizing land or power or desire for wreaking vengeance or ethnic cleansing.
- Duly empowered legal authorities should decide on war according to proper procedure and inform public and the enemy state.
- War should be a last resort after exhausting all avenues of peaceful settlement.
- War should not be undertaken unless there is reasonable chance of success.
- War should be considered if the benefits are proportional and the costs are worth the benefits.

Jus In Bello

Jus in bello refers to justice in war, to right conduct in war. Military commanders, officers and soldiers who formulate and execute the war policy of a particular state are responsible for strict adherence to jus in bello norms. They are to be held responsible for any breach of the norms. Those who violate the norms may be tried for war crimes, either by their national military justice system or even by the newly-formed International Criminal Court (under the 1998 Treaty of Rome).

There are several rules of jus in bello:

- No weapons like chemical and biological weapons prohibited under international law should be used. Use of nuclear weapons, though not prohibited, would be cataclysmic.
- Only legitimate political, military and industrial targets should be attacked, and civilians should not be deliberately attacked.
- Use of arms should be proportional to objects, and weapons of mass destruction are hardly proportional.
- Prisoners of war should be treated fairly in accordance with the Geneva Convention.
- Evil campaigns like mass rapes, genocide and ethic cleansing should be absolutely avoided.
- There should be no reprisals of any kind.

Jus Post Bellum

Jus post bellum refers to justice during the phase of war termination. It covers the manner of ending war and smoothly transiting from war to peace. International law scarcely touches upon this area; however, the following principles can be mentioned.

- Peace agreements should be reasonable and moderate and not be vengeful; nor should unconditional surrender be sought or enforced.
- Peace agreement should rectify the wrongs that led to the war.
- All groups in vanquished country should be fairly treated without exacting revenge on any one.
- Civilians unconnected with war decisions should not be penalized.
- Those responsible for blatant human rights violations and war crimes should be punished.
- Financial losses suffered by nations who are victims of aggression may be compensated without however overburdening the vanquished nation.
- Humane political, administrative and judicial reforms may be introduced in the defeated nation.

PACIFISM

Pacifism totally opposes war. While pacifists oppose all killing, they particularly abhor the mass killing which usually accompanies war. They object to this type and scale of killing. Pacifists believe that no moral grounds can justify war, and that it is always wrong. Many thinkers disagree with this blanket opposition to war.

The pacifist position has been criticized from many sides, including by Just war theorists. Some critics argue that the pacifist shies away from the brutal measures needed for defending himself and his country in order to maintain his own inner moral purity. The pacifist is a type of free-rider who while enjoying the benefits of citizenship refuses to share its burdens. Some argue that a pacifist is an internal threat to the over-all security of his state.

But this criticism appears to be harsh. Morality is premised on the belief that moral agents ought to do what they consider good or just and to avoid what they consider bad or unjust. This view weakens the criticism of pacifism. Further, the view that pacifists are morally or spiritually selfish is difficult to maintain. Many pacifists have braved social boycott and prison terms in war times. Genuine pacifists arc perhaps more interested in promoting a humane world than in preserving their inner moral purity.

Some writers consider pacifism's idealism as over optimistic, and its vision of a nonviolent world as an empty dream. Practical statesmen and people have to adopt a less utopian moral outlook on war. One has to recognise that sometimes war is morally justified in the real world. Nazis could not have been defeated by any means other than war.

Another criticism of pacifism is that failure to effectively resist international aggression rewards aggression as it fails to protect defenseless people. Pacifists argue that armed invasion can be effectively countered by an organized and committed campaign of non-violent civil disobedience, accompanied by international diplomatic and economic sanctions. No invader could administer the conquered nation when met with such systematic isolation, non-cooperation and non-violent resistance. The invaders cannot carry on work in factories, fields and stores or run the infrastructure.

In this context, the commonly cited examples are Mahatma Gandhi's campaign against the British rule in the late 1940s and Martin Luther King's civil rights crusade in the 1960s on behalf of African-Americans. Walzer argues that effective non-violent resistance depends upon the scruples of those against whom it is aimed. It was only because the British and the Americans had some scruples, and were moved by the determined idealism of the non-violent protesters, that they acquiesced to their demands. But aggressors will not always be so moved. A tyrant like Hitler, for example, might interpret non-violent resistance as weakness, deserving contemptuous crushing.

This sort of civil disobedience relies on the scruples of the invader, and fails if the aggressor is totally ruthless. The invader can displace the local population with people from home country. (China seems to have done this partly in Tibet and Sinkiang.) Under certain circumstances the defence of people's lives and rights against such invaders of various hues will need use of force. Under such conditions, (as Walzer says), adherence to pacifism might even amount to "a disguised form of surrender."

Moral thinkers have extended debates - from deontological and consequentialist perspectives - on whether pacifism is justifiable. In the real world, it is neither reasonable nor fair to require a political community not to avail itself of the most effective means available for resisting an aggressive invasion which threatens the lives and rights of its citizens. It is simply not reasonable to require a state to stand down while an aggressor—be it state or terrorist—wreaks havoc, murder and mayhem upon its people.

Coercive Regime Change

There is considerable controversy on coercive regime change - changing the government of a nation through external military intervention. Recent events in Afghanistan, Iraq, Libya, Egypt and the civil war in Syria involve this question. Can coercive regime change ever be justified, or is it essentially an act of imperialism? One view is that UN mandated sovereign-equality of nations prohibits external intervention in the internal affairs of a state.

Some advocates of human rights and democracy justify coercive regime change in the following circumstances. (1) The war resulting in regime change should be just and conducted properly. (2) The regime sought to be replaced should be illegitimate. (Any such regime forfeits its state rights). (3) The goal of the reconstruction should be to build a reasonably just regime. (4) Human rights should be respected during the war and the transformation process.

Sceptics argue that it is often impossible to transplant liberal democratic institutions in societies which are steeped in religiously sanctioned authoritarian social structures. But optimists point to the coercive regime change for creation of rights respecting states as was actually done in Germany and Japan from 1945-55. Hence, the idea is neither conceptually nor empirically impossible. But it is very difficult, and in some instances, well nigh impossible.

NEW DIMENSIONS OF INTERNATIONAL MORALITY

In recent years, political thinkers have widened the scope of discussions on international morality. Changes in theory and contemporary events contributed to this trend. The new topics which now figure in discussions of international morality are the following:

- Transfer of resources from rich countries to less developed nations
- Removing inequities in economic exchanges (trade, commerce and finance) between developed and less developed countries
- Giving greater voice to developed countries in the working of international agencies
- Humanitarian assistance to countries in the grip of famine and immiserization
- Intervention in states which carry out genocide, ethnic cleansing or war on their own people
- Naturalization of people who migrate into a country and settle there
- Adopting a cosmopolitan as opposed to a national approach to morals.

We will discuss these questions in the rest of the chapter.

International Economic Equity: Promoting Equitable Development

The world is divided into a few rich and many poor nations. During the imperialist phase of the world history, many poor nations were the colonies of the rich nations. The poverty of the poor countries is largely due to the exploitation of the imperialist nations. While the imperialist nations progressed economically, the poor countries stagnated. The historically unequal relations between rich and poor nations have got embedded into the international economic system, and continue to persist in new forms.

Many international economic institutions are under the hegemony of the rich nations. These nations dominate the management structures of the international institutions such as IMF, World Bank and WTO, and significantly influence their policies and processes. International morality in the economic sphere implies that rich nations should help the poor nations. Such help can consist of providing concessional economic aid, changing the international economy to the advantage of the poor, and giving the poor nations a greater representation in the international economic institutions. Many of these questions form part of international economic relations. They are on the agenda of "North south dialogue" which refers to the negotiations between the rich and poor nations on economic matters.

The disparities between North and South or the gap between rich and poor has doubled in the recent decades. Presently, 20% of world's people consume more than 80% of its wealth. During the

1980s, per capita incomes declined in many developing countries especially in sub-Saharan Africa. Poverty, famine, and disease remain widespread. Third World countries cannot cope with these problems, and in a global economy need help from the industrial North.

Economic development has a moral component in that it enhances the quality of life. Ideally, development promotes a suitable environment for people to develop their full potential and lead productive and creative lives. This also underlies the ethical end of human self realisation. As a prerequisite to this end, development has to generate employment, and provide social services covering health, education and sanitation. Rich nations have a moral duty to help the poor nations in their developmental efforts.

After the Second World War, there was a general recognition that peace requires economic integration between nations. Multilateral institutions like the World Bank, and IMF were set up around that time to promote international cooperation and assistance. This architecture exists till today. Initially, the multilateral institutions had two goals: helping in the post war reconstruction of the war ravaged countries; and promoting development in poor countries. Afterwards, some rich nations created their own agencies for aiding poor countries. Many NGOs were also active advocates of aid to poor nations.

The ideal way of assisting the development efforts of poor nations is through grants which have no repayment obligations. Soft loans with low interest and long repayment period come next. International aid or official development assistance (ODA) is a grant from donor nations to poor countries. Unlike loans, it places no burden on its recipients.

The developed nations made certain commitments to assist the poor countries. The World Council of Churches in 1958 called on the rich countries to allocate 1 percent of their national income as aid for developing countries. The Development Assistance Group of the Organisation for Economic Co-operation and Development (OECD) later endorsed this recommendation. UN General Assembly in 1970 agreed to a target of 0.7 percent. But very few rich countries are meeting this target.

FOREIGN AID DURING THE COLD WAR

From the 1950s to the fall of the Berlin Wall in 1989, there was intense cold War between the West and the Soviet Union. The relations between the two blocs were marked by mutual suspicion, intense hostility and political competition. Aid became enmeshed in foreign policy and geopolitical calculations. After the breakup of the USSR, aid to Eastern Europe and Central Asia to help them in their transition to market economy was also guided by political considerations.

Western nations also extended food aid to poor and needy nations. But this was not motivated by pure philanthropy, rather it was partly the outcome of their domestic policies towards agriculture. Under these policies, they subsidized agriculture, which led to surpluses. These were dumped on world markets and used for food aid. The whole process has retarded agricultural growth in poor countries. The rich countries have been protecting their markets from competitive imports. Poor countries are denied access to markets in the West through various means. These unequal relations harmed the poor nations. Despite various rounds of discussions between rich and poor nations under the aegis of the World Trade Organization negotiations, agricultural protectionism is still high in the West.

In the 1970s aid was linked to structural adjustment or to changes in the macroeconomic policy of aid receiving countries. This approach aimed at supporting the poor countries which faced severe macroeconomic imbalances characterised by high balance of payments deficits, fiscal deficits and excessive debt. Aid was used to push neoliberal economic reform and to bolster the private sector. The recipient country had to accept conditions that sought to enforce macroeconomic and trade reforms, and to facilitate private (particularly foreign) investment. Donors insisted on structural economic reforms without simultaneous attention to institutional reform, social sector investments or social cohesion. Structural reform policies harshly impacted on the poor people. By the mid-1990s, the public opinion turned against externally imposed market based structural reforms which ignored the state of the poor and the need for social services.

POVERTY REDUCTION AND RECENT DEVELOPMENT MODELS

By the late 1990s, the goals of development began to embrace the elimination of poverty in all its dimensions. The earlier approach concentrated mainly on increasing the income and consumption of the poor people. The new approach also focuses on improving education, health, and other human capacities of the poor - not simply on increasing their income levels. Poor people have to be helped not only by creating opportunities for employment and income earning but also by empowering them through a combination of education, health, and greater participation in politics and community decisions.

Millennium Development Goals

In 2000 heads of state of both rich and poor countries committed themselves to achieving the Millennium Development Goals (MDGs). These are:

- eradicate extreme poverty
- achieve universal primary education
- promote gender equality and empower women
- reduce child mortality
- improve maternal health
- combat HIV/AIDS, malaria, and other diseases
- ensure environmental sustainability
- develop a global partnership for development

Based on this declaration, the 2002 Monterrey Conference established a new partnership for development. The rich countries promised to increase aid to poor countries. The developing countries agreed to undertake reforms to improve aid effectiveness. Neither side could fulfil its commitments. Aid flows have increased, but these remain far short of the agreed targets. There is also an ongoing debate between strong advocates and opponents of the need for development assistance from the rich to the poor.

Resource transfers alone cannot help developing countries overcome their poverty. Rich countries can reform their trade and other policies to help poor countries. They can change their protectionist policies - especially in agriculture and textiles - and allow market access to the exports of poor countries. Changes in trade, investment, migration, environment, and technology policies in rich countries would help people from poor countries. For example, advanced countries should allow liberal entry (through appropriate visa procedures) to knowledge workers - engineers, doctors, nurses, programmers, accountants and the like - from developing countries. Rich nations have to bear the main burden for carrying out measures for protecting environment. This is known as "common but differentiated responsibility". Rich nations need to be liberal in their policies for transferring technologies to poor nations. They have to assist poor countries many of whom are caught in severe external debt problems.

Despite the progress made in the past 50 years, poverty remains a great challenge. Approximately 1 billion people still live on less than one dollar per day. Aid is essential for supporting growth and reducing poverty. Raising the volume and the quality of aid is a moral, strategic, and economic imperative.

MORAL ROOTS OF INDIA'S FOREIGN POLICY

Although, it was Jawaharlal Nehru who shaped India's foreign policy, Mahatma Gandhi's thinking and philosophy influenced it greatly. India's foreign policy is based on the Gandhian values of its freedom struggle. It was Gandhian ideas that set the tone of India's foreign policy in the early decades of its independence. These were:

- Non-alignment or the right to follow an independent foreign policy and to decide foreign policy issues on merits;
- Moral, diplomatic and economic support for the struggle against colonialism, racialism and apartheid;
- Non-violence and the quest for nuclear disarmament; and
- India's role as an international peacemaker.

India's stand on international problems was based on moral clarity and courage. Many nations admired this approach. It won for India the leadership of the developing countries. It gave India an influence in world affairs out of proportion to its real economic and political strength. Gandhi's message greatly influenced the perceptions of outsiders about India. From the beginning, while formulating its foreign policy, India focused not only on its own narrow national interests, but also on the impact its policy would have on other similarly placed Asian and African countries. India's foreign policy had a strong idealist streak in this sense, and expressed solidarity with the other nations which shared its colonial past.

Both supporters and critics of Indian foreign policy invariably focus attention on Panchsheel. It goes back to a stage long past in Indian foreign policy. Nehru perhaps thought it a centerpiece of policy which also held up a moral torch in the cynical environment of diplomacy. While some praise Panchsheel for its idealism, others condemn it for its unrealism.

The Panchsheel Treaty (from Sanskrit, panch: five, sheel: virtues) is considered the high watermark of the diplomacy of this period. Panchsheel consists of five principles for peaceful coexistence between nations or for governing relations between states. Their first formal codification in treaty form was in an agreement between China and India in 1954. The five principles to which states have to subscribe are:

1. Mutual respect for each other's territorial integrity and sovereignty
2. Mutual non-aggression
3. Mutual non-interference in each other's internal affairs
4. Equality and mutual benefit and
5. Peace and coexistence.

Panchsheel is premised on the belief that the states which became independent after colonial era would be able to develop a new and more principled approach to international relations. About Panchsheel, Pandit Jawaharlal Nehru said: "If these principles were recognised in the mutual relations of all countries, then indeed there would hardly be any conflict and certainly no war." The five principles were later included in a revised form in the ten principles of Asian-African Conference (1955) in Bandung. The Five Principles formed the basis of the Non-Aligned Movement, which began in Belgrade in 1961.

Panchsheel ended as a sad story for India. The boundary dispute between India and China resulted in outbreak of open war in 1962. Panchsheel (April 1954) agreement was set to last for eight years. When it lapsed, the provision for renewal of the agreement was not taken up.

Some writers have been critical of the Five Principles. According to, Peter Lyon, a British writer on international relations: "Though neutralists in general, and at that time Mr Nehru in particular, seemed to regard these principles as being a special contribution to world politics, they were not at all original, were repetitious, and really boiled down to the edict that a state's independence should not be infringed." Any criticism of Panchsheel may seem like flogging a dead horse. But its strong strain of naiveté and misconceived idealism divorced from harsh realities continue to plague India's foreign policy.

The lack of hard realism in India's foreign policy has cost us dear. "Among the mistakes that India made in its Gandhi-inspired and Nehru-directed foreign policy were the referral of the Kashmir issue to the United Nations in 1948, the 'bhai-bhai' (brother-brother) policy towards China and the missed opportunity in Nepal to fully integrate it into the Indian security system." Indian Policy makers, in referring the Kashmir issue to UN, appear to have shown simple mindedness and credulity. UN is a political organ, and not an impartial judicial body. Indian policy makers also made a grievous error in failing to support the autonomous status of Tibet vis-a-vis China. With these two errors, India threw away forever the strategic bargaining chips it could have used against China. Perhaps Nehru was more concerned with his image as a messiah of peace and as an anti-imperialist crusader than with India's geostrategic interests in its neighbourhood.

These errors arose at least partly from misguided application of Gandhian principles to India's external relations. There is another instance in which Mahatma Gandhi forced the Indian government to sacrifice national financial interest to grand moral principles. After Pakistan's invasion of Kashmir, many people argued that India should hold on to the Rs 55 crores that India owed Pakistan. Gandhi went on a fast unto death to force government to pay the amount to Pakistan. Ultimately the government relented. The point is not that India should have reneged on its commitment. This could have been used as a means to wring some concessions from Pakistan.

This mindset continues to afflict India's policy towards Pakistan. This has become an in-built feature of Indian foreign policy establishment. Many observers argue that India showed the same softness at the Simla Conference in 1972 after the war over Bangladesh. India had at that time more than 90,000 Pakistani prisoners of war. While they cannot be housed permanently in India, some concessions could have been secured for their return. Although we mention this point of criticism we would like to add that no Indian can refrain from praising Srimati Indira Gandhi for her grit and determination during the Bangladesh crisis. Critics complain that India's responses to terrorist attacks are confined to hand wringing and breast beating. India is seen as amiable and ineffectual - a soft target to foreign and indigenous terrorist groups. In these areas, the legacy of Gandhian morality seems to have ill served the interests of the people and the nation. As students would be aware, India's stand on Pakistan and terrorism became much tougher after the NDA government came to power in 2014. Some of the namby-pamby approaches of earlier times have been given the go by.

The second area where Gandhi's thinking had an enduring impact on India's foreign policy is Palestine. Gandhi's editorial in the Harijan of 11 November 1938 was a major policy statement that guides India's policy on Palestine to this day. Despite his sympathy for the Jews who had been subjected to discrimination and persecution for centuries, Gandhi was clear about the rights of the Palestinians. "*My sympathy,*" he said, *"does not blind me to the requirements of justice. The cry for the national home for the Jews does not make much appeal to me... Why should they not, like other peoples of the earth, make that country their home where they are born and where they earn their livelihood? Palestine belongs to the Arabs in the same sense that England belongs to the English or France to the French. It is wrong and inhuman to impose the Jews on the Arabs... Surely it would be a crime against humanity to reduce the proud Arabs so that Palestine can be restored to the Jews partly or wholly as their national home."*

We need not enter into the merits of Indian foreign policy stance on the complex Palestine issue. There is, however, a surprising moral inconsistency in Mahatma Gandhi's formulation. It appears that the English, French and the Arabs are entitled to homelands. But the Jews are advised to live wherever historical circumstances have placed them. Possibly, Mahatma Gandhi's views on Jews and Palestine are also based on the strategic imperatives of Indian Independence movement. He was perhaps trying to appeal to the sentiments of Muslim masses, and enlist their support for the national movement. Indian foreign policy on Palestine is guided not only by the views of Mahatma Gandhi but also by India's geopolitical interests in Middle East. India has also recognised Israel as a nation. It is also a large buyer of military supplies from Israel. In this way, the Indian foreign policy makers certainly kept national interests in view.

Our intention is not to assess or criticize India's foreign policy. It is rather to touch upon certain moral ideas which went into its making. In studying international morality, one examines whether and in what manner morals influence international relations. In contrast, the process of foreign policy formulation, its implementation and its impacts are studied in the theory and history of diplomatic practice. This area falls outside the scope of our discussion. Our remarks on the results of Indian foreign policy are incidental and are for purposes of rounding off the discussion.

COSMOPOLITANISM IN MORALS

Liberalism believes in moral egalitarianism - the doctrine that human beings deserve equal moral consideration. Thus race, ethnicity, sex, language or religion cannot be used to discriminate between people. Now, traditionally liberals applied this principle of non discrimination only within national boundaries. Some liberal thinkers believe that egalitarian guarantees should not be confined to national boundaries or to territorial states. They consider an individual's nationality also an accident of birth like his/her race, gender, or social class. It cannot therefore be made a basis for differentiation in dispensing administrative justice. This leads to the vexing problem of the moral status of national boundaries.

In many cases, this is not just an esoteric theoretical problem. It has the following consequences.

¤ It undermines the legitimacy of national boundaries of nations.

¤ It obliterates the distinction between citizens and foreigners.

¤ It will confer rights on the hordes of illegal aliens or immigrants who move into and settle in a country.

USA is currently facing these questions in regard to illegal Latin American immigrants. Liberals represented by the Democratic Party are in favour of conferring citizenship on these immigrants. Republican Party which represents conservative opinion opposes this proposal, partly because the immigrants after acquiring citizenship may form a permanent support group of Democrats.

This is a highly sensitive issue in India. There is continuous and unchecked immigration from Bangladesh into Assam, West Bengal and North East. It is claimed that this infiltration has taken place with the connivance of some political parties. This infiltration has also led to an agitation from the Assamese people. This is one of the main reasons for the frequent violent eruptions in the north east. This infiltration is massive enough to undermine the political standing of the local peoples and their way of life. Our limited interest in the subject is from the point of view of ethical theory. We can only touch upon these practical issues, and interested readers can study the matter further on their own.

From a theoretical angle, this raises the question: can moral egalitarianism be confined to national boundaries? There are three reasons for restricting it to the citizens of the nation.

(A) Duties towards fellow nationals differ in kind from those owed to others because national community is the source of language and values used in making moral judgments.

(B) Distinct duties to one's fellow nationals arise because it is necessary for well being and protection of the national community.

(C) Men find themselves located in a particular society, share a culture and are determined to live within it. This national or local community has to preserve its distinct identity. This gives it a right to close its borders against outsiders, even if those outsiders are needier than its members. Admission and exclusion of outsiders or foreign nationals are at the core of national independence. They constitute the meaning of self-determination. Otherwise, there would be no nations. Patriotism belongs to a class of loyalty-exhibiting virtues; other such virtues include - love of one's own family and of relatives, friendship and loyalty to cherished institutions.

Patriotism conflicts with universalism in morals. Many TV anchors and talkers they assemble sneer at patriotism and describe it as tribalism. We have given above the moral reasons which support patriotism. There is no need to teach patriotic virtues to common people. They are ingrained in them. We need to consider this question since many pseudo intellectuals try to demoralize ordinary folks by dismissing their attachment to their nation, religion, language and culture as barbarian parochialism.

MacIntyre argues that a flourishing community of people with shared moral norms and values is a necessary precondition of one's continued existence as a moral agent; therefore, patriotism–understood as involving special obligations to maintain and defend one's nation–is a precondition of morality. He mentions that the ends in terms of which morality is justified to human beings arise in the shared understandings of the community. No one can remain as a lone moral hero without any community of shared moral understanding. MacIntyre observes, "We are unlikely to flourish as moral agents if deprived of a community of shared moral understandings. Hence, morality and patriotism cannot be meaningfully contrasted as distinct strands of normative thinking; patriotism is the precondition of moral functioning." He adds that some parts of the national project must be treated as permanently exempt from critical examination. If a national community systematically disowns its true history or substitutes a fictitious history for it (for various reasons) or tries to replace national ties derived from shared history with bonds of reciprocal self-interest, it will disintegrate.

INTERVENTION IN OTHER NATIONS

There is one more aspect of international morality which needs a brief discussion. We referred to it briefly earlier. The basic norm of international political order is respect for independence and sovereignty of nations. This implies that outside powers should not intervene in the internal affairs of a nation. Such intervention is countenanced when in certain emergencies the Security Council of UN authorizes intervention.

The emergencies can originate from many causes. But we may consider two important circumstances. An emergency can arise when a state conducts genocide against its own population. The most notorious example is the killing of six million Jews by the Nazis under Hitler. Another example is genocide in Kampuchea under Pol Pot. Genocide means massive killing of people.

Another emergency arises due to 'ethnic cleansing'. This means that in an area inhabited by a diverse population, a particular section is forcibly ejected. The section of population targeted for eviction is selected on the basis of its race, ethnicity or religion. A recent example is from the state of Yugoslavia during its phase of disintegration. From their areas of dominance, Serbs tried to drive out Croats; Croats did the same with Serbs. The whole process was accompanied by war crimes and unspeakable atrocities to force ethnic cleansing. NATO forces intervened on humanitarian grounds.

A state has a right to preserve itself against domestic rebellion. Many countries are made up of diverse populations. The divesities relate to ethnicity, race, language, religion or denominational differences within the same religion. When any particular community in a country is populous and occupies a definite geographic area in that country, it may harbour ambitions of independence. It may want to secede, and start a violent struggle with military and material support from outside states. The current struggles in the Middle East have their origin in these causes. They involve clashes between Sunnis and Shias, moderate and radical Islamic groups and rival tribal formations. The details are irrelevant for our present discussion.

UN charter does not authorize such secessionist movements. UN has adopted an interpretation of 'self determination' which excludes any claims of secessionist groups within a nation state. The state has to however treat the different groups within its population fairly and impartially. It has to respect their minimum human rights. Some states have to engage in military conflict to overcome and crush secessionist movements. At times, they violate the international law which governs warfare. Recently, the Assad regime in Syria used chemical weapons against rebel held areas and caused widespread civilian damages. USA considered it a sufficient ground to militarily attack Syria in violation of its sovereignty. The matter ended after Assad agreed to the destruction of his chemical weapon stockpile under UN supervision.

Besides humanitarian intervention, powerful nations have also brought about 'regime changes' in a state. Regime change means replacing the existing government of a state by another government which agrees to abide by canons of internationally recognised norms of behaviour. The well known examples are the regime changes which occurred in Iraq, Libya and Egypt. This raises a tricky question of what are the preconditions which warrant regime change and who determines whether the preconditions are met in any particular case. Both in Iraq and Egypt, Western powers led by USA decided these moral issues.

Before concluding, we may briefly discuss two instances which involved India. One is the Indian intervention when Pakistan used brutal military force to crush the democratic movement in what was then East Pakistan. Apart from human costs in terms of lost lives, Pakistan's brutalities forced 8 million refugees into India. At that critical stage in our history, Shrimati Indira Gandhi acted with admirable grit and determination and withstood the American pressure from President Nixon and Secretary of state, Henry Kissinger. During that emergency, Russia (erstwhile USSR) stood by India's side. The operation was completed even as the US Seventh fleet entered the Bay of Bengal.

One cannot help comparing India's above mentioned decisive response to its utterly tepid response to the massacre of Sri Lankan Tamils. By many accounts, it was a major episode of genocide. However, the humanitarian aspect was taken up by Scandinavian nations especially Norway. India was reluctant to support resolutions in UN which condemned the human rights violations against Tamils in Sri Lanka. India abstained even on the most recent resolution in UN on this subject of human rights violations. It is not our intention to suggest that India should have acted as it did in response to events in the then East Pakistan. At a minimum, India should have halted the massacre. It is possible that India might not have succeeded. But the point is that the Indian policy makers just stood in silence while the Sri Lankan army went on its rampage.

We need not get into the details of the matter. But its moral aspects need a brief mention. It is difficult to fathom India's acquiescence in the massacre. One may argue that Sri Lankan Tamilians are foreigners, and not Indian citizens. But then so were the people of Bangladesh. But since our foreign policy owes so much to Gandhian legacy, should we not have tried to prevent the carnage in our immediate neighbourhood?

A more interesting feature is the total lack of outrage at any stage in the media or among opinion makers or in political establishment. Historically speaking, migration of Sri Lankan Tamils is recent; to all intents and purposes, they are like other Indians. Regrettably, we have to conclude that the spark of fellow feeling and solidarity for erstwhile members of our national community has become weak in us. This is the reason why we have discussed what may be considered a well worn theme - the need for solidarity born out of national fellow feeling. Without this feeling, neither nations nor their citizens can survive.

Summary

- International morality refers to morals or codes of conduct governing relations between nations.
- 'Sovereignty' is the ultimate authority or power possessed by a state as an embodiment of its political community. Sovereignty represents the will of the people which is theoretically absolute and unfettered.
- A nation is a group which thinks of itself as 'a people,' usually because they share many things in common. These consist of a common territory, history, culture, language, religion and way of life. The state has a narrower meaning referring to the constitutional arrangements which determine how a nation is governed.
- The main theories of IR are - realism, idealism, their variants and a collection of views drawn from other schools of thought. Neorealism and neoliberalism have become popular in the twentieth century.
- Idealism advocates the moral point of view or 'what ought to be' in politics.
- Machiavellianism is a radical type of political realism. It denies the relevance of morality in politics, and claims that all means (moral and immoral) are justified to achieve certain political ends. This is the doctrine of raison d'état which implies that rulers should follow whatever is good for the state and not ethical scruples or norms.
- In the nineteenth-century, Hegel and Treitschke, pushed Machiavellian realism to even further extremes, and applied it to international relations.
- Realpolitik is a national policy having a sole principle-advancement of the national interest.
- For realists, the world of (nation) states is anarchic, and security is the overriding goal of any state. Realists doubt the relevance of morality to international politics.
- Descriptive realism claims that in real world states do not behave morally. Either they lack the moral motivation, or are unable to act morally due to competitive struggles
- Prescriptive realism advocates that states should be prudent in their international conduct.
- Immanuel Kant is among those who anticipated many modern themes of idealism in international morals.
- The idealists of the 1920s and 1930s are also known as liberal internationalists or utopians. They upheld values like peace, international law, common interests of nations, human rationality and morality.

- ¤ In his *The Twenty Years' Crisis*, E. H. Carr attacks idealism.
- ¤ Hans J. Morgenthau is another famous writer who formulated an international relations theory based on realism. He identifies unquenchable human lust for power, the desire to dominate, as the main cause of conflict.
- ¤ Morgenthau uses six principles to show how realism underlies international relations.
- ¤ Kenneth Waltz, who proposed neorealism, regards the international order of nations as a system, and argues that states in the international system, like firms in a domestic economy, seek survival.
- ¤ Waltz explains that states continue to behave uniformly over long periods because of the constraints which the structure of the international system imposes on them.
- ¤ Liberal institutionalists (another name for neoliberal thinkers) believe that states can seek security through construction of international agreements, regimes and structures such as arms control agreements (like START I and START II) and multilateral economic institutions like the WTO. States can engage each other through these structures, learning norms of peaceful cooperation and developing a common interest in the status quo.
- ¤ For some time, neo liberalism became influential in international relations, at the expense of realism. But major international developments like disintegration of USSR weakened it greatly.
- ¤ Feminism has influenced international morality to some extent.
- ¤ Tenets of international morality are found in UN Charter. The principles embodied in UN Charter form the norms or maxims of currently accepted international morality.

UN prescribes that for achieving its aims member states should adopt the following principles of conduct:

- * Sovereign equality of all Members
- * Fulfilling in good faith the obligations assumed by Members in accordance with the Charter.
- * Settling by members of their international disputes by peaceful means so as not to endanger international peace and security, and justice
- * Avoidance by Members of the threat or use of force against the territorial integrity or political independence of any state, or in any other manner inconsistent with the Purposes of the United Nations
- * Assisting UN in its actions under the present Charter, and refraining from assisting any state against which the UN is taking preventive or enforcement action
- * Ensuring by UN that non UN member states comply with these Principles to the extent necessary for the maintenance of international peace and security.
- * Non intervention by UN in internal affairs of members nor requiring them to submit such matters for settlement under the Charter

- ¤ John Rawls discusses the morality of international politics in his book *The Law of Peoples*. His list of international moral norms is based on his version of political liberalism. States have to comply with these norms (code of conduct) to qualify as members of good standing in the international political community.

- Rawls is concerned here with proposing an international framework in which states with different internal political regimes (i.e. liberal and non liberal) can live in peace and harmony. In this framework, liberal states will not insist that all states should follow full blown liberalism; and illiberal regimes will adopt some watered down principles of liberalism.
- States which do not meet the minimum requirements are termed outlaw regimes. Rawls regards their existence as an unfortunate fact.
- Rawls's framework implies that states should avoid ideological crusades and struggles against other nations with divergent regimes.
- Rawls also mentions that some countries face extremely unfavourable circumstances like famine and immiseration. Rawls urges that well-ordered societies should help these countries.
- There are three main schools of thought on the ethics of war and peace - Realism; Pacifism; and Just War Theory.
- Just war theory is divided into three parts which have Latin names. These parts are:
  1. *jus ad bellum*, which is about the justice of resorting to war in the first place;
  2. *jus in bello*, which is about justice of conduct within war; and
  3. *jus post bellum*, which is about the justice of peace agreements and the termination phase of war.
- Pacifism totally opposes war. While pacifists oppose all killing, they particularly abhor the mass killing which usually accompanies war. They object to this type and scale of killing. Pacifists believe that no moral grounds can justify war, and that it is always wrong.
- There is considerable controversy on coercive regime change - changing the government of a nation through external military intervention. It involves the question – Can coercive regime change ever be justified, or is it essentially an act of imperialism? One view is that UN mandated sovereign equality of nations prohibits external intervention in the internal affairs of a state.
- New dimensions of international morality are:
  - (i) Transfer of resources from rich countries to less developed nations
  - (ii) Removing inequities in economic exchanges (trade, commerce and finance) between developed and less developed countries
  - (iii) Giving greater voice to developed countries in the working of international agencies
  - (iv) Humanitarian assistance to countries in the grip of famine and immiserization
  - (v) Intervention in states which carry out genocide, ethnic cleansing or war on their own people
  - (vi) Naturalization of people who migrate into a country and settle there
  - (vii) Adopting a cosmopolitan as opposed to a national approach to morals
- Although, it was Jawaharlal Nehru who shaped India's foreign policy, Mahatma Gandhi's thinking and philosophy influenced it greatly. India's foreign policy is based on the Gandhian values of freedom struggle. It was Gandhian ideas that set the tone of India's foreign policy in the early decades of its independence.

- India's stand on international problems was based on moral clarity and courage. Many nations admired this approach. It won for India the leadership of the developing countries. It gave India an influence in world affairs out of proportion to its real economic and political strength
- Both supporters and critics of Indian foreign policy invariably focus attention on Panchsheel. It goes back to a stage long past in Indian foreign policy. Nehru perhaps thought it a centerpiece of policy which also held up a moral torch in the cynical environment of diplomacy. While some praise Panchsheel for its idealism, others condemn it for its unrealism.
- Some liberal thinkers believe that egalitarian guarantees should not be confined to national boundaries or to territorial states. They consider an individual's nationality also an accident of birth like his/her race, gender, or social class. It cannot therefore be made a basis for differentiation in dispensing administrative justice. This leads to the vexing problem of the moral status of national boundaries.
- Moral egalitarianism should be confined to national boundaries.
- Indian foreign policy makers acted vigorously during the crisis leading to the birth of Bangladesh. But their response to the killing of Sri Lankan Tamils has been tepid.

PRACTICE QUESTIONS

1. What are the main aspects or components of international morality?
2. What is sovereignty? Explain its significance in international relations.
3. Outline the main principles of idealism in relation to international relations.
4. Briefly discuss the concept of realism in international relations.
5. What is Descriptive realism? What is Prescriptive realism? How will you distinguish between the two?
6. What according to the idealists of the 1920s and 1930s are the main principles which should guide the conduct of nations in international affairs?
7. What are the main points of EH Carr's criticism of idealism of the 1920s and 1930s?
8. Outline the theory of neorealism.
9. State the main ideas of neoliberalism in respect of international relations.
10. What are the tenets of international morality enumerated in the UN Charter?
11. State the principles of morality of international politics according to John Rawls.
12. What are three main schools of thought on the ethics of war and peace?
13. State the principles which according to the Just War theory should be followed in the declaration of war, conduct of war and the termination of war.
14. Discuss the merits and demerits of pacifism.
15. What are the new dimensions of international morality?

16. Discuss the economic aspects of international morality.
17. Comment on the role of idealism in India's foreign policy. To what extent has it been modified by realist principles and for what reasons?
18. Outline the principles of Panchsheel and comment on them.
19. Discuss the view that moral egalitarianism should be confined to national boundaries in the context of large scale migration of people from one nation to another.

REFERENCES

- W. Julian Korab-Karpowicz Political realism in International Relations.
- Michael Blake, International Justice
- Orend, Brian, War } articles from Stanford Encyclopaedia of Philosophy
- Rajiv Sikri, Mahatma Gandhi's Influence on India's Foreign Policy (Available on website)

CASE STUDIES

INTRODUCTION

Strategy for Solution of Case Studies

A careful reader of this book must have recognised that taking an ethically correct decision is a challenge in itself. Of course, there is no denying that most moral decisions men make, are simple and straightforward. They are based on common school copy book maxims such as, "Always tell truth", "Be kind to animals", "Be non-violent", and "Treat others with kindness and consideration". If human morality depended on elaborate intellectual analysis, there would be little scope for common human decency. But men generally behave decently though they lack formal tutoring in ethics.

However, at times the course of morality becomes muddied. Men and women face situations in which moral decisions are neither apparent nor clear cut. Moral decision making then ceases to be a simple matter. There are a wide variety of considerations to take into account and often the guiding principles do not completely accord with one other. When the applicable standards are equally valid, the moral agent faces a dilemma. As we discussed earlier, the moral agent then has to pursue what appears to him as the primary duty. Although ethical dilemmas are interesting areas of ethical discussion, they are not that common in one's official, social and personal life. They crop up in exceptional circumstances.

The more common situation is that a moral agent's moral principles and his other life goals come into conflict. This may be described as the clash between one's morality and one's desire for material advancement or personal advantage. Thus, the broad set of objectives and principles which a moral agent chooses for himself may lack internal harmony. As a consequence, his moral principles and material objectives often pull in opposite directions. An individual's moral strength is put to the toughest test when he has to reconcile his principles and objectives with his personal goals dictate such as material comfort, wealth and power. We are not suggesting that such objectives are not worth pursuing. However, the means of realising these objectives ethically matter a lot - and that is the crux in ethical choices.

Because of the above factors and some others we mention below, things tend to become unclear or complicated in work situations especially in civil services and corporate management. People may find themselves surrounded by troubling circumstances. They have to contain, harmonise and manage numerous internal mental conflicts. At the basic level, officials seek career progression in order to satisfy their self-actualisation needs and ensure economic sustenance for family. This is a legitimate aspiration. On the other end, giving wings to greed and fast track career climb at a price of doing wrong things, is an ever present temptation.

So far, we have mentioned two issues: one concerns ethical dilemmas; and the other is the risk of sacrificing morality in pursuit of self-interest. Morality may be overlooked not only because of selfish interests but also due to other reasons. One may lack adequate knowledge of moral principles. But this is not an excuse which can be condoned in civil servants. They can be imparted moral training and encouraged to increase their moral sensitivity. At times, even experienced public officials may fail to recognise the moral dimensions of a situation. Hence, officials have to hone their skills in this area.

In any situation, officials have to look for a choice which satisfies the requirements of fair play, equity and justice. Prejudice, bias, malice, and other vices should not come into play. Officials are motivated not only by greed or power. Often, they abandon the correct path due to cowardice. They may look to their personal advantage and avoid rubbing their political or administrative bosses on the wrong side. They may fail to show courage of conviction. Officials sometimes act arbitrarily or abuse their office. They may overreact to small violations which common people may make. They may fail to show a sense of proportion in handling matters. They may be insensitive to the problems of the poor and the weak.

What we have narrated above may be the context of cases that will surface in the examination situation. To discuss these cases, a systematic approach is very essential. In the case studies in previous chapters you would have noticed how we analysed a situation taking different perspectives. To an extent, it is difficult to give a framework for analysis which will be universally applicable since ethical issues are mostly case-specific. Nevertheless, we will attempt to outline a framework which will help you to think in an organised manner and respond quickly in an examination situation. We are conscious that the approach we are taking may appear to be an over simplification; we are doing this not on the basis of rigorous intellectual standards but only with a view to provide a tool to help thinking in practice and particularly in the examination hall.

Two Types of Cases

Cases can be divided into two broad types. The first type consists of cases which confront an individual who has no position of authority or official obligation. This is the situation of every human being who is called upon to decide upon a course of action in a given situation and the situation is not linked with any office or position of authority. The second categroy of cases results from official environment. Here the ethical decision maker is not merely an individual (often called moral agent in Ethics) but has an official duty cast upon him. Clearly, the second type of situation is more complex because there is a call of duty to be answered in addition to one's moral inclinations. Professional duty brings more matters into consideration than private moral behaviour.

Test of Ethical Soundness of an Action

Social Situation

As a social being, you have to take the following steps for analyzing any decision choice. First examine, whether the suggested decision or the decision which comes to your mind is legal at all. You do not need a great deal of expertise in law to understand what kinds of acts are illegal. Punishable offences under IPC are well known - murder, injury to other persons, rape, cheating, misappropriation and fraud, etc. fall in this class. It is unlikely that any suggested alternative in examinations will present any of these. There are other kinds of laws too: laws pertaining to prohibition, smuggling, taking of dowry, dealing in drugs and the like. These matters are commonly understood and do not need elaboration. Laws of a sovereign have ethical sanction in the context of that society. No doubt what is illegal in one country may occasionally be legal in another country. But you have to imagine the context of the particular situation which is country specific. Unless you are specifically called upon to discuss legitimacy of the law itself, the rule is straightforward: Follow the Law of the Land. Thus, any course of action that suggests or implies transgression of law is unethical in the context of that state or location.

Thus, though enjoying a mug of beer in any season is normal in Germany, in Gujarat even in summer one cannot do that without a permit. The sanction in Gujarat is strictly speaking not derived from purely ethical canons, but from a perception of public good or well-being in Gujarat society. By an extension of the notion of what is good or bad, the restriction becomes a binding principle so long as one resides within the state. Since law is mandatory, there is no practical sense in questioning its legitimacy - though such questions may be perfectly legitimate in academic or intellectual contexts.

After this test of legal conformity is cleared, one enters a more complex domain where guiding principles come from two powerful and potent sources. The first source undoubtedly is ethics, and the second consists of all manner of cultural norms including religion. While reading this book you have acquainted yourself with the various approaches or guidelines to test the ethical soundness of an action. To repeat: these tests follow the tracks of utilitarianism, deontology, virtue ethics, and all the deeply ingrained universal values such as truthfulness, compassion, and empathy among others. Our general approach is that if an action clears the talisman of morality it should be acceptable. Whether such an action complies with cultural guidance or norms is a secondary consideration. If it does, so much the better; if it does not, the ethical consideration would prevail. In short, cultural norms yield to ethics in case of conflict between the two.

Let us give a simple example. In all societies that we know, there is a last rites custom to pay respects to the deceased. Customs differ, but generally speaking, friends and close relatives (often only male members) accompany the mortal remains of the departed soul to the cremation ground whatever be the method of cremation. Consider the case of a socially reputed but an ordinary business person X. X is passing through a bad patch and has suffered substantial loss in his business recently. On top of it, he has just lost his wife. To make things more difficult for him, he has two marriageable daughters and the marriage of the elder daughter has been fixed and he has to prepare for it socially and financially. X comes from a conservative Bengali Hindu family wherein according to custom the family not only performs last rites, but also has to do a Shraddha (a manner of religious prayer cum ceremonial offerings to Gods) followed by a feast for at least all those who had paid last respects to the departed. X is in a fix; if he spends money for elaborate Shraddha and feast, his financial condition will be further weakened. However, skipping the practice is not easy because social convention does not enjoin non-compliance. If he does skip, many friends and family members will be talking unpleasant things behind his back. On the other hand, social compliance will compel him to take loans for daughter's marriage. So X is in a dilemma.

Clearly, skipping feast and scaling down Shraddha ceremony is ethically permissible. In fact, taking loan for daughter's marriage may later exhaust his bankability to finance his business thus, jeopardising his livelihood. As a father he has ethical responsibility to his family. Thus, an ethical course of action would be to do Shraddha at the minimal level and skip feast altogether. However, he should address the perception issue of society by talking honestly to good friends and family members and only hope they would understand and sympathise.

Now we have come to a stage where we can describe the tests of moral action in a logical scheme, which you can use in most situations. To appreciate the scheme you may have a look at the flow diagram below.

Test of Ethical Soundness of an Action – Social Situation

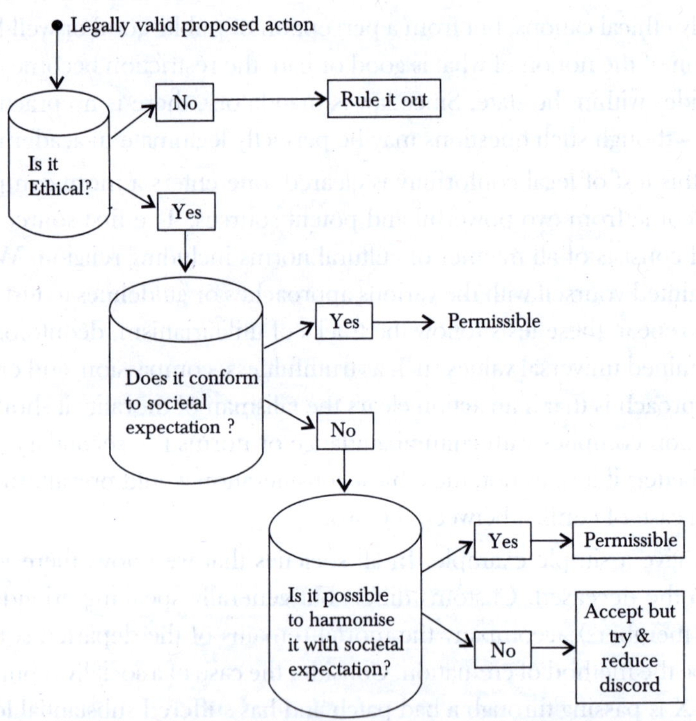

The diagram tells you to make the proposed action pass through the sequential tests in the cylindrical test rooms so to say. Each test asks a straightforward question which is already written there. After each test, there are two outcomes 'yes' or 'no'. You begin at the top and sequentially go down. If the first test throws up 'no' answer i.e. the proposed action is not legal, you have to simply rule out that action. If the test yields 'yes' result, then you go down for the next test and so on. At the end, you will always get an answer.

Now in essay type examination, two types of possibilities arise. First, the answer choice is given in black and white and the examinee has no flexibility. In that situation, in case of conflict between ethical principles and cultural practice, the first dominates. One has to choose answer on that basis. However, if the examinee has flexibility in selecting or modifying the answer choice he/she should try to select a course of action where the conflict is narrowed in scope or severity. Like in the given example, Mr. X should explain in advance to family members and close friends why he is compelled to scale down Shraddha ceremony.

Test of Ethical Soundness of An Action

In a Professional Situation

Now let us turn to the category of situations where the decision maker holds some position of power or control over others. This does not mean that the moral agent we are thinking is necessarily a civil servant or a corporate manger. He can be a doctor or nurse as well because they have some measure of influence and control on the behaviour of patients. The applicable professional code depends on the profession and policy of the institution in which the moral agent is working. In the case of government servants in India, there are codes made by both the Central and state governments. The spirit and the flavour of the codes whether made by the government of India or a state government run parallel and so do the important principles; they differ in respect of minor operational details. These details are not relevant from the standpoint of civil services examination.

Similarly, corporate managers also follow the codes determined by the respective company. Those codes, though may differ from one company to another, share common values which are ethical in nature such as courage, trust, teamwork, commitment, integrity and so forth. Code of a company may lay special emphasis on sharing sensitive information so that information having commercial potential is not lost to competition. Code may elaborate on sexual harassment also. We hope you get the theme and an appreciation of what a code generally stipulates.

We shall describe this class of cases where the decision maker has some measure of influence, control, or authority over others as professional situation. Now let us see how the test will progress in case of a professional moral agent. As previously made out, here also the first test is whether the contemplated action is legally permissible or not. For 'no' outcome the moral agent shall not proceed with execution of contemplated action. If test result is 'yes', then he/she should go for further filtration or the sequential next tests. To keep the diagram simpler, here we begin with a proposed course of action which is legally permissible.

The next test as shown below will be whether the proposed action is in conformity with professional code. The flow diagram will be identical after that stage. In other words, when the proposed action, besides being legal, is also consistent with professional code, the next question to test will be whether the action is likely to be valid from the standpoint of ethical considerations. In other words after 'professional codes' test, next two stages are similar to the process adopted for social situation.

Test of Ethical Soundness of an Action – Professional Situation

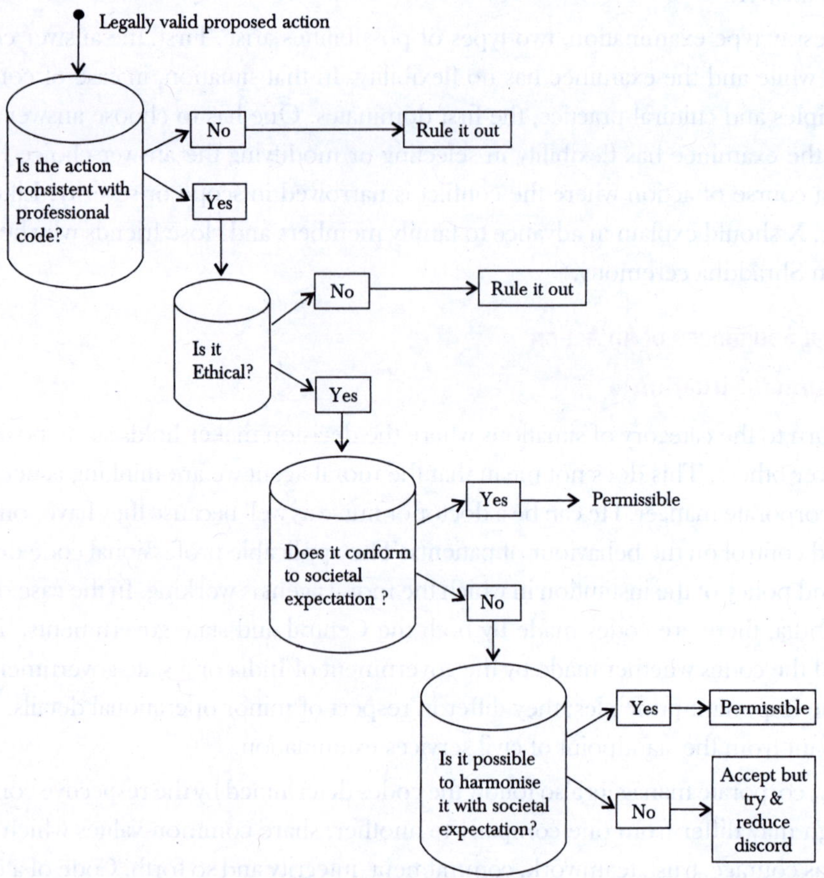

Before we conclude this discussion a we would like to mention that there are situations when the professional etiquette and cultural/religious norms can come in conflict. Professional code will dominate in such situation. However, a conscientious professional sometimes gets over this conflict in a smart way as the following illustration will demonstrate. Like most cases in this book, this illustration mirrors a real life episode.

Jainul Haq is a middle level IAS officer of excellent standing in a state that has a strong current of Hindutva. Tapping into that popular sentiment to build political capital, the chief minister of the state has brought in direct or indirect participation of the government in celebration of Hindu festivals. He has also marketed the festivities as a prominent cultural event nationally and internationally. In one particular festival, there are substantial cultural components interlaced with religious symbolism and prayer. The people of the state enjoy these celebrations hugely.

In this particular festival, at the end of inauguration ceremony, there is a prayer called *aarti* for mother goddess. During *aarti* the entire audience, including ministers and top brass of administration, stand up respectfully holding a lit lamp on a plate and executing traditional yet simple hand movements making the *aarti* a grand public event. The invitations to attend the ceremony go to all the IAS officers, MLAs, MPs and who's who of the city. In this milieu, Jainul's position is a bit tricky, as his religion does not permit doing *aarti* before any image or idol. At the same time the general etiquette in public service is that officers do not absent themselves when the CM and his ministerial colleagues and senior officers are present.

Jainul can, of course, skip this celebration all together, and he cannot be called to explain his absence. Service rules will be in his favour in such situation. However, he reconciles the opposite pulls in his unique way. He would attend to the celebration punctually, and when *aarti* starts, he and his spouse will respectfully stand up with others but not do the actual *aarti* and, in fact, they would not take the lamp at all. No wonder, he is popular with both his official colleagues and political bosses.

I hope you get the strategy we have just elaborated. Happy reading of the cases that follow!

Case Studies

CASE 1 Gift for Sister's Marriage

T.N. Reddy, Municipal commissioner, is in a momentary dilemma. Hailing from a poor but cultured family in Srikakulam District, he came out with flying colours in M.Sc. Psychology from Osmania University and joined the IAS after post-graduation. Over the years, he has built reputation for efficiency and integrity.

This morning one Amarchand, a successful builder, just called on him at his official residence. Mr. Reddy had met Amarchand on the occasion of inauguration of a school for the visually challenged which Amarchand had financed fully. In the inaugural function, Amarchand had sought Mr. Reddy's permission to meet [him] at home to talk about other socially useful charitable projects he was organising and funding.

This morning Amarchand did talk about a number of projects to which his total donation in aggregate would not be less than 20 crore rupees. While narrating all these, Amarchand profusely thanked Reddy for timely clearance of his "Epitome" commercial complex in the heart of Business district of state capital which he said was the only one he could get cleared without having to meet the Municipal Commissioner. At the end of the meeting while preparing to leave, Amarchand mentioned that he had come to know of the marriage of Reddy's sister slated next month and requested Reddy to accept a small token of appreciation. Reddy said "No, thanks", but Amarchand swiftly went to his parked car and returned with a jewel box and put it on the table with folded hands and slightly bent posture.

His sister's marriage has been a matter of financial concern for Reddy for he did not have enough savings. The still prevalent evil of dowry in his community added to his anxiety. Given his reputation, Reddy never expected to receive such expensive gift from a builder, and so for a few seconds, he seemed to be at a loss as to how to deal with this situation.

Question

In the above narrated situation, what should Reddy do?

1. He should abuse Amarchand, throw the jewel box at him, and ask him to leave his residence.
2. He should ask Amarchand to take a seat, proceed to another room, inform Anti-Corruption Bureau (ACB), and get Amarchand arrested.
3. He should keep the gift, and try to return to Amarchand its cash equivalent later whenever he can
4. He should tell Amarchand that conduct rules prohibit officers from accepting expensive gifts, and immediately hand over the jewel box to Amarchand.

Discussion

The course of action in this case (and similar others) is quite clear. Reddy cannot accept the gift under the prescribed codes of civil service conduct. As this position is very clear, he should reject the gift outright. This is what may be called an open and shut case which admits of no ambiguity. No second thoughts can be entertained in matters of this nature. Reddy does not face any dilemma. Hence (4) is the answer.

What are the reasons for excluding the other alternatives? In (1), the behaviour of Reddy would be crude. As a senior officer, he should behave with dignity and composure. Although Amarchand's conduct is reprehensible (in offering the thinly disguised bribe for what he thought was a favour), Reddy should behave calmly and refrain from uncouth conduct.

As for (2), Reddy would be within his rights to put ACB onto to Amarchand. Some people would argue that Amarchand is guilty of an offence and that Reddy would have to alert ACB to take cognizance of it. But in the ordinary course of affairs, this response would be excessive. Further, Amarchand is showing his (misguided sense of) gratitude to Reddy. There is no specific transaction for which the gift is offered as a bribe.

The third option is a tricky one. It will be a way of rationalizing an action which is ab initio inadmissible. It is patently wrong. Although Reddy may have good intention of returning the gift in the form of cash, with passage of time, he is likely to forget about it. He will be stepping on morally slippery ground. It will gradually lead him more and more into morally dubious acts.

CASE 2 Lying to Please

Mr. Raghavan had indeed a pleasant surprise in his bathroom. He just heard daughter Suchitra shouting "Achan, I am at home." Mr. Raghavan, a philosophy professor, retired last year and is presently settled in Cochin.

He has a small family of his wife Sujatha, daughter Suchitra and his son Madhavan. Twenty-five year old Madhavan, the elder of the two children, is working in USA. He has come home on a vacation. Suchitra is a Post Graduate student in Delhi. Mr. Raghavan had no inkling that Suchitra would arrive that morning; it was a surprise to him.

He was in fact expecting a friend of Madhavan to join them for breakfast. A couple of days back Madhavan had told his father that one of his friends could be visiting them during this vacation. Madhavan had already told his mother that his friend is a vegetarian, does not like eggs and prefers a particular type of Rasam and Idli. Sujatha had instantly commented that Madhavan's sister also likes that particular Rasam.

That Friday was Eid day and the first of a long weekend of three holidays in a row for Suchitra. In the morning, Madhavan had accompanied the driver in the family car to receive his friend and the family was expecting a friend of Madhavan to come at home for breakfast.

Generally, when the daughter visits home, Raghavan buys air-tickets, as he always knows in advance about her programme. This time Madhavan had purchased air-ticket for Suchitra's trip from his own funds. He made up a false story about his friend visiting Cochin in connection with his work. The whole idea of Madhavan was to give a pleasant surprise to the family by creating a dramatic situation.

Question

Notwithstanding Madhavan's desire to gift his sister a costly trip to home and create a pleasant surprise to parents, he had fabricated lies to make an appearance as if his university classmate was to visit his home. How should Mr. Raghavan respond to his son's harmless falsehood?

1. He should express his displeasure to Madhavan and reprimand him severely.
2. He should just ignore the whole incident as of no consequence.
3. He should tell Madhavan gently to avoid all forms of lies, even harmless ones, in future.
4. He should give Madhavan a long lecture on how philosophers analyse the virtue of truth telling

Discussion

In the situation outlined above, one needs to look at four aspects. The basic issue is that Madhavan told a lie in order to create a pleasant situation within the family. His lie is completely harmless and intended to increase the feeling of happiness in the family. There is a second issue which involves a parent's duty to morally guide his children—though Madhavan is an adult. The third question has to do with whether and how Mr. Raghavan should express his feelings and reaction to the incident. This will involve communication method and appreciation of human psychology. Finally, Mr. Raghavan should show a sense of proportion about the matter. If we consider all these issues, (3) will be the correct course of action.

Getting angry over the matter and reprimanding will obviously be an overreaction. In any case, no parent will get annoyed over such a matter. The principle of truth telling should not be escalated to an absolutely high level in innocent matters of common family life. At the same time, Mr. Raghavan should not completely ignore Madhavan's falsehood. Lies have to be avoided whether in important or trivial matters. Since Madhavan is in a foreign land, he needs to avoid all forms of improper conduct. It will be best if Mr. Raghavan mildly tells his son to avoid lies even in small and apparently inconsequential matters. Finally, no useful purpose will be served by giving a long philosophical lecture on truth. This is a matter of applying ethical principles in an ordinary family situation.

CASE 3 Reflections on Power of Words

Balbir had been soft spoken and sober unlike many of his loud classmates in Chandigarh. Few would have believed that he could opt for an IPS career. He is currently posted as District SP in a coastal district with rich lime stone deposits, sanctuary and port facilities. Good infrastructure for coastal transport and lime stone mines had accelerated industrialization in this district and in its neighboring distinct neighbouring district, generating in response a good deal of environmental activism.

Last ten years have witnessed the phenomenal rise of one time school dropout Baldeo Patil – popularly called 'Patilboss' in the district. Baldeo failed twice in XIIth standard and thereafter dabbled in Panchayat politics of the district. Quickly learning the fundamentals of environmental laws from his lawyer uncle, he specialized in finding out minor and substantial violations of environmental laws committed by mines and industrial units. Profusely using RTI to his advantage, he could nail most of the mines and industries compelling them to pay a 'Monthly Instalment of Lakhs of Rupees'. Occasionally, when specific units have shown audacity to challenge his authority he would drag them to different courts and stall their projects. But the courts and law have not been the only tools of Baldeo. For the last two years he has developed muscle power and often resorted to obstructionist agitation against miners and cement producers for extortion. Frequently, he has indulged in war of words with police and executive magistrates. Once he had even threatened the DSP that his career may be in jeopardy if he tried "to keep peace at the cost of common people". Common people of course meant his henchmen and associates.

Five days ago Baldeo started an agitation against a miner on some alleged violation of environmental law which High Court decided in favour of the miner. Baldeo and his men stopped truck movement of this miner now and then. After two days of agitation which paralysed operations of mines, Police HQ asked Mr. Balbir Singh to clear the road block.

This morning Balbir had briefed his Dy. SP and team of Police Inspectors on how to address this problem. He had told them "To teach Baldeo a lesson as he has crossed all limits". On reaching the spot, police had faced a severe public order problem while clearing road block. Baldeo had slapped a PI and seeing this policeman shot at Baldeo and he succumbed to the injury. Some more were injured in police firing. The area became tense.

Question

How can one evaluate the situation leading to firing by police?

1. DSP should not have used the expression 'teach him a lesson" while briefing the police.
2. Baldeo was an anti-social and no tears need be shed over his death.
3. Such incidents sometimes occur in law and order situations.
4. The police man was gravely provoked when Baldeo slapped a police inspector.

Discussion

The central issue involved relates to use of force by police to control violence and lift the road blockade. Use of force is justified to some extent. But minimal force should be used so as to effectively eliminate or thwart the imminent threat. It is from this angle one has to evaluate the conduct of Baldeo and his supporters at the scene of the event. Were they armed and close to attacking police? This does not seem to be the case. Or is it just the case that arrogant Baldeo lost self-control and slapped a police officer? This is what seems to have happened. This conduct even without anything more is criminal and deserves punishment. But it will not justify firing to kill Baldeo.

Based on the above analysis, the alternatives (2) and (3) have to be rejected. Although Baldeo is an anti-social, he has to be brought to book through legal means. Any punishment meted out to him has to be legal and based on a court's order. The incident resulting in death is unfortunate, and such incidents have to be avoided even in difficult law and order situations.

It is true that Baldeo's action of slapping a police inspector was provocative. But the police man's reaction was excessive. He need not have shot Baldeo, but he could have apprehended and dealt with Baldeo in other ways.

But was Balbir's briefing of policemen with the comment of teaching a lesson appropriate? It is difficult to judge that comment in isolation without considering the overall demeanour of Balbir. Police men who have to handle many criminals day in and out often use much stronger and filthy language. But then, Balbir is the head of the District Police organization. The same words spoken by a constable and the head of the District Police would have different impacts. The obvious reason is that leaders can create forceful motivation and charge up their followers to overreact to situations. Therefore, Balbir should have avoided use of those words. Teaching a lesson was not the task before him; he should have asked police to clear the road blockade.

CASE 4 Clean-sweep Plan against Corruption in Interstate Check-posts

S. K. Anantham an IAS officer was posted as Transport Commissioner. The whole of Transport department including its Minister are steeped in corruption. While posting Anantham, the Chief Minister had privately told him to clean up the department. Anantham faced a tough task. It is widely believed that the Minister of the Department has arranged posting of 'bad elements' to sensitive jobs with the sole objective of facilitating rent seeking.

Corrupt practices take place mainly in check-posts. There is heavy vehicle traffic to the neighbouring state which has many ports. Check-posts work on an age old system. There is parking area where the drivers of the trucks first park the vehicle. They then collect 'challans' (demand note) after standing in a long queue before the window of the challan issuing officers. The driver may have to wait in the queue anywhere between 15 minutes to an hour to collect the challan from the clerk. Along with the challan amount, the truck drivers also paid 'extra' amount as indicated in a coded sign language by the challan issuing staff.

In case the supervisor of the check-post has any doubt about the weight or the nature of goods in a truck, he would ask the driver to get the weight verified in the weigh- bridges. If the details do not tally with the challan prepared on the basis of driver's report, he has to go back to the payment counter and pay the shortfall amount including a penalty which sometimes could go as high as 100% of normal charges. Because of manual systems, vehicles are held up for considerable time at the check-posts.

Question

In Anantham's place how would you try to improve the system?

1. Conduct surprise raids on check-posts, seize unauthorized, unaccounted cash and prosecute check-post officials.
2. Set a high personal example of honesty, efficiency and dedication to duty.
3. Create a system of informers at check-post to know about the shady activities.
4. Introduce a system of complete automation, minimising retention time of vehicles, computerizing collection of tax and increasing weighbridges and by establishing real time video linkage between check-posts and transport commissioner's office.

Discussion

This problem of corruption has to be tackled by changing the present system. It has built-in features which create opportunities and incentives for bribe-takers and bribe-givers. The truckers want to avoid taxes and speed the movement of their vehicles through the check-posts. Since the system is manual and inefficient, truckers gain by paying some bribes. If the system is speeded up through computerization and automation with arrangements for live monitoring, the systemic faults can be removed. Thereafter, truckers will have no reason to pay bribes. Fearing detection, the staff at check posts will be on their guard.

The first alternative relies on trying to catch the wrong doers. It may have a limited impact. But it cannot be continuously put into practice. It attacks the symptoms rather than the disease.

The second alternative is based on wrong premises. Sometimes, honest officers make the mistake of thinking that by restraining themselves from being corrupt and dealing with corrupt subordinates with stern hand they can automatically reform the system. That does not happen for the simple reason that in an organisation like the check-post network predominant majority of personnel are corrupt and they mutually protect one other. These organisations settle to an operational methodology where outwardly everything would look fine and the transactions would be good for the bureaucracy and the corrupt clients---in this case the community of transporters. Another point to note is that any action to interfere with this large scale and systemic corruption will be opposed tooth and nail by the officers of the transport department and the interested politicians. Therefore, the focus should be on tackling the systemic roots of the problem.

The third alternative is also based on a crime detection approach. The so called informers may also join the racket.

The root of corruption lies in the fact that there is no universal weighing of vehicles. This gives opportunity for under reporting. There is no memory of the vehicle passing through the check post and hence any follow up on its movements is not possible.

Anantham will have to persuade Government to automate the working of the check-post so that all the vehicles are weighed without fail and their destinations clearly recorded. When a computer server keeps tracking the behaviour of errant vehicles, habitual cheaters will be quickly identified. Automated high quality weighing machines along a layout of sufficient number of gates will solve the problem. Of course, this will need further investment, but given the high quantum of leakage this upfront investment will be recovered quickly. Hence, the fourth alternative is the most feasible solution.

CASE 5 Governance Failure in Worldwide Biologicals

Well wishers of Kushagra Iyer read with regret that morning the news of his downfall from the prestigious post of CEO, Indian Operations of Worldwide Biologicals. Kushagra had transformed his company from the 'Indian backyard' of pharmacy research into a highly respected Indian multi-national corporation.

Kushagra had a brilliant educational career. He topped the Higher Secondary Board Examination, and represented India in Physics and mathematics Olympiads. He joined IIT, Chennai and then IIM Bangalore.

In the IIT, his personality developed an odd streak. He developed excessive fascination towards fair sex so much so that his 'girl friend circle' extended far beyond IIT. On a few occasions, some girls had complained about his offensive behaviour in public places. But despite these diversions, his extraordinary sharpness enabled him to come among the top three of his B tech in Bio-technology class. A couple of times a few female students of the IIT had also complained about his offensive behaviour, but the faculty had been soft on him and got the matters amicably settled.

The pattern of his behaviour was no different in IIM. However, he could pass out with flying colours without any major event and joined a US based corporation. Within a short span of eight years he rose to become the site head of the formulation and discovery unit of that corporation. During these eight years he dated many young women including unmarried colleagues and juniors. His bosses cautioned him to be careful about flirting relationships with women and the danger inherent in frequently changing partners. But they valued him for his contribution. There was no serious complaint; the few matters that arose were amicably settled.

In the tenth year something went out of control, and a lady working in the site office initiated a sexual harassment case in US court. The court found Kushagra guilty of sexual harassment. Kushagra according to the code of conduct of the company was required to inform management of any such relationship with subordinate staff, but he did not do so. The company paid handsome compensation to Kushagra and asked him to leave.

Kushagra returned to India, and after a little while was chosen as CEO, Indian Operations of Worldwide Biologicals. The company, ignoring the unsavoury behaviour of Kushagra, selected him for the post of CEO, Indian Operations. Once again, he achieved great success in his new assignment. Meanwhile, though he had lately married and had a family, his old predatory sexual habits continued. After six years of his stint as Indian CEO, when he was at the threshold of being chosen as Chief of Operations of the European Continent, a scandal broke out. One married female employee of the company registered a FIR in police station alleging that Kushagra had flirted with her and promised a quick promotion. She also revealed that there was yet another woman in the same company who was also cheated in a similar manner. She alleged that the president, HR department of the Company knew this and yet gave Kushagra latitude in view of his position by ignoring complaints. Kushagra was subsequently arrested and released on bail.

Question

What are the moral issues involved in this case?

1. Would it be right to say that there was Corporate Governance failure in Worldwide Biologicals?
2. Could IIT professors have done a better job of disciplining Kushagra?
3. Can we hold the women employees who developed relations with Kushagra as also responsible?
4. Can Kushagra be held entirely responsible for his misdeeds?

Discussion

1. There can be little doubt about the lack of good corporate governance in World Wide Biologicals. While selecting Kushagra, they knew of the unsavoury episodes involving him. The Company had its eye on profits or the bottom line rather than on maintaining wholesome environment in office. After all, it was not selecting a manager in the shop floor level, but the CEO of Indian Operations. In view of the earlier record of Kushagra, he should have been cautioned and kept under careful watch. But the company was obviously insensitive to issues of sexual harassment.
2. Some blame certainly also attaches to the student disciplinary authorities in IIT. Kushagra was then at an impressionable age, and harsh words and no nonsense action from authorities, short of rustication form IIT, would have perhaps done the trick. But they allowed the academic performance of Kushagra to influence their judgement. His misdeeds went unchecked and unpunished. As the Biblical proverb says "Whoever spares the rod hates his son, but he who loves him is diligent to discipline him". This is not to be interpreted literally, and there are different ways of punishing an errant student. Had such punishment been promptly meted out, Kushagra being very sharp, would have known how to curb his deplorable impulses.
3. It is easy to get confused over this matter. We can ignore the minor lapses involving the college/university girls since none of them has come to any harm. As regards other women, one can argue that it takes two willing individuals to form 'relationship', and that adult women enter into 'relationships' with their eyes fully open. In this case, some of them may have been willing to sacrifice morals to advance their career.

   But the issue is different. Office codes of conduct expressly prohibit senior managers from contracting such relationships. Hence, the onus lies on them to avoid such behaviour. There is a more general issue. In such situations, senior managers are in a position of trust; they are guardians of the women employees in the workplace. Further, as feminist writers point out, situations of this type are parts of power relationships. The women employees are in a subordinate position, and may often find it difficult, for various reasons, to rebuff the advances of their bosses. It is for senior managers, in line with official codes and general morality, to refrain from such conduct. In these situations, women are invariably the victims.

4. Kushagra is obviously guilty of serious and criminal misconduct. He completely failed to rein in his sexual cravings. This shows complete lack of moral self-discipline. He failed to realise his role (arising from his high managerial status) as a moral custodian. He was not entering into relationships with individuals of same rank and position. He was exploiting gullible and dependent women. No excuse that his actions are part of irresistible psychological urges can be accepted. If he suffers from such compulsions, he is unfit to hold responsible positions. Kushagra ended up ruining his life along with those of many others.

CASE 6 The Winter of Discontent

Winter is the season of discontent in the city in which P.K. Pal is Food and Civil Supplies Controller. Pal's organization deals with all issues of essential items that are covered under India's Public Distribution System (PDS). He was appointed to this position in July last year. Because of failure of PDS to supply 100% Kerosene (SKO) to the households, he had to face torrid time during November to February last year. Besides nasty media comments, he had to face demonstrations of angry housewives, which were often accompanied by beating of cooking utensils. He wants to avoid the problem this time around.

He carefully studied the supply situation. The city had 9.71 lakh ration cards. 4.75 lakh of these cardholders had no gas connection. 4.96 lakh cardholders had gas connection. The ration card holders were supplied through 865 fair price shops (FPS). SKO was distributed only through the FPS. LPG connection holders are concentrated in the economically better off areas. Thus unused kerosene could have been added to the distribution channel to fulfil the needs of middle class, lower middle class and below poverty line (BPL) card holders.

The problem was the unauthorized diversion of kerosene for other uses. Industrial users are not given permits to buy LPG because it is a subsidized item. Government did not encourage expansion of LPG supply for industrial and commercial uses. Restaurants were not able to buy SKO because it is a subsidized item in short supply. In the circumstances, small eating joints and restaurants try to procure Kerosene illegally from PDS. There is no CNG supply in the city except for auto rickshaws and city transport buses.

The real culprits of the system were the suppliers of petrol in the city and in outskirts. Those dealers particularly in the outskirts bought SKO for mixing with petrol. As the retail price of petrol is much higher than that of PDS kerosene, adulteration of petrol with kerosene is profitable.

The SKO was supplied by a relatively small number of wholesalers (42 only) who deployed close to 50 tankers used for supply of kerosene to the fair price shops. Incidentally, fifteen of the SKO wholesalers were also owners of petrol pumps selling both petrol and diesel in retail in the city and the outskirts.

Question

Given the above broad scenario, suggest four courses of action which Pal can follow and identify the optimum course.

1. Conduct continuous raids on the premises of restaurants, petrol pumps and fair price shops.
2. Make a proposal to government to stop supplying kerosene to 4.96 lakh people who have gas connections.
3. Computerize the system with biometric identification of beneficiaries and introduce GPS in the tankers of wholesalers which supply kerosene to FPSs.
4. Run a press campaign and appeal to dealers, wholesalers and restaurants to refrain from misusing the system meant for the poor.

Discussion

The first alternative will yield limited results. It is a heavy handed administrative method which fails to tackle the root of the issue. The problem is one of plain black marketing on a significant scale. The incentive for black marketing and adulteration will remain since government cannot increase the price of PDS kerosene. It is, therefore, necessary to consider managerial and technical means of plugging the leakages.

The second alternative will improve the situation. A careful survey has to be done before stopping supply of kerosene to LPG connection holders. Although Pal can make a recommendation to government, he cannot take a final decision since this is a policy level decision. This is not a matter within Pal's area of authority.

In the given situation, Pal must think strategically to bring about fundamental changes. It is given that a relatively small number of tankers are involved in kerosene delivery from wholesalers to FPSs. These tankers, instead of delivering material to the FPSs, must be occasionally off-loading the highly subsidised SKO in petrol pumps. In modern times, GPS technology can address this problem very well. Each of the wholesale suppliers has a list of FPSs to which he has to supply SKO. So if the route of the tanker which supplies kerosene to FPSs is fixed well in advance and notified by official order then the only task is to monitor whether the tanker is going to wrong places. Government can easily pass an order adding a condition to Wholesale supply licence that every tanker should be GPS equipped. Then only one or two persons can monitor the movements of the tankers throughout the day on screen and make sure that they follow the right path. Attendant instructions to drivers will also be needed or else they would make flimsy excuses to go to the wrong destination. If the diversion to petrol pumps and other industry gets significantly eliminated, the situation will improve greatly. The situation will further improve since biometric identity will ensure that no person without entitlement gets the supply. This is the best solution.

The fourth option may be well intentioned, but is unlikely to be effective. There are powerful interests who are gaining a substantially from the malpractices. They will not listen to such appeals. This approach will be unrealistic and naive.

CASE 7 Dilemma of Director General, LBSNAA

Director General of LBSNAA is in a dilemma. Its decision context arose in the following way.

One morning, during the time probationers do horse riding, PT or Yoga, an elderly couple knocked at the door of course director Dr. Tripathi. The couple were dishevelled, and with trembling hand the gentleman brought out a fax which simply read:

"Dear Mr. ....

We are extremely grieved to inform that your son Ramesh Chandra IRS probationer is no more. He accidentally fell from a horse and had head injury. He was given immediate medical attention and taken to hospital forthwith where he breathed his last yesterday evening."

Dr. Tripathi

Course Director

The fax carried the number of a connection at Deharadun. It bore no Seal of LBSNAA. Reading the fax Dr. Tripathi's surprise and shock knew no limits. For, Ramesh Chandra was absolutely fine and he knew that somebody had played a cruel joke with the couple and their family.

LBSNAA and Dr. Tripathi lost no time in entrusting investigation on the matter to CID crimes of the then Uttar Pradesh state. Ramesh Chandra revealed that his father's office fax number was available only from one of the personal effects he had; and that there was no other source. Naturally only probationers who went to his room frequently could have access to this detail. From there, locating the number from which the fax was sent, CID took only a few days to find out that Rakesh had in person gone to the telephone vendor and sent the fax.

On being questioned Rakesh admitted guilt and expressed grief. Apparently, his motive was to play some cruel joke with the family of the co-probationer.

LBSNAA administration viewed this conduct of Rakesh with the seriousness it deserved, and after getting explanation to formal 'showcase notice' proposed 'tough measure' in respect of this severe misconduct. This is the matter engaging DG's attention now.

Question

In DG's position what would you decide and why?

1. DG should recommend to Government of India that Rakesh should be summarily removed from service.
2. DG should recommend a moderate punishment.
3. DG should regard the whole matter as a prank, though cruel, and opine that no official rules have been violated.
4. DG should recommend that Rakesh should be subjected to psychological evaluation in order to determine whether it is a one-off event or reveals a deep seated malady.

Prima facie (1) appears a very harsh course to adopt. As Rakesh is a probationer, it may be difficult to judge his action however deplorable as warranting outright removal from service.

The course of action at (3) would not be correct since Rakesh's action appears quite abnormal. He caused great mental agony to the elderly parents of Ramesh Chandra. Further, his action shows an attitude which is highly unbecoming of a government official. The matter requires a deeper probe.

Alternative (2) is also unacceptable. It is necessary to consider what prompted Rakesh to act in that highly improper manner. Without making a professional psychological assessment of Rakesh's personality, no recommendation should be made.

The course of action at (4) is the most appropriate. Without a professional psychological assessment of Rakesh's personality, no further action is possible. Does Rakesh's personality contain pronounced pathological streaks? If so, can they be cured? Is the malady likely to recur or will Rakesh be cured with proper counselling? Can he be entrusted with responsibilies of public office? DG should make his recommendation after getting a report covering the above issues.

CASE 8 Hard Choice for the District Magistrate

Ramjibhai Rachch is a farmer of Umanteerth taluka of Jaybahar district and lives in a medium-sized village. He was a onetime elected President of the Taluka Panchayat. Besides two married daughters, Ramjibhai has a 25 year old young son Jitubhai. Being the only son of the family, Jitubhai was pampered and became spoilt. He was arrogant, always wanted to have his way and would pick up a fight at the slightest opportunity. At the age of 17, Jitubhai had got into the habit of drinking. Village elders had advised Ramjibhai to discipline his son, but Ramjibhai paid no heed to them.

By the time he was 21, the people in the village talked in whispers, that Dhanjibhai Barot had been shot at by Jitubhai. While Jitubhai was arrested along with five others, it was rumoured that the major burden of the incident had been shifted on to another person. A few years later, Shanabhai the money-lender, was also shot at in suspicious circumstances, which was also rumoured to have been done by Jitubhai. It is known in the village that Jitubhai had cast his evil eyes on Shanabhai's beautiful daughter and against this Shanabhai had vehemently protested. Jitubhai was arrested, but once again some of the witnesses retracted from their statements. The final turning point was the third murder, which occurred of Kalabhai, the primary school teacher. He was shot in the head by Jitubhai in full view of a large number of persons. This time there was no escape for Jitubhai. He was arrested and remained in jail, despite several attempts to come out.

The district is represented in the state cabinet by a Minister whose constituency includes the Umanteerth Taluka. Ramjibhai happens to be a long time political associate of the Minister who is currently very influential in the government. The present District Magistrate, Srikant Jana has directly worked under this Minister in the secretariat before he came to this district. The Minister is very well educated, Gandhian in leaning in a right of centre political party, and without any moral blemish. In fact, he had recommended Srikant's posting as the DM.

Yesterday, five MLAs of the district, met the District Magistrate, with a joint application for recommending to government grant of parole for three months to Jitubhai since his mother died three days ago and since the ailing Ramjibhai needed his help to carry out agricultural activities.

Later, the cabinet Minister from the District called Srikant for recommending parole to Jitubhai. The Minister did not claim that Jitubhai is innocent; his pleading was restricted to the circumstances the family was passing thorough. The Minister's request has created a somewhat difficult situation for Srikant. This Minister rarely intervenes in any administrative day-to-day functions. Any application received during his tour is always discussed on its merits with officials and then the officials take appropriate decisions.

Question

Which of the following courses should Srikant follow and why?

1. He should reject the request and send an adverse opinion to government.
2. He should also tell the minister that his intervention in the matter is unwarranted.
3. He should recommend parole for three months.
4. He should recommend parole for a short period of 10 days with due precautionary conditions.

Discussion

1. An outright rejection may not go well with the Minister. He seems decent, and well disposed towards Srikant. It may make perfect sense for Srikant to remain in the Minister's good books if the cost of doing so is acceptable and involves no illegality or impropriety. Administrative actions, within an acceptable range, need to be pragmatic. Further, Indian law enforcement based on western rule of law and our own traditions has been soft. We are not expressing any opinion on what is desirable; we are only mentioning how our culture shapes policy and criminal jurisprudence. For these reasons, the first option is undesirable
2. This course of action will be needlessly offensive. Being public representatives, ministers have a tendency of making various recommendations. Civil servants can take their decisions after examining the matter, but there is no need to unnecessarily offend the minister.
3. This option is improper. It is tantamount to simply accepting without examination the application of Jitubhai.
4. Jitubhai cannot be allowed to roam freely. First, people will get a wrong signal that criminals with political connections are privileged. Second and worse, he may try to break witnesses to his crimes as he had done earlier. He may misdirect investigation if charge sheet under IPC is not already filed. He may even try to assault deceased Shanabhai's daughter, who must be now more vulnerable. To prevent such possibilities the DSP and DM must be careful. Jitubhai is a Hindu and there are Hindu customs to follow after one loses parents. DM might show inclination to recommend parole for only ten days so that social customs may be followed. This would show sensitivity and should satisfy the minister He should also make it a condition that two armed guards would accompany Jitubhai all the time so that he does not run away. He should also ask DSP to put plains clothes police to check if Jitubhai is approaching the witnesses. Circumscribed in this way, the ten days of parole may pass peacefully.

CASE 9 Politics of Flood Relief – Large Scale Rent-seeking Opportunity

Prakash Jha is the State Relief commissioner. Being earnest, he is concerned about the malpractices in administration of relief in the State. The typical situation that recurs every year is narrated below. Many perennial rivers pass through the State. However, the State is very poorly administered; every time there is a heavy rainfall in the upper catchment areas of its rivers. It reels under floods. The drainage system of the riparian areas is in shambles. If there is simultaneous heavy rain in the upper catchment and in the rural areas of the state, water cannot simply get drained out through the river system. This results in flooding and stagnation of water for weeks in the rural areas and in submergence of cultivated crops.

From such catastrophes, mischievous men have developed a notorious enterprise of making illicit gains. As soon as the news of floods is flashed in news papers and television channels, state/ central ministers do reconnaissance of the "Flood Situation" in helicopters. Patwari Offices all over the affected districts get flooded with requests for flood relief. Even if 10% of landmass of a village is affected, it will have literally 95 - 99% people applying for flood relief. It is only the exceptionally upright person who will not fall into the temptation of making false claims.

These days, the wave of sympathy for the poor is very strong nationwide and relief package has been extended to include more and more cash payments for items such as, giving cash-doles for the period of hardship, cost for refurbishing homes, cost for repair of residences, compensation of loss of crop and compensation for loss of sheep, goats and cattle.

The most pitiable part is that the losses are surveyed only on paper. Survey teams are not allowed to do any actual survey. The Panchayat functionaries and bullies of the village surround the small visiting survey team and compel them to write whatever they say. The poor surveyors have no choice but to record all the falsehood narrated by the villagers. In some places, the Tehsildars recognizing the problem had tried to get systematic survey done, but they were promptly dissuaded by MLAs and other important leaders not to go against wishes of 'suffering masses.' It is said that Panchayat leaders through whom money for relief passes take a cut depending on the extent of falsehood in the claim.

This being a large state with a host of MPs, the CM tries to wrest special package every year there is a flood and often the Union Government obliges. The relief fund can be spent for repairs and rebuilding capital assets also. Jha received forecast of heavy rains in the upper catchments next week, and is wondering whether he should allow 'business as usual' or even at the cost of heavy opposition try some fundamental reform in administration of relief that would really help the economy and indeed the poor.

Question

Which of the following action pathways would you suggest for Prakash Jha? Evaluate their merits and recommend the most desirable line of action.

1. Arrange for armed escorts for the survey teams
2. In any flood affected district, deploy surveyors from other districts.
3. Take action against Panchayat members under the relevant laws if they encourage malpractices.
4. Cross check magnitude claims of relief in any village by using satellite imagery to assess the extent of submergence.

Discussion

1. This approach treats the problem as one of law and order. It is true that survey teams are not allowed to report truthfully. But it will be difficult to spare police from their other duties. As it is, Police are understaffed. It is desirable to identify the lacunae in the system and try to find managerial and technology-based solutions. It is necessary to expose the malpractices clearly so that people will support such solutions.
2. Deploying surveyors from other districts will make it harder for villagers to influence them easily. They will be outsiders. However, even outside surveyors will face intense pressure from mobs in villages bent upon gaining from the floods.
3. This alternative treats the problem as one of violation of laws. To be effective, many cases will have to be made out. But in that process, the administration will get bogged down in lengthy, time consuming legal battles with panchayat functionaries. This will create other problems since administration has to work harmoniously with local self government bodies.
4. The problem is that people are not compensated in part or whole on the basis of actual loss suffered. Local politicians have shut out the information by ruling out real surveys. Loss takes place mostly because of inundation of areas, swift flow of steams eroding agricultural fields and stagnation of water in the low lying areas. But these days one may completely bypass survey by human agents. If satellite imagery is procured from National Remote Sensing Agency, one can very clearly see how flooding had taken place, and how water has stagnated in a particular village. Images should be procured to cover before and after the flood situation. It is true that while interpreting images, one must allow a margin of error because the image will not give very precise details of the field. After providing for a reasonable margin of error the technology can be used to rule out false claims. For this the staff must be also trained to interpret the satellite images.

Panchayats may raise a hue and cry trying to discredit the technology. For meeting such opposition the power of the technology must be demonstrated to the leaders of the panchayat. People can be warned that false claims can lead to prosecution (though no one may be prosecuted.) The political establishment can be convinced that savings from preventing malpractices can be productively used for flood mitigation works. Thus alternative 4 is the correct choice.

CASE 10 Plunder by Mining Mafia; when enough is enough

Till yesterday Shri H. R. Khanna, Commissioner, was agonizing over an ugly episode in which one of his Assistant Directors, Geology & Mining (G&M) along with one Range Forest Officer got killed by Mining Mafia. After the incident, the Chief Minister had told him to control the mafia in the 'X' region of the State. He had also assured Khanna of full support from other Departments of Government. Khanna knew about the political aspect of the problem; in the last election this CM had given assembly tickets to one mafia leader and his associates.

Mining mafia had played havoc with many Reserved Forests. Organized on caste lines, a couple of families became leaders of their caste brethren. Initially they exploited the factories which came into the region because of its rich deposits of limestone and bauxite. Having got a complete hold on the transport, construction and labour supply business, these families became wealthy and their influence penetrated deep into society. Slowly they became involved in politics by flexing muscle and using money power.

The mafias realised that they can enrich themselves quickly by grabbing state resources. Cement factories and other miners took license either from District Collector or the Commissioner of Geology & Mines at the state capital. The mafias began capturing areas that are not yet licensed and started mining in those areas. The mafias first took over government lands, and then slowly started entering into Reserved Forest areas.

At this stage, the Forest Department started confronting them but met with only partial success. It did not have enough strength of Beat Guards and Rangers to intercept and seize hundreds of trucks and earth moving equipments which kept ravaging the forest for procuring minerals. Realising the danger of permanently losing the forest areas, Forest Department was eager to collaborate with Geology and Mining Department to jointly control the menace. Local magistrates and the police were also supportive.

Major chunk's of state mineral resources are concentrated in some pockets; one of these pockets, region 'X' has high mafia presence. There is no surveyed inventory of mineral resources of the State. Some estimates of rough indicative areas and of available minerals exist. But there is no exact survey and there are no boundary marks for the important licenses that have been issued. So the criminal elements also take licenses for one or two areas and then keep exploiting surrounding areas, because the area is not sharply demarcated. The Department does not have enough surveyors who could complete the survey of mine areas and arrange for demarcation.

The situation in the 'X' region is such that unarmed surveyors and inspectors are very fearful to enter the area. There are no strong disincentives for criminals stealing resources. Loaded trucks seized with material would be released by the Department on payment of nominal fine. This liberal attitude may be the result of collusive corruption between departmental staff and the mafia. Some of the ill-gotten wealth has been channelized into procurement of guns, well equipped vehicles, material handling equipments and purchase of politicians.

Khanna wanted to proceed systematically, conscious that he is in a very weak position for following reasons:

1. The mafia is very well entrenched politically.
2. They have muscle power to overwhelm G &M Dept.
3. They have money power to infiltrate within ranks of G & M Dept.
4. G&M Department is inadequately staffed and poorly equipped.
5. It is not technically savvy to detect theft and to get information.

Question

In Commissioner Khanna's position what kind of strategy would you adopt?

1. Informally request police officers to arrange fake encounters to kill the main leaders of the mining mafia

2. Initiate proceedings for arresting mafia leaders under available preventive detention laws
3. Ask the chief minister to use his influence with mafia leaders to end their depredations.
4. Arrange strong interdepartmental coordination under Collector; survey and fix boundaries of mining leases; use satellite imagery to monitor encroachments in forest areas; install GIS in vehicles and equipment of lease operators to track their movement and prevent entry of unauthorised vehicles.

Discussion

The first alternative is absolutely unacceptable. It amounts to taking law into one's own hands. No officer should ever think of proposing or joining in acts which are patently illegal or improper. Killing people—even hardened vicious criminals in fake encounters—is illegal and should not be countenanced.

Some laws such as the Prevention of Anti-Social Activities Act or those for curbing organized crime permit arrest of criminals engaged in certain activities. It is difficult to act under such laws since courts and Tribunals allow wide leeway to offenders from human rights angle. Hence, the approach suggested in answer choice (2) will have limited impact.

This approach is both naive and improper. Even if there is strong reason to suppose that the chief minister is politically close to undesirable elements, no officer should refer to such matters either with the chief minister or with others. An officer can depose on such matters if he has personal knowledge and authentic information, if called upon to do so by competent courts and judicial authorities. In any case, no chief minister will admit to having influence on mafias and other anti-socials.

The appropriate answer choice is the last one. Survey Operations can be outsourced; important mining licensed area can be surveyed; and boundary marks should be fixed in these surveyed areas. Every miner should be asked to give the list of his trucks along with registration details and equipments they use and circulate those lists so that unauthorized trucks could be easily identified. Heavy fines should be imposed for releasing of seized trucks so that they act as a deterrent. Satellite technology should be used to detect the state of exploitation in the Reserved Forest pockets. When the licensed areas are properly marked in Satellite based maps, unauthorised mining could be detected and surprise raids and action could be taken. Forest and mining department personnel should be armed.

CASE 11 Employee's Personal Life – When Does it Become a Matter of Official Concern

Chandrakala Nair is the Municipal Commissioner Bodhpur municipal corporation. Partha Chaudhary works as a maintenance engineer of Water Supply facilities in the Corporation. Chandrakala just received a complaint in her mailbox about him. Three days ago Partha, along with his wife and young kid had gone to Avkar restaurant in the city. That evening the restaurant was full, but Partha asked for two tables to celebrate the birthday of his small son. According to the complaint, the manager present there requested him to wait for some time because no tables were vacant. After fifteen minutes, Partha again went to the manager and threateningly asked him why he was not arranging for the tables. Further according to the complaint, the manager told him that as no customer had since vacated a table he must wait. Hearing this Partha got annoyed and told the manager to ask the customers to finish bloody fast, and then arrange tables. He threatened that he knew the Sanitation Department officials of the corporation and could get the licence of the Avkar restaurant suspended. He shouted a lot calling the Avkar staff as useless jokers. Meanwhile his guests arrived, calmed him and took him out of the premises. The complaint also suggests that Partha was a bit inebriated that evening. The state does not have a prohibition law.

Question

The following courses of action strike Chandrakala as possible alternatives.

1. To immediately suspend Partha and start a disciplinary inquiry for his conduct unbecoming of a public servant.
2. To ask an officer of the Municipal Corporation to informally inquire into the veracity of the complaint, and initiate action against Partha if the complaint happens to be broadly true.
3. Try to personally contact the complainant and find out the facts.
4. Ignore the complaint altogether as the matter does not pertain to Partha's behaviour as a public servant.

What would be your advice to Chandrakala?

Discussion

Undeniably the conduct of Partha is unacceptable. It is not the case that tables were vacant and that the manager was not offering him a table. As a mature person he should have known that it is pointless to ask the manager to get tables vacated quickly. Customers presently occupying the tables are valuable for repeat business and as such the manager has no good reason to tell somebody to vacate quickly.

Partha also had no business whatsoever to threaten the manager that he would use the influence of Sanitation Department of the corporation to cancel the licence. Licences cannot be just cancelled like that unless some violation of conditions of the licence takes place. No such violation is pointed out or known to us. Also it is not proper to settle private scores by bringing public authority into picture. Any sensible officer should know this and Partha should not have even thought in that direction.

In view of the above, Chandrakala should not ignore the complaint. Although the incident is in one sense trivial, Partha as a public servant should not misbehave with the hotel staff. Nor should he threaten them using his official contacts.

But there is no need for her to personally contact the complainant. As she is the administrative head of the corporation, she should entrust the inquiry to an officer of the appropriate level in the organization. The primary task of ascertaining facts of the incident can be performed at lower levels.

Before initiating any action in the matter, the relevant facts have to be ascertained. In public life it is not uncommon to get complaints that exaggerate matters to attract notice. One does not know whether the details narrated in the complaint give a faithful account of the event. If there is exaggeration in the complaint, to that extent Partha's moral culpability would be lower. We are saying moral culpability because the misdemeanour does not attract any provisions of criminal law. Avkar staff has also not lodged a police complaint either. Thus the Commissioner should not take any hasty steps as suggested in (1).

However she should get the matter first inquired to ascertain the facts. She should also ascertain from office record whether Partha is an ill tempered and impatient person. If Partha has such a record then he needs a formal warning. If he does not have any such record and the allegation turns out to be correct, the appropriate action should be to caution him for the future. This is a matter which has arisen from private life and commissioner should not jump to any conclusion to declare the case to be one of behaviour unbecoming of a public servant without a proper inquiry.

CASE 12 An Anonymous Application

Samyukta Nair has early in her career developed a formidable reputation for personal integrity and efficiency. She has succeeded in setting right matters in many corrupt organisations. She is now the chief vigilance officer of the successful State Mineral Development Corporation (SMDC). However, with the surfacing of scams recently, the reputation of SMDC has become sullied.

This morning Samyukta received a letter which reads:

"Respected Madam,

I am writing this letter knowing that you have the courage and rectitude to fight corruption in your organisation. I regret to mention that there are a few monsters in SMDC who are looting the corporation. One of them is Mahendra Dash, the General Manger (contracts). He never signs any big contract without taking a cut on the basis of transaction value. Transporters are his big time clients.

Over the last four years since his entry into this corporation on deputation from the state civil services, he has looted the corporation rapaciously. All the carting rates are inflated as inflated prices only increase his share. He has acquired a number of properties in the state capital and at least two properties in the NCR. When he had joined the services his family was of only moderate means. The following are the lists of the properties:

1. XYZ details
2. PQR details
3. LMN details
4. NCR Property: Details of one property and one suspected ownership for which only the area is mentioned

The value of the properties would easily exceed 10 crores at current market prices.

This officer is not just corrupt, he is a debauch also. Though he is married and has a family, he stays most of the time with one Manohari Prandi (address). Manohari is a divorcee and it is said that her affair with Mahendra Dash was at the root of marital discord resulting in her divorce. Recently, they had gone to Goa on X'mas vacation and stayed in Taj.

I sincerely hope that you would take appropriate action in the matter.

Your anonymous applicant Pro Bono Publico"

The state government instructions suggest that anonymous complaints should be investigated only if they contain verifiable facts. Incidentally, Samyukta knew Mahendra when she was CEO of the Zilla Parishad and he used to work in the office of the District Magistrate. Back then, she had never heard anything adverse about him.

Question

Samyukta thinks of the following lines of action.

1. Ignore the application since it is anonymous.
2. Find out about Dash's reputation from her contacts in Anti-corruption Bureau (ACB), and then consider what to do.
3. Confront Dash with the application and demand his explanation.
4. Consult the MD, SMDC, and order an open investigation into the facts alleged in the application.

Discussion

Alternative (1) will be an inappropriate choice. Government instructions lay down that even anonymous applications should be investigated if they contain verifiable details. As the application gives specific details of properties, it needs to be looked into.

Alternative (2) is also not worth pursuing. Any information she gets will be based on impressions of officers in case some matters concerning Dash reached ACB. But it will be unfair to rely on such impressionistic views while deciding on whether or not to order an investigation. Incidentally, such inputs may not be directly relevant to investigation into the present application. In law, each separate offence becomes a separate proceeding.

As regards alternative (3), no useful purpose will be served by confronting Mahendra. He is certainly not going to accept any of the allegations. On the flip side, he will be alerted to the risk of an impending investigation. Frequently, it happens that when an officer loses fear of getting caught he lowers guard, makes mistakes and finally gets caught. Such a denouement may be waiting for Mahendra. He should not be cautioned or alerted.

It will be appropriate to follow alternative (4). It is easy to verify whether a particular property in a city is registered in somebody's name. It is not even difficult to determine whether the property is held benami. It is also possible to uncover whether Mahendra is having extra marital affair as alleged. But this may have to be treated as a personal matter, though some may consider this as moral turpitude.

Samyukta should inform the MD about the contents of the letter and seek his advice in the matter. This is required in public interest so that MD does not agree with proposals from Mahendra without thorough scrutiny. In government, higher officers have heavy workload and often they tend to trust subordinates. The MD may even take into account his past knowledge of matters dealt with by the General Manager (contracts) and analyse if something was amiss. He would be much better equipped to deal with proposals coming from the General Manager (contracts).

CASE 13 Environmental Entrepreneurship

Kapil and Vasant are from a business family. Both have been very bright since childhood. Both brothers did Masters in Environmental engineering from USA and are currently in the Central Pollution Control Board (CPCB) serving as Deputy Directors in two different areas. Both are known for their expertise and spotless integrity.

Recently, the brothers have been facing pressure from their wives who wanted them to augment the family incomes. They were comparing their lifestyles with those of their business relatives. Vasant proposed to Kapil that they could render valuable service in many areas of environmental management to individual businesses, corporate clients and to large consulting firms. Kapil was initially hesitant but Vasant assured him that they would not do it from office but mostly utilise time at home. Later, they could employ a few good professionals to work under their guidance. With these ground rules, they were planning to float 'VAKA Envirotech' for providing services in environment field.

Question

They think of the following alternatives. Which is the preferable course of action?

1. They will register the firm in the names of their wives and brothers-in-law, and ensure that their own names figure nowhere in the documents.
2. The firm will avoid accepting any work that may involve dealings with their employer organization CPCB.
3. They will register the firm in partnership with a few close consultant friends from their college far away from Delhi in some city like Pune or Thiruvananthapuram.
4. Drop the project since it involves conflict of interest, and they may land in official trouble if their association with the firm comes to light.

Discussion

At the outset, we may note that the whole enterprise involves devious and covert attempts at circumventing codes of official conduct. Public service in India creates a legal fiction that public servants are to be all the time in government service. Physically a public servant may be anywhere but he shall have only one professional preoccupation— service in his specific duties. It is because of this legal fiction that government servants may be called on duty at any odd hours provided the circumstances legitimately demand that. This would rule out even doing any kind of job outside of duty hours for remuneration. No doubt with prior permission of superiors one can engage in charitable activities of apolitical nature. But in this matter there is no charitable purpose involved. It is business pure and simple and that is not permitted. Further, the enterprise involves conflict of interest since issues even those unconnected with pollution may get referred to CPCB.

Against the above clear cut position, we can evaluate the alternatives.

1. Alternative (1) involves setting up a benami firm or a front organization—at best a dubious procedure. The brothers will be working secretly for the firm. This violates the official code of conduct binding them. There are inherent risks of exposure from disgruntled employees or whistleblowers.

Alternative (2) involves taking an extra precaution to keep things under wraps. But as CPCB has a wide mandate, what at sight may seem a project outside its ambit, may get referred to it. This will create serious embarrassment to the brothers.

Alternative (3) is another way of trying to hide things. Again the problem is that one cannot guess when things may come unstuck. Relations between partners may sour; then they may threaten the brothers with exposure. All the above three alternatives illustrate the risks of leaving the straight and narrow moral path. There are no fail safe safeguards in these matters. The Bible cautions that even the wary transgressor will be found out.

As stated in alternative (4), the brothers will be well advised to give up the project. It is fraught with unknown and uncontrollable risks. Once the matters surface, as sooner or later they are bound to, the investigative agencies will go after them. Their name will be mud. They should convince their wives that the expected returns can in no way compensate the risks. Alternatively, they should resign from their jobs and take to business. Hence alternative (4) is the best option.

CASE 14 Decision-making conundrum

Bhupal was secretary of the energy department of a state which like many others is short of power. The state is plagued with power cuts, and these often lead to loud and periodic protests from different consumer groups. The state government has embarked upon an ambitious programme of increasing the power generation capacity within the next five years.

Power projects are huge enterprises with enormous capital costs. They involve tricky technical, commercial and financial problems. With the opening of the power sector to private enterprise, the problems have multiplied. The power which private companies generate has to be purchased usually by public enterprises i.e. state electricity boards. Such purchases are based on power purchase agreements which are concluded for long periods stretching over 20 years. The private parties quote their rates for selling power separately for each of the 20 years. As electricity boards have to conclude agreement with the lowest bidder, the rates quoted for different years have to be made comparable by calculating present values through a process of discounting. Electricity boards also have to look at the sources from which the private generating companies obtain fuels like coal, gas or lignite.

The selection of the final bidder is based on a two stage process. In the first stage, the bidders who want to set up the generating plant are prequalified based on their technical, financial, and organizational skills and track record in setting up and operating power plants. In the second phase, the bidder is selected from the prequalified firms based on their financial quotations. At both stages, the process involves study of detailed documents and massive data. Those preparing the documents can tweak them in various ways to favour certain parties. It is rumoured that the whole process involves large scale corruption. CAG often comes out with scathing criticism highlighting huge losses to public due to faulty selection of projects.

A meeting has been proposed for the ostensible purpose of deciding upon the commercial offers for building a 600 MW power plant at a cost of nearly 2000 crores in a remote tribal location with coal deposits. The meeting will be between the Minister (in chair), chairman of the electricity board, a political appointee, chief engineer (Projects) and the Secretary of the Energy Department.

Bhupal is a senior officer who is shortly expecting a promotion to the top rung of the state administration. He knows from experience that many decisions on power project selection invariably get mired in controversy. He carefully goes through the project documents. He realises that the electricity board has departed from many standard conditions which should go into such documents. He sees that a clever and surreptitious attempt is being made to favour a particular bidder. He suspect this to be the handiwork of the board's chairman and officials with the minister's connivance. Bhupal is wary of the whole proposal not least because of his impending promotion.

Question

Bhupal was wondering what he should do in the situation. He thought of the following alternatives.

1. Proceed on sick leave and rejoin duty after the meeting is over.
2. Pretend to be stuck in some unavoidable business and send a junior officer to attend the meeting
3. Meet the minister privately and caution him that the proposal is dubious and will create a huge stink
4. Attend the meeting, point out the faults in the analysis of tenders and ask for a fresh analysis.

What do you think is the correct alternative?

Discussion

Alternative (1) implies that Bhupal is ducking the issue. He is evading his responsibility. Proceeding on leave for feigned illness is a form of malingering or work avoidance. It is hardly expected from a senior officer. He has to face the issue squarely instead of choosing an escapist route.

Alternative (2) is also unacceptable, and in a way is worse than alternative (1). Bhupal as a senior officer should not expose to risk a junior officer who may be unaware of the serious problems involved in accepting the board's proposal. Further, a junior will not be able to stand up to the pressures which others will put on him during the meeting.

Alternative (3) is unlikely to work. Most probably, the minister will side with the board. He may argue that they will be only endorsing a proposal of the board, which is supposed to know its business. They are not the prime movers of the proposal and can blame the board if things go wrong. In any case, they are not indulging in any wrong doing. This argument is, of course, invalid since all the participants in the decision will become liable.

Alternative (4) is the most appropriate choice. In this option, Bhupal will be taking action in line with public interest. He will be performing his duty faithfully. Once he points out the lacunae in the tender evaluation and records his views, the board will be forced to rework the proposals in accordance with acceptable criteria. The chances of deviating from correct procedure will be eliminated. In this process, he may incur the minister's displeasure. That is a cross he has to carry as part of his job as a public servant.

CASE 15 Aftermath of an accident

Prakasam is the driver of Bhujanga Rao, an upcoming industrialist who also dabbles in politics. Recently, from the proceeds of his flourishing business he has purchased a luxury brand car. He is a fast driver who likes to cut through traffic leaving little margin for errors which he, other drivers or pedestrians may make.

Normally, Prakasam drives the vehicle. But one day, Bhujanga Rao was driving the vehicle. As he was expecting a business team at his factory, and as he was getting late, he started speeding up. Prakasam cautioned him to drive slowly since though they were on a highway, some of its stretches are adjacent to villages without separating barricades. On those stretches, people have a tendency to cross the highway or get onto it with little concern for the rushing traffic. Most drivers slowed down on those stretches. But Bhujanga Rao was driving fast ignoring the cautious words of Prakasam.

Then, all of a sudden, a motor cyclist entered the highway from the side on which Bhujanga Rao was driving. He applied the brakes, but as the vehicle was moving too fast, it hit the motor cyclist, and injured him grievously. Bhujanga Rao went into a panic. He knew that he would, considering the present harsh attitude of judges towards to rash drivers, get a stiff sentence. While he was waiting, an ambulance (responding to the call of a passerby) came and removed the injured motorcyclist to a hospital. After some time, to his relief, he came to know that the accident victim though seriously injured is out of danger.

Question

He began to think of how best to handle the situation, and the following alternatives occur to him. Which do you think is the correction one?

1. He should bribe the traffic police, and induce them to prepare a case blaming the motorcyclist of careless driving and absolving him since he was driving on the highway.
2. He should contact his political friends to whom he has made donations to intervene in the case in his favour.
3. He should induce Prakasam to claim that he was driving the vehicle, and offer him (Prakasam) full financial help and large upfront payment.
4. He should help the injured motor cyclist and his family, engage a good lawyer to fight his case, and hope for the best.

Discussion

The first alternative can be ruled out straightaway. Bhujanga Rao will be compounding the initial offence by committing another criminal act. While making decisions whether in office or at home illegal or immoral actions should never be considered. They are not real decision choices.

The second alternative is also an improper course of action. It is an example of trying to use undue influence on public servants---in this case on police. This is called 'influence pedalling' and it is an unhealthy, if not an illegal, practice.

The third alternative is also totally wrong. It is just fastening guilt on an innocent person. It is tampering with evidence and falsifying the case which itself is an offence. Even if Prakasam agrees to the inducement, he will be running the risk of facing a jail term depending on the outcome of the case. Depending on how the case is proceeding, Prakasam, if he becomes nervous, may retract his statement and tell the truth. These three alternatives are really unsatisfactory even from a prudential (as opposed to moral) point of view.

The fourth alternative is the most appropriate. Bhujanga Rao cannot and should not try to escape the legal consequences of his action. He has to act within the confines of law. He should try to put up the best defence along lines that he had the right of way, that he was not driving recklessly and that the motorcyclist suddenly came onto the highway unmindful of the traffic. By financially helping the motorcyclist, he would earn some goodwill and the motorcyclist may soften his stand in the court.

CASE 16 Land for cultural centre

Seshachari is working as deputy secretary in Revenue department on the desk dealing with grants of government land for various purposes. As land has become very scarce and very expensive, such grants have to be carefully made. Government has formulated a policy for grant of its land for public purposes. The policy has been embodied in an official resolution. Government lands are granted for purposes such as public educational institutions, hostels, hospitals, charitable institutions, government offices and rural infrastructure.

One day a proposal for granting land to a cultural centre proposed in a prime urban location reached Seshachari's desk. The centre was not proposed by state culture department, but by a private group. As Seshachari was reading the file, he received a phone from Revenue minister's private secretary that the person who wants to set up the centre is closely related to a prominent central leader of the ruling political establishment. The private secretary added that the proposal was cleared by the lower levels in the department and that Seshachari should also endorse it positively.

Seshachari saw that the proposal could not be cleared under the government's policy. Land could be given to private parties in a few cases for institutions which undertake programmes of education, health and skill upgradation for weaker sections of society. The lower level staff justified the proposal since the official policy resolution contained a residual phrase that grant can be made for "other public purposes as may be decided by government". Seshachari feared that grant of valuable land to a private person with political connections could lead to controversy.

Question

He wondered what to do with the proposal, and the following alternatives occurred to him.

1. He should oppose the proposal tooth and nail, and even if government approves it, he should not issue the order.
2. He should clearly point out that the cultural centre is not eligible for land under the present policy and that the proposal should be rejected.
3. Since the proposal has emanated from a lower level and as he is only a supervisory officer, he may sign on the proposal.
4. He should raise queries (questions and doubts) on the file, and at the same time engineer RTI application or letter to Lokayukta about the matter.

What in your view is the correct course of action and why?

Discussion

Alternative (1) will represent an overreaction. If Seshachari believes that the grant of land cannot be made, he should record his views clearly on the file outlining the factual, legal and policy dimensions. Thereafter, he should implement whatever orders government decides to pass.

Alternative (2) is the correct line of action. The role of civil servants in secretariat is to advise government. In other words, they should study proposals and recommend courses of actions which can be justified on factual, legal and proprietary grounds and which are within the accepted policy framework. Once officers perform this task, they would have discharged their duty adequately. Thereafter, they have to follow government decision. They will not be answerable to any illegal or improper actions of government.

Alternative (3) is unacceptable. Affixing signature on a proposal in a file means that the official accepts it. He becomes responsible for the decision. The only defence, if the decision is later questioned, is to claim that he has been misled. But this is possible if the earlier analysis misstates or omits to mention material facts which have a vital bearing on the decision. Another defence can be that the relevant legal provisions and policy issues have been left out of analysis. This defence seldom works since officers are supposed to know about relevant laws and policies. It is their job to get matters analysed properly. Their job is not just to put signatures on files.

The fourth alternative is mischievous. When queries are raised on files, they go back to lower levels again, and are returned with answers to the queries. This delays decision-making and can be used as a delaying tactic. Genuine questions about matters missed out in analysing a proposal can be raised, but no attempt should be made to deliberately delay matters by raising unnecessary queries. RTI and other avenues have been created for common citizens, and officers should not abuse those provisions in any way for collateral ends.

CASE 17 Vasumathi in a quandary

Vasumathi completed B.Com (Hons) and various computer certificate courses on accounting and audit. She was delighted when she was offered employment on contract basis in the Accounts wing of a public works department. She could have got better jobs, but had no desire to leave her hometown in South India.

Her job consisted in verifying the bills which contractors submitted for the projects they were implementing. The works had numerous components such as digging foundations, depositing excavated materials at designated points, spreading earth or materials for roads under construction and laying concrete for foundation work. The contracts specified the quantum of work in physical quantities such as M^3 or M^2 of earth spreading or depositing. Rates for payment were specified for such physical quantities, and contractors put in claims on the basis of the work done. Vasumathi had to make sure that the quantities, rates and claims were in line with the approved contract document. As she was proficient in the accounting software, she could do the job effortlessly.

She has been given a cubicle in a corridor with an open office layout. Vasumathi kept to herself as she was preparing for competitive examinations. After checking the bills received by her, she would start working for her exams.

She had a completely unexpected experience in the middle of the second month. One well dressed person came and gave her a cover. Taking it to be a letter, she opened and found that it contained Rs. 5000. Taken aback, she tried to return the amount thinking that it was for someone else. He told her that it is a normal routine payment which the contractors made to staff as part of goodwill. He assured her that others are paid such amounts and that she should not hesitate in taking it for it carries no obligation whatsoever. Vasanthi realised that it is part of institutionalized corruption.

Question

What do you think should she do in this situation?

1. She should create a big scene so that the bribe giver would never approach her again
2. She should accept the amount since she does not have to do any wrong in return.
3. She should refuse the payment, and also inform a senior officer in the organization about the incident
4. She should just refuse the payment and tell the bribe giver not to approach her again.

Discussion

Vasumathi should not create a scene. It will serve no purpose. If others in the organization are accepting the payment, her creating a scene may turn them against her. Incidentally, the bribe giver may make a counter allegation against her, and try to put her in the dock.

The second alternative is patently wrong. By accepting the payment, though not of her seeking, she would be embroiled in a criminal act. She would be violating the Prevention of Corruption Act. Hence, she should firmly reject the proffered payment. A quid pro quo from her side is not necessary to land her in trouble. She will be as guilty as the others accepting the payment

The third alternative is the most appropriate response. She has unwittingly come to know of illegal goings on in the organization. She does not have the power or authority to initiate action against the persons involved in the illegalities. It is for the duly empowered authorities to initiate necessary administrative and legal actions. But as she has become cognizant of the wrong deeds, she has to inform the senior officers, and leave it to them to take suitable actions. She can request them to keep her role in the matter secret.

The fourth alternative is correct up to a point. But as a responsible citizen and office worker, she has to bring the matter to the notice of the concerned senior officers.

CASE 18 Problems at election time

Elections have been declared in the state. According to the election code of conduct, all major decisions have been put on hold. In this situation, chief secretary, Prakash Godbole faced a delicate problem which arose from failure of rains in some parts of the state. Extra power has to be supplied to farmers to enable them to run irrigation pump sets. Power was also needed to tackle drinking water supply problems. The situation led to public dissatisfaction and the Chief Minister knew that it would affect the party's election prospects. He asked Godbole to do something about the matter.

Things were a bit complicated. As the state had no generation capacity, power has to be purchased at a high cost. Further, the state electricity board had no money. Funds can be given to the board only by withdrawing a large sum from contingency fund. Finance department would not agree to such withdrawals since the election process is in progress. Large purchases of supply of power may be interpreted as an attempt by the state administration to support the government facing elections.

Godbole knew that money can be provided to the board by way of temporary loan from a state investment corporation. It is in joint sector with 51% private share and is outside normal CAG audit. Its operations are not part of government transactions. Power secretary and the electricity board agree to purchase power and supply it to farmers and water supply board if a temporary loan is arranged. Incidentally, Godbole was appointed as chief secretary by the present chief minister. He also dealt with him in a friendly manner.

Question

Godbole thinks of the following alternative lines of action.

1. Tell the Chief Minister that because of the ongoing election process, he cannot do anything.
2. Advise the Chief Minister to approach the Election Commission for necessary approval
3. Arrange temporary loan to the electricity board and give extra power supply to the areas of the state which are actually facing the adverse effects of inadequate rains.
4. Arrange a liberal loan and make power available on a large scale all over the state.

Discussion

By adopting alternative (1), Godbole would be playing safe. Since he is not taking any initiative, and postponing a decision till the completion of elections, no political party will accuse him of partiality. The Election Commission would not raise any issue. This approach is inappropriate since state administration (and its head chief secretary) cannot ignore the genuine hardships of people simply because the election process is in progress.

The second alternative is unacceptable since the chief secretary should not just leave the matter to Election Commission. Obviously, he should try his utmost first to help farmers and the people. This advice is pointless since the Chief Minister will be aware of the position and wants the chief secretary to do something.

The third alternative is appropriate. It leads to quick action and avoids the detailed and time consuming financial scrutiny. It concentrates on the genuine needs of the affected people. No one can reasonably object to this action. While remaining within the ambit of law and propriety, the chief secretary will be implementing the Chief Minister's instructions to the extent feasible.

The last alternative is improper. As elections are going on, no extra facilities and advantages should be given to people. It may amount to offering inducement to people and polishing the image of government. The normal levels of power supply, along with any routine power cuts, should be continued. Any decision regarding enhancement to supply in these areas with normal rainfall should be left to the elected government which will take office after elections.

CASE 19 Playboys in office

Sujatha joined her office recently. She was trying to learn the work and get used to the official procedures. Her boss Sudarshan was a nice guy and gave her the background material for getting acquainted with the work and alerted het to the critical issues which can crop up from time to time. He assured her that he would help her in case she was unable to cope with any work problems. Sujatha was settling down in her job.

Soon, she realised that all was not well in the office. A senior officer and a couple of his favourites were in the habit of misbehaving with lady staff in the office. It is rumoured that the favourites facilitated the out of way actions of the senior. It is also believed that he has the patronage of the higher ups.

The favourites did not of course (mercifully) physically assault any lady worker. But they would start uninvited and unsolicited conversation with them. They would invite the ladies to accompany them to dinners in expensive hotels. They would hint on how the sexual mores of the society have changed and how prudery is out of place. They would ask them many personal questions. They would introduce romantic themes into the conversation. They would at times block the way of ladies in the corridor.

They tried this with Sujatha once or twice. She rebuffed them quite roughly. They left dropping hints about their influence and clout in the organization and of their proximity to bosses who matter. Sujatha felt diffident about mentioning the matter to Sudarshan. She discussed the matter with her lady friends. They shrugged off the issue and said that such things were common in offices, that the behaviour of the favourites was not criminal and that no effective response would result from their complaints. It could end up souring their relations with others in office and create greater tensions for them.

Question

Given the above situation, what should Sujatha do?

1. She should accept the situation as a necessary part of the office eco-system and "go with the flow".
2. She should lodge a complaint of sexual harassment with the concerned senior officer and insist on speedy action.
3. She should appeal to the good sense of the favourites and tell them not to disturb their fellow lady workers.
4. She should complain about the matter to the MLA of her constituency and ask him to take it up with higher authorities.

Discussion

The first alternative is passive and smacks of defeatism. It is this passivity of the victims which encourages the aggressors. If they do not fear any strong reaction to their misconduct, they will continue to misbehave. It is necessary for an individual to assert his/her right in the face of unprovoked misbehaviour of others. Unless the victims air the grievances, the custodians of official discipline will have no cause for action. They will have an excuse for inaction.

The second alternative is appropriate. Once Sujatha makes a complaint, the wheels will start moving. The concerned officers would not like to overlook a complaint of sexual harassment. Even the senior officer and his favourites will become cautious. The top level officers may be unaware of the goings on in the office. They will usually come down with a heavy hand since they would not like to answer the Women's Commission or get embroiled (if matters go out of hand) in legal tangles.

The third alternative is unlikely to succeed. Those who behave in this way are insensitive to the rights, feelings and sensitivities of other people. It is a form of unselfconscious anti-social behaviour. Had they been brought up properly, they would not behave in this manner.

The fourth alternative is also improper. According to a legal principle, an aggrieved person should, in the first place, seek redressal from the first level of authority empowered to act in the matter. Naturally, it will be the concerned authorities in the organization who are entrusted with the task of handling sexual harassment complaints. In case they fail to act, then Sujatha can explore other avenues.

CASE 20 Sneha's courage of conviction

Sneha hails from a medium sized town in eastern India. After completing a course in communications, she got a job with a small advertising agency in a metropolis. Finding accommodation is a great problem in any megacity. Luckily, an elderly couple, allowed her to stay with them as a paying guest.

Sneha became friendly with a few girls working with her and occasionally joined them for spending the leisure hours she got from her heavy schedule. They have been staying in the metropolis since quite some time. Initially, Sneha was fascinated by their behaviour which seemed to be free from the inhibition and diffidence of small town girls. The anonymity of girls in the metropolis and its permissiveness added to their sense of freedom. She noticed that people tended to generally ignore one another, and that each person remained within the cocoon of his narrow personal world.

Gradually, Sneha began to feel uneasy about her friends. They seemed to ridicule, though not in so many words, her conventional and rustic background. They were amused by the bindi she put on. They hinted that she should dress in modern style. Sneha was really troubled when she came to know that they consumed alcohol and some of them even experimented with drugs. Her real shock came when she learned that two of the girls were living with male partners without formal ties of marriage.

Realising the risks of friendship with her new found friends, she cut down her contacts with them under the pretext of heavy work pressure. Most of the girls left her alone, but one of them confronted her. She accused Sneha of avoiding them deliberately. She advised her that their jobs are unconventional and creative and presuppose play of spontaneous artistic impulses. She added that their creativity can blossom and their work can be original only when they rid themselves of conventional behaviour patterns. She went on to add that such morals are shackles which a patriarchal society puts on women. She concluded by urging Sneha to give up her small town mind set and adopt the life style of the artistic groups in the metropolis.

Question

How should Sneha respond to this piece of advice from her friend?

1. Sneha should change her behaviour on the lines suggested by her friend.
2. Sneha should ignore the advice of her friend.
3. Sneha should pack her bags and leave the metropolis.
4. Sneha should change her job and move to conventional journalism.

Discussion

The first alternative should be rejected. The girls are misguided and have fallen into the tempting snares which they face in large cities. She should not give in to the undesirable influences of her friends---which is called "peer pressure". The life style they adopted can land them in serious troubles. Young people acquire many bad habits from the company they keep. They consider that it is fashionable to do so; this gives them a sense of being inside a closed group with solidarity. But one should not rely on such false psychological props.

This is the correct option. Basically, Sneha has a wholesome personality. There is nothing fake about her and she has a sense of decency and of what is right and wrong. The other girls perhaps realise this. They may be feeling a sense of moral unease in the presence of a person observing conventional codes. By converting her to their way of thinking, they can reduce their feeling of moral dissonance which may be unconscious. . But Sneha has to remain steadfast to her values. A large part of being moral consists in firmly resisting such pressures. It is not enough to know what morals are; one has to practise them continuously.

Sneha need not leave the metropolis. Her problem is not with the city, but with a set of undesirable friends. In such situations, it is better to maintain a distance from the sources of unwholesome influences. We cannot dub metropolises as bad places, though large crowded urban areas do create problems of isolated human beings leading atomized lives. As in any other place, metropolises contain good people and groups.

Sneha need not change her job. One should not leave a job unless it is too full of intractable problems or it is psychologically burdensome. At a time when jobs are insufficient, it will be imprudent to leave a job. One should leave a job only after finding another one. Of course, if a job is hopelessly intolerable, one has no choice.

CASE 21 Dealing with systematic overpayments

The state government has a scheme for giving subsidies to industries set up in backward areas. The subsidy is paid on eligible fixed investments mainly for purchase of land and physical equipment. In order to avoid disputes, the state government prepared an exhaustive list of eligible items entitled to subsidy; it also prepared a negative list clearly identifying the ineligible items such as good will and patents. Calculation of subsidies for large projects is laborious and troublesome since thousands of items of machinery have to be checked for eligibility. There is a high level team of officials which examines the claims of subsidy after getting the scrutiny report for each project.

Pramod has recently joined the division which scrutinizes subsidy claims. He is responsible for ensuring the accuracy of the report prepared for the high level official team. Pramod found that the work of scrutiny is being done manually with someone marking the items as eligible and ineligible. He noticed that subsidies were allowed and disallowed for same items in some cases. He noticed that overall, the subsidy amounts were being inflated systematically. He was worried that the excess payments, if continued, could involve him in trouble if auditors object to them. He realised that most of the process, barring that which needed judgemental assessments, can be computerized. This would also eliminate the problem of overpayments.

Pramod wanted to engage an agency to quickly prepare a project for computerization. But his proposal met with stiff resistance. Pramod has a degree in IT. He decided to prepare the programme with the help of a few willing staff members. Even then, some people were trying to derail the scheme. Pramod was puzzled until one day a staff member told him that the proposals were being systematically inflated and that the inflated amounts were being shared at various levels including political levels. He was told that it would be very difficult to change the system.

Question

Pramod wants to get over the problem. He thinks of the following alternatives. Which of them is the appropriate one in your view?

1. He should meet the chairman of the high level official team, apprise him about overpayments that have been made and tell him that it would be necessary to computerize the system for ensuring greater accuracy and avoiding inconsistencies and overpayments.
2. Leak a story to press that there may be large scale irregularities in subsidy payments.
3. Provide information to a whistle blower about the wrong payments that may have been made earlier
4. Quietly tip off audit and ask them to scrutinize files with exorbitant ineligible subsidy payments.

Discussion

The first option is appropriate. When any irregularity comes to an officer's knowledge, he has to immediately inform his supervisory officer. Government organisations (and many others) are hierarchies; in such systems organisational discipline requires that an officer has to report problems to his supervisor and seek his instructions. Pramod should not assume that the high level team is involved in wrong doing. To come to that conclusion, he should have valid grounds and not be guided by verbal statements of staff. In all likelihood, the chairman would agree with Pramod and ensure that no overpayments are made in future. He may order recovery of excess payments made in the past.

The second alternative is inappropriate. Organisations (including governments) designate officers and procedures for dealing with media. Pramod should not violate that procedure. Further, it involves devious conduct. In adopting that course, Pramod would not be acting in a straightforward manner.

The third alternative suffers from the same defects as the second one. Of course, nowadays whistle blowing is being encouraged. But the officers should resort to it only in extreme situations. Essentially, it is a remedy which should be used only when the whole organisation or large parts of it are hopelessly corrupt, and even honest officers are dragged into corruption against their wishes.

The fourth alternative is also devious. Audit is an independent function. An organisation has to provide audit with all the information and documentation it seeks. But officers should not try to influence the audit one way or the other. They should answer the questions which audit raises fully. Officers should not use audit, even if it is willing, for other purposes.

CASE 22 Unsuitable match

Ponnuswamy is in a state of mental turmoil. He has a mid-sized farm and lives with his daughter and two young sons in a municipal town. He is comfortably off, and his children are in degree colleges. But a little while ago, his wife told him that their daughter was romantically involved with Selwaraj. Selwaraj is known to be a feckless young man with no steady job or income. Ponnuswamy is slightly acquainted with Selwaraj's family. Their family is pretty low, as compared to ponnuswamy's family, in the caste hierarchy. He knew that his caste panchayat would take umbrage at the marriage proposal.

Ponnuswamy was not at all keen on his daughter tying up with Selwaraj. He told his wife to reason with their daughter. But their daughter was adamant. Ponnuswamy tried to convince his daughter to abandon the proposal. He told her that he would find a good match in their caste or a higher caste. He told her that Selwaraj had no job and would be unable to provide her with any material comforts.

His daughter refused to listen to his advice. She said that she had given her heart to Selwaraj, and that he is a wonderful person. He planned to start a self employment venture, and she would support him in the venture. She expressed idealistic sentiments about love.

Question

Ponnuswamy was wondering what to do in the situation. He thinks of the following alternatives.

1. He could forcibly marry her to a person of his caste.
2. He could shift to his village home and confine her movements to the village.
3. He can buy time by asking her to wait till Selwaraj makes a success of his business or gets a good job, and extract a promise from her not to meet Selwaraj till such time.
4. He can hire thugs from his caste group and they can threaten Selwaraj with dire consequences if he continues to meet Ponnuswamy's daughter.

Discussion

The situation depicted in this case is delicate and troublesome. Often, young girls are idealistic, sentimental and highly impressionable. They often fall for the first scoundrel who comes along. Unscrupulous individuals can easily take advantage of them. In fact, this is a reason why they should be cautious about whom they choose as their friends. Parents of young girls also need to be careful and ensure that their daughters do not fall into bad company. From the facts given in the case, the choice of Ponnuswamy's daughter appears foolish. Selwaraj has neither qualifications nor a job. His self employment idea is woolly and is unlikely to provide economic security.

The idea of forced marriage should not be pursued. Marriage is too important a relationship to admit of any compulsions. It has to result from free and voluntary consent of the two partners. Compulsorily marrying someone against his/her desire can be an offence, and bring woes in future.

Forcibly confining the movements of a person---even of one's daughter---is an offence. It will have very undesirable consequences on the person thus confined. No father should put his daughter through such situation. It may end up by creating a permanent rift between the father and the daughter. The whole procedure is of doubtful legality.

The third option appears to be the best under the circumstances. Ponnuswamy should be able to convince his daughter that the whole idea of marrying a person without job or any future prospects is unthinkable for a girl. It can ruin her life. He can tell her that it would be a source of great mental anguish to her parents. His daughter is likely to hear this argument. After sometime, if Selwaraj fails to make the grade, she will lose her interest in him. If Ponnuswamy can convince her not to meet Selwaraj, her infatuation may slowly come to an end. In this option, Ponnuswamy is not doing anything which he should not do as a father or as a law abiding citizen. If by chance Selwaraj finds a good job or succeeds in his business venture, then Ponnuswamy can agree to the marriage.

The last alternative is obviously illegal. In addition to the problem of his daughter's ill chosen match, Ponnuswamy will end up facing the law. If Selwaraj makes a police complaint, they will question Ponnuswamy. Then the anti-social elements will immediately tell police that they had acted on Ponnuswamy's instructions.

CASE 23 Public stance and private morality

Vidhushi is a prominent socialist intellectual. She was a professor of sociology in a prominent university. She was no ivory tower academic. She actively espoused---in the name of Marxian praxis---causes of labour, tribals, minorities and oppressed women. Her work on pedagogy for the oppressed won acclaim in liberal western universities.

The political establishment found that her writings provided some theoretical support for their populist agendas. She was offered a position in the think tank of their party. Vidhushi appeared in TV shows and wrote articles in support of the party's programmes. In one of the argumentative debates, Vidhushi condemned the admission procedures of public schools and suggested that the political, social and academic elites should send their children only to government schools. This procedure, Vidhushi argued, would raise the standards of government schools.

After some time, during the schools opening season, there were heated debates about admission procedures to elite schools. There were allegations of large scale influence peddling and of how the rich and the powerful manage to secure admissions to their wards in prestigious schools. During one of the debates, it came out that Vidhushi was seeking admission for her daughter in a top school. This was followed by lot of criticism that Vidhushi is guilty of hypocrisy and that she should admit her daughter in government school near her school.

Question

Which one of the following decisions should Vidhushi make?

1. Vidhushi should withdraw her daughter's admission application from the prestigious school and admit her in a government school.
2. Vidhushi should stop appearing on TV shows and let the issue fade away
3. She should try to get admission to her daughter in the prestigious school.
4. She should ask her party colleagues to stoutly defend her stand.

Discussion

The first alternative need not be pursued. There is no doubt about inconsistency, if not hypocrisy, in the behaviour of Vidhushi. But it does not mean that she should adopt in her personal life the principles she advocated in her academic and political roles. In this case, she has to act as a mother, and not as a party ideologue. She should do what she considers is the best for her daughter.

The second alternative will temporarily save Vidhushi's embarrassment. After some time, the story will no longer be newsworthy and just be forgotten. In any case, most people will recognise that she has a right to secure admission for her daughter in the best possible school. She should appear on the news channels and defend her position on logical and factual grounds.

This is the correct course of action. We have mentioned some reasons while discussing the first alternative. In addition, we should note the distinction between one's private and public life. Vidhushi cannot impose her publicly proclaimed principles and policies on her daughter. Family members cannot be brought within the ambit of public political stance unless it is a matter of law or policy. Of course, examples of this type show that it is easy to proclaim public principles, but hard to put them into practice in private life.

This alternative is quite irrelevant to the issue. In fact, if Vidhushi so desires, she should personally defend her position.

CASE 24 Filing a false affidavit

Akshay found himself in a difficult spot during a discussion with the ministerial group. The group was set was set up to examine the serious irregularities which occurred in the purchase of relief materials in the aftermath of a major cyclone which lashed the state. The relief materials did not arrive on time when needed. Many of the samples which were checked for quality failed to conform to the tender specifications. The orders were placed by a purchase committee after taking the approval of the Relief commissioner under emergency purchase procedures. The file was also seen by the concerned cabinet minister.

The matter led to wide adverse media coverage. It created uproar in the state assembly, and the opposition forced many adjournments. The Chief Minister promised to have the whole question of malpractices examined and take action against those found responsible. In the meanwhile, an application for public interest litigation was also filed in the High court in the matter.

Akshay was assisting the group. After carefully going through the files relating to the purchases, he found that in some cases the officers at lower level failed to clearly specify the standards for the materials being procured. He also saw that in many instances, the concerned staff failed to carry out the necessary quality checks. Because of the distress of the people and the urgency of the needs, everyone was in a hurry to just get hold of the relief materials.

Akshay explained these matters to the group. He pointed to some lower staff as responsible for not correctly laying down specifications and for not performing quality checks as required. The group was, however, not satisfied with this approach. They wanted to fix the responsibility on the Relief Commissioner. They also wanted Akshay to file an affidavit in the high court blaming the Relief Commissioner for the malpractices. When he pointed out that it would be difficult to do so, they told him to treat it as Group's order and implement it.

Question

What should Akshay do in these circumstances?

1. He should file the affidavit blaming the Relief Commissioner.
2. He should politely decline to file the affidavit.
3. He should file a diluted affidavit vaguely hinting at the indirect responsibility of the Relief Commissioner.
4. He should apprise the Relief Commissioner of the matter so that he can approach the group

Discussion

The first alternative will be wrong. An affidavit is a sworn statement which affirms facts. If it is not true, the person swearing it can be prosecuted for perjury. In official contexts, affidavits are mostly based on facts which are found in files or statements which can be supported by materials contained in official records. In this case, the Relief Commissioner endorsed a recommendation of the purchase committee. He had no direct role; nor is there any statement about his mala fide involvement. He cannot delay matters in a crisis situation.

The second alternative is the appropriate course of action. An affidavit has to be based on one's direct, personal knowledge and on facts revealed by available records. An affidavit cannot be filed on the basis of what some else tells one to do. Hence in this case Akshay cannot legally follow the group's order. Being illegal, it is not binding on him. So he should politely decline to file the affidavit on the suggested lines---though it may cause unpleasantness.

For the reasons discussed above, the third alternative is improper. In any case, affidavits cannot be vague or airy statements.

The fourth alternative is also inappropriate. Akshay should perform his official role to the best of his judgement. Tipping off the Relief Commissioner may mean improper communication of the proceedings of the group.

CASE 25 Irregular Industrial Plot allotments

State industrial development corporation (SIDC) looks after allotment of industrial plots. SIDC creates industrial estates in acquired land by providing infrastructure such as roads, water supply, drainage, power, waste disposal, transport parking lots, bank branches and so on. The demand for plots far exceeds supply and offers scope for corruption. The chairman of SIDC is an influential politician who wants to gain from the situation. MD also joins hands with him.

To further their purposes, they create an opaque system with built-in discretionary powers. Outwardly, the allotment of plots was based on first-come-first served basis. But there was no system of promptly recording the date and time of receipt of applications - especially using tamper proof computer based system. The chairman assumed the power of discretionary or out-of-turn allotments under the pretext of helping highly deserving or hard pressed entrepreneurs. By making arbitrary allotments of industrial plots and through other means, the chairman and the MD made money. They resisted the attempts of some board members to introduce a system plot allotment through public auctions.

After a while, some of the applicants who were denied plots instigated some dummy applicants to send complaints to government and vigilance commission. They also mounted pressure in other ways. Government was forced to institute an inquiry into the whole matter.

The inquiry reveals various irregularities. Plots have been allotted to non industrialists. Most of the out-of-turn allotments went to influential individuals. Many plots were much larger than the permissible size. No reliable records were available to show the application dates, or any reliable queue system for making allotments. Many allotments were made without consulting the Board. In the meanwhile based on a tip off, anti corruption police raided the residences of the chairman and MD, and recovered large amounts of cash. They registered a case against them under the PC Act.

Question

What can we say about the nature of corruption in this case? How can it be tackled?

1. It is due to the excessive greed of the chairman.
2. Corruption can be traced to the fact that the chairman is a politician.
3. Corruption is basically due to systemic causes and needs systemic remedies.
4. Corruption was made possible as MD also joined the game.

Discussion

1. The first alternative will be a simplistic answer. Corruption may arise in one sense from individual greed and lack of moral strength. But corruption also requires an administrative environment which creates opportunities for officials to exploit the weaknesses of the system.

2. The second alternative is off the mark. It is an over generalization and paints all politicians with the same brush. It is called stereotyping of a whole group ignoring the significant differences among its members.
3. Unfortunately, corruption in this case has originated from the top of SIDC. It reminds one of a proverb that a rotten fish stinks from the head. The corruption is collusive in nature since both bribe givers and bribe takers benefit from the transaction at the cost of genuine entrepreneurs. The economic source of corruption here lies in scarcity of industrial plots. In such scarcity situations, people are willing to pay 'on money' over official price for commodities. In this regard, economists and political thinkers have spoken of two types of irregularities. In 'profit seeking' behaviour, politicians seek gains through promoting genuine industrial enterprises as illustrated by the experience of Japan, South Korea and Singapore. Here, though there may be underhand dealings or cronyism between industrialists and politicians, there is also economic or industrial growth. The other form of irregularity involves 'rent seeking' behaviour. Here, entrepreneurs and politicians combine to skim off the surplus (called rent in economics) which exists between the official and market prices of scarce resources. If political leaders adopt rent seeking behaviour as in India, industrial growth invariably takes a hit.

   The following measures can be adopted

   - Government should dispose of scarce natural and other resources through open competitive bidding or auctions.
   - If any other process like 'first come first served' is adopted, it should be transparent and be backed by full, reliable documentation to avoid malpractices.
   - In these situations, the macroeconomic remedies consist of supply side interventions for enhancing production and availability of scarce commodities.
   - There should be deregulation of economy to the maximum feasible extent - with due regard to social concerns - to allow free play to market forces, and to remove unnecessary administrative controls.
   - Administrative processes should be simplified and put on web sites. In this case, the date wise receipt of applications for industrial plots and their processing in SIDC should be kept on web site.
4. The fourth option is a partial answer. MD could have made it hard for the Chairman to indulge in malpractices. But the root of the problem is systemic.

Glossary of Terms

Abortion

Abortion refers to the termination of the unborn entity (or termination of pregnancy) at any of its growing stages. Abortions at times occur due to internal biochemical processes of the pregnant woman or due to injuries suffered by her. These are known as miscarriages and create no moral issues. Debates on abortion centre on induced abortions which are brought about by human action.

Abortion debates involve two broad issues: (i) the value of life, both of mother and foetus; and (ii) individual freedom and rights of women over their bodies. These debates also cover the rights of foetus or unborn baby, definitions of human life and the point at which life begins.

Prior to 1971, under the Indian Penal Code, induced abortion was illegal. Abortion in India is now covered under the Medical Termination of Pregnancy (MTP) Act 1971. According to MTP Act, Pregnancies not exceeding 12 weeks may be terminated based on a single doctor's opinion formed in good faith. In case of pregnancies exceeding 12 weeks but less than 20 weeks, termination needs opinion of two doctors. Abortion is allowed subject to various conditions.

Accountability

Accountability means the answerability of officials for due discharge of functions assigned to them. James Fessler and Don Kettl divide accountability into two dimensions: 'One is [formal or legal] accountability; faithful obedience to the law, to higher officials' directions, and to standards of efficiency. The other is ethical behaviour; adherence to moral standards and avoidance even of the appearance of unethical actions.

Accountability can be enforced through external and internal controls. External controls include: legislative supervision of administrative actions; judicial scrutiny of administrative decisions and procedures; and participation of citizens in administrative processes. Internal controls include: the use of rules and procedures, making administration transparent, provision for whistle blowers, democratizing organizations and promotion of professional and ethical standards. Over strict enforcement of accountability can prove counterproductive. There is a conflict between the value of accountability and the values of originality, experimentation, inventiveness and risk-taking.

(Paul C. Light, Federal Inspectors General and the Path to Accountability)

Accounts

Accounts of a company contain complete and comprehensive details of its financial transactions. Financial transactions result in revenue and expenditure. Revenue consists of various forms of income. All revenues have to be promptly put into company's accounts. Expenditures incurred have to be properly vouched or backed by receipts for their authentication. Expenditures are classified into categories such as revenue and capital expenditure. Revenue expenditures cover day to day items like payments for wages and raw materials. Capital expenditures lead to creation of physical or financial assets like buildings or fixed deposits in banks. Accounts have to be prepared according to a prescribed format (conforming to accounting standards) to correctly classify transactions and reflect their true nature. The two main financial statements of a company are - profit and loss account and the balance sheet.

Administrative Ethics

John A. Rohr makes a distinction between two categories of public administrative ethics. One category is legally enforceable and the other is aspirational or is supposed to form part of a civil servant's moral aspirations or ideals. The first category deals almost entirely with financial irregularities in such matters as bribery, conflict of interest and financial disclosure. In the Indian context, administrative ethics in this sense are found in the codes of conduct for civil servants. The second category goes beyond legal obligation and looks for practical ways in which public servants can fulfill their oath to uphold the constitution. In the Indian context, this will mean that civil servants should work towards realisation of constitutional values.

(John R. Rohr, Constitutionalism and Administrative ethics)

Administrative Ethos

These are traditionally understood as civil service codes and traditions. In recent times, public administration theorists have added rather exalted moral principles to this concept. Among these are – Rawls's concept of social equity, allegiance to a higher law beyond both individual and government, a moral framework applicable both to public and private domains, or a notion of a lasting moral order. Although these are abstract ideas, we should look at their general drift.

Adultery

Adultery consists in having sexual relations with an individual other than one's spouse. Adultery was an offence under Section 497 of the Indian Penal Code. A man is guilty under this section when he has consensual sexual intercourse with another man's wife without his consent or connivance. This section does not apply if a man has consensual relations with an unmarried adult woman. Supreme Court scrapped section 497 of the IPC on 27 September 2018.

Aesthetics

Aesthetics studies values in art and beauty. Ethics studies values against the background of morals.

Affective

Affective refers to that aspect of human psyche or personality which is connected with emotions and feelings.

Affirmative Action

Affirmative action (phrase used in USA) seeks to remove or correct discrimination in education, employment and politics practised against some groups on account of their race, religion, and gender. This is analogous to reservation policies in India.

Altruism

Altruism is based on beneficence and selflessness; it is other regarding and the opposite of self-interest and self-love. An altruistic act is one which is done with the ultimate aim of benefiting another person. An act that is done in order to benefit another, but only with a view to one's own late benefit, is not an altruistic act. C. D. Broad defines altruism as "the doctrine that each of us has a special obligation to benefit others."

Amoral

Amoral signifies indifference to morals. An amoral person has no concern for morality, and ignores the moral aspects in deciding things or in performing actions. He refuses to look at objects and events through the prism of morality. He may act viciously not because he is bad but because he lacks a sense of morality. Amoral persons could be psychopaths.

Anarchism

There are many forms of non-Marxist communism. The most influential of these is anarchism, or anarcho-communism. It advocates not only communal ownership of property but also the abolition of the state. Anarchists argue that the state and private property are interdependent institutions. The state exists to protect private property, and the owners of private property protect the state. If property is to be owned communally and distributed equally, the state must be smashed once and for all.

Analytic Ethics: *See metaethics*

Animal Rights

Traditionally, philosophers excluded animal kingdom and nature from moral discourse. From early 1970s, environmental issues and animal rights became popular topics of discussion both among philosophers and lay public. In 1975, Peter Singer published his work*Animal Liberation*. Its basic message is---'All animals are equal'. It implies that human beings are also (biologically speaking) animals, and should not ill treat or abuse other animals. These views have led to considerable argumentation in support of and against animal rights.

Appetite

Appetite is a blind tendency towards a particular end. Satisfactions of appetite are frequently referred to simply as pleasures, while unsatisfied appetites are called pains. A pleasure-seeker is one who seeks the satisfaction of his animal appetites, or of human impulses which are akin to these appetites.

Applied Ethics

Applied ethics uses ethical theories, concepts and principles for studying practical moral problems. Applied ethics studied a wide range of tricky moral questions that emerged in recent time in the west.

These include: abortion, same sex marriage, gun control (in USA), stem cell research, predetermining desired qualities in unborn babies, sexual behaviour, sex and gender identity, discrimination in its various forms, criteria for distribution of scarce resources, religious freedom, medically-assisted suicide and euthanasia, freedom expression, animal rights and humanitarian aid especially to countries affected by war and natural calamities. These issues dominate debates in western nations, but are also picked up and followed elsewhere in the world. Business and biomedical ethics are also important areas studied in applied ethics.

Approaches to Ethics

There are three theoretical perspectives or approaches to the study of ethics. One is deontology, a rule-based ethics which identifies our moral duties and recommends that they should be obeyed irrespective of their consequences. Kant was a well-known deontologist philosopher. The second approach is consequentialism, an ethics based on outcomes of actions, which recommends the right thing to do as that which will lead to the best consequences. Utilitarianism recommends maximization of happiness or utility as the criterion for actions. The third approach is virtue ethics, according to which the fundamental question in is 'What kind of person should I be?'. It revolves around moral character (of individuals) than around acts or their consequences. Aristotle was the seminal thinker on virtue ethics.

Aptitude: Nature and Measurement

Intelligence tests assess general mental ability. Aptitude refers to special abilities in a particular field of activity. It is a combination of characteristics that indicates an individual's capacity to acquire some specific knowledge or skill after training. We assess aptitude with the help of selected tests. The knowledge of aptitude can help us to predict an individual's future performance. While assessing intelligence, psychologists often found that people with similar intelligence differed widely in acquiring certain knowledge or skills. There are certain areas in which some intelligent students do not do well. Students are able to perform well in certain areas of study and activity.

These specific skills and abilities are called aptitudes. With proper training, these abilities can be considerably enhanced. In order to be successful in a particular field, a person must have both aptitude and interest. Interest is a preference for a particular activity; aptitude is the potentiality to perform that activity. A person may be interested in a particular job or activity, but may not have the aptitude for it. Similarly, a person may have the potentiality for performing a job, but may not be interested in doing that. In both cases, the outcome will be unsatisfactory. A student with high mechanical aptitude and strong interest in engineering is more likely to be a successful mechanical engineer.

Aptitude tests are available in two forms: independent (specialized) aptitude tests and multiple (generalized) aptitude tests. Clerical Aptitude, Mechanical Aptitude, Numerical Aptitude, and Typing Aptitude are independent aptitude tests. Multiple Aptitude Tests exist in the form of test batteries (tests covering multiple aptitudes), which measure aptitude in several separate but homogeneous areas. Differential Aptitude Tests (DAT), the General Aptitude Tests Battery (GATB), and the Armed Services Vocational Aptitude Battery (ASVAB) are well-known aptitude test batteries. Among these, DAT is most commonly used in educational settings. It consists of 8 independent subtests: (i) Verbal Reasoning, (ii) Numerical Reasoning, (iii) Abstract Reasoning, (iv) Clerical Speed and Accuracy, (v) Mechanical Reasoning, (vi) Space Relations, (vii) Spelling, and (viii) Language Usage.

Assessment of Intelligence

In 1905, Alfred Binet and Theodore Simon made the first successful attempt to formally measure intelligence. In 1908, when the scale was revised, they gave the concept of Mental Age (MA), which is a measure of a person's intellectual development relative to people of her/his age group. A mental age of 5 means that a child's performance on an intelligence test equals the average performance level of a group of 5-yearold children. Chronological Age (CA) is the biological age from birth.

A bright child's MA is more than her/his CA; for a dull child, MA is below the CA. Retardation was defined by Binet and Simon as being two mental age years below the chronological age. In 1912, William Stern, a German psychologist, devised the concept of Intelligence Quotient (IQ). IQ refers to mental age divided by chronological age, and multiplied by 100. The number 100 is used as a multiplier to avoid the decimal point. When the MA equals the CA, the IQ equals 100. If MA is more than the CA, IQ is more than 100. IQ becomes less than 100 when the MA is less than the CA. For example, a 10-year-old child with a mental age of 12 would have an IQ of 120 (12/10 * 100), whereas the same child with an MA of 7 would have an IQ of 70 (7/10 * 100). The average IQ in the population is 100, irrespective of age.

(From NCERT class XII text for psychology)

Attitudes

Social psychologists reserve the term attitude to refer to our relatively enduring evaluation of something, where the something is called the attitude object. The attitude object might be a person, a product, or a social group. Attitudes involve a preference for or against the attitude object, as commonly expressed in such terms as prefer, like, dislike, hate, and love. When we express our attitudes–for instance, when we say, "I love rasagullas," or "I hate snakes," or "I like Biharis"– we are expressing the relationship (either positive or negative) between the self and an attitude object. Statements such as these make it clear that attitudes are an important part of the self-concept. Attitudes tie the self-concept to the attitude object, and so our attitudes are an essential part of us. This perspective has generated a number of conceptual models of the attitude concept.

The most influential model of attitude has been the multi-component model. According to this perspective, attitudes are summary evaluations of an object that have Cognitive, Affective, and Behavioural components.

(i) Affective Component

The affective component of attitudes refers to feelings or emotions linked to an attitude object. Affective responses influence attitudes in a number of ways. Emotions shape attitudes through feelings that are aroused in response to an attitude object. For instance, many people indicate that spiders make them feel scared. This negative affective response is likely to cause a negative attitude toward spiders.

(ii) Behavioural Component

Behaviour is one of the three components of an attitude directed towards an object. The behavioural component of attitudes refers to past behaviours or experiences regarding an attitude object. For instance, people might guess that they must have a negative attitude toward child labour, if they remember having signed a petition against depriving children of their educational and playing opportunities.

The idea that people might infer their attitudes from their previous actions was formulated by Daryl Bem. According to Bem's self-perception theory, individuals do not always have access to their opinions about different objects, and sometimes infer their attitudes by thinking about how they have behaved with respect to the attitude object in the past.

(iii) Cognitive Component

The cognitive component of attitudes refers to the beliefs, thoughts, and attributes we associate with an object. In many cases, a person's attitude might be based primarily upon the positive and negative attributes they associate with an object. For example, when one author recently bought a new car, he devoted considerable attention to different vehicles' safety records, gas mileage, and repair costs. In this example, attitudes toward the different cars were formed through a methodical consideration of the positive and negative characteristics of each car.

Audit

The annual audit is one of the cornerstones of corporate governance. It provides an external and objective check on the way in which the financial statements have been prepared and presented by the directors of the company. It has to ensure that accounts provide a true and fair view of company's financial statements. Auditors' role is to design audit in such a manner that it provides a reasonable assurance that the financial statements are free of material misstatements.

Audit Committee

Every listed company and some other specified companies have to constitute an audit committee. Audit committee shall have not less than three independent directors; at least two of them should be able to understand financial statements like balance sheets, profit and loss accounts, cash flow statements and statements of changes in equity. The chairperson should have this ability. The terms of reference or jurisdiction of an audit committee shall include all matters relating to finance, accounts, commercial transactions, investments and audit. The directors and employees can report to the audit committee their genuine concerns or apprehensions about things happening in the company. Any person who uses such mechanism shall have direct access to chairperson of the audit committee.

Avarice

Avarice is covetousness or greed. It is a desire to possess more than one has need or use for or excessive love of money. Avarice may extend to power and to various material possessions. People desire wealth because it is a means of acquiring other material comforts. Avarice is a morbid excess of the propensity to seek wealth.

Behaviourism

Behaviourism is an approach to study of psychology developed by J.B. Watson and B.F. Skinner. It argues that manifest or observable human behaviour can only be scientifically studied. It rejects reliance on mentalistic concepts such as mind, soul, spirit or self. It concentrates on body and brain which respond to stimuli. Behaviourism underplays the role of psycho-analytic techniques which seek to understand the mental processes of psychologically troubled individuals.

Belief

Belief is a concept used both in psychology and ethics. Alexander Bain, a Scottish psychologist, defined belief as 'that upon which a man is prepared to act'. In this sense, belief stands for true conviction. According to Bain, it is natural for men to believe, and doubt is an uncomfortable condition. Inquiry frees men from this uncomfortable state by leading them into a 'serene, satisfying, and happy tone of mind' which is believing.

American philosopher Peirce regarded that the purpose of enquiry is to produce stable and enduring beliefs. We consider such beliefs as true and regard 'reality' as what they are about. Peirce argued that science (and not reliance on authority or on speculative reasoning) is the source of such beliefs. Even when scientific inquiries appear to differ, they ultimately converge. We may hold false beliefs. The only safeguard is to scrutinize our beliefs based on science and factual evidence. John Dewey considered beliefs to be instruments we create for navigating the social reality we face. What validates the belief as true is the agreement in society to regard it as such, based on society's approval of it. Dewey's view is applicable to moral beliefs which represent a society's consensus. Moral beliefs are values and not facts.

(Based on A.C. Grayling, A history of Philosophy)

Benami Transactions

Corrupt public servants try to hide their illegitimate wealth through 'Benami' transactions. In these transactions, the government servant holds property in someone else's name. The Law Commission recommended enactment of a legislation for prohibiting Benami transactions and acquiring properties held Benami. A law entitled The Benami Transactions (Prohibition) Act was passed in 1988. The Act precludes the person who acquired the property in the name of another person from claiming it as his own. The Act prohibits Benami transactions and prohibits the acquirer from recovering the property from the Benamidar. The Act permits acquisition of property held Benami.

Beneficent

Beneficent or beneficial is anything good or produces goodness. Principle of beneficence is the same as principle of good.

Benevolence

Benevolence is a disposition, habit, quality, trait of the person or soul, which an individual either has or seeks to have. The philosopher Schopenhauer has taken benevolence and justice as the cardinal virtues. Benevolence is the love of others. It means the desire to do good and to be kind and generous. The philosophers of Scottish Enlightenment [such as Hutcheson, Hume and Adam Smith] emphasised benevolence as a virtue and regarded it as central to the attainment of their version of good society.

(William Frankena op.cit, & David K. Hart, Administration and Ethics of Virtue)

Canons of Financial Propriety

Every officer incurring or authorizing expenditure from public moneys should be guided by high standards of financial propriety. Every officer should also enforce financial order and strict economy and see that all relevant financial rules and regulations are observed, by his own office and by subordinate disbursing officers. Among the principles on which emphasis is generally laid are the following: -

(i) Every officer is expected to exercise the same vigilance in respect of expenditure incurred from ppublic moneys as a person of ordinary prudence would exercise in respect of expenditure of his own money.

(ii) The expenditure should not be prima facie more than the occasion demands.

(iii) No authority should exercise its powers of sanctioning expenditure to pass an order which will be directly or indirectly to its own advantage.

(iv) Expenditure from public moneys should not be incurred for the benefit of a particular person or a section of the people, unless (a) a claim for the amount could be enforced in a Court of Law, or (b) the expenditure is in pursuance of a recognised policy or custom.

(v) The amount of allowances granted to meet expenditure of a particular type (e.g. travelling allowance or house rent allowance) should be so regulated that the allowances are not on the whole a source of profit to the recipients.

Capital Punishment (Death Penalty)

Since long many people have been arguing for abolition of capital punishment or death penalty. Those who support reinstituting or retaining capital punishment are called retentionists. They believe that capital punishment is justified in heinous crimes like premeditated or cold blooded murder. Abolitionists believe that capital punishment is never morally justified.

IPC prescribes death penalty for grave crimes such as murder, rape resulting in victim's death and waging war against the State. Similarly, The Arms Act, The Narcotic Drugs and Psychotropic Substances Act, The Scheduled Caste and Scheduled Tribes (Prevention of Atrocities) Act, The Commission of Sati (Prevention) Act, The Army/Air Force/navy Acts, contain capital punishment for serious offences.

The Supreme Court upheld the constitutional validity of capital punishment in "rarest of rare" cases. It ruled that if capital punishment is provided in the law and if the procedure is fair, just and reasonable, death sentence is constitutional. "Rarest of rare" cases imply that courts should specify "special reasons" while awarding death penalty.

Cardinal Virtues

Cardinal virtues are defined as a group of virtues such that (1) they cannot be derived from one another and (2) all other virtues can be derived from them or shown to be forms of them. Ancient Greek philosophers identified four cardinal virtues: wisdom, courage, temperance and justice. Christianity has seven cardinal virtues. Three of these - faith, hope and charity (love) - are theological virtues. Four virtues - prudence, fortitude, temperance and justice - are human. Schopenhauer regarded benevolence and justice as cardinal virtues. The commonly recognised virtues like love, courage, kindness, temperance, honesty and gratitude can all be derived from cardinal virtues.

Care Ethics

Some writers refer to feminist ethics as care ethics, based on a perception that women tend to respond more sympathetically and readily than men to people in distress.

Categorical Imperative, Hypothetical Imperative

Kant says that moral value is to be found in the good will of an individual who acts not out of inclination, or desire for a particular end, but from a sense of duty, which consists in obeying a moral law, which reason recognizes as appropriate in the circumstances. This law is not a hypothetical imperative. A hypothetical imperative recommends that if the agent wants to achieve a certain end, he should act in a particular manner, as in, 'If you want to strengthen your shoulder muscles, do weight lifting'. A hypothetical imperative is such that if the agent does not desire the end mentioned in the 'If' part, he does not have to obey the command contained in the 'then' part. If one does not want to strengthen his shoulder muscles, he need not lift weights.

A genuinely moral law, on the other hand, assumes the form of a categorical imperative, plainly commanding 'do so-and-so'. It is an absolute and unconditional command with no 'ifs' attached. Kant formulates this view by distinguishing between subjective and objective action-guiding principles. Subjective action-guiding principles apply only to the agent himself; objective principles apply to all rational beings. Kant calls the former maxims, and the latter laws. Appetites and passions often prevent people from acting according to moral laws. They have rely on duty and obligation, and imperatives as guides to what they ought to do. According to A.C. Grayling, command of reason refers to a kind of objective principle which exercises a compelling force on the will, and the formula of such command is called an imperative.

The most common version of Categorical imperative is: 'I ought never to act in any way other than according to a maxim which I can at the same time will should become a universal law.' A universal law is one which applies to everyone and not just to a single moral agent. Another formulation of categorical imperative is: 'Act in such a way that you always treat humanity, whether in your own person or in the person of any other, never simply as a means, but always at the same time as an end.' Some writers mention a third form of categorical imperative: 'An individual should act as if the principles underlying his actions can serve as moral laws for the community'.

(Based on A.C. Grayling, A History of Philosophy)

Character

Character implies possession of virtues or desirable moral qualities. When we say that Jane is a lady of character, we mean that Jane is virtuous. Aristotle believed that virtue is not an inborn quality or original endowment in human beings. Virtues and therefore character have to be acquired or cultivated through constant practice or by being constantly good in one's behaviour. Thus, one becomes courageous by performing brave deeds regularly and generous by performing acts of charity regularly. Character and virtues are matters of habit. Aristotle differs in this regard from Socrates who regarded that mere knowledge of virtue is sufficient to make a man virtuous. Besides, character requires that one is habitually able to overcome temptations and weakness of will.

This conception of character makes it the central tenet of morality. Actions of a person shed light on his character. Utilitarians do not ground ethics in character because they think that it is subjective. Only moral agents can know the intentions and desires prompting their actions. Sometimes people don't understand their own motives. Hence, Utilitarianism looks at the consequences of actions and not at the intentions of actors. A good action is one that produces good consequences irrespective of the moral agent's intentions. Deontology on the other hand sees the essence of morality in the obedience of moral agents to their duty in the given circumstances.

It is necessary to make a distinction between a person's character and her personality. Character is mainly an ethical concept whereas personality is mainly a psychological concept. Personality traits of people refer to qualities such as short temper or even temper and being introverted or extroverted. These are not primarily ethical categories.

Characteristics of Emotionally Intelligent Persons

- ¤ Perceive and be sensitive to your feelings and emotions.
- ¤ Perceive and be sensitive to various types of emotions in others by noting their body language, voice and tone, and facial expressions.
- ¤ Relate your emotions to your thoughts so that you take them into account while solving problems and taking decisions.
- ¤ Understand the powerful influence of the nature and intensity of your emotions. ¤ Control and regulate your emotions and their expressions while dealing with self and others to achieve harmony and peace.

Cheating

Cheating is a vice which consists in cunning, deception, in acting fraudulently or misleadingly, and in trickery and dishonesty.

Citizen's Charters

The functions of government fall into two broad heads: legal exercise of authority and provision of services. Modern states are welfare States and provide a wide range of public services to their citizens. The services cover areas such as education, health, housing and transport. Services also include meeting needs of citizens for a driving license, telephone connection, gas connection, tax refund, Aadhaar card, passport, and extracts from public records of one's property, educational qualification and date of birth. Citizens often experience considerable difficulty in securing timely, reliable and quality services from government agencies. Citizen Charters are a means of solving the day to day problems which citizens experience while dealing with organisations providing public services.

Class Action

If shareholders, depositors or any class of them are of the opinion that the affairs of a company are being conducted in a manner prejudicial to the interest of the company, its members or depositors, they may file an application before tribunal. The class action can also cover the auditors. Class action differs from individual litigation. Class action means a representative suit and the court judgement delivered in such a suit will apply to all the members of that class - even to those who did not join the suit.

Classical Conditioning

Classical conditioning can be used to create in people positive emotional reactions to a person, object or event. This is done by associating positive feelings which the audience experience in a different context with a target object. Commercial advertisements use classical conditioning to create a favourable impression about a product in the minds of readers or viewers. For example, it will show popular cricket stars consuming a particular brand of soda while having fun. It influences the audience by carrying over their favourable feelings about cricketers to the particular soda brand.

Cloning

A clone is an exact genetic copy of a molecule, cell, plant, or animal. It is no novel phenomenon but common in nature. Whenever single cell organisms like bacteria reproduce by cell division, the resultant cells are clones of the original cells. Similarly, when a worm is divided into two parts, each part will regenerate into a full genetic duplicate of the original worm. Identical twins resulting from separated embryos in uterus are natural clones.

Scientists extract DNA from the cell of an adult mammal and insert it into a hollowed out donor egg. By jump-starting the egg with a jolt of electricity, they can create an embryo that would become, if implanted into a surrogate mother, the patient's identical twin. As for human beings, no cloning is allowed.

The first law regulating cloning is UK's Human Fertilisation Embryology Act (1990). It permits licensed research using human embryos only for very limited purposes involving studies into infertility treatment, congenital diseases, and causes of miscarriages, contraception techniques and the detection of genetic abnormalities.

Codes of Ethics

Codes of ethics usually contain general values while codes of conduct clearly spell out the principles which are derived from values. In the words of Jeremy Bentham, a principle is "a general law or rule that guides behaviour or decisions," whereas values articulate "an aspiration of an ideal moral state."

Values refer to political and social visions and exalted goals which societies seek to achieve. In contrast, codes of conduct have a narrow focus. Codes of conduct are particular rules of conduct either imposed from higher levels of an organization or voluntarily accepted as the requirements of a profession or occupation.

A code of ethics differs from a code of conduct in another way. A code of ethics or a code of morality has a wide canvas. It may virtually cover all aspects of a man's life. It will contain prescriptions and prohibitions which cover one's personal, social, economic, political and religious life. Codes of ethics apply to the culture, education, and religion of a whole society. Codes of conduct generally cover an individual's official or professional conduct.

Cognitive

Cognitive refers to processes involved in human knowledge acquisition including rationality and thinking.

Cognitive Dissonance

In simple terms, cognitive dissonance is an unpleasant internal (psychological) state that exists when we notice inconsistency in our attitudes or between attitudes and behaviour. People reduce dissonance by:

- Changing attitudes or behaviour to make them consistent with one another.
- Acquiring new information that supports an attitude or behaviour, or
- Trivializing the inconsistency

In general, people will reduce dissonance by whichever method requires the least effort.

Collusive Corruption

An act of corruption has two players: the bribe-giver and the bribe-taker. In cases of coercive corruption, the bribe-giver is a victim of extortion. Bribe-taker forces bribe-giver to make the payment. Besides this coercive corruption, there is also collusive corruption in which the bribe-giver and bribe-taker act as partners and rob society. In this situation, the bribe-giver is as great an offender as the bribe-taker. The acts involved in these situations defraud public exchequer and also harm public welfare. Among such instances are–execution of substandard works, distortion of competition, robbing the public exchequer, kickbacks or commissions in public procurement, tax evasion by collusion, and causing direct harm to people by spurious drugs and violation of safety norms.

Commercial Audit

There is a secial arrangement for the audit of companies where the equity participation by Government is 51 percent or more. The primary auditors of these companies are Chartered Accountants, appointed by the Comptroller and Auditor General of India, who gives the directions to the auditors on the manner in which the audit should be conducted by them. The Comptroller and Auditor General of India is also empowered to comment upon the audit reports of the primary auditors. In addition, the Comptroller and Auditor General of India conducts a test audit of the accounts of such companies and reports the results of his audit to Parliament and State Legislatures.

Committee on Public Undertakings (COPU)

COPU is a parliamentary committee. The Committee on Public Undertakings exercises the same powers on the public sector undertakings as the Public Accounts Committee exercises over CAG'S audit reports of the Government Departments.

Communism

Communism is used in two senses. First, it refers to a political and economic doctrine propounded originally by Karl Marx and Frederic Engels. The original Marxist ideas went through many changes in the hands of Lenin, Trotsky, Stalin, Mao, Althusser, Gramsci and others. Secondly, communism refers to a totalitarian political and economic system as existed in the erstwhile USSR. Communism as an economic system differs sharply from capitalism. Capitalism is based on individual or private enterprise and theoretically free markets. Communism is a centrally planned economy. It has no place for private entrepreneurs. Capital and land---representing natural resources---are owned collectively by the state. Private ownership of any form is very limited. Communism has no parliamentary democracy based on multiple parties and free elections. It does not allow civil liberties or freedoms. There is no independent judiciary. There is no free press. Government exercises censorship for regulating free thinking in many spheres. It is a centralized totalitarian system of government.

Communitarian Ethics

Communitarian ethics refers to several views which share a general orientation. These are communitarian, neo-Aristotelian, and character or virtue ethics. They reflect a new perspective on morals. Communitarians refuse to consider human beings as solitary beings in isolation from society. Traditionally, Western thinkers regarded the essence of human self as consciousness, thought and reason. Communitarians go back to the Aristotelian notion of man as a social animal whose moral development can take place only within an ideal community (polis). They reject the idea of a universal and independent human self.

Communitarians hold that human beings are born into actual historical societies; they share the values and aims of such societies. Individual judgements and decisions-to-act should not be seen as autonomously determined. They are the outcomes of reciprocal interaction between human beings and society. In this regard, communitarians speak of man's "situatedness" in society. They deny 'individual primacy' and accord due role to social influences on men. Communitarians do not regard human beings as wholly self-seeking rationalist decision-makers – a model which underlies modern market based economic theory. They emphasise community based sentiments such as benevolence, altruism, loyalty, and group-based sentiments. This view has important implications for perspectives on public administration and public policy.

Communitarianism focuses on character or virtue ethics. Morality is expressed not in terms of rules but as virtues. For example, 'Kill not' is an expression of a rule. But 'Hate not' prescribes a virtue which we need to cultivate. Communitarianism also calls for practical wisdom instead of rigid codes or rules.

Communitarian ethics has four weaknesses. First, neither all communities nor all their features are benign. Secondly, community based ethics tend to be particular or parochial and lack universality. Thirdly, communitarianism, in overemphasizing group virtues and solidarity, can usher intotalitarian trends. Fourthly, communitarianism seems like a form of "idealistic stained-glass window nostalgia" for societies which exited human history long ago.

(Charles J. Fox, The Use of Philosophy in Administrative Ethics)

Conditioning

Behaviourism uses conditioning as a term to designate the process through which human beings are made to behave in certain ways by a controller who wants to modify their behaviour. This term was first used by Pavlov to describe the idea of a conditioned reflex, and later by Skinner in the theory of operant conditioning. Conditioning has a bad odour because it is often used surreptitiously on people to manipulate their conduct without their knowledge.

Conduct

The habitual modes of action that accompany a formed or stable character are described by the term conduct.

Conflict Management

In most conflicts, neither party is right or wrong; instead, different perceptions collide to create disagreement. Conflict is natural and managers have to respond to conflict situations quickly and professionally. Conflict can be positive; if managers deal with it openly, they can strengthen the organization by correcting problems. Conflicting views give managers an opportunity to learn more about themselves, explore views of others, and develop productive relationships. Clear and open communication is the cornerstone of successful conflict resolution.

Conflict management refers to the practice of recognizing and dealing with disputes in a rational, balanced and effective way. Conflict management, within a business environment usually involves effective communication, problem resolving abilities and good negotiating skills to restore the focus on the company's overall goals.

To manage conflict effectively, one has to be a skilled communicator. One has to create an open communication environment in the organization by encouraging employees to talk about work issues. Listening to employee concerns will foster an open environment. One has to really understand what employees are saying by asking questions and focusing on their perception of the problem

Conflict of Interest

Public servants have to decide various matters in the course of their work. In doing so, they have to act in a detached and disinterested manner keeping in view only the relevant facts and law. Sometimes, it may so happen that a public servant has a personal interest in a matter he or she has to decide. Then he is said to have a conflict of interest. In other words, his personal interest and official duties are in conflict. He should not decide such matters, but should recuse himself from them.

Conscience

According to Joseph Butler, conscience is a God-given ability to reason, our 'natural guide' with ultimate authority. Conscience is a form of intuition. In making judgements based on our conscience, we do not rely on logic or conceptual thinking. This concept conscience to which moral thinkers of earlier times subscribed has an ocular quality. It is not empirical. It resembles a mysterious faculty distinct from the mental operations with which men are familiar. Yet the moral agent regards judgements based on his conscience as unquestionable. But the consciences of different individuals may speak differently.

Modern writers maintain that conscience refers to codes of morality which are inculcated in men during the process of upbringing in family and through education. These represent social values and mores. The psychoanalyst Freud divided human consciousness into three parts. Id represents the primitive drives of man which seek satisfaction unmindful of consequences. Ego is a more rational part of consciousness that recognises that one has to regulate or check one's selfish pleasureseeking impulses considering the social norms and codes. This is a part of prudence which can be regarded as the reality principle that guides human actions. Reality principle can be contrasted with pleasure principle, which underlies the primitive impulses of id. Superego, the third part of consciousness, consists of the moral codes which men acquire. Conscience can be considered as the analogue of superego.

Consequentialism

Consequentialism refers to those ethical theories which trace moral worth or value of actions to their consequences. An old philosophical name for consequentialism is teleology, derived from telos that means end or purpose in Greek. Utilitarianism is a well-known consequentialist theory.

Conservatism

Conservatism is a political doctrine that emphasises the value of traditional institutions and practices. It regards society as a living organism with organically interlinked parts. Conservatives value institutions which evolved slowly for they promote social stability and continuity. Government should guard existing ways of life and not attempt to transform society rapidly. Suspicion of government activism separates conservatism from liberalism and radicalism.

Constitutional Protection to Civil Servants – Article 311

Article 311 gives job security to government servants. It provides procedural safeguards to them against arbitrary dismissal or removal or reduction to a lower rank. These provisions are enforceable in a court of law. Any order which a disciplinary authority passes in violation of Article 311 will be ab initio void or flawed or invalid from its very inception. The provisions of Articles 311 apply to all government servants.

Conventional or Customary Morality

Conventional morality refers to those customs, laws, and judgments on which there is common social agreement. This agreement or common feeling is the starting point of ethics and of ethical thought. This agreement is itself a source of authority and a test of right and wrong. Conventional morality changes partially over time due to changes in society, economy, culture and general intellectual climate.

Corporate Governance

Corporate governance refers to the processes, and the related organisational structures, by which organisations are directed, controlled and held to account. It involves a set of relationships between an organisation's management, its board, its shareholders and other stakeholders. It can also be viewed as the laws, rules, regulations, systems, principles and processes which regulate companies. Three areas are of particular importance for corporate governance – finance, audit and corporate law (which ensures compliance with regulations). Chief financial officer and company secretary play critical parts in corporate governance.

Corporate Social Responsibility (CSR)

If a company a) has a net worth of rupees five hundred crore or more, or b) turnover of rupees one thousand crore or more, or c) a net profit of rupees five crore or more in a financial year, then it has to constitute a Corporate Social Responsibility Committee of the Board. The committee should have three or more directors, with at least one independent director. The Board's report to share holders should disclose the composition of the Corporate Social Responsibility Committee. CSR policy has to be formulated and monitored by the board's CSR committee. CSR can cover health, education, poverty alleviation, skill development and other similar programmes which help the poor and needy.

Corruption

Corruption is generally understood as misusing public office for private gain. Corruption includes:

(i) Demanding and/or accepting [by any public servant] of gratification other than legal remuneration with respect to an official act or for using his influence with any other official.

(ii) Obtaining a valuable thing, without consideration or with inadequate consideration from a person with whom he has or is likely to have official dealings or with whom his subordinates have official dealings or where he can exert influence.

(iii) Obtaining for himself or for any other person any valuable thing or pecuniary advantage by corrupt or illegal means or by abusing his position as a public servant.

(iv) Possessing assets disproportionate to his known sources of income

(v) Cases of misappropriation, forgery or cheating or other similar criminal offences.

Cynics

The classical Greek and Roman Cynics regarded virtue as the only requirement for happiness. They sought to free themselves from conventions; become self-sufficient; and live only in accordance with nature. They rejected conventional notions of happiness involving money, power and fame, and sought happiness in the pursuit of virtue. In rejecting conventional social values, they criticised the types of behaviour, such as greed, which they viewed as causes of suffering.

The modern view of cynicism sees it as "an attitude of scornful or jaded negativity, especially a general distrust of the integrity or professed motives of others." This modern definition of cynicism is in marked contrast to the ancient philosophy, which emphasized "virtue and moral freedom in liberation from desire". Early Cynics were not mere social critics; they were public advocates of cosmopolitanism, freedom of speech, a woman's right to select her spouse, and constitutional law.

Cyrenaics

Cyrenaics are ancient Greek philosophers who advocated that pleasure is the only good for men. They rejected other higher ideals. Unlike Epicureans who advocated long term happiness as the desirable human goal, Cyrenaics recommended that men should chase momentary pleasures or make the best of every moment of life. They had no concern for the morrow.

Deontology

Deontology means rule-based or duty-based ethics. In deontology an action is moral only if it accords with the duty of the moral agent in the given circumstances, irrespective of the consequences or outcomes of the action. Right and wrong involve an agent's intentions, and whether the behaviour they lead to conforms to universalizable moral rules independently of their consequences. Kant's moral theory based on the categorical imperative is a deontological theory. Kant opposes telling of lies even for saving innocent lives.

Deontology is usually contrasted with consequentialism. Consequentialism does not consider any action as intrinsically right or wrong. It evaluates the moral worth of an action based on its good or bad, desirable or undesirable, outcomes or results. Utilitarianism is an example of a consequentialist theory.

Desire

Will is a faculty of the mind. Desires and wants are cravings for things we seek to possess and enjoy. Some moral philosophers distinguish desire from wish. In this view, desires far outnumber our wishes. Many desires are filtered out by will, leaving out some that we actually seek. These desires we pursue are wishes.

According to Spinoza, desires are cravings which our emotions drive us to get. These things or objects of desire lie beyond our control. Hence, the more our desires, the less they are likely to be satisfied, and the more unhappy, and the less free we will be. Spinoza refers to the inability of men to moderate and restrain their emotions and desires as bondage or slavery. If we can moderate our desires (whose fulfillment depends on circumstances outside our control), to that extent we liberate ourselves. Regulating our desires is also an aspect of ethics which Epicureanism, Stoicism, and Buddhism emphasize.

From a different perspective, economists describe human wants and desires as limitless, and resources available for their satisfaction as scarce. This is the root of economic problems.

Determinism (See Free Will)

Discretionary Decision-Making

In theory, government decisions at various levels are objective in the sense that they rely on a set of impersonal rules and operate equally as between similarly situated individuals. However, in practice no set of rules, no matter how exhaustive, can cover all possible cases. Hence, rules cannot entirely guide decisions. In such situations officials have to use their individual discretion in decision making. But discretionary power has to be minimised. There is a tendency for corruption to follow in the wake of discretion.

Doctrine of Double Effects (DDE)

The doctrine of double effects (DDE) examines a problem moral agents face when the action they contemplate has both good and bad consequences. When are such actions permissible morally? They are permissible when they satisfy the following conditions:

(i) The action should be either good or at least indifferent, and not intrinsically bad.

(ii) The intention of the moral agent should be good.

(iii) The good effects of the act should not flow from its badness.

(iv) The good effects must be proportionately more than the bad effects.

(v) There must initially be a valid reason for performing the action.

These principles can be applied to a nation engaging in a defensive war.

Domino Argument or Slippery Slope Argument

This is the view that often even seemingly trivial moral lapses can set off a train of events leading to grave moral wrongs. What may start as a harmless consumption of liquor on social occasions can lead one to alcoholism. Slippery slope argument applies to policies also. Thus, legalization of abortion, by weakening a society's adherence to the principle of sanctity of life, can lead to acceptance of infanticide (or termination of relatively advanced pregnancy) and mercy killing over time.

Duty

Duty commonly means what a moral agent ought to do in given circumstances. Thus, a soldier has to defend his post from attack; a nurse has to attend to the sick; and a teacher has to provide instruction to his pupils. Deontological theories consider duty as the central question in morality. Stoics have assigned a major role to duty in their stern morals. Kant describes duty as consisting in obedience to moral laws which are universal in that they apply to all rational beings. According to Hegel, men are free when they do their duty because that liberates them from the tyranny of their impulses and desires. Actions based on the latter represent subjective freedom. Incidentally, codes of official conduct represent (at a mundane level) the concrete duties of government servants. Non deontological theories trace morality to good actions, good intentions, divine commands, and to virtues of moral agents.

Duty Ethics

Kant believed that ethical acts arise from a moral agent's obedience to call of duty, and not from his inclinations or sentiments. Consequently, his system of ethics is sometimes called duty ethics.

Ego Defence Mechanisms

According to Freud, much of human behaviour reflects an attempt to deal with or escape from anxiety. Thus, how the ego deals with anxiety largely determines how people behave. Freud believed that people avoid anxiety mainly by developing defence mechanisms that try to defend the ego in situations threatening their self-esteem. Thus, defence mechanism is a way of reducing anxiety by distorting reality.

Although some defence against anxiety is normal and adaptive, people who use these mechanisms to such an extent that reality is truly distorted develop various forms of maladjustment. Freud has described many different kinds of defence mechanisms. The most important is repression, in which anxiety provoking behaviours or thoughts are totally repressed by the unconscious. When people repress a feeling or desire, they become totally unaware of that wish or desire. Repressing one's feelings can lead to psychological problems. Freud's early studies in Vienna were about hysteria in ladies caused by their repression of their sexual impulses and embarrassments. Freud cured them by making them aware of their repressed feelings through psycho analysis. Other major defence mechanisms are projection, denial, reaction formation and rationalization. In projection, people attribute their own traits to others. Thus, a person who has strong aggressive tendencies may see other people as acting in an excessively aggressive way towards her/him. In denial, a person totally refuses to accept reality. Thus, someone suffering from HIV/AIDS may altogether deny her/his illness. In reaction formation, a person defends against anxiety by adopting behaviours opposite to her/his true feelings. A person with strong sexual urges, who channels her/his energy into religious fervour, presents a classical example of reaction formation. In rationalization, a person tries to make unreasonable feelings or behaviour seem reasonable. For example, when someone buys a set of new pens after doing poorly in an examination, she/he may try to rationalize her/his behaviour by asserting "I will do much better with these pens".

People who use defence mechanisms are often unaware of doing so. Each defence mechanism is a way for the ego to deal with the uncomfortable feelings produced by anxiety. However, Freud's ideas about the role of defence mechanisms have been questioned.

Egoism

Egoism is the view that human beings seek their own self-interest by way of their own pleasure or happiness. There are two versions of egoism---psychological egoism and ethical egoism. Psychological egoism says that men always and inevitably pursue their own happiness. Their psychological constitution is such that they cannot act otherwise. This view undercuts the very possibility of ethics. Ethics tells people what they ought to do. But if men pursue self-interest compulsively or obsessively, there is no point in saying what they ought to do.

Another criticism of psychological egoism is that men do not always follow their own self-interest. Altruistic or philanthropic behaviour is cited as a counter example to psychological egoism. A further problem with psychological egoism is that men do not always pursue pleasure. Masochistic behaviour, though uncommon, shows that some people derive pleasure by inflicting pain on themselves. Further, men often try to satisfy their desires, and this leads to happiness. Satisfaction of hunger or quenching of thirst lead to pleasure. Thus, happiness is what follows from other pursuits. At times, men aim exclusively or directly at pleasure as when they sit before TV to watch a favourite programme. Psychological egoism does not explain the complexity of human motivations.

Ethical egoism is the view that men should in fact follow their own self-interest but often fail to do so. This view leads to universally selfish behaviour. Further, one cannot disclose that one is an ethical egoist. Then, others will be on their guard to protect their interests. A way out could in practice be enlightened self-interest which makes a moral agent take into account what is due to others even while following his interests.

Emotional Intelligence

Daniel Goleman explains emotional intelligence as consisting of "abilities such as being able to motivate oneself and persist in the face of frustrations; to control impulse and delay gratification; to regulate one's moods and keep distress from swamping the ability to think; to empathize and hope." We can regard these as positive qualities which help us in steadfastly pursuing goals which ultimately lead to success and happiness. Except empathy, the other qualities are directed towards one's own self.

According to Howard Gardener, interpersonal intelligence is the ability to understand other people: what motivates them, how they work, how to work cooperatively with them. Successful sales people, politicians, teachers, clinicians, and religious leaders are all likely to be individuals with high degrees of interpersonal intelligence. Intrapersonal intelligence is a correlative ability, turned inward. It is a capacity to form an accurate, veridical [true] model of oneself and to be able to use that model to operate effectively in life.

In another formulation, Howard Gardener mentions that the core of interpersonal intelligence includes "the capacities to discern and respond appropriately to the moods, temperaments, motivations, and desires of other people". In intrapersonal intelligence, the key to self- knowledge is "access to one's own feelings and the ability to discriminate among them and draw upon them to guide one's behaviour."

Emotional intelligence can also be considered as a set of skills that underlie accurate appraisal, expression, and regulation of emotions. It is the feeling side of intelligence. A good IQ and scholastic record is not enough to be successful in life. You may find many people who are academically talented, but are unsuccessful in their own life. They experience problems in family, workplace and in interpersonal relationships. What do they lack? Some psychologists believe that the source of their difficulty may be a lack of emotional intelligence. Salovey and Mayer consider emotional intelligence as "the ability to monitor one's own and other's emotions, to discriminate among them, and to use the information to guide one's thinking and actions". Emotional Quotient (EQ) is used to express emotional intelligence in the same way as IQ is used to express intelligence. In simple terms, emotional intelligence refers to the ability to process emotional information accurately and efficiently.

Emotional Literacy

According to Claude Steiner, Emotional Literacy is made up of 'the ability to understand your emotions, the ability to listen to others and empathize with their emotions, and the ability to express emotions productively. Emotional literacy improves relationships, creates loving possibilities between people, makes co-operative work possible, and facilitates the feeling of community.

He breaks emotional literacy into 5 parts:

1. Knowing one's feelings.
2. Having a sense of empathy.
3. Learning to manage one's emotions.
4. Repairing emotional damage; and
5. Emotional interactivity.

According to Steiner, emotional literacy involves understanding one's feelings and those of others to facilitate relationships, including using dialogue and self-control to avoid negative arguments. The ability to be aware and read other people's feelings enables one to interact with them effectively so that powerful emotional situations can be handled in a skillful way. Steiner calls this "emotional interactivity".

Emotivism

Emotivism is a doctrine about the logical status of moral judgements. According to emotivism, moral judgements are not statements or propositions in a logical sense; they are neither true nor false. In logic, a statement is either true or false. Objective properties of things and states of affairs in the world can be verified through observation and experiment. Mathematical and logical statements can be demonstrated or proved. Moral judgements can neither be verified nor proved. Moral statements are simply expressions of one's attitudes or subjective mental feelings. Moral exhortations resemble pure expressions of emotion or prescriptions for action A.J. Ayer elaborated this view in his book Language, Truth and Logic.

Empathy

The dictionary meaning of empathy is the ability to understand and share the feelings of another. People often confuse the words empathy and sympathy. Empathy means 'the ability to understand and share the feelings of another' whereas sympathy means 'feelings of pity and sorrow for someone else's misfortune' (example: sympathy for the flood victims).

In psychology, empathy refers to the ability to imagine oneself in another's place and understand the other's feelings, desires, ideas, and actions. It is a term coined in the early 20th century, equivalent to the German Einfühlung and modelled on "sympathy." The term is used with special (but not exclusive) reference to aesthetic experience. The most obvious example, perhaps, is that of the actor or singer who genuinely feels the part he is performing. With other works of art, a spectator may, by a kind of introjection, feel himself involved in what he observes or contemplates. The use of empathy is an important part of the counselling technique developed by the American psychologist Carl Rogers. This ability helps managers and administrators to deal effectively with workers and general public.

Ends and Means

Human actions can be seen as made-up of two parts. One part consists of the objective or aim of action - also called its end. The other part consists of methods or mechanisms - usually called means in ethics - used for achieving the ends.

Moral discussions often involve questions about the relation between ends and means. The end of an action is that for the sake of which it is performed; the means is the way in which the end is to be achieved. The distinction arises also in connection with various moral principles. Some of these are - you may not do evil for the sake of good; who wills the end wills the means; people must always be treated as ends, never merely as means. One perennial debate in ethics is whether bad means can be used to secure good ends. The general view of most moralists is that no good can result from evil. If achieving a goal necessarily involves bad means, it has to be given up. There is a general consensus that good ends can be or should be reached only through good means. It is vehemently argued that evil means inevitably defeat even good ends. Or in trying to reach certain ideals (as it happened in Soviet Union) one may end up inflicting enormous harm.

Working out how to adapt means to ends is one characteristic function of reason. According to Hume and Weber, the place of reason in practical affairs consists in instrumental or technical rationality. In other words, reasoning is concerned only with the best or efficient means of reaching social goals. On such an account, questions of ends are not subject to reason, but are non-rational matters of emotion or desire; reason therefore cannot adjudicate between conflicting ends, but only tell us how to achieve them. Many writers regard that the equation of reason with instrumental reasoning is typically a feature of industrial, technical societies. They argue that human rationality helps in suitable choice of individual and social goals.

(Oxford Dictionary of Philosophy)

Environmental Ethics

Definition

Environmental Ethics or Ethics of Nature is a branch of applied ethics that discusses values, rules, norms and criteria for responsibly handling non-human natural entities. It provides the groundwork for social policy on issues of environmental protection, animal protection, nature protection, animal rights and sustainability.

Environmental ethics cover three main areas:

1. Resource Ethics : responsible management of scarce and non-renewable resources and environmental media such as water, soil, air and climate
2. Animal Ethics : Responsible treatment of animals, particularly those which can experience pain
3. Ethics of Nature Protection : responsible treatment of collective biotic entities e.g. populations, species and ecosystems.

Major strands of thought

1. Anthropocentrism (Greek: Anthropo = human being) holds that animals, plants, or organisms have no intrinsic value. They deserve protection only if they serve human purposes as resources, or as sources of joy or of recreation/sports. Human beings are seen as at the top of 'nature's ladder' by virtue of their reasoning abilities. Classical Western philosophers like Bacon, Descartes and Kant believed in this view which is based on dualism (body/soul; body/ spirit; body/brain).
2. Pathocentrism (Greek: pathos = suffering, pain) assumes that all life is of the same origin and thus related. As a consequence, all living beings have the capacity to experience pain. In Christian tradition, this leads back to an 'ethics of compassion'.
3. Holism: It is the doctrine that the whole is more than the sum of its parts or that in certain contexts one has to look at the system as a whole than at its parts.

The following three doctrines provide the basis for many environmental themes and values.

(a) Biocentrism

Albert Schweitzer advocates that we should have reverence for life. "All life wants to live, like me". Paul Taylor says that all living has intrinsic value, and a will of life. Living beings have own interests and strive for their own good. Biocentrism can be either individualistic or holistic. It generally excludes ecosystems and non-living nature, like ozone layer.

(b) Ecocentrism

Aldo Leopold's Land Ethics argues that the land/ecosystem forms a community as if it was an organism or living being. It is self-regulating. People should not conquer the land but protect it for the sake of themselves.

(c) Deep Ecology

Norwegian philosopher Arne Naess propounded Deep Ecology. The term 'deep' implies asking deeper questions concerning 'why' and 'how'. This approach is thus concerned with the fundamental philosophical questions about the impacts of human life as one part of the ecosphere, rather than with a narrow view of ecology as a branch of biological science. Incidentally, most holistic positions have been concerned with wilderness and its preservation.

In this connection, we may mention GAIA hypothesis. James Lovelock formulated GAIA in the mid-1960s and published it in a book in 1979. The Gaia Hypothesis says that earth functions as a single organism that maintains conditions necessary for its survival. This idea (which has it critics) has led to several theories and many new fields of research. While this hypothesis is still unsubstantiated, it provides many useful lessons about the interaction of physical, chemical, geological, and biological processes on Earth.

The following ethical issues arise in environmental policies.

(i) Inter-generational equity or protecting interests of future generations

(ii) Justice to poor (and to women) who suffer most from environmental decay

(iii) Equity between rich and poor nations; since richer nations historically caused most of environmental damage, they should bear a correspondingly greater burden in environmental restoration

[Dr. Nicole Karafyllis, Technical University, Braunschweig, Germany]

Envy

Envy is resentment of others for their wealth and success. Envy is a perversion in which desire for one's own good turns to a desire to deprive other people of their good. An envious person wishes ill of others. He is unable to bear their success and happiness. Often, he is unable to take active measures for harming others. But their very success and happiness become the source of his misery.

Epicureanism

Epicurus considered pleasure as the beginning and end of a blessed life. Pleasure is our 'first and native good'. Epicurean ethic consists in seeking pleasure and avoiding pain. Epicureanism does not advocate indiscriminate pursuit of pleasure. It recognizes that some pleasures are followed by greater pains; and that some pain could result later in greater pleasure. Epicureanism does not equate pleasure with immoderate sensuality. Pleasure has to do with absence of bodily pain and mental disquiet. Epicurus regarded friendship as one the greatest pleasures of life.

A happy life depends on prudent thinking, making rational choices, and on avoiding things that cause mental turmoil. Epicureans highly valued ataraxia or peace of mind. Epicurus also believed that men live in a state of constant anxiety because of the fears that religion and superstations implant in them. He held that the world is material and that men do not survive in any sense after death. They will not face hell or any posthumous punishments.

The purpose of philosophy, according to Epicurus, is to enunciate what constitutes the best life, and why. Philosophy is an 'education of the mind, and a therapy of the soul'. The happy life is one of ataraxia, and men can reach it by understanding the true nature of things, and living according to that understanding.

Estimates Committee

While PAC considers the regularity, propriety and legality of expenditure, the Estimates committee looks at the accuracy of the budget estimates. (Incidentally, budget is a forecast of income and expenditure for the coming financial year.) In other words, its focus is on how accurate the forecasts of the budget proved to be. This aspect can be called 'the targeting' of budget.

Ethical Dilemma

Ethical dilemmas are situations in which decisions involve conflicts between two or more moral principles. In these situations, moral agents (who have to make decisions) find themselves in a quandary since they have to choose between two ethical norms (N1and N2) which have equal status. If the moral agent selects N1, he has to give up N2 and vice versa. In other words, the decision involves a trade-off between two moral criteria which have equal status. Similarly, it may be possible to pass two opposite judgments - say J1 and J2 - on action using two different moral standards.

Ethical dilemmas can at times arise due to the different roles which men have in life. An individual may be, for example, a father, soldier, judge, farmer and the like. Sometimes, his role, for example, as a police officer may conflict his role as a brother if his sibling is caught in a crime. That is why codes of conduct prescribe, that officers should not, especially in financial matters, get into conflict-of-interest situations.

How to resolve ethical dilemmas? Simply put, the moral agent should act according to that prima facie duty or moral norm that deserves greater priority in the given circumstances.

Ethical Monism

This theory holds that there is only a single intrinsic moral principle or value in life. Thus, hedonism locates moral good only in pleasure or happiness.

Ethical Pluralism

This is the view that there are multiple worthwhile moral ends we can pursue in life.

Ethics

There are two ways of spelling ethics---Ethics and ethics. 'Ethics' when spelled with an upper case 'E', means a part or branch of philosophy. It is a study of the ideas and theories of what is good, of what is right and wrong, of moral choice and action. In this context, it also discusses various moral standards that should guide a moral agent's decisions and choices. The word 'ethics' (spelled with lower case 'e' as here) refers to the outlook and attitudes of individuals and organizations about their values, how they act, and how they look upon themselves.

The usage of the terms 'ethics', 'ethical' and 'moral 'varies among writers. Some consider them as more or less synonymous whereas others regard them as different. A. C. Grayling (in A history of philosophy) distinguishes between 'ethics' and 'morals' based on their etymology. The Greek word ethos, which means character, is the root of 'ethics'. The Latin word mos, moris (plural mores), which means 'custom, is the root of 'moral'. This distinction implies that morality is about the duties, obligations and actions of human beings whereas ethics is about what type of person one is.

This distinction spills over into discussion of ethical theories. Thus, in trying to locate where the value of a moral action resides, some theories focus on the character (or virtues) of a moral agent, others on the consequences of the action, and some others on whether it conforms to the moral agent's duty. When the focus is on the character of the agent, the discussion is ethical; when the discussion is on the consequences of an action or its conformity to the agent's duty, the discussion is moral.

One major topic of ethics is what constitutes the best life, why, and how to lead it. There are many views on this question. The ideal life is said to consist in pursuing happiness, following duty, or in seeking knowledge or in working on creative arts. Some writers emphasize moral self-perfection, spiritual self-realization, liberation from mental bondage, and seeking divine grace and salvation--- as among the higher moral ideals.

Eudemonia (or Eudaimonia)

This is a term from ancient Greek philosophy. Plato defined it as: "The good composed of all goods; an ability which suffices for living well; perfection in respect of virtue; resources sufficient for a living creature." In his *Nicomachean Ethics*, Aristotle says that everyone agrees that eudemonia is the highest good for human beings, but that there is substantial disagreement on what sort of life counts as doing and living well. Both ordinary men and philosophers identify living well and faring well with being happy. But ordinary people think that happiness consists of things like pleasure, wealth or honour.

Aristotle points out that it is difficult to specify just what sort of activities enable one to live well. He mentions three popular conceptions of the best life for human beings - (1) a life of pleasure, (2) a life of political activity [active citizenship in a city state] and (3) a philosophical life. Aristotle links another concept virtue as needed for achieving eudemonia. He says that the happy life is one of "virtuous activity in accordance with reason".

(Eudaimonia, Wikipedia)

Euthanasia

Euthanasia is a Greek word which means 'good death' or 'noble death'. It now means that human life can be terminated in certain circumstances. It may include mercy killing and assisted suicide. Those who believe that human life is sacrosanct oppose euthanasia.

Facts Versus Morals (or Values)

When we judge an action as moral or immoral, we approve or disapprove of it; we consider it praiseworthy or blameworthy. Our judgement is based on the feelings and emotions the action evokes in us. The praise or blame we associate with the action may also arise from the moral standards implanted in us. In other words, our moral judgements are not based on objective facts connected with the action, but with the sentiments it engenders in us.

Moral judgements are not based, to use an expression of David Hume, on 'matter of fact or of real existence'. This is something in the world which exists independently of anyone's choices and preferences. This leads to the conclusion that one cannot derive a prescription (moral maxim) from a description: one cannot derive a prescription for action or what one ought to do by observing some aspect of the world. Another way of expressing this idea is that one cannot get an 'ought' conclusion from an 'is' premise. Facts and morals or values are distinct categories. Factual accounts and moral discourse are different things

False Claims Act

SARC recommended that a law on the model of the US False Claims Act should be passed in India with the following main provisions:

- Citizens and civil society groups can seek legal relief when people defraud governments by filing false claims against government.
- Any citizen can file a suit against any person or agency that makes a false claim against the government.
- If the false claim is proved, then the person/agency responsible shall be liable for penalty equal to five times the loss sustained by the exchequer or society.
- The person who brought the suit should be suitably rewarded out of the damages recovered.

Fascism

Fascism is a totalitarian ideology. It opposes liberalism, conservatism, and socialism. Fascism claims to be an elitist response to modern social and political problems which other ideologies are unable to resolve. The main attributes of Fascism are: totalitarianism, omnipotent state, subordination of individuals and institutions to state, opposition to equality, and commitment to nationalism and racial superiority.

Fatalism

Fatalism is the belief that future events are preordained and follow an inexorable course. This belief implies that human efforts cannot influence the course of future events.

Feminism

Feminism is the belief that men and women should have equal rights and opportunities; it is organized activity in support of women's rights and interests. The movement witnessed three waves. In the first, women sought full legal equality with men, including full educational opportunity, equal compensation and the right to vote. In 1950s, a second wave of feminism arose challenging the restricted role assigned to women in the workplace and the tendency to confine women to the household arena. A third wave of feminism arose in the late 20th century and was notable for challenging middle-class white feminists and for broadening feminism's goals to encompass equal rights for all people, regardless of race, creed, economic or educational status, physical appearance or ability, or sexual orientation.

Feminist Ethics

Feminist ethics is an offshoot of contemporary feminist movement. This movement aims at promoting women's flourishing and opposes forces which tend to harm women's well being. Feminist ethics specifically factor in women's experience as a way to understand what flourishing means for women and men.

Feminist ethics revises traditional ethical frameworks in order to provide new ways of dealing with moral issues. It finds fault with traditional ethics for various reasons. "Malestream" ethics underrates women's moral abilities and ignores issues which are of special concern to women. More fundamentally, it is vitiated by a masculine perspective. Traditional ethics, while picturing moral life and analyzing ethical reasoning leaves out women, treating men as the only moral agents.

In traditional society, women are considered inferior to men. They are confined to spheres and activities of life that men choose for them. Men are placed in the public realm and women in the private realm. The cognitive traits of the two are seen as different. Men are regarded as reasonable, rational, and logical, whereas women as intuitive, illogical, and emotional. Emotions and sentiments as feminine attributes are treated with supercilious disdain.

Arising from this mindset, many traditional moral theories gave primacy to reason and relegated emotions to the background. Further, traditional academic ethics conceived good with the good of its predominantly male practitioners in mind. Its conception causes mental anguish to women who are excluded from the formulation of the good.

Arising from the above critique, feminine ethics adopts three approaches. One approach is based on liberalism. Feminism is understood in this approach as a political movement that is concerned with the rights of women - equal rights of women

The second approach concentrates on the liberation of women. Women are seen as trapped in many social structures and practices that are oppressive. From this viewpoint, feminist ethics focus on removing such oppressive structures and practices, and reshaping society so as to encourage realisation of the full creative potential of women.

The third approach of feminist ethics consists in "a commitment to the distinctiveness of women's perspective and insight." Traditional ethics ignore the experiences of women which are important sources of moral insight. Women also feel the bonds of human relationships more intensely than men, and better understand the interdependence of human beings. They show great sensitivity to and concern for human suffering. Feminist ethics cover the three preceding broad areas, and several individual elements within each area.

Source: Chaitanya Motupalli, Feminist Ethics

Forgiveness

'Forgiveness' means pardoning of an offence, wrongdoing, or obligation. The victim of the wrongdoing pardons the wrong doer. The wrong doer sincerely repents and tries to alleviate the victim's hurt feelings. The phrase 'forgive and forget' sums up the idea.

Fortitude

Fortitude means courage, bravery and endurance. It is opposite of cowardice. Courage reflects indifference to physical danger. Courage implies not only physical bravery but also courage of conviction. Courage protects other moral qualities. In the absence of courage, people will be too afraid to act virtuously or in line with their principles.

Free Will

The question whether human beings have free will arose first in religious discussions. Many believe that God is omnipotent (all-powerful) and omniscient (all knowing). God created the world, and is responsible (at least partly because He created human beings with unique attributes) for the course of events in the world. God has foreknowledge of future course of worldly events. If God knows the future, it must be fixed in advance, and there can be no such thing as free will. If everything in the world is preordained, free will and human agency become irrelevant in human affairs. This leads to religious doctrines of predestination.

Determinism, which is a scientific or philosophical, and not a religious doctrine, also contradicts free will. Determinism is the view that prior causes result in particular events and no others. Physical and biological world (the locale of human beings) is governed by invariant laws of nature. Determinism has two versions---strong and weak. Strong determinism says that human freedom or free will is incompatible with universal causation. Weak determinism holds that all events are caused but that some causes can be attributed to human beings.

Leaving aside the philosophical issues, one needs to recognize from a practical point of view the considerable leeway for autonomous, voluntary human actions possible in many areas and circumstances. Even while recognizing the operations of chance events and random factors, one should steadfastly pursue one's chosen ends and ideals. Adopting a passive or fatalistic attitude based on determinism or predestination will be a form of 'lazy sophism'.

Functions of Attitudes

Daniel Katz proposed a functionalist theory of attitudes. He takes the view that attitudes are determined by the functions they serve for us. People hold given attitudes because these attitudes help them achieve their basic goals. Katz distinguishes four types of psychological functions that attitudes subserve.

A. Instrumental

We develop favourable attitudes towards things that aid or reward us. We want to maximise rewards and minimize penalties. Katz says we develop attitudes that help us meet this goal. We favour political parties that will advance our economic lot - if we are in business, we favour the party that will keep our taxes low, and if unemployed we favour one that will increase social welfare benefits. We are more likely to change our attitudes, if doing so allows us to fulfil our goals or avoid undesirable consequences.

B. Knowledge

Attitudes partly enable us to understand the world and see our environment as structured and meaningful.'; delete 'provide ... environment. Attitudes help us understand society, and adjust and respond to events around us. They are part of the frame of reference we use in our thinking, and which makes our ideas consistent.

C. Value-expressive

This psychological function expresses an individual's basic values and reinforces his/her self-image. For example: if you view yourself as a Catholic, you can reinforce that image by adopting Catholic beliefs and values. For example: We may have self-images of ourselves as enlightened conservatives or militant radicals, and we therefore cultivate attitudes that we believe indicate such a core value.

D. Ego-defensive

Some attitudes serve to protect us from acknowledging basic truths about ourselves or the harsh realities of life. They serve as defence mechanisms. For example: Those with feelings of inferiority may develop an attitude of superiority.

Katz's functionalist theory also offers an explanation as to why attitudes change. According to Katz, an attitude changes when it no longer serves its function and the individual feels blocked or frustrated. Thus, attitude change is achieved not so much by changing a person's information or perception about an object, but rather by changing the person's underlying motivational and personality needs.

Example : As your social status increases, your attitudes toward your old car may change - you need something that better reflects your new status. (For that matter, your attitudes toward your old friends may change as well).

Gene Therapy

Gene therapy is based on genetics which studies transmission of hereditary traits from one generation to later generations. Defects in genes present within cells can cause inherited diseases like cystic fibrosis, sickle-cell anemia, and hemophilia. If some chromosomes are missing in a cell, diseases like Down syndrome are caused. A change in proper genetic sequence can cause diseases like atherosclerosis and cancer. Gene therapy replaces missing genes or provides copies of functioning genes to replace defective ones. The inserted genes can be naturally-occurring genes that produce the desired effect or may be genetically engineered (or altered) genes.

Gene Therapy

Gene therapy is based on genetics which studies transmission of hereditary traits from one generation to later generations. Defects in genes present within cells can cause inherited diseases like cystic fibrosis, sickle-cell anemia, and hemophilia. If some chromosomes are missing in a cell, diseases like Down syndrome are caused. A change in proper genetic sequence can cause diseases like atherosclerosis and cancer. Gene therapy replaces missing genes or provides copies of functioning genes to replace defective ones. The inserted genes can be naturally-occurring genes that produce the desired effect or may be genetically engineered (or altered) genes.

Good

Good is a basic ethical term. It is used either as a noun or as an adjective in many contexts. When used as an adjective as in 'good sailor', 'good teacher', or 'good nurse', good refers to skill or dexterity in work. In ethics, good as an adjective refers to a quality, property, or behaviour which is morally commendable or praiseworthy. Virtues as for example, courage, kindness, wisdom, are good. Vices like cruelty, malice, and envy, are bad. Good is often associated with excellence, and promotion of harmony and creativity.

According to R.B. perry, "Good" means being an object of favourable interest' (desire). However, not all desires are good; only wholesome desires are good. F.C. Sharp defines '"Good" as "desired upon reflection". This definition is more acceptable since it implies that people consider something good and desire it after thinking rationally about it.

What is a good life? How to lead such a life? These two questions mainly serve as background for the discussion of Socrates on good. Aristotle regards happiness as the ultimate end of life men seek. In his conception, happiness is a good, and is associated with a life of reason and virtue. Plato's view of good is metaphysical. He thought that the form of supreme Good can be perceived by human souls in only their disembodied state after death. For Stoics, good consists in leading a life according to nature and virtue. Some Stoics preached that virtue can be reached only through asceticism. Kant associates the idea of good with human will. According to Kant, nothing is higher or more valuable in the world than the good will of human beings. What marks out human beings with such good will is that they invariably obey moral laws.

According to Utilitarianism, what is good is happiness. Happiness consists of pleasure and absence of pain. Utilitarianism regards happiness is the greatest good. Moral agents should strive for the greatest happiness of the greatest number.

Good Temper and Temperance

Anger reflects the vice of intemperance. Anger has to be rationally controlled since it overwhelms reason and self-control. Anger controlled by reason reflects virtue, whereas anger ungoverned by reason, or wild rage, is a vice. Moral indignation which leads to constructive responses deseves praise.

Group IQ

Research has shown that work teams have a collective intelligence. It does not depend on the intelligence of the team's individual members. Group intelligence depends neither on the average intelligence of the members or on that of its smartest member. Group intelligence predicts how well a group handles a complex task such as the computer checkers game and on the Legos task.

Research found evidence for the following conclusions:

- ¤ Group or collective intelligence exists.
- ¤ A group's motivation, satisfaction, and unity are important for its collective intelligence.
- ¤ In a group with a high level of collective intelligence, the members tended to score well on a test that measured how good they were at reading other people's emotions. ¤ Groups with overbearing leaders who were reluctant to cede the floor and let the others talk did worse than those in which participation was better distributed and people took turns speaking.
- ¤ The proportion of women in the group was a predictor of collective intelligence – arising from women's generally superior social sensitivity.

(From Carolyn Y. Johnson's article in Boston Globe, December 19, 2010)

Happiness

Aristotle identifies happiness as the ultimate end of all human pursuits. Many people associate happiness with wealth, health, honour, glory and the like. A little reflection shows that these are intermediate goals or instrumentalities for a final end. That final end is happiness which is sought for its own sake and not for anything else. Aristotle uses the Greek term eudaimonia to refer to happiness. However, according to many writers the more accurate meaning of eudaimonia is 'well-doing and well-being' or 'flourishing'.

At first sight, pursuit of happiness seems an ignoble moral end. However, ancient Greek philosophers propounded an elevated conception of happiness. Thus, Aristotle connects happiness with what he regards as the highest function of men, what is unique and distinctive about humanity, which is reason. Happiness for human beings consists in leading a virtuous and rational life. Happiness is not found in base joys or dissipation, or worse still, in vile pursuits.

People differ on what constitutes happiness and on how to attain happiness. It is said to consist variously- –in simple and natural living; in escaping from fears and anxieties or more generally in ataraxia or peace of mind; in austere and ascetic habits; and in abandoning desires and goals beyond one's reach. Many religions deny the possibility of happiness in man's earthly life, which Martin Luther says consists of "Suffering, Suffering, Cross, Cross".

Modern secular philosophers like J.S. Mill observed that happiness will elude us if we seek it consciously. Happiness arises as a byproduct when we immerse ourselves in impersonal activities. Mill identified 'the internal culture of the individual' as the source of happiness. It will foster refined tastes in people and enable them to be happy in pursuits like art and culture. Happiness can also be found in helping people in distress, in friendships, in harmonious family life and in commitment to one's chosen profession.

Happiness and Pleasure

No hard and fast distinction is often made between happiness and pleasure. Happiness is considered as pleasure and absence of pain. Utilitarianism recommends that moral agents should so act as to promote the greatest happiness of the greatest number. Bentham looks at the amount or quantity happiness as if it is made up of uniform and measurable units. Critics attacked utilitarianism as 'pig' philosophy since it could imply that a pig fed with enough mud and muck will be happier than a Socrates. Mill answered this criticism by introducing a qualitative dimension in happiness. He distinguished between 'higher' and 'lower' pleasures, and held that people of refined culture who know both can readily make the distinction. He argued that it was better to be a human being dissatisfied than a pig satisfied, better to be a Socrates dissatisfied than a fool satisfied. This view in turn can be considered elitist. Not many people can enjoy a dance recital by Birju Maharaj or a music recital by Kishori Amonkar. They would prefer to settle down in a sofa watching their favourite soap opera. But as rational beings we should seek higher pleasures.

It is possible to distinguish pleasure and happiness in another way. Pleasure is momentary or has a short time horizon. Happiness has a long-term perspective. From this standpoint, happiness includes prudence. Happiness excludes excessive indulgence which may be unhealthy, and also pleasures which are harmful.

Hedonism

Hedonism is the general term for those theories that regard happiness or pleasure as the supreme end of life. These theories have taken many different forms. Some theorists maintain (as a matter of fact) that men always seek pleasure, i.e. that pleasure in some form is always the ultimate object of desire. Other hedonists confine themselves to the view that men ought always to seek pleasure. The former theory is known as psychological hedonism, because it simply affirms the seeking of pleasure as a psychological fact; whereas the latter theory is called ethical hedonism.

Psychological Hedonism is the theory that the ultimate object of desire is pleasure. Following are the three ways of expressing psychological hedonism:

- Pleasure is always that which serves as the inducement to action.
- Pleasure and pain are the only possible motives to action.
- They are the only ends at which we can aim.

Hierarchical Model of Ideology

Sociologists have formulated a hierarchical model of political attitudes consisting of four tiers: specific opinions, habitual opinions, attitudes and ideology. We can illustrate this hierarchical model from Eysenck's studies of social attitudes. The following example shows the manifestation of anti-Semitism or anti-Jewish sentiment at four levels in the attitudinal hierarchy. Incidentally, anti-Jewish sentiment prevailed for long in Europe and Russia.

1. IDEOLOGY (Conservatism)
2. ATTITUDES (Anti-Semitic)
3. HABITUAL OPINIONS ("Jews are inferior.")
4. SPECIFIC OPINIONS ("Finkelstein is a an unreliable Jew!")

Incidentally, all conservatives cannot be dubbed as anti-Jewish, and the above list has only an illustrative value.

Homosexuality

Section 377 of the Indian Penal Code (IPC) makes homosexual sex punishable with life imprisonment. Many people have been urging government to decriminalize homosexuality. Supreme Court upheld the constitutionality of Section 377 of the IPC. Supreme Court however declared that Section 377, to the extent it criminalizes consensual sexual acts of adults in private, violates Articles 21, 14 and 15 of the Constitution. But it upheld the provisions of Section 377 covering non-consensual homosexuality and homosexual acts involving minors. Supreme Court also suggested that Parliament should suitably amend Sec377. Supreme Court added that it would refer petitions to scrap Section 377 to a five-member constitutional bench.

Honesty

Honesty can be regarded as truthfulness in financial matters. Individuals in positions of fiduciary trust–accountants, custodians of cash, wealth managers, and guardians of minors, trustees of charitable bodies, bankers and treasury officers–have to be scrupulously honest. Honesty in public administration implies that civil servants should discharge their duties in a bona fide manner without giving into monetary temptations or inducements. Businessmen should avoid all forms of deception, cheating and fraud.

Humanism

'Humanist' in modern times means an individual with a non-religious or secular ethical outlook. Humanism implies a morality which consciously disassociates itself from religious doctrines. Humanist morality is not grounded in religion. At the same time, humanists accept many virtues and vices as identified by religions.

Humanism in another sense denotes an intellectual movement of the Renaissance period. Humanist scholars of this period believed that humanistic studies---grammar, rhetoric, history, poetry and ethics---would help in developing well rounded and effective citizenry. Classic works of ancient Greece and Rome were considered as the sources of such study. They would help students in acquiring intellectual discipline, moral orientation, and refined taste. Petrarch (14th century) is considered as the 'Father of Humanism'.

Humanism is also associated with ideas about the dignity of man. In medieval Europe, gloomy religious views which regarded human nature as depraved, and the world as a valley of tears, dominated. Renaissance humanism softened this view, and recognized the possibility of finding joy in this world through aesthetic and artistic pursuits. Human dignity is also associated with Kant's view that human beings are ends in themselves and should never be treated as means for achieving any putative higher ends.

Human Responsibility

Freedom of human will always seemed something of a riddle. Theologically, men and women were seen as merely created, finite, and dependent beings, and therefore endowed with limited choices of life patterns and activities. Even if human beings are considered self-determined, the formation of 'self' is seen as dependent on influences - divine, social and psychological - over which they have no control. On the other hand, some argued that God endows men with reason and the ability to make rational choices. Men can shape their character and life substantially on their own. In this view, men are held responsible for the kinds of lives they lead, and the habitual types of actions they take. Men have stable elements of character. Sometimes, they may act on momentary impulses out of tune with their character. But by and large, a man's actions follow from his basic, stable character. In this sense, his actions are free.

This issue is seen in modern times keeping in view the relation of the individual to society. In one sense, an individual cannot shape or form his own character. He is naturally endowed with certain aptitudes and tendencies. Further, the pattern of his life is set by the moral atmosphere into which he is born or in which he is placed. We have no control over our inherited traits or our environment. To what extent can society hold individuals responsible for their actions or offences?

The answer is that human beings cannot be regarded as wholly determined by external forces and causes and absolved of responsibility. As rational beings living within a society, they have to be regarded as governed by common human ideals. Once they recognise the ideal, they are under an obligation to work towards that ideal through appropriate conduct. This is the way in which a man or a society of men must judge human conduct. Men cannot abdicate common morals on vague philosophical grounds. "There is no stone wall in the way of a man's moral progress. There is only himself. And he cannot accept himself as a mere fact, but only as a fact ruled by an ideal."

Humility

Humility is recognised as a virtue in all religions. Many other virtues spring from or gather lustre from it. Humility does not mean self-debasement or denying one's merits, talents and accomplishments. It means that we should not place ourselves on a higher pedestal than others -even when we far exceed them in talents and achievements. Traditionally vanity, pride and arrogance have been regarded as the vices opposed to humility. Humility is especially a virtue in those vested with power. Humility will serve to ward off the insolence that usually goes with power.

Inclinations

Inclinations are human proclivities or the common ways in which men tend to feel and act. Immanuel Kant believed that human inclinations lead men morally astray and grounded morality in duty.

Idealism

Idealism advocates the moral point of view or "what ought to be" in politics. Till Machiavelli's times, political thinkers generally believed that politics, including the relations among states, should be virtuous, and that the methods of warfare should remain subordinated to ethical standards. However, realism has been the dominant trend in politics and diplomacy.

Ideology

According to Middendorp, ideology consists of: "A system of general ideas on man and society, centered around one or a few general values, which has manifested itself historically as a doctrine adhered to by some major groups and categories, and which expresses the interests of some important category e.g. a social class".

Ideology may be loosely defined as any kind of action-oriented theory or approach to politics based on a system of ideas. Ideology, in Destutt de Tracy's original conception, has five characteristics:

- It contains a comprehensive explanatory theory about human experience and the external world. It is based on a few underlying general values.
- It proposes a general programme for social and political organization.
- It believes that the programme can only be realized through a struggle
- It seeks not merely to persuade but to recruit loyal adherents with commitment. ¤ It addresses a wide public but assigns special leadership role to intellectuals.

Immoral

Immoral refers to whatever is bad or wrong like bad people or wrong actions. Immoral and unethical have the same meaning.

Independent Directors

The independent directors are the custodians of corporate governance and the conscience keepers of the board of directors of a company. The qualities expected of an independent director include: integrity and probity; objective and constructive approach; bonafides of action; banishing extraneous considerations that threaten his objective, independent judgment; refraining from abuse of his office and from any action that would lead to loss of his independence. The Companies Act includes a code as a guide to professional conduct for independent directors.

Individual Differences in Ideology

Many factors are cited to explain ideological differences among individuals. Standard 'background' variables, such as age, education, occupation, rural versus urban residence, and occasionally income are used to explain individual differences. The influence of these variables is explained through effects of socialization, or economic interests. Thus, policies which individuals prefer (or policy preferences) are explained based on tangible benefits they expect or derive from policies.

Individual freedom

Individual moral freedom means that people should be free to pursue their own values and morality so long as they do not harm others or violate core ethical norms.

Integrity

One meaning of integrity in public administration is financial honesty. A public servant with integrity shows financial probity and rectitude. Integrity also means that the moral agent acts according to his inner convictions. His conduct is free from hypocrisy and deception. His actions are in conformity with his stated values. Integrity implies wholeness or harmony of self in the sense that that one lives according to certain self-professed principles and values. All social interaction depends on integrity and trust. Integrity is especially relevant in public administration in which cooperative, corroborative and collective efforts are needed to solve interconnected problems. Hence, character, particularly integrity, is essential in public leaders.

Integrity Pact

Integrity pact is an agreement between the public agency procuring goods and services and the bidder for a public contract. Through the pact the bidders give assurances that they have not paid and shall not pay any illegal gratification to secure the contract in question. From its side, the public agency calling for bids commits to ensuring a level playing field and fair play in the procurement process. Such pacts often involve supervision and scrutiny by independent, outside observers. Such pacts increase transparency and confidence in the processes through which Government and public sector units conclude major deals. Many national legal systems now recognise such pacts.

Intention and Behaviour

Many social psychologists regard that the nearest cognitive antecedent of actual behavioural performance is the agent's intention than his attitude. It means that one can accurately predict specific behaviours of people from their intentions.

Intention and Motive

The words intention and motive, though often used interchangeably, have different meanings. 'Intend' means being resolved to do or decided about doing something on purpose. Intention is the purpose with which an act is done. Motive gives rise to intention. A hits B with a stick with an intent to hurt him. The motive of A's action may be hatred or a desire to wreak vengeance.

International Morality

International morality refers to morals or codes of conduct governing relations between nations.

Justice

One meaning of justice is to give each person his due or what he/she is entitled to get. People make claims about resources, opportunities, and the like. These may create conflicts, and justice is invoked to resolve such conflicts by determining what each person is properly entitled to have. Justice involves impartial, uniform and consistent application of rules. Justice is the opposite of arbitrariness. It requires that where two cases are alike, they should be treated in the same way. Justice is embodied or finds expression in the rule of law, where laws are understood as general rules impartially applied.

Four distinctions are commonly made in discussions on justice. (1) Conservative versus radical justice: Conservative justice respects people's rights under existing law or moral rules. Radical justice may invoke ideals like equality and merit for determining rights and resource distribution in society. (2) Distributive versus retributive Distributive justice is a principle for assigning resources or distributable goods of various sorts to individuals. Retributive or corrective justice is a remedial principle that applies when one person wrongly interferes with another's legitimate holdings or harms him in any way. (3) Procedural versus substantive justice: Procedural justice refers to fairness of the procedures used in courts for settling disputes. Substantive justice means the justice rendered in a case based on its merits through a judicial order. (4) Comparative versus non comparative justice:e Comparative justice means that for determining what is due to one person, we need to look at what others can also claim. Non-comparaive justice means that we can determine what is due to a person merely by knowing relevant facts about that particular person.

In economics and politics, Justice involves discussion on fairness in distribution of wealth, income and power in society. Conservatives believe that rights of property owners are based on principles of just acquisition and consequent entitlement. These principles severely limit possibilities of redistribution of wealth and income. Even when these principles lead to gross inequality, it has to be tolerated as a price for justice. In contrast, egalitarians argue that principles of just distribution limit property rights, and would justify state interference to curtail property claims hitherto regarded sacrosanct in society.

Keeping Promises

Keeping promises, honesty and integrity are virtues which are part of veracity. Gandhiji regards breaking a promise as equivalent to abandoning truth. No one should light heartedly make a promise. One should not enter into immoral or illegal promises.

Kindness

Aristotle defines kindness as helpfulness towards someone in need, not in return for anything, nor for the advantage of the helper himself, but for that of the person helped. Kindness is the quality of being friendly, generous, and considerate. It is the bedrock of humanist as well as religious ethics.

Knowledge Worker

Peter Drucker, the doyen among management theorists, coined the term "knowledge worker" and predicted that more than a third of the American workforce would soon consist of knowledge workers. He mentions that their productivity consists in adding value to information. Knowledge workers are people such as financial analysts, writers and computer programmers. Their knowledge is highly specialized and their productivity depends on their individual work getting integrated into the work of a work team. For example, novelists are not publishers; and nor are hardware designers sellers of computer parts. In knowledge - based work, team replaces the individual as the work unit.

Laissez faire

Laissez faire is a view which holds that government should not interfere in the working of private enterprises and allow economic markets to operate freely.

Law and Ethics (or Morals)

Law and ethics share some common features but differ in others. Both law and ethics lay down norms or standards for human action. The objective of any law is to lay down within its specific sphere what is legal and what is illegal. Jurisprudence explains the basis or rationale of law. Law and jurisprudence presuppose ethics. Historically law emerged from ethics. Law is codified custom which represents the mores or morals of society.

Law is related not only historically but also logically to ethics. The primary principles or norms of law go back to or presuppose ethics. For example, laws protecting life, liberty and property are based on rights or claims which are essentially moral. In fact, jurists observe that law is 'the minimum of moral performance and disposition required of members of society'. Law is regarded as the ethical minimum required to maintain a society.

From this angle, the scope of law is far narrower than that of ethics. Ethics is more extensive and covers many more areas of human life than law. The scope of law is limited to the statutes enacted by a sovereign or legislature. In this sense, law is formal and is embodied in written public documents. Though moral maxims are found in books and religious texts, morals are also part of uncodified social conventions and traditions.

Laws are enforced by government under threat of punishment. Obedience to law is mandatory or compulsory. Ethics are voluntary, though their violation may attract social opprobrium. Compliance with morals is not obligatory or compulsory. In old textbooks, morals are referred to as merit, virtue, or nobleness.

Positive laws are laws passed by legislature. They include rules, regulations and judicial pronouncements. Sometimes, a distinction is made between positive law and natural law and God's law. Unlike statutory law, natural law is derived from nature and reason, and divine law from God's commandments. In modern times, law refers to positive or statutory law.

Sometimes, a distinction is made between legal justice and moral justice. Legal justice is based on existing laws. These may at times be unethical such as laws which at one time sanctioned racial segregation. Contrarily, some enlightened laws may reflect morals more refined than those found in contemporary society. An example is law decriminalizing homosexuality between consenting adults or limiting death penalty to really heinous crimes.

Laziness

Laziness is aversion to work or exertion. Indolent individuals can be effective in no field of human life. A lazy child can make no progress in studies. Fortunately, by and large, children are seldom lazy. Indolence is a vice which adults acquire. It may start as love of ease, the tendency to take things easy and avoid strenuous effort of any kind. Lazy people shun both physical and mental labour. After completing studies and joining a job with security, people may fall into easy ways. Hard work may seem unnecessary since they may be under no great compulsion to perform and deliver results. Those who try to avoid work are not smart or clever. Shirkers get sidelined in organizations.

Learning Theory of Attitude Change

Psychologists mention three learning theories of attitude change: classical conditioning; operant conditioning; and observational learning.

Liberalism

Liberalism aims primarily at protecting and increasing an individual's freedom. Liberals believe that government is necessary to protect individuals from being harmed by others; but they also fear that government itself, by usurping excessive power, can threaten individual liberty. Early liberals argued that government should have minimum economic role and allow markets to function freely. Both from political and economic perspectives, liberals wanted to limit government activity.

Over time, liberalism got divided into classical liberalism and modern liberalism. Classical liberalism argues that government should merely protect individual liberty. Modern liberalism believes that government should enhance individual freedom by promoting conditions for its enjoyment by the poor. T.H. Green argued that excessive government powers which hindered freedom earlier shrank by mid-19th century, but that other hindrances such as poverty, disease, discrimination, and ignorance have emerged. Governments should positively help needy individuals to overcome these problems and enjoy their freedom. Modern liberalism enlists government to establish public schools and hospitals, aid the needy, and regulate working conditions to promote workers' health and well-being. It is only through public support that the poor and powerless can truly become free. Classical liberalism is said to be based on negative freedom or liberty and modern liberalism on positive freedom. Neo-liberalism is closer to conservatism, and modern liberalism to socialism.

Marriage of Information and Predisposition

According to one view, values provide the underpinnings to political attitudes of people. John Zaller, in The Nature and Origins of Mass Opinion, outlines the role of values (in shaping political attitudes)along lines similar to accounts found in political psychology According to Zaller, every opinion is "a marriage of information and predisposition: information to form a mental picture of the given issue, and predisposition to motivate some conclusion about it". He explains mass opinion or political attitudes as based on (i) elite discourse which provides political information to people and (ii) the 'predisposition' of individuals who receive the information. The role of predispositions is critical in this process.

Meta Ethics

Meta ethics or analytical ethics is an approach to ethics which refrains from advocating or prescribing or preaching any system of morality. It studies the language (terminology), logic and doctrines of ethics. Normative or prescriptive ethics is the opposite of meta ethics. Normative ethics prescribes the desirable moral behaviour which men should adopt. To this end, it proposes norms or value systems that prescribe how men and women should behave. Utilitarianism, virtue ethics, and duty ethics---are all normative.

Model of Moral Decision-Making

In simple terms, moral decisions involve a moral agent, an action (of his own or of someone else), judgement on action, a criterion used for judgement and the source of the criterion. These elements are shown below.

- ¤ Moral agent X
- ¤ Voluntary action or conduct X picks Y's pocket
- ¤ X's action is morally wrong judgment
- ¤ It is wrong to steal moral standard
- ¤ Religion, custom, law, social norm and the like are sources of standard
- ¤ In administrative situations, codes of conduct and ethics are often the sources of moral standards.

Models of Reasoned Action

These theories consider immediate prior intentions as reliable predictors of likely behaviour of individuals; they discuss factors that lead to formation of intentions.

The decision to adopt a particular behaviour will be determined by:

(i) positive or negative consequences of behaviour;

(ii) approval or disapproval of behaviour by respected individuals or groups; and

(iii) factors that may facilitate or impede behaviour.

This model assumes:

1. Intention is the immediate antecedent of actual behaviour.
2. Intention, in turn, is determined by attitude toward the behaviour, subjective norm, and perceived behavioural control.
3. These determinants are themselves a function, respectively, of underlying behavioural, normative, and control beliefs.
4. Behavioural, normative, and control beliefs can vary as a function of a wide range of background factors.

Moderates

Moderates occupy the middle ground in political spectrum. In any ideological grouping, moderates avoid extreme positions. They are not ideologically driven. For example, socialists represent the middle ground between capitalism and communism.

Moral

Moral is commonly used interchangeably with ethical. It signifies what is good and right such as a good person or a right action.

Moral Autonomy, Moral Heteronomy

Kant emphasized that human beings should be morally autonomous. It means that they should cultivate independence of thought, and take matters in their hands when deciding how to lead their life especially in the moral realm. Autonomy implies self-direction based on reason. Moral autonomy is an idea that gained prominence during the European Enlightenment movement.

Heteronomy in contrast stands for direction or government by someone or something outside one self, by some external agency. Heteronomy implies that a moral agent allows his will to become subject to or dependent on someone else's will. Traditionally, men accepted authorities such as God, organized religion, and academic establishment. In modern times, one dimensional discourse orchestrated by ideologically driven media and academia (and trivia uploaded on social media which big tech giants control and censor) tend to undermine one's moral autonomy. Genuine moral freedom requires that men should free themselves from such fetters.

Moral Ends or Ideals Which Various Philosophies Prescribe

Different schools of moral philosophy prescribe different ideals or ends in life The common ends of life which moral thinkers have proposed are shown in the table below:

Philosophy or theory	Prescribed end of life
Cyrenaics	Pursuit of gross pleasures and enjoyments; 'drink life to the dregs' Hedonism
Epicureanism	Pursuit of happiness or refined pleasures
Stoicism	Living in harmony with nature; self-control; endurance; being untroubled in adversity
Materialism	Accumulation of wealth and material comforts
Humanism	Well-being of people of individual nations or of world at large
Spiritualism	Undergoing self-discipline to realise God
Utilitarianism	Maximizing social utility or welfare
Deontology	Following moral law; duty
Virtue ethics	Cultivating a virtuous character through practice
Natural law ethics	Valuing (especially human life) and promoting growth of species, its preservation and welfare

Moral Hazard

Economic agents and organizations, while making decisions try to cover the risks which their decisions carry. An example is insuring goods in transit. Moral hazard is a situation which reduces the incentive to economic agents to guard against risk by insulating or protecting them from the consequences of risk-taking. Such a situation could arise when a householder after fully insuring his house and belongings becomes less cautious about their security. In economic sphere, moral hazard may be created by governments and regulators through their policies and actions. If central banks have a policy of protecting systematically important banks and financial institutions, it may embolden them paradoxically to assume greater risk in search of higher profits. Another example is of US Federal Reserve which consistently maintained extremely low interest rates which bolstered stock markets effectively providing them with a back-stop. This led to excessive risk taking by investors and a stock market bubble. Situations of moral hazard can also be created by economic players other than governments and regulators.

Moral Intuition

Logic and experience are the two cognitive routes to knowledge. Knowledge based on logic is also called demonstrative. Mathematics is an example of logical or demonstrative knowledge. Knowledge based on logic is contrasted with empirical knowledge which is derived from observation, experience or experiment. Scientific knowledge is empirical but also relies on mathematics and logic.

Philosophers also speak of intuitive knowledge, something which is directly perceived, which is seen as obviously evident or true. Intuitions are considered indubitable (cannot be doubted) and infallible (cannot be wrong). In ethics, intuition means that we directly recognize what is good in things or goodness, and what is the right thing to do in a given situation. G. E. Moore considered good as an indefinable quality. This raises the question how we can identify or recognize good when we see it. Moore's answer is that we intuit good. Intuitions can be the basis for ethical behaviour.

Intuition is a difficult idea. What is the nature of intuition? How does it operate? As people's moral judgements differ, which one should we consider as correct? If moral judgements are directly given in intuition, the intuiting moral agent may see no need for justifying them. Intuitions being nonlogical categories are not amenable to discussion. Moral disagreements become undecidable, and moral consensus becomes impossible.

Moral Noncognitivism

Moral noncognitivism is the view that moral judgements are not about things which are true or false. Moral judgements do not refer to properties of things in the world or about any existing states of affairs. Moral judgements, though they purport to be about good and bad, or right and wrong, simply express the feelings and preferences of people, what they approve and disapprove, and reflect their psychological states

Moral Realism

This is the view that morality is derived from nature and is not merely a matter of social convention, or human agreement or custom. This was part of the ancient Greek distinction between nature and convention. In modern ethical discussions, the concept of moral intuition, associated among others with G.E. Moore, implies moral realism. It is the idea that moral judgements refer to objective properties of entities or states of affairs in the world. It is their existence or nonexistence which makes moral judgements true or false. This view is rejected by logical positivists who argue that moral judgments are nor verifiable statements but are only expressions of our emotions and preferences.

Moral Relativism

Relativism is the view that different views, different modes of thinking, and different truths are equally valid. This implies that competing and contradictory statements are true. Relativism runs counter to both logic and commonsense. In logic, a statement cannot be both true and false. Of course, there could be differences even in scientific matters. But it is believed that various scientific investigations on a subject tend to converge. People accept that divergent viewpoints have to submit to common standards of reason and evidence.

In ethics, relativism means that there is no objective morality or standpoint. Truth for one individual may not be truth for another. Truth, and this holds for morality, is relative to or conditioned by the experiences and circumstances which individuals face. Subjective moral relativism means that two people can subscribe to opposing views with equal justification on the same question. In that situation, one cannot say which is the acceptable or more valid position. Moral relativism denies the possibility of having universally valid ethical norms. Morality is relative to particular societies, historical periods, and even to individuals.

Moral Scepticism

In epistemology (i.e., theory of knowledge), scepticism means a doctrine that questions the very possibility of knowledge. Moral scepticism denies or doubts possibility of moral knowledge (or truth), justified moral belief, and reasons to be moral. It assumes two forms. First, no moral belief is justified. Secondly, it is not possible to say whether a particular moral belief is or is not justified. This version implies that one should not take sides in moral disputes but suspend judgement or belief. Moral relativism is one form of scepticism. Sophists believed that one can find cogent reasons for both sides of a dispute. This raises the question, 'Which side is really right?' It then becomes difficult to have common ground or consensus on moral issues. Moral scepticism is an arm-chair theoretical view. No society can function without some form of moral consensus.

Moral Subjectivism

This is the doctrine that there are no moral facts existing outside human minds, in the external physical or material world 'out there'. Morality is a matter of human thought and choices and consists of our attitudes, beliefs and judgements. Morality is a representation of our feelings and sentiments on to the world and society. This view is now known as moral subjectivism. It was called sentimentalism in the eighteenth century and was propounded by David Hume among others. According to this view, what we call good is what we approve, and what we regard as bad is what we disapprove. Morality is grounded in our emotions, feelings and sentiments, not in reason nor in any concept of religion or divinity.

Moral Universalism (or Moral Objectivism)

Moral universalism is the opposite of moral relativism. It is the view that morality is the same for all individuals, for all societies, at all places, and at all times.

Nation

A nation is a group which thinks of itself as 'a people,' usually because they share many things in common. These consist of a common territory, history, culture, language, religion and way of life.

National Financial Reporting Authority (NFRA)

NFRA will formulate the accounting and auditing standards for companies. The Institute of Chartered Accounts has earlier prescribed the existing 'accounting standards' or the correct ways of writing accounts. Now, NFRA will formulate the accounting and auditing standards by revisiting the existing standards prescribed by the institute of chartered accountants. It will monitor and enforce compliance of these standards. To this end, it will oversee the quality of the professions like accountancy, auditing and financial analysis connected with these matters. The Authority will investigate professional and other misconduct of chartered accounts or of their firms.

Naturalistic Fallacy

Moore believed that that good is an indefinable quality. People perceive it directly without relying on any intervening logical processes just as they recognize colour yellow when they see it. Although good is indefinable, some philosophers identify it with a natural property such as pleasure which men experience. This identification of good with some natural property results in an error which Moore calls 'naturalistic fallacy'.

Nature of Audit

Audit means examination of accounts, transactions and records which CAG does in pursuance of duties and exercise of powers under the Constitution and the CAG Act. It also includes performance audit or any other type of audit determined by CAG. The CAG examines various aspects of Government expenditure. Conduct of audit is done based on such accounts, vouchers and records as may be received in the audit office and/or in the accounts office and may include online data, information and documents of the auditable entity. It may also be done in the office of the auditable entity or at the site where the relevant records for audit are available. The CAG audit is broadly classified into Regularity Audit and Performance Audit.

New Politics - The Emergence of New Issues and Conflicts

Themes known as 'new politics' issues and new social movements have recently emerged in political science. This literature focuses on the consequences of massive economic and social changes sweeping the Western democracies. In this view, new social and political developments have shaken the classic Western ideological structures. Schools of thought such as New Politics, the post-materialist left and the radical right question the former ideas of unidimensional ideological structure which mainly revolved around economic factors. Many writers have recognised that traditional socio-economic cleavages can no longer explain political behaviour.

Nolan Committee's List of Values

The 'Seven Principles of Public Life' enunciated by the Nolan committee are - selflessness, integrity, objectivity, accountability, openness, honesty and leadership.

Objective

'Objective' when used as an adjective refers to something that is outside of or external to human mind. An objective morality exists in a sense outside human mind or subjective realm.

Obligations

Obligations are responsibilities that men have towards to one another in virtue of law, morality, or tradition to ensure that their just rights are protected and accorded to them.

Ombudsman

An ombudsman is usually appointed by the government or by parliament but with a significant degree of independence, and is charged with representing the interests of the public by investigating and addressing complaints of maladministration or violation of rights. The modern use of the term began in Sweden, with the Swedish Parliamentary Ombudsman being instituted by the Instrument of Government of 1809, to safeguard the rights of citizens by establishing a supervisory agency independent of the executive branch. Lokpal is an ombudsman.

Observational Learning

One way in which people form attitudes is by observing people around them. People are particularly enced by the attitudes of those whom they admire. Children observe the attitudes of their parents and imitate their ways including attitudes. Some psychologists believe that learning is the source of most of our attitudes

Outputs and Outcomes

The purpose of fund utilization is to realise value for money, and achieve the programme objectives. Achievement of these objectives depends on provision of facilities, inputs and services. Physical targets of programmes are necessary but not sufficient for achieving its ultimate goals. As a result, there is considerable emphasis in recent times on the final outcomes of the programmes. It is necessary to distinguish between outputs and outcomes. To take an example, the goals of health programmes are now stated in terms of reducing infant mortality rates, maternal mortality rates and total fertility rates. Earlier, they were stated in physical terms such as number of hospitals, doctors, nurses or supply of medicines and nutrients.

Pacifism

Pacifism totally opposes war. While pacifists oppose all killing, they particularly abhor the mass killing which usually accompanies war. They object to this type and scale of killing. Pacifists believe that no moral grounds can justify war, and that it is always wrong. Many thinkers disagree with this blanket opposition to war.

Panchsheel

The Panchsheel Treaty (from Sanskrit, panch: five, sheel: virtues) is considered the high watermark of the Indian diplomacy of fifties. Panchsheel consists of five principles for peaceful coexistence between nations or for governing relations between states. Their first formal codification in treaty form was in an agreement between China and India in 1954.The five principles to which states have to subscribe are:

1. Mutual respect for each other's territorial integrity and sovereignty
2. Mutual non-aggression
3. Mutual non-interference in each other's internal affairs
4. Equality and mutual benefit and
5. Peace and coexistence.

Paradox of Hedonism

Hedonism is the doctrine that men should seek pleasure. But human desires are not always directed towards pleasure. To experience pleasure, men have to seek something else. To experience the joy of success, people have to toil at something, and the committed people derive pleasure from the effort. Further, physical pleasures soon begin to pall so that pursuit of pleasure becomes self-defeating. This is known as paradox of hedonism. Pleasure has to be derived as a byproduct by following avidly one's creative, intellectual and cultural interests.

Performance Audit

The objective of performance audit is to see that Government programmes have achieved the desired objectives at the lowest cost and produced the intended benefits.

The three Es of performance audit are economy, efficiency and effectiveness. Economy is minimizing the cost of resources used for an activity, having regard to appropriate quality. Efficiency is the relationship between the output, in terms of goods, services or other results and the resources used to produce them. Efficiency exists where the use of financial, human, physical and information resources is such that output is maximised for any given set of resource inputs, or input is minimized for any given quantity and quality of output. Effectiveness is the extent to which objectives are achieved and the relationship between the intended impact and the actual impact of an activity. Effectiveness addresses the issue of whether the scheme, programme or organization has achieved its objectives.

Personality

Personality is characterised by the following features:

1. It has both physical and psychological components.
2. Its expression in terms of behaviour is fairly unique in a given individual.
3. Its main features do not easily change with time.
4. It is dynamic in the sense that some of its features may change due to internal or external situational demands. Thus, personality is adaptive to situations.

Once we are able to characterize someone's personality, we can predict how that person will probably behave in a variety of circumstances. An understanding of personality allows us to deal with people in realistic and acceptable ways.

Personality and Ideological Orientation

Marxists rely on economic variables such as economic class of an individual to explain his ideological orientation.

Individual personality is largely moulded by family dynamics [events in family from one's childhood to adulthood], cultural forces, work experiences, and educational experiences. Personality differences have a significant bearing on political attitudes and behaviour. According to modern psychologists, there are five major personality traits (the Big Five) - agreeableness, openness to experience, emotional stability (or alternatively its inverse, neuroticism), conscientiousness, and extraversion. These are also known as dispositional personality traits and are used to explain an individual's ideological orientation.

Social psychology uses the SR mechanism model to explain political attitudes and behaviour. According to this view, political attitudes are characteristic adaptations that are the product of essential dispositional traits and environmental factors. McCrae and Costa describe characteristic adaptations as "acquired skills, habits, attitudes, and relationships that result from the interaction of individual and environment". In this framework, political issues and ideological labels are "stimuli"[stimuli come from environment] to which the Big Five traits shape responses. The meaning of these stimuli is shaped by environmental factors such as political context.

Extraversion implies an energetic approach to the social and material world and includes traits such as sociability, activity, assertiveness, and positive emotionality. Agreeableness refers to a pro social and community orientation toward others and includes traits such as altruism, tender-mindedness, trust, and modesty. Conscientiousness describes socially prescribed impulse control that facilitates task and goal-directed behaviour, such as thinking before acting, delaying gratification, following norms and rules, and planning, organizing, and prioritizing tasks. Emotional Stability describes even-temperedness and contrasts with negative emotionality, such as feeling anxious, nervous, sad, and tense. Openness to Experience (versus closed-mindedness) describes the breadth, depth, originality, and complexity of an individual's mental and experiential life. Social psychologists explained the relationship of the Big Five psychological traits to an individual's ideological preferences.

Personality-related Terms

- Temperament : Biologically based characteristic way of reacting.
- Trait : Stable, persistent and specific way of behaving.
- Disposition : Tendency of a person to react to a given situation in a particular way.
- Character : The overall pattern of regularly occurring behaviour.
- Habit : Over-learned modes of behaving.
- Values : Goals and ideals that are considered important and worthwhile to achieve.

Persuading People to Change Attitudes

In order to be effective persuaders, we must first get people's attention, then send an effective message to them, and then ensure that they process the message in the way we would like them to. Furthermore, to accomplish these goals, persuaders must take into consideration the cognitive, affective, and behavioural aspects of their methods. Persuaders also must understand how the communication they are presenting relates to the message recipient–his or her motivations, desires, and goals.

People process the message – like advertisements – in two ways. Spontaneous attitude change occurs as a direct or affective response to the message, whereas thoughtful attitude change is based on our cognitive elaboration of the message. The messages that we deliver may be processed in two ways: spontaneously or thoughtfully. Other terms for 'spontaneously' are 'peripherally 'or' heuristically. Other terms for 'thoughtfully' are 'centrally 'and systematically'.

(a) Spontaneous Message Processing

Spontaneous processing is direct, quick, and often involves affective responses to the message. We may simply accept the message without thinking about it very much. In these cases, we engage in spontaneous message processing, in which we accept a persuasion attempt because we focus on whatever is most obvious or enjoyable without much attention to the message itself.

(b) Thoughtful Message Processing

Thoughtful processing, on the other hand, is more controlled and involves a more careful cognitive elaboration of the meaning of the message.

The route that we take when we process a communication is important in determining whether or not a particular message changes our attitudes.

Political Attitudes

In simple terms, political attitudes can be defined as relatively stable views, either favourable or unfavourable, which individuals or groups have about events, movements, policies and issues in the public sphere. These targets towards which attitudes are directed are described in literature as "attitude objects."

Political Spectrum

Political attitudes are best understood based on the idea of political spectrum. Political spectrum is a graphic, or more specifically, a straight line along which political positions are shown from left to right. These positions are radical, liberal, moderate, conservative and reactionary. These terms are generic descriptions of political attitudes. They also refer to specific ideologies.

Positive Thinking

"The power of positive thinking" is the idea that thinking positively helps people meet their goals and keeps them healthy, happy, and able to effectively cope with the negative events that they experience. It turns out that positive thinking really works. People who think positively about their future, who believe that they can control future outcomes, and who are willing to open up and share with others, are healthier people.

The power of positive thinking appears in many beneficial ways.. Some researchers have focused on optimism, a general tendency to expect positive outcomes, and have found that optimists are happier and have less stress. Others have focused on self-efficacy, the belief in our ability to carry out actions that produce desired outcomes. People with high self-efficacy respond to environmental and other threats in an active, constructive way–by getting information, talking to friends, and attempting to face and reduce the difficulties they are experiencing. These people, too, are better able to ward off their stresses in comparison with people with less self-efficacy. It helps in part because it leads us to perceive that we can control the potential stressors that may affect us. Workers who have control over their work environment (e.g., by being able to move furniture and control distractions) experience less stress, as do patients in nursing homes who are able to choose their everyday activities.

Practical Imperative

This is a name for Kant's principle that human beings should always be treated as ends in themselves and never as instruments for any other supposedly higher ends

Predestination

Predestination is determinism as formulated in a religious context. It says that God sees the future and has preordained it to follow certain course which human beings can in no way influence.

Pride

Pride is excessive love of self so much so that one develops contempt for others. This goes against the brotherhood of humanity which all religions preach. Besides, pride can be harmful, as indicated in the saying, 'pride goes before a fall

Prima Facie Duty

W. D. Ross coined this term. It says that some duties and obligations have priority over others. Thus, Ross believed that avoiding doing harm to others is more important than trying to do good.

Professional Codes of Conduct

These are regulations which are voluntarily adopted by members of various professions and occupations. They define the standard practices which all members follow to ensure uniformity and acceptable quality of service which maintains their reputation and credibility. For example, various professionals such as nurses, doctors, engineers, accountants, auditors and lawyers have professional codes. Such standards, also known as professional standards, are also prescribed by regulatory agencies for some professions.

Professional Ethics

Professional ethics cover the personal and job-related standards of behaviour expected of professionals. Professionals possess and use specialist knowledge and skill. The manner of using such knowledge while providing a service to the public is considered a moral issue and is termed as professional ethics. Professionals can make informed judgments in various situations based on their skills. The general public is unable to make such decisions for want of relevant training.

Promise

Promise or vow is to solemnly state that one will do or not do a thing. It is a basic moral maxim. Breach of promise is to violate such statement. Contract is a legal concept which in principle is analogous to a promise.

Prudence

The dictionary meaning of prudence is discretion, cautiousness, care, forethought or good sense. Prudent individuals avoid rashness and recklessness and tend to be wary of needless risk taking. They tend to be conventional and stick to the well-trodden path. They may not be adventurous, and instead seek safety and comfort. Mere calculating prudence or a desire for social conformity should not be the basis of morality. A prudent individual may simply observe the external forms of religion without putting his heart into it. Aristotle, however, considered prudence as eminently desirable practical wisdom. It is a habit of intellectual perception that enables the virtuous man to discover the golden mean of moral virtue. Prudence in the sense of moderation and practical wisdom is a highly desirable virtue in civil servants.

Public Accounts Committee (PAC)

The Public Accounts Committee satisfies itself that the moneys (shown in the accounts) were used legally on the service or purpose to which they were applied; that the expenditure was authorized; and that re-appropriation (i.e. whether reallocation of funds from one programme or budget head to another programme or budget head) was appropriate. The PAC also examines the statement of accounts of autonomous and semi-autonomous bodies, the audit of which is conducted by the CAG.

Public Sphere

Public sphere is the arena in which the policies and actions of political parties, government and civil society are formulated and enacted. This concept of public sphere applies best to open democratic societies; it is inapplicable to states in which oligarchies and coteries hold the levers of power.

Radicalism

"Radical" refers to individuals, parties, and movements that seek to drastically alter any existing practice, institution, or social system. As radicals are highly dissatisfied with the society, they want immediate and revolutionary changes. Extreme leftists challenge the most cherished values and assumptions of society. They reject the institutions of the establishment, and seek a more humane, egalitarian, and idealistic social and political system. Many radicals espouse violence.

Realism

Realists doubt the relevance of morality to international politics. This usually leads them to the following conclusions: there is no place for morality in international relations; morality and successful conduct of international relations of a nation are incompatible; morality of States is different from customary morality; and morality, if any, is merely used instrumentally to justify states' conduct.

Regularity Audit (Financial)

In regularity (financial) audit and in other types of audit when applicable, auditors should analyse the financial statements to establish whether acceptable accounting standards for financial reporting and disclosure are complied with.

Related Party Transactions

Related transactions are those in which board directors or their immediate family members have a personal financial interest. These transactions place them in conflict of interest situations. Their gain may depend on company's loss. It is a cardinal principle that they should keep a safe distance from such transactions.

Reward

Reward is given or received by someone for good behaviour. Rewards are commonly based on merit, desert or what people deserve, or ability. Reward serves as incentive to morality while punishment serves as a deterrent to bad behaviour.

Right

Right has two meanings. First, it means what is the correct action for a moral agent in a given situation. Secondly, it means what is due to a person under law, morality, or tradition. Ownership of property and freedom of expression are rights.

Sanction

Sanction means an authoritative permission or approval to do something. It could include prohibitions. Religious and social sanctions are often mentioned in ethical discussions.

Secretarial Audit

The purpose of this audit is to ensure that the company duly complies with all the legal requirements as specified in the Companies Act and other relevant laws. Every listed company and/or specified Company has to attach to its Board's report to share holders a secretarial audit report given by a company secretary in practice. The task of a company secretary who heads its secretariat is to ensure that the company duly complies with all the legal requirements as specified in the Companies Act and other relevant laws.

Self-Awareness

Self-awareness indicates how far we are currently fixing our attention on our own self-concept. The self-concept becomes highly accessible to us when we think that others are observing and judging us. In that situation, we experience the publicly induced self-awareness known as self- consciousness. We feel anxious and embarrassed mainly because the self-concept becomes highly accessible, and such feelings serve as a signal to monitor and perhaps change our behaviour. People are more likely to act morally when they are self-aware. This implies that while trying to study harder, or engage in other difficult behaviours, one should try to focus on oneself and the importance of the goals one is pursuing.

Further, people who lose their self-awareness are likely to violate acceptable social norms. When people are in large crowds, such as a mass demonstration or a riot, they may become so much a part of the group that they lose their individual self-awareness and experience deindividuation–the loss of self-awareness and individual accountability in groups. They are more prone to violent actions.

Self-Complexity

Our self-concept is a rich and complex social representation. Besides thoughts about who we are right now, self-concept includes thoughts about our past self–our experiences, accomplishments, and failures–and about our future self–our hopes, plans, goals, and possibilities. The self-concept also includes thoughts about our relationships with others. Although every human being has a complex self-concept, there are nevertheless individual differences in self-complexity. Some selves are more complex than others, and such individual differences affect people's behaviour and how they think about themselves. For example, a woman's self-concept could include social identities of student, wife, daughter, economics graduate, and tennis player with a wide variety of life experiences. She has high self-complexity. In comparision, someone who sees himself only as a student or as a member of the hockey team and who has had a relatively narrow range of life experiences would have low self-complexity. People with more complex self-concepts have been found to have lower levels of stress and illness and more positive and less negative reactions to events that they experience. They may be better able to adjust to such adverse events by turning to other interests.

Self-Concept

The self-concept is a cognitive representation that contains knowledge about us, including our beliefs about our personality traits, physical characteristics, abilities, values, goals, and roles, as well as our sense of individuality. During childhood and adolescence, the self-concept becomes more abstract and complex. It is organized into many cognitive aspects, known as self-schemas. The self-schemas cover our appearance, skills and many other aspects. Adults have many self-schemas, and can analyse their thoughts, feelings, and behaviours, and realise that these differ from those of others. At times, having a sense of self may seem unpleasant–as when we are unhappy our looks, actions, or relationships with others. Bu our thoughts about our past and likely future are adaptive in that we can modify our behaviour in the light of our missteps and plan for future activities.

Although each individual has a unique self-concept, it contains common items. Three aspects go into the self-concept. One's physical characteristics form an important part. component of the self-concept. A second characteristic reflects our memberships in the social groups we belong to and our social identity .Finally, personality traits–the specific and stable personality characteristics of an individual–are part of his/her self-concept.

Self-Realisation

Many writers maintain that the moral end of a human being must consist in some form of self-realisation i.e. in some form of the development of character. In short, man's end ought to be called perfection than happiness. In this view, moral life is, in its very essence, a growth or development. Hindu, Buddhist and Jain religious thought also emphasizes the idea of self-realization culminating in salvation, enlightenment or Nirvana..

We can find other roots of this view. St. Thomas Aquinas, who fully formulated the Christian moral philosophy, borrowed heavily from Aristotle's thought. Like Aristotle, he believed that everything in nature, every created thing, has its own good and its own perfection and strives towards that perfection. The good of man consists in the perfection of his rational or spiritual nature, and ultimately in the beatific vision of God from whom his being and reason are derived.

Philosophers such as Leibnitz and Spinoza subscribed to this conception of the moral life. Despite his formalism, Kant's moral philosophy, taken as a whole, contains an element of perfectionism, and Hegel has expressed it most completely for modern times. English idealistic philosophers such as T. H. Green, F. H. Bradley, Bernard Bosanquet and others also held this moral view. They were influenced by classic Greek thought and Christian philosophy, and opposed the hedonism and utilitarianism of the English empirical school.

Self-Regulation

We need to learn how to control our emotions and to prevent our emotions from letting our behaviour get out of control. The process of setting goals and using our cognitive and affective capacities to reach those goals is known as self-regulation, and a good part of self-regulation involves regulating our emotions. To be the best people that we possibly can, we have to work hard at it. Succeeding at school, at work, and in our relationships with others takes a lot of effort. When we are successful at self-regulation, we are able to move toward or meet the goals that we set for ourselves. When we fail at self-regulation, we are not able to meet those goals. People who are better able to regulate their behaviours and emotions are more successful in their personal and social encounters and thus self-regulation is a skill we should seek to master.

Sex Selective Abortions

Indian couples have a strong preference for a male child. This led to misuse of the provisions of MTP Act for conducting abortions of female foetuses. Subsequently, new technologies such as sonography made sex detection easier, and increased sex-selective abortions. To control these abortions, the Pre-natal Diagnostic Techniques (PNDT) Act, was passed in 1994. It prohibits sex determination tests on fetus.

Situation Ethics

Situation ethics is the doctrine that particular judgements are fundamental to ethical conduct. Particular judgements in this view are contrasted with general moral principles or maxims. For example, one may take pity on a famished beggar and give him money for food. This action is based simply on considerations connected with finding a famished beggar. One may also view the act as following from the general principle that those in distress should be helped. Situation ethics says that such general principles are irrelevant or of no use. It may also maintain that general moral principles are inductive generalizations based on observing several similar individual occurrences. Thus the generalization, 'barking dogs do not bite' may be an inductive generalization based on observing many barking dogs.

Sleeper Effect

People are generally aware that communicators may deliver messages that are inaccurate or misleading, and tend to discount messages that come from untrustworthy sources. But there is one interesting situation in which people may be fooled by communicators. This occurs when a message is presented by someone that people think is untrustworthy. On first hearing that person's communication, people discount it and it therefore has little influence on their opinions. However, over time there is a tendency to remember the content of a communication to a greater extent than the source of the communication. As a result, people may forget over time to discount the remembered message. This attitude change that occurs over time is known as the sleeper effect.

Social Audit

While financial audit is conducted by qualified accountants and auditors, social audit is done through people's participation. It is particularly useful in ascertaining the true state of affairs about programmes which benefit large groups such as local public works, distribution of welfare payments, and procurement of products and services for government and delivery of services to people. Provisions for social audit should be made a part of the operational guidelines of all such schemes. It has already been adopted in many schemes.

Social Cleavage Model

Sociologists apply the notion (idea) of primary social groups to explain ideologies. Social groups are based on common group interests or seen as a reflection of social cleavages. In this perspective, cleavage is defined as social division, accompanied by specific group identities and attitudes (specific group ideology), and politicization of the division by specific political parties.

Sophists

Sophists are ancient Greek philosophers. They were peripatetic teachers who travelled from one city to another and gave lectures. Sophists primarily taught rhetoric (writing skills. oratory and grammar), argumentation and ethics. Sophists taught their students how to succeed in their professional career and practical life. Arguing cases in law courts and swaying mobs in political meetings were among the skills sophists taught. In the process, sophists taught students demagogic skills and how to win arguments by hook or crook. They earned the scorn of philosophers who believed that inquiries and arguments should aim at reaching truth. The term 'sophism' which means a clever but false argument is derived from the supposed practices of sophists. Sophists were also the first to advocate moral relativism. The approach of Socrates who sought objective definitions of ethical terms is a response to moral relativism. The relativism of sophists can be traced to differences in laws and governing practices among city states.

Sovereignty

Political theorists commonly use sovereignty in three contexts. From an international legal perspective it refers to the terms of the reciprocal recognition that states accord one another in the international political order. In its reference to domestic polity of a state, it means the ultimate source of legal or constitutional authority. Empirically, it means effective capacity to exercise unilateral control over various fields of activity and to formulate policies unilaterally.

Standards or Norms

Standards or norms are defined as principles of right action binding upon members of a group and serving to guide, control, or regulate proper and acceptable behaviour. Standards and norms are the codification of group, organizational, community, or governmental values. Laws, regulations, codes of ethics, and rules—all these are typical examples of standards and norms.

(H. George Frederickson & Jeremy Davis Walling, Research and Knowledge in Administrative Ethics)

State

The state has a narrower meaning referring to the constitutional arrangements which determine how a nation is governed. Or 'state' refers to the machinery of government which organizes life in a given territory. Whereas governments come and go, state is an enduring entity and permanent, barring cataclysmal changes.

Stealing

Stealing or theft or pilfering is both a moral and legal offence. It means taking away someone else's property or belongings secretively without their knowledge or permission.

Stem Cells

A stem cell is a unique type of cell with remarkable qualities. It can differentiate into other types of functional cells like nerve cells or skin cells. It can renew itself, and also form other cells. However, most stem cells reside in particular organs and tissues, and produce a limited range of cells. Thus, bone marrow cells only produce blood cells. These are known as adult stem cells.

Embryonic stem (ES) cells are much more potent. They can produce any other type of cell–blood, brain, intestine, muscles, bone and skin. Hence, they are known as pluripotent. They can be isolated from embryo, and grown in Petri dishes in laboratory. They can grow continuously in culture.

Stem Cell Research

This is research conducted based on cells taken either from human beings or human embryos.

Strength of Attitudes

The importance of an attitude, as assessed by how quickly it comes to mind, is known as attitude strength. Some of our attitudes are strong attitudes, in the sense that we find them important, hold them with confidence, do not change them very much, and use them frequently to guide our actions. These strong attitudes often operate without people being consciously aware of them. Strong attitudes are attitudes that are more cognitively accessible–they come to mind quickly, regularly, and easily. We can easily measure attitude strength by assessing how quickly our attitudes are activated when we are exposed to the attitude object. If we can state our attitude quickly, without much thought, then it is a strong one. If we are unsure about our attitude and need to think about it for a while before stating our opinion, the attitude is weak. Attitudes become stronger when we have direct positive or negative experiences with the attitude object. Other attitudes are weaker and have little influence on our actions.

Summum Bonum

Plato and Aristotle introduced this concept. It is the highest good, especially as the ultimate goal according to which values and priorities are established in an ethical system. Individual actions of men aim at particular ends. The particular ends are in turn means for achieving other ends. However, this means-ends series finds closure in a final or ultimate end which has no reference to any other end. This ultimate value or end is summum bonum. Aristotle identified it with serene philosophical contemplation.

Aquinas took from Aristotle this notion of an ultimate end, or goal–a summum bonum–at which all human action is directed; and, like Aristotle, he conceived of this end as necessarily connected with happiness. This conception was Christianized, however, by the idea that happiness is to be found in the love of God.

(Partly from Encyclopaedia Britannica)

Surrogacy

Surrogacy means a practice whereby one woman bears and gives birth to a child for an intending (mainly infertile) couple with the intention of handing over such child to the intending couple after the birth. The Surrogacy regulation Bill (which union cabinet recently approved) makes a distinction between altruistic and commercial surrogacy. In altruistic surrogacy, no monetary incentives of whatever nature (other than medical insurance and expenses) are given to the surrogate mother or her dependents or her representative. Commercial surrogacy refers to commercialisation either in whole or part of surrogacy services or procedures. Commercialization may cover selling or buying of human embryo or trading in the sale or purchase of human embryo or gametes or selling or buying or trading the services of surrogate motherhood by giving incentives in cash or kind, to the surrogate mother or her dependents or her representative.

System of Human Values

Human moral values can be arranged in a hierarchy from the lower to the higher.

THE TABLE OF VALUES (ascending order)

I. Bodily Values

II. Economic Values

III. Values of Recreation

IV. Values of Association

V. Character Values

VI. Aesthetic Values

VII. Intellectual Values

VIII. Religious Values

The values in this table of values fall into three distinct groups.

The bodily, economic and recreation values go together since they all involve the satisfaction of wants connected with what we may call the bodily self. The character values and the values of association form a distinct group because they are connected with the social self and arise only in relation of the self to others. The aesthetic, intellectual and religious values also go together. They are no doubt related to the bodily and social self, and conditioned by them. But these values arise only in some functioning of the self that goes beyond man's bodily and social self.

The values arise from certain dispositions or tendencies which may be taken as fundamental springs of action. The dispositions can be instincts or cultivated habits. There are certain dispositions or tendencies which, whether innate or acquired, are fundamental and universal enough to be made the basis of human values. All these values correspond to fundamental instinctive needs or wants of men.

Self-realisation requires the satisfaction of all these tendencies, or the realisation of all these values. It is only an ideal, in the sense that it describes only a direction in which man's conscious activity may be directed. There is no such thing as total self-realisation, realisation of the self all at once, or in one act. Life is a process.

Systemic Reforms

Government procedures or methods of work often have an inbuilt scope for corrupt operations. The operating environment is marked by monopolistic structures, opaque procedures, discretionary decision-making, dilatory processes and lack of accountability to public. Further, government tends to allocate public or natural resources at much below their market price. This environment reduces the chances of speedy detection of malfeasance and creates incentives for collusive corruption. Systemic reforms can follow four main routes: deregulation and reducing government controls; creating competition by providing alternative service providers; speeding up work and increasing transparency through use of ICT; and streamlining work procedures.

Stoicism

Stoicism is a strict, harsh, and ascetic ethical doctrine. Still, stoics like other ancient Greek moral schools, consider happiness as the end or goal of life. Stoic view of happiness or good consists in living according to nature. The good is beneficial in all circumstances. Stoics called things sometimes good and sometimes bad, like wealth, as 'indifferent'. The things always good are virtues like moderation, prudence, courage and justice. Men prefer these things with value---wealth, health and honour--- to their opposites---poverty, sickness and dishonour. However, these things of value, may at times militate against good as such, and should be then eschewed.

Living well involves choosing unqualified good, and things of value consistent with good. Men may face misfortunes; things of value like wealth and honour may elude them. Even then, men can be happy by adopting virtues like courage, prudence and moderation. In this regard, Stoics distinguish between things within our control---appetites, desires and fears, and things beyond our control such as illness and misfortunes. Adverse events outside our control agitate our passions. We need to endure the troubling passions bravely. We should not allow them to overpower us, but be apathetic or indifferent to them. We should bear with fortitude what are beyond our control such as illness and misfortunes. This is the Stoic recipe for dealing with troubling external circumstances. Happiness or at least putting up with adversity, depends on our attitudes which our reason can regulate. Acceptance of the inevitable is freedom; it is the 'price paid for a quiet mind'.

Stoicism argues that mental disquiet ultimately arises not from outward events but the way they affect our minds, which we can control. One should be indifferent to what one cannot control, and at the same time rationally govern one's emotions. Happiness consists in not feeling oppressed by fears and anxieties, whether real or imaginary or anticipated, and in not striving for things one cannot achieve or gain.

Stoics believed that all men are endowed with reason, and therefore make up a single community. Stoics are the first to propound the idea of cosmopolitanism.

Subjective

'Subjective' means to emanate from or traceable to or related to (individual) human mind and not to external world. Thus, human feelings and emotions are subjective. It is the opposite of objective.

Teleology (See consequentialism)

Teleological or End-based Ethics (from teleology or end-based)

Some moral standards propose that the actions of moral agents should serve harmonious social ends, or lead to maximum social welfare. Such standards are in fact saying that an action should be judged based on the end or objective which it seeks. This type of moral justification of an act based on the end which the moral agent has in view is called teleological. In modern times, it is called consequentialist. The classic example of teleological ethics is utilitarianism. Deontology on the other hand holds that moral agents should obey their duty or moral commands without worrying about the likely consequences.

Temperance

Temperance is a virtue which brings to bear the judgement of reason on human cravings for food, drink and sex. Temperance promotes self-control and checks other rash impulses like anger. Men naturally tend to overindulge in matters which delight them. By cultivating the habit of temperance, one can avoid the harm which excessive indulgence causes.

Terrorism

Terrorism is defined in many ways. Its main attributes are the following:

- A type of violence harming people and damaging property
- Specific use of violence for achieving social and political ends
- Creating great fear, alarm and a sense of panic among people
- Reliance on random or arbitrary use of violence
- Targeting innocent people or non-combatants

Another definition of terrorism which Caleb Carr gave is: "... the contemporary name given to, and the modern permutation of, warfare deliberately waged against civilians with the purpose of destroying their will to support either leaders or policies that agents of such violence find objectionable." It is noteworthy that terrorism is warfare and aims at undermining peoples' will and belief in their way of living.

The Freedom of The Will

There is an age old ethical debate in on whether men are free or dependent beings. Some philosophers argued that real human freedom does not exist, since men are determined by circumstances. Others considered this as a "lazy sophism" or an excuse to avoid moral effort.

Moral judgement maintains that we ought to act in one way rather than in another, that one manner of action is good or right, and another bad or evil. As Kant remarked, there would be no meaning in an 'ought' if it were not accompanied by a 'can' – i.e., if men have no freedom or ability to act. But ability or habit needed for moral action cannot be instantaneously generated. The 'can' may not be an immediate possibility. A man ought to be wise, for instance; but wisdom is a quality that can only be gradually developed. Thus, virtues have to be cultivated over time.

Now if a man's will be absolutely determined by his circumstances, it would be strictly impossible for him to become anything but that which he does become. Moral imperatives ('ought to') would cease to have any meaning. If the moral imperative is to operate, human will must in some sense be free.

The Golden Rule

The Golden rule is a principle common to many religions. It says "We must treat others as we wish others to treat us". Many writers assert that the golden rule forms the essence of any morality. It is an ethic of equity. If there are two individuals X and Y, their conduct towards each other should be governed by identical principles. Human beings like to be treated by others with kindness and consideration. Therefore, according to the Golden Rule, each will treat the other kindly. The Golden Rule will automatically lead to ethical behaviour. If people adopt the golden rule, they need not refer to any elaborate moral codes.

The MODE Model

This model depicts how general attitudes of people affect their evaluations of the attitude object. General attitudes introduce bias in perceiving and judging information relevant to the attitude object. The bias depends on how strong or weak the general attitude is. If the general attitude is strong, the bias will be high. If it is weak, bias will be low.

The Nine Types of Intelligence

1. Naturalist Intelligence (Nature Smart)

   This refers to the human ability to discriminate among living things (plants, animals) as well as sensitivity to other features of the natural world (clouds, rock configurations). This ability was clearly of value in our evolutionary past as hunters, gatherers, and farmers; it continues to be central in such roles as botanist or chef. Present day consumer society exploits the naturalist intelligence by creating discriminating tastes among cars, dresses, shoes, different types of makeup, and the like.

2. Musical Intelligence ("Musical Smart"):

   Musical intelligence is the capacity to follow musical qualities like pitch, rhythm, timbre, and tone. Composers, conductors, musicians, vocalists, and sensitive listeners are endowed with these qualities. Many thinkers have commented on the link between music and the emotions, and between mathematical and musical aptitudes.

3. Logical-Mathematical Intelligence (Number/Reasoning Smart):

   Logical-mathematical intelligence denotes skills of calculation, quantification and problem solving. It involves the ability to visualize relationships and connections and to use abstract, symbolic thought. It is also reflected in sequential reasoning as well as in inductive and deductive thinking. Logical intelligence is associated with mathematicians, physical scientists, statisticians and computer programmers.

4. Existential Intelligence:

This indicates sensitivity and capacity to tackle deep questions about human existence, such as the what life means, why do we die, and how did we get here and why we are born on earth. In this concept, Martin Gardner is referring to philosophical, theological and metaphysical interests of people. Adi Sankara, Plato, Pascal, Spinoza and Kant will fall in this category.

5. Interpersonal Intelligence (People Smart):

Interpersonal intelligence is the ability to understand and interact effectively with others. It involves effective verbal and nonverbal communication, the ability to appreciate differences among people, awareness of the moods and temperaments of others, and the capacity for viewing matters from multiple perspectives. These skills are usually present in teachers, social workers, actors, and politicians.

6. Bodily-Kinesthetic Intelligence (Body Smart):

This involves the ability to manipulate objects and use various bodily skills. It includes a sense of timing and fine tuning skills through mind-body coordination. These skills are commonly found among athletes, dancers, surgeons, and various categories of craftsmen.

7. Linguistic Intelligence (Word Smart):

These skills relate to verbal thinking and linguistic usages for expressing complex and difficult involved ideas. This forms the essence of written communication skills. It enables one to express and communicate ideas clearly and coherently. Masters of prose and poetry use this intelligence to create appropriate ambience in fiction, drama and verse.

8. Intra-personal Intelligence (Self Smart):

Intra-personal intelligence signifies self-understanding – one's personality, abilities, motives and aptitudes. By understanding our thoughts and feelings we can plan and direct our life. This skill also involves understanding the human predicament or the general situation of man in society and nature, and the common course of man's life. Psychologists, spiritual leaders, philosophers and great literary artists possess this type of intelligence.

9. Spatial Intelligence (Picture Smart):

Spatial intelligence refers to skills in visualizing three dimensional entities. It involves imaginative faculty and configuration of things in three dimensional spaces. The specific skills which fall into this category include: mental imagery, spatial reasoning, image manipulation and graphic and artistic skills. Sailors, pilots, sculptors, painters, and architects all have these skills.

The Principle of Beneficence

William Frankena defines beneficence as the obligation to do good and prevent harm. Beneficence implies four things.

1. One ought not to inflict harm or evil. (What is bad)
2. One ought to prevent harm or evil.
3. One ought to remove evil.
4. One ought to promote or do good.

Morality strictly prohibits doing harm to anyone. However, helping others, except when they are in dire need or extreme difficulty (covered in 3), may not be obligatory though desirable.

(William Frankena, Ethics)

The Theory of Persuasion

This theory posits that attitudes of people on any subject can be changed by suitably communicating appropriate information to them. Many aspects are relevant in trying to persuade people to change their attitude on any subject. These are:

(i) object of the attitude i.e. thing, person, group or idea towards which an attitude is directed;

(ii) the message or information;

(iii) the manner in which it is delivered;

(iv) the messenger and

(v) the target audience i.e., individuals whose attitudes need change.

The Theory of Planned Behaviour

Although there is generally consistency between attitudes and behaviour of people, the relationship is stronger in certain situations, for certain people, and for certain attitudes. The theory of planned behaviour outlines many of the important variables that affect the attitude-behaviour relationship (summarized in the list that follows).

- When attitudes are strong, rather than weak
- When we have a strong intention to perform the behaviour
- When the attitude and the behaviour both occur in similar social situations
- When the same components of the attitude (either affect or cognition) are accessible
- When the attitudes are measured at a specific, rather than a general, level
- For low self-monitors (rather than for high self-monitors)

The above factors determine whether attitudes lead to corresponding behaviours.

The Three Selves of Man

From moral point of view, man's rational self alone counts as his real self. Man's genuine freedom consists in acting from this rational self. The man who acts irrationally is said to be "enslaved by his passions." He is thus not really free.

There can be said to be three selves in every man. One is the self, as revealed in momentary impulses which men cannot subdue. The second is the man's permanent character which habitually guides his actions. The third is the true or rational self which expresses what is best in man. These ideas find expression in modern terms in Freud's concepts id, ego and superego.

Topics discussed in Ethics

Ethical discussions fall broadly into four categories. First, sociology, anthropology and history give factual or descriptive accounts of morals in existing and past societies. These are observational or neutral studies of societies and not normative ethical discussions.

Secondly, Ethics discusses what is good, right, or obligatory. Such discussions recommend moral maxims like 'Wealth should be equitably distributed in society' and 'women should have equal rights with men'. Such maxims are supported with reasoned arguments. Ethical discussions also cover what moral agents ought to do in a given situation based on applicable ethical criteria.

Thirdly, some ethical discussions may not cover substantial questions like what moral principles an individual or society should adopt or how one should lead one's life. Thus, many philosophers in early twentieth century concentrated only on the language, terminology or concepts used in ethics. They discussed or interpreted the meanings of moral terms based on how they are used by common people in ordinary language or by past or contemporary philosophers in their writings. Such discussions cover questions like—What is the meaning of good and right? What are the logical implications of act utilitarianism? And how can moral judgements be justified if at all? This approach is known as meta ethics and the questions it raises are called second-order questions since they are not primarily moral.

There is another related way of classifying the subject matter of ethics.

1. Ethical or moral psychology which discusses a moral agent's desires, drives and dispositions.
2. Sociology of morals or a factual objective study of prevailing morals in a society
3. Theories of moral standard such as utilitarianism or deontology or virtue ethics
4. Application of ethics in individual life, social life, public administration and in various professions.

Transparency

Transparency signifies openness and accountability of administration. An organization is transparent when its decision-making and mode of working is open to public and media scrutiny and public discussion. A transparent system of administration encourages public participation in government's decision-making processes. It is especially useful in promoting grass root level democracy. RTI Act is the foremost measure that government took for promoting transparency in administration.

Triage

Triage in medicine usually refers to a disastrous situation in which doctors are forced to decide whom to treat first or in what order of priority based on chances of survival of the injured victims. Such situations may arise during wars, terrorist attacks, or natural calamities.

Truth-telling

Veracity or telling the truth is an intrinsic virtue, and is not based on rights of others or on any external circumstances. It is fit and proper that one should state facts, opinions and truths to the best of his knowledge without mixing any falsehoods. Aristotle says that: "to say of what is that it is, and of what is not that it is not, is true." Romans similarly spoke of Veritas as a factual representation of events. Social existence of human beings depends on truth telling. There are many synonyms of truth such as veracity, fact, reality, integrity, honesty, candour, fidelity and honesty. Keeping one's promise is also part of truthfulness. Truthfulness also implies that a moral agent should never betray trust placed in him.

Two Types of Moral Judgements

In some of our moral judgements we say that a certain action or kind of action is morally right, wrong, obligatory, or ought or ought not to be done. In others, we talk not about action or kind of action, but about persons, motives, intentions, character traits and the like. We may say that they are morally good, bad, virtuous, vicious, responsible, blameworthy, etc. The things talked about in these two kinds of judgement and what is said about them is different. The former judgements are called judgements of moral obligation (deontic) and the latter as judgements of moral value (aretaic). It is better to avoid expressions like 'good actions' and call them instead 'correct actions'.

Two Types of Self Awareness

Two particular types of individual differences in self-awareness have been found to be important: self-concern and other-concern. Private self-consciousness refers to the tendency to introspect about our inner thoughts and feelings. People who are high in private self-consciousness tend to think a great deal about themselves and to be attentive to their inner feelings. People who are high on private self-consciousness are likely to base their behaviour on their own inner beliefs and values–they let their inner thoughts and feelings guide their actions–and they are likely to strive to succeed in areas that demonstrate their own personal accomplishments

Public self-consciousness, in contrast, refers to the tendency to focus on our outer public image and to be particularly aware of the extent to which we are meeting the standards set by others. These are the people who check their hair in a mirror they pass and devote considerable time getting ready in the morning; they are more likely to let the opinions of others, (rather than their own opinions) guide their behaviours and are particularly concerned with making good impression on others.

Universalistic Hedonism

This is another way of describing utilitarianism.

UN Charter

UN Charter can be regarded as embodying the currently accepted code of international morality. The preamble refers to the great human misery which the First World War and the Second World War caused and to the need to end wars. It emphasises the value of human rights, and also the rights of small (and weak) nations. It highlights that all nations should abide by treaties and should observe international law.

The Charter mentions the following as requirements for achieving the aims set out in the preamble.

- An environment of peace, tolerance and good neighbourly relations
- A commitment to act together for collective or international security
- Adoption of principle and institutions for avoiding use of armed forces

The main purpose of UN is to maintain international peace and security. This purpose leads to two instrumental objectives to act collectively to prevent and remove threats to peace; and to suppress acts of aggression or other breaches of peace. An allied purpose is to settle peacefully, and in accordance with the principles of justice and international law, international disputes or situations which can disrupt peace.

Utilitarianism (doctrine)

Utilitarianism recommends that an act or application of rule by a moral agent should seek to maximize the net balance of good over evil (the "greatest good") for as many members of the society as possible (the "greatest number"). Utilitarianism requires measuring and aggregating (at least in rough quantity) the relative benefits and burdens to an entire community of people of some act or rule. Consequences may be judged as good or bad from the individual moral agent's perspective or on the basis of welfare or happiness or utility. (Gerald M. Pops, A Teleological Approach to Administrative Ethics)

Bentham, who propounded Utilitarianism, believed that legislators and common people have an obligation to promote general happiness. This obligation is 'paramount to and inclusive of every other'. Bentham used 'utility' to mean '[whatever] tends to benefit, advantage, good, or happiness'. He considered these four words as having the same meaning.

Utilitarianism is a consequentialist theory of morality. It attaches moral values only to the [good] consequences of actions. It ignores the intentions of the moral agents and/or their personal character. Bentham valued each individual's happiness equally. No individual or group has any privileged status in the matter of happiness. This implies that everyone has to impartially pursue the greatest happiness of the greatest number.

Utilitarianism, Act

Utilitarianism recommends that people should seek the greatest happiness of the greatest number. Act utilitarianism says that every decision and action of an individual should be based on this aim. This prescription creates two problems. First, a moral agent has to undertake, every time he takes a decision or performs an action, an impracticable burden of evaluating its effect on the happiness and unhappiness of all the people it impacts. Secondly, act utilitarianism leads to odd conclusions; actions that harm a few but benefit many become morally permissible. Thus, researchers may experiment with a dangerous drug on a few patients, if as a result, they can develop a safe drug for treating a widely prevalent disease afflicting many people.

Utilitarianism, Rule

Rule utilitarianism prescribes that a moral agent should be guided in his behaviour by such rules as tend to promote the greatest happiness of the greatest number. The moral agent is not required to apply the utilitarian criterion to every time he takes an action or makes a decision. He should rather adopt rules of behaviour, which common experience shows, lead to maximum happiness in society. Rule utilitarianism frees people from the burden of scrutinizing each and every one of their moral actions and decisions. It avoids a criticism against act utilitarianism that it may sacrifice the interests of small social groups in the name of greater social welfare.

Values

According to William Frankena, "values" in the narrower sense refer to that which is considered good, desirable or worthwhile, and in the broader sense, to "all kinds of rightness, obligation, virtues, beauty, truth, and holiness". The anthropologist Clyde Kluckhohn says: "A value is a conception, explicit or implicit, distinctive of an individual or characteristic of a group, of the desirable which influences the selection from available modes, means, and ends of action." David Hume refers to values as the 'oughts' and 'ought nots' of the world.

According to sociologists values are not strictly individual. Thomas McCullough defines values as:

Values ... are communal. They are public in that they are standards transcending individual taste, carrying a claim to be recognised by the community. They can be discussed, analysed, ordered, and justified in a rational discourse. A meaningful discussion about values presupposes a common lifeworld, a shared cultural context within which persons respect one another and care about ideas and values as determinants of life together.

Max Weber referred to "value pluralism" and observed that ultimately the possible attitudes towards life are innumerable and irreconcilable. However, as pointed out by Durkheim, human beings in society achieve some convergence in their values through "collective sentiments and collective ideas".

(Harold F. Gortner, Values and Ethics)

There can be values in different spheres of society as shown in the table

Social	Bureaucratic	Economic*	Democratic**	Professional
Humanitarianism Security, comfort Equality External conformity Efficiency Practicality	Competence & specialization Externally established goals Impersonality in action Rationality, stability Career in organization Hierarchical obligation & accountability	Rationality Economic efficiency Measurability of values in material or monetary terms Quantifiable goals Minimum interference with market forces	Individual worth & dignity Personal achievement Minority rights Liberty, Freedom Efficacy, empowerment	Expertise Rejection of self interest in action Independent decisions Beneficence for clients Recognition, identification by community Lifetime work commitment Social obligation & self regulation within profession

*The reference to minimum market interference is derived from economic liberalism. Socialist can have different ideas.

**For a statement of these values in Indian context, refer to constitutional values in the text.

*** The table does not include the character virtues mentioned in Ethics. We have referred to them elsewhere in the text.

Vice

Vices are the opposites of virtues. Obviously, we have to shun vices; otherwise, they harm us both physically and psychologically. Once, we get into the grip of a vice, it is hard to escape. It becomes a settled habit, and we can give up the habit, if at all, with great effort of will. Hence, it is best to watch our responses and nip in the bud any bad or immoral thoughts and responses that enter our mind.

Vigilance

Vigilance is a generic term for the mechanisms and procedures followed in government organizations to curb corruption. Government agencies can adopt three broad approaches to reduce corruption. The three approaches are (i) Preventative vigilance; (ii) Punitive vigilance; and (iii) Surveillance and detection. Preventive vigilance refers to measures which are taken to reduce or eliminate the likelihood of corruption in an organization. Punitive vigilance refers to actions including award of punishment which arise after commission of acts of corruption. Surveillance vigilance refers to ongoing monitoring of vigilance cases.

Virtue

Aristotle refers to virtues as arete, a Greek word which means excellence, particularly excellence of character. Virtues are eminently desirable character traits. These include: honesty, integrity, courage, prudence, kindness, a sense of justice, and self-restraint. Each of these virtues leads to a corresponding virtuous behaviour. A virtuous person acts not out of a sense of duty or from a recognition that better consequences flow from following virtue than from violating it. He acts from a habitual or ingrained tendency to follow virtue. Aristotle considers that virtues are not innate but have to be cultivated or acquired through continuous, sustained practice.

Virtues: Intellectual and Moral

According to Aristotle, human beings possess two kinds of virtues, intellectual and moral, the former corresponding to mind, and the latter corresponding to character. Intellectual virtues fall into two categories: practical wisdom and theoretical wisdom. Theoretical wisdom is learnt from teachers. Practical wisdom is gained with age and life experiences.

Moral virtues are acquired through habit. Human beings become just by performing just acts, and similarly through practice acquire other virtues. By being compelled to acquire good habits, we shall in time, Aristotle thinks, come to find pleasure in performing good actions. By good habits Aristotle means a settled disposition to feel and act appropriately. Aristotle rejects the Socratic view that knowledge is virtue or results automatically in good behaviour. Human will is weak, and virtuous behaviour can be ensured only by strong habits acquired through constant practice.

Virtue as a Mean

In his ethical discussions, Aristotle focuses on character, because by improving it, he thought men could also cultivate their virtues. Aristotle considered that virtue represents a balance between extremes. For example, courage is the middle between one extreme of deficiency (cowardice) and the other extreme of excess (recklessness). A coward would be a warrior who flees from the battlefield and a reckless warrior would charge at fifty enemy soldiers. This doesn't mean that the golden mean is the exact arithmetical middle between extremes, but that the middle depends on the situation. There is no universal middle that would apply to every situation. Because of the difficulty the balance in certain situations can represent, constant moral improvement of the character is crucial for recognizing it. The golden mean applies only for virtues, not vices. Certain emotions and actions (hate, envy, jealousy, theft, and murder) are always wrong, regardless of their degree.

The importance of virtue aa the mean is that it re-affirms the balance needed in life. It was recognised in ancient Greek: "Nothing in Excess". This approach is very relevant to modern society which suffers from excessive wealth accumulation and consumption and neglect of education, healthy sports activities and of intellectual pursuits.

Virtue Ethics or Character Ethics

This is an approach to Ethics which regards notion of virtue (often conceived as excellence) as fundamental. Virtue ethics is primarily concerned with traits of character that are essential to human flourishing, not with the enumeration of duties. It considers that morality consists not in adhering certain principles (like hedonism), but consists in cultivating good character traits. According to virtue ethics, an ideal moral life can be led by cultivating good character.

This can be viewed as another approach to Ethics - along with deontological ethics and consequentialism. It has a closer affinity to deontological ethics in that it views morally right actions are constitutive of the end itself and are not mere instrumental means to the end.

(From Britannica Concise Encyclopaedia)

Virtue, unity of

Unity of virtue is a Socratic idea. It means that if a person has one virtue, he will have all virtues. This view, though appealing in some ways, is implausible. A brave person may be cruel; a courageous individual could be unjust; and a just person could be timid. Another logical difficulty with the idea of unity of virtue is that qualities like wisdom and temperance are not single universals. Thus, a wise father could be unwise in business dealings; a person moderate in alcohol consumption may be intemperate in eating Rosagullas.

Whistleblower

The term "whistle blowing" is a newly coined expression. It refers to an individual who makes public the illegal or dark secrets carefully hidden within an organization.

Widening The Definition of Corruption

SARC recommended widening the definition to include:

- Gross perversion of the Constitution and democratic institutions amounting to wilful violation of oath of office
- Abuse of authority unduly favouring or harming someone
- Obstruction of justice
- Squandering public money

Will

Will is mental faculty by which one deliberately chooses or decides upon a course of action. Kant believed that morality can exist only if voluntary or freely-willed actions of men are governed by laws of morality. The task of Ethics is to show that reason governs and directs the will. The will is truly autonomous when it obeys laws it rationally prescribes for itself. It then expresses the highest good there can be which is freedom. Kant adds that moral value is to be found in individuals who act not out of inclination or desires or passions but in obedience to a law prescribed by their reason.

Weakness of human will is a recurring theme in morality. Common examples are inability to resist temptations, or to follow exercise schedules, or to give up bad habits like smoking and drinking. Socrates wondered how men could do something they know is wrong. Socrates apparently failed to notice that common experience shows that people do it all the time.

Schopenhauer looks at will differently. It is a blind force of nature which expresses itself in human beings as desire, craving, yearning, and as it is seldom satisfied, causes suffering and misery. To secure release from suffering, human beings should seek release from the blind will and thralldom to desire. This view echoes Buddhist thought.

TACKLING THEORY QUESTIONS

TIPS FOR TACKLING THEORY QUESTIONS

Pattern of GS IV question paper

Let us begin with the structure of the GS question paper IV. It now seems to have acquired a stable format.

- **Time :**3 hours
- **Marks :** 250
- **Parts :** 2 (A & B)
- Types and number of questions:

  Part A : Theory 8 Questions

  Part B : Case Studies 6 Questions (Questions suggest 3-4 answer choices; and the examinee has to evaluate them to generate and discuss possible options.)

- *Length of answers*

  Part A : approximately 2000 words (5 × 300 plus 3 × 150)

  Part B : approximately 1500 words

Students should absorb this information, since it helps in adopting a proper method of examination preparation.

Common Errors in Students' Answers

Students make the following errors while answering questions.

- They do not answer questions as they are worded. They cover the general area of the question, but not the exact points which questions embody or paper-setters have in mind.

- Students leave out some parts of the questions/sub-questions
- Answers far exceed the prescribed word limits.
- Answers are unstructured and unorganised; ideas are not arranged logically or sequentially.
- Language is loose and flabby, and ungrammatical.

A few words of explanation are needed on these errors. For simplicity's sake, we discuss the first three errors by using examples from UPSC question papers.

Relevance of Answers

Example I

What is 'emotional intelligence' and how can it be developed in people? How does it help an individual in taking ethical decisions? (150 words)

The examiner is **not** asking you to write a mini-essay on emotional intelligence. He/she has three aspects of emotional intelligence in mind: (a) its definition; (b) the ways it can be fostered in people; and (c) the manner it aids in taking ethical decisions. Write about these sub-questions distributing the 150 words among them suitably.

Example II

Differentiate between the following (200 words):

(i) Law and Ethics

(ii) Ethical management and Management of ethics

(iii) Discrimination and Preferential treatment

(iv) Personal ethics and Professional ethics

Each sub-question has two terms, and the entire question has eight terms. The examiner is **not** asking you to write about the eight terms individually or separately. If you go on writing about the terms individually, the answer will be wrong, for that is not what you are asked to do. Briefly define each term in the pair and show how they differ.

Example III

Public servants are likely to confront with the issues of 'Conflict of Interest'. What do you understand by the term 'Conflict of Interest' and how does it manifest in the decision making by public servants? If faced with the Conflict of Interest situation, how would you resolve it? Explain with the help of examples.

The scope of the question covers four aspects: definition of conflict of interest; explaining how it arises; how officers should respond to it; and illustrative examples. Your answer should cover these four issues, and not trail off into irrelevancies.

In brief, students should analyse the question and understand its scope. Their answer should be relevant to the question and sub-questions; and be based on the focus and thrust of the question.

Quotations and direction words/sentences

Many theory questions contain a quotation which is followed by a direction word/sentence for candidates. Pay special attention to these direction words/sentences which tell you what the central themes of the answer should be. Let us look at a few examples.

Corporate social responsibility makes companies more profitable and sustainable. **Analyse**

Strength, peace and security are considered to be the pillars of international relations. **Elucidate**

The crisis of ethical values in modern times is traced to a narrow perception of the good life. **Discuss**

"Increased national wealth did not result in equitable distribution of its benefits. It has created only some "enclaves of modernity and prosperity for a small minority at the cost of the majority". **Justify**

Without commonly shared and widely entrenched moral values and obligations, neither the law, nor democratic government, nor even the market economy will function properly.

What do you understand by this statement? Explain with illustration in the contemporary times.

We have italicized the quotations or statements and highlighted the direction word or sentence. "Analyse" means that the answer should explain the logic or rationale of the statement or specify its various aspects. "Elucidate" indicates that the answer should elaborate the statement or expand its content. "Discuss" suggests that the answer should deal with both sides of an issue or all its dimensions. "Justify" means that answer should give reasons or facts in support of the statement. For example, it should not refute the statement. "What do you understand by this statement?" indicates that students should expand the statement showing what it conveys to them.

The short point is that students should comment on the quotation or statement in the light of the direction word or sentence. They should avoid merely giving a descriptive account unrelated to the direction word/sentence. Students should carefully look at the answers we gave to these questions later in the chapter.

Covering all parts of a question

The second common error in students' answers is inadequate coverage. What we mean is that they forget about some question parts. They may not miss out the sub-questions which carry tag like (a) or (b). Some questions with such tags are also divided into bits. The bits should also be answered.

We can use one of the previous examples to explain the point. Thus in example III, the question as worded seems to have three parts. But it also seeks examples. Students have to write about all the three parts and also give examples in the answer. If they omit any part, they will lose marks. They can decide how to distribute the 150 word limit among the parts.

Sticking to prescribed word limits

As regards word limit, interestingly this is the only material point on which UPSC's instructions advise students on how to write answers. We quote from 2014 paper:

Word limit in questions, wherever specified, should be adhered to.

Answer questions in NOT MORE than the word limit specified for each in the parenthesis. Content of the answer is more important than its length.

Normally, each theory question (found in Part A of the paper), consisting of two parts (a) and (b) has to be answered in 150 words. If (a) or (b) has parts, the words have to be distributed between such parts. What is a proper word limit? It could exceed (or fall short of) the prescribed word limit by 5% to 7%.

What happens when students write?

Before discussing ways of avoiding poorly structured and badly worded answers, we should understand the sources of such errors. They can be traced to bad reading and study practices. Students read superficially. They fail to grasp and firm up ideas in their mind in clear language. On most topics, they have hazy and vague ideas, often irrelevant, trivial and repetitive. They float in their mind in loose, long and ungrammatical sentences. Students tend to reproduce such ideas in raw form just as they occur to them as answers. Thus they write incoherent or jumbled up answers.

How to tackle the problem?

The difficulties have to be handled in two stages. First students should practise constantly before examinations for cultivating right techniques of answering questions. Secondly, students should answer questions, matching as closely as they can the expectations of the examiners. No adequate coverage of reading skills and study methods is possible within the short space available to us. But the tips mentioned in this chapter will prove helpful.

Let us consider a few examples of topics on which questions can be expected. One set could be: *money bill, habeas corpus, feminism, surrogacy, balance of trade, current account deficit, inclusive growth, monetary policy committee, poverty line, good governance, cloud computing, Make in India* **and** *Start-up* **and** *acorns.* **Another set from Ethics syllabus could be:** *corporate governance, ethical dilemma, good life, virtue ethics, cognitive dissonance, rationalization, and difference between the pairs such as integrity and honesty, happiness and pleasure, and duty and obligation.*

There is no point, as students doubtless know from their experience from examinations, in scratching one's head in examination hall, and try to find words for such terms or concepts. It means that one's preparation is inadequate. Students should remember these terms in readymade, memorized phrases, and use them in writing answers quickly. If there is a question on a concept, definition, doctrine or administrative principle, students should be able to answer it based on clearly memorized materials. These are topics included in the syllabus which students are supposed to learn. They should be able to recall such basic terms and theories in standard phrases. This knowledge should be at their fingertips. A store of suitably worded key ideas should be present in their mind. Then students will not struggle for expression. Their thoughts will be in a presentable form.

Are we suggesting memorization? The answer is partially in the affirmative, but such memorization will be with understanding and confined to critical terms and ideas. As they have to be used often in answers, it will save labour, and they need not keep thinking of new ways of writing them every time.

If they are memorized, the task becomes easier.

Application-based questions need a different approach. In answering such questions also, memorized phrases can be selectively used. But answers to these questions should otherwise be in one's words. Students will gain needful insights through practice in this matter.

To conclude:

- **Never allow ideas to float vaguely in your mind. Firm them up in clear and concrete words.**
- **Keep a store of suitably worded basic terms, concepts, definitions, theories and key ideas in your mind.**

Analysing questions

Students should analyse questions quickly in examinations. It has to be a reflex or automatic process. In preparatory stage, students should master the process. Analysis involves looking at the following:

(i) What exactly is the question asking?

(ii) What are the ideas I know about the question?

(iii) What is the most logical way of arranging them in a serial order?

(iv) How can I express them in effective sentences?

To see what analysis involves, let us consider the following example from 2014 UPSC question paper:

What do you understand by 'probity' in public life? What are the difficulties in practising it in the present times? How can these difficulties be overcome? (10 marks/150 words)

Here, the examiner wants students to (i) define probity; (ii) mention difficulties officers face in practicing it now; and (iii) suggest means of handling such difficulties.

If a question has three parts as in this example, students have to mentally recollect 4-7 ideas on each part, arrange them in a sequence, and write the answer. If the question has two parts, each part will have 6-9 ideas. Finally, if the question has one part only, the answer will have 15-18 ideas. These numbers are illustrative and the actual numbers can vary from question to question.

Practising Answer Writing

The next step is to arrange the ideas in a logical order. Students should make sure that the ideas are distinct and separate and not repetitive. After deciding on 4-7 ideas of a part, they can arrange them sequentially. They can start with the most important points.

Finally, students need to write out the answer. They should practise writing answer to each part along following lines:

- Think of the first idea

- What is the **sentence in my mind** which expresses the idea?
- Is it clear or vague? If it is vague, sharpen it.
- Is it long or short? If it is long make it short. This is the simplest way of improving one's language.
- Is it grammatical or ungrammatical? If it is ungrammatical, correct it.
- Follow similar procedure for all the other ideas of the answer.
- Reread all the sentences and make further revisions you think are necessary.
- Then write down the final draft as answer.
- Then go to second part and answer it following above steps.
- Follow same procedure for the third part.
- To begin with, watch answer length roughly. (Number of lines × approximate words per line)
- In the end, count the words for the entire answer.
- Trim the answer by omitting inessential ideas or by cutting words or by omitting examples.

Obviously, the above steps are designed to help students in writing answers and in improving them. This process of writing answers and revising them will improve the content and language of student answers. With constant practice, students will learn how to polish the answers. This will become a habit and improve their answers.

Study and practice in the above manner will help in the examination. Students will analyse questions and write relevant and effective answers. They will get used to tackling questions correctly. They will have clear ideas in their mind which they can readily apply.

Answering in the examination

However, there is a world of difference between (a) practising in the manner suggested in the preceding section and (b) in actually writing answers in the examination hall. In actual examinations, many students feel tense and anxious. The time pressure will be intense. The process of thinking about 14-15 questions and their parts and writing answers will be mentally fatiguing.

How to cope with these problems? The commonsense approach consists in intensely practising before examinations. Students have to follow the aforementioned techniques for mastering course materials and for writing answers. They need to answers as many mock tests as they can before the actual examinations.

These tests should be taken in conditions identical to an examination situation. These trial runs will condition students to the examination situation and atmosphere. Of course, they should not look at mock test papers beforehand so that they experience the element of surprise as in real examinations. Mock test will work best if taken after completing substantial parts of syllabus and after learning to write answers along the previously outline lines. By doing so, students will have a fair idea of the problems they will face in examinations. Students can work on rectifying those problems.

Students may run into a few common difficulties in examinations. It is easy to overshoot the prescribed word limits for answers. It will be awkward, for example, if 380 words are written as against the word limit of 250 words. Examiners are unlikely to be harsh if the answer exceeds the word limit by a tolerable margin. But during their answer practice sessions, students need to practise writing answers of varying length ranging from 250 words, 150 words, 50 words and 30 words. They will then have a rough idea of how long an answer is becoming.

Adopting a Simple Writing Style

Normally, we tend to use wordy expressions and sentence forms. By learning about such wordy expressions and ways of trimming them, students can write better. Conscious and regular practice can help in removing this weakness. A few simple rules are:

- Use active voice instead of passive voice.
- Express ideas directly instead of using indirect or roundabout expressions.
- Wherever possible, replace clauses with phrases and phrases with single words.
- Learn to express your thoughts in short sentences with simple construction.
- Avoid writing convoluted or awkward sentences.
- Avoid use of adjectives and jargon.
- Cut out repetitive words, expressions and ideas.
- Restrict use of words which modify other words and phrases.
- Write sentences using mainly subject-verb form severely restricting use of modifiers and adjuncts.
- Express only one idea (as far as possible) in a sentence

These rules can be easily followed while practising answer writing. As mentioned earlier, the first drafts of answers have to be rewritten using the above listed rules. In this way, students can critically scrutinize their answers. Such scrutiny should also cover the material content and logical structure of the answer.

Self-evidently, aforementioned procedures are for use during the preparatory stages, and not in the examination. There will be no time for such revisions. Students have to quickly determine the focus of the question, mentally recall and group ideas, and start writing. At the most, they can jot down main points very briefly and note their possible sequence. Their best bet would be to write down those points in simple grammatical sentences, and especially avoiding glaring errors. There will be no time for mulling over things and polishing language.

Students should not get bogged down in the examination. Questions have to be answered within time. Too much time cannot be spent on a few questions at the cost of others. Extra marks gained on the former will be far fewer than marks lost on the latter. There is a famous saying that the best is the enemy of good. This has a special relevance in the context of writing answers in examinations.

